Visual Basic® 2010

HOW TO PROGRAM

Deitel® Ser

How To Program Series

C How to Program, 6/E

C++ How to Program, 7/E

Java How to Program, 8/E, Early Objects Version

Java How to Program, 8/E, Late Objects Version

Internet & World Wide Web How to Program, 4/E

Visual Basic® 2010 How to Program

Visual C#® 2008 How to Program, 3/E

Visual C++® 2008 How to Program, 2/E

Small Java™ How to Program, 6/E

Small C++ How to Program, 5/E

Simply Series

Simply C++: An Application-Driven
   Tutorial Approach

Simply Java™ Programming: An
   Application-Driven Tutorial
   Approach

Simply C#: An Application-Driven
   Tutorial Approach

Simply Visual Basic® 2008, 3/E: An
   Application-Driven Tutorial
   Approach

CourseSmart Web Books

www.deitel.com/books/CourseSmart/

C++ How to Program, 5/E, 6/E & 7/E

Java How to Program, 6/E, 7/E & 8/E

Simply C++: An Application-Driven
   Tutorial Approach

Simply Visual Basic 2008: An
   Application-Driven Tutorial
   Approach, 3/E

Small C++ How to Program, 5/E

Small Java How to Program, 6/E

Visual Basic® 2008 How to Program

Visual Basic® 2010 How to Program

Visual C#® 2008 How to Program, 3/E

ies Page

Deitel® Developer Series

AJAX, Rich Internet Applications and
   Web Development for Programmers

C++ for Programmers

C# 2008 for Programmers, 3/E

iPhone for Programmers:
   An App-Driven Approach

Java for Programmers

Javascript for Programmers

LiveLessons Video Learning Products

www.deitel.com/books/LiveLessons/

Java Fundamentals Parts 1 and 2

C# Fundamentals Parts 1 and 2

C++ Fundamentals Parts 1 and 2

iPhone App Development
   Fundamentals Parts 1 and 2

JavaScript Fundamentals Parts 1 and 2

To receive updates on Deitel publications, Resource Centers, training courses, partner offers and more, please register for the free *Deitel® Buzz Online* e-mail newsletter at:

www.deitel.com/newsletter/subscribe.html

follow us on Twitter®

@deitel

and Facebook®

www.deitel.com/deitelfan/

To communicate with the authors, send e-mail to:

deitel@deitel.com

For information on government and corporate *Dive-Into® Series* on-site seminars offered by Deitel & Associates, Inc. worldwide, visit:

www.deitel.com/training/

or write to

deitel@deitel.com

For continuing updates on Prentice Hall/Deitel publications visit:

www.deitel.com
www.pearsonhighered.com/deitel

Check out our Resource Centers for valuable web resources that will help you master Java, other important programming languages, software and Internet- and web-related topics:

www.deitel.com/ResourceCenters.html

Library of Congress Cataloging-in-Publication Data
On file

Vice President and Editorial Director, ECS: *Marcia J. Horton*
Editor-in-Chief, Computer Science: *Michael Hirsch*
Associate Editor: *Carole Snyder*
Vice-President, Production: *Vince O'Brien*
Managing Editor: *Jeff Holcomb*
Associate Managing Editor: *Robert Engelhardt*
Art Director: *Kristine Carney*
Cover Design: *Abbey S. Deitel, Harvey M. Deitel, Francesco Santalucia, Kristine Carney*
Interior Design: *Harvey M. Deitel, Kristine Carney*
Manufacturing Manager: *Alexis Heydt-Long*
Manufacturing Buyer: *Lisa McDowell*
Director of Marketing: *Margaret Waples*

Prentice Hall
is an imprint of

PEARSON

© 2011 by Pearson Education, Inc., publishing as Prentice Hall
Upper Saddle River, New Jersey 07458

10 9 8 7 6 5 4 3 2 1

ISBN-10:   0-13-255160-8 (Instructor's Edition)
ISBN-13: 978-0-13-255160-1 (Instructor's Edition)

ISBN-10:   0-13-215213-4 (Student Edition)
ISBN-13: 978-0-13-215213-6 (Student Edition)

Pearson Education Ltd., *London*
Pearson Education Australia Pty. Ltd., *Sydney*
Pearson Education Singapore, Pte. Ltd.
Pearson Education North Asia Ltd., *Hong Kong*
Pearson Education Canada, Inc., *Toronto*
Pearson Educación de Mexico, S.A. de C.V.
Pearson Education–Japan, *Tokyo*
Pearson Education Malaysia, Pte. Ltd.
Pearson Education, Inc., *Upper Saddle River, New Jersey*

Visual Basic® 2010

HOW TO PROGRAM

P. J. Deitel
Deitel & Associates, Inc.

H. M. Deitel
Deitel & Associates, Inc.

Prentice Hall
is an imprint of

Upper Saddle River, New Jersey 07458

Trademarks

In memory of Dolores "Deen" Mars:

We will always remember you as the epitome of grace, friendship, caring and kindness.

Paul, Harvey, Abbey and Barbara

Deitel Resource Centers

Our Resource Centers focus on the vast amounts of free content available online. Find resources, downloads, tutorials, documentation, books, e-books, journals, articles, blogs, RSS feeds and more on many of today's hottest programming and technology topics. For the most up-to-date list of our Resource Centers, visit:

> www.deitel.com/ResourceCenters.html

Let us know what other Resource Centers you'd like to see! Also, please register for the free *Deitel®* *Buzz Online* e-mail newsletter at:

> www.deitel.com/newsletter/subscribe.html

Computer Science
Functional Programming
Regular Expressions

Programming
ASP.NET 3.5
Adobe Flex
Ajax
Android
Apex
ASP.NET Ajax
ASP.NET
C
C++
C++ Boost Libraries
C++ Game Programming
C#
Code Search Engines and Code Sites
Computer Game Programming
CSS 2.1
Dojo
Facebook Developer Platform
Flash 9
Functional Programming
Java
Java Certification and Assessment Testing
Java Design Patterns
Java EE 5
Java SE 6
Java SE 7 (Dolphin) Resource Center
JavaFX
JavaScript
JSON
Microsoft LINQ
Microsoft Popfly
.NET
.NET 3.0
.NET 3.5
OpenGL
Perl
PHP
Programming Projects
Python
Regular Expressions
Ruby
Ruby on Rails
Silverlight

UML
Visual Basic
Visual C++
Visual Studio Team System
Web 3D Technologies
Web Services
Windows Presentation Foundation
XHTML
XML

Apple
iPhone
iPhone Apps Development
Objective-C
Cocoa

Games and Game Programming
Computer Game Programming
Computer Games
Mobile Gaming
Sudoku

Internet Business
Affiliate Programs
Competitive Analysis
Facebook Social Ads
Google AdSense
Google Analytics
Google Services
Internet Advertising
Internet Business Initiative
Internet Public Relations
Link Building
Location-Based Services
Online Lead Generation
Podcasting
Search Engine Optimization
Selling Digital Content
Sitemaps
Web Analytics
Website Monetization
YouTube and AdSense

Java
Java
Java Certification and Assessment Testing

Java Design Patterns
Java EE 5
Java SE 6
Java SE 7 (Dolphin) Resource Center
JavaFX

Microsoft
ASP.NET
ASP.NET 3.5
ASP.NET Ajax
C#
DotNetNuke (DNN)
Internet Explorer 7 (IE7)
Microsoft LINQ
.NET
.NET 3.0
.NET 3.5
SharePoint
Silverlight
Visual Basic
Visual C++
Visual Studio Team System
Windows Presentation Foundation
Windows Vista
Microsoft Popfly

Open Source & LAMP Stack
Apache
DotNetNuke (DNN)
Eclipse
Firefox
Linux
MySQL
Open Source
Perl
PHP
Python
Ruby

Software
Apache
DotNetNuke (DNN)
Eclipse
Firefox
Internet Explorer 7 (IE7)
Linux
MySQL
Open Source

Search Engines
SharePoint
Skype
Web Servers
Wikis
Windows Vista

Web 2.0
Alert Services
Attention Economy
Blogging
Building Web Communities
Community Generated Content
Facebook Developer Platform
Facebook Social Ads
Google Base
Google Video
Google Web Toolkit (GWT)
Internet Video
Joost
Location-Based Services
Mashups
Microformats
Recommender Systems
RSS
Social Graph
Social Media
Social Networking
Software as a Service (SaaS)
Virtual Worlds
Web 2.0
Web 3.0
Widgets

Dive Into® Web 2.0 eBook
Web 2 eBook

Other Topics
Computer Games
Computing Jobs
Gadgets and Gizmos
Ring Tones
Sudoku

Contents

Chapters 16–27 and Appendix F are PDF documents posted online at the book's Companion Website (located at www.pearsonhighered.com/deitel/).

Companion Website Online Content

Chapters 16–27 and Appendix F are PDF documents posted online at the book's Companion Website (located at www.pearsonhighered.com/deitel).

Contents

Chapters 16–27 and Appendix F are PDF documents posted online at the book's Companion Website (located at **www.pearsonhighered.com/deitel/**).

10 Object-Oriented Programming: Inheritance and Polymorphism 355

11 Introduction to LINQ 386

12 Databases and LINQ 403

13 Web App Development with ASP.NET 443

14 Windows Forms GUI: A Deeper Look 495

Companion Website Online Content

Chapters 16–27 and Appendix F are PDF documents posted online at the book's Companion Website (located at www.pearsonhighered.com/deitel).

Preface

Welcome to the Visual Basic® 2010 programming language and the world of Microsoft® Windows® and Internet programming with Microsoft's .NET platform!

At the heart of the book is the Deitel signature "live-code approach." Concepts are presented in the context of working programs, rather than in code snippets. Each code example is accompanied by one or more sample executions. All the source code is available at www.deitel.com/books/vb2010htp/.

As you read the book, if you have questions, send an e-mail to deitel@deitel.com; we'll respond promptly. For updates on this book and its supporting Visual Basic software, visit www.deitel.com/books/vb2010htp/, follow us on Facebook (www.deitel.com/deitelfan) and Twitter (@deitel), and subscribe to the *Deitel® Buzz Online* newsletter (www.deitel.com/newsletter/subscribe.html).

New and Updated Features

Here are the updates we've made for *Visual Basic® 2010 How to Program*:

- *Late objects approach.* We now defer the discussion of creating custom classes until Chapter 9, but in the early chapters, we still use lots of existing objects. Chapter 10 discusses how to create powerful new classes quickly by using inheritance to "absorb" the capabilities of existing classes, and presents the crucial concepts of polymorphism, abstract classes and interfaces.

- *Shorter printed book with optional online advanced chapters.* The printed book contains the core content for introductory Visual Basic courses. Several *optional* online chapters are included for second courses and professionals. These are available in searchable PDF format on the book's password-protected Companion Website—see the access card in the front of this book. If you are an instructor with a complimentary review copy that did not come with an access card, contact your Pearson Education/Prentice-Hall representative.

- *Focus on business and personal utility examples.*

- *Windows Forms GUI is integrated throughout the core chapters.* We replaced all console applications in the core content with GUI applications.

- *Making a Difference exercises set.* We encourage you to use computers and the Internet to research and solve problems that of social significance. These new exercises are meant to increase awareness of important issues the world is facing. We hope you'll approach them with your own values, politics and beliefs.

- *Up-to-date with Visual Basic 2010, the Visual Studio 2010 IDE and .NET 4.0.*

- The code will run on *Windows 7, Windows Vista* and *Windows XP.* We'll post any issues on www.deitel.com/books/vb2010htp/.

- We include *VideoNotes* for most of the programs in the core book.

- *Integrated Using the Debugger sections and exercises* in the core printed book. Students use the debugger to locate and fix logic errors.

- *Files and databases are covered earlier. ASP.NET is in the core book.*

- *New design.* The book has a new interior design that graphically organizes, clarifies and highlights the information, and enhances the book's pedagogy.

- We added *new exercise types* including "What does this code do?", "What's wrong with this code?" and "Using the Debugger."

- We added *multiple-choice Self-Review Exercises and answers* to many of the chapters in the printed book.

- We added a *multiple-choice Quick Quiz* in many chapters.

- *We now present graphics in the context of Windows* **Forms** *with GDI+.* We moved the WPF graphics chapter to the online section.

- *We titled the programming exercises* to help instructors select assignments.

- *Larger programs are presented in small increments.*

Other features of *Visual Basic 2010 How to Program* include:

- *We use LINQ (Language Integrated Query) to query files, databases, XML and collections.* The introductory LINQ chapter in the core printed book is intentionally brief to encourage instructors to cover this important technology. The online chapters continue the discussion of LINQ.

- *Databases.* We use Microsoft's free SQL Server Express (which installs with the free Visual Basic Express) to teach the fundamentals of database programming. Chapters 12, 13, 22 and 23 use database and LINQ fundamentals in the context of an address-book desktop application and web-based guestbook, bookstore and airline reservation system applications, respectively.

- *ASP.NET 4.0.* Microsoft's .NET server-side technology, ASP.NET, enables you to create robust, scalable web-based applications. In Chapter 13, you'll build several applications, including a web-based guestbook application that uses ASP.NET, LINQ and a LinqDataSource to store data in a database and display data in a web page. The chapter also discusses the ASP.NET Development Server for testing your web applications on your local computer.

- *Local type inference.* When you initialize a local variable in its declaration, you can now omit the variable's type—the compiler infers it from the initializer value.

- *Optional parameters.* You can specify method parameters with default values— if a corresponding method argument is not provided in the method call, the compiler inserts the optional parameter's default value in the call.

- *Object initializers.* For new objects, you can use object initializer syntax (similar to array initializer syntax) to assign values to the new object's properties.

- *"Quick Fix" window.* We show how to use the IDE's **Error Correction Options** window to quickly fix certain common programming errors simply by clicking the suggested fix, which is displayed in a window in the code editor.

- *We emphasize the IDE's* **IntelliSense** *feature* that helps you write code faster and with fewer errors.

- *We show how to use* **DataTips** *and visualizers* to view object contents in the code window during debugging.

- *Appendix F, Creating Console Applications.* This online appendix is referenced by the online chapters that contain some console applications.

Our Text + Digital Approach to Content

We surveyed hundreds of instructors teaching Visual Basic courses and learned that most want a book with content focused on their introductory courses. With that in mind, we moved many of the intermediate and advanced chapters to the web. Having this content in digital format makes it easily searchable, and gives us the ability to fix errata and add new content as appropriate. The book's Companion Website at

```
www.pearsonhighered.com/deitel/
```

(see the access card at the front of the book) contains the following chapters and appendices in *searchable* PDF format:

- Chapters 16–18 extend the core coverage of *exception handling, strings and files.*

- The .NET framework provides an extensive set of *pre-built collections*, so you rarely need to create your own data structures. Chapter 25 discusses collections.

- *WPF (Windows Presentation Foundation) GUI, graphics and multimedia.* We extend the core book's coverage of GUI and graphics in Chapters 19–20, respectively, with an introduction to Windows Presentation Foundation (WPF)—Microsoft's new framework that integrates GUI, graphics and multimedia capabilities. We implement a painting application, a text editor, a color chooser, a book-cover viewer, a television video player, various animations, and speech synthesis and speech recognition applications.

- *ASP.NET 4.0 and ASP.NET AJAX.* Chapter 22 extends Chapter 13's ASP.NET discussion with a case study on building a password-protected, web-based bookstore application. We also introduce ASP.NET AJAX controls and use them to add AJAX functionality to web applications to improve their responsiveness.

- *WCF (Windows Communication Foundation) Web Services (Chapter 23).* Web services enable you to package application functionality in a manner that turns the web into a library of reusable software components. We include case studies on building an airline reservation web service, a blackjack web service and a math question generator web service that's called by a math tutor application.

- *Silverlight.* Chapter 24 introduces Silverlight, which enables you to create visually stunning, multimedia-intensive user interfaces for web applications. The chapter presents powerful multimedia applications, including a weather viewer, Flickr photo viewer, deep zoom book-cover collage and video viewer.

- *Visual Basic XML capabilities.* Use of the Extensible Markup Language (XML) is exploding in the software-development industry and in e-business, and is pervasive throughout the .NET platform. Visual Basic has many features that integrate XML with the language. In Chapter 21, we use XML axis properties to manipulate elements of an XML document by their element names. We also demonstrate Visual Basic's new support for XML literals—this enables you to embed XML documents and elements directly in your Visual Basic code. In addition, we use LINQ to manipulate XML data.

- *Optional Case Study: Using the UML to Develop an Object-Oriented Design of an ATM.* The UML™ (Unified Modeling Language™) has become the preferred graphical modeling language for designing object-oriented systems. This edition includes an optional online case study on object-oriented design using the UML. We design and implement the software for a simple automated teller machine (ATM). We analyze a typical requirements document that specifies the system to be built. We determine the classes needed to implement that system, determine the attributes the classes need to have, determine the behaviors the classes need to exhibit and specify how the classes must interact with one another to meet the system requirements. From the design we produce a working Visual Basic implementation.

- *Index.* The index posted on the Companion Website includes the content from the printed book *and* the online content. The print book index covers only the material in the printed book.

Dependency Charts

The charts in Figs. 1–2 show the dependencies among the chapters to help instructors plan their syllabi. The core printed book focuses on introductory courses (Fig. 1). The online chapters include intermediate and advanced content for second courses (Fig. 2).

Teaching Approach

Visual Basic 2010 How to Program contains a rich collection of examples. We concentrate on building good software, and stress program clarity.

Live-Code Approach. The book is loaded with "live-code" examples. Most new concepts are presented in the context of complete working Visual Basic applications, followed by one or more executions showing program inputs and outputs.

Syntax Shading. For readability, we syntax shade the code, similar to the way most integrated-development environments and code editors syntax color code. Our syntax-shading conventions are:

```
comments appear like this
keywords appear like this
constants and literal values appear like this
all other code appears in black
```

Code Highlighting. We place gray rectangles around each program's key code.

Using Fonts for Emphasis. We place the key terms and the index's page reference for each defining occurrence in bold blue text for easy reference. We emphasize on-screen components in the **bold Helvetica** font (for example, the **File** menu) and Visual Basic program text in the Lucida font (for example, Dim count As Integer = 5).

Objectives. The opening quotes are followed by a list of chapter objectives.

Dependency Chart for Print Chapters

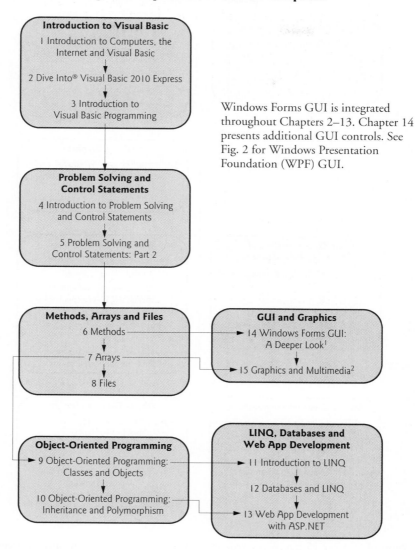

Windows Forms GUI is integrated throughout Chapters 2–13. Chapter 14 presents additional GUI controls. See Fig. 2 for Windows Presentation Foundation (WPF) GUI.

1. Section 14.7 requires the `Using` statement, which is presented in Chapter 8. Section 14.14 requires concepts presented in Chapter 9. Section 14.15 requires inheritance concepts from Chapter 10.

2. Several Chapter 15 examples override `Form` method `OnPaint`. Method overriding is presented in Chapter 10. To use graphics sooner, students can mimic `OnPaint` as shown in the examples. Sections 15.9 and 15.12 use `Imports` statements, which are introduced in Chapter 8.

Fig. I | Chapter dependency chart.

Dependency Chart for Online Chapters

1. Most of Chapter 16 can be covered after Chapter 6. Section 16.8 requires concepts from Chapter 9.

2. Most of Chapter 17 can be covered after Chapter 6, but a couple of examples require one-dimensional arrays (Chapter 7).

3. Chapter 21 depends on the introduction to XML in Sections 19.3–19.5.

4. Online Appendix F shows how to create console applications. Parts of Chapters 16, 17, 21 and 27 use console applications.

Fig. 2 | Chapter dependency chart for the online chapters.

Illustrations/Figures. Abundant tables, line drawings, UML diagrams, programs and program outputs are included.

Programming Tips. We include programming tips to help you focus on important aspects of program development. These tips and practices represent the best we've gleaned from a combined seven decades of programming and teaching experience.

Good Programming Practice

The Good Programming Practices *call attention to techniques that will help you produce programs that are clearer, more understandable and more maintainable.*

Common Programming Error

Pointing out these Common Programming Errors *reduces the likelihood that you'll make them.*

Error-Prevention Tip

These tips contain suggestions for exposing and removing bugs from your programs; many describe aspects of Visual Basic that prevent bugs from getting into programs.

Performance Tip

These tips highlight opportunities for making your programs run faster or minimizing the amount of memory that they occupy.

Portability Tip

The Portability Tips *help you write code that will run on a variety of platforms.*

Software Engineering Observation

The Software Engineering Observations *highlight architectural and design issues that affect the construction of software systems, especially large-scale systems.*

Look-and-Feel Observation

These observations help you design attractive, user-friendly graphical user interfaces that conform to industry norms.

Summary Bullets. We present a section-by-section, bullet-list summary of each chapter.

Terminology. We include an alphabetized list of the important terms defined in each chapter with the page number of each term's defining occurrence for easy reference.

Self-Review Exercises and Answers. Extensive self-review exercises *and* answers are included for self-study. We've added many new multiple-choice exercises and answers.

Exercises. Each chapter concludes with additional exercises including:

- simple recall of important terminology and concepts
- What's wrong with this code?
- What does this code do?
- Using the Debugger

- writing individual statements and small portions of methods and classes
- writing complete methods, classes and programs
- major projects.

Please do not write to us requesting access to the Pearson Instructor's Resource Center which contains the book's instructor supplements, including the exercise solutions. Access is limited strictly to college instructors teaching from the book. Instructors may obtain access only through their Pearson representatives. Solutions are *not* provided for "project" exercises. Check out our Programming Projects Resource Center for lots of additional exercise and project possibilities (www.deitel.com/ProgrammingProjects/).

Index. We've included an extensive index for reference. Defining occurrences of key terms are highlighted with a **bold blue** page number.

Student Resources and Software

This book includes the Microsoft® Visual Studio® 2010 Express Editions All-in-One DVD, which contains the Visual Basic® 2010 Express Edition (and other Microsoft development tools). These tools are also downloadable from

> www.microsoft.com/express/Windows

We wrote *Visual Basic 2010 How to Program* using Visual Basic® Express Edition. You can learn more about Visual Basic® at msdn.microsoft.com/en-us/vbasic/default.aspx.

Deitel Online Resource Centers

Our website www.deitel.com provides Resource Centers on various topics of interest to our readers—see the list of Resource Centers in the first few pages of this book and visit www.deitel.com/ResourceCenters.html. We've found many exceptional resources online, including tutorials, documentation, software downloads, articles, blogs, podcasts, videos, code samples, books, e-books and more—most are free. Some of the Resource Centers you might find helpful while studying this book are Visual Basic, ASP.NET, ASP.NET AJAX, LINQ, .NET, Silverlight, SQL Server, Web Services, Windows Communication Foundation, Windows Presentation Foundation, Windows 7, UML, Code Search Engines and Code Sites, Game Programming and Programming Projects.

Instructor Supplements

The following supplements are available to qualified instructors only through Pearson Education's Instructor Resource Center (www.pearsonhighered.com/irc):

- *Solutions Manual* with solutions to most of the end-of-chapter exercises.
- *Test Item File* of multiple-choice questions (approximately two per book section)
- *Customizable PowerPoint® slides* containing all the code and figures in the text, plus bulleted items that summarize key points. The slides also include links to the project files for the code examples so that you can click to open the corresponding project in Visual Basic Express or Visual Studio and execute the program.

If you're not a registered faculty member, contact your Pearson representative or visit www.pearsonhighered.com/educator/replocator/.

CourseSmart Web Books

Today's students and instructors have increasing demands on their time and money. Pearson has responded to that need by offering digital texts and course materials online through CourseSmart. CourseSmart allows faculty to review course materials online saving time and costs. It is also environmentally sound and offers students a high-quality digital version of the text for as much as 50% off the cost of a print copy of the text. Students receive the same content offered in the print textbook enhanced by search, note-taking, and printing tools. For more information, visit www.coursesmart.com.

Microsoft Developer Network Academic Alliance (MSDNAA) and Microsoft DreamSpark

Microsoft Developer Network Academic Alliance (MSDNAA)—Free Microsoft Software for Academic and Research Purposes
The MSDNAA provides free software for academic and research purposes. For software direct to faculty, visit www.microsoft.com/faculty. For software for your department, visit www.msdnaa.com.

Microsoft DreamSpark—Professional Developer and Designer Tools for Students
Microsoft provides many of its developer tools to students for free via a program called DreamSpark (www.dreamspark.com). See the website for details on verifying your student status so you take advantage of this program.

Acknowledgments

Many people at Deitel & Associates, Inc., devoted long hours to this project—thanks especially to Abbey Deitel and Barbara Deitel. We would also like to thank the participants of our Honors Internship and Co-op programs who contributed to this publication—Jesse Errico, a Computer Science Masters candidate at Brown University, and Michael Morgano, a Computer Science Masters graduate from Northeastern University.

We are fortunate to have worked on this project with the dedicated team of publishing professionals at Pearson. We appreciate the guidance, savvy and energy of Michael Hirsch, Editor-in-Chief of Computer Science, and Margaret Waples, Director of Marketing, Engineering and Computer Science. Carole Snyder recruited the book's reviewers team and managed the review process. Kristine Carney and Francesco Santalucia (an independent artist) designed the book's cover. Bob Engelhardt managed the book's production.

Reviewers
We wish to acknowledge the efforts of our reviewers. Adhering to a tight schedule, they scrutinized the text and the programs and provided countless suggestions for improving the presentation: Huanhui Hu (Microsoft Corporation), Narges Kasiri (Oklahoma State University), Charles Liu (University of Texas at San Antonio), Dr. Hamid R. Nemati (The University of North Carolina at Greensboro), Jeffrey P. Scott (Blackhawk Technical College) and José Antonio González Seco (Parliament of Andalusia, Spain).

Previous Edition Reviewers
Douglas B. Bock (MCSD.NET, Southern Illinois University Edwardsville), Dan Crevier (Microsoft), Amit K. Ghosh (University of Texas at El Paso), Marcelo Guerra Hahn (Microsoft), Kim Hamilton (Software Design Engineer at Microsoft and co-author of *Learn-*

ing UML 2.0), Huanhui Hu, Vitek Karas (Microsoft), James Edward Keysor (Florida Institute of Technology), Helena Kotas (Microsoft), Chris Lovett (Software Architect at Microsoft), Bashar Lulu (INETA Country Leader, Arabian Gulf), John McIlhinney (Spatial Intelligence; Microsoft MVP 2008 Visual Developer, Visual Basic), Ged Mead (Microsoft Visual Basic MVP, DevCity.net), Anand Mukundan (Architect, Polaris Software Lab Ltd.), Timothy Ng (Microsoft), Akira Onishi (Microsoft), José Antonio González Seco (Parliament of Andalusia), Joe Stagner (Senior Program Manager, Developer Tools & Platforms), Erick Thompson (Microsoft) and Jesús Ubaldo Quevedo-Torrero (University of Wisconsin–Parkside, Department of Computer Science)

Well, there you have it! Visual Basic 2010 is a powerful programming language that will help you write programs quickly and effectively. It scales nicely into the realm of enterprise-systems development to help organizations build their business-critical and mission-critical information systems. As you read the book, we'd appreciate your comments, criticisms, corrections and suggestions for improvement. Please address all correspondence to:

deitel@deitel.com

We'll respond promptly. We hope you enjoy working with *Visual Basic 2010 How to Program* as much as we enjoyed writing it!

Paul Deitel and Harvey Deitel
February 2010 Maynard, Massachusetts

About the Authors

Paul J. Deitel, CEO and Chief Technical Officer of Deitel & Associates, Inc., is a graduate of MIT's Sloan School of Management, where he studied Information Technology. Through Deitel & Associates, Inc., he has delivered Visual Basic, C#, Java, C++, C and Internet programming courses to industry clients, including Cisco, IBM, Sun Microsystems, Dell, Lucent Technologies, Fidelity, NASA at the Kennedy Space Center, the National Severe Storm Laboratory, White Sands Missile Range, Rogue Wave Software, Boeing, SunGard Higher Education, Stratus, Cambridge Technology Partners, One Wave, Hyperion Software, Adra Systems, Entergy, CableData Systems, Nortel Networks, Puma, iRobot, Invensys and many more. He and his co-author, Dr. Harvey M. Deitel, are the world's best-selling programming-language textbook authors.

Dr. Harvey M. Deitel, Chairman and Chief Strategy Officer of Deitel & Associates, Inc., has 48 years of experience in the computer field. Dr. Deitel earned B.S. and M.S. degrees from MIT and a Ph.D. from Boston University. He has extensive college teaching experience, including earning tenure and serving as the Chairman of the Computer Science Department at Boston College before founding Deitel & Associates, Inc., with his son, Paul J. Deitel. He and Paul are the co-authors of dozens of books and multimedia packages and they are writing many more. With translations published in Japanese, German, Russian, Chinese, Spanish, Korean, French, Polish, Italian, Portuguese, Greek, Urdu and Turkish, the Deitels' texts have earned international recognition. Dr. Deitel has delivered hundreds of professional seminars to major corporations, academic institutions, government organizations and the military.

Before You Begin

This section contains information you should review before using this book and instructions to ensure that your computer is set up properly for use with this book. We'll post updates to this Before You Begin section (if any) on the book's website:

    www.deitel.com/books/vb2010htp/

Font and Naming Conventions

We use fonts to distinguish between features, such as menu names, menu items, and other elements that appear in the program-development environment. Our convention is to emphasize IDE features in a sans-serif bold Helvetica font (for example, **Properties** window) and to emphasize program text in a sans-serif Lucida font (for example, `Private x As Boolean = True`).

Software for the Book

This textbook includes a DVD which contains the Microsoft® Visual Studio® 2010 Express Edition Integrated Development Environments for Visual Basic 2010, Visual C# 2010, Visual C++ 2010, Visual Web Developer 2010 and SQL Server 2008. (You do not need Visual C# or Visual C++ for use with this book.) These IDEs are also downloadable from `www.microsoft.com/express`. The Express Editions are fully functional, and there is no time limit for using the software. We discuss the setup of this software shortly. The system requirements for these editions can be found at:

    www.microsoft.com/express/Support/

Viewing File Extensions

Several screenshots in *Visual Basic 2010 How to Program* display file names with file-name extensions (for example, `.txt`, `.vb` or `.png`). Your system's settings may need to be adjusted to display file-name extensions. Follow these steps to configure your computer:

1. In the **Start** menu, select **All Programs**, then **Accessories**, then **Windows Explorer**.

2. In Windows Vista and Windows 7, press *Alt* to display the menu bar, then select **Folder Options...** from **Windows Explorer**'s **Tools** menu. In Windows XP, simply select **Folder Options...** from **Windows Explorer**'s **Tools** menu.

3. In the dialog that appears, select the **View** tab.

4. In the **Advanced settings:** pane, uncheck the box to the left of the text **Hide extensions for known file types**. [*Note*: If this item is already unchecked, no action needs to be taken.]

Notes to Windows XP Users Regarding the Segoe UI Font

With Windows® Vista, Microsoft released a new font called Segoe UI to make graphical user interfaces (GUIs) more readable. Our GUI examples use this font, which is installed with Windows® Vista and Windows® 7, but not available by default on Windows® XP. XP users can get it by installing Windows Live™ Mail or Windows Live™ Messenger. Both are free downloads from

```
download.live.com
```

XP users must also enable ClearType; otherwise, the font will not display correctly. ClearType is a technology for smoothing the edges of fonts displayed on the screen. To enable ClearType, perform the following steps:

1. Right click your desktop and select **Properties...** from the popup menu to view the **Display Properties** dialog.

2. In the dialog, click the **Appearance** tab, then click the **Effects...** button to display the **Effects** dialog.

3. In the **Effects** dialog, ensure that the **Use the following method to smooth edges of screen fonts** checkbox is checked, then select **ClearType** from the combobox below the checkbox.

4. Click **OK** to close the **Effects** dialog. Click **OK** to close the **Display Properties** dialog.

Obtaining the Code Examples

The examples for *Visual Basic 2010 How to Program* are available for download at

```
www.deitel.com/books/vb2010htp/
```

If you're not already registered at our website, go to www.deitel.com and click the **Register** link below our logo in the upper-left corner of the page. Fill in your information. There is no charge to register, and we do not share your information with anyone. After registering, you'll receive a confirmation e-mail with your verification code. You need this code to sign in at www.deitel.com for the first time.

Next, go to www.deitel.com and sign in using the **Login** link below our logo in the upper-left corner of the page. Then, go to www.deitel.com/books/vb2010htp/. Click the **Examples** link to download the Examples.zip file to your computer. Write down the location where you choose to save the file on your computer.

We assume the examples are located at C:\Examples on your computer. Extract the contents of Examples.zip using a tool such as WinZip (www.winzip.com) or the built-in capabilities of Windows Explorer.

Installing the Software

Before you can run the applications in *Visual Basic 2010 How to Program* or build your own applications, you must install a development environment. We used Microsoft's free Visual Basic 2010 Express Edition in the examples for most chapters and Visual Web Developer 2010 Express Edition for Chapter 13 and online Chapters 22–24. Chapters 12–13 and online Chapters 22–23 require SQL Server 2008 Express Edition, which is installed with Visual Basic 2010 Express. The Visual Studio Express Editions are included on the DVD bundled with this book and can also be downloaded from:

```
www.microsoft.com/express/
```

To install the Visual Basic 2010 and Visual Web Developer 2010 Express Editions, insert the DVD that accompanies this book into your computer's DVD drive to launch the software installer, then click the name of the product you wish to install and follow the on-screen instructions. If the setup window does not appear, use Windows Explorer to view the contents of the DVD drive and double click `Setup.exe` to launch the installer.

Differences Between Visual Studio 2010 and the Express Editions
There are differences between the full versions of Visual Studio 2010 and the Express Editions we use in this book—for example, there are often more options in the Visual Studio 2010 menus and dialogs. One key difference is that the **Database Explorer** we refer to in Chapters 12–13 and online Chapters 22–23 is called the **Server Explorer** in the full Visual Studio 2010 products.

You're now ready to begin your Visual Basic studies with *Visual Basic 2010 How to Program*. We hope you enjoy the book!

Introduction to Computers, the Internet and Visual Basic

The chief merit of language is clearness.
——Galen

Our life is frittered away with detail. . . . Simplify, simplify.
—Henry David Thoreau

Man is still the most extraordinary computer of all.
—John F. Kennedy

Objectives

In this chapter you'll learn:

- Basic hardware and software concepts.
- The different types of programming languages.
- The history of the Visual Basic programming language.
- Some basics of object technology.
- The history of the Internet and the World Wide Web.
- About Microsoft's .NET initiative, which involves the Internet in developing and using software systems.
- To test-drive a Visual Basic 2010 drawing application.

1.1 Introduction

Welcome to Visual Basic 2010 which, from this point forward, we'll refer to simply as Visual Basic. Computer use is increasing in almost every field. Computing costs have been decreasing dramatically due to rapid developments in hardware, software and communications technologies. Computing has become so economical that billions of computers are in use worldwide, helping people in business, industry and government, and in their personal lives.

Computers process **data**, using sets of instructions called **computer programs**. These programs guide computers through orderly sets of calculations and other actions that are specified by people known as **computer programmers**. Todays personal computers can perform billions of these calculations and actions per second. A person operating a desk calculator might require a lifetime to complete the same amount of work! Today's fastest **supercomputers** work so quickly that they can perform the equivalent of 150,000 actions and calculations per second for every person on the planet!

A computer consists of various devices referred to as **hardware** (for example, the keyboard, screen, mouse, hard drive, memory, DVDs and processing units). The programs that run on a computer are referred to as **software** (for example, applications such as word processors, payroll systems, spreadsheets, e-mail systems, games, etc.).

Object-oriented programming (which models real-world objects with software counterparts), available in Visual Basic and other major programming languages, is a significant breakthrough that can greatly enhance your productivity. The core of this book emphasizes achieving program clarity through the proven techniques of object-oriented programming (OOP) and event-driven programming.

1.2 Computer Organization

Regardless of differences in physical appearance, virtually every computer may be envisioned as divided into various logical units or sections:

1. *Input unit*. This "receiving" section obtains information (data and computer programs) from **input devices** and places it at the disposal of the other units so that it can be processed. Most information is entered into computers through keyboards and mouse devices. Information also can be entered in many other ways, including by speaking to your computer, scanning images and barcodes, reading from secondary storage devices (like hard drives, CD drives, DVD drives and USB drives—also called "thumb drives") and having your computer receive information from the Internet (such as when you download videos from You-Tube™, e-books from Amazon, and the like).

2. *Output unit*. This "shipping" section takes information that the computer has processed and places it on various **output devices** to make it available for use outside the computer. Most information that is output from computers today is displayed on screens, printed on paper, played on audio players (such as Apple's popular iPods), or used to control other devices. Computers also can output their information to networks, such as the Internet.

3. *Memory unit*. This rapid-access, relatively low-capacity "warehouse" section retains information that has been entered through the input unit, making it immediately available for processing when needed. The memory unit also retains processed information until it can be placed on output devices by the output unit. Information in the memory unit is **volatile**—it's typically lost when the computer's power is turned off. The memory unit is often called either **memory** or **primary memory**.

4. *Arithmetic and logic unit (ALU)*. This "manufacturing" section performs calculations, such as addition, subtraction, multiplication and division. It also contains the decision mechanisms that allow the computer, for example, to compare two items from the memory unit to determine whether they're equal. In today's systems, the ALU is usually implemented as part of the next logical unit, the CPU.

5. *Central processing unit (CPU)*. This "administrative" section coordinates and supervises the operation of the other sections. The CPU tells the input unit when information should be read into the memory unit, tells the ALU when information from the memory unit should be used in calculations and tells the output unit when to send information from the memory unit to certain output devices. Many of today's computers have multiple CPUs and, hence, can perform many operations simultaneously—such computers are called **multiprocessors**. A **multicore processor** implements multiprocessing on a single integrated circuit chip—for example a dual-core processor has two CPUs and a quad-core processor has four CPUs.

6. *Secondary storage unit*. This is the long-term, high-capacity "warehousing" section. Programs or data not actively being used by the other units normally are placed on secondary storage devices (for example, your hard drive) until they're needed again, possibly hours, days, months or even years later. Therefore, infor-

mation on secondary storage devices is said to be **persistent**—it is preserved even when the computer's power is turned off. Secondary storage information takes much longer to access than information in primary memory, but the cost per unit of secondary storage is much less than that of primary memory. Examples of secondary storage devices include CDs, DVDs and flash drives (sometimes called memory sticks), which can hold hundreds of millions to billions of characters.

1.3 Personal Computing, Distributed Computing and Client/Server Computing

In the early years of computing, computer systems were too large and expensive for individuals to own. In the 1970s, silicon chip technology made it possible for computers to be much smaller and so economical that individuals and small organizations could own these machines. In 1977, Apple Computer—creator of today's popular Mac personal computers, iPod digital music players and iPhones—popularized **personal computing**. In 1981, IBM, the world's largest computer vendor, introduced the IBM Personal Computer, legitimizing personal computing in business, industry and government organizations.

These computers were "stand-alone" units—people transported disks back and forth between computers to share information (creating what was often called "sneakernet"). These machines could be linked together in computer networks, sometimes over telephone lines and sometimes in **local area networks** (**LANs**) within an organization. This led to the phenomenon of **distributed computing**, in which an organization's computing, instead of being performed only at some central computer installation, is distributed over networks to the geographically dispersed sites where the organization's work is performed.

Today's personal computers are as powerful as the million-dollar machines of a few decades ago; complete personal computer systems often sell for as little as a few hundred dollars. The most powerful desktop machines provide individual users with enormous capabilities. Information is shared easily across computer networks, where computers called **servers** offer a common data store and various services that may be used by **client** computers distributed throughout the network, hence the term **client/server computing**. In Chapter 13, you'll learn how to build Internet- and web-based applications; we'll talk about web servers (computers that distribute content over the web) and web clients (computers that request and receive the content offered up by web servers).

1.4 Hardware Trends

For decades, hardware costs have been falling rapidly. Every year or two, the computing power of computers has approximately doubled without any increase in price. This often is called **Moore's Law**, named after the person who first identified and explained the trend, Gordon Moore, co-founder of Intel—the company that manufactures the vast majority of the processors in today's personal computers. Moore's Law is especially true in relation to the amount of memory that computers have for programs and data, the amount of secondary storage (such as disk storage) they have, and their processor speeds—the speeds at which computers execute their programs (that is, do their work). Similar growth has occurred in the communications field, in which costs have plummeted as enormous demand for communications bandwidth has attracted intense competition. Such phenomenal improvement in the computing and communications fields is truly fostering the so-called Information Revolution.

1.5 Microsoft's Windows® Operating System

Microsoft became the dominant software company in the 1980s and 1990s. In the mid-1980s, Microsoft developed the **Windows operating system**, consisting of a graphical user interface built on top of DOS (a personal computer operating system that users interacted with by typing commands). The Windows operating system became incredibly popular after the 1993 release of Windows 3.1, whose successors, Windows 95 and Windows 98, virtually cornered the desktop operating systems market by the late 1990s. These operating systems, which borrowed from many concepts (such as icons, menus and windows) popularized by early Apple Macintosh operating systems, enabled users to navigate multiple applications simultaneously. Microsoft entered the corporate operating systems market with the 1993 release of Windows NT. Windows XP, was released in 2001 and combined Microsoft's corporate and consumer operating system lines. Windows Vista, released in 2007, offered the attractive new Aero user interface, many powerful enhancements and new applications. A key focus of Windows Vista was enhanced security. Windows 7 is Microsoft's latest operating system—its features include enhancements to the Aero user interface, faster startup times, further refinement of Vista's security features, touch screen and multi-touch support, and more. This book is intended for Windows XP, Windows Vista and Windows 7 users. Windows is by far the world's most widely used operating system.

1.6 Machine Languages, Assembly Languages and High-Level Languages

Although hundreds of computer languages are in use today, they can be divided into three general types:

1. Machine languages
2. Assembly languages
3. High-level languages

Machine Languages

A computer can directly understand only its own **machine language**, which is defined by the computer's hardware design. Machine languages generally consist of streams of numbers (ultimately reduced to 1s and 0s) that instruct computers how to perform their most elementary operations. People normally work in the decimal number system with digits in the range 0–9. The number system with only 1s and 0s is called the binary number system. Machine-language programs are sometimes called "binaries" for that reason. Machine languages are *machine dependent*—a particular machine language can be used on only *one* type of computer. The following section of an early machine-language program, which adds *overtime pay* to *base pay* and stores the result in *gross pay*, demonstrates the incomprehensibility of machine language to humans:

```
+1300042774
+1400593419
+1200274027
```

Assembly Languages

As the popularity of computers increased, machine-language programming proved to be slow and error prone. Instead of using the strings of numbers that computers could directly understand, programmers began using English-like abbreviations (called mnemonics) to represent the computer's basic operations. These abbreviations formed the basis of **assembly languages**. **Translator programs** called **assemblers** convert assembly-language programs to machine language at computer speeds. The following section of an assembly-language program also adds *overtime pay* to *base pay* and stores the result in *gross pay*, but the steps are clearer to humans than in the machine-language example:

```
LOAD    BASEPAY
ADD     OVERPAY
STORE   GROSSPAY
```

High-Level Languages

The speed at which programmers could write programs increased rapidly with the creation of assembly languages, but these languages still require many instructions to accomplish even simple tasks. To speed up the programming process, **high-level languages** (in which single program statements accomplish more substantial tasks) were developed. Translator programs called **compilers** convert high-level-language programs into machine language. High-level languages enable programmers to write instructions that look almost like everyday English and contain common mathematical notations. For example, a payroll application written in a high-level language might contain a statement such as

```
grossPay = basePay + overTimePay
```

From these examples, it's clear why programmers prefer high-level languages. Visual Basic is one of the world's most popular high-level programming languages.

1.7 Visual Basic

Visual Basic evolved from **BASIC** (Beginner's All-purpose Symbolic Instruction Code), developed in the mid-1960s at Dartmouth College as a language for introducing novices to fundamental programming techniques.

When Bill Gates founded Microsoft Corporation in the 1970s, he implemented BASIC on several early personal computers. In the late 1980s and the early 1990s, Microsoft developed the Microsoft Windows **graphical user interface (GUI)**—the *visual* part of the operating system with which users interact. With the creation of the Windows GUI, the natural evolution of BASIC was to **Visual Basic**, introduced by Microsoft in 1991 to make programming Windows applications easier.

Until Visual Basic appeared, developing Microsoft Windows-based applications was a difficult process. Visual Basic programs are created with the use of a collection of software tools called an **Integrated Development Environment (IDE)**. With Microsoft's **Visual Studio 2010** IDE, you can write, run, test and debug Visual Basic programs quickly and conveniently.

The latest versions of Visual Basic are fully *object oriented*—you'll learn some basics of object technology shortly and will study a rich treatment later in the book. Visual Basic is **event driven**—you'll write programs that respond to user-initiated **events** such as mouse clicks, keystrokes and timer expirations. It's a *visual programming language*—in addition to writing program statements to build portions of your applications, you'll also use Visual Studio's graphical user interface to conveniently drag and drop predefined objects like buttons and textboxes into place on your screen, and label and resize them. Visual Studio will write much of the GUI code for you.

1.8 Some Other Key Programming Languages

The C programming language was developed in the early 1970s. C first gained widespread recognition as the development language of the UNIX operating system. C is a hardware-independent language, and, with careful design, it is possible to write C programs that are portable to most computers.

C++, developed in the early 1980s, provides several features that "spruce up" the C language, and, more importantly, capabilities for **object-oriented programming** (OOP). **Objects** are reusable software **components** that model items in the real world. A modular, object-oriented approach to design and implementation can make software development groups much more *productive* than is possible using earlier programming techniques.

The **Objective-C** programming language, also developed in the early 1980s, added capabilities for object-oriented programming (OOP) to the C programming language. It eventually became the software development language for Apple's Macintosh. Its use has exploded as the app development language for Apple's wildly popular iPod, iPhone and iPad consumer devices. Objective-C has access to the Cocoa frameworks (powerful libraries of prebuilt components), enabling you to develop apps quickly.

Microprocessors are having a profound impact in intelligent consumer electronic devices. Recognizing this, Sun Microsystems in 1991 funded an internal corporate research project that resulted in the development of a C++-based language, which Sun eventually called **Java**. As the World Wide Web exploded in popularity in 1993, Sun saw the possibility of using Java to add **dynamic content** (for example, interactivity, animations and the like) to web pages. Sun announced the language in 1995. This generated immediate interest in the business community because of the commercial potential of the web. Java is now used to develop large-scale enterprise applications, to enhance the functionality of web servers (the computers that provide the content we see in our web browsers), to provide applications for consumer devices (such as cell phones, pagers and personal digital assistants) and for many other purposes. Visual Basic 2010 is similar in capability to Java.

In 2000, Microsoft announced the **C#** (pronounced "C-Sharp") programming language—created specifically for the .NET platform (discussed in Section 1.11). C# has roots in C, C++ and Java. Like Visual Basic, C# is object oriented and has access to a powerful **class library** of prebuilt components, enabling programmers to develop applications quickly—Visual Basic and C# *share* the .NET Framework Class Library. Both languages have similar capabilities to Java and are appropriate for the most demanding application development tasks, especially for building today's enterprise applications, and web-based and mobile applications.

1.9 The Internet and the World Wide Web

In the late 1960s, ARPA—the Advanced Research Projects Agency of the Department of Defense—rolled out plans to network the main computer systems of some ARPA-funded universities and research institutions. Academic research was about to take a giant leap forward. ARPA proceeded to implement what quickly became known as the ARPAnet, the grandparent of today's Internet.

Things worked out differently from the original plan. Although the ARPAnet enabled researchers to network their computers, its main benefit proved to be the capability for quick and easy communication via what came to be known as electronic mail (e-mail). This is true even on today's Internet, with e-mail, instant messaging and file transfer allowing billions of people worldwide to communicate with each other.

Businesses rapidly realized that by using the Internet, they could improve their operations and offer new and better services to their clients. Companies started spending large amounts of money to develop and enhance their Internet presence. This generated fierce competition among communications carriers and hardware and software suppliers to meet the increased infrastructure demand. As a result, bandwidth—the information-carrying capacity of communications lines—on the Internet has increased tremendously, while hardware costs have plummeted.

The World Wide Web is a collection of hardware and software associated with the Internet that allows computer users to locate and view multimedia-based documents (documents with various combinations of text, graphics, animations, audios and videos) on almost any subject. In 1989, Tim Berners-Lee of CERN (the European Organization for Nuclear Research) began to develop a technology for sharing information over the Internet via "hyperlinked" text documents. Berners-Lee called his invention the Hyper-Text Markup Language (HTML). He also wrote communication protocols such as HyperText Transfer Protocol (HTTP) to form the backbone of his new hypertext information system, which he referred to as the World Wide Web.

In 1994, Berners-Lee founded an organization, called the World Wide Web Consortium (W3C, www.w3.org), devoted to developing technologies for the World Wide Web. One of the W3C's primary goals is to make the web universally accessible to everyone regardless of disabilities, language or culture.

In the past, most computer applications ran on "stand-alone" computers (computers that were not connected to one another). Today's applications can be written with the aim of communicating among the world's computers via the Internet and the web. In fact, as you'll see, this is the focus of Microsoft's .NET strategy. Later in this book we discuss how to build web-based applications with Visual Basic.

1.10 Extensible Markup Language (XML)

As the popularity of the web exploded, HTML's limitations became apparent. HTML's lack of extensibility (the ability to change or add features) frustrated developers, and its ambiguous definition allowed erroneous HTML to proliferate. The need for a standardized, fully extensible and structurally strict language was apparent. As a result, XML was developed by the W3C.

Data independence, the separation of content from its presentation, is the essential characteristic of XML. Because XML documents describe data, any application conceivably can process them. Software developers are integrating XML into their applications to improve web functionality and interoperability.

XML is not limited to web applications. For example, it is increasingly being employed in databases—the structure of an XML document enables it to be integrated easily with database applications. As applications become more web enabled, it's likely that XML will become the universal technology for data representation. All applications employing XML would be able to communicate with one another, provided that they could understand their respective XML markup schemes, or vocabularies. Microsoft's .NET technologies use XML to mark up and transfer data over the Internet, and to enable software components to interoperate.

1.11 Introduction to Microsoft .NET

In 2000, Microsoft announced its .NET initiative (www.microsoft.com/net), a broad new vision for using the Internet and the web in the development, engineering, distribution and use of software. Rather than forcing developers to use a single programming language, the .NET initiative permits developers to create .NET applications in *any* .NET-compatible language (such as Visual Basic, C# and others). Part of the initiative includes Microsoft's ASP.NET technology, which allows you to create web applications.

The .NET strategy extends the idea of software reuse to the Internet by allowing programmers to concentrate on their specialties without having to implement every component of every application. Visual programming (which you'll learn throughout this book) has become popular because it enables you to create Windows and web applications easily, using such prepackaged controls as buttons, textboxes and scrollbars.

The Microsoft .NET Framework is at the heart of the .NET strategy. This framework executes applications, contains a class library (called the .NET Framework Class Library) and provides many other programming capabilities that you'll use to build Visual Basic applications.

1.12 The .NET Framework and the Common Language Runtime

The details of the .NET Framework are found in the Common Language Infrastructure (CLI), which contains information about the storage of data types (that is, data that has predefined characteristics such as a date, percentage or currency amount), objects and so on. The CLI has been standardized, making it easier to create the .NET Framework for other platforms. This is like publishing the blueprints of the framework—anyone can build it by following the specifications.

The Common Language Runtime (CLR) is another central part of the .NET Framework—it executes .NET programs. Programs are compiled into machine-specific instructions in two steps. First, the program is compiled into Microsoft Intermediate Language (MSIL), which defines instructions for the CLR. Code converted into MSIL from other languages and sources can be woven together by the CLR. The MSIL for an application's components is placed into the application's executable file. When the application executes, another compiler (known as the just-in-time compiler or JIT compiler) in the CLR translates the MSIL in the executable file into machine-language code (for a particular platform), then the machine-language code executes on that platform.

If the .NET Framework exists (and is installed) for a platform, that platform can run any .NET program. The ability of a program to run (without modification) across multiple platforms is known as platform independence. Code written once can be used on another type of computer without modification, saving time and money. In addition, software can target a wider audience—previously, companies had to decide whether converting their programs to different platforms (sometimes called **porting**) was worth the cost. With .NET, porting programs is no longer an issue (at least once .NET itself has been made available on the platforms).

The .NET Framework also provides a high level of **language interoperability**. Programs written in different languages (for example, Visual Basic and C#) are all compiled into MSIL—the different parts can be combined to create a single unified program. MSIL allows the .NET Framework to be **language independent**, because .NET programs are not tied to a particular programming language.

The .NET Framework Class Library can be used by any .NET language. The library contains a variety of reusable components, saving you the trouble of creating new components. This book explains how to develop .NET software with Visual Basic.

1.13 Test-Driving the Visual Basic Advanced Painter Application

In this section, you'll "test-drive" an existing application that enables you to draw on the screen using the mouse. The **Advanced Painter** application allows you to draw with different brush sizes and colors. The elements and functionality you see in this application are typical of what you'll learn to program in this text. The following steps show you how to test-drive the application. You'll run and interact with the working application.

1. *Checking your setup.* Confirm that you've set up your computer properly by reading the Before You Begin section located after the Preface.

2. *Locating the application directory.* Open a Windows Explorer window and navigate to the C:\Examples\ch01 directory (Fig. 1.1)—we assume you placed the examples in the C:\Examples folder.

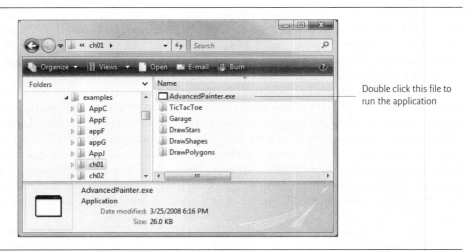

Double click this file to run the application

Fig. 1.1 | Contents of C:\Examples\ch01.

3. *Running the Advanced Painter application.* Now that you're in the proper directory, double click the file name AdvancedPainter.exe (Fig. 1.1) to run the application (Fig. 1.2). [*Note:* Depending on your system configuration, Windows Explorer might not display file name extensions. To display file name extensions (like .exe in Fig. 1.1), type *Alt + T* in Windows Explorer to open the **Tools** menu, then select **Folder options...**. In the **Folder Options** window, select the **View** tab, uncheck **Hide extensions for known file types** and click **OK**.]

Fig. 1.2 | Visual Basic **Advanced Painter** application.

Figure 1.2 labels several graphical elements—called **controls**. These include GroupBoxes, RadioButtons, a Panel and Buttons (these controls and many others are discussed in depth throughout the text). The application allows you to draw with a red, blue, green or black brush of small, medium or large size. You can also undo your previous operation or clear the drawing to start from scratch.

By using existing controls—which are objects—you can create powerful applications much faster than if you had to write all the code yourself.

The brush's properties, selected in the RadioButtons labeled **Black** and **Medium**, are *default settings*—the initial settings you see when you first run the application. You'll program default settings in your applications to provide visual cues for users to choose their own settings. Now you'll choose your own settings as a user of this application.

4. *Changing the brush color and size.* Click the RadioButtons labeled **Red** to change the color of the brush and **Small** to change the size of the brush. Position the mouse over the white Panel, then press and hold down the left mouse button to draw with the brush. Draw flower petals, as shown in Fig. 1.3. Then click the RadioButton labeled **Green** to change the color of the brush again.

Fig. 1.3 | Drawing with a new brush color.

5. *Changing the brush size.* Click the `RadioButton` labeled **Large** to change the size of the brush. Draw grass and a flower stem, as shown in Fig. 1.4.

Fig. 1.4 | Drawing with a new brush size.

6. *Finishing the drawing.* Click the **Blue** and **Medium** `RadioButtons`. Draw raindrops, as shown in Fig. 1.5, to complete the drawing.

Fig. 1.5 | Finishing the drawing.

7. *Closing the application.* Close your running application by clicking its **close box**, ▣ (Fig. 1.5).

1.14 Introduction to Object Technology

When object-oriented programming became widely used in the 1980s and 1990s, it dramatically improved the software development process.

What are objects, and why are they special? **Object technology** is a packaging scheme for creating meaningful software units. There are date objects, time objects, paycheck objects, invoice objects, automobile objects, people objects, audio objects, video objects, file objects, record objects and so on. On your computer screen, there are button objects, textbox objects, menu objects and many more. In fact, almost any *noun* can be reasonably represented as a software object. Objects have **attributes** (also called **properties**), such as color, size, weight and speed; and perform **actions** (also called **methods** or **behaviors**), such as moving, sleeping or drawing.

Classes are types of related objects. For example, all cars belong to the "car" class, even though individual cars vary in make, model, color and options packages. A class specifies the general format of its objects, and the attributes and actions available to an object depend on its class. An object is related to its class in much the same way as a building is related to its blueprint from which the building is constructed. Contractors can build many buildings from the same blueprint; programmers can instantiate (create) many objects from the same class.

With object technology, properly designed classes can be *reused* on future projects. Some organizations report that another key benefit they get from object-oriented programming is the production of software that's better organized and has fewer maintenance requirements than software produced with earlier technologies.

Object orientation allows you to focus on the "big picture." Instead of worrying about the minute details of how reusable objects are implemented, you can focus on the behaviors and interactions of objects. A road map that showed every tree, house and driveway would be difficult, if not impossible, to read. When such details are removed and only the essential information (roads) remains, the map becomes easier to understand. In the same way, an application that is divided into objects is easy to understand, modify and update because it hides much of the detail.

It's clear that object-oriented programming will be the key programming methodology for the next several decades. Visual Basic is one of the world's most widely used object-oriented languages.

Basic Object-Technology Concepts

Object-oriented design (OOD) models software in terms similar to those that people use to describe real-world objects. It takes advantage of class relationships, where objects of a certain class, such as a class of vehicles, have the same characteristics—cars, trucks, little red wagons and roller skates have much in common. OOD takes advantage of **inheritance** relationships, where new classes of objects are derived by absorbing characteristics of existing classes and adding unique characteristics of their own. An object of class "convertible" certainly has the characteristics of the more general class "automobile," but more specifically, the roof goes up and down.

Object-oriented design provides a natural and intuitive way to view the software design process—namely, modeling objects by their attributes, behaviors and interrelationships, just as we describe real-world objects. OOD also models communication between objects. Just as people send messages to one another (for example, a sergeant commands a soldier to stand at attention), objects also communicate via messages. A bank-account object may receive a message to decrease its balance by a certain amount because the customer is withdrawing that amount of money.

OOD **encapsulates** (that is, wraps) attributes and **operations** (behaviors) into objects—an object's attributes and operations are intimately tied together. Objects have the property of **information hiding**. This means that objects may know how to communicate with one another across well-defined **interfaces,** but normally they're not allowed to know how other objects are implemented—implementation details are hidden within the objects themselves. You can drive a car effectively, for example, without knowing the details of how engines, transmissions, brakes and exhaust systems work internally—as long as you know how to use the accelerator pedal, the brake pedal, the steering wheel and so on. Information hiding, as you'll see, is crucial to good software engineering.

Classes, Fields and Methods

As a Visual Basic programmer, you'll concentrate on creating your own classes. Each class contains data as well as the set of methods that manipulate that data and provide services to **clients** (that is, other classes that *use* the class). The data components of a class are called attributes or **fields**. For example, a bank account class might include an account number and a balance. The operation components of a class are called methods. For example, a bank-account class might include methods to make a deposit (increase the balance), make a withdrawal (decrease the balance) and inquire what the current balance is.

Classes are to objects as blueprints are to houses—a class is a "plan" for building objects of the class. Just as we can build many houses from one blueprint, we can instantiate (create) many objects from one class. You *cannot* cook meals in the kitchen of a blueprint, but you *can* cook meals in the kitchen of a house. Packaging software as classes makes it possible for future software systems to reuse the classes.

> **Software Engineering Observation 1.1**
>
> *Reuse of existing classes when building new classes and programs saves time, money and effort. Reuse also helps you build more reliable and effective systems, because existing classes and components often have gone through extensive testing, debugging and performance tuning.*

You won't build your own classes until Chapter 9, but you will be *using existing classes and making objects of those classes* throughout the entire book, including the early chapters.

With object technology, you can build much of the new software you'll need by *combining existing classes*, just as automobile manufacturers combine *standardized interchangeable parts*. Each class you create will have the potential to become a valuable *software asset* that you and other programmers can reuse to speed future software development efforts.

Introduction to Object-Oriented Analysis and Design (OOAD)

Soon you'll be writing programs in Visual Basic. How will you create the code for your programs? Perhaps, like many beginning programmers, you'll simply turn on your computer and start typing. This approach may work for small programs (like the ones we present in the early chapters of the book), but what if you were asked to create a software system to control thousands of automated teller machines for a major bank? Or what if you were asked to work on a team of thousands of software developers building the next generation of the U.S. air traffic control system? For projects so large and complex, you could not simply sit down and start writing programs.

To create the best solutions, you should follow a detailed process for determining your project's **requirements** (that is, *what* your system is supposed to do) and developing a **design** that satisfies them (that is, deciding *how* your system should do it). Ideally, you would go through this process and carefully review the design (and have your design reviewed by other software professionals) before writing any code. If this process involves analyzing and designing your system from an object-oriented point of view, it's called **object-oriented analysis and design** (**OOAD**). Experienced programmers know that proper analysis and design can help avoid an ill-planned system development approach that has to be abandoned partway through its implementation, possibly wasting considerable time, money and effort. Although many different OOAD processes exist, a single graphical language known as the **UML** (**Unified Modeling Language**) for communicating the results of *any* OOAD process has come into wide use. We introduce some simple UML diagrams in the early chapters and present a richer treatment in the optional ATM OOD case study.

1.15 Wrap-Up

This chapter introduced basic hardware and software concepts and basic object-technology concepts, including classes, objects, attributes and behaviors. We discussed the different types of programming languages and some widely used languages. We presented a brief history of Microsoft's Windows operating system, and the Internet and the web. We presented a brief history of Visual Basic programming and Microsoft's .NET initiative, which allows you to program Internet and web-based applications using Visual Basic (and other languages). You learned the steps for executing a Visual Basic application. You test-drove a sample Visual Basic application similar to the types of applications you'll learn to program in this book.

In the next chapter, you'll use the Visual Studio IDE (Integrated Development Environment) to create your first Visual Basic application, using the techniques of visual programming. You'll also become familiar with Visual Studio's help features.

1.16 Web Resources

The Internet and the web are extraordinary resources. This section includes links to interesting and informative websites.

www.deitel.com/books/vb2010htp/

Visit this site for code downloads, updates, corrections and additional resources for *Visual Basic 2010 How To Program*—such as links to our Resource Centers for Visual Basic and other related Visual Studio 2010 technologies. Our Resource Centers provide links to downloads, tutorials, documentation, books, e-books, journals, articles, blogs and more that will help you develop Visual Basic applications.

www.pearsonhighered.com/deitel

The Deitel & Associates page on the Prentice Hall website contains information about our publications and code downloads for this book.

Summary

Section 1.1 Introduction
- Computers process data, using sets of instructions called computer programs.
- A computer consists of various devices referred to as hardware.
- The programs that run on a computer are referred to as software.

Section 1.2 Computer Organization
- The input unit obtains information (data and computer programs) from input devices and places it at the disposal of the other units so that it can be processed.
- The output unit takes information that the computer has processed and places it on various output devices to make it available for use outside the computer.
- The memory unit temporarily retains information that has been entered through the input unit, making it immediately available for processing when needed. The memory unit also retains processed information until it can be placed on output devices by the output unit.
- The arithmetic and logic unit (ALU) performs calculations and makes decisions.
- The central processing unit (CPU) is the "administrative" section of the computer, which coordinates and supervises the operation of the other sections.
- Many of today's computers have multiple CPUs and, hence, can perform many operations simultaneously—such computers are called multiprocessors.
- A multi-core processor implements multiprocessing on a single integrated circuit chip.
- The secondary storage unit is the long-term, high-capacity "warehousing" section. Programs or data not actively being used by the other units normally are placed on secondary storage devices (for example, your hard drive) until they're needed again. Information on secondary storage devices is persistent.

Section 1.3 Personal Computing, Distributed Computing and Client/Server Computing
- Silicon chip technology made it possible for computers to be much smaller and more economical—individuals and small organizations could own these machines.
- In 1977, Apple Computer—creator of today's popular Macintosh personal computers and iPod digital music players—popularized personal computing.
- In 1981, IBM, the world's largest computer vendor, introduced the IBM Personal Computer, legitimizing personal computing in business, industry and government organizations.
- Personal computers could be linked together in computer networks, sometimes over telephone lines and sometimes in local area networks (LANs) within an organization. This led to the phenomenon of distributed computing, in which an organization's computing is distributed over networks to the geographically dispersed sites where the organization's work is performed.
- Information is shared easily across computer networks, where computers called file servers offer a common data store and various services that may be used by client computers distributed throughout the network, hence the term client/server computing.

Section 1.4 Hardware Trends
- Moore's Law states that the computing power of computers approximately doubles every year or two, without any increase in price. Similar growth has occurred in the communications field.

Section 1.5 Microsoft's Windows® Operating System

- In the mid-1980s, Microsoft developed the Windows operating system, a graphical user interface built on top of DOS (a personal computer operating system that users interacted with by typing commands).

- The Windows operating system became incredibly popular after the 1993 release of Windows 3.1, whose successors, Windows 95 and Windows 98, virtually cornered the desktop operating systems market by the late 1990s.

- Windows XP was released in 2001 and combined Microsoft's corporate and consumer operating system lines.

- Windows Vista, released in 2007, offered the attractive new Aero user interface, many powerful enhancements and new applications. A key focus of Windows Vista was enhanced security.

- Windows 7 is Microsoft's latest operating system. Some new features include enhancements to the Aero user interface, faster startup times, further refinement of Vista's security features, touch screen and multi-touch support, and much more.

Section 1.6 Machine Languages, Assembly Languages and High-Level Languages

- Computer languages can be divided into three general types—machine languages, assembly languages and high-level languages.

- A computer can directly understand only its own machine language, which is defined by the computer's hardware design.

- Machine languages generally consist of streams of numbers (ultimately reduced to 1s and 0s) that instruct computers how to perform their most elementary operations.

- The number system with only 1s and 0s is called the binary number system. Machine-language programs are sometimes called "binaries" for that reason.

- A particular machine language can be used on only one type of computer.

- Programmers began using English-like abbreviations (called mnemonics) to represent the computer's basic operations. These abbreviations formed the basis of assembly languages. Translator programs called assemblers convert assembly-language programs to machine language at computer speeds.

- High-level languages enable programmers to write instructions that look almost like everyday English and contain common mathematical notations. Translator programs called compilers convert high-level-language programs into machine language.

Section 1.7 Visual Basic

- BASIC's was developed to teach novices fundamental programming techniques.

- Visual Basic made programming Windows applications easier.

- With Microsoft's Visual Studio Integrated Development Environment (IDE), you can write, run, test and debug Visual Basic programs quickly and conveniently.

- Visual Basic is an object-oriented, event-driven language.

- Visual Studio's graphical user interface enables you to conveniently drag and drop predefined objects like buttons and textboxes into place on your screen, and label and resize them.

Section 1.8 Some Other Key Programming Languages

- The C programming language was developed in the early 1970s and gained widespread recognition as the development language of the UNIX operating system.

- C++ provides a number of features that "spruce up" the C language and provides capabilities for object-oriented programming (OOP).

- Objects are reusable software components that model items in the real world.
- A modular, object-oriented approach to design and implementation can make software development groups much more productive.
- Sun Microsystems developed Java, a C++-based language, which is used to develop large-scale enterprise applications, to enhance the functionality of web servers, to provide applications for consumer devices and for many other purposes.
- C#, created by Microsoft specifically for the .NET platform, has roots in C, C++ and Java.

Section 1.9 The Internet and the World Wide Web

- In the late 1960s, ARPA—the Advanced Research Projects Agency of the Department of Defense—rolled out plans to network the main computer systems of some ARPA-funded universities and research institutions. This became known as the ARPAnet, the grandparent of today's Internet.
- ARPAnet's main benefit proved to be the capability for quick and easy communication via what came to be known as electronic mail (e-mail).
- Bandwidth—the information-carrying capacity of communications lines—on the Internet has increased tremendously, while hardware costs have plummeted.
- The World Wide Web is a collection of hardware and software associated with the Internet that allows computer users to locate and view multimedia-based documents on almost any subject.
- HyperText Markup Language (HTML) is a technology for sharing information via "hyperlinked" text documents on the World Wide Web.
- The Internet and the web make information instantly and conveniently accessible to billions of people worldwide.

Section 1.10 Extensible Markup Language (XML)

- Data independence, the separation of content from its presentation, is the essential characteristic of XML.
- As applications become more web enabled, it is likely that XML will become the universal technology for data representation.

Section 1.11 Introduction to Microsoft .NET

- In 2000, Microsoft announced its .NET initiative, a broad new vision for using the Internet and the web in the development, engineering, distribution and use of software.
- You can create .NET applications in any .NET-compatible languag.
- ASP.NET technology allows you to create web applications.
- The .NET strategy extends the idea of software reuse to the Internet by allowing programmers to concentrate on their specialties without having to implement every component of every application.
- The .NET Framework executes applications, contains a class library (called the .NET Framework Class Library) and provides many other programming capabilities that you'll use to build Visual Basic applications.

Section 1.12 The .NET Framework and the Common Language Runtime

- The details of the .NET Framework are found in the Common Language Infrastructure (CLI), which contains information about the storage of data types, objects and so on.
- The Common Language Runtime (CLR) executes .NET programs.
- Programs are compiled into machine-specific instructions in two steps. First, the program is compiled into Microsoft Intermediate Language (MSIL), which defines instructions for the

CLR. When the application executes, a just-in-time (JIT) compiler in the CLR translates the MSIL in the executable file into machine-language code, then the machine-language code executes on that platform.

- If the .NET Framework exists (and is installed) for a platform, that platform can run any .NET program. The ability of a program to run (without modification) across multiple platforms is known as platform independence.

Section 1.13 Test-Driving the Visual Basic *Advanced Painter* Application

- You can use existing controls—which are objects—to get powerful applications running in Visual Basic much faster than if you had to write all of the code yourself.

- The default settings for controls are the initial settings you see when you first run the application. Programmers include default settings to provide reasonable choices that the application will use if the user chooses not to change the settings.

Section 1.14 Introduction to Object Technology

- Object technology is a packaging scheme for creating meaningful software units.

- Objects have attributes (also called properties) and perform actions (also called methods or behaviors).

- Classes are types of related objects. A class specifies the general format of its objects, and the attributes and actions available to an object depend on its class.

- Programmers can instantiate (create) many objects from the same class.

- Properly designed classes can be reused on future projects.

- An application that is divided into objects is easy to understand, modify and update because it hides much of the detail.

- Visual Basic is one of the world's most widely used object-oriented languages.

- Object-oriented design (OOD) models software in terms similar to those that people use to describe real-world objects. It takes advantage of class relationships, where objects of a certain class have the same characteristics.

- OOD takes advantage of inheritance relationships, where new classes of objects are derived by absorbing characteristics of existing classes and adding unique characteristics of their own.

- Object-oriented design provides a natural and intuitive way to view the software design process—namely, modeling objects by their attributes, behaviors and interrelationships, just as we describe real-world objects.

- OOD also models communication between objects.

- Objects have the property of information hiding—objects may know how to communicate with one another across well-defined interfaces, but normally they're not allowed to know how other objects are implemented.

- Languages like Visual Basic are object oriented. Programming in such a language is called object-oriented programming (OOP), and it allows you to conveniently implement an object-oriented design as a working software system.

- Visual Basic classes contain methods that implement operations, and data that implements attributes.

- The data components of a class are called attributes or fields.

- The operation components of a class are called methods.

- With object technology, you can build much of the new software you'll need by combining existing classes.

Terminology

actions (verbs) 13
arithmetic and logic unit (ALU) 3
ARPAnet 8
ASP.NET 9
assembler 6
assembly language 6
attribute 13
bandwidth 8
BASIC (Beginner's All-purpose Symbolic Instruction Code) 6
behavior 13
button 9
C programming language 7
C# programming language 7
C++ programming language 7
central processing unit (CPU) 3
class 13
class library 7
client computer 4
client of a class 14
client/server computing 4
close box 13
Common Language Infrastructure (CLI) 9
Common Language Runtime (CLR) 9
compiler 6
component 7
computer program 2
computer programmer 2
controls 11
data 2
data independence 8
design 15
distributed computing 4
dynamic content 7
encapsulate 14
event 6
event driven 6
extensibility 8
field 14
graphical user interface (GUI) 6
hardware 2
high-level language 6
HyperText Markup Language(HTML) 8
HyperText Transfer Protocol (HTTP) 8
information hiding 14
inheritance 13
input device 3
input unit 3
Integrated Development Environment (IDE) 6

interface 14
Internet 8
just-in-time (JIT) compiler 9
language independent 10
language interoperability 10
local area network (LAN) 4
machine language 5
memory 3
memory unit 3
method 13
Microsoft Intermediate Language (MSIL) 9
Moore's Law 4
multi-core processor 3
multiprocessor 3s
.NET Framework 9
.NET Framework Class Library 9
.NET Initiative 9
object (or instance) 7
object-oriented analysis and design (OOAD) 15
object-oriented design (OOD) 13
object-oriented programming (OOP) 2
object technology 13
operation 14
output device 3
output unit 3
personal computer 4
platform independence 9
porting 10
primary memory 3
programmer 2
property of a class 13
requirements 15
scrollbars 9
server 4
software 2
software reuse 9
supercomputer 2
textbox 9
translator program 6
Unified Modeling Language (UML) 15
Visual Basic 6
Visual Studio 2010 6
volatile information 3
Windows operating system 5
World Wide Web (WWW) 8
World Wide Web Consortium (W3C) 8
XML (Extensible Markup Language) vocabulary 9

Self-Review Exercises

1.1   Fill in the blanks in each of the following statements:
  a) Computers can directly understand only their native _____ language, which is composed only of 1s and 0s.
  b) Computers process data under the control of sets of instructions called computer _____.
  c) The three types of computer programming languages discussed in the chapter are machine languages, _____ and _____.
  d) Programs that translate high-level-language programs into machine language are called _____.
  e) Visual Studio is a(n) _____ in which Visual Basic programs are developed.
  f) Visual Basic is a(n) _____, event-driven language.
  g) _____ is a programming language that was created by Microsoft specifically for the .NET platform.
  h) _____ is a language for sharing information via "hyperlinked" text documents on the World Wide Web.
  i) The _____ executes .NET programs.
  j) Objects have _____ (also called properties) and perform actions (also called methods or _____).
  k) _____ models software in terms similar to those that people use to describe real-world objects.
  l) With _____, you can build much of the new software you'll need by combining existing classes.

1.2   State whether each of the following is *true* or *false*. If *false*, explain why.
  a) The UML is used primarily to implement object-oriented systems.
  b) Visual Basic is an object-oriented language.
  c) Visual Basic is the only language available for programming .NET applications.
  d) Computers can directly understand high-level languages.
  e) MSIL is the common intermediate format to which all .NET programs compile, regardless of their original .NET language.
  f) The .NET Framework is portable to non-Windows platforms.

Answers to Self-Review Exercises

1.1   a) machine. b) programs. c) assembly languages, high-level languages. d) compilers. e) IDE. f) object-oriented. g) C#. h) HyperText Markup Language (HTML). i) Common Language Runtime (CLR). j) attributes, behaviors. k) Object-oriented design (OOD). l) object technology.

1.2   a) False. The UML is used primarily to design object-oriented systems. b) True. c) False. Visual Basic is one of many .NET languages (others are C# and Visual C++). d) False. Computers can directly understand only their own machine languages. e) True. f) True.

Exercises

1.3   Categorize each of the following items as either hardware or software:
  a) CPU
  b) Compiler
  c) Input unit
  d) A word-processor program
  e) A Visual Basic program

1.4   Translator programs, such as assemblers and compilers, convert programs from one language (referred to as the source language) to another language (referred to as the target language). Determine which of the following statements are *true* and which are *false*:

    a) An assembler translates source-language programs into machine-language programs.

    b) High-level languages are generally machine dependent.

    c) A machine-language program requires translation before it can be run on a computer.

    d) The Visual Basic compiler translates high-level-language programs into SMIL.

1.5   Expand each of the following acronyms:

    a) W3C

    b) XML

    c) OOP

    d) CLR

    e) CLI

    f) MSIL

    g) UML

    h) IDE

1.6   What are the key benefits of the .NET Framework and the CLR? What are the drawbacks?

1.7   What are the advantages to using object-oriented techniques?

1.8   You are probably wearing on your wrist one of the world's most common types of objects—a watch. Discuss how each of the following terms and concepts applies to the notion of a watch: object, attributes and behaviors.

1.9   What was the key reason that Visual Basic was developed as a special version of the BASIC programming language?

1.10   What is the key accomplishment of the UML?

1.11   What did the chief benefit of the early Internet prove to be?

1.12   What is the key capability of the web?

1.13   What is the key vision of Microsoft's .NET initiative?

1.14   How does the .NET Framework Class Library facilitate the development of .NET applications?

1.15   What is the key advantage of standardizing .NET's CLI (Common Language Infrastructure)?

1.16   Besides the obvious benefits of reuse made possible by OOP, what do many organizations report as another key benefit of OOP?

1.17   Why is XML so crucial to the development of future software systems?

Making a Difference Exercises

1.18   *(Test Drive: Carbon Footprint Calculator)* Some scientists believe that carbon emissions, especially from the burning of fossil fuels, contribute significantly to global warming and that this can be combatted if individuals take steps to limit their use of carbon-based fuels. Organizations and individuals are increasingly concerned about their "carbon footprints." Websites such as TerraPass

    www.terrapass.com/carbon-footprint-calculator/

and Carbon Footprint

    www.carbonfootprint.com/calculator.aspx

provide carbon footprint calculators. Test drive these calculators to determine your carbon footprint. Exercises in later chapters will ask you to program your own carbon footprint calculator. To prepare for this, use the web to research the formulas for calculating carbon footprints.

1.19   *(Test Drive: Body Mass Index Calculator)* By recent estimates, two-thirds of the people in the United States are overweight and about half of those are obese. This causes significant increases in illnesses such as diabetes and heart disease. To determine whether a person is overweight or obese, you can use a measure called the body mass index (BMI). The United States Department of Health and Human Services provides a BMI calculator at `www.nhlbisupport.com/bmi/`. Use it to calculate your own BMI. An exercise in Chapter 3 will ask you to program your own BMI calculator. To prepare for this, use the web to research the formulas for calculating BMI.

1.20   *(Attributes of Hybrid Vehicles)* In this chapter you learned some basics of classes. Now you'll "flesh out" aspects of a class called "Hybrid Vehicle." Hybrid vehicles are becoming increasingly popular, because they often get much better mileage than purely gasoline-powered vehicles. Browse the web and study the features of four or five of today's popular hybrid cars, then list as many of their hybrid-related attributes as you can. Some common attributes include city-miles-per-gallon and highway-miles-per-gallon. Also list the attributes of the batteries (type, weight, etc.).

1.21   *(Gender Neutrality)* Many people want to eliminate sexism in all forms of communication. You've been asked to create a program that can process a paragraph of text and replace gender-specific words with gender-neutral ones. Assuming that you've been given a list of gender-specific words and their gender-neutral replacements (e.g., replace "wife" with "spouse," "man" with "person," "daughter" with "child" and so on), explain the procedure you'd use to read through a paragraph of text and manually perform these replacements. How might your procedure generate a strange term like "woperchild?" In Chapter 4, you'll learn that a more formal term for "procedure" is "algorithm," and that an algorithm specifies the steps to be performed and the order in which to perform them.

2

Dive Into® Visual Basic 2010 Express

Seeing is believing.
—Proverb

Form ever follows function.
—Louis Henri Sullivan

Intelligence ... is the faculty of making artificial objects, especially tools to make tools.
—Henri-Louis Bergson

Objectives

In this chapter you'll learn:

- The basics of the Visual Studio Integrated Development Environment (IDE) that assists you in writing, running and debugging your Visual Basic programs.

- Visual Studio's help features.

- Key commands contained in the IDE's menus and toolbars.

- The purpose of the various kinds of windows in the Visual Studio 2010 IDE.

- What visual programming is and how it simplifies and speeds program development.

- To create, compile and execute a simple Visual Basic program that displays text and an image using the Visual Studio IDE and the technique of visual programming.

2.1 Introduction

Visual Studio 2010 is Microsoft's Integrated Development Environment (IDE) for creating, running and debugging programs (also called **applications**) written in various .NET programming languages. This chapter provides an overview of the Visual Studio 2010 IDE and shows how to create a simple Visual Basic program by dragging and dropping predefined building blocks into place—a technique known as visual **programming**.

2.2 Overview of the Visual Studio 2010 IDE

There are many versions of Visual Studio available. This book's examples are based on the Microsoft Visual Basic 2010 Express Edition, which supports only the Visual Basic programming language. See the Before You Begin section that follows the Preface for information on installing the software. Microsoft also offers a full version of Visual Studio 2010, which includes support for other languages in addition to Visual Basic, such as Visual C# and Visual C++. Our screen captures and discussions focus on the IDE of the Visual Basic 2010 Express Edition. The examples will work on most other current versions of Visual Basic. We assume that you have some familiarity with Windows.

Introduction to Microsoft Visual Basic 2010 Express Edition
We use the > character to indicate the selection of a menu item from a menu. For example, we use the notation **File > Open File...** to indicate that you should select the **Open File...** menu item from the **File** menu.

To start Microsoft Visual Basic 2010 Express Edition, select **Start > All Programs > Microsoft Visual Basic 2010 Express**. Once the Express Edition begins execution, the **Start Page** displays (Fig. 2.1) Depending on your version of Visual Studio, your **Start Page** may look different. The **Start Page** contains a list of links to Visual Studio 2010 IDE resources and web-based resources. From this point forward, we'll refer to the Visual Studio 2010 IDE simply as "Visual Studio" or "the IDE." At any time, you can return to the **Start Page** by selecting **View > Start Page**.

Links on the Start Page
The **Start Page** links are organized into sections—**Recent Projects, Get Started** and **Latest News**—that contain links to helpful programming resources. Clicking any link on the **Start Page** displays relevant information associated with the specific link. [*Note:* An Inter-

net connection is required for the IDE to access some of this information.] We refer to single clicking with the left mouse button as selecting or clicking. We refer to double clicking with the left mouse button simply as double clicking.

New Project button   Start Page tab   Latest News tab   Solution Explorer (no projects open)

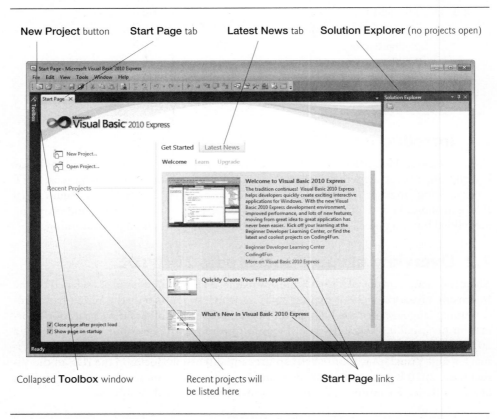

Collapsed **Toolbox** window   Recent projects will   **Start Page** links
                                       be listed here

Fig. 2.1 | **Start Page** in Visual Basic 2010 Express Edition.

The **Recent Projects** section contains information on projects you've recently created or modified. You can also open existing projects or create new ones by clicking the links above this section. The **Get Started** section focuses on using the IDE for creating programs and learning Visual Basic.

The **Latest News** tab provides links to the latest Visual Basic developments (such as updates and bug fixes) and to information on advanced programming topics. To access more extensive information on Visual Studio, you can browse the **MSDN** (**Microsoft Developer Network**) library at msdn.microsoft.com/en-us/library/default.aspx. The MSDN site contains articles, downloads and tutorials on technologies of interest to Visual Studio developers. You can also browse the web from the IDE by selecting **View > Other Windows > Web Browser** or by typing *<Ctrl> <Alt> R*. To request a web page, type its URL into the location bar (Fig. 2.2) and press the *Enter* key—your computer, of course, must be connected to the Internet. The web page that you wish to view appears as another tab in the IDE (Fig. 2.2).

Web browser window tab   Location bar

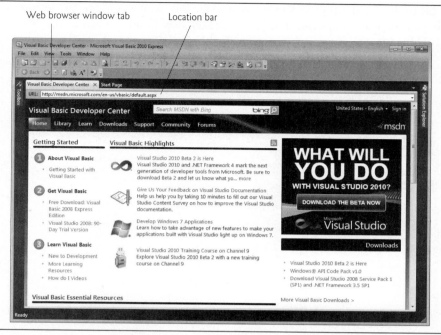

Fig. 2.2 | Displaying a web page in Visual Studio.

Customizing the IDE and Creating a New Project

To begin programming in Visual Basic, you must create a new project or open an existing one. Select either **File > New Project...** to create a new project or **File > Open Project...** to open an existing project. From the **Start Page**, above the **Recent Projects** section, you can also click the links **New Project...** or **Open Project....** A **project** is a group of related files, such as the Visual Basic code and any images that might make up a program. Visual Studio 2010 organizes programs into projects and **solutions**, which contain one or more projects. Multiple-project solutions are used to create large-scale programs. Each program we create in this book consists of a single project.

When you select **File > New Project...** or click the **New Project...** link on the **Start Page**, the **New Project** dialog (Fig. 2.3) displays. **Dialogs** are windows that facilitate user–computer communication.

Visual Studio provides several templates (Fig. 2.3). **Templates** are the project types users can create in Visual Basic—Windows Forms applications, console applications, WPF applications and others. In this chapter, we build a **Windows Forms Application**. A **Windows Forms application** is a program that executes within a Windows operating system (such as Windows 7 or Windows Vista) and typically has a **graphical user interface** (**GUI**)—the visual part of the program with which the user interacts. Windows applications include Microsoft software products like Microsoft Word, Internet Explorer and Visual Studio; software products created by other vendors; and customized software that you and other programmers create. You'll create many Windows applications in this text.

By default, Visual Studio assigns the name **WindowsApplication1** to a new **Windows Forms Application** project and solution (Fig. 2.3). Select **Windows Forms Application**, then click **OK** to display the IDE in **Design view** (Fig. 2.4), which contains the features that enable you to create programs. The IDE's Design view is also known as the **Windows Forms Designer**.

Visual Basic **Windows Forms Application** (selected)

Default project name (provided by Visual Studio)

Description of selected project (provided by Visual Studio)

Fig. 2.3 | New Project dialog.

Menu in the menu bar

Active tab

Solution Explorer window

Form (Windows Forms application)

Properties window

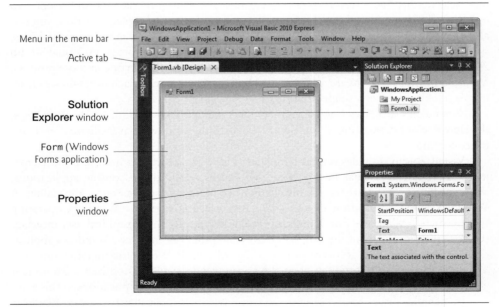

Fig. 2.4 | Design view of the IDE.

The rectangle in the **Design** area titled **Form1** (called a **Form**) represents the main window of the Windows Forms application that you're creating. Visual Basic applications can have multiple Forms (windows)—however, most applications you'll create in this text will use only one Form. You'll learn how to customize the Form by adding GUI **controls**— in this example, you'll add a **Label** and a **PictureBox** (as you'll see in Fig. 2.25). A **Label** typically contains descriptive text (for example, "Welcome to Visual Basic!"), and a **PictureBox** displays an image, such as the Deitel bug mascot. Visual Basic Express has many preexisting controls and other components you can use to build and customize your programs. Many of these controls are discussed and used throughout the book. Other controls are available from third parties.

In this chapter, you'll work with preexisting controls from the .NET Framework Class Library. As you place controls on the Form, you'll be able to modify their properties (discussed in Section 2.4). For example, Fig. 2.5 shows where the Form's title can be modified and Fig. 2.6 shows a dialog in which a control's font properties can be modified.

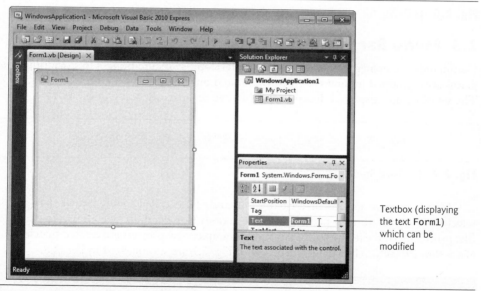

Fig. 2.5 | Textbox control for modifying a property in the Visual Studio IDE.

Collectively, the Form and controls make up the program's GUI. Users enter data (**inputs**) into the program by typing at the keyboard, by clicking the mouse buttons and in a variety of other ways. Programs use the GUI to display instructions and other information (**outputs**) for users to view. For example, the **New Project** dialog in Fig. 2.3 presents a GUI where the user clicks the mouse button to select a template type, then inputs a project name from the keyboard (the figure is still showing the default project name **WindowsApplication1** supplied by Visual Studio).

Each open document's name is listed on a tab. To view a document when multiple documents are open, click its tab. Tabs facilitate easy access to multiple open documents. The **active tab** (the tab of the currently displayed document) is highlighted in yellow (for example, **Form1.vb [Design]** in Fig. 2.4).

Fig. 2.6 | Dialog for modifying a control's font properties.

2.3 Menu Bar and Toolbar

Commands for managing the IDE and for developing, maintaining and executing programs are contained in **menus**, which are located on the **menu bar** of the IDE (Fig. 2.7). The set of menus displayed depends on what you're currently doing in the IDE.

File	Edit	View	Project	Debug	Data	Format	Tools	Window	Help

Fig. 2.7 | Visual Studio menu bar.

Menus contain groups of related commands (also called **menu items**) that, when selected, cause the IDE to perform specific actions (for example, open a window, save a file, print a file and execute a program). For example, new projects are created by selecting **File > New Project...**. The menus depicted in Fig. 2.7 are summarized in Fig. 2.8.

Menu	Description
File	Contains commands for opening, closing, adding and saving projects, as well as printing project data and exiting Visual Studio.
Edit	Contains commands for editing programs, such as cut, copy, paste, undo, redo, delete, find and select.
View	Contains commands for displaying IDE windows (for example, **Solution Explorer, Toolbox, Properties** window) and for adding toolbars to the IDE.
Project	Contains commands for managing projects and their files.
Debug	Contains commands for compiling, debugging (that is, identifying and correcting problems in programs) and running programs.

Fig. 2.8 | Summary of Visual Studio 2010 IDE menus. (Part 1 of 2.)

Menu	Description
Data	Contains commands for interacting with databases (that is, organized collections of data stored on computers), which we discuss in Chapter 12, Databases and LINQ.
Format	Contains commands for arranging and modifying a Form's controls. The **Format** menu appears only when a GUI component is selected in **Design** view.
Tools	Contains commands for accessing additional IDE tools and options for customizing the IDE.
Window	Contains commands for hiding, opening, closing and displaying IDE windows.
Help	Contains commands for accessing the IDE's help features.

Fig. 2.8 | Summary of Visual Studio 2010 IDE menus. (Part 2 of 2.)

You can access many of the more common menu commands from the **toolbar** (Fig. 2.9), which contains graphics, called **icons**, that graphically represent commands. By default, the standard toolbar is displayed when you run Visual Studio for the first time—it contains icons for the most commonly used commands, such as opening a file, adding an item to a project, saving files and running applications (Fig. 2.9). The icons that appear on the standard toolbar may vary, depending on the version of Visual Studio you're using. Some commands are initially disabled (grayed out or unavailable to use). These commands are enabled by Visual Studio only when they're necessary. For example, Visual Studio enables the command for saving a file once you begin editing a file.

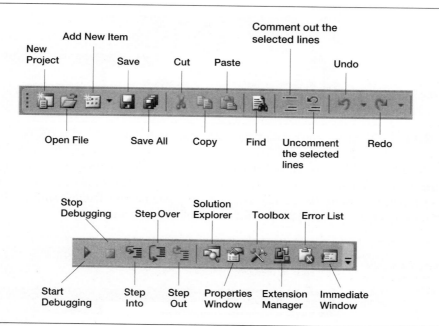

Fig. 2.9 | Standard Visual Studio toolbar.

You can customize the IDE's toolbars. Select **View > Toolbars** (Fig. 2.10). Each toolbar you select is displayed with the other toolbars at the top of the Visual Studio window. To execute a command via the toolbar, click its icon. Some icons contain a down arrow that you can click to display related commands, as shown in Fig. 2.11.

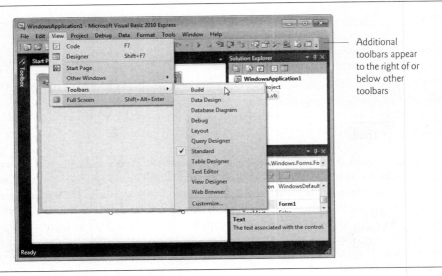

Fig. 2.10 | Adding the **Build** toolbar to the IDE.

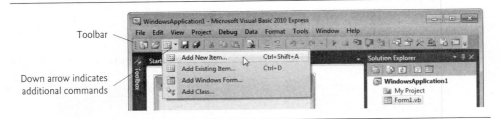

Fig. 2.11 | IDE toolbar icon showing additional commands.

It can be difficult to remember what each toolbar icon represents. Hovering the mouse pointer over an icon highlights it and, after a brief pause, displays a description of the icon called a tool tip (Fig. 2.12). **Tool tips** help you become familiar with the IDE's features and serve as useful reminders for each toolbar icon's functionality.

Fig. 2.12 | Tool tip demonstration.

2.4 Navigating the Visual Studio IDE

The IDE provides windows for accessing project files and customizing controls. This section introduces several windows that you'll use frequently when developing Visual Basic programs. These windows can be accessed via the toolbar icons (Fig. 2.13) or by selecting the desired window's name in the **View** menu.

Fig. 2.13 | Toolbar icons for four Visual Studio windows.

Visual Studio provides a space-saving feature called **auto-hide**. When auto-hide is enabled, a tab appears along either the left, right or bottom edge of the IDE window (Fig. 2.14). This tab contains one or more icons, each of which identifies a hidden window. Placing the mouse pointer over one of these icons displays that window (Fig. 2.15). Moving the mouse pointer outside the window's area hides the window. To "pin down" a window (that is, to disable auto-hide and keep the window open), click the pin icon. When auto-hide is enabled, the pin icon is horizontal (Fig. 2.15)—when a window is "pinned down," the pin icon is vertical (Fig. 2.16).

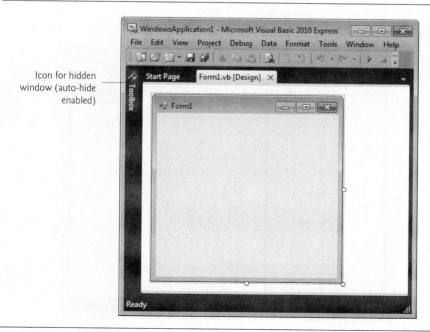

Fig. 2.14 | Auto-hide feature demonstration.

Horizontal orientation for pin icon
when auto-hide is enabled

Toolbox
title bar

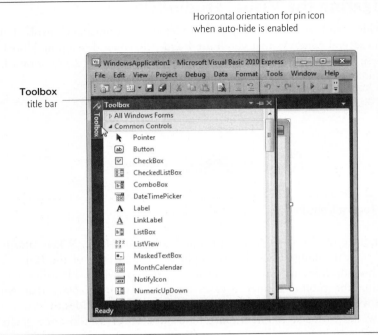

Fig. 2.15 | Displaying a hidden window when auto-hide is enabled.

Toolbox
"pinned down"

Vertical orientation for pin icon
when window is "pinned down"

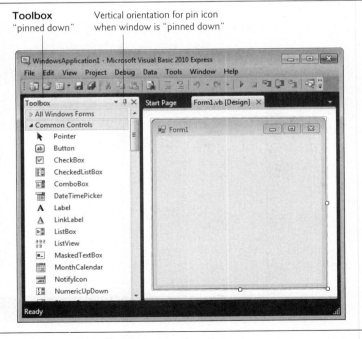

Fig. 2.16 | Disabling auto-hide ("pinning down" a window).

The next few sections cover three of Visual Studio's main windows—the **Solution Explorer**, the **Properties** window and the **Toolbox**. These windows display project information and include tools that help you build your programs.

2.4.1 Solution Explorer

The **Solution Explorer** window (Fig. 2.17) provides access to all of a solution's files. If it's not shown in the IDE, click the **Solution Explorer** icon in the IDE (Fig. 2.13), select **View > Other Windows > Solution Explorer** or type *<Ctrl> <Alt> L*. When you open a new or existing solution, the **Solution Explorer** displays the solution's contents.

Fig. 2.17 | Solution Explorer window with an open project.

The solution's **startup project** is the one that runs when you select **Debug > Start Debugging** (or press the *F5* key). For a single-project solution like the examples in this book, the startup project is the only project (in this case, **WindowsApplication1**) and the project name appears in bold text in the **Solution Explorer** window. When you create an application for the first time, the **Solution Explorer** window lists only the project's My Project and Form1.vb files (Fig. 2.17). The Visual Basic file that corresponds to the Form shown in Fig. 2.4 is named Form1.vb (selected in Fig. 2.17). Visual Basic files use the .vb file-name extension, which is short for "Visual Basic."

By default, the IDE displays only files that you may need to edit—other files that the IDE generates are hidden. The **Solution Explorer** window includes a toolbar that contains several icons. Clicking the **Show All Files** icon (Fig. 2.17) displays all the solution's files, including those generated by the IDE (Fig. 2.18). Clicking the arrows to the left of a file

Fig. 2.18 | Solution Explorer with the **References** node expanded.

or folder expands or collapses the project tree's nodes. Try clicking the arrow to the left of **References** to display items grouped under that heading (Fig. 2.18). Click the arrow again to collapse the tree. Other Visual Studio windows also use this convention.

2.4.2 Toolbox

The **Toolbox** (**View > Other Windows > Toolbox**) contains icons representing controls used to customize Forms (Fig. 2.19). With visual programming, you can "drag and drop" controls onto the Form and the IDE will write the code that creates the controls for you. This is faster and simpler than writing this code yourself. Just as you do not need to know how to build an engine to drive a car, you do not need to know how to build controls to use them. Reusing preexisting controls saves time and money when you develop programs. You'll use the **Toolbox** when you create your first program later in the chapter.

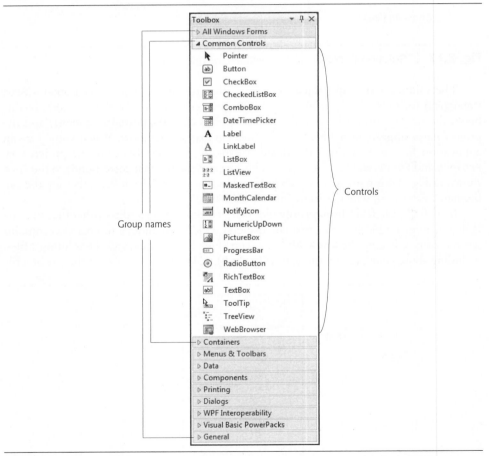

Fig. 2.19 | **Toolbox** window displaying controls for the **Common Controls** group.

The **Toolbox** groups the prebuilt controls into categories—**All Windows Forms, Common Controls, Containers, Menus & Toolbars, Data, Components, Printing, Dialogs,**

WPF Interoperability, **Visual Basic PowerPacks** and **General** are listed in Fig. 2.19. Again, note the use of arrows, which can expand or collapse a group of controls. We discuss many of the **Toolbox**'s controls and their functionality throughout the book.

2.4.3 Properties Window

To display the **Properties** window, select **View > Other Windows > Properties Window**, click the **Properties** window toolbar icon shown in Fig. 2.13, or press the *F4* key. The **Properties window** displays the properties for the currently selected Form (Fig. 2.20), control or file in **Design** view. **Properties** specify information about the Form or control, such as its size, color and position. Each Form or control has its own set of properties—a property's description is displayed at the bottom of the **Properties** window whenever that property is selected.

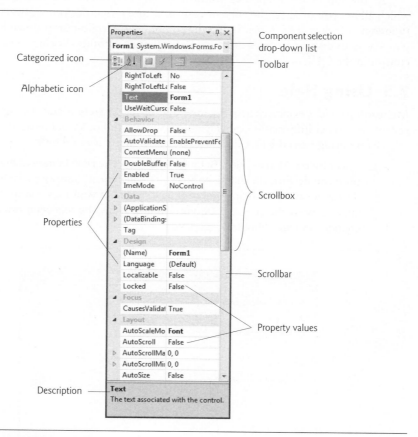

Fig. 2.20 | **Properties** window.

Figure 2.20 shows Form1's **Properties** window. The left column lists the Form's properties—the right column displays the current value of each property. You can sort the properties either alphabetically (by clicking the **Alphabetical** icon) or categorically (by clicking the **Categorized** icon). The properties can be sorted alphabetically from A–Z or

Z–A—sorting by category groups the properties according to their use (that is, **Appearance**, **Behavior**, **Design**, etc.). Depending on the size of the **Properties** window, some of the properties may be hidden from view on the screen. Users can scroll through the list of properties by **dragging** the **scrollbox** up or down inside the **scrollbar**, or by clicking the arrows at the top and bottom of the scrollbar. We show how to set individual properties later in this chapter.

The **Properties** window is crucial to visual programming—it allows you to modify a control's properties visually, without writing code. You can see which properties are available for modification and, in many cases, can learn the range of acceptable values for a given property. The **Properties** window displays a brief description of the selected property, helping you understand its purpose. A property can be set quickly using this window, and no code needs to be written.

At the top of the **Properties** window is the **component selection drop-down list**, which allows you to select the **Form** or control whose properties you wish to display in the **Properties** window (Fig. 2.20). Using the component selection drop-down list is an alternative way to display a **Form**'s or control's properties without clicking the actual **Form** or control in the GUI.

2.5 Using Help

Microsoft provides extensive help documentation via the **Help menu**. Using **Help** is an excellent way to get information quickly about Visual Studio, Visual Basic and more.

Before using **Help** the first time, you must configure it as follows:

1. Select **Help > Manage Help Settings** to display the **Help Library Manager**. The first time you do this, the dialog in Fig. 2.21 will appear. Simply click **OK** to select the default location for help content that is stored on your local computer. If a dialog appears with the message **Do you want to allow the following program to make changes to this computer?**, click **Yes**.

Fig. 2.21 | **Help Library Manager** window the first time you select **Help > Manage Help Settings**.

2. In the **Help Library Manager** window, click **Choose online or local help** (Fig. 2.22). Accessing online help requires an Internet connection, but gives you access to the most up-to-date documentation, as well as tutorials, downloads, support, forums and more. Accessing local help requires that you first download the help files, which can take considerable time and use a significant amount of disk space. If possible, we recommend that you use the online help.

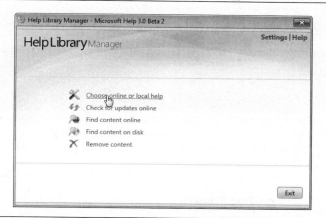

Fig. 2.22 | Preparing to select online or local help.

3. Select **I want to use online help**, then click **OK**. Next, click **Exit** in the **Help Library Manager** window. Your IDE is now configured to use online help.

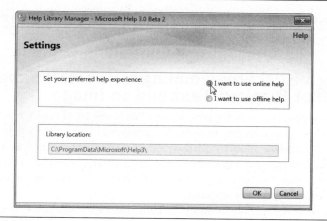

Fig. 2.23 | Selecting online help.

Context-Sensitive Help
Visual Studio provides **context-sensitive help** pertaining to the "current content" (that is, the items around the location of the mouse cursor). To use context-sensitive help, click an item, such as the Form, then press the *F1* key. The help documentation is displayed in a

web browser window. To return to the IDE, either close the browser window or select the icon for the IDE in your Windows task bar. Figure 2.24 shows the help page for a Form's Text property. You can view this help by selecting the Form, clicking its Text property in the **Properties** window and pressing the *F1* key.

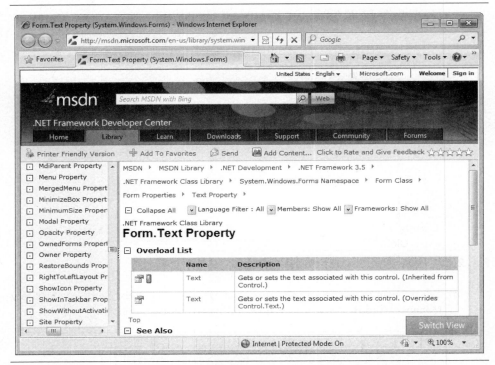

Fig. 2.24 | Using context-sensitive help.

2.6 Using Visual Programming to Create a Simple Program that Displays Text and an Image

Next, we create a program that displays the text "Welcome to Visual Basic!" and an image of the Deitel & Associates bug mascot. The program consists of a single Form that uses a Label and a PictureBox. Figure 2.25 shows the result of the program as it executes. The program and the bug image are available with this chapter's examples. You can download the examples from www.deitel.com/books/vb2010htp/. We assume the examples are located at C:\examples on your computer.

You won't write a single line of program code. Instead, you'll use visual programming techniques. Visual Studio processes your actions (such as mouse clicking, dragging and dropping) to generate program code. Chapter 3 begins our discussion of writing program code. Throughout the book, you produce increasingly substantial and powerful programs that usually include a combination of code written by you and code generated by Visual Studio. The generated code can be difficult for novices to understand—but you'll rarely need to look at it.

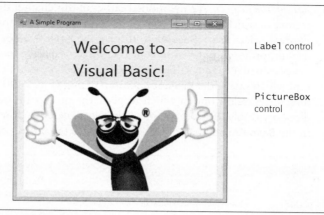

Fig. 2.25 | Simple program executing.

Visual programming is useful for building GUI-intensive programs that require a significant amount of user interaction. To create, save, run and terminate this first program, perform the following steps:

1. *Closing the open project.* If a project is already open, close it by selecting **File > Close Project**. A dialog asking whether to save the current project might appear. Click **Save** to save your changes or **Discard** to ignore them.

2. *Creating the new project.* To create a new Windows Forms application for the program, select **File > New Project...** to display the **New Project** dialog (Fig. 2.26). Select **Windows Forms Application**. Name the project **ASimpleProgram** and click **OK**.

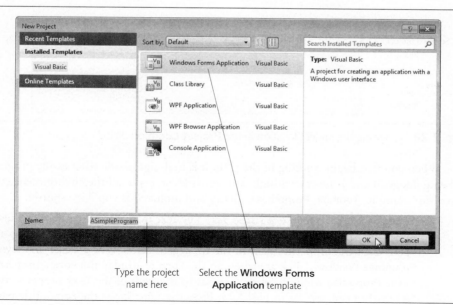

Fig. 2.26 | New Project dialog.

3. *Saving the project.* We mentioned earlier in this chapter that you must set the directory in which the project is saved. To specify the directory in Visual Basic 2010 Express, select **File > Save All** to display the **Save Project** dialog (Fig. 2.27). By default, projects are saved to your user directory in the folder `Documents\Visual Studio 2010\Projects`. To change the project location, click the **Browse...** button, which opens the **Project Location** dialog (Fig. 2.28). Navigate through the directories, select one in which to place the project (in our example, we use the directory **C:\MyVBProjects**) and click **Select Folder** to close the dialog. Click **Save** in the **Save Project** dialog (Fig. 2.27) to save the project and close the dialog.

Fig. 2.27 | **Save Project** dialog.

Selected project location

Click to set project location

Fig. 2.28 | Setting the project location in the **Project Location** dialog.

When you first begin working in the IDE, it is in **design mode** (that is, the program is being designed and is not executing). This provides access to all the environment windows (for example, **Toolbox**, **Properties**), menus and toolbars, as you'll see shortly.

4. *Setting the text in the Form's title bar.* The text in the Form's title bar is determined by the Form's **Text property** (Fig. 2.29). If the **Properties** window is not open, click the properties icon in the toolbar or select **View > Other Windows > Properties Window**. Click anywhere in the Form to display the Form's properties in the **Properties** window. In the textbox to the right of the Text property, type "A Simple Program", as in Fig. 2.29. Press the *Enter* key—the Form's title bar is updated immediately (Fig. 2.30).

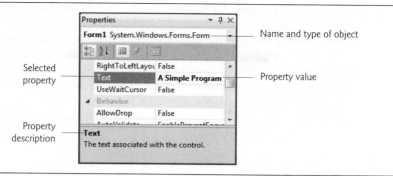

Fig. 2.29 | Setting the Form's Text property in the **Properties** window.

Fig. 2.30 | Form with enabled sizing handles.

5. *Resizing the Form.* Click and drag one of the Form's enabled **sizing handles** (the small white squares that appear around the Form, as shown in Fig. 2.30). Using the mouse, select the bottom-right sizing handle and drag it down and to the right to make the Form larger (Fig. 2.31).

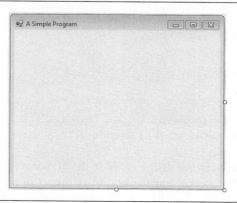

Fig. 2.31 | Resized Form.

6. *Changing the* ***Form's*** *background color.* The **BackColor** property specifies a Form's or control's background color. Clicking BackColor in the **Properties** window causes a down-arrow button to appear next to the value of the property (Fig. 2.32). When clicked, the down-arrow button displays other options, which vary depending on the property. In this case, the arrow displays tabs for **Custom**, **Web** and **System** (the default). Click the **Custom tab** to display the **palette** (a grid of colors). Select the box that represents light blue. Once you select the color, the palette closes and the Form's background color changes to light blue (Fig. 2.33).

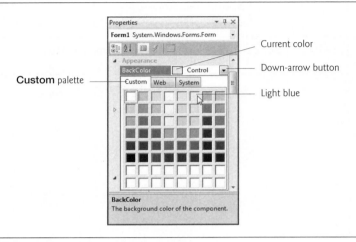

Fig. 2.32 | Changing the Form's BackColor property.

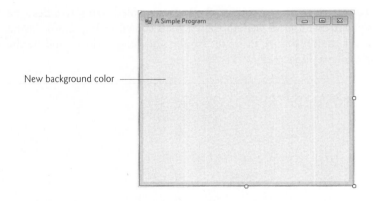

Fig. 2.33 | Form with new BackColor property applied.

7. *Adding a* ***Label*** *control to the* ***Form.*** If the **Toolbox** is not already open, select **View > Other Windows > Toolbox** to display the set of controls you'll use for creating your programs. For the type of program we're creating in this chapter, the typical controls we use are located in either the **All Windows Forms** group of the

Toolbox or the **Common Controls** group. If either group name is collapsed, expand it by clicking the arrow to the left of the group name (the **All Windows Forms** and **Common Controls** groups are shown in Fig. 2.19). Next, double click the Label control in the **Toolbox**. This action causes a Label to appear in the upper-left corner of the Form (Fig. 2.34). [*Note:* If the Form is behind the **Toolbox**, you may need to hide the **Toolbox** to see the Label.] Although double clicking any **Toolbox** control places the control on the Form, you also can "drag" controls from the **Toolbox** to the Form—you may prefer dragging the control because you can position it wherever you want. The Label displays the text **Label1** by default. The Label's background color is the same as the Form's background color. When a control is added to the Form, its BackColor property is set to the Form's BackColor. You can change the Label's background color by changing its BackColor property.

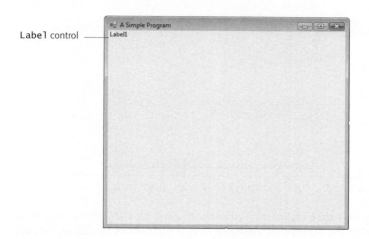

Label control

Fig. 2.34 | Adding a Label to the Form.

8. *Customizing the Label's appearance.* Select the Label by clicking it. Its properties now appear in the **Properties** window. The Label's Text property determines the text (if any) that the Label displays. The Form and Label each have their own Text property—Forms and controls can have the same types of properties (such as Back-Color, Text, etc.) without conflict. Set the Label's Text property to Welcome to Visual Basic!. The Label resizes to fit all the typed text on one line. By default, the **AutoSize property** of the Label is set to True, which allows the Label to update its size to fit all of the text if necessary. Set the AutoSize property to False (Fig. 2.35) so that you can resize the Label on your own. Resize the Label (using the sizing handles) so that the text fits. Move the Label to the top center of the Form by dragging it or by using the keyboard's left and right arrow keys to adjust its position (Fig. 2.36). Alternatively, when the Label is selected, you can center the Label control horizontally by selecting **Format > Center In Form > Horizontally**.

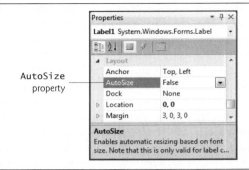

Fig. 2.35 | Changing the Label's AutoSize property to False.

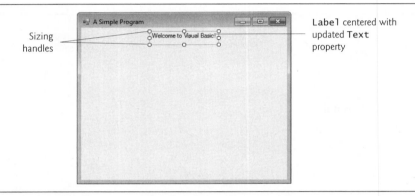

Fig. 2.36 | GUI after the Form and Label have been customized.

9. *Setting the Label's font size.* To change the font type and appearance of the Label's text, select the value of the **Font property**, which causes an **ellipsis button** to appear next to the value (Fig. 2.37). When the ellipsis button is clicked, a dialog that provides additional values—in this case, the **Font dialog** (Fig. 2.38)—is displayed. You can select the font name (the font options may be different, depending on your

Fig. 2.37 | **Properties** window displaying the Label's Font property.

system), font style (**Regular**, **Italic**, **Bold**, etc.) and font size (**16**, **18**, **20**, etc.) in this dialog. The **Sample** text shows the selected font settings. Under **Font**, select **Segoe UI**, Microsoft's recommended font for user interfaces. Under **Size**, select **24** points and click **OK**. If the Label's text does not fit on a single line, it wraps to the next line. Resize the Label vertically if it's not large enough to hold the text. You may need to center the Label horizontally again after resizing.

Fig. 2.38 | **Font** dialog for selecting fonts, styles and sizes.

10. *Aligning the Label's text.* Select the Label's **TextAlign** property, which determines how the text is aligned within the Label. A three-by-three grid of buttons representing alignment choices is displayed (Fig. 2.39). The position of each button corresponds to where the text appears in the Label. For this program, set the TextAlign property to MiddleCenter in the three-by-three grid—this selection causes the text to appear centered in the middle of the Label, with equal spacing from the text to all sides of the Label. The other TextAlign values, such as Top-Left, TopRight, and BottomCenter, can be used to position the text anywhere within a Label. Certain alignment values may require that you resize the Label larger or smaller to better fit the text.

Fig. 2.39 | Centering the Label's text.

11. *Adding a **PictureBox** to the Form.* The PictureBox control displays images. The process involved in this step is similar to that of *Step 7*, in which we added a Label to the Form. Locate the PictureBox in the **Toolbox** (Fig. 2.19) and double click it to add it to the Form. When the PictureBox appears, move it underneath the Label, either by dragging it or by using the arrow keys (Fig. 2.40).

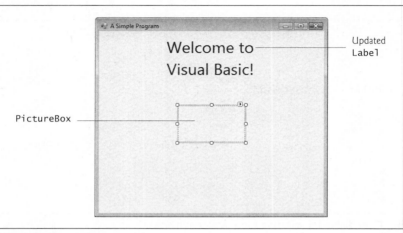

Fig. 2.40 | Inserting and aligning a PictureBox.

12. *Inserting an image.* Click the PictureBox to display its properties in the **Properties** window (Fig. 2.41). Locate the **Image property**, which displays a preview of the selected image or **(none)** if no image is selected. Click the ellipsis button to display the **Select Resource** dialog (Fig. 2.42), which is used to import files, such as images, for use in a program. Click the **Import...** button to browse for an image to insert, select the image file and click **OK**. We used bug.png from this chapter's examples folder. The image is previewed in the **Select Resource** dialog (Fig. 2.43). Click **OK** to use the image. Supported image formats include PNG (Portable Network Graphics), GIF (Graphic Interchange Format), JPEG (Joint Photographic Experts Group) and BMP (Windows bitmap). To scale the image to the PictureBox's size, change the **SizeMode property** to **StretchImage** (Fig. 2.44). Resize the PictureBox, making it larger (Fig. 2.45).

Fig. 2.41 | Image property of the PictureBox.

Fig. 2.42 | **Select Resource** dialog to select an image for the PictureBox.

Image file name

Fig. 2.43 | **Select Resource** dialog displaying a preview of selected image.

SizeMode property

SizeMode property set to StretchImage

Fig. 2.44 | Scaling an image to the size of the PictureBox.

Fig. 2.45 | PictureBox displaying an image.

13. *Saving the project.* Select **File > Save All** to save the entire solution. The solution file (which has the file name extension .sln) contains the name and location of its project, and the project file (which has the file name extension .vbproj) contains the names and locations of all the files in the project. If you want to reopen your project at a later time, simply open its .sln file.

14. *Running the project.* Recall that up to this point we have been working in the IDE design mode (that is, the program being created is not executing). In **run mode**, the program is executing, and you can interact with only a few IDE features—features that are not available are disabled (grayed out). The text **Form1.vb [Design]** in the

Fig. 2.46 | Debugging a solution.

project tab (Fig. 2.46) means that we're designing the Form visually rather than programmatically. If we had been writing code, the tab would have contained only the text **Form1.vb**. If there is an * at the end of the text in the tab, the file has been changed and should be saved. Select **Debug > Start Debugging** to execute the program (or you can press the *F5* key). Figure 2.47 shows the IDE in run mode (indicated by the title-bar text **ASimpleProgram (Running) – Microsoft Visual Basic 2010 Express Edition**). Many toolbar icons and menus are disabled, since they cannot be used while the program is running. The running program appears in a separate window outside the IDE as shown in the lower-right portion of Fig. 2.47.

IDE displays text **Running**, which
signifies that the program is executing

Fig. 2.47 | IDE in run mode, with the running program in the foreground.

15. *Terminating execution.* Click the running program's close box (the **X** in the top-right corner of the running program's window). This action stops the program's execution and returns the IDE to design mode. You can also select **Debug > Stop Debugging** to terminate the program.

2.7 Wrap-Up

In this chapter, we introduced key features of the Visual Studio Integrated Development Environment (IDE). You used the technique of visual programming to create a working Visual Basic program without writing a single line of code. Visual Basic programming is a mixture of the two styles: Visual programming allows you to develop GUIs easily and avoid tedious GUI programming. Conventional programming (which we introduce in Chapter 3) allows you to specify the behavior of your programs.

You created a Visual Basic Windows Forms application with one Form. You worked with the **Solution Explorer**, **Toolbox** and **Properties** windows, which are essential to developing Visual Basic programs. The **Solution Explorer** window allows you to manage your solution's files visually.

You explored Visual Studio's help features. You learned how to set **Help** options to display help resources internally or externally in a web browser. We also demonstrated context-sensitive help, which displays help topics related to selected controls or text.

You used visual programming to design the GUI portions of a program quickly and easily, by dragging and dropping controls (a Label and a PictureBox) onto a Form or by double clicking controls in the **Toolbox**.

In creating the **ASimpleProgram** program, you used the **Properties** window to set the Text and BackColor properties of the Form. You learned that Label controls display text and that PictureBoxes display images. You displayed text in a Label and added an image to a PictureBox. You also worked with the AutoSize, TextAlign and Font properties of a Label and the Image and SizeMode properties of a PictureBox.

In the next chapter, we discuss "nonvisual," or "conventional," programming—you'll create your first programs that contain Visual Basic code that you write, instead of having Visual Studio write the code. You'll study console applications (programs that display only text and do not have a GUI). You'll also learn memory concepts, arithmetic, decision making and how to use a dialog to display a message.

2.8 Web Resources

Please take a moment to visit each of these sites briefly.

`www.deitel.com/VisualBasic2010/`
This site lists many of the key web resources we used as we were preparing to write this book. There's lots of great stuff here to help you become familiar with the world of Visual Basic 2010.

`msdn.microsoft.com/vstudio`
This site is the home page for Microsoft Visual Studio. The site includes news, documentation, downloads and other resources.

`msdn.microsoft.com/en-us/vbasic/default.aspx`
This site provides information on the newest release of Visual Basic, including downloads, community information and resources.

`social.msdn.microsoft.com/forums/en-US/category/visualbasic/`
This site provides access to the Microsoft Visual Basic forums, which you can use to get your Visual Basic language and IDE questions answered.

`msdn.microsoft.com/en-us/magazine/default.aspx`
This is the Microsoft Developer Network Magazine site. This site provides articles and code on many Visual Basic and .NET programming topics. There is also an archive of past issues.

Summary

Section 2.1 Introduction

- Visual Studio is Microsoft's Integrated Development Environment (IDE) for creating, running and debugging programs written in a variety of .NET programming languages.

- Creating simple programs by dragging and dropping predefined building blocks into place is called visual programming.

Section 2.2 Overview of the Visual Studio 2010 IDE

- The **Start Page** contains links to Visual Studio 2010 IDE resources and web-based resources.
- A project is a group of related files that compose a program.
- The Visual Studio 2010 IDE organizes programs into projects and solutions—a solution may contain one or more projects.
- Dialogs are windows that facilitate user–computer communication.
- Visual Studio provides templates for the project types you can create, including Windows Forms applications and console applications.
- A **Form** represents the main window of the Windows Forms application that you're creating.
- Collectively, the **Form** and controls constitute the program's graphical user interface (GUI), which is the visual part of the program with which the user interacts.

Section 2.3 Menu Bar and Toolbar

- Commands for managing the IDE and for developing, maintaining and executing programs are contained in the menus, which are located on the menu bar.
- Menus contain groups of commands (menu items) that, when selected, cause the IDE to perform actions (for example, open a window, save a file, print a file and execute a program).
- Tool tips help you become familiar with the IDE's features.

Section 2.4 Navigating the Visual Studio IDE

- The **Solution Explorer** window lists all the files in the solution.
- The **Toolbox** contains controls for customizing **Forms**.
- By using visual programming, you can place predefined controls onto the **Form** instead of writing the code yourself.
- Moving the mouse pointer over a hidden window's icon opens that window. Moving the mouse out of that window hides it. This feature is known as auto-hide. To "pin down" a window (that is, to disable auto-hide), click the pin icon.
- The **Properties** window displays the properties for a **Form**, control or file (in **Design** view). Properties are information about a **Form** or control, such as size, color and position. The **Properties** window allows you to modify **Forms** and controls visually, without writing code.
- Each control has its own set of properties. The left column of the **Properties** window shows the property names and the right column displays the property values. This window's toolbar contains options for organizing properties alphabetically when the **Alphabetic** icon is selected or categorically (for example, **Appearance**, **Behavior**, **Design**) when the **Categorized** icon is selected.

Section 2.5 Using Help

- Extensive help documentation is available via **Help** menu.
- Context-sensitive help brings up a list of relevant help articles. To use context-sensitive help, select an item and press the *F1* key.

Section 2.6 Using Visual Programming to Create a Simple Program that Displays Text and an Image

- Visual Basic programming usually involves a combination of writing a portion of the program code and having Visual Studio generate the remaining code.

- The text that appears at the top of the Form (the title bar) is specified in the Form's Text property.
- To resize the Form, click and drag one of the Form's enabled sizing handles (the small squares around the Form). Enabled sizing handles appear as white boxes.
- The BackColor property specifies the background color of a Form. The Form's background color is the default background color for any controls added to the Form.
- Double clicking any **Toolbox** control icon places a control of that type on the Form. Alternatively, you can drag and drop controls from the **Toolbox** to the Form.
- The Label's Text property determines the text (if any) that the Label displays. The Form and Label each have their own Text property.
- A property's ellipsis button, when clicked, displays a dialog containing additional options.
- In the **Font** dialog, you can select the font for a Form's or Label's text.
- The TextAlign property determines how the text is aligned within a Label's boundaries.
- The PictureBox control displays images. The Image property specifies the image to displayed.
- Select **File > Save All** to save the entire solution, including all of its files.
- A program that is in design mode is not executing.
- In run mode, the program is executing—you can interact with only a few IDE features.
- When designing a program visually, the name of the Visual Basic file appears in the project tab, followed by **[Design]**.
- Terminate execution by clicking the close box.

Terminology

active tab 29
Alphabetical icon 37
application 25
auto-hide 33
AutoSize property of Label 45
BackColor property of Form 44
Categorized icon 37
component selection drop-down list 38
context-sensitive help 39
control 29
Custom tab 44
design mode 42
Design view 28
dialog 27
dragging 38
ellipsis button 46
Font dialog 46
Font property of Label 46
Form 29
graphical user interface (GUI) 27
Help menu 38
icon 31
Image property of PictureBox 48
input 29
Label 29
menu 30

menu bar in Visual Studio 30
menu item 30
MSDN (Microsoft Developers Network) 26
New Project dialog 27
output 29
palette 44
PictureBox 29
project **27**
Project Location dialog 42
Properties window 37
property of a Form or control 37
run mode 50
Save Project dialog 42
scrollbar 38
scrollbox 38
Select Resource dialog 48
Show All Files icon 35
SizeMode property of PictureBox 48
sizing handle 43
solution 27
Solution Explorer in Visual Studio 35
Start Page 25
startup project 35
StretchImage value 48
templates for projects 27
Text property 42

Self-Review Exercises

2.1 Fill in the blanks in each of the following statements:
a) The technique of _____ allows you to create GUIs without writing any code.
b) A(n) _____ is a group of one or more projects that collectively form a Visual Basic program.
c) The _____ feature hides a window when the mouse pointer is moved outside the window's area.
d) A(n) _____ appears when the mouse pointer hovers over an icon.
e) The _____ window allows you to browse solution files.
f) The properties in the **Properties** window can be sorted _____ or _____.
g) A Form's _____ property specifies the text displayed in the Form's title bar.
h) The _____ allows you to add controls to the Form in a visual manner.
i) Using _____ displays relevant help articles, based on the current context.
j) The _____ property specifies how text is aligned within a Label's boundaries.

2.2 State whether each of the following is *true* or *false*. If *false*, explain why.
a) The title bar of the IDE displays the IDE's mode.
b) The **X** box toggles auto-hide.
c) The toolbar icons represent various menu commands.
d) The toolbar contains icons that represent controls you can drag onto a Form.
e) Both Forms and Labels have a title bar.
f) Control properties can be modified only by writing code.
g) PictureBoxes typically display images.
h) Visual Basic files use the file extension .bas.
i) A Form's background color is set using the BackColor property.

Answers to Self-Review Exercises

2.1   a) visual programming. b) solution. c) auto-hide. d) tool tip. e) **Solution Explorer**. f) alphabetically, categorically. g) Text. h) **Toolbox**. i) context-sensitive help. j) TextAlign.

2.2   a) True. b) False. The pin icon toggles auto-hide. The **X** box closes a window. c) True. d) False. The **Toolbox** contains icons that represent such controls. e) False. Forms have a title bar but Labels do not (although they do have Label text). f) False. Control properties can be modified using the **Properties** window. g) True. h) False. Visual Basic files use the file extension .vb. i) True.

Exercises

2.3 Fill in the blanks in each of the following statements:
a) When an ellipsis button is clicked, a(n) _____ is displayed.
b) To save every file in a solution, select _____.
c) Using _____ help immediately displays a relevant help article.
d) GUI is an acronym for _____.

2.4 State whether each of the following is *true* or *false*. If *false*, explain why.
a) You can add a control to a Form by double clicking its control icon in the **Toolbox**.
b) The Form, Label and PictureBox have identical properties.

c) If your machine is connected to the Internet, you can browse the Internet from the Visual Studio IDE.
d) Visual Basic programmers usually create complex programs without writing any code.
e) Sizing handles are visible during execution.

2.5   Some features that appear throughout Visual Studio perform similar actions in different contexts. Explain and give examples of how the ellipsis buttons, down-arrow buttons and tool tips act in this manner. Why do you think the Visual Studio IDE was designed this way?

2.6   Fill in the blanks in each of the following statements:
a) The _____ property specifies which image a PictureBox displays.
b) The _____ menu contains commands for arranging and displaying windows.

2.7   Briefly describe each of the following terms:
a) toolbar
b) menu bar
c) **Toolbox**
d) control
e) **Form**
f) solution

[*Note:* In the following exercises, you're asked to create GUIs using controls that we have not yet discussed in this book. The exercises give you practice with visual programming only—the programs do not perform any actions. You place controls from the **Toolbox** on a Form to familiarize yourself with what each control looks like. We have provided step-by-step instructions for you. If you follow these, you should be able to replicate the screen images we provide.]

2.8   *(Notepad GUI)* Create the GUI for the notepad as shown in Fig. 2.48.

Fig. 2.48 | Notepad GUI.

a) *Manipulating the Form's properties.* Change the Text property of the Form to My Notepad. Change the Font property to 9pt Segoe UI.
b) *Adding a MenuStrip control to the Form.* Add a MenuStrip to the Form. After inserting the MenuStrip, add items by clicking the **Type Here** section, typing a menu name (for example, **File**, **Edit**, **View** and **About**) and then pressing *Enter*.
c) *Adding a RichTextBox to the Form.* Drag this control onto the Form. Use the sizing handles to resize and position the RichTextBox as shown in Fig. 2.48. Change the Text property to Enter text here.

2.9 *(Calendar and Appointments GUI)* Create they GUI for the calendar as shown in Fig. 2.49.

Fig. 2.49 | Calendar and appointments GUI.

a) *Manipulating the Form's properties.* Change the Text property of the Form to My Scheduler. Change the Font property to 9pt Segoe UI. Set the Form's Size property to 275, 400.

b) *Adding Labels to the Form.* Add two Labels to the Form. Both should be of equal size (231, 23; remember to set the AutoSize property to False) and should be centered in the Form horizontally, as shown. Set the Label's Text properties to match Fig. 2.49. Use 12-point font size. Also, set the BackColor property to Yellow.

c) *Adding a MonthCalendar control to the Form.* Add this control to the Form and center it horizontally in the appropriate place between the two Labels.

d) *Adding a RichTextBox control to the Form.* Add a RichTextBox control to the Form and center it below the second Label. Resize the RichTextBox accordingly.

2.10 *(Calculator GUI)* Create the GUI for the calculator as shown in Fig. 2.50.

Fig. 2.50 | Calculator GUI.

a) *Manipulating the Form's properties.* Change the Text property of the Form to Calculator. Change the Font property to 9pt Segoe UI. Change the Size property of the Form to 258, 210.

b) *Adding a TextBox to the Form.* Set the TextBox's Text property in the **Properties** window to 0. Stretch the TextBox and position it as shown in Fig. 2.50. Set the TextAlign property to Right—this right aligns text displayed in the TextBox.

c) *Adding the first **Panel** to the Form.* Panel controls are used to group other controls. Add a Panel to the Form. Change the Panel's BorderStyle property to Fixed3D to make the inside of the Panel appear recessed. Change the Size property to 90, 120. This Panel will contain the calculator's numeric keys.

d) *Adding the second **Panel** to the Form.* Change the Panel's BorderStyle property to Fixed3D. Change the Size property to 62, 120. This Panel will contain the calculator's operator keys.

e) *Adding the third (and last) **Panel** to the Form.* Change the Panel's BorderStyle property to Fixed3D. Change the Size property to 54, 62. This Panel contains the calculator's **C** (clear) and **C/A** (clear all) keys.

f) *Adding **Buttons** to the Form.* There are 20 Buttons on the calculator. Add a Button to the Panel by dragging and dropping it on the Panel. Change the Text property of each Button to the calculator key it represents. The value you enter in the Text property will appear on the face of the Button. Finally, resize the Buttons, using their Size properties. Each Button labeled 0–9, *, /, -, = and . should have a size of 23, 23. The **00** Button has size 52, 23. The **OFF** Button has size 54, 23. The **+** Button is sized 23, 81. The **C** (clear) and **C/A** (clear all) Buttons are sized 44, 23.

2.11 *(Alarm Clock GUI)* Create the GUI for the alarm clock as shown in Fig. 2.51.

Fig. 2.51 | Alarm clock GUI.

a) *Manipulating the **Form's** properties.* Change the Text property of the Form to Alarm Clock. Change the Font property to 9pt Segoe UI. Change the Size property of the Form to 438, 170.

b) *Adding **Buttons** to the Form.* Add six Buttons to the Form. Change the Text property of each Button to the appropriate text. Align the Buttons as shown.

c) *Adding a **GroupBox** to the Form.* GroupBoxes are like Panels, except that GroupBoxes display a title. Change the Text property to AM/PM, and set the Size property to 100, 50. Center the GroupBox horizontally on the Form.

d) *Adding **AM/PM** RadioButtons to the GroupBox.* Place two RadioButtons in the GroupBox. Change the Text property of one RadioButton to AM and the other to PM. Align the RadioButtons as shown.

e) *Adding the time **Label** to the Form.* Add a Label to the Form and change its Text property to 00:00:00. Change the BorderStyle property to Fixed3D and the BackColor to Black. Use the Font property to make the time bold and 12pt. Change the ForeColor to Silver (located in the **Web** tab) to make the time stand out against the black background. Position the Label as shown.

2.12 *(Radio GUI)* Create the GUI for the radio as shown in Fig. 2.52. [*Note:* The image used in this exercise is located in the examples folder for Chapter 2.]

a) *Manipulating the **Form's** properties.* Change the Font property to 9pt Segoe UI. Change the Form's Text property to Radio and the Size to 427, 194.

Fig. 2.52 | Radio GUI.

b) *Adding the **Pre-set Stations** GroupBox and Buttons.* Set the GroupBox's Size to 180, 55 and its Text to Pre-set Stations. Add six Buttons to the GroupBox. Set each one's Size to 23, 23. Change the Buttons' Text properties to 1, 2, 3, 4, 5, 6, respectively.

c) *Adding the **Speakers** GroupBox and CheckBoxes.* Set the GroupBox's Size to 120, 55 and its Text to Speakers. Add two CheckBoxes to the GroupBox. Set the Text properties for the CheckBoxes to Rear and Front.

d) *Adding the **Power On/Off** Button.* Add a Button to the Form. Set its Text to Power On/Off and its Size to 75, 55.

e) *Adding the **Volume Control** GroupBox, the **Mute** CheckBox and the **Volume** TrackBar.* Add a GroupBox to the Form. Set its Text to Volume Control and its Size to 180, 70. Add a CheckBox to the GroupBox. Set its Text to Mute. Add a TrackBar to the GroupBox.

f) *Adding the **Tuning** GroupBox, the radio station Label and the **AM/FM** RadioButtons.* Add a GroupBox to the Form. Set its Text to Tuning and its Size to 120, 70. Add a Label to the GroupBox. Set its AutoSize to False, its Size to 50, 44, its BackColor to Black, its ForeColor to Silver, its font to 12pt bold and its TextAlign to MiddleCenter. Set its Text to 92.9. Place the Label as shown in the figure. Add two RadioButtons to the GroupBox. Set the Text of one to AM and of the other to FM.

g) *Adding the image.* Add a PictureBox to the Form. Set its SizeMode to StretchImage and its Size to 55, 70. Set the Image property to MusicNote.gif (located in the examples folder for Chapter 2).

3

Introduction to Visual Basic Programming

Comment is free, but facts are sacred.
—C. P. Scott

The creditor hath a better memory than the debtor.
—James Howell

When faced with a decision, I always ask, "What would be the most fun?"
—Peggy Walker

Objectives

In this chapter you'll learn:

- To write simple Visual Basic programs.
- To use the Windows Forms designer to position, size and align controls.
- To write statements that input data from the user and display results to the user.
- To declare and use data of various types.
- To use variables to store data for later use in a program.
- To use arithmetic operators to perform calculations.
- How the precedence of arithmetic operators determines the order in which they're applied.
- To write decision-making statements.
- To use equality and relational operators to compare operands.

3.1 Introduction

In this chapter, we introduce Visual Basic programming with program code and present examples to demonstrate how programs can display information on the screen and obtain information from the user at the keyboard for processing. You'll use graphical user interfaces (GUIs) to allow users to interact visually with your programs. A GUI (pronounced "GOO-ee") gives a program a distinctive look-and-feel.

Sample GUI
GUIs are built from GUI controls (which are sometimes called **components or widgets**—short for **window gadgets**). GUI controls are objects that can display information on the screen or enable users to interact with an application via the mouse, keyboard or other forms of input (such as voice commands). Figure 3.1 shows a Visual Basic 2010 Express window that contains various GUI controls.

Near the top of the window is a menu bar containing the menus **File, Edit, View, Tools, Window** and **Help**. Below the menu bar is a tool bar of buttons, each with a defined task, such as creating a new project or opening an existing project. Scrollbars are located at the right side of the **Start Page**'s **Recent Projects** and **Get Started** sections. Usually, scrollbars appear when there is more information than can be displayed in certain types of controls. Scrollbars enable a user to view different portions of a control's contents, in this case the list of recent projects or information about getting started with the IDE.

The **Start Page** is shown on a tab—if multiple documents are open, the user can click a document's tab to view it. These controls form a user-friendly interface through which you've been interacting with the Visual Basic 2010 Express IDE. As you'll see, the .NET framework provides many predefined controls.

Look-and-Feel Observation 3.1
Consistent user interfaces enable a user to learn new applications faster because the applications have the same look-and-feel.

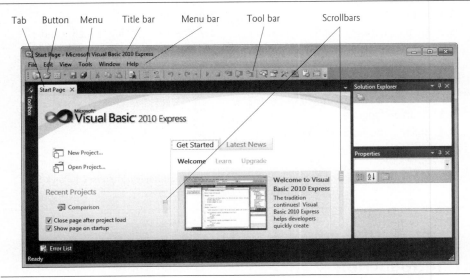

Fig. 3.1 | GUI controls in the Visual Basic 2010 Express window.

3.2 Programmatically Displaying Text in a Label

In Chapter 2, we showed how to create a simple GUI application using *visual* programming. We defined the application's appearance by dragging and dropping GUI controls onto a Form and setting properties in design mode—without writing *any* program code. The application you created in Section 2.6 displayed text and an image but did not perform any other actions.

Most Visual Basic programmers use a combination of visual programming and conventional programming techniques. In this section, you'll modify the Label's text programmatically, causing the text displayed on the Form to change when you execute the program. You'll also learn how to write code that performs an action when the Form loads—that is, when the program executes and displays the Form.

We begin by considering the program's code and sample execution (Fig. 3.2). Later in this section, we guide you step-by-step through the process of creating this program by modifying the one you created in Section 2.6.

```
1   ' Fig. 3.2: ASimpleProgram.vb
2   ' Programmatically changing a Label's text.
3   Public Class ASimpleProgram
4       ' called when the program loads the Form
5       Private Sub ASimpleProgram_Load(ByVal sender As System.Object,
6           ByVal e As System.EventArgs) Handles MyBase.Load
7
8           Label1.Text = "Visual Basic is fun!"
9       End Sub ' ASimpleProgram_Load
10  End Class ' ASimpleProgram
```

Fig. 3.2 | Programmatically changing a Label's text. (Part 1 of 2.)

Fig. 3.2 | Programmatically changing a Label's text. (Part 2 of 2.)

3.2.1 Analyzing the Program

Line Numbers

All of our program listings include line numbers—these are not part of Visual Basic. The line numbers help us refer to specific parts of a program. In Section 3.2.2, you'll learn how to display line numbers in program files. Each program in the book is followed by one or more sample outputs that demonstrate the program's execution.

Comments

Line 1 of Fig. 3.2 begins with a **single-quote character** ('), which indicates that the remainder of the line is a **comment**. Comments improve the code's readability—you can write anything you want in a comment. Comments can be placed either on their own lines (we call these "**full-line comments**"; as in lines 1–2) or at the end of a line of Visual Basic code (we call these "**end-of-line comments**"; as in lines 9 and 10). The compiler ignores comments—they do not cause the computer to perform any actions when a program runs. The comment in line 1 simply indicates the figure number (Fig. 3.2) and the file name (ASimpleProgram.vb) in which we stored this program. The comment in line 2 provides a brief description of the program. By convention, we begin each program this way.

Classes

Windows Forms applications consist of pieces called **classes**, which are logical groupings of methods and data that simplify program organization. **Methods** perform tasks and can return information when the tasks are completed. Lines 3–10 define a class that represents our Form. These lines collectively are called a **class declaration**. We discuss the method in lines 5–9 shortly. Every Windows Forms application consists of at least one class that typically contains one or more methods that perform tasks.

Keywords

The words **Public** and **Class** (line 3) are examples of keywords. **Keywords** are words reserved for use by Visual Basic. The complete list of keywords can be found at:

```
msdn.microsoft.com/en-us/library/dd409611(VS.100).aspx
```

Class Names and Identifiers

The name of the Class—ASimpleProgram in line 3—is an **identifier**, which is a series of characters consisting of letters, digits and underscores (_). Identifiers cannot begin with a digit and cannot contain spaces. Examples of valid identifiers are value1, Welcome1, xy_coordinate, _total and grossPay. The name 7Welcome is not a valid identifier because it begins with a digit; input field is not valid because it contains a space.

Good Programming Practice 3.1

By convention, every word in a class name should begin with an uppercase letter—this is known as "Pascal case."

Common Programming Error 3.1

You cannot use a keyword as an identifier, so it's an error, for example, to use the keyword Double as a class name. The Visual Basic compiler helps you locate such errors in your programs. Though keywords cannot be used as identifiers, they can be used in comments.

Visual Basic Is Not Case Sensitive

Visual Basic keywords and identifiers are not **case sensitive**. Uppercase and lowercase letters are considered to be identical, so asimpleprogram and ASimpleProgram are interpreted as the same identifier. Although keywords appear to be case sensitive, they're not. Visual Basic Express applies its "preferred" case (that is, the casing used in Fig. 3.2) to each letter of a keyword, so when you type class, for example, the IDE changes the lowercase c to uppercase, as in Class, even though class would be correct.

Blank Lines and Whitespace

Line 7 (Fig. 3.2) is a blank line. Blank lines, space characters and tab characters are used throughout a program to make it easier to read. These are called **whitespace**. Blank lines are ignored by the compiler.

The Form's Load Event and Method ASimpleProgram_Load

GUIs are **event driven**. When the user interacts with a GUI component, the interaction—known as an **event**—causes the program to perform a task by "calling" a method. Common events (user interactions) include clicking a Button, selecting an item from a menu, closing a window and moving the mouse. All GUI controls, including Forms, have events associated with them. A method that performs a task in response to an event is called an **event handler**, and the process of responding to events is known as **event handling**. Most of a GUI application's functionality executes based on events. Event handling methods are called automatically. You'll learn how to call existing methods yourself later in this chapter. You'll learn how to create and call your own methods in Chapter 6.

A common event for a Form is its **Load event**, which occurs just before a Form is displayed on the screen—typically as a result of executing the program. Lines 5–9 define the method ASimpleProgram_Load as the Form's Load event handler. When this event is **raised** (that is, the event occurs), method ASimpleProgram_Load executes to perform its task—changing the text in the Label. At the end of line 6, the clause

```
Handles MyBase.Load
```

indicates that method ASimpleProgram_Load is the one that will be called to handle the Form's Load event. The IDE automatically inserts this clause for you when you create the event handler. We'll discuss the contents inside the parentheses in lines 5–6 in later chapters.

Defining a Method

The keyword **Sub** (line 5) begins the **method declaration** (the code that will be executed by this method). The keywords **End Sub** (line 9) close the method declaration. The **body of the method declaration** appears between the keywords Sub and End Sub. The keyword Sub is short for "subroutine"—an early term for method. Methods are also sometimes called **procedures**. The end-of-line comments in lines 9 and 10 improve readability by indicating which method or class ends at those lines.

Good Programming Practice 3.2

Follow a method's End Sub with an end-of-line comment containing the name of the method that the End Sub terminates.

Indentation

Lines 4–9 are indented three spaces relative to lines 3 and 10. Indentation improves program readability—in this case making it clear that method ASimpleProgram_Load is part of the class ASimpleProgram. We show how to set the IDE's indent size in Section 3.2.2.

Line 8 in the method body is indented three additional spaces to the right relative to lines 5 and 9. This emphasizes that line 8 is part of method ASimpleProgram_Load's body. The indentation is whitespace and is ignored by the compiler.

Good Programming Practice 3.3

Indent the entire body of each method declaration one additional "level" of indentation. This emphasizes the structure of the method, improving its readability. In this text, one level of indentation is set to three spaces—this keeps the code readable yet concise. The IDE automatically uses "pretty listing" to perform indentation for you as you type your code.

Modifying a Label's Text with Code

Line 8 in Fig. 3.2 does the "real work" of the program, displaying the phrase Visual Basic is fun!. Line 8 instructs the computer to perform an **action**—namely, to change the text on the Label to the characters contained between the double quotation marks. These characters and the surrounding double quotes are called **strings**, **character strings** or **string literals**.

The entire line is called a **statement**. When this line executes, it changes the Label's Text property to the message Visual Basic is fun!. This updates the text on the Form (Fig. 3.2). The statement uses the **assignment operator** (=) to give the Text property a new value. The statement is read as, "Label1.Text *gets* the value "Visual Basic is fun!"."

The expression Label1.Text contains two identifiers (that is, Label1 and Text) separated by the **dot separator** (.). The identifier to the right of the dot separator is the **property name**, and the identifier to the left of the dot separator is the name of the Label control. When you add a Label to a Form, the IDE gives it the name Label1 by default for the first Label you add—you'll learn how to change the IDE-assigned names in Section 3.4. After the statement in line 8 executes, the program reaches the keywords **End Sub**, which indicate that this method has completed performing its task. The keywords **End Class** (line 10), indicate the end of the Class.

Note About *Public* and *Private*

We did not discuss the keywords Public (line 3) and Private (line 5). Most classes you'll define begin with keyword Public and most event-handling methods begin with the keyword Private. We'll discuss each of these keywords in detail when we formally present classes in Chapter 9, Object-Oriented Programming: Classes and Objects.

3.2.2 Modifying ASimpleProgram to Programmatically Change the Label's Text Property

Now that we've presented the program (Fig. 3.2), we provide a step-by-step explanation of how to modify the version of ASimpleProgram you created in Section 2.6.

Loading the Project

Load the project ASimpleProgram from your Chapter 3 examples folder into the IDE. You can do this by selecting **File > Open Project...** in the IDE and locating the project's .sln file or by double-clicking the .sln file in Windows Explorer. This is the same program you created in Chapter 2.

Naming the Form Class

In larger programs, you might have several Forms—giving each one a name helps programmers understand the purpose of each Form and improves program clarity. Change the name of the file from Form1.vb to ASimpleProgram.vb by right clicking the file in the **Solution Explorer**, selecting **Rename** and typing the new file name. Next, double click this file to open it in design mode. Select the Form by clicking it. Notice in the **Properties** window that the IDE changed the Form's name from Form1 to ASimpleProgram when you changed the file name. You can also rename a file by selecting it in the **Solution Explorer**, then changing the **File Name** property in the **Properties** window.

Viewing the Form's Code

There are several ways to view the code for ASimpleProgram:

1. Right click the Form and select **View Code**.

2. Right click the ASimpleForm.vb file in the **Solution Explorer** and select **View Code**.

3. Press the *F7* key.

4. Select **Code** from the **View** menu.

Figure 3.3 shows ASimpleProgram.vb's initial contents. The editor window contains some Visual Basic code generated by the IDE.

Fig. 3.3 | ASimpleProgram.vb's initial contents.

Syntax Shading

The code coloring scheme used by the IDE is called **syntax-color highlighting** and helps you visually differentiate program elements. Keywords appear in dark blue. When present, comments are colored green. Other program elements use different colors. In this book, we simulate the IDE's syntax coloring with syntax shading—bold dark blue for keywords, gray for comments, bold light blue for literals and constants, and black for all other text. One example of a literal is the string assigned to `Label1.Text` in line 8 of Fig. 3.2. You can customize the colors shown in the code editor by selecting **Tools > Options...** to display the **Options** dialog. Then select **Fonts and Colors** to display the options for changing the fonts and colors of various code elements.

Modifying the Editor Settings to Display Line Numbers

Visual Basic 2010 Express provides many ways to personalize your coding experience. You'll now learn how to change the editor's settings. To display line numbers, select **Tools > Options....** In the dialog that appears (Fig. 3.4), ensure that the **Show all settings** check box in the dialog's lower-left corner is unchecked. Expand the **Text Editor Basic** category in the left pane and select **Editor**. Under **Interaction**, check the **Line Numbers** check box. Keep the **Options** dialog open for the next step.

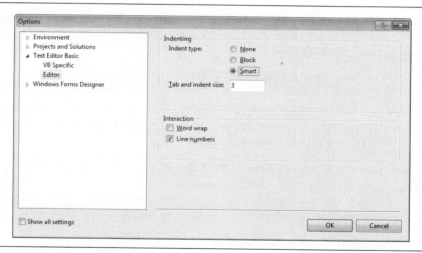

Fig. 3.4 | Modifying the IDE settings.

Setting Code Indentation to Three Spaces per Indent

In the **Options** dialog that you opened in the previous step, enter **3** in the **Tab Size** textbox (Fig. 3.4). Any new code you add will now use three spaces for each level of indentation. Click **OK** to save your settings, close the dialog and return to the editor window. As you type your code, the IDE will update the code to conform to various Visual Basic code conventions and your current IDE settings.

Creating the Event Handler Method `ASimpleProgram_Load`

Click the **ASimpleProgram.vb [Design]** tab in the IDE to view the Windows Forms designer. Double clicking any control creates that control's default event handler (if it does not already exist) and switches to code view. For a Form, the default is the Load event handler. Double click the blue background of the Form to create the event handler now. The IDE automatically names an event handler with the name of the control (ASimpleForm), an underscore (_) and the name of the event that the method handles (Load). Figure 3.5 shows the code editor with the new event handler method.

```
ASimpleProgram.vb* ×  ASimpleProgram.vb [Design]*
ASimpleProgram                              (Declarations)
  1  Public Class ASimpleProgram
  2
  3      Private Sub ASimpleProgram_Load(ByVal sender As System.Object, ByVal e
  4
  5      End Sub
  6  End Class
  7
100 %
```

Fig. 3.5 | ASimpleProgram.vb's initial contents.

Line 3 is too long to fit on a single line in our book, so we split the line into two lines as shown in lines 5–6 of Fig. 3.2. To improve readability, long statements may be split over several lines. In earlier versions of Visual Basic, you had to use the **line-continuation character** (_) to do this as follows:

```
Private Sub ASimpleProgram_Load(ByVal sender As System.Object, _
    ByVal e As System.EventArgs) Handles MyBase.Load
```

As of Visual Basic 2010, line-continuation characters are not required in most cases, so we'll use them only when necessary. For the few cases in which they're still required, the compiler will tell you if you do not include them.

Common Programming Error 3.2
Splitting a statement over several lines without including the line-continuation character is sometimes a syntax error. If you get error messages after splitting a long line of code, insert a line-continuation character.

Common Programming Error 3.3
Failure to precede the line-continuation character (_) with at least one whitespace character is a syntax error.

Writing Code and Using IntelliSense
In the editor window, add the comments from lines 1, 2, 4, 9 and 10 of Fig. 3.2. Also, split the first line of method ASimpleProgram_Load's first line as shown in Fig. 3.2. Then click the line before End Sub, press *Enter* and type the code contained in line 8 of Fig. 3.2. As you begin typing, a small window appears (Fig. 3.6). This IDE feature, called *IntelliSense*, lists keywords, class names, **members** of a class (which include property and method names) and other features that start with the same characters you've typed so far. Tabs (**Common** and **All**) are provided in the *IntelliSense* window so that you can view either the most commonly used matches or all available matches.

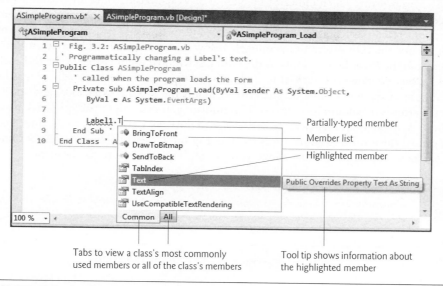

Tabs to view a class's most commonly used members or all of the class's members

Tool tip shows information about the highlighted member

Fig. 3.6 | *IntelliSense* feature of Visual Basic Express.

As you type characters, *IntelliSense* highlights the most commonly used item that matches the characters typed, then displays a tool tip containing information about that item. You can type the complete item name (for example, `Label1` or `Text`), or you can let the IDE insert the complete name for you by double clicking the item's name in the list. or by pressing the *Space* or *Tab* keys. When the complete name is provided, the *IntelliSense* window closes. Notice that once you type the dot (`.`) after `Label1`, the *IntelliSense* window shows only the members of class `Label` that can be used on the right side of the dot. This also helps you learn about the control or class you're using.

While the *IntelliSense* window is displayed, pressing the *Ctrl* key makes the window transparent so you can see the code behind the window. Also, if you accidentally close *IntelliSense* (normally by pressing the *Esc* key), you can display it at any time by pressing *Ctrl* and the *Spacebar*.

Compiling and Running the Program
You're now ready to compile and run the program. To do so, select **Debug > Start Debugging** (or press *F5* or the toolbar button ▶). The statement in line 8 displays `Visual Basic is fun!` on the `Label`. When you run a program, the IDE first compiles it. You can also compile the program without running it by selecting **Debug > Build ASimpleProgram** (this menu option's name changes based on your project's name). This creates a new file with the project's name and the `.exe` file-name extension (`ASimpleProgram.exe`). This file contains the program's Microsoft Intermediate Language (MSIL) code, which executes on the .NET Framework. The **.exe file extension** indicates that the file is **executable**.

Syntax Errors, Error Messages and the Error List Window
Go back to the application in Visual Basic Express. When you type a line of code and press the *Enter* key, the IDE responds either by applying syntax-color highlighting or by gener-

ating a **syntax error**, which indicates a violation of Visual Basic's rules for creating correct programs (that is, one or more statements are not written correctly). Syntax errors occur for various reasons, such as missing parentheses and misspelled keywords. When a syntax error occurs, the IDE places a blue squiggle below the error and provides a description of the error in the **Error List** window. If the **Error List** window is not visible in the IDE, select **View > Other Windows > Error List** to display it. In Fig. 3.7, we intentionally omitted the parenthesis at the end of line 6. The error contains the text **"')' expected."** and specifies that the error is in column 33 of line 6. This informs you that a right parenthesis is missing in line 6. You can double click an error message in the **Error List** to jump to the line of code that caused the error. For some errors (such as this one), the IDE shows the **Error Correction Options** drop-down list and allows you to simply click a link to fix the error.

Error-Prevention Tip 3.1

One syntax error can lead to multiple entries in the **Error List** *window. Fix the errors in the order they appear—fixing one error might make the others disappear.*

Omitted parenthesis character (syntax error)

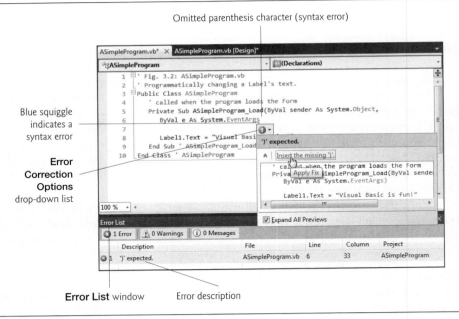

Blue squiggle indicates a syntax error

Error Correction Options drop-down list

Error List window   Error description

Fig. 3.7 | Syntax error indicated by the IDE.

3.3 Addition Program

We'll now build an Addition program (Fig. 3.8) that allows the user to enter two integers (whole numbers) then click an **Add** Button to calculate their sum and display the result. First, we'll discuss the GUI and the application's code. Then, we'll show how to lay out the GUI and create the addButton_Click event handler (lines 5–16) that is called when the user clicks the button. The sample output that follows the code shows the GUI after the user has entered two integers and clicked the **Add** button to display the result.

```
 1   ' Fig. 3.8: Addition.vb
 2   ' Addition program that adds two integers entered by the user.
 3   Public Class Addition
 4      ' adds two integers and displays the result
 5      Private Sub addButton_Click(ByVal sender As System.Object,
 6         ByVal e As System.EventArgs) Handles addButton.Click
 7
 8         Dim number1 As Integer ' first number entered by the user
 9         Dim number2 As Integer ' second number entered by the user
10         Dim total As Integer ' sum of the two integers
11
12         number1 = number1TextBox.Text ' get the first number entered
13         number2 = number2TextBox.Text ' get the second number entered
14         total = number1 + number2 ' add the two numbers
15         resultLabel.Text = "The sum is " & total ' display the total
16      End Sub ' addButton_Click
17   End Class ' Addition
```

Fig. 3.8 | Addition program that adds two integers entered by the user.

The Addition Program's GUI

The GUI for this program consists of three Labels, two TextBoxes and a Button. As you've seen, Labels display text information. The application user cannot directly modify the text on a Label, but as you saw in Fig. 3.2, a Label's text can be changed programmatically by modifying the Label's Text property. The Labels **Enter first integer:** and **Enter second integer:** are called **prompts**, because they direct the user to take a specific action.

A **TextBox** is an area in which a program can display text or the user can type text via the keyboard. TextBoxes are typically used to obtain information from the application's user. Like a Label, a TextBox's **Text property** can be used to change the text that is displayed in a TextBox. As you'll see in this program, the Text property can also be used to get information the user types in a TextBox.

A **Button** is a control that the user clicks to trigger a specific action in the program. When the user clicks the **Add** Button, this program reads the values typed by the user in the two TextBoxes, adds the values and displays the result. The text displayed on a Button is specified using its Text property.

Variable Declarations and Naming

Lines 8–10 are **declarations**, which begin with keyword **Dim**. The words number1, number2 and total are identifiers for **variables**—locations in the computer's memory where values can be stored for use by a program. *All variables must be declared before they can be used in a program.* The declarations in lines 8–10 specify that the variables number1, number2 and total are data of type **Integer**; that is, these variables store **integer** values (that is, whole numbers such as 919, −11, 0 and 138624). Types defined as part of the Visual Basic language, such as **Integer**, are known as **primitive types** and their type names are keywords. The primitive types are listed in Fig. 3.9.

Primitive types				
Boolean	Byte	Char	Date	Decimal
Double	Integer	Long	SByte	Short
Single	String	UInteger	ULong	UShort

Fig. 3.9 | Primitive types.

A variable name can be any valid identifier. Variables of the same type can be declared in separate statements or they can be declared in one statement with each variable in the declaration separated by a comma. The latter format uses a **comma-separated list** of variable names.

You should choose meaningful variable names to make your programs "self-documenting." This helps other people understand your code.

By convention, the first word in a variable-name identifier begins with a lowercase letter. Every word in the name after the first should begin with an uppercase letter—this is known as "camel case." For example, identifier firstNumber has a capital N beginning its second word, Number. Although identifiers are not case sensitive, using this convention helps make your programs more readable.

Using Variables to Store the Values Entered by the User

Line 12 uses an assignment operator (=) to give a value to variable number1. The statement is read as, "number1 *gets* the value returned by number1TextBox.Text." We call the entire statement an **assignment statement** because it assigns a value to a variable. The expression number1TextBox.Text gets the value that the user typed in the TextBox. Line 13 assigns number2 the value that the user entered in the number2TextBox.

What if the User Doesn't Enter an Integer?

Technically, the user can type any character into a TextBox as input. For this program, if the user types a noninteger value, such as "hello," a **runtime error** (an error that has its effect at execution time) occurs. The message displayed in Fig. 3.10 appears when you run the application using **Debug > Start Debugging** (or press *F5*). In this case, you can terminate the program by selecting **Debug > Stop Debugging** or typing *Ctrl + Alt + Break*. In Chapter 7, we'll introduce how to handle such errors to make programs more robust—that is, able to handle runtime errors and continue executing.

Using Variables in a Calculation

The assignment statement in line 14 (Fig. 3.8) calculates the sum of the Integer variables number1 and number2 and assigns the result to variable total. The statement is read as, "total *gets* the value of number1 + number2." The expression to the right of the = is always evaluated first before the assignment occurs. The addition (+) operator is called a **binary operator**, because it has two **operands**—number1 and number2.

Error message

Fig. 3.10 | Dialog displaying a runtime error.

Good Programming Practice 3.4

The Visual Basic IDE places a space on either side of a binary operator, such as the addition operator, to make the operator stand out and improve the statement's readability.

Displaying the Result in `resultLabel`

Line 15 displays the total of the two values by assigning a new value to the `resultLabel`'s `Text` property. The expression

```
"The sum is " & total
```

uses the **string concatenation operator**, **&**, to combine the string literal `"The sum is "` and the value of the variable `total` (the `Integer` variable containing the sum calculated in line 14). The string concatenation operator is a binary operator that joins two strings together. This operation results in a new, longer string. If one of the operands is a number, the program automatically creates a string representation of the number.

3.4 Building the Addition Program

Follow the steps in Section 2.6 to create a new Windows Forms application. Name the application `Addition`. In the **Solution Explorer**, right click `Form1.vb` and select **Rename**, then rename the file `Addition.vb`.

Changing the Names of Controls

Figure 3.11 shows the `Addition` program's GUI with the names we used for each control. When you build a GUI, you'll typically want to rename each control. The name of a control is actually a variable that can be used to interact with that control. For example, in Fig. 3.2 we used `Label1.Text` to access and change the `Label`'s `Text` property. In that expression, `Label1` is the variable name that you can use to interact with the control programmatically. You can change a control's variable name by selecting the control and modifying its **Name** property (listed in the **Properties** window as **(Name)**). We'll use this technique to change the names of all the controls in this GUI, which will enable us to easily identify the `Form`'s controls in the program code.

Fig. 3.11 | `Addition` program's GUI with the variable names of the controls.

Setting the Form's Text Property

In the Windows Forms designer, click the Form to select it. Then use the **Properties** window to change the Form's Text property to Addition. This is displayed in the Form's title bar.

Creating the number1Label

Next, you'll create the number1Label. Visual Studio provides design tools that help you lay out a GUI. When you drag a control across a Form, **snap lines** appear to help you position the control with respect to the Form's edges and other controls. As you move a control close to another control or close to the edge of the Form, the IDE moves it a bit for you—and quickly—hence the term "snap into place." Drag a Label from the **Toolbox** onto the Form and position it near the Form's upper-left corner. Figure 3.12 shows the two snap lines that appear when you drag the Label near the upper-left corner. These snap lines indicate the recommended minimum distance that you should place the control from the top and left of the Form. After releasing this Label, set its Name property to number1Label and its Text property to Enter first integer:.

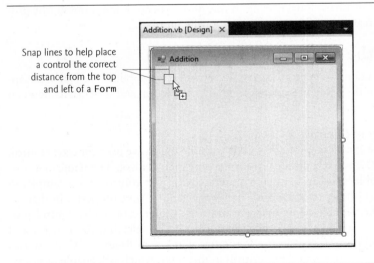

Fig. 3.12 | Snap lines for positioning a Label near the upper-left corner of the Form.

Look-and-Feel Observation 3.2

A Label used to describe the purpose of a control should use sentence-style capitalization—only the first word should be capitalized—and end with a colon. This is called a descriptive Label.

Control Naming Convention

You'll notice that, by convention, each variable name we create for a control ends with the control's type. For example, the variable name number1Label ends with Label. This is a widely used naming practice in the Visual Basic community. For example, the **Enter first integer:** Label's name could be lblNumber1.

Good Programming Practice 3.5

Append the control's type to the end of the variable name for a control. This helps you know the control's type when reading your code.

Creating the *number2Label*

Next, drag another Label onto the Form. Set its Name property to number2Label and its Text property to Enter second integer:. Drag the Label near the top of the Form and to the right of number1Label as shown in Fig. 3.13.

Look-and-Feel Observation 3.3

Align the bottoms of a group of descriptive Labels if they're arranged horizontally. Align the left or right sides of a group of descriptive Labels if they're arranged vertically.

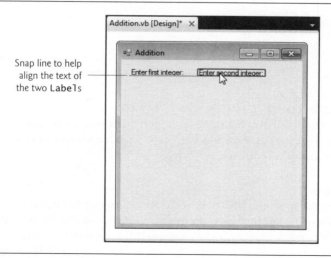

Snap line to help align the text of the two Labels

Fig. 3.13 | Snap line for aligning the text of two Labels.

Creating the *number1TextBox*

Next, drag a TextBox from the **Toolbox** onto the Form. Set its Name property to number1TextBox. Drag the TextBox below the number1Label as shown in Fig. 3.14. Snap lines help you align the left sides of the TextBox and Label, and help you position the TextBox the recommended distance from the Label.

Look-and-Feel Observation 3.4

Place each descriptive Label either above or to the left of the control that it identifies.

Look-and-Feel Observation 3.5

A descriptive Label and the control it identifies should be aligned on the left if they're arranged vertically. The text in a descriptive Label and the text in the control it identifies should be aligned on the bottom if they're arranged horizontally.

Snap lines to help align the TextBox with the left side of the Label and to position the TextBox the recommended distance below the Label

Fig. 3.14 | Snap lines for positioning number1TextBox below number1Label.

Creating the *number2TextBox*
Drag another TextBox onto the Form. Set its Name property to number2TextBox. Drag the TextBox below the number2Label as shown in Fig. 3.15. Snap lines help you position the TextBox with respect to the other controls.

Creating the *addButton*
Drag a Button from the **Toolbox** onto the Form. Set its Name property to addButton and its Text property to Add. Drag the Button below the number1TextBox so that the two controls are aligned at the left side and the Button is the recommended distance from the TextBox. Then use the Button's sizing handles to resize the Button as shown in Fig. 3.16. Snap lines help you size the Button so that it aligns with the right side of number2TextBox.

Look-and-Feel Observation 3.6

A Button's text should use book-title capitalization—each significant word should start with an uppercase letter. The text should be concise, but meaningful to the user.

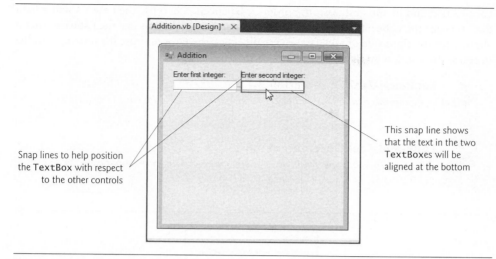

Fig. 3.15 | Snap lines for positioning `number2TextBox` below `number2Label`.

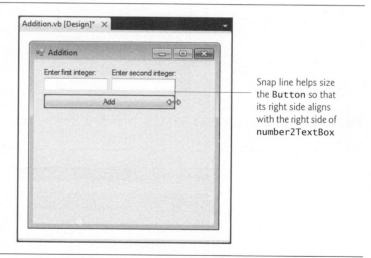

Fig. 3.16 | Snap line for sizing `addButton`.

Creating the `resultLabel` and Resizing the `Form`

Drag a `Label` onto the `Form`. Set its `Name` property to `resultLabel` and delete the value of the `Text` property so that the `Label` is blank when the application begins executing— remember that we set this text programmatically when the user clicks the **Add** button to add the numbers. Set the `Label`'s `AutoSize` property to `False` so that you'll be able to size the `Label`. Set the `Label`'s **BorderStyle property** to **Fixed3D** to give the `Label` a three-dimensional appearance. We use this style to highlight the fact that the `Label` displays the program's results. Set the `Label`'s `TextAlign` property to **MiddleLeft** as shown in Fig. 3.17. This centers the text vertically on the `Label`, so that the distance between the

Label's text and its top and bottom borders is balanced. Then use the Label's sizing handles to resize the Label as shown in Fig. 3.18. Snap lines help you size the Label so that it aligns with the right side of addButton. Finally, click the Form and use it's resizing handles to resize the window so that it appears as shown in Fig. 3.11.

 Look-and-Feel Observation 3.7
Place controls that display output below and/or to the right of a Form's input controls.

 Look-and-Feel Observation 3.8
Distinguish output Labels from descriptive Labels by setting each output Label's Border-Style property to Fixed3D (see resultLabel in Fig. 3.11).

Fig. 3.17 | Setting a Label's TextAlign property to MiddleLeft.

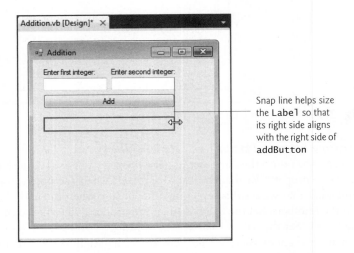

Snap line helps size the Label so that its right side aligns with the right side of addButton

Fig. 3.18 | Snap line for sizing resultLabel.

Creating the **addButton_Click** Event Handler

Recall from Section 3.2.2 that double clicking any control creates that control's default event handler. For a Button, the default event is the Click event. Double click the add-Button now to create its addButton_Click event handler. The IDE automatically switches to the code editor window. The IDE automatically names the event handler with the control's name (addButton), an underscore (_) and the name of the event that the method handles (Click). Notice that the first line of the method ends with

> **Handles** addButton.Click

This indicates that the method will be called when the user clicks the addButton, which raises a Click event.

Entering the Code from Fig. 3.8 into the **addButton_Click** Event Handler

You can now enter the code in the event handler to read the numbers, perform the calculation and display the result. To ensure that your line numbers match with those shown in Fig. 3.8, enter the comments on lines 1–2 of Fig. 3.8 and split the first line of the method definition as shown in lines 5–6.

Good Programming Practice 3.6

If a single statement must be split across lines, choose breaking points that make sense, such as after a comma in a comma-separated list or after an operator in a lengthy expression. If a statement is split across two or more lines, indent all subsequent lines with one level of indentation.

Testing the Program

When you're done entering the code, test the program to ensure that it works correctly. Enter 45 for the first number and 72 for the second, then click the **Add** Button. The result should be 117. Now, type 10 in the number1TextBox. Notice that the resultLabel still shows the previous calculation's result (Fig. 3.19). This can be confusing to the application user. For this reason, we should clear the resultLabel when the user starts typing a new number in either TextBox. We show how to do this in the program of Section 3.7.

resultLabel showing incorrect result after user enters 10 in number1TextBox and before user clicks **Add**

Fig. 3.19 | Addition program showing old result as new numbers are entered.

3.5 Memory Concepts

Variable names, such as number1, number2 and total, correspond to locations in the computer's memory. Every variable has a **name**, **type**, **size** and **value**. In the addition program of Fig. 3.8, when the statement (line 12)

```
number1 = number1TextBox.Text ' get the first number entered
```

executes, the data input by the user in number1TextBox is placed into a memory location to which the name number1 has been assigned by the compiler. Suppose the user enters the characters 45. This input is returned by number1TextBox.Text and assigned to number1. The program places the Integer value 45 into location number1, as shown in Fig. 3.20. Whenever a value is placed in a memory location, this value replaces the value previously stored in that location. The previous value is lost.

number1   45

Fig. 3.20 | Memory location showing the name and value of variable number1.

Suppose that the user then enters the characters 72 in number2TextBox. Line 13

```
number2 = number2TextBox.Text ' get the second number entered
```

places the Integer value 72 into location number2, and memory appears, as shown in Fig. 3.21.

number1   45

number2   72

Fig. 3.21 | Memory locations after values for variables number1 and number2 have been input.

Once the program has obtained values for number1 and number2, it adds these values and places their total into variable total. The statement (line 14)

```
total = number1 + number2 ' add the two numbers
```

performs the addition and replaces total's previous value. After total is calculated, memory appears, as shown in Fig. 3.22. The values of number1 and number2 appear *exactly* as they did before they were used in the calculation of total. Although these values were used when the computer performed the calculation, they remain unchanged. As this illustrates, when a value is *read* from a memory location, the value is retained in memory.

number1   45

number2   72

total   117

Fig. 3.22 | Memory locations after an addition operation.

3.6 Arithmetic

Programs often perform arithmetic calculations. The **arithmetic operators** are summarized in Fig. 3.23. Note the use of various special symbols not used in algebra. For example, the **asterisk** (*) indicates multiplication, and the keyword **Mod** represents the **Mod operator** (also known as the **modulus** or **modulo operator**), which we'll discuss shortly. Most of the arithmetic operators in Fig. 3.23 are binary operators, because each operates on two operands. For example, the expression sum + value contains the binary operator + and the two operands sum and value. Visual Basic also provides **unary operators** that take only one operand. For example, unary versions of plus (+) and minus (–) are provided, so that you can write expressions such as +9 and –19.

Visual Basic operation	Arithmetic operator	Algebraic expression	Visual Basic expression
Addition	+	$f + 7$	f + 7
Subtraction	–	$p - c$	p – c
Multiplication	*	bm	b * m
Division (floating point)	/	x / y or $\frac{x}{y}$ or $x \div y$	x / y
Division (integer)	\	none	v \ u
Modulus	Mod	$r \bmod s$	r Mod s
Exponentiation	^	q^p	q ^ p
Unary minus	–	$-e$	–e
Unary plus	+	$+g$	+g

Fig. 3.23 | Arithmetic operators.

Division Operators

Visual Basic has separate operators for **integer division** (the backslash, \) and **floating-point division** (the forward slash, /). Integer division takes two Integer operands and yields an Integer result; for example, the expression 7 \ 4 evaluates to 1, and the expression 17 \ 5 evaluates to 3. Any fractional part in an Integer division result simply is truncated (that is, discarded)—no rounding occurs. When floating-point numbers (that is, numbers that contain a decimal point, such as 2.3456 and –845.7840) are used with the integer division operator, the numbers are first rounded to the nearest whole number, *then* divided. This means that, although 7.1 \ 4 evaluates to 1 as expected, the statement 7.7 \ 4 evaluates to 2, because 7.7 is rounded to 8 before the division occurs. To divide floating-point numbers *without* rounding the operands (which is normally what you want to do), use the floating-point division operator.

> **Common Programming Error 3.4**
> *Using the integer division operator (\) when the floating-point division operator (/) is expected (that is, when one or both of the operands is a floating-point value) can lead to incorrect results.*

Error-Prevention Tip 3.2

Ensure that each integer division operator has only integer operands.

Common Programming Error 3.5

Neither division operator allows division by zero. If your code divides by zero, a runtime error occurs. By default, this error terminates the application.

Mod *Operator*

The Mod operator yields the *remainder* after division. The expression x Mod y yields the remainder after x is divided by y. Thus, 7 Mod 4 yields 3, and 17 Mod 5 yields 2. You use this operator mostly with Integer operands, but it also can be used with other types. When you add 1 to 59 you normally expect the result to be 60. But in an application that keeps time, adding 1 to 59 *seconds* should cause the seconds to reset to zero and the *minutes* to be incremented by 1. The Mod operator is helpful in this situation. In later chapters, we consider other interesting applications of the Mod operator, such as determining whether one number is a multiple of another.

Arithmetic Expressions in Straight-Line Form

Arithmetic expressions must be entered into the computer in **straight-line form**. Thus, expressions such as "a divided by b" must be written as a / b, so that all constants, variables and operators appear in a straight line. The algebraic notation

$$\frac{a}{b}$$

is generally *not* acceptable to compilers, although some special-purpose software packages do exist that support more natural notation for complex mathematical expressions.

Parentheses for Grouping Subexpressions

Parentheses are used in Visual Basic expressions in the same manner as in algebraic expressions. For example, to multiply a times the quantity b + c, we write a * (b + c).

Rules of Operator Precedence

Operators in arithmetic expressions are applied in a precise sequence determined by the **rules of operator precedence** (Fig. 3.24), which are similar to those in algebra. Operators in the same row of the table are said to have the same level of precedence. When we say

Operator(s)	Operation	Order of evaluation (precedence)
^	Exponentiation	Evaluated first. If there are several such operators, they're evaluated from left to right.
+, −	Sign operations (unary)	Evaluated second. If there are several such operators, they're evaluated from left to right.
*, /	Multiplication and Division	Evaluated third. If there are several such operators, they're evaluated from left to right.

Fig. 3.24 | Precedence of arithmetic operators. (Part 1 of 2.)

Operator(s)	Operation	Order of evaluation (precedence)
\	Integer division	Evaluated fourth. If there are several such operators, they're evaluated from left to right.
Mod	Modulus	Evaluated fifth. If there are several such operators, they're evaluated from left to right.
+, –	Addition and Subtraction (binary)	Evaluated sixth. If there are several such operators, they're evaluated from left to right.

Fig. 3.24 | Precedence of arithmetic operators. (Part 2 of 2.)

operators are evaluated from left to right, we're referring to the operators' **associativity**. All binary operators associate from left to right. If there are multiple operators, each with the same precedence, the order in which the operators are applied is determined by the operators' associativity.

Operators in expressions contained within a pair of parentheses are evaluated before those that are outside the parentheses. Parentheses can be used to group expressions and change the order of evaluation to occur *in any sequence you desire*. With **nested parentheses**, the operators contained in the innermost pair of parentheses are applied first.

Not all expressions with several pairs of parentheses contain *nested* parentheses. For example, although the expression

```
a * (b + c) + c * (d + e)
```

contains multiple sets of parentheses, none are nested. Rather, these sets are said to be "on the same level." Appendix A contains a complete operator-precedence chart.

Sample Algebraic and Visual Basic Expressions

Now consider several expressions in light of the rules of operator precedence. Each example lists an algebraic expression and its Visual Basic equivalent. The following is an example of an arithmetic mean (average) of five terms:

Algebra: $m = \dfrac{a + b + c + d + e}{5}$

Visual Basic: `m = (a + b + c + d + e) / 5`

The parentheses are required, because division has higher precedence than addition. The entire quantity (a + b + c + d + e) is to be divided by 5. If the parentheses are erroneously omitted, we obtain a + b + c + d + e / 5, which evaluates as

$$a + b + c + d + \frac{e}{5}$$

The following is the equation of a straight line:

Algebra: $y = mx + b$

Visual Basic: `y = m * x + b`

No parentheses are required. The multiplication is applied first, because multiplication has a higher precedence than addition.

Evaluation of a More Complex Expression
To develop a better understanding of the rules of operator precedence, consider how the expression $y = ax^2 + bx + c$ is evaluated:

The circled numbers under the statement indicate the order in which Visual Basic applies the operators. In Visual Basic, x^2 is represented as x ^ 2. The exponentiation is applied first. The multiplication operators are evaluated next in left-to-right order (that is, they associate from left to right). The addition operators are evaluated next from left to right.

Now, suppose that a, b, c and x in the preceding expression are initialized as follows: a = 2, b = 3, c = 7 and x = 5. Figure 3.25 illustrates the order in which the operators are applied.

Step 1.   y = 2 * 5 ^ 2 + 3 * 5 + 7   *(Exponentiation first)*
                          5 ^ 2 is 25

Step 2.   y = 2 * 25 + 3 * 5 + 7   *(Leftmost multiplication)*
                       2 * 25 is 50

Step 3.   y = 50 + 3 * 5 + 7   *(Multiplication before addition)*
                            3 * 5 is 15

Step 4.   y = 50 + 15 + 7   *(Leftmost addition)*
                       50 + 15 is 65

Step 5.   y = 65 + 7   *(Last addition)*
                       65 + 7 is 72

Step 6.   y = 72   *(Last operation—place 72 in y)*

Fig. 3.25 | Order in which operations are evaluated.

Redundant Parentheses
As in algebra, it is acceptable to place unnecessary parentheses in an expression to make the expression clearer—these are called **redundant parentheses**. For example, many people might parenthesize the preceding assignment statement for clarity as

```
y = (a * x ^ 2) + (b * x) + c
```

Good Programming Practice 3.7

Using redundant parentheses in complex arithmetic expressions can make them easier to read.

Error-Prevention Tip 3.3

When you are uncertain about the order of evaluation in a complex expression, you can use parentheses to force the order, as you would in an algebraic expression, or you can break complex expressions into several simpler ones. Doing so can help avoid subtle bugs.

3.7 Decision Making: Equality and Relational Operators

This section introduces Visual Basic's If...Then statement, which allows a program to make a decision based on the truth or falsity of some expression. The expression in an If...Then statement is called a **condition**. If the condition *is* met (that is, the condition is true), the statement in the If...Then statement's body executes. If the condition *is not* met (that is, the condition is false), the body statement does not execute. Conditions in If...Then statements can be formed by using the **equality operators** and **relational operators** (also called **comparison operators**), which are summarized in Fig. 3.26. The relational and equality operators all have the same level of precedence and associate from left to right.

Standard algebraic equality operator or relational operator	Visual Basic equality or relational operator	Example of Visual Basic condition	Meaning of Visual Basic condition
Equality operators			
=	=	x = y	x is equal to y
≠	<>	x <> y	x is not equal to y
Relational operators			
>	>	x > y	x is greater than y
<	<	x < y	x is less than y
≥	>=	x >= y	x is greater than or equal to y
≤	<=	x <= y	x is less than or equal to y

Fig. 3.26 | Equality and relational operators.

Comparing Integers with the Equality and Relational Operators

The Comparison program uses six If...Then statements to compare two numbers entered into a program by the user. If the condition in any of these statements is true, the statement associated with that If...Then executes. The user enters these values, which are stored in variables number1 and number2, respectively. Then the comparisons are performed and the results are displayed in a multiline TextBox. Figure 3.27 shows the program and sample outputs.

```vb
 1   ' Fig. 3.27: Comparison.vb
 2   ' Comparing integers with the equality and relational operators.
 3   Public Class Comparison
 4      ' compares two integers using the relational and equality operators
 5      Private Sub compareButton_Click(ByVal sender As System.Object,
 6         ByVal e As System.EventArgs) Handles compareButton.Click
 7
 8         ' declare Integer variables to store user input
 9         Dim number1 As Integer
10         Dim number2 As Integer
11
12         number1 = number1TextBox.Text ' get first number entered by user
13         number2 = number2TextBox.Text ' get second number entered by user
14
15         If number1 = number2 Then ' number1 is equal to number2
16            resultTextBox.AppendText(number1 & " = " & number2)
17         End If
18
19         If number1 <> number2 Then ' number1 is not equal to number2
20            resultTextBox.AppendText(number1 & " <> " & number2)
21         End If
22
23         If number1 < number2 Then ' number1 is less than number2
24            resultTextBox.AppendText(vbCrLf & number1 & " < " & number2)
25         End If
26
27         If number1 > number2 Then ' number1 is greater than number2
28            resultTextBox.AppendText(vbCrLf & number1 & " > " & number2)
29         End If
30
31         ' number1 is less than or equal to number2
32         If number1 <= number2 Then
33            resultTextBox.AppendText(vbCrLf & number1 & " <= " & number2)
34         End If
35
36         ' number1 is greater than or equal to number2
37         If number1 >= number2 Then
38            resultTextBox.AppendText(vbCrLf & number1 & " >= " & number2)
39         End If
40      End Sub ' compareButton_Click
41
42      ' clears resultTextBox when the user begins typing in number1TextBox
43      Private Sub number1TextBox_TextChanged(ByVal sender As System.Object,
44         ByVal e As System.EventArgs) Handles number1TextBox.TextChanged
45
46         resultTextBox.Clear() ' clears the resultTextBox
47      End Sub ' number1TextBox_TextChanged
48
49      ' clears resultTextBox when the user begins typing in number2TextBox
50      Private Sub number2TextBox_TextChanged(ByVal sender As System.Object,
51         ByVal e As System.EventArgs) Handles number2TextBox.TextChanged
52
```

Fig. 3.27 | Comparing integers with the equality and relational operators. (Part 1 of 2.)

```
53           resultTextBox.Clear() ' clears the resultTextBox
54        End Sub ' number2TextBox_TextChanged
55     End Class ' Comparison
```

Fig. 3.27 | Comparing integers with the equality and relational operators. (Part 2 of 2.)

Getting the Values Entered By the User

Lines 9–10 declare the variables that are used in the compareButton_Click event handler. The comment that precedes the declarations indicates the purpose of the variables in the program. Lines 12–13 get the numbers that the user entered and assign the values to Integer variables number1 and number2, respectively.

The If...Then Statement

The If...Then statement in lines 15–17 compares the values of the variables number1 and number2 for equality. If the values are equal, the statement in line 16 outputs a string indicating that the two numbers are equal. The keywords **End If** (line 17) end the body of the If...Then statement. Assignment and the equality operator both use the = symbol. When a condition is expected (such as after the If keyword in an If...Then statement), the = is used as an equality operator.

*Displaying Text in a Multiline **TextBox***

In this program, we display several lines of text in a TextBox. To enable this functionality, we set the TextBox's MultiLine property to True in the Properties window. We also use the TextBox's **AppendText method**, which enables us to add more text to what is already displayed in a TextBox. The statement in line 16 is known as a **method call** because it "calls" a method (that is, method AppendText of class TextBox) to ask the method to perform its task. Sometimes you give a method values—known as **arguments**—that the method uses while performing its task. In line 16 of Fig. 3.27, the expression number1 & " = " & number2 in parentheses is the argument to method AppendText.

In line 16, if number1 contains the value 333 and number2 contains the value 333, the expression inside the parentheses following AppendText evaluates as follows: number1 is converted to a string and concatenated with the string " = ", then number2 is converted to a string and concatenated with the resulting string from the first concatenation. At this point, the string "333 = 333" is appended to the TextBox's Text property by method AppendText. As the program proceeds through the remaining If...Then statements (lines 19–39), additional strings are appended by the resultTextBox.AppendText statements.

For example, when given the value 333 for number1 and number2, the conditions in lines 32 and 37 also are true, resulting in the third output of Fig. 3.27.

Lines 24, 28, 33 and 38 also append the value vbCrLf to the TextBox. This predefined value, known as a constant, positions the **output cursor** (the location where the next output character will be displayed) at the beginning of the next line in the TextBox. This behavior is similar to what happens when you press the *Enter* key when typing in a text editor window—the cursor is repositioned at the beginning of the next line.

Indentation in If...Then Statements

Notice the indentation of the body statements within the If...Then statements throughout the program. Such indentation enhances program readability.

Good Programming Practice 3.8

Visual Basic indents the statements in the body of an If...Then statement to emphasize the body statements and enhance program readability.

Handling the TextChanged Events for number1TextBox and number2TextBox

After comparing two numbers and clicking the **Compare** Button, the resultTextBox shows the results of comparing the two values. If the user wishes to compare different values and starts typing in number1TextBox or number2TextBox, the previous results will still be displayed in the resultTextBox. This can be confusing to the program's user. To prevent this problem, you can handle number1TextBox's and number2TextBox's TextChanged events and use them to clear the contents of the resultTextBox. The **TextChanged** event is a TextBox's default event. Lines 43–47 and 50–54 show the TextChanged event handlers for number1TextBox and number2TextBox, respectively. These methods are called when the user types in the corresponding TextBoxes. In both cases, we call the resultTextBox's **Clear** method, which removes the text that is currently displayed in the TextBox. You can also clear a Label's or TextBox's Text property by assigning it the value String.Empty, which represents a string that does not contain any characters.

Building the GUI

Use the techniques you learned in Section 3.4 to build the GUI for the Comparison program. Figure 3.28 shows the GUI with all of its variable names. To allow the resultText-Box to display multiple lines, set its MultiLine property to True. In the Windows Forms

Fig. 3.28 | Comparison program GUI with variable names.

designer, double click the compareButton to create its event handler. To create the Text-Changed event handlers for the number1TextBox and number2TextBox, double click each one in the Windows Forms designer—TextChanged is the default event for a TextBox.

Entering the Code; Introducing the Parameter Info Window

Enter the code from Fig. 3.27 into the three event handlers to complete the application. When you're typing line 16, the IDE displays the *Parameter Info* window (Fig. 3.29) as you type the opening left parenthesis character, (, after resultTextBox.AppendText. This window contains information about the method and the information that the method needs to perform its task—its so-called parameter (methods can have several parameters). In this case, the *parameter info* window shows that the method requires you to give it the text to append to the current contents of the TextBox. The information you provide when you call the method is the method's argument.

Testing the Program

Be sure to test your program. Enter the values shown in the sample outputs of Fig. 3.27 to ensure that the program is working properly.

Fig. 3.29 | *Parameter Info* window for the TextBox's AppendText method.

Operator Precedence

Figure 3.30 shows the precedence of the operators introduced in this chapter. The operators are displayed from top to bottom in decreasing order of precedence.

Operators	Type
^	exponentiation
+ -	sign operations (unary)
* /	multiplication and floating-point division
\	Integer division
Mod	modulus
+ -	addition and subtraction (binary)
= <> < <= > >=	equality and relational

Fig. 3.30 | Precedence of the operators introduced in this chapter.

3.8 Wrap-Up

You learned many features of Visual Basic in this chapter, including displaying data on Labels, inputting data from TextBoxes and declaring variables of primitive type Integer. You used GUIs to build simple interactive programs. We demonstrated how to use event handling to respond to a Form's Load event, a Button's Click event and a TextBox's Text-Changed event. You learned how to position, size and align controls using the IDEs Windows Forms designer. We explained how values are stored in and retrieved from variables in memory. You learned how to use arithmetic operators to perform calculations, and the order in which Visual Basic applies these operators (that is, the rules of operator precedence and associativity). We demonstrated how Visual Basic's If...Then statement allows a program to perform actions based on a condition. You learned how to create conditions using the equality and relational operators.

In the next chapter, we begin our discussion of structured programming. We demonstrate creating applications using pseudocode, an informal language that helps you develop programs. We study how to specify and vary the order in which statements are executed—this is called **flow of control**. You'll learn how to use control statements to select between alternative actions based on the truth or falsity of a condition, or to perform actions repeatedly based on a condition. You'll see several case studies that demonstrate the types of repetition.

Summary

Section 3.1 Introduction

- Graphical user interfaces (GUIs) allow users to interact visually with programs.
- A GUI (pronounced "GOO-ee") gives a program a distinctive look-and-feel.
- GUI controls can display information on the screen or enable users to interact with an application via the mouse, keyboard or another form of input.
- The .NET framework provides many predefined controls.

Section 3.2 Programmatically Displaying Text in a Label

- Most programmers use a combination of visual programming and conventional programming.

Section 3.2.1 Analyzing the Program

- A single-quote character (') indicates that the remainder of the line is a comment.
- The compiler ignores comments.
- Classes are logical groupings of methods and data that simplify program organization.
- Every Windows Forms application consists of at least one class containing one or more methods.
- Keywords like Public and Class are reserved for use by Visual Basic.
- An identifier is a series of characters consisting of letters, digits and underscores (_). Identifiers cannot begin with a digit and cannot contain spaces.
- Visual Basic keywords and identifiers are not case sensitive.
- Whitespace (spaces, tabs and blank lines) makes programs easier to read.
- GUIs are event driven. When the user interacts with a GUI component, the interaction—known as an event—causes the program to perform a task by calling a method. Common events include clicking a Button, selecting an item from a menu, closing a window and moving the mouse.

- A method that performs a task in response to an event is called an event handler, and the overall process of responding to events is known as event handling.
- A Form's Load event occurs just before a Form is displayed on the screen.
- The keyword Sub begins a method declaration; End Sub closes it.
- Indentation improves program readability.
- A series of characters between double quotation marks is called a string.
- The assignment operator (=) can be used to give a new value to a property.
- The dot separator (.) is used to programmatically access a control's properties and methods.

Section 3.2.2 Modifying ASimpleProgram to Programmatically Change the Label's Text Property

- To load an existing project, select **File > Open Project…** in the IDE and locate the project's .sln file, or double click the .sln file in Windows Explorer.
- To view the code for a Form: Right click the Form and select **View Code**; right click the .vb file in the **Solution Explorer** and select **View Code**; press the *F7* key; or select **Code** from the **View** menu.
- Syntax-color highlighting helps you visually differentiate program elements in the IDE.
- The IDE will often update your code to conform to various Visaul Basic code conventions.
- Double clicking any control creates that control's default event handler (if it does not already exist) and switches to code view. For a Form, the default is the Load event handler.
- To improve readability, long statements may be split over several lines. In earlier versions of Visual Basic, you were required to use the line-continuation character (_) to do this. When used, the line-continuation character *must* be preceded by a space.
- As you begin typing code, *IntelliSense* lists keywords, class names, members of a class and other features that start with the same characters you've typed so far.
- *IntelliSense* highlights the most commonly used item that matches the characters typed, then displays a tool tip with information about that item. You can either type the complete item name, double click the item name in the list or press the *Tab* key to complete the name.
- Once you type a dot (.) after a variable name, the *IntelliSense* window shows the members that can be used on the right of the dot.
- While the *IntelliSense* window is displayed, pressing the *Ctrl* key makes the window transparent so you can see the code behind it. You can display *IntelliSense* by pressing *Ctrl* and the *Spacebar*.
- To run a program, select **Debug > Start Debugging** (or press *F5* or the toolbar button ▶). When you run a program, the IDE first compiles it. You can also compile the program without running it by selecting **Debug > Build** *YourProjectName*. This creates a new file with the project's name and a .exe file-name extension, which indicates that the file is executable.
- When you type a line of code and press the *Enter* key, the IDE responds either by applying syntax-color highlighting or by generating a syntax error, which indicates a violation of Visual Basic's rules for creating correct programs.
- When a syntax error occurs, the IDE places a blue squiggle below the error and provides a description of the error in the **Error List** window. You can double click an error message in the **Error List** to jump to the line of code that caused the error. For some errors, the IDE shows the **Error Correction Options** drop-down list and allows you to simply click a link to fix the error.

Section 3.3 Addition Program

- A Label's text can be changed programmatically by modifying the Label's Text property.
- Labels that direct the user to take a specific action are called prompts.

- A TextBox's Text property can be used to change the text that is displayed in a TextBox or to get information the user types in a TextBox.
- The user clicks a Button to trigger a specific action. The text displayed on a Button is specified using its Text property.
- Variable declarations begin with keyword Dim and specify identifiers for variables. All variables must be declared before they can be used in a program.
- Types defined as part of the Visual Basic language, such as Integer, are known as primitive types and their type names are keywords.
- A variable name can be any valid identifier.
- The assignment operator (=) is used to give a value to a variable. The expression to the right of the = is always evaluated first before the assignment occurs.
- The string concatenation operator, &, is a binary operator that joins two strings together, resulting in a new, longer string. If one of the operands is a number, the program creates a string representation of the number before performing the concatenation.

Section 3.4 Building the Addition Program
- You can rename a control by modifying its (Name) property.
- Snap lines help you position a control with respect to the Form's edges and other controls.
- Set a Label's BorderStyle property to Fixed3D to give the Label a three-dimensional appearance.
- For a Button, the default event is the Click event.

Section 3.5 Memory Concepts
- Every variable has a name, type, size and value.
- A value placed in a memory location replaces the value previously stored there.
- When a value is read from a memory location, the value is retained unmodified.

Section 3.6 Arithmetic
- Most arithmetic operators are binary operators—they take two operands.
- Unary operators take only one operand. Unary versions of plus (+) and minus (-) are provided, so that you can write expressions such as +9 and -19.
- Integer division (\) takes two Integer operands and yields an Integer result. Any fractional part in an Integer division result is truncated. When floating-point numbers are used with the integer division operator, the numbers are rounded to the nearest whole number, then divided. To divide floating-point numbers without rounding, use the floating-point division operator (/).
- The Mod operator yields the remainder after division.
- Parentheses are used in Visual Basic expressions in the same manner as in algebraic expressions.
- Operators in arithmetic expressions are applied in a precise sequence determined by the rules of operator precedence, which are similar to those in algebra.
- Multiple operators with the same precedence are applied in the order determined by the operators' associativity. Binary operators associate from left to right.
- Operators in expressions contained in parentheses are evaluated before those that are outside the parentheses. Parentheses can be used to change the order of evaluation. With nested parentheses, the operators contained in the innermost pair of parentheses are applied first.
- As in algebra, it's acceptable to place redundant parentheses in an expression to make the expression clearer.

Section 3.7 Decision Making: Equality and Relational Operators

- The If...Then statement allows a program to make a decision based on a condition. If the condition is true, the body statements execute; otherwise, they do not.

- Conditions can be formed by using the equality operators and relational operators. These operators all have the same level of precedence and associate from left to right.

- Assignment and the equality operator both use the = symbol. When a condition is expected, = represents the equality operator.

- To display several lines of text in a TextBox, set its MultiLine property to True.

- TextBox method AppendText adds more text to what is already displayed in a TextBox.

- A method call asks a method to perform its task. Sometimes a method receives values, known as arguments, from its caller—it uses these arguments while performing its task.

- A TextBox's TextChanged event occurs when the text in a TextBox changes. This is the default event for a TextBox.

- TextBox method Clear removes the text that is currently displayed in a TextBox.

- The IDE displays the *Parameter Info* window as you type the opening left parenthesis character, (, in a method call. This window contains information about the method and the information that the method needs to perform its task—its so-called parameters.

Terminology

_ line-continuation character 68
. dot separator 65
* multiplication operator 81
+ addition operator 81
- subtraction operator 81
/ floating-point division operator 81
\ integer division operator 81
& string concatenation operator 73
= assignment operator 65
action 65
AppendText method of a TextBox 87
arithmetic operator 81
assignment statement 72
associativity of operators 83
asterisk (*) indicating multiplication 81
binary operator 72
book-title capitalization 76
BorderStyle property of a Label 77
Button class 71
case sensitive 64
character string 65
class 63
class declaration 63
Class...End Class keywords 63
Clear method of a TextBox 88
comment 63
comparison operator 85
component 61

condition 85
declaration 71
Dim keyword 71
End Class keywords 65
End If keywords 87
End Sub keywords 65
equality operators (=, <>) 85
Error List window 70
event 64
event driven 64
event handler 64
.exe file extension 69
executable file 69
File Name property of a file in the **Solution Explorer** 66
Fixed3D value for BorderStyle property 77
floating-point number 81
flow of control 90
Handles keyword 64
identifier 64
If...Then selection statement 85
Integer primitive type 72
IntelliSense 68
keyword 63
Load event of a Form 64
member of a class 68
method 63
method call 87

Self-Review Exercises

3.1 Answer each of the following questions:

a) The Form's _____ property specifies the text that is displayed in the Form's title bar.

1. Title
2. Text
3. (Name)
4. Name

b) Property _____ specifies how text is aligned within a Label's boundaries.

1. Alignment
2. AlignText
3. Align
4. TextAlign

c) A Button's text should use _____ capitalization.

1. book-title
2. complete
3. no
4. sentence-style

d) An output Label should _____.

1. be distinguishable from other Labels
2. initially have an empty Text property or a default value (e.g., 0)
3. use Fixed3D for the BorderStyle property
4. All of the above

e) A Button's _____ property sets the text on the face of the Button.

1. Name
2. Text
3. Title
4. Face

f) If there are errors in an application, they appear in a window known as the _____.

1. Task List
2. Output
3. Properties
4. Error List

g) When a value is placed into a memory location, the value _____ the previous value in that location.

1. copies
2. replaces
3. adds itself to
4. moves

h) When a value is read from memory, that value is _____.
   1. overwritten   2. replaced with a new value
   3. moved to a new location in memory   4. not overwritten

i) Arithmetic expressions in must be written _____ to facilitate entering applications into the computer.
   1. using parentheses   2. on multiple lines
   3. in straight-line form   4. None of the above

j) The expression to the right of an assignment operator (=) is evaluated _____ the assignment occurs.
   1. before   2. after
   3. at the same time   4. None of the above

3.2 State whether each of the following is *true* or *false*. If *false*, explain why.
   a) Comments cause the computer to print the text after the ' on the screen when the program executes.
   b) All variables must be declared before they can be used in a Visual Basic program.
   c) Visual Basic considers the variable names `number` and `NuMbEr` to be different.
   d) The arithmetic operators *, /, + and - all have the same level of precedence.
   e) A string of characters contained between double quotation marks is called a phrase or phrase literal.
   f) Integer division yields an `Integer` result.

Answers to Self-Review Exercises

3.1 a) 2. b) 4. c) 1. d) 4. e) 2. f) 4. g) 2. h) 4. i) 3. j) 1.

3.2 a) False. Comments do not cause any action to be performed when the program executes. They're used to document programs and improve their readability. b) True. c) False. Identifiers are not case sensitive, so these variable names are identical. d) False. The operators * and / are on the same level of precedence, and the operators + and - are on a lower level of precedence. e) False. A string of characters is called a string or string literal. f) True.

Quick Quiz

3.3 Answer each of the following questions:
   a) A `Label`'s `BorderStyle` property can be set to _____.
      1. `Fixed3D`   2. `Single`
      3. `3D`   4. All of the above
   b) A(n) _____ helps the user understand a control's purpose.
      1. `Button`   2. descriptive `Label`
      3. output `Label`   4. title bar
   c) A _____ is a control in which the user can enter data from a keyboard.
      1. `Button`   2. `TextBox`
      3. `Label`   4. `PictureBox`
   d) A descriptive `Label` uses _____.
      1. sentence-style capitalization   2. book-title capitalization
      3. a colon at the end of its text   4. Both a and c
   e) A(n) _____ represents a user action, such as clicking a `Button`.
      1. statement   2. event
      3. application   4. function

f) Code that performs the functionality of an application _____.
1. normally is provided by the programmer
2. can never be in the form of an event handler
3. always creates a graphical user interface
4. is always generated by the IDE

g) Comments _____.
1. help improve program readability
2. are preceded by the single-quote character
3. are ignored by the compiler   4. All of the above

h) A(n) _____ contains code that performs a specific task.
1. variable   2. method
3. operand   4. identifier

i) Visual Basic keywords are _____.
1. identifiers   2. reserved words
3. case sensitive   4. properties

j) An example of a whitespace character is a _____ character.
1. space   2. tab
3. newline   4. All of the above

k) Parentheses added to an expression simply to make it easier to read are known as _____ parentheses.
1. necessary   2. redundant
3. embedded   4. nested

l) The _____ operator performs integer division.
1. \   2. +
3. Mod   4. ^

m) Every variable has a _____.
1. name   2. value
3. type   4. All of the above

n) Variable declarations in event handlers begin with the keyword _____.
1. Declare   2. Dim
3. Sub   4. Integer

o) Entering a value in a TextBox causes a _____ event.
1. TextAltered   2. ValueChanged
3. ValueEntered   4. TextChanged

p) Variables that store integer values should be declared as an _____.
1. Integer   2. Int
3. IntVariable   4. None of the above

q) The data type in a variable declaration is immediately preceded by keyword _____.
1. IsA   2. Type
3. Dim   4. As

Exercises

3.4 Write Visual Basic statements that accomplish each of the following tasks:
a) Display the message "Hello" in resultTextBox.
b) Assign the product of hourlySalary and hoursWorked to variable earnings.
c) State that a program performs a sample payroll calculation (that is, use text that helps to document a program).

3.5   *(What does this code do?)* This code modifies variables number1, number2 and result. What are the final values of these variables?

```
1    Dim number1 As Integer
2    Dim number2 As Integer
3    Dim result As Integer
4
5    number1 = 5 * (4 + 6)
6    number2 = 2 ^ 2
7    result = number1 \ number2
```

3.6   *(What's wrong with this code?)* Find the error(s) in the following code, which uses variables to perform a calculation.

```
1    Dim number1 As Integer
2    Dim number2 As Integer
3    Dim result As Integer
4
5    number1 = (4 * 6 ^ 4) / (10 Mod 4 - 2)
6    number2 = (16 \ 3) ^ 2 * 6 + 1
7    result = number1 - number2
```

3.7   *(Temperature Converter Application)* Write an application that converts a Celsius temperature, *C*, to its equivalent Fahrenheit temperature, *F*. Figure 3.31 displays the completed application. Use the following formula:

$$F = \frac{9}{5}C + 32$$

Fig. 3.31 | Completed **Temperature Converter**.

a) *Creating the application.* Create a new Windows Forms application named TemperatureConverter. Rename its Form1.vb file as TemperatureConverter.vb. Set the Form's Font property to Segoe UI 9pt and its Text property to Temperature Converter.

b) *Coding the Click event handler.* Perform the conversion in the **Convert** Button's Click event handler. Display the Fahrenheit equivalent of the Celsius temperature.

c) *Clearing the result.* When the user starts typing in the **Enter a Celsius temperature:** TextBox, use the TextBox's TextChanged event to clear the previous result. You can do this by assigning the value String.Empty to the output Label's Text property. String.Empty is equivalent to a string literal with no characters—that is, "".

d) *Running the application.* Select **Debug > Start Debugging** to run your application. Enter the value 20 into the **Enter a Celsius temperature:** TextBox and click the **Convert** Button. Verify that the value 68 is displayed in the output Label. Enter other Celsius temperatures; click the **Convert** Button after each. Verify that the proper Fahrenheit equivalent is displayed each time.

3.8 *(Simple Calculator Application)* Write a simple calculator application (Fig. 3.32). The calculator allows a user to enter two integers in the TextBoxes. There are four Buttons labeled +, -, / and *. When the user clicks one of these Buttons, the application performs that operation on the integers in the TextBoxes and displays the result. The calculator also should clear the calculation result when the user enters new input.

Fig. 3.32 | Result of **Calculator** application.

a) *Creating the application.* Create a new Windows Forms application named SimpleCalculator. Rename its Form1.vb file as SimpleCalculator.vb. Set the Form's Font property to Segoe UI 9pt and its Text property to Simple Calculator.

b) *Coding the addition Click event handler.* This event handler should add the two numbers and display the result.

c) *Coding the subtraction Click event handler.* This event handler should subtract the second number from the first number and display the result.

d) *Coding the multiplication Click event handler.* This event handler should multiply the two numbers and display the result.

e) *Coding the division Click event handler.* This event handler should divide the first number by the second number and display the result.

f) *Clearing the result.* Write event handlers for the TextBoxes' TextChanged events. Write code to clear resultLabel after the user enters new input into either TextBox.

g) *Running the application.* Run your application. Enter a first number and a second number, then verify that each of the Buttons works by clicking each and viewing the output.

3.9 *(Average Calculator Application)* Write an application that takes three numbers as input in TextBoxes, stores the three integers in variables, then calculates and displays the average of the numbers. The output is displayed in a Label. Figure 3.33 shows the completed application.

Fig. 3.33 | Result of **Average Calculator** application.

a) *Creating the application.* Create a new Windows Forms application named Average-Calculator. Rename its Form1.vb file as AverageCalculator.vb. Set the Form's Font property to Segoe UI 9pt and its Text property to Average Calculator.

b) *Coding the Click event handler.* Perform the average calculation in the **Calculate** Button's Click event handler. Display the average in the resultLabel.

c) *Clearing the result.* Write event handlers for the TextBoxes' TextChanged events. Write code to clear resultLabel after the user enters new input into any of the TextBoxes.

d) *Running the application.* Select **Debug > Start Debugging** to run your application. Enter three integers, then verify that the average is calculated properly.

Solve Exercises 3.10–3.15 using the same techniques as in Exercises 3.7–3.9.

3.10 *(Diameter, Circumference and Area)* Write an application that inputs from the user the radius of a circle and displays the circle's diameter, circumference and area. Use the following formulas (*r* is the radius): *diameter* = 2*r*, *circumference* = 2π*r*, *area* = π*r*². Use the predefined constant Math.PI from class Math for π. Figure 3.34 shows the completed application.

Fig. 3.34 | Completed circle information application.

3.11 *(Multiples)* Write an application that reads two integers and determines and prints whether the first is a multiple of the second. For example, if the user inputs 15 and 3, the first number is a multiple of the second. If the user inputs 2 and 4, the first number is not a multiple of the second. [*Hint:* Use the Mod operator.] Figure 3.35 shows the completed application.

Fig. 3.35 | Completed multiples application.

3.12 *(Displaying Tabular Data)* Write a program that calculates the squares and cubes of the numbers from 0 to 5 and displays the resulting values in table format as shown in Figure 3.36. Set the TextBox's MultiLine property to True and its Font property to the fixed-width font Lucida Console. You can use the Visual Basic constant vbTab to create the tabular output by placing tabs between each column. In Chapter 4, we study repetition, which will make this much easier.

Fig. 3.36 | Displaying tabular data in a `TextBox`.

3.13   *(Find the Largest and Smallest Sales Figures)* Write an application that reads integers representing the total sales for three sales people then determines and prints the largest and the smallest integers in the group. Figure 3.37 shows the completed application.

Fig. 3.37 | Completed largest and smallest application.

3.14   *(Concatenating Strings)* Write a program that reads a first name and a last name from the user as two separate inputs and concatenates the first name and last name, separating them by a space. Display the concatenated name in a `Label`. You can store the user input in variables of type `String`, a primitive type used to represent string data. Figure 3.38 shows the completed application. You can create variables of type `String` just as you created variables of type `Integer`, except using the keyword `String`:

```
Dim firstName As String
Dim lastName As String
```

Fig. 3.38 | Completed string concatenation application.

3.15   *(Digit Extraction)* Write an application that allows the user to enter a five-digit number into a `TextBox`. The application then separates the number into its individual digits and displays each digit in a separate Label. The application should look and behave similarly to Figure 3.39. [*Hint:* You can use the Mod operator to extract the ones digit from a number. For instance, 12345 Mod 10 is 5. You can use integer division (\) to "peel off" digits from a number. For instance, 12345 \ 100 is 123. This allows you to treat the 3 in 12345 as a ones digit. Now you can isolate the 3 by using the Mod operator. Apply this technique to the rest of the digits.]

Fig. 3.39 | Digit Extractor application GUI.

Making a Difference Exercises

3.16 *(Body Mass Index Calculator)* We introduced the body mass index (BMI) calculator in Exercise 1.19. The formulas for calculating the BMI are

$$BMI = \frac{weightInPounds \times 703}{heightInInches \times heightInInches}$$

or

$$BMI = \frac{weightInKilograms}{heightInMeters \times heightInMeters}$$

Create a BMI calculator application that reads the user's weight in pounds and height in inches (or, if you prefer, the user's weight in kilograms and height in meters), then calculates and displays the user's body mass index. Also, the application should use a multiline TextBox with its Enabled property set to False and its Font property set to Lucida Console to display the following information from the Department of Health and Human Services/National Institutes of Health so the user can evaluate his/her BMI:

```
BMI VALUES
Underweight: less than 18.5
Normal:      between 18.5 and 24.9
Overweight:  between 25 and 29.9
Obese:       30 or greater
```

Figure 3.40 shows the completed application.

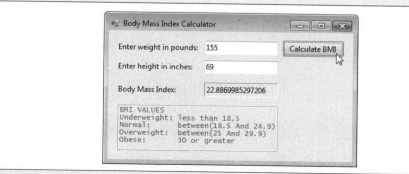

Fig. 3.40 | Completed BMI application.

3.17   *(Car-Pool Savings Calculator)* Research several car-pooling websites. Create an application that calculates your daily driving cost, so that you can estimate how much money could be saved by car pooling, which also has other advantages such as reducing carbon emissions and reducing traffic congestion. The application should input the following information and display the user's cost per day of driving to work:

    a)   Total miles driven per day.
    b)   Cost per gallon of gasoline.
    c)   Average miles per gallon.
    d)   Parking fees per day.
    e)   Tolls per day.

Figure 3.41 shows the completed application.

Fig. 3.41 | Completed BMI application.

Introduction to Problem Solving and Control Statements

4

Let's all move one place on.
—Lewis Carroll

The wheel is come full circle.
—William Shakespeare

How many apples fell on Newton's head before he took the hint?
—Robert Frost

Objectives

In this chapter you'll learn:

- Basic problem-solving techniques.

- To develop algorithms through the process of top-down, stepwise refinement.

- To use the If...Then and If...Then...Else selection statements to choose among alternative actions.

- To use the Do While...Loop, While...End While and Do Until...Loop repetition statements to execute statements in a program repeatedly.

- To use the compound assignment operators to abbreviate assignment operations.

- To use counter-controlled repetition.

- To use nested control statements.

- To use the debugger to locate logic errors in a program.

4.1 Introduction

Before writing a program to solve a problem, you should have a thorough understanding of the problem and a carefully planned approach. When writing a program, it's also important to know the available building blocks and to use proven program-construction principles. In this chapter and the next, we present the theory and principles of structured programming with control statements. We introduce the If...Then, If...Then...Else, Do While...Loop, While...End While and Do Until...Loop statements—five of the building blocks that allow you to specify the logic required for methods to perform their tasks. We introduce the ListBox control and use it to display and process data, such as a list of grades in a class-average program. We also demonstrate how to "stack" and "nest" control statement to solve problems. The chapter concludes with an introduction to the Visual Studio debugger. You'll learn how to view the values of variables during a program's execution, how to step through code one statement at a time and how the debugger can help you locate logic errors in your programs.

4.2 Algorithms

Any computing problem can be solved by executing a series of actions in a specific order. A **procedure** for solving a problem, in terms of

   1. the **actions** to be executed and

   2. the **order** in which these actions are to be executed

is called an **algorithm**. The following example demonstrates the importance of getting the order right.

Consider the "rise-and-shine algorithm" followed by one junior executive for getting out of bed and going to work: (1) get out of bed, (2) take off pajamas, (3) take a shower, (4) get dressed, (5) eat breakfast and (6) carpool to work. This routine prepares the executive for a productive day at the office.

However, suppose that the same steps are performed in a slightly different order: (1) get out of bed, (2) take off pajamas, (3) get dressed, (4) take a shower, (5) eat breakfast, (6) carpool to work. In this case, our junior executive shows up for work soaking wet.

Specifying the order in which statements (actions) execute in a program is called **program control**. This chapter investigates program control using **control statements**.

Software Engineering Observation 4.1

Experience has shown that the most difficult part of solving a problem on a computer is developing the algorithm for the solution. Once a correct algorithm has been specified, the process of producing a working program from the algorithm is normally straightforward.

4.3 Pseudocode

Pseudocode is an informal language that helps you develop algorithms. It's similar to everyday English; it's convenient and user friendly, but not an actual computer programming language. The pseudocode we present is particularly useful for developing algorithms that will be converted to structured portions of Visual Basic programs.

Pseudocode programs are not executed on computers. Rather, they help you "think out" a program before writing it in a programming language. You can easily convert a carefully prepared pseudocode program to a corresponding Visual Basic program.

Pseudocode normally describes only statements representing the actions that occur after you convert a program from pseudocode to Visual Basic and run the program on a computer. Such actions might include input, output or calculations.

4.4 Control Structures

Normally, statements in a program are executed one after another in the order in which they're written. This is called **sequential execution**. A **transfer of control** occurs when an executed statement does *not* directly follow the previously executed statement.

During the 1960s, it became clear that the indiscriminate use of transfers of control was causing difficulty for software development groups. A key problem was the **GoTo statement**, which allows you to specify a transfer of control to one of a wide range of possible destinations in a program. The excessive use of GoTo statements caused programs to become quite unstructured and hard to follow—such disorganized programs were referred to as "spaghetti code." Since then, the notion of **structured programming** has become almost synonymous with "GoTo elimination."

Research demonstrated that all programs could be written in terms of only three **control structures**—the **sequence structure**, the **selection structure** and the **repetition structure**. The term "control structures" comes from the field of computer science. When we introduce Visual Basic's implementation of control structures, we'll refer to them as "control statements."

Sequence Structure

Unless directed otherwise, the computer executes statements sequentially. The UML **activity diagram** in Fig. 4.1 illustrates a sequence structure that performs two calculations in order. You can have as many actions as you want in a sequence structure. Anywhere a single action may be placed, you may place several actions in sequence.

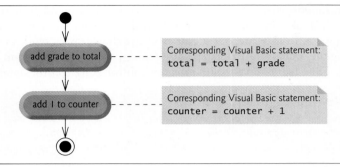

Fig. 4.1 | Sequence-structure activity diagram.

The two statements in Fig. 4.1 involve adding a grade to a `total` variable and adding the value 1 to a `counter` variable. Such statements might appear in a program that takes the average of several student grades. To calculate an average, the total of the grades being averaged is divided by the number of grades. A counter variable would be used to keep track of the number of values being averaged.

UML Activity Diagrams

Like pseudocode, activity diagrams help you develop and represent algorithms. An activity diagram models the workflow (also called the activity) of a portion of a software system. A workflow may include a portion of an algorithm, such as the sequence structure in Fig. 4.1. Activity diagrams are composed of special-purpose symbols, such as the action state symbol (a rectangle with its left and right sides replaced with arcs curving outward), the diamond symbol and the small circle symbol; these symbols are connected by transition arrows, which represent the flow of the activity.

Activity diagrams clearly show how control structures operate. The sequence-structure activity diagram in Fig. 4.1 contains two action states that represent actions to perform. Each action state contains an action expression—"add grade to total" or "add 1 to counter"—that specifies a particular action to perform. Other actions might include calculations or input/output operations. The arrows represent transitions that indicate the order in which the actions occur—the program that implements the activities illustrated by the activity diagram in Fig. 4.1 first adds `grade` to `total`, then adds 1 to `counter`.

The solid circle symbol located at the top of the activity diagram represents the activity's initial state—the *beginning* of the workflow before the corresponding program performs the activities. The solid circle surrounded by a hollow circle at the bottom of the activity diagram represents the final state—the *end* of the workflow after the corresponding program performs its activities.

Figure 4.1 also includes rectangles with the upper-right corners folded over. These are called notes in the UML. Notes are optional comments that describe the purpose of symbols in the diagram. A dotted line connects each note with the element the note describes.

Each activity diagram contains one initial state and one final state, which represent the control statement's entry and exit point, respectively. These single-entry/single-exit control statements make it easy to build programs—the control statements are "attached" to one another by "connecting" the exit point of one control statement to the entry point of the next (which we accomplish simply by following one control statement immediately by another). This is similar to stacking building blocks, so we call it **control-statement stacking**. There is only one other way to connect control statements, and that is through **control-statement nesting**, where one control statement is placed inside another.

Selection Statements

Visual Basic provides three types of selection statements.

- The `If...Then` selection statement either performs (selects) an action (or sequence of actions) if a condition is true, or *skips* the action (or sequence of actions) if the condition is false. The `If...Then` statement is called a **single-selection statement** because it selects or ignores a single action (or a sequence of actions).

- The `If...Then...Else` selection statement performs an action (or sequence of actions) if a condition is true, and performs a *different* action (or sequence of actions) if the condition is false. The `If...Then...Else` statement is called a **double-selection statement** because it selects between *two* different actions (or sequences of actions).

- The `Select...Case` selection statement performs one of *many* possible actions (or sequences of actions), depending on the value of an expression. For this reason, the `Select...Case` statement is called a **multiple-selection statement**.

Repetition Statements

Visual Basic provides seven types of repetition statements (also called **looping statements** or **loops**) that enable programs to perform statements repeatedly based on the value of a condition.

- The `Do While...Loop` and `While...End While` repetition statements execute a set of statements while a condition—known as the **loop-continuation condition**—remains true. If the condition is initially false, the set of statements does not execute.

- The `Do Until...Loop` repetition statement executes a set of statements until a condition—known as the **loop-termination condition**—becomes true. If the condition is initially true, the set of statements does not execute.

- The `Do...Loop While` repetition statement executes a set of statements while its loop-continuation condition remains true. The set of statements is guaranteed to execute at least once.

- The `Do...Loop Until` repetition statement executes a set of statements until its loop-termination condition becomes true. The set of statements is guaranteed to execute at least once.

- The `For...Next` repetition statement executes a set of statements a specified number of times—this is known as counter-controlled (or definite) repetition.

- The `For Each...Next` repetition statement (introduced in Chapter 7) performs a set of statements for every element of a so-called array or collection of values.

The words `If`, `Then`, `Else`, `End`, `Select`, `Case`, `While`, `Do`, `Until`, `Loop`, `For`, `Next` and `Each` are all keywords. By providing many repetition statements, the designers of Visual Basic make it more convenient for you to express certain types of algorithms. Theoretically, however, you need only one repetition statement that enables you to loop zero or more times based on the truth or falsity of a condition—both `Do While...Loop` and `While...End While` allow you to do this. In this book, we typically use the `Do While...Loop`, `For...Next` and `For Each... Next` repetition statements.

4.5 If...Then Selection Statement

A selection statement chooses among alternative courses of action. Suppose that the passing grade on an examination is 60 (out of 100). Then the pseudocode statement

> *If student's grade is greater than or equal to 60 then*
> > *Display "Passed"*

determines whether the condition "student's grade is greater than or equal to 60" is true or false. If the condition is true, then "Passed" is displayed, and the next pseudocode statement in order is "performed" (remember that pseudocode is not a real programming language). If the condition is false, the display statement is ignored, and the next pseudocode statement in order is "performed."

The preceding pseudocode *If* statement may be written in Visual Basic as

```
If studentGrade >= 60 Then
    resultLabel.Text = "Passed" ' display "Passed"
End If
```

The code corresponds closely to the pseudocode, showing the usefulness of pseudocode as a program-development tool. The statement in the body of the `If...Then` statement displays the string `"Passed"` on `resultLabel`.

Whitespace
The compiler ignores whitespace, such as spaces, tabs and blank lines used for indentation and vertical spacing, unless the whitespace is contained in strings. Some whitespace is required, however, such as the space between variable names and keywords. You can insert extra whitespace characters to enhance program readability.

Single Line *If...Then statement*
The preceding `If...Then` selection statement also could be written on a single line as

```
If studentGrade >= 60 Then resultLabel.Text = "Passed"
```

In the multiple-line format, all statements (there can be many) in the `If...Then`'s body execute if the condition is true. In the single-line format, only the statement immediately after the `Then` keyword executes if the condition is true.

UML Activity Diagram for the *If...Then Selection Statement*
Figure 4.2 is an activity diagram for the single-selection `If...Then` statement. It contains what is perhaps the most important symbol in an activity diagram—the diamond, or **decision symbol**, which indicates that a decision is to be made. A decision symbol indicates that the workflow will continue along a path determined by the symbol's associated **guard conditions**, which can be true or false. Each transition arrow emerging from a decision symbol has a guard condition (specified in square brackets above or next to the transition arrow). If a particular guard condition is true, the workflow enters the action state to which that transition arrow points. Exactly *one* of the guard conditions associated with a decision

symbol must be true when a decision is made. In Fig. 4.2, if the grade is greater than or equal to 60, the program displays "Passed" on the screen, then transitions to the final state of this activity. If the grade is less than 60, the program immediately transitions to the final state without displaying a message.

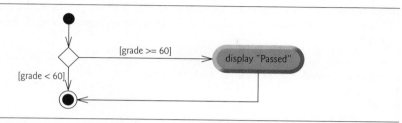

Fig. 4.2 | If...Then single-selection statement activity diagram.

4.6 If...Then...Else Selection Statement

The If...Then...Else selection statement allows you to specify that a *different* action (or sequence of actions) is to be performed when the condition is *true* than when the condition is *false*. For example, the pseudocode statement

> *If student's grade is greater than or equal to 60 then*
> > *Display "Passed"*
> *Else*
> > *Display "Failed"*

displays "Passed" if the student's grade is greater than or equal to 60, and displays "Failed" if the student's grade is less than 60. In either case, after the display occurs, the next pseudocode statement in sequence is "performed."

The preceding pseudocode *If...Else* statement may be written in Visual Basic as

```
If studentGrade >= 60 Then
    resultLabel.Text = "Passed" ' display "Passed"
Else
    resultLabel.Text = "Failed" ' display "Failed"
End If
```

The body of the **Else** clause is indented so that it lines up with the body of the If clause.

UML Activity Diagram for the If...Then...Else Selection Statement
Figure 4.3 illustrates the flow of control in the If...Then...Else statement.

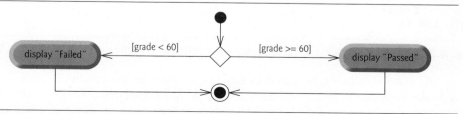

Fig. 4.3 | If...Then...Else double-selection statement activity diagram.

4.7 Nested If...Then...Else Statements

Nested **If...Then...Else statements** test for multiple conditions by placing If...Then ...Else statements *inside* other If...Then...Else statements. For example, the pseudocode in Fig. 4.4 displays "A" for exam grades greater than or equal to 90, "B" for grades in the range 80–89, "C" for grades in the range 70–79, "D" for grades in the range 60–69 and "F" for all other grades. The pseudocode may be written in Visual Basic as shown in Fig. 4.5.

```
 1    If student's grade is greater than or equal to 90 then
 2        Display "A"
 3    Else
 4        If student's grade is greater than or equal to 80 then
 5            Display "B"
 6        Else
 7            If student's grade is greater than or equal to 70 then
 8                Display "C"
 9            Else
10                If student's grade is greater than or equal to 60 then
11                    Display "D"
12                Else
13                    Display "F"
```

Fig. 4.4 | Pseudocode for nested If...Then...Else statements that display a letter grade based on a numeric grade value.

```
 1   If studentGrade >= 90 Then
 2       resultLabel.Text = "A" ' display "A"
 3   Else
 4       If studentGrade >= 80 Then
 5           resultLabel.Text = "B" ' display "B"
 6       Else
 7           If studentGrade >= 70 Then
 8               resultLabel.Text = "C" ' display "C"
 9           Else
10               If studentGrade >= 60 Then
11                   resultLabel.Text = "D" ' display "D"
12               Else
13                   resultLabel.Text = "F" ' display "F"
14               End If
15           End If
16       End If
17   End If
```

Fig. 4.5 | nested If...Then...Else statements that correspond to the pseudocode in Fig. 4.4.

If studentGrade is greater than or equal to 90, the first four conditions are true, but only the statement at line 2 executes (causing "A" to be displayed). After that statement executes, the Else part of the "outer" If...Then...Else statement (line 3–17) is skipped, and the program proceeds with the next statement after the last End If.

ElseIf

Most programmers prefer to write the nested If...Then...Else statements from Fig. 4.5 using the **ElseIf keyword** as shown in Fig. 4.6. Both forms are equivalent, but the latter is popular because it avoids deeply indenting the code and makes it more readable. In nested If...Then...Else statements, if you type Else If on one line, the Visual Basic editor will automatically convert it to ElseIf and indent the code as in Fig. 4.6.

```
 1   If grade >= 90 Then
 2       resultLabel.Text = "A" ' display "A"
 3   ElseIf grade >= 80 Then
 4       resultLabel.Text = "B" ' display "B"
 5   ElseIf grade >= 70 Then
 6       resultLabel.Text = "C" ' display "C"
 7   ElseIf grade >= 60 Then
 8       resultLabel.Text = "D" ' display "D"
 9   Else
10       resultLabel.Text = "F" ' display "F"
11   End If
```

Fig. 4.6 | Nested If...Then...Else statements from Fig. 4.5 reimplemented using ElseIf.

4.8 Repetition Statements

A **repetition statement** (also called a looping statement, an iteration statement or a loop) allows you to specify that an action should be repeated, depending on the value of a loop-continuation condition or a loop-termination condition. The pseudocode statements

> *While there are more items on my shopping list*
> *Put next item in cart*
> *Cross it off my list*

describe the repetitive actions on a shopping trip. The loop-continuation condition "there are more items on my shopping list" can be true or false. If it's true, the actions "Put next item in cart" and "Cross it off my list" are performed. These actions execute repeatedly while the condition remains true. The statement(s) contained in the *While* repetition statement constitute the body of the *While*. Eventually, the condition becomes false (when the last remaining item on the shopping list has been purchased and crossed off the list). Then, the repetition terminates, and the first statement after the repetition statement executes.

Performing a Calculation in a Do While...Loop Repetition Statement

Consider a program segment designed to find the first power of 3 larger than 100. Suppose that the Integer variable product is initialized to 3. When the following Do While...Loop statement finishes executing, product contains the result:

```
Do While product <= 100
    product = product * 3 ' compute next power of 3
Loop
```

When the Do While...Loop statement begins execution, product is 3. The body statement repeatedly multiplies product by 3, so it takes on the values 3, 9, 27, 81 and 243, successively. When product becomes 243, the condition product <= 100 becomes false. This *ter-*

minates the repetition with 243 as product's final value. Then, execution continues with the next statement after the keyword `Loop`. If the condition in a `Do While...Loop` is initially false, the body statement(s) do not execute.

UML Activity Diagram for the *Do While...Loop* Repetition Statement

The activity diagram of Fig. 4.7 illustrates the preceding `Do While...Loop` statement's flow of control. Once again, the symbols in the diagram (besides the initial state, transition arrows, a final state and three notes) represent an action state and a decision. This diagram also introduces the UML's **merge symbol**, which joins two activity flows into one. The UML represents *both* the merge symbol *and* the decision symbol as diamonds (this can be confusing). In this diagram, the merge symbol joins the transitions from the initial state and the action state, so they both flow into the decision that determines whether the loop should begin (or continue) executing. The decision and merge symbols can be distinguished by the number of "incoming" and "outgoing" transition arrows. A decision symbol has one transition arrow pointing to the diamond and two or more transition arrows pointing out from the diamond to indicate possible transitions from that point. In addition, each transition arrow pointing out of a decision symbol has a guard condition next to it (exactly *one* of which must be true when a decision is made). A merge symbol has two or more transition arrows pointing to the diamond and only one transition arrow pointing from the diamond, to indicate multiple activity flows merging to continue the activity. The transition arrows associated with a merge symbol do not have guard conditions.

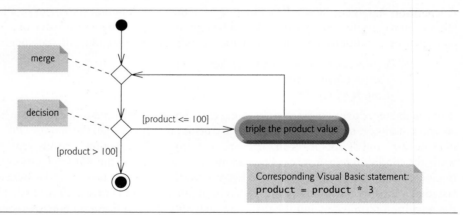

Fig. 4.7 | Do While...Loop repetition statement activity diagram.

Figure 4.7 clearly shows the repetition of the preceding `Do While...Loop` statement. The transition arrow emerging from the action state connects back to the merge, which transitions back to the decision that's tested each time through the loop until the guard condition `product > 100` becomes true. Then the `Do While...Loop` statement exits (reaches its final state) and control passes to the next statement in sequence.

Common Programming Error 4.1

Failure to provide the body of a Do While...Loop statement with an action that eventually causes the loop-continuation condition to become false is a logic error. Normally, such a repetition statement never terminates, resulting in a logic error called an "infinite loop."

Error-Prevention Tip 4.1
Whereas syntax errors are caught by the compiler, logic errors affect the program only at execution time. A fatal logic error causes a program to fail and terminate prematurely (or go into an infinite loop). A nonfatal logic error does not terminate a program's execution but causes the program to produce incorrect results.

While...End While *Repetition Statement*

The `While...End While` repetition statement behaves identically to the `Do While...Loop` repetition statement, so their activity diagrams are also identical. For consistency, you should choose one or the other. In this book, we use the `Do While...Loop` statement. The following `While...End While` statement reimplements the preceding `Do While...Loop`:

```
While product <= 100
    product = product * 3 ' compute next power of 3
End While
```

Do Until...Loop *Repetition Statement*

Unlike the preceding repetition statements, the `Do Until...Loop` repetition statement executes its body statement(s) repeatedly as long as the condition (known as the **loop-termination condition**) evaluates to *false*. You can write the preceding `Do While...Loop` statement as a `Do Until... Loop` statement as follows:

```
Do Until product > 100
    product = product * 3 ' compute next power of 3
Loop
```

The activity diagram of Fig. 4.7 also illustrates the flow of control in the preceding statement; however, we focus on the *leftmost* guard condition—product > 100—the loop-termination condition for our control statement. Because we're using a `Do Until...Loop` statement, the statement's action is performed when the statement's loop-termination condition is false (that is, product is less than or equal to 100). When the loop-termination condition (product > 100, the leftmost guard condition) is true, the statement exits. If the condition in a `Do Until...Loop` is initially true, the body statement(s) do not execute. In general, you can use a `Do While...Loop` statement with the condition expressed differently (in this case product <= 100), rather than using a `Do Until...Loop`.

4.9 Compound Assignment Operators

The **compound assignment operators** enable you to abbreviate assignment statements. For example, the statement

```
value = value + 3
```

which mentions the variable value on *both* sides of the assignment, can be abbreviated with the **addition assignment operator**, += as

```
value += 3
```

The += operator adds the value of the right operand to the value of the left operand and stores the result in the left operand's variable. Figure 4.8 summarizes the compound assignment operators.

Compound assignment operator	Sample expression	Explanation	Assigns
Assume: c = 4, d = "He"			
+=	c += 7	c = c + 7	11 to c
-=	c -= 3	c = c - 3	1 to c
*=	c *= 4	c = c * 4	16 to c
/=	c /= 2	c = c / 2	2 to c
\=	c \= 3	c = c \ 3	1 to c
^=	c ^= 2	c = c ^ 2	16 to c
&=	d &= "llo"	d = d & "llo"	"Hello" to d

Fig. 4.8 | Compound assignment operators.

The variable on the left side of an assignment operator must be an *lvalue* ("left value")—a modifiable variable or property that can appear on the *left* side of an assignment statement. We'll learn how to declare constants in Section 6.10—constants cannot be *lvalues*.

The =, +=, -=, *=, /=, \=, ^= and &= operators are always applied *last* in an expression. When an assignment (=) is evaluated, the expression to the right of the operator is always evaluated first, then the value is assigned to the *lvalue* on the left. When a compound assignment is evaluated, the appropriate operator is applied to the *lvalue*'s original value and the value to the operator's right, then the resulting value is assigned to the *lvalue* on the left.

Demonstrating the ^= Compound Assignment Operator

Figure 4.9 calculates a power of 2 using the exponentiation assignment operator. In line 8, we take advantage of a Visual Basic feature that allows variable initialization to be incorporated into a declaration. In this case, we initialize variable exponent to the value of exponentTextBox's Text property. Lines 12 and 17 each raise variable result to the value of variable exponent. The results of these two calculations are identical as shown in the sample output.

```
 1   ' Fig. 4.9: PowerOf2.vb
 2   ' Calculates 2 raised to the exponent entered by the user.
 3   Public Class PowerOf2
 4      ' calculates 2 raised to the exponent entered by the user.
 5      Private Sub calculateButton_Click(ByVal sender As System.Object,
 6         ByVal e As System.EventArgs) Handles calculateButton.Click
 7
 8         Dim exponent As Integer = exponentTextBox.Text ' get the exponent
 9         Dim result As Integer ' stores the calculation result
10
11         result = 2 ' number to raise to a power
12         result ^= exponent ' same as result = result ^ exponent
```

Fig. 4.9 | Exponentiation using a compound assignment operator. (Part 1 of 2.)

```
13      resultLabel.Text = "result = 2" & vbCrLf &
14         "result ^= " & exponent & ": " & result & vbCrLf & vbCrLf
15
16      result = 2 ' reset result to 2 for next calculation
17      result = result ^ exponent ' same as result ^= exponent
18      resultLabel.Text &= "result = 2" & vbCrLf &
19         "result = result ^ " & exponent & ": " & result
20   End Sub ' calculateButton_Click
21
22   ' clear results when user types in the exponentTextBox
23   Private Sub exponentTextBox_TextChanged(ByVal sender As System.Object,
24      ByVal e As System.EventArgs) Handles exponentTextBox.TextChanged
25      resultLabel.Text = String.Empty ' clears the resultLabel's text
26   End Sub ' exponentTextBox_TextChanged
27 End Class ' PowerOf2
```

Fig. 4.9 | Exponentiation using a compound assignment operator. (Part 2 of 2.)

4.10 Formulating Algorithms: Counter-Controlled Repetition

To illustrate how algorithms are developed, we solve a problem that averages student grades. Consider the following problem statement:

> *A class of students took a quiz. The grades (integers in the range 0 to 100) for this quiz are available to you. Determine the class average on the quiz.*

The class average is equal to the sum of the grades divided by the number of students. The algorithm for solving this problem on a computer must input each grade, keep track of the total of all grades input, perform the averaging calculation and display the result.

GUI for the Class-Average Application

Figure 4.10 shows this application's GUI. For this example, we introduce the **ListBox** control, which we use to display the grades the user enters and to manipulate those grades to perform the class-average calculation. Each grade that the user enters into the program by pressing the **Submit Grade** Button is placed in the ListBox. We calculate the class average when the user presses the **Calculate Average** Button. We also provide a **Clear Grades** Button to remove all the grades from the ListBox and clear the results, so the user can enter a new set of grades.

Fig. 4.10 | GUI for the class-average problem.

Setting the **Form's** Default Button

When you execute this program, notice that the **Submit Grade** Button has a blue highlight around it. This Button is the Form's default Button—the one that will be pressed when the user presses the *Enter* key. In this program, the user can type a value in the TextBox and press *Enter* to press the **Submit Grade** Button rather than clicking it with the mouse. This convenience feature enables the user to rapidly enter grades. You can specify a Form's default Button in the **Properties** window by setting the Form's **AcceptButton** property to the appropriate Button. For this program, we set the AcceptButton property to the submitGradeButton.

Pseudocode Algorithm with Counter-Controlled Repetition

Let's use pseudocode to list the actions to execute and specify the order of execution for calculating the class average. After the user enters the grades and presses the **Calculate Average** Button, we use counter-controlled repetition to get the grades from the ListBox and process them one at a time. This technique uses a variable called a **counter** (or **control variable**) to specify the number of times that a set of statements will execute. This is also called **definite repetition** because the number of repetitions is known before the loop begins executing. In this example, repetition terminates when the counter exceeds the number of grades in the ListBox. Figure 4.11 presents a fully developed pseudocode algorithm and Fig. 4.12 presents the program that implements the algorithm. In the next section, you'll learn how to develop pseudocode algorithms and convert them to Visual Basic. (In Exercise 4.15, you'll use counter-controlled repetition to output a table of values.)

1	*Set total to zero*
2	*Set grade counter to zero*
3	
4	*While grade counter is less than the number of grades*
5	*Get the next grade*
6	*Add the grade into the total*
7	*Add one to the grade counter*

Fig. 4.11 | Pseudocode algorithm that uses counter-controlled repetition to solve the class-average problem. (Part 1 of 2.)

8	
9	*If the grade counter is not equal to zero then*
10	*Set the class average to the total divided by the number of grades*
11	*Display the class average*
12	*Else*
13	*Display "No grades were entered"*

Fig. 4.11 | Pseudocode algorithm that uses counter-controlled repetition to solve the class-average problem. (Part 2 of 2.)

Note the references in the pseudocode algorithm (Fig. 4.11) to a total and a counter. A **total** is a variable used to accumulate the sum of several values. A counter is a variable used to count—in this case, the grade counter records the number of grades input by the user. It's important that variables used as totals and counters have appropriate initial values before they're used. Counters usually are initialized to 0 or 1, depending on their use. Totals generally are initialized to 0. Numeric variables are initialized to 0 when they're declared, unless another value is assigned to the variable in its declaration.

Software Engineering Observation 4.2

Many algorithms can be divided logically into an initialization phase *that initializes the program variables, a* processing phase *that inputs data values and adjusts program variables accordingly and a* termination phase *that calculates and displays the results.*

In the pseudocode, we add one to the grade counter only in the body of the loop (line 7). If the user does not enter any grades, the condition *"grade counter is less than the number of grades"* (line 4) will be false and grade counter will be zero when we reach the part of the algorithm that calculates the class average. We test for the possibility of division by zero—a logic error that, if undetected, would cause the program to fail.

Error-Prevention Tip 4.2

When performing division by an expression whose value could be zero, explicitly test for this case and handle it appropriately in your program. Such handling could be as simple as displaying an error message. Sometimes more sophisticated processing is required, such as using the exception-handling techniques introduced in Chapter 7.

Implementing Counter-Controlled Repetition

The ClassAverage class (Fig. 4.12) defines the Click event handlers for the submit-GradeButton, calculateAverageButton and clearGradesButton. The calculate-AverageButton_Click method (lines 19–49) implements the class-averaging algorithm described by the pseudocode in Fig. 4.11.

Method submitGradeButton_Click

When the user presses the **Submit Grade** Button, method submitGradeButton_Click (lines 5–16) obtains the value the user typed and places it in the gradesListBox. Line 9 first ensures that the gradeTextBox is not empty by comparing its Text property to the constant String.Empty. This prevents the program from inserting an empty string in the ListBox, which would cause the program to fail when it attempts to process the grades.

This is the beginning of our efforts to validate data entered by the user. In later chapters, we'll ensure that the data is in range (for example, an `Integer` representing a month needs to be in the range 1–12) and that data meets various other criteria. For this program, we assume that the user enters only `Integer` values—noninteger values could cause the program to fail when the grades are processed.

```vbnet
 1   ' Fig. 4.12: ClassAverage.vb
 2   ' Counter-controlled repetition: Class-average problem.
 3   Public Class ClassAverage
 4      ' place a grade in the gradesListBox
 5      Private Sub submitGradeButton_Click(ByVal sender As System.Object,
 6         ByVal e As System.EventArgs) Handles submitGradeButton.Click
 7
 8         ' if the user entered a grade
 9         If gradeTextBox.Text <> String.Empty Then
10            ' add the grade to the end of the gradesListBox
11            gradesListBox.Items.Add(gradeTextBox.Text)
12            gradeTextBox.Clear() ' clear the gradeTextBox
13         End If
14
15         gradeTextBox.Focus() ' gives the focus to the gradeTextBox
16      End Sub ' submitGradeButton_Click
17
18      ' calculates the class average based on the grades in gradesListBox
19      Private Sub calculateAverageButton_Click(ByVal sender As System.Object,
20         ByVal e As System.EventArgs) Handles calculateAverageButton.Click
21
22         Dim total As Integer ' sum of grades entered by user
23         Dim gradeCounter As Integer ' counter for grades
24         Dim grade As Integer ' grade input by user
25         Dim average As Double ' average of grades
26
27         ' initialization phase
28         total = 0 ' set total to zero before adding grades to it
29         gradeCounter = 0 ' prepare to loop
30
31         ' processing phase
32         Do While gradeCounter < gradesListBox.Items.Count
33            grade = gradesListBox.Items(gradeCounter) ' get next grade
34            total += grade ' add grade to total
35            gradeCounter += 1 ' add 1 to gradeCounter
36         Loop
37
38         ' termination phase
39         If gradeCounter <> 0 Then
40            average = total / gradesListBox.Items.Count ' calculate average
41
42            ' display total and average (with two digits of precision)
43            classAverageLabel.Text = "Total of the " & gradeCounter &
44               " grade(s) is " & total & vbCrLf & "Class average is " &
45               String.Format("{0:F}", average)
```

Fig. 4.12 | Counter-controlled repetition: Class-average problem. (Part 1 of 2.)

```
46          Else
47              classAverageLabel.Text = "No grades were entered"
48          End If
49      End Sub ' calculateAverageButton_Click
50
51      ' clear grades from gradeListBox and results from classAverageLabel
52      Private Sub clearGradesButton_Click(ByVal sender As System.Object,
53          ByVal e As System.EventArgs) Handles clearGradesButton.Click
54
55          gradesListBox.Items.Clear() ' removes all items from gradesListBox
56          classAverageLabel.Text = String.Empty ' clears classAverageLabel
57      End Sub ' clearGradesButton_Click
58  End Class ' ClassAverage
```

Fig. 4.12 | Counter-controlled repetition: Class-average problem. (Part 2 of 2.)

If the gradeTextBox is not empty, line 11 uses the ListBox's **Items** property to add the grade to the ListBox. This property keeps track of the values in the ListBox. To place a new item in the ListBox, call the Items property's Add method, which adds the new item at the end of the ListBox. Line 12 then clears the value in the gradeTextBox so the user can enter the next grade. Line 15 calls the gradeTextBox's **Focus** method, which makes the TextBox the **active control**—the one that will respond to the user's interactions. This allows the user to immediately start typing the next grade, without clicking the TextBox.

Method calculateAverageButton_Click; Introducing Type Double and Floating-Point Numbers

Method calculateAverageButton_Click (lines 19–49) uses the algorithm in Fig. 4.11 to calculate the class average and display the results. Lines 22–24 declare variables total, gradeCounter and grade to be of type Integer. Line 25 declares variable average to be of type Double. Although each grade is an Integer, the average calculation uses division, so it is likely to produce a number with a fractional result. Such numbers (like 84.4) contain decimal points and are called **floating-point numbers**. Type **Double** is typically used to store floating-point numbers. All the floating-point numbers you type in a program's source code (such as 7.33 and 0.0975) are treated as Double values by default and are known as **floating-point literals**. Values of type Double are represented approximately in memory. For precise calculations, such as those used in financial calculations, Visual Basic provides type Decimal (discussed in Section 5.4).

Variable `total` accumulates the sum of the grades entered. Variable `gradeCounter` helps us determine when the loop at lines 32–36 should terminate. Variable `grade` stores the most recent grade value obtained from the `ListBox` (line 33). Variable `average` stores the average grade (line 40).

The declarations (in lines 22–25) appear in the body of method `calculateAverage-Button_Click`. Variables declared in a method body are so-called local variables and can be used only from their declaration until the end of the method declaration. A local variable's declaration must appear before the variable is used in that method. A local variable cannot be accessed outside the method in which it is declared.

The assignments (in lines 28–29) initialize `total` and `gradeCounter` to 0. Line 32 indicates that the `Do While...Loop` statement should continue looping (also called iterating) while `gradeCounter`'s value is less than the `ListBox`'s number of items. `ListBox` property `Items` keeps track of the `ListBox`'s number of items, which you can access via the expression `gradesListBox.Items.Count`. While this condition remains true, the `Do While...Loop` statement repeatedly executes the statements in its body (lines 33–35).

Line 33 reads a grade from the `ListBox` and assigns it to the variable `grade`. Each value in the `ListBox`'s `Items` property has a position number associated with it—this is known as the item's **index**. For example, in the sample output of Fig. 4.12, the grade 65 is at index 0, 78 is at index 1, 89 is at index 2, and so on. The index of the last item is always one less than the total number of items represented by the `ListBox`'s `Items.Count` property. To get the value at a particular index, we use the expression:

```
gradesListBox.Items(gradeCounter)
```

in which `gradeCounter`'s current value is the index.

Line 34 adds the new `grade` entered by the user into the variable `total` using the `+=` compound assignment operator. Line 35 adds 1 to `gradeCounter` to indicate that the program has processed another grade and is ready to input the next grade from the user. Incrementing `gradeCounter` eventually causes the loop to terminate when the condition `gradeCounter < gradesListBox.Items.Count` becomes false.

When the loop terminates, the `If...Then...Else` statement at lines 39–48 executes. Line 39 determines whether any grades have been entered. If so, line 40 performs the averaging calculation using the floating-point division operator (`/`) and stores the result in `Double` variable `average`. If we used the integer division operator (`\`), the class average would not be as precise because any fractional part of the average would be discarded. For example, 844 divided by 10 is 84.4, but with integer division the result would be 84. Lines 43–45 display the results in the `classAverageLabel`. If no grades were entered, line 47 displays a message in the `classAverageLabel`.

Method `clearGradesButton_Click`

When the user presses the **Clear Grades** Button, method `clearGradesButton_Click` (lines 52–57) prepares for the user to enter a new set of grades. First, line 55 removes the grades from the `gradesListBox` by calling the `Item`'s property's **Clear** method. Then, line 56 clears the text on the `classAverageLabel`.

Control Statement Stacking

In this example, we see that control statements may be stacked on top of one another (that is, placed in sequence) just as a child stacks building blocks. The `Do While...Loop` statement (lines 32–36) is followed in sequence by an `If...Then...Else` statement (lines 39–48).

Formatting for Floating-Point Numbers

The statement in lines 43–45 outputs the class average. In this example, we decided to display the class average rounded to the nearest hundredth and to output the average with exactly two digits to the right of the decimal point. To do so, we used the expression

```
String.Format("{0:F}", average)
```

which indicates that average's value should be displayed as a number with a specific number of digits to the right of the decimal point—called a **fixed-point number**. This is an example of **formatted output**, in which you control how a number appears for display purposes. The `String` class's **Format method** performs the formatting. The first argument to the method (`"{0:F}"`) is the format string, which acts as a placeholder for the value being formatted. The numeric value that appears before the colon (in this case, 0) indicates which of `Format`'s arguments will be formatted—0 specifies the first argument *after* the format string passed to `Format`, namely average. As you'll see in later examples, additional values can be inserted into the string to specify other arguments. The value after the colon (in this case, F) is known as a **format specifier**, which indicates how a value is to be formatted. The format specifier F indicates that a fixed-point number should be rounded to *two decimal places* by default. The entire placeholder (`{0:F}`) is replaced with the formatted value of variable average. You can change the number of decimal places to display by placing an integer value after the format specifier—for example, the string `"{0:F3}"` rounds the number to three decimal places.

4.11 Formulating Algorithms: Nested Control Statements

We've seen that control statements can be stacked on top of one another (in sequence). We now examine the only other structured way that control statements can be combined—by *nesting* one control statement inside another.

Problem Statement and Notes

Consider the following problem statement:

> *A college offers a course that prepares students for the state real estate broker licensing exam. Last year, 10 of the students who completed this course took the exam. The college wants to know how well its students did. You've been asked to write a program to summarize the results. You've been given a list of the 10 students. Next to each name is written a "P" if the student passed the exam and an "F" if the student failed the exam.*
>
> *Your program should analyze the results of the exam as follows:*
>
> *1. Input each exam result (that is, a "P" or an "F").*
>
> *2. Count the number of passes and the number of failures.*
>
> *3. Display a summary of the exam results, indicating the number of students who passed and the number who failed.*
>
> *4. If more than eight students passed the exam, display the message "Bonus to Instructor."*

After reading the problem statement carefully, we make the following observations:

1. The program must process exam results for 10 students. A counter-controlled loop can be used because the number of test results is known in advance.

2. Each exam result is a string—either a "P" or an "F." When the program reads an exam result, it must determine whether the result is a "P" or an "F." We test for a "P" in our algorithm. If the input is not a "P," we assume it's an "F." An exercise at the end of the chapter considers the consequences of this assumption. For instance, consider what happens when the user enters a lowercase "p."

3. Two counters store the exam results—one counts the number of students who passed the exam and the other counts the number of students who failed.

4. After the program has processed all the exam results, it must determine whether more than eight students passed the exam, and, if so, bonus the instructor.

GUI for the Licensing-Exam Analysis Application

Figure 4.13 shows this application's GUI. Each result is placed in the `ListBox` when the user presses the **Submit Result** `Button`. We process all 10 results when the user presses the **Analyze Results** `Button`. We also provide a **Clear Results** `Button` to reset the GUI so the user can enter a new set of results. As in the previous example, we used the Form's `Accept-Button` property to set the **Submit Result** `Button` as the default `Button`. We disabled the **Analyze Results** `Button` initially by setting its **Enabled** property to `False`.

Fig. 4.13 | GUI for the licensing-exam analysis problem.

Developing the Pseudocode Algorithm with Top-Down, Stepwise Refinement: The Top and the First Refinement

We approach this program with **top-down, stepwise refinement**, a technique for developing well-structured algorithms. We begin with a pseudocode representation of the **top**—a single statement that conveys the overall function of the program:

Analyze exam results and decide if the instructor should receive a bonus

The top is a *complete* representation of a program. Unfortunately, the top rarely conveys enough detail from which to write a program, so we conduct the refinement process. We divide the top into a series of smaller tasks and list them in the order in which they must be performed, resulting in the following **first refinement**:

> *Initialize variables*
> *Input the 10 exam results, and count passes and failures*
> *Display a summary of the exam results and decide if the instructor should*
> *   receive a bonus*

Proceeding to the Second Refinement

To proceed to the second refinement, we commit to specific variables. In this example, counters are needed to record the passes and failures. A counter controls the looping process and a variable stores the user input. The pseudocode statement

> *Initialize variables*

can be refined as follows:

> *Initialize passes to zero*
> *Initialize failures to zero*
> *Initialize student to zero*

Only the counters for the number of passes, number of failures and number of students need to be initialized before they're used. The variable we use to store each value the user enters does not need to be initialized because the assignment of its value does not depend on its previous value, as is the case for the counter variables.

The pseudocode statement

> *Input the 10 exam results, and count passes and failures*

requires a repetition statement (that is, a loop) that successively inputs the result of each exam. We know in advance that there are 10 exam results, so counter-controlled looping is appropriate. Inside the loop (that is, *nested* inside the loop), a double-selection statement will determine whether each exam result is a pass or a failure and will increment the appropriate counter. The refinement of the preceding pseudocode statement is then

> *While student counter is less than or equal to 10*
> *   Get the next exam result*
>
> *   If the student passed then*
> *   Add one to passes*
> *   Else*
> *   Add one to failures*
>
> *   Add one to student counter*

Note the use of blank lines to set off the *If…Else* control statement to improve readability. The pseudocode statement

> *Display a summary of the exam results and decide if the instructor should*
> *   receive a bonus*

may be refined as follows:

> *Display the number of passes*
> *Display the number of failures*
>
> *If more than eight students passed then*
> *   Display "Bonus to instructor!"*

Complete Second Refinement of Pseudocode
The complete second refinement of the pseudocode appears in Fig. 4.14. Blank lines are also used to set off the *While* loop (lines 5–13) for readability. This pseudocode is now sufficiently refined for conversion to Visual Basic.

Software Engineering Observation 4.3

Each refinement, including the top, is a complete *version of the algorithm; only the level of detail in each refinement varies.*

1	*Initialize passes to zero*
2	*Initialize failures to zero*
3	*Initialize student to zero*
4	
5	*While student counter is less than or equal to 10*
6	*Get the next exam result*
7	
8	*If the student passed then*
9	*Add one to passes*
10	*Else*
11	*Add one to failures*
12	
13	*Add one to student counter*
14	
15	*Display the number of passes*
16	*Display the number of failures*
17	
18	*If more than eight students passed then*
19	*Display "Bonus to instructor!"*

Fig. 4.14 | Pseudocode for examination-results problem.

Class Analysis
The program that implements the pseudocode algorithm and the sample outputs are shown in Fig. 4.15. We defined the Click event handlers for the submitResultButton, analyzeResultsButton and clearResultsButton. The analyzeResultsButton_Click method (lines 24–55) implements the class-averaging algorithm described by the pseudocode in Fig. 4.14.

```
1  ' Fig. 4.15: Analysis.vb
2  ' Nested control statements: Examination-results problem.
3  Public Class Analysis
4     ' place a result in the resultsListBox
5     Private Sub submitResultButton_Click(ByVal sender As System.Object,
6        ByVal e As System.EventArgs) Handles submitResultButton.Click
7
```

Fig. 4.15 | Nested control statements: Examination-results problem. (Part 1 of 3.)

```
 8        If resultsListBox.Items.Count < 10 Then
 9            ' add the grade to the end of the resultsListbox
10            resultsListBox.Items.Add(resultTextBox.Text)
11            resultTextBox.Clear() ' clear the resultTextBox
12            resultTextBox.Focus() ' select the resultTextBox
13        End If
14
15        ' determine whether to prevent the user from entering more results
16        If resultsListBox.Items.Count = 10 Then
17            submitResultButton.Enabled = False ' disables submitResultButton
18            resultTextBox.Enabled = False ' disables resultTextBox
19            analyzeResultsButton.Enabled = True ' enable analyzeResultsButton
20        End If
21    End Sub ' submitResultButton_Click
22
23    ' analyze the results
24    Private Sub analyzeResultsButton_Click(ByVal sender As System.Object,
25        ByVal e As System.EventArgs) Handles analyzeResultsButton.Click
26
27        ' initializing variables in declarations
28        Dim passes As Integer = 0 ' number of passes
29        Dim failures As Integer = 0 ' number of failures
30        Dim student As Integer = 0 ' student counter
31        Dim result As String ' one exam result
32
33        ' process 10 students using counter-controlled loop
34        Do While student < 10
35            result = resultsListBox.Items(student) ' get a result
36
37            ' nested control statement
38            If result = "P" Then
39                passes += 1 ' increment number of passes
40            Else
41                failures += 1 ' increment number of failures
42            End If
43
44            student += 1 ' increment student counter
45        Loop
46
47        ' display exam results
48        analysisResultsLabel.Text =
49            "Passed: " & passes & vbCrLf & "Failed: " & failures & vbCrLf
50
51        ' raise tuition if more than 8 students passed
52        If passes > 8 Then
53            analysisResultsLabel.Text &= "Bonus to instructor!"
54        End If
55    End Sub ' analyzeResultsButton_Click
56
57    ' clears the resultsListBox and analysisResultsLabel
58    Private Sub clearResultsButton_Click(ByVal sender As System.Object,
59        ByVal e As System.EventArgs) Handles clearResultsButton.Click
60
```

Fig. 4.15 | Nested control statements: Examination-results problem. (Part 2 of 3.)

```
61         resultsListBox.Items.Clear() ' removes all items
62         analysisResultsLabel.Text = String.Empty ' clears the text
63         submitResultButton.Enabled = True ' enables submitResultButton
64         resultTextBox.Enabled = True ' enables resultTextBox
65         analyzeResultsButton.Enabled = False ' disables analyzeResultsButton
66         resultTextBox.Focus() ' select the resultTextBox
67      End Sub ' clearResultsButton_Click
68   End Class ' Analysis
```

Fig. 4.15 | Nested control statements: Examination-results problem. (Part 3 of 3.)

Method *submitResultButton_Click*

When the user presses the **Submit Result** button, method submitResultButton_Click (lines 5–21) executes. The problem statement specified that the user can enter only 10 results, so we need to keep track of the number of results that have been entered. Since the ListBox property Items keeps track of the ListBox's total number of items, we use its Count property in line 8 to determine whether 10 results have been entered. If not, line 10 adds the next result to the ListBox, line 11 clears the TextBox and line 12 gives the TextBox the focus so the user can enter the next result. The last result entered could have been the 10th result (line 16). If so, lines 17–18 disable the submitResultButton and the resultTextBox by setting their Enabled properties to False. This prevents the user from interacting with these two controls, so the user cannot enter more than 10 results. Line 19 enables analyzeResultsButton by setting its Enabled property to True so the user can tell the program to analyze the results.

Method *analyzeResultsButton_Click*

Method analyzeResultsButton_Click (lines 24–55) uses the algorithm in Fig. 4.14 to calculate the class average and display the results. Lines 28–31 declare the variables the algorithm uses to process the examination results. Several of these declarations incorporate variable initialization—passes, failures and student are all initialized to 0.

The Do While...Loop statement (lines 34–45) loops 10 times. During each iteration, the loop inputs and processes one exam result from the ListBox. The If...Then...Else statement (lines 38–42) for processing each result is nested in the Do While...Loop statement. If the result is "P", the If...Then...Else statement increments passes; otherwise, it assumes the result is "F" and increments failures. Strings are case sensitive by default—uppercase and lowercase letters are different. Only "P" represents a passing grade. In Exercise 4.13, we ask you to enhance the program by processing lowercase inputs such as "p" and "f".

Line 44 increments student before the loop condition is tested again at line 34. After 10 values have been processed, the loop terminates and lines 48–49 display the number of passes and failures. The If...Then statement at lines 52–54 determines whether more than eight students passed the exam and, if so, displays "Bonus to instructor!". In the first sample execution, the condition at line 52 is True—more than eight students passed the exam, so the program outputs the bonus message.

Method clearResultsButton_Click

When the user presses the **Clear Results** Button, method clearResultsButton_Click (lines 58–67) prepares for the user to enter a new set of results. Line 61 removes the results from the resultsListBox by calling the Item property's Clear method. Line 62 clears the text on the analysisResultsLabel. Lines 63 and 64 enable the submitResultButton and the resultTextBox by setting their Enabled properties to True—the user can now interact with these controls again. Line 65 disables the analyzeResultsButton by setting its Enabled property to False so the user cannot click it. Line 66 gives the focus to the resultTextBox so the user can begin typing the next result immediately.

4.12 Using the Debugger: Locating a Logic Error

You'll now begin learning about the Visual Basic 2010 Express tools that can help you find and correct logic errors (also called **bugs**). Such errors do not prevent a program from compiling successfully, but can cause a running program to produce incorrect results. Visual Studio includes a tool called a **debugger** that can be used to monitor the execution of your programs so you can locate and remove logic errors. A program must successfully compile before it can be used in the debugger. Some of the debugger's features include:

- suspending program execution so you can "step" through the program one statement at a time
- examining and setting variable values
- watching the values of variables and expressions
- viewing the order in which methods are called

To illustrate some of the debugger's capabilities, let's use a modified version of the class-average program from Fig. 4.12. In the modified version (located in the Debugging folder with this chapter's examples), the condition in line 32 uses the <= rather than the < operator. This bug causes the loop in calculateAverageButton_Click to execute its statements one extra time. The program fails at line 33 when it attempts to access a grade that does not exist. The modified event handler is shown in Fig. 4.16.

```
18   ' calculate the class average based on the grades in gradesListBox
19   Private Sub calculateAverageButton_Click(ByVal sender As System.Object,
20      ByVal e As System.EventArgs) Handles calculateAverageButton.Click
21
```

Fig. 4.16 | Modified calculateAverageButton_Click event handler that contains a logic error. (Part 1 of 2.)

```
22      Dim total As Integer ' sum of grades entered by user
23      Dim gradeCounter As Integer ' counter for grades
24      Dim grade As Integer ' grade input by user
25      Dim average As Double ' average of grades
26
27      ' initialization phase
28      total = 0 ' set total to zero before adding grades to it
29      gradeCounter = 0 ' prepare to loop
30
31      ' processing phase
32      Do While gradeCounter <= gradesListBox.Items.Count
33         grade = gradesListBox.Items(gradeCounter) ' get next grade
34         total += grade ' add grade to total
35         gradeCounter += 1 ' add 1 to gradeCounter
36      Loop
37
38      ' termination phase
39      If gradeCounter <> 0 Then
40         average = total / gradesListBox.Items.Count ' calculate average
41
42         ' display total and average (with two digits of precision)
43         classAverageLabel.Text = "Total of the " & gradeCounter &
44            " grade(s) is " & total & vbCrLf & "Class average is " &
45            String.Format("{0:F}", average)
46      Else
47         classAverageLabel.Text = "No grades were entered"
48      End If
49   End Sub ' calculateAverageButton_Click
```

Fig. 4.16 | Modified `calculateAverageButton_Click` event handler that contains a logic error. (Part 2 of 2.)

The Off-By-One Logic Error

Execute this program with **Debug > Start Debugging** (or by pressing *F5* or the toolbar button ▶). Enter several grades and press the **Calculate Class Average** Button. The program does not display the class average. Rather, you get a dialog in the IDE showing a runtime error known as an `ArgumentOutOfRangeException` (Fig. 4.17). This indicates that the argument in parentheses (`gradeCounter`) is out of range. As you'll soon see, `gradeCounter`'s value is one higher than the index of the last grade in the `gradesListBox`, so the program attempts to get a value that does not exist. This logic error—commonly known as an **off-by-one error**—is frequently caused by using the incorrect relational operator in a loop's condition. The debugger highlights the line of code (line 33) that caused the problem.

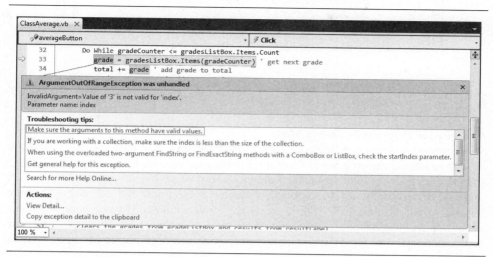

Fig. 4.17 | IDE showing the line of code that caused an `ArgumentOutOfRangeException`.

In the following steps, you'll use various debugger commands to examine the values of the variables used in the `calculateAverageButton_Click` event handler and to study the flow of control in the `Do While...Loop` repetition statement. This will help us locate and correct the logic error.

4.12.1 Breakpoints and Running the Program

Breakpoints are special markers that you can set at any *executable* line of code. You cannot place them on comments or whitespace. When a running program reaches a breakpoint, execution pauses, allowing you to examine the values of variables to help determine whether logic errors exist. For example, you can examine the value of a variable that stores a calculation's result to determine whether the calculation was performed correctly. You can also examine the value of an expression. Once the debugger pauses program execution, you can use various debugger commands to execute the program one statement at a time—this is called "single stepping" or simply "stepping." We'll examine the code in the `averageButton_Click` event handler. Before proceeding, if you ran the program to cause the logic error, stop the debugger by selecting **Debug > Stop Debugging**.

Inserting a Breakpoint

To insert a breakpoint, left click in the **margin indicator bar** (the gray margin at the left of the code window in Fig. 4.18) next to line 28, or right click in line 28 and select **Breakpoint > Insert Breakpoint**. Additionally, you can click a line of code then press *F9* to toggle a breakpoint on and off for that line of code. You may set as many breakpoints as you like. A solid circle appears in the margin indicator bar where you clicked and the entire code statement is highlighted, indicating that a breakpoint has been set.

Margin indicator bar   Breakpoints

Fig. 4.18 | Breakpoint set at line 28.

Running the Program in Debug Mode

After setting breakpoints in the code editor, select **Debug > Start Debugging** (or press the *F5* key) to rebuild the program and begin the debugging process. Enter the grades 100, 97 and 88, then press the **Calculate Class Average** button. When the debugger reaches line 28 (the line that contains the breakpoint), it suspends execution and enters **break mode** (Fig. 4.19). At this point, the IDE becomes the active window. The yellow arrow to the left of line 28—called the **instruction pointer**—indicates that this line contains the next statement to execute. The IDE also highlights the line as well to emphasize the line that is about to execute.

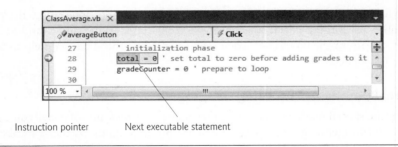

Instruction pointer   Next executable statement

Fig. 4.19 | Program execution suspended at the first breakpoint.

4.12.2 *Quick Info* Box

In break mode, you can place the mouse cursor over any variable and its value will be displayed in a *Quick Info* **box** (Fig. 4.20). This can help you spot logic errors.

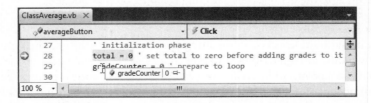

Fig. 4.20 | *Quick Info* box displays value of variable `gradeCounter`.

4.12.3 Locals Window

While in break mode, you can also explore the values of a method's local variables using the debugger's **Locals** window (Fig. 4.21). To view the **Locals** window, select **Debug > Windows > Locals**. Recall that all variables in Visual Basic get initialized, so even though lines 28–29 have not executed yet, variables `total` and `gradeCounter` currently have the value 0 (the default for `Integer` variables). In Fig. 4.21, we call out only the variables declared in lines 22–25.

Good Programming Practice 4.1

Explicitly initialize variables rather than relying on default initialization. This makes your programs more readable and easier to understand.

Variables we declared in the event handler method

Fig. 4.21 | Locals window showing the values of the variables in the event-handler method `calculateAverageButton_Click`.

4.12.4 Using the Step Over Command to Execute Statements

You'll now execute the program one statement at a time using the debugger's **Step Over** command. You can access this command by selecting **Debug > Step Over**, by pressing *Shift + F8* or by pressing the **Step Over** command's toolbar icon ( ). Do this *twice* now. The instruction pointer arrow now points to the Do While...Loop statement's first line. If you position the mouse over the word Count in `gradesListBox.Items.Count` (Fig. 4.22), you can see in the *Quick Info* window that the number of items in the ListBox is 3. Similarly, you can place the mouse over variable `gradeCounter` to see that its value is currently 0.

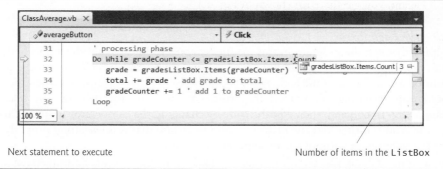

Next statement to execute

Number of items in the ListBox

Fig. 4.22 | Stepping over a statement in the `calculateAverageButton_Click` method.

At this point in the program's execution, the user cannot add more items to the ListBox because we've disabled the TextBox and Button that allow the user to enter a grade, so gradesListBox.Items.Count will remain as 3. Thus, the loop should execute the statements at lines 33–35 a total of three times to process the three grades.

First Iteration of the Loop

Since gradeCounter's value is less than or equal to 3, the condition in line 32 is true. Thus, when you use the **Step Over** command again, the instruction pointer moves to line 33 in the loop's body. Now use the **Step Over** command to execute line 33. The first item in the ListBox (100) is assigned to variable grade, which you can see in the *Quick Info* box and in the **Locals** window. Whenever a variable's value is modified as a result of the last statement to execute, the **Locals** window highlights that value in red.

Now, **Step Over** lines 34 and 35 to add the grade to the total and to add 1 to the gradeCounter. The instruction pointer is now aimed at line 36. When you use the **Step Over** command now, the instruction pointer moves back to the top of the loop so the condition can be tested again.

Second Iteration of the Loop

Variable gradeCounter's value is now 1, so the condition is still true, thus the loop's body will execute again. Use the **Step Over** command *five* times to step through this iteration of the loop, which adds the grade 97 to the total, increments gradeCounter to 2 and positions the instruction counter at the top of the loop.

Third Iteration of the Loop

Variable gradeCounter's value is now 2, so the condition is still true, thus the loop's body will execute again so we can process the last grade. Use the **Step Over** command five times to step through this iteration of the loop, which adds the grade 88 to the total, increments gradeCounter to 3 and positions the instruction counter at the top of the loop.

Fourth Iteration of the Loop

At this point, we've processed all three grades and the loop should terminate. However, gradeCounter's value is 3, which is less than *or equal to* 3. The condition is *still* true—even though we are done processing the three grades. Thus, the loop will attempt to process another grade, even though one does not exist. This is the logic error. When you **Step Over** line 33 again, you get the error shown in Fig. 4.17.

Fixing the Logic Error

Stepping through the program in this manner enables you to see that the loop's body executes *four* times when it should only execute *three* times. So we can focus on the loop's condition as the source of the logic error, because the condition determines when the loop should stop executing. To correct the error, you can stop the debugger by selecting **Debug > Stop Debugging**, then edit the code by changing the <= operator in line 32 to a < operator. You can then test the program again to ensure that it is executing properly. To execute the program without the breakpoints, you can:

1. Disable each breakpoint by right clicking in the line of code with the breakpoint and selecting **Breakpoint > Disable Breakpoint**, then run the program;

2. Remove each breakpoint by right clicking the breakpoint and selecting **Delete Breakpoint**, then run the program; or

3. Execute the program without debugging by pressing *Ctrl + F5*.

4.13 Wrap-Up

This chapter presented basic problem-solving techniques that you use to build programs. We demonstrated how to develop an algorithm in pseudocode, evolving it through several refinements until it is ready to be translated to Visual Basic code that can be executed. This process is called top-down, stepwise refinement.

You learned that only three types of control structures—sequence, selection and repetition—are needed to develop an algorithm. We demonstrated the If...Then single-selection statement and the If...Then...Else double-selection statement. The If...Then statement is used to execute an action (or sequence of actions) based on a condition—if the condition is true, the statements execute; if it is false, the statements are skipped. The If...Then...Else double-selection statement is used to execute one set of statements if a condition is true, and another set if the condition is false.

We discussed the Do While...Loop and While...End While repetition statements that execute sets of statements repeatedly as long as a loop-continuation condition remains true. We discussed the Do Until...Loop repetition statement, where a set of statements executes repeatedly as long as a loop-termination condition remains false. You studied the UML activity diagrams that represent each control statement presented in the chapter.

We introduced compound assignment operators, which can be used for abbreviating assignment statements. We used control-statement stacking to compute a class average with counter-controlled repetition then display the results, and we used control-statement nesting to analyze and make decisions based on a set of exam results. You also learned how to use the debugger to view the values of variables during program execution and to step through a program to help locate a logic error. In Chapter 5, Problem Solving and Control Statements: Part 2, we present additional selection and repetition statements.

Summary

Section 4.2 Algorithms
- Computing problems are solved by executing actions in a specific order.
- An algorithm is a procedure for solving a problem in terms of the actions to be executed and the order in which these actions are to be executed.
- Program control refers to the task of ordering a program's statements correctly.

Section 4.3 Pseudocode
- Pseudocode is an informal language that helps you develop algorithms and "think out" a program before attempting to write it in a programming language.
- Carefully prepared pseudocode can be converted easily to a corresponding Visual Basic program.

Section 4.4 Control Structures
- Normally, statements in a program execute sequentially in the order in which they're written.

- Various Visual Basic statements enable you to specify that the next statement to be executed might not be the next one in sequence. This is called a transfer of control.
- All programs can be written in terms of the sequence, selection and repetition structures.
- The sequence structure is built into Visual Basic. Unless directed otherwise, the computer executes Visual Basic statements one after the other in the order in which they're written.
- A UML activity diagram models the workflow (also called the activity) of a software system.
- Like pseudocode, activity diagrams help you develop and represent algorithms.
- An action state is represented as a rectangle with its left and right sides replaced by arcs curving outward. An action expression appears inside the action state.
- The arrows in an activity diagram represent transitions that indicate the order in which the actions represented by action states occur.
- The solid circle in an activity diagram represents the initial state—the beginning of the workflow before the program performs the modeled actions.
- The solid circle surrounded by a hollow circle in an activity diagram represents the final state—the end of the workflow after the program performs its actions.
- UML notes are optional explanatory remarks that describe the purpose of symbols in the diagram. A dotted line connects each note with the element that it describes.
- Single-entry/single-exit control statements make it easy to build programs.
- In control-statement stacking, the control statements are attached to one another by connecting the exit point of one control statement to the entry point of the next.
- In control-statement nesting, one control statement is placed inside another.
- The `If...Then` single-selection statement selects or ignores an action (or group of actions) based on the truth or falsity of a condition.
- The `If...Then...Else` double-selection statement selects between two different actions (or groups of actions) based on the truth or falsity of a condition.
- A multiple-selection statement selects among many different actions or groups of actions.
- The `Do While...Loop` and `While...End While` repetition statements execute a set of statements while a loop-continuation condition remains true. If the condition is initially false, the set of statements does not execute.
- The `Do Until...Loop` repetition statement executes a set of statements until a loop-termination condition becomes true. If the condition is initially true, the set of statements does not execute.
- The `Do...Loop While` repetition statement executes a set of statements while its loop-continuation condition remains true. The set of statements is guaranteed to execute at least once.
- The `Do...Loop Until` repetition statement executes a set of statements until a loop-termination condition becomes true. The set of statements is guaranteed to execute at least once.
- The `For...Next` repetition statement executes a set of statements a specified number of times.
- The `For Each...Next` repetition statement performs a set of statements for every element of a an array or collection of values.

Section 4.5 If...Then Selection Statement

- Syntax errors are caught by the compiler. Logic errors affect the program only at execution time. Fatal logic errors cause a program to fail and terminate prematurely. Nonfatal logic errors do not terminate a program's execution but cause the program to produce incorrect results.
- The diamond or decision symbol in an activity diagram indicates that a decision is to be made. A decision symbol indicates that the workflow will continue along a path determined by the symbol's associated guard conditions, which can be true or false.

- Each transition arrow emerging from a decision symbol has a guard condition (specified in square brackets above or next to the transition arrow). If a particular guard condition is true, the workflow enters the action state to which that transition arrow points.

Section 4.6 If...Then...Else Selection Statement
- The If...Then...Else selection statement allows you to specify that a different action (or sequence of actions) is to be performed when the condition is true than when the condition is false.

Section 4.7 Nested If...Then...Else Selection Statements
- Nested If...Then...Else statements test for multiple conditions by placing If...Then...Else statements inside other If...Then...Else statements.
- Keyword ElseIf can be used in nested If...Then...Else statements to make them more readable.

Section 4.8 Repetition Statements
- The UML's merge symbol joins two flows of activity into one flow of activity. The UML represents both the merge symbol and the decision symbol as diamonds.
- The Do While...Loop repetition statement allows you to specify that an action is to be repeated while a specific condition remains true.
- Eventually, the loop-continuation condition in a Do While...Loop statement becomes false. At this point, the repetition terminates, and continues with the next statement in sequence.
- Failure to provide the body of a Do While...Loop statement with an action that eventually causes the loop-continuation condition to become false is a logic error. Normally, such a repetition statement never terminates, resulting in an error called an "infinite loop."
- The While...End While repetition statement operates identically to Do While...Loop.
- Statements in the body of a Do Until...Loop are executed repeatedly as long as the loop-termination condition evaluates to false.

Section 4.9 Compound Assignment Operators
- Visual Basic provides the compound assignment operators +=, -=, *=, /=, \=, ^= and &= for abbreviating assignment statements.

Section 4.10 Formulating Algorithms: Counter-Controlled Repetition
- Many algorithms can be divided logically into an initialization phase, a processing phase and a termination phase.
- The ListBox control can be used to display a list of values that your program manipulates.
- A Form's default Button is the one that will be pressed when the user presses the *Enter* key and is specified by setting the Form's AcceptButton property to the appropriate Button.
- Counter-controlled repetition uses a variable called a counter (or control variable) to specify the number of times that a set of statements will execute. Counter-controlled repetition also is called definite repetition because the number of repetitions is known before the loop begins executing.
- Variables used as totals and counters should be initialized before they're used. Counters usually are initialized to 0 or 1, depending on their use. Totals generally are initialized to 0.
- Numeric variables are initialized to 0 when they're declared, unless another value is assigned to the variable in its declaration.
- A ListBox's Items property keeps track of the values in the ListBox. To place a new item in a ListBox, call the Items property's Add method.
- Calling a control's Focus method makes the control the active control—the one that will respond to the user's interactions.

- Type `Double` is typically used to store floating-point numbers. Floating-point literals in a program's source code are treated as `Double` values by default.
- Local variables can be used only from their declaration until the end of the method declaration. A local variable's declaration must appear before the variable is used in that method.
- `ListBox` property `Items.Count` keeps track of the `ListBox`'s number of items.
- Each value in a `ListBox` has a position number associated with it—this is known the item's index.
- For a `ListBox`, calling the `Item`'s property's `Clear` method removes all the items in the `ListBox`.
- Formatted output allows you to control how a number appears for display purposes. The `String` class's `Format` method performs formatting.
- In the format string `"{0:F}"`, the numeric value that appears before the colon indicates which of `Format`'s arguments will be formatted—0 specifies the first argument *after* the format string passed to `Format`. The F is as a format specifier which indicates that a fixed-point number should be rounded to two decimal places by default.

Section 4.11 Formulating Algorithms: Nested Control Statements

- Control statements can be stacked or nested within one another.
- Top-down, stepwise refinement is a technique for developing algorithms.
- The top is a single statement that conveys the overall function of the program. As such, the top is a complete representation of a program.
- Through the process of refinement, we divide the top into a series of smaller tasks, listed in the order in which they must be performed. Each refinement, including the top, is a complete specification of the algorithm; only the level of detail in each refinement varies.
- You terminate the top-down, stepwise refinement process when the pseudocode algorithm is specified in sufficient detail for the pseudocode to be converted to a Visual Basic program.

Section 4.12 Using the Debugger: Locating a Logic Error

- Logic errors are also called bugs. Such errors do not prevent a program from compiling successfully, but can cause a running program to produce incorrect results.
- Visual Studio's debugger can be used to monitor the execution of your programs so you can locate and remove logic errors.
- An off-by-one error is often caused by using the incorrect relational operator in a loop condition.
- Breakpoints can be set at any executable line of code.
- Once the debugger pauses program execution, you can use various debugger commands to execute the program one statement at a time—this is called "single stepping" or simply "stepping."
- To insert a breakpoint, left click in the margin indicator bar or select **Breakpoint > Insert Breakpoint**. You can also click a line of code then press *F9* to toggle a breakpoint on and off.
- After setting breakpoints in the code editor, select **Debug > Start Debugging** (or press the *F5* key) to rebuild the program and begin the debugging process.
- When the debugger reaches a breakpoint, it suspends execution and enters break mode. A yellow instruction-pointer arrow in the IDE indicates the next statement to execute.
- While in break mode, you can place the mouse cursor over any variable and its value will be displayed in a *Quick Info* box. You can also explore the values of a method's local variables using the debugger's **Locals** window. To view the **Locals** window, select **Debug > Windows > Locals**.
- To execute a program one statement at a time, use the **Step Over** command. You can access this command by selecting **Debug > Step Over**, by pressing *Shift + F8* or by pressing the **Step Over** command's toolbar icon (🖳).

Terminology

Self-Review Exercises

4.1 Answer each of the following questions.

a) _____ refer(s) to the task of ordering an application's statements correctly.
   1. Actions
   2. Program control
   3. Control structures
   4. Visual programming

b) A(n) _____ is a plan for solving a problem in terms of the actions to be executed and the order in which these actions are to be executed.
   1. chart
   2. control structure
   3. algorithm
   4. ordered list

c) _____ is an informal language that helps you develop algorithms.
   1. Pseudocode
   2. VB-Speak
   3. Notation
   4. None of the above

d) Pseudocode _____.
   1. usually describes only declarations
   2. is executed on computers
   3. usually describes only executable lines of code
   4. usually describes declarations and executable lines of code

e) All Visual Basic applications can be written in terms of _____ types of control structures.
   1. one
   2. two
   3. three
   4. four

f) The process of application statements executing one after another in the order in which they are written is called _____.
   1. transfer of control
   2. sequential execution
   3. workflow
   4. None of the above

g) Which of the following `If...Then` statements correctly displays that a student received an A on an exam if the score was 90 or above?

```
1. If studentGrade <> 90 Then
       displayLabel.Text = "Student received an A"
   End If
```
```
2. If studentGrade > 90 Then
       displayLabel.Text = "Student received an A"
   End If
```
```
3. If studentGrade = 90 Then
       displayLabel.Text = "Student received an A"
   End If
```
```
4. If studentGrade >= 90 Then
       displayLabel.Text = "Student received an A"
   End If
```

h) The symbol _____ is not a Visual Basic operator.
   1. *
   2. ^
   3. %
   4. <>

i) `If...Then...Else` is a _____-selection statement.

    1. single   2. double

    3. triple   4. nested

j) Placing an `If...Then...Else` statement inside another `If...Then...Else` statement is an example of _____.

    1. nesting `If...Then...Else` statements   2. stacking `If...Then...Else` statements

    3. creating sequential `If...Then...Else` statements   4. None of the above

k) The `*=` operator _____.

    1. squares the value of the right operand and stores the result in the left operand

    2. adds the value of the right operand to the value of the left operand and stores the result in the left operand

    3. creates a new variable and assigns the value of the right operand to that variable

    4. multiplies the value of the left operand by the value of the right operand and stores the result in the left operand

l) If `number` is initialized with the value 5, what value will `number` contain after the expression `number -= 3` executes?

    1. 3   2. 5

    3. 7   4. 2

m) Method `String.Format` is used to _____.

    1. create constants   2. control how text is formatted

    3. format Visual Basic statements   4. All of the above

n) An application enters break mode when _____.

    1. **Debug > Start** is selected   2. a breakpoint is reached

    3. there is a syntax error   4. None of the above.

o) The body of a `Do While...Loop` statement executes _____.

    1. at least once   2. never

    3. while its condition is true   4. while its condition is false

p) The UML represents both the merge symbol and the decision symbol as _____.

    1. rectangles with rounded sides   2. diamonds

    3. small black circles   4. ovals

q) A `Do Until...Loop` repetition statement differs from a `Do While...Loop` repetition statement in _____.

    1. that a `Do While...Loop` repetition statement loops as long as the loop-continuation condition remains `False`, whereas a `Do Until...Loop` repetition statement loops as long as the loop-continuation condition remains `True`

    2. that a `Do Until...Loop` repetition statement loops as long as the loop-termination condition remains `False`, whereas a `Do While...Loop` repetition statement loops as long as the loop-continuation condition remains `True`

    3. that a `Do Until...Loop` repetition statement always executes at least once

    4. no way. There is no difference between the `Do Until...Loop` and `Do While...Loop` repetition statements

r) Statements in the body of a `Do Until...Loop` execute repeatedly for as long as the _____ remains `False`.

    1. loop-continuation condition   2. do-loop condition

    3. loop-termination condition   4. until-loop condition

    s) Counter-controlled repetition is also called _____ because the number of repetitions is known before the loop begins executing.
        1. definite repetition   2. known repetition
        3. sequential repetition   4. counter repetition

4.2 State whether each of the following is *true* or *false*. If *false*, explain why.
    a) It's difficult to convert pseudocode into a Visual Basic program.
    b) Sequential execution refers to statements in a program that execute one after another.
    c) The If...Then statement is called a single-selection statement.
    d) Pseudocode closely resembles actual Visual Basic code.
    e) The Do While statement is terminated with the keywords End While.

4.3 Write two different Visual Basic statements that each add 1 to Integer variable number.

4.4 Write a statement or a set of statements to accomplish each of the following:
    a) Sum the odd integers between 1 and 15 using a While statement. Use Integer variables sum and count.
    b) Sum the squares of the even integers between 1 and 15 using a Do While...Loop repetition statement. Use Integer variables sum and count and initialize them to 0 and 2, respectively.
    c) Display the numbers from 5 to 1 in resultListBox using a Do Until...Loop and Integer counter variable counterIndex. Initialize counterIndex to 5.
    d) Repeat Exercise 4.4 (c) using a Do While...Loop statement.

4.5 Write a Visual Basic statement to accomplish each of the following tasks:
    a) Declare variables sum and number to be of type Integer.
    b) Assign 1 to variable number.
    c) Assign 0 to variable sum.
    d) Total variables number and sum, and assign the result to variable sum.
    e) Display "The sum is: " followed by the value of variable sum in resultLabel.

4.6 Combine the statements that you wrote in Exercise 4.5 into a program that calculates and displays the sum of the Integers from 1 to 10. Use a Do While...Loop statement to loop through the calculation and increment statements. The loop should terminate when the value of control variable number becomes 11.

4.7 Identify and correct the error(s) in each of the following (you may need to add code):
    a) The following loop should total the values from 1 to 50. Assume that value is 50.

```
Do While value >= 0
   sum += value
Loop
```

    b) The following code should display the squares of 1 to 10 in resultListBox.

```
Dim number As Integer = 1

Do While number < 10
   resultListBox.Items.Add(number ^ 2)
End While
```

    c) This segment should display the integers from 888 to 1000 in resultListBox. Initialize variable value to 888.

```
Dim value As Integer = 888

Do While value <= 1000
   value -= 1
Loop
```

4.8   State whether each of the following is *true* or *false*. If the answer is *false*, explain why.
   a) Pseudocode is a structured programming language.
   b) The body of a Do While...Loop is executed only if the loop-continuation test is false.
   c) The body of a While...End While is executed only if the loop-continuation test is false.
   d) The body of a Do Until...Loop is executed only if the loop-termination condition is false.

Answers to Self-Review Exercises

4.1   a) 2. b) 3. c) 1. d) 3. e) 3. f) 2. g) 4. h) 3. i) 2. j) 1. k) 4. l) 4. m) 2. n) 2. o) 3. p) 2. q) 2. r) 3. s) 1.

4.2   a) False. Pseudocode normally converts easily into Visual Basic code. b) True. c) True. d) True. e) False. It's terminated with the keyword Loop.

4.3
```
number = number + 1
number += 1
```

4.4   a)
```
Dim sum As Integer = 0
Dim count As Integer = 1

While count <= 15
   sum += count
   count += 2
End While
```
   b)
```
Dim sum As Integer = 0
Dim count As Integer = 2

Do While count <= 15
   sum += count ^ 2
   count += 2
Loop
```
   c)
```
Dim counterIndex As Integer = 5

Do Until counterIndex < 1
   resultListBox.Items.Add(counterIndex)
   counterIndex -= 1
Loop
```
   d)
```
Dim counterIndex As Integer = 5

Do While counterIndex >= 1
   resultListBox.Items.Add(counterIndex)
   counterIndex -= 1
Loop
```

4.5   a)
```
Dim sum As Integer
Dim number As Integer
```
   b) `number = 1`
   c) `sum = 0`
   d) `sum += number or sum = sum + number`
   e) `resultLabel.Text = "The sum is: " & sum`

4.6 See the code below:

```
 1   ' Ex. 4.6: CalculateSum.vb
 2   ' Calculates the sum of the integers from 1 to 10.
 3   Public Class CalculateSum
 4      ' performs the calculation
 5      Private Sub CalculateSum_Load(ByVal sender As System.Object,
 6         ByVal e As System.EventArgs) Handles MyBase.Load
 7
 8         Dim sum As Integer
 9         Dim number As Integer
10
11         sum = 0
12         number = 1
13
14         Do While number <= 10
15            sum += number
16            number += 1
17         Loop
18
19         resultLabel.Text = "The sum is: " & sum
20      End Sub ' CalculateSum_Load
21   End Class ' CalculateSum
```

Sum of 1 to 10

The sum is: 55

4.7 a) Error: Repetition condition never becomes false, resulting in an infinite loop.

```
While value >= 0
   sum += value
   value -= 1
End While
```

b) Errors: The counter is never incremented, resulting in an infinite loop. The repetition condition uses the wrong relational operator. Keywords End While are used instead of keyword Loop.

```
Dim number As Integer = 1

Do While number <= 10
   resultListBox.Items.Add(number ^ 2)
   number += 1
Loop
```

c) Error: The values are never displayed and are decremented instead of incremented.

```
value = 888

While value <= 1000
   resultListBox.Items.Add(value)
   value += 1
End While
```

4.8 a) False. Pseudocode is not a programming language.
b) False. The loop condition must evaluate to true for the body to be executed.
c) False. The loop condition must evaluate to true for the body to be executed.
d) True.

Quick Quiz

4.9 Answer each of the following questions.

a) The _____ operator returns `False` if the left operand is larger than the right operand.

    1. =   2. <

    3. <=   4. All of the above

b) A _____ occurs when an executed statement does not directly follow the previously executed statement in the written application.

    1. transition   2. flow

    3. logical error   4. transfer of control

c) The `If...Then` statement is called a _____ statement because it selects or ignores one action (or group of actions).

    1. single-selection   2. multiple-selection

    3. double-selection   4. repetition

d) The three types of control structures are sequence, selection and _____.

    1. repeat   2. looping

    3. redo   4. repetition

e) In an activity diagram, a rectangle with curved sides represents _____.

    1. a complete algorithm   2. a comment

    3. an action   4. the termination of the application

f) The `If...Then...Else` selection statement ends with the keywords _____.

    1. `End If Then Else`   2. `End If Else`

    3. `End Else`   4. `End If`

g) The _____ operator assigns the result of adding the left and right operands to the left operand.

    1. +   2. =+

    3. +=   4. None of the above

h) The _____ statement executes until its loop-termination condition becomes `True`.

    1. `Do While...Loop`   2. `Do Until...Loop`

    3. `Do`   4. `Loop`

i) The _____ statement executes until its loop-continuation condition becomes `False`.

    1. `Do While...Loop`   2. `Do Until...Loop`

    3. `Do`   4. `Do While`

j) A(n) _____ loop occurs when a condition in a `Do While...Loop` never becomes `False`.

    1. infinite   2. undefined

    3. nested   4. indefinite

k) A _____ is a variable that helps control the number of times that a set of statements executes.

    1. repeater   2. counter

    3. loop   4. repetition control statement

l) The _____ control allows users to add and view items in a list.

    1. `ListItems`   2. `SelectBox`

    3. `ListBox`   4. `ViewBox`

m) In a UML activity diagram, a(n) _____ symbol joins two flows of activity into one flow of activity.

    1. merge   2. combine

    3. action state   4. decision

n) Property _____ maintains all the values in a ListBox.

1. All
2. List
3. ListItemValues
4. Items

o) Items's method _____ deletes all the values in a ListBox.

1. Remove
2. Delete
3. Clear
4. Del

p) Items's method _____ adds an item to a ListBox.

1. Include
2. Append
3. Add
4. None of the above

Exercises

Selection Statement Exercises

4.10 What does this code do? Assume that the user entered the value 27 into ageTextBox.

```
1   Dim age As Integer
2
3   age = ageTextBox.Text
4
5   If age < 0 Then
6       ageLabel.Text = "Enter a value greater than or equal to zero."
7   ElseIf age < 13 Then
8       ageLabel.Text = "Child"
9   ElseIf age < 20 Then
10      ageLabel.Text = "Teenager"
11  ElseIf age < 30 Then
12      ageLabel.Text = "Young Adult"
13  ElseIf age < 65 Then
14      ageLabel.Text = "Adult"
15  Else
16      ageLabel.Text = "Senior Citizen"
17  End If
```

4.11 *(Wage Calculator with Tax Calculations)* Develop an application that calculates an employee's earnings, as shown in Fig. 4.23. The user should provide the hourly wage and number of hours worked per week. When the **Calculate** Button is clicked, the employee's gross earnings should display in the **Gross earnings:** TextBox. The **Less FWT:** TextBox should display the amount deducted for federal taxes and the **Net earnings:** TextBox should display the difference between the gross earnings and the federal tax amount. You can use the format specifier C with String method Format, to

Fig. 4.23 | Wage Calculator GUI.

format the result as currency. Assume that overtime is calculated for hours over 40 hours worked, overtime wages are 1.5 times the hourly wage and federal taxes are 15% of gross earnings. The **Clear** Button should clear all fields. Set the TextAlign properties of the Labels that show the results to MiddleRight so that the values are aligned at their decimal points. [*Note:* In the next chapter, we'll introduce the data type Decimal for financial calculations.]

4.12   *(Credit Checker Application)* Develop an application (as shown in Fig. 4.24) that determines whether a department-store customer has exceeded the credit limit on a charge account. Each customer enters an account number (an Integer), a balance at the beginning of the month (a Double), the total of all items charged this month (a Double), the total of all credits applied to the customer's account this month (a Double), and the customer's allowed credit limit (a Double). The application should input each of these facts, calculate the new balance (= *beginning balance – credits + charges*), display the new balance and determine whether the new balance exceeds the customer's credit limit. You can use the format "{0:C}" with String method Format, to format the result as currency (see Fig. 4.24). If the customer's credit limit is exceeded, display a message (in messageLabel at the bottom of the Form) informing the customer of this fact; otherwise, display the customer's remaining credit amount. If the user presses the **Clear Fields** Button, the application should clear the TextBoxes and Labels. [*Note:* In the next chapter, we'll introduce the data type Decimal for financial calculations.]

Fig. 4.24 | Credit Checker GUI.

Repetition Statement Exercises

4.13   *(Enhanced Exam Analysis Application)* Modify the program of Fig. 4.15 to process the four Strings: "P", "p", "F" and "f". If any other String input is encountered, increment a counter that tracks the number of invalid inputs. Display a message indicating the number of invalid inputs. Test your new program.

4.14   *(Miles Per Gallon Application)* Drivers are concerned with the mileage obtained by their automobiles. One driver has kept track of several tankfuls of gasoline by recording the miles driven and the gallons used for each tankful. Each time the user enters the miles driven and gallons used (both as Doubles) for a tankful and presses the **Calculate MPG** Button, the program should calculate the miles per gallon then display the miles driven, gallons used and miles per gallon in ListBoxes as shown in Fig. 4.25. The program should also display the total miles per gallon. (Be careful—this is not the average of the miles per gallon for each tankful.) All average calculations should produce floating-point results. Avoid division by zero—if the user enters zero for the number of gallons, inform the user that the input value for gallons must be greater than zero.

Fig. 4.25 | Miles Per Gallon GUI.

4.15   *(Table of Powers Application)* Write an application that displays a table of numbers from 1 to an upper limit, along with each number's squared value (for example, the number *n* to the power 2, or *n* ^ 2) and cubed value (the number *n* to the power 3, or *n* ^ 3). The user specifies the upper limit, and the results are displayed in a ListBox, as in Fig. 4.26.

Fig. 4.26 | Table of Powers GUI.

4.16   *(Using the Debugger: Odd Numbers Application)* The **Odd Numbers** application should display all of the odd integers between one and the number input by the user. Open the **Odd Numbers** application from the ex04_16 folder located with this chapter's examples. Run the application. Note that an infinite loop occurs after you enter a value into the **Upper limit:** TextBox and click the **Display** Button. Select **Debug > Stop Debugging** to close the running application. Use the debugger to find and fix the error(s) in the application. Figure 4.27 displays the correct output for the application.

Making a Difference Exercises

4.17   *(World Population Growth)* World population has grown considerably over the centuries. Continued growth could eventually challenge the limits of breathable air, drinkable water, arable cropland and other limited resources. There is evidence that growth has been slowing in recent years and that world population could peak some time this century, then start to decline.

Fig. 4.27 | Correct output for the **Odd Numbers** application.

For this exercise, research world population growth issues online. *Be sure to investigate various viewpoints.* Get estimates for the current world population and its growth rate (the percentage by which it is likely to increase this year). Write a program that calculates world population growth each year for the next 75 years, *using the simplifying assumption that the current growth rate will stay constant.* Display the results in a `ListBox` (Fig. 4.28). The first column should display the year from year 1 to year 75. The second column should display the anticipated world population at the end of that year. The third column should display the numerical increase in the world population that would occur that year. Using your results, determine the year in which the population would be double what it is today, if this year's growth rate were to persist. [*Hint:* Use `Double` variables because `Integer` variables can store values only up to approximately two billion.]

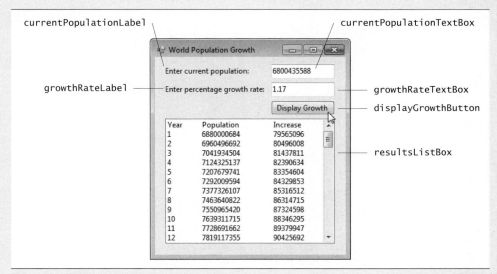

Fig. 4.28 | World Population Growth GUI.

4.18 *(Enforcing Privacy with Cryptography)* The explosive growth of Internet communications and data storage on Internet-connected computers has greatly increased privacy concerns. The field of cryptography is concerned with coding data to make it difficult (and hopefully—with the most advanced schemes—impossible) for unauthorized users to read. In this exercise you'll investigate a simple scheme for encrypting and decrypting data. A company that wants to send data over the Internet has asked you to write a program that will encrypt it so that it may be transmitted more securely. All the data is transmitted as four-digit integers. Your application (Fig. 4.29) should read a four-digit integer entered by the user and encrypt it as follows: Replace each digit with the result of adding 7 to the digit and getting the remainder after dividing the new value by 10. Then swap the first digit with the third, and swap the second digit with the fourth. Then display the encrypted integer. Write a separate application that inputs an encrypted four-digit integer and decrypts it (by reversing the encryption scheme) to form the original number.

Fig. 4.29 | Encryption GUI.

Problem Solving and Control Statements: Part 2

Who can control his fate?
—William Shakespeare

The used key is always bright.
—Benjamin Franklin

Not everything that can be counted counts, and not every thing that counts can be counted.
—Albert Einsteins

Objectives

In this chapter you'll learn:

- Problem solving with additional control statement building blocks.

- The essentials of counter-controlled repetition.

- To use the **For...Next**, **Do...Loop While** and **Do...Loop Until** repetition statements.

- To perform multiple selection using the **Select...Case** selection statement.

- To use the **Exit** statement to break out of a repetition statement.

- To use the **Continue** statement to terminate the current iteration of a loop and proceed with the next iteration.

- To use logical operators to form more complex conditions for decision making.

5.1 Introduction

Chapter 4 began our introduction to the types of building blocks that are available for problem solving. We used those building blocks with proven program-construction techniques. In this chapter, we continue our study of control statements. We demonstrate the For...Next, Select...Case, Do...Loop While and Do...Loop Until control statements. We explore the essentials of counter-controlled repetition and demonstrate nested repetition statements. We use a Select...Case multiple-selection statement to count the number of A, B, C, D and F grades in a set of letter grades entered by the user. We introduce the Exit program control statement for terminating a control statement immediately, and we introduce the Continue program control statement for terminating the current iteration of a repetition statement. Finally, we discuss the logical operators, which enable you to form more powerful conditional expressions in control statements.

5.2 For...Next Repetition Statement

In Chapter 4, we introduced counter-controlled repetition with the Do While...Loop statement. Counter-controlled repetition requires:

    1. the **name** of a control variable (or loop counter) that is used to determine whether the loop continues to iterate

    2. the **initial value** of the control variable

    3. the **increment** (or **decrement**) by which the control variable is modified each time through the loop

    4. the condition that tests for the **final value** of the control variable (that is, whether looping should continue).

The **For...Next repetition statement** specifies counter-controlled repetition details in a single line of code. In general, counter-controlled repetition should be implemented with For...Next. Figure 5.1 illustrates the power of For...Next statement by displaying the even integers from 2 to 10. The ForCounter_Load event handler is called when you execute the program.

```
1    ' Fig. 5.1: ForCounter.vb
2    ' Counter-controlled repetition with the For…Next statement.
3    Public Class ForCounter
4        ' display the even Integers from 2 to 10
5        Private Sub ForCounter_Load(ByVal sender As System.Object,
6           ByVal e As System.EventArgs) Handles MyBase.Load
7
8           ' initialization, repetition condition and
9           ' incrementing are all included in the For...Next statement
10          For counter As Integer = 2 To 10 Step 2
11              ' append counter value to outputLabel's Text property
12              outputLabel.Text &= counter & "  " ' display counter
13          Next
14      End Sub ' ForCounter_Load
15  End Class ' ForCounter
```

Even Integers from 2 to 10

2 4 6 8 10

Fig. 5.1 | Counter-controlled repetition with the For...Next statement.

When the For...Next statement (lines 10–13) is reached, the control variable counter is declared as an Integer and initialized to 2, thus addressing the first two elements of counter-controlled repetition—the control variable's *name* and its *initial value*. Next, the *implied* loop-continuation condition counter <= 10 is tested. The **To keyword** is required in the For...Next statement. The optional **Step keyword** specifies the increment, that is, the amount that's added to counter after each time the For...Next body is executed. If Step and the value following it are omitted, the increment defaults to 1. You typically omit the Step portion for increments of 1. The increment of a For...Next statement could be negative, in which case it's called a decrement, and the loop actually counts downward. If the loop-continuation condition is initially false (for example, if the initial value is greater than the final value and the increment is positive), the For...Next's body is *not* performed. Instead, execution proceeds with the first statement after the For...Next.

Error-Prevention Tip 5.1

Use a For...Next loop for counter-controlled repetition. Off-by-one errors (which occur when a loop is executed for one more or one less iteration than is necessary) tend to disappear, because the initial and terminating values are clear.

First Iteration of the Loop
In Fig. 5.1, the initial value of counter is 2, so the implied loop-continuation condition (counter <= 10) is true, and the counter's value 2 is appended to outputLabel's Text property (line 12). The required **Next keyword** (line 13) marks the end of the For...Next repetition statement. When Next is reached, variable counter is incremented by the Step value (2), and the implied loop-continuation test is performed again.

Second and Subsequent Iterations of the Loop
Now, the control variable is equal to 4. This value still does not exceed the final value, so the program performs the body statement again. This process continues until the counter value 10 has been displayed and the control variable counter is incremented to 12, causing the implied loop-continuation test to fail and the loop to terminate. The program continues by performing the first statement after the For...Next statement (line 14).

Good Programming Practice 5.1
Some programmers place the control variable name after Next as in Next counter. This is particularly useful in nested For...Next statements to identify the statement to which the Next belongs.

5.2.1 For...Next Statement Header Components

Figure 5.2 takes a closer look at the For...Next statement of Fig. 5.1. The first line of the For...Next statement sometimes is called the **For...Next header**. It specifies each of the items needed for counter-controlled repetition with a control variable.

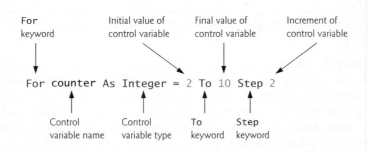

Fig. 5.2 | For...Next header components.

5.2.2 General Form of a For...Next Statement

The general form of the For...Next statement is

```
For initialization To finalValue Step increment
    statement
Next
```

where the *initialization* expression initializes the loop's control variable, *finalValue* determines whether the loop should continue executing and *increment* specifies the amount the control variable should be incremented (or decremented) each time through the loop.

5.2.3 Declaring the Control Variable Before a For...Next Statement

In Fig. 5.1, the counter variable is declared and initialized *in* the For...Next header. The counter variable may be declared *before* the For...Next statement. For example, the code in Fig. 5.1 could have been written as

```
Dim counter As Integer
For counter = 2 To 10 Step 2
    outputLabel.Text &= counter & "  "
Next
```

Although both forms are correct, declaring the control variable in the For...Next header is clearer and more concise. The difference between the two forms is that if the *initialization* expression in the For...Next statement header declares the control variable (as we've done in Fig. 5.1), the control variable can be used *only* in the body of the For...Next statement—it will be unknown outside the For...Next statement. This restricted use of the control-variable name is known as the variable's **scope**, which specifies where the variable can be used in a program. If the control variable is declared before the For...Next control statement, it can be used from the point of declaration, inside the control statement's body and after the control statement as well.

5.2.4 Using Expressions in the For...Next Statement's Header

The starting value, ending value and increment portions of a For...Next statement can contain arithmetic expressions. The expressions are evaluated once (when the For...Next statement begins executing) and used as the starting value, ending value and increment of the For...Next statement's header. For example, assume that x = 2 and y = 10. The header

```
For j As Integer = x To 4 * x * y Step y \ x
```

is equivalent to the header

```
For j As Integer = 2 To 80 Step 5
```

Common Programming Error 5.1

Counter-controlled loops should not be controlled with Double or Single variables. Values of these types are represented only approximately in the computer's memory. This can lead to imprecise counter values and inaccurate tests for termination.

5.2.5 For...Next Statement UML Activity Diagram

The activity diagram of the For...Next statement in Fig. 5.1 is shown in Fig. 5.3. This activity diagram makes it clear that the initialization occurs only once and that incrementing occurs *after each* execution of the body statement.

5.2.6 Local Type Inference

In each For...Next statement presented so far, we declared the control variable's type in the For...Next statement's header. For any local variable that is initialized in its declaration, the variable's type can be determined based on its initializer value—this is known as **local type inference**. Recall that a local variable is any variable declared in the body of a method. For example, in the declaration

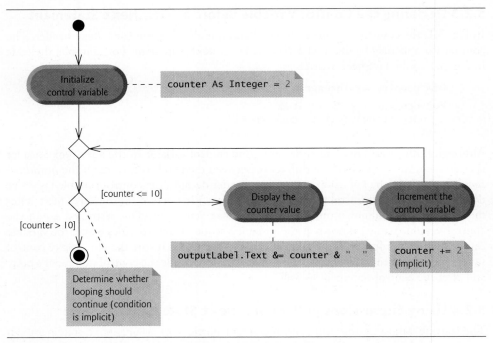

Fig. 5.3 | For...Next repetition statement activity diagram.

```
Dim x = 7
```

the compiler infers that the variable x should be of type Integer, because the compiler assumes that whole-number values, like 7, are Integer values. In the declaration

```
Dim y = -123.45
```

the compiler infers that the variable y should be of type Double, because the compiler assumes that floating-point literals, like -123.45, are Double values. In the declaration

```
Dim z = 987.65D
```

the compiler infers that the variable z should be of type Decimal, because the value 987.65 is followed by the **literal type character D**, which indicates that the value is of type Decimal. Some common literal type characters include C for Char ("T"C), F for Single (123.45F), S for Short (123S) and L for Long (123L).

You can also use local type inference with control variables in the header of a For...Next statement. For example, the For...Next header

```
For counter As Integer = 1 To 10
```

can be written as

```
For counter = 1 To 10
```

In this case, counter is of type Integer because it is initialized with an Integer literal (1).

5.3 Examples Using the For...Next Statement

The following examples demonstrate different ways of varying the control variable in a For...Next statement. In each case, we write the appropriate For...Next header using local type inference.

a) Vary the control variable from 1 to 100 in increments of 1.

```
For i = 1 To 100 or For i = 1 To 100 Step 1
```

b) Vary the control variable from 100 to 1 in increments of -1 (decrements of 1).

```
For i = 100 To 1 Step -1
```

c) Vary the control variable from 7 to 77 in increments of 7.

```
For i = 7 To 77 Step 7
```

d) Vary the control variable from 20 to 2 in increments of -2 (decrements of 2).

```
For i = 20 To 2 Step -2
```

e) Vary the control variable over the sequence of the following values: 2, 5, 8, 11, 14, 17, 20.

```
For i = 2 To 20 Step 3
```

f) Vary the control variable over the sequence of the following values: 99, 88, 77, 66, 55, 44, 33, 22, 11, 0.

```
For i = 99 To 0 Step -11
```

5.4 Application: Interest Calculator

Consider the following problem statement:

A person invests $1000.00 in a savings account. Assuming that all the interest is left on deposit, calculate and print the amount of money in the account at the end of each year for up to 10 years. Allow the user to specify the principal amount, the interest rate and the number of years. To determine these amounts, use the following formula:

$$a = p \, (1 + r)^{\,n}$$

where

> *p is the original amount invested (that is, the principal)*
> *r is the annual interest rate (for example, .05 stands for 5%)*
> *n is the number of years*
> *a is the amount on deposit at the end of the nth year.*

This problem involves a loop that performs the indicated calculation for each of the years that the money remains on deposit. Figure 5.4 shows the GUI for this application. We introduce the **NumericUpDown** control, which limits a user's choices to a specific range of values—this helps to avoid data entry errors. In this program, we use the control to allow the user to choose a number of years from 1 to 10. The control's **Minimum** property specifies the starting value in the range. Its **Maximum** property specifies the ending value in the range. Its **Value** property specifies the current value displayed in the control. You can also use this property programmatically to obtain the current value displayed. The control provides up and down arrows that allow the user to scroll through the control's range of values. In this example, we use 1 as the minimum value, 10 as the maximum value and 1 as the initial value for this control. The **Increment** property specifies by how much the current number in the NumericUpDown control changes when the user clicks the control's up (for incrementing) or down (for decrementing) arrow. We use the Increment property's default value, 1. When the user changes the value in a NumericUpDown control, a **ValueChanged** event occurs. If you double click the yearUpDown control in design mode, the IDE generates the event handler yearUpDown_ValueChanged to handle the Value-Changed event. The **Interest Calculator** program is shown in Fig. 5.5.

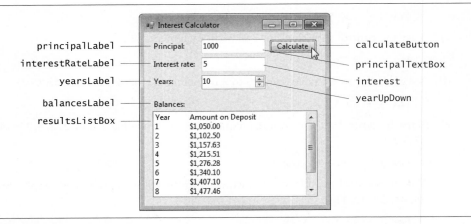

Fig. 5.4 | GUI for the **Interest Calculator** application.

```
1    ' Fig. 5.5: InterestCalculator.vb
2    ' Compound interest calculation using For...Next.
3    Public Class InterestCalculator
4        ' handles Calculate Button's Click event
5        Private Sub calculateButton_Click(ByVal sender As System.Object,
6            ByVal e As System.EventArgs) Handles calculateButton.Click
7
8            ' store the principal and the interest rate
9            Dim principal As Decimal = Val(principalTextBox.Text)
10           Dim rate As Decimal = Val(interestRateTextBox.Text)
11
12           ' display the output header
13           resultsListBox.Items.Add(
14               "Year" & vbTab & "Amount on Deposit")
15           Dim amount As Decimal ' amount on deposit after each year
16
17           ' calculate amount after each year and add to resultListBox
18           For yearCounter As Integer = 1 To yearUpDown.Value
19               amount = principal * ((1 + rate / 100) ^ yearCounter)
20               resultsListBox.Items.Add(yearCounter & vbTab &
21                   String.Format("{0:C}", amount))
22           Next
23       End Sub ' calculateButton_Click
```

Fig. 5.5 | Compound interest calculation using For...Next. (Part 1 of 2.)

```
24
25      ' clear resultListBox when principal changes
26      Private Sub principalTextBox_TextChanged(ByVal sender As System.Object,
27         ByVal e As System.EventArgs) Handles principalTextBox.TextChanged
28         resultsListBox.Items.Clear() ' empty ListBox when inputs change
29      End Sub ' principalTextBox_TextChanged
30
31      ' clear resultListBox when interest rate changes
32      Private Sub interestRateTextBox_TextChanged(
33         ByVal sender As System.Object,
34         ByVal e As System.EventArgs) Handles interestRateTextBox.TextChanged
35         resultsListBox.Items.Clear() ' empty ListBox when inputs change
36      End Sub ' interestRateTextBox_TextChanged
37
38      ' clear resultListBox when number of years changes
39      Private Sub yearUpDown_ValueChanged(ByVal sender As System.Object,
40         ByVal e As System.EventArgs) Handles yearUpDown.ValueChanged
41         resultsListBox.Items.Clear() ' empty ListBox when inputs change
42      End Sub ' yearUpDown_ValueChanged
43   End Class ' InterestCalculator
```

Fig. 5.5 | Compound interest calculation using For…Next. (Part 2 of 2.)

Decimal *Variables*

Lines 9–10 in the `calculateButton_Click` event handler declare and initialize two `Decimal` variables. Type **Decimal** should be used for monetary calculations such as those required in the **Interest Calculator** application. Line 9 declares `pricipal` as type `Decimal`. Variable `principal` is initialized to the value in `principalTextBox` and `rate` (line 10) is initialized to the value in `interestRateTextBox`. Line 15 declares amount as a `Decimal`. This variable stores the amount on deposit at the end of each year.

Using the **Val** Function to Convert *Strings to Numbers*

This application uses TextBoxes to read numeric input. Unfortunately, we cannot prevent users from accidentally entering nonnumeric input, such as letters and special characters like $ and @ in the TextBoxes. Lines 9–10 use the built-in **Val** function to prevent inputs like this from terminating the application. Previously, you've used the method `Format`, which is part of class `String`. When a method not part of a class, it's called a function.

Function `Val` obtains a value from a `String` of characters, such as a `TextBox`'s `Text` property. The value returned is *guaranteed* to be a number. We use `Val` because this application is not intended to perform arithmetic calculations with characters that are not numbers. `Val` reads its argument one character at a time until it encounters a character that is not a number. Once a nonnumeric character is read, `Val` returns the number it has read up to that point. `Val` ignores whitespace (for example, "33 5" will be converted to 335). `Val` recognizes the decimal point as well as plus and minus signs that indicate whether a number is positive or negative (such as -123). `Val` does not recognize such symbols as commas and dollar signs. If `Val` receives an argument that cannot be converted to a number (for example, "b35", which begins with a nonnumeric character, or an empty string), it returns 0.

Performing the Interest Calculations
The `For...Next` statement (lines 18–22) varies the control variable `yearCounter` from 1 to `yearUpDown.Value` in increments of 1. Line 19 performs the calculation from the problem statement

$$a = p \, (1 + r) \,^n$$

where *a* is the `amount`, *p* is the `principal`, *r* is the `rate` and *n* is the `yearCounter`.

Formatting Currency Output
Lines 20–21 display the amount on deposit at the end of each year in the `resultsListBox`. The text includes the current `yearCounter` value, a tab character (`vbTab`) to position to the second column and the result of the method call `String.Format("{0:C}", amount)`. The `C` ("currency") **format specifier** indicates that its corresponding value (`amount`) should be displayed in monetary format—with a dollar sign to the left and commas in the proper locations. For example, the value `1334.50`, when formatted using the `C` format specifier, will appear as "`$1,334.50`." This may differ based on your locale throughout the world. Other commonly used format specifiers include:

- `F` for floating-point numbers—sets the number of decimal places to two (introduced in Section 4.10).

- `N` for numbers—separates every three digits with a comma and sets the number of decimal places to two.

- `D` for integers

A Warning About Function `Val`
Although the value returned by `Val` is always a number, it's not necessarily the value the user intended. For example, the user might enter the text `$10.23` to represent a monetary amount, which `Val` evaluates to 0 without reporting an error. A common mistake like this causes the application to execute incorrectly. Visual Basic provides two ways to handle invalid input. One way is to use string-processing capabilities to examine input. We discuss these throughout this book. The other form of handling invalid input is called exception handling, where you write code to handle errors that may occur as the application executes. You'll learn about exception handling in Chapter 7.

5.5 Formulating Algorithms: Nested Repetition Statements

Consider the following problem statement:

> Write a program that displays in a TextBox a filled square consisting solely of one type of character, such as the asterisk (*). The side of the square and the character to be used to fill the square should be entered by the user. The length of the side should be in the range 1 to 20.

Your program should draw the square as follows:

1. Input the fill character and side length of the square.

2. Ensure that the side is in the range 1 to 20 by using a NumericUpDown control to specify the exact range of allowed values.

3. Use repetition to draw the square by displaying only one fill character at a time.

After reading the problem statement, we make the following observations:

- The program must draw *side* rows, each containing *side* fill characters, where *side* is the value entered by the user. Counter-controlled repetition should be used.

- Four variables should be used—one that represents the length of the side of the square, one that represents (as a String) the fill character to be used, one that represents the row in which the next symbol should appear and one that represents the column in which the next symbol should appear.

GUI for the Square of Characters Application

Figure 5.6 shows the GUI for this application. We use a NumericUpDown control to allow the user to specify a side length in the range 1 to 20. The output is displayed in a TextBox with its MultiLine property set to True and its Font property set to the fixed-width font Lucida Console.

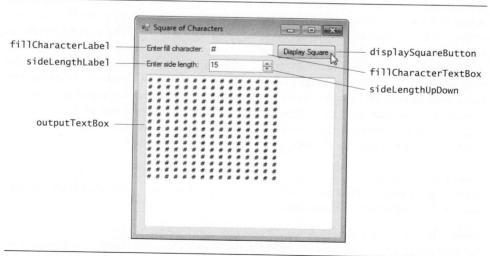

Fig. 5.6 | GUI for the **Square of Characters** application.

Evolving the Pseudocode

Let's proceed with top-down, stepwise refinement. We begin with a pseudocode representation of the top:

> *Display a square of fill characters*

Our first refinement is

> *Input the fill character*
> *Input the side of the square*
> *Display the square*

Here, too, even though we have a complete representation of the entire program, further refinement is necessary.

Displaying the Square

The pseudocode statement

> *Display the square*

can be implemented by using one loop nested inside another. In this example, it is known in advance that there are *side* rows of *side* fill characters each, so counter-controlled repetition is appropriate. One loop controls the row in which each fill character is to be displayed. A nested loop displays each fill character (one at a time) for that row. The refinement of the preceding pseudocode statement is

> *For row from 1 to the number of characters in a side*
>
> > *For column from 1 to the number of characters in a side*
> > *Display the fill character*
>
> *Move to the next line of output*

The outer *For* statement initializes *row* to one to prepare to display the square's first row and loops while the implied condition *row is less than or equal to the number of characters in a side* remains true—that is, for each row of the square. Within this *For* statement, the nested *For* statement initializes *column* to one to prepare to display the first fill character of the current row. The nested (or inner) loop executes while the implied condition *column is less than or equal to the number of characters in a side* remains true. Each iteration of the inner loop displays one fill character. After each row of characters, we move to the next line in the TextBox to prepare to display the next row of the square. At this point, the outer loop increments variable *row* by 1. If the outer loop's condition is still true, *column* is reset to 1, and the inner loop executes again, displaying another row of fill characters. Then, the outer loop increments *row* by 1 again. This process repeats until the value of *row* exceeds *side*, at which point the square of fill characters is complete.

Completed Pseudocode

The complete second refinement appears in Fig. 5.7. The pseudocode now is refined sufficiently for conversion to Visual Basic.

Visual Basic Code for the Square of Characters Application

We implement the pseudocode algorithm in the displaySquareButton_Click event handler (Fig. 5.8, lines 5–25). The nested For...Next statements (lines 15–24) display the

1	*Input the fill character*
2	*Input the side of the square*
3	
4	*For each row from 1 to the number of characters in a side*
5	
6	*For each column from 1 to the number of characters in a side*
7	*Display the fill character*
8	
9	*Move to the next line of output*

Fig. 5.7 | Second refinement of the pseudocode.

square of characters. The outer loop specifies which row is being displayed and the inner loop (lines 18–21) displays the current row of characters. We follow each fill character by a space (line 20) to make the output look more like a square. Line 23 in the outer loop moves the cursor to the next line in the TextBox to begin the next line of output.

```vb
 1  ' Fig. 5.8: SquareOfCharacters.vb
 2  ' Nested repetition statements used to display a square of characters.
 3  Public Class SquareOfCharacters
 4     ' display a square of characters
 5     Private Sub displaySquareButton_Click(ByVal sender As System.Object,
 6        ByVal e As System.EventArgs) Handles displaySquareButton.Click
 7
 8        outputTextBox.Clear() ' clears the output
 9
10        ' get the fill character and side length
11        Dim fillCharacter As String = fillCharacterTextBox.Text
12        Dim sideLength As Integer = sideLengthUpDown.Value
13
14        ' this For...Next controls the row being displayed
15        For row As Integer = 1 To sideLength
16           ' this For...Next controls the column being displayed;
17           ' this loop is nested in the For...Next at lines 13-22
18           For column As Integer = 1 To sideLength
19              ' display fill character and a space
20              outputTextBox.AppendText(fillCharacter & " ")
21           Next column
22
23           outputTextBox.AppendText(vbCrLf) ' move to next line
24        Next row
25     End Sub ' displaySquareButton_Click
26
27     ' clear outputTextBox when the fill character is changed by the user
28     Private Sub fillCharacterTextBox_TextChanged(
29        ByVal sender As System.Object, ByVal e As System.EventArgs) _
30        Handles fillCharacterTextBox.TextChanged
31        outputTextBox.Clear() ' clears the output
32     End Sub ' fillCharacterTextBox_TextChanged
```

Fig. 5.8 | Nested repetition statements used to display a square of characters. (Part 1 of 2.)

```
33
34        ' clear outputTextBox when the side length is changed by the user
35        Private Sub sideLengthUpDown_ValueChanged(
36           ByVal sender As System.Object, ByVal e As System.EventArgs) _
37           Handles sideLengthUpDown.ValueChanged
38           outputTextBox.Clear() ' clears the output
39        End Sub ' sideLengthUpDown_ValueChanged
40     End Class ' TextBox_TextChanged
```

Fig. 5.8 | Nested repetition statements used to display a square of characters. (Part 2 of 2.)

5.6 Select…Case Multiple-Selection Statement

Occasionally, an algorithm contains a series of decisions that test a variable or expression separately for each value that the variable or expression might assume. The algorithm then takes different actions based on those values. The **Select…Case** multiple-selection statement handles such decision making. Figure 5.9 enhances the **Class Average** application of Fig. 4.12 by using a Select…Case statement to determine whether each grade is the equivalent of an A, B, C, D or F and to increment the appropriate grade counter. The program also displays a summary of the number of students who received each grade. An extra counter is used to display the number of students who received a perfect score of 100 on the exam. The GUI uses the same controls as in Fig. 4.12, but we've made the class-AverageLabel taller to display more output and resized the gradesListBox so that it extends to the bottom of the clearGradesButton.

Instance Variables

For the first time in this example, we declare a variable in the class, but *outside* all of the class's event-handling methods. Such variables—called **instance variables**—are special because they can be used by all of the class's methods. They also retain their values, so a value set by one method in the class can be used by another method. We do this so that we can increment the letter-grade counters declared in lines 6–11 in the submitGrade-Button_Click event handler, then use those variables' values to display a grade report in the calculateAverageButton_Click event handler. The variable perfectScoreCount (line 11) counts the number of students who received a perfect score of 100 on the exam.

```vb
1   ' Fig. 5.9: ClassAverage.vb
2   ' Counter-controlled repetition: Class-average problem.
3   Public Class ClassAverage
4      ' variables declared in the class, but not inside the class's methods
5      ' can be used in all of the class's methods
6      Dim aCount As Integer ' count of A grades
7      Dim bCount As Integer ' count of B grades
8      Dim cCount As Integer ' count of C grades
9      Dim dCount As Integer ' count of D grades
10     Dim fCount As Integer ' count of F grades
11     Dim perfectScoreCount As Integer ' count of perfect scores
12
13     ' places a grade in the gradesListBox
14     Private Sub submitGradeButton_Click(ByVal sender As System.Object,
15        ByVal e As System.EventArgs) Handles submitGradeButton.Click
16
17        Dim grade As Integer = Val(gradeTextBox.Text) ' get grade
18
19        ' add the grade to the end of the gradesListBox
20        gradesListBox.Items.Add(grade)
21        gradeTextBox.Clear() ' clear the gradeTextBox
22
23        ' add 1 to appropriate counter for specified grade
24        Select Case grade ' determine which grade was entered
25           Case 100 ' perfect score
26              perfectScoreCount += 1 ' increment perfectScoreCount
27              aCount += 1 ' increment aCount
28           Case 90 To 99 ' grade was between 90 and 99
29              aCount += 1 ' increment aCount
30           Case 80 To 89 ' grade was between 80 and 89
31              bCount += 1 ' increment bCount
32           Case 70 To 79 ' grade was between 70 and 79
33              cCount += 1 ' increment cCount
34           Case 60 To 69 ' grade was between 60 and 69
35              dCount += 1 ' increment dCount
36           Case Else ' grade was less than 60
37              fCount += 1 ' increment fCount
38        End Select
39
40        gradeTextBox.Focus() ' gives the focus to the gradeTextBox
41     End Sub ' submitGradeButton_Click
42
43     ' calculates the class average based on the grades in gradesListBox
44     Private Sub calculateAverageButton_Click(ByVal sender As System.Object,
45        ByVal e As System.EventArgs) Handles calculateAverageButton.Click
46
47        Dim total As Integer ' sum of grades entered by user
48        Dim gradeCounter As Integer ' counter for grades
49        Dim grade As Integer ' grade input by user
50        Dim average As Double ' average of grades
51
52        ' initialization phase
53        total = 0 ' set total to zero before adding grades to it
```

Fig. 5.9 | Counter-controlled repetition: Class-average problem. (Part I of 2.)

```
54          gradeCounter = 0 ' prepare to loop
55
56       ' processing phase
57       Do While gradeCounter < gradesListBox.Items.Count
58          grade = gradesListBox.Items(gradeCounter) ' get next grade
59          total += grade ' add grade to total
60          gradeCounter += 1 ' add 1 to gradeCounter
61       Loop
62
63       ' termination phase
64       If gradeCounter <> 0 Then
65          average = total / gradeCounter ' calculate average
66
67          ' display total and average (with two digits of precision)
68          classAverageLabel.Text = "Total of the " & gradeCounter &
69             " grade(s) is " & total & vbCrLf & "Class average is " &
70             String.Format("{0:F}", average) & vbCrLf & vbCrLf
71
72          ' display summary of letter grades
73          classAverageLabel.Text &=
74             "Letter grade summary:" & vbCrLf & "A: " & aCount &
75             vbCrLf & "B: " & bCount & vbCrLf & "C: " & cCount &
76             vbCrLf & "D: " & dCount & vbCrLf & "F: " & fCount &
77             vbCrLf & "Perfect scores: " & perfectScoreCount
78       Else
79          classAverageLabel.Text = "No grades were entered"
80       End If
81    End Sub ' calculateAverageButton_Click
82
83    ' clears grades from gradeListBox and results from classAverageLabel
84    Private Sub clearGradesButton_Click(ByVal sender As System.Object,
85       ByVal e As System.EventArgs) Handles clearGradesButton.Click
86
87       gradesListBox.Items.Clear() ' removes all items from gradesListBox
88       classAverageLabel.Text = String.Empty ' clears classAverageLabel
89    End Sub ' clearGradesButton_Click
90 End Class ' ClassAverage
```

Fig. 5.9 | Counter-controlled repetition: Class-average problem. (Part 2 of 2.)

Method submitGradeButton_Click

In this version of the program, we no longer check whether the user entered a grade before pressing the **Submit Grade** Button. Instead, we now use the Val function to convert the user's input into a number. If the TextBox is empty, 0 will be added to the ListBox.

Lines 24–38 in submitGradeButton_Click use a Select...Case statement to determine which counter to increment. A grade in the range 90–100 represents an A, 80–89 represents a B, 70–79 represents a C, 60–69 represents a D and 0–59 represents an F. We assume that the user enters a grade in the range 0–100.

Line 24 begins the Select...Case statement. The expression following the keywords Select Case (in this case, grade) is called the **controlling expression**. It is compared in order with each Case. If a matching Case is found, the code in the Case executes, then program control proceeds to the first statement after the Select...Case statement (line 40).

The first Case (line 25) determines whether the value of grade is equal to 100. If so, the statements in lines 26–27 execute, incrementing both aCount (because a grade of 100 is an A) and perfectScoreCount. A Case statement can specify multiple actions—in this case, incrementing both aCount and perfectScoreCount. The next Case statement (line 28) determines whether grade is between 90 and 99, inclusive. In this case, only aCount is incremented (line 29). Keyword To specifies the range; lines 30–35 use this keyword to present a series of similar Cases. Each case increments the appropriate counter.

If no match occurs between the controlling expression's value and a Case label, the optional **Case Else** (lines 36–37) executes. We use the Case Else in this example to process all controlling-expression values that are less than 60—that is, all failing grades. If no match occurs and the Select...Case does not contain a Case Else, program control simply continues with the first statement after the Select...Case. Case Else commonly is used to deal with *invalid* values. In this example, we assume all values entered by the user are in the range 0–100. When used, the Case Else must be the last Case. The required **End Select** keywords (line 38) terminate the Select...Case statement.

Common Programming Error 5.2
Duplicate Case statements are logic errors. At runtime, the first matching Case executes.

Common Programming Error 5.3
If the value on the left side of keyword To in a Case statement is larger than the value on the right side, the Case is ignored during program execution; this is typically a logic error.

Error-Prevention Tip 5.2
Provide a Case Else in Select...Case statements. Cases not handled in a Select...Case statement are ignored unless a Case Else is provided. Including a Case Else statement can facilitate the processing of exceptional conditions.

Types of Case Statements

Case statements also can use relational operators to determine whether the controlling expression satisfies a condition. For example

```
Case Is < 0
```

uses keyword **Is** along with the relational operator, <, to test for values less than 0.

Multiple values can be tested in a Case statement by separating the values with commas, as in

```
Case 0, 5 To 9
```

which tests for the value 0 or values in the range 5–9. Also, Cases can be used to test String values.

Select...Case *Statement UML Activity Diagram*
Figure 5.10 shows the UML activity diagram for the general Select...Case statement.

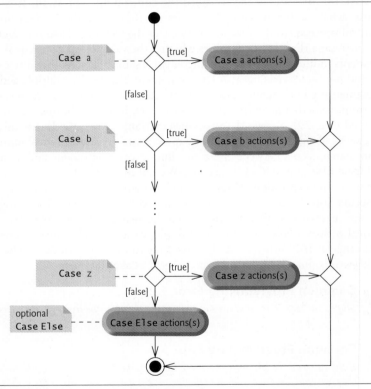

Fig. 5.10 | Select...Case multiple-selection statement UML activity diagram.

5.7 Do...Loop While and Do...Loop Until Repetition Statements

The **Do...Loop While** repetition statement is similar to the While...End While statement and Do While...Loop statement. In the While...End While and Do While...Loop statements, the loop-continuation condition is tested at the *beginning* of the loop, *before* the body of the loop is performed, so these are referred to as pre-test loops. The Do...Loop While statement tests the loop-continuation condition *after* the loop body is performed, so it's referred to as a post-test loop. In a Do...Loop While statement, the loop body is always executed *at least once*. When a Do...Loop While statement terminates, execution continues with the statement after the Loop While clause. The program in Fig. 5.11 uses a Do...Loop While statement to output the even integers from 2 to 10.

```
 1    ' Fig. 5.11: DoLoopWhile.vb
 2    ' Do...Loop While repetition statement.
 3    Public Class DoLoopWhile
 4       ' display the even Integers from 2 to 10
 5       Private Sub DoLoopWhile_Load(ByVal sender As System.Object,
 6          ByVal e As System.EventArgs) Handles MyBase.Load
 7
 8          Dim counter As Integer = 2 ' initialize counter
 9
10          Do
11             outputLabel.Text &= counter & "  " ' display counter value
12             counter += 2 ' increment counter
13          Loop While counter <= 10
14       End Sub ' DoLoopWhile_Load
15    End Class ' DoLoopWhile
```

Even Integers from 2 to 10

2 4 6 8 10

Fig. 5.11 | Do...Loop While repetition statement.

Lines 10–13 demonstrate the Do...Loop While statement. When program control enters the loop, lines 11–12 execute, displaying the value of counter (at this point, 2), then incrementing counter by 2. Then the loop-continuation condition in line 13 is evaluated. Variable counter is 4, which is less than or equal to 10, so the Do...Loop While statement executes lines 11–12 again. In the fifth iteration of the statement, line 11 outputs the value 10, and line 12 increments counter to 12. At this point, the loop-continuation condition in line 13 evaluates to false, and the program exits the Do...Loop While statement.

Do...Loop While *Statement Activity Diagram*
The Do...Loop While activity diagram (Fig. 5.12) shows that the loop-continuation condition is not evaluated until *after* the statement body executes *at least once*.

Do...Loop Until *Repetition Statement*
The **Do...Loop Until** repetition statement is similar to the Do Until...Loop statement, except that the loop-termination condition is tested *after* the loop body is performed; therefore, the loop body executes *at least once*. When a Do...Loop Until terminates, execution continues with the statement after the Loop Until clause. The following code uses a Do...Loop Until statement to reimplement the Do...Loop While statement of Fig. 5.11

```
Do
   outputLabel.Text &= counter & "  " ' display counter value
   counter += 2 ' increment counter
Loop Until counter > 10
```

The Do...Loop Until statement activity diagram is the same as the one in Fig. 5.12. The loop-termination condition (counter > 10) is not evaluated until *after* the loop body executes *at least once*. If this condition is true, the statement exits. If the condition is false (that is, the condition `counter <= 10` is true), the loop continues executing.

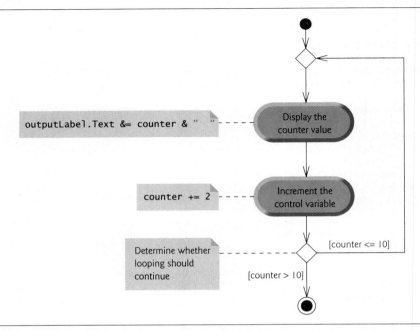

Fig. 5.12 | Do...Loop `While` repetition statement activity diagram.

5.8 Using `Exit` to Terminate Repetition Statements

There are many forms of the **Exit** statement, designed to terminate different types of repetition statements. When the **Exit Do** statement executes in a `Do While...Loop`, `Do...Loop While`, `Do Until...Loop` or `Do...Loop Until` statement, the program terminates that repetition statement and continues execution with the first statement after the repetition statement. Similarly, the **Exit For** statement and the **Exit While** statement cause immediate exit from `For...Next` and `While...End While` loops, respectively. The **Exit Select** statement causes immediate exit from a `Select...Case` statement.

5.9 Using `Continue` in Repetition Statements

A **Continue** statement terminates *only the current iteration* of a repetition statement and continues execution with the next iteration of the loop. The **Continue Do** statement can be executed in a `Do While...Loop`, `Do...Loop While`, `Do Until...Loop` or `Do...Loop Until` statement. Similarly, the **Continue For** statement and **Continue While** statement can be used in `For...Next` and `While...End While` statements, respectively.

When `Continue For` is encountered in a `For...Next` statement, execution continues with the statement's increment expression, then the program evaluates the loop-continuation test. When `Continue` is used in another type of repetition statement, the program evaluates the loop-continuation (or loop-termination) test immediately after the `Continue` statement executes. If a control variable's increment occurs in the loop body after the Continue statement, the increment is skipped.

Exit *and* Continue *in Nested Control Statements*

Exit and Continue also can be used in nested control statements. For instance, Exit For or Continue For can be used in a While...End While statement, as long as that statement is nested in a For...Next statement. In such an example, the Exit or Continue statement would be applied to the proper control statement based on the keywords used in the Exit or Continue statement—in this example, the For keyword is used, so the For...Next statement's flow of control will be altered. If there are nested loops of the same type (for example, a For...Next statement within a For...Next statement), the statement that immediately surrounds the Exit or Continue statement is the one affected.

5.10 Logical Operators

A condition is an expression that results in a Boolean value—**True** or **False**. So far, we've studied only **simple conditions**, such as count <= 10, total > 1000 and number <> -1. Each selection and repetition statement evaluated only *one* condition with *one* of the operators >, <, >=, <=, = and <>. To make a decision that relied on the evaluation of multiple conditions, we performed these tests in separate statements or in nested If...Then or If...Then...Else statements.

To handle multiple conditions more efficiently, the **logical operators** can be used to form complex conditions by combining simple ones. The logical operators are And, Or, AndAlso, OrElse, Xor and Not.

Logical And *Operator*

Suppose we wish to ensure that two conditions are *both* True in a program before a certain path of execution is chosen. In such a case, we can use the logical **And** operator as follows:

```
If gender = "F" And age >= 65 Then
    seniorFemales += 1
End If
```

This If...Then statement contains *two* simple conditions. The condition gender = "F" determines whether a person is female and the condition age >= 65 determines whether a person is a senior citizen. The two simple conditions are evaluated first, because the precedences of = and >= are both higher than the precedence of And. The If...Then statement then considers the combined condition

```
gender = "F" And age >= 65
```

This condition evaluates to True if and only if *both* simple conditions are True. When this combined condition is True, the seniorFemales count is incremented by 1. However, if either or both simple conditions are False, the program skips the increment and proceeds to the statement following the If...Then statement. The readability of the preceding combined condition can be improved by adding redundant (that is, unnecessary) parentheses:

```
(gender = "F") And (age >= 65)
```

Figure 5.13 illustrates the effect of using the And operator with two expressions. The table lists all four possible combinations of True and True values for *expression1* and *expression2*. Such tables often are called **truth tables**. Expressions that include relational operators, equality operators and logical operators evaluate to `True` or `False`.

expression1	expression2	expression1 And expression2
False	False	False
False	True	False
True	False	False
True	True	True

Fig. 5.13 | Truth table for the logical And operator.

Logical *Or Operator*

Now let's consider the **Or** operator. Suppose we wish to ensure that *either or both* of two conditions are `True` before we choose a certain path of execution. We use the `Or` operator as in the following program segment:

```
If (semesterAverage >= 90 Or finalExam >= 90) Then
    resultLabel.Text = "Student grade is A"
End If
```

This statement also contains *two* simple conditions. The condition `semesterAverage >= 90` is evaluated to determine whether the student deserves an "A" in the course because of an outstanding performance throughout the semester. The condition `finalExam >= 90` is evaluated to determine whether the student deserves an "A" in the course because of an outstanding performance on the final exam. The `If...Then` statement then considers the combined condition

```
(semesterAverage >= 90 Or finalExam >= 90)
```

and awards the student an "A" if *either or both* of the conditions are `True`. The text `"Student grade is A"` is displayed, unless *both* of the conditions are `False`. Figure 5.14 shows the `Or` operator's truth table. The `And` operator has a higher precedence than `Or`.

expression1	expression2	expression1 Or expression2
False	False	False
False	True	True
True	False	True
True	True	True

Fig. 5.14 | Truth table for the logical Or operator.

Logical *AndAlso and OrElse Operators*

The **logical AND operator with short-circuit evaluation** (`AndAlso`) and the **logical inclusive OR operator with short-circuit evaluation** (`OrElse`) are similar to the `And` and `Or` operators, respectively, with one exception—an expression containing `AndAlso` or `OrElse` operators is evaluated only until its truth or falsity is known. For example, the expression

```
(gender = "F" AndAlso age >= 65)
```

stops evaluating immediately if `gender` is not equal to "F" (that is, the entire expression is `False`); the second expression is irrelevant because the first condition is `False`. Evaluation of the second condition occurs if and only if `gender` is equal to "F" (that is, the entire expression could still be `True` if the condition age >= 65 is `True`). This performance feature for the evaluation of `AndAlso` and `OrElse` expressions is called short-circuit evaluation.

Performance Tip 5.1

In expressions using operator `AndAlso`, if the separate conditions are independent of one another, place the condition most likely to be `False` as the leftmost condition. In expressions using operator `OrElse`, make the condition most likely to be `True` the leftmost condition. Each of these suggestions can reduce a program's execution time.

Logical *Xor* Operator

A condition containing the logical exclusive OR (`Xor`) operator is `True` if and only if one of its operands results in a `True` value and the other results in a `False` value. If both operands are `True` or both are `False`, the entire condition is `False`. Figure 5.15 presents a truth table for the logical exclusive OR operator (`Xor`). This operator always evaluates *both* of its operands—there is no short-circuit evaluation.

expression1	expression2	expression1 Xor expression2
False	False	False
False	True	True
True	False	True
True	True	False

Fig. 5.15 | Truth table for the logical exclusive OR (`Xor`) operator.

Logical *Not* Operator

The `Not` (logical negation) operator enables you to "reverse" the meaning of a condition. Unlike the logical operators `And`, `AndAlso`, `Or`, `OrElse` and `Xor`, which each combine *two* conditions, the logical negation operator is a unary operator, requiring only one operand. The logical negation operator is placed before a condition to choose a path of execution if the original condition (without the logical negation operator) is `False`. The logical negation operator is demonstrated by the following program segment:

```
If Not (value = 0) Then
    resultLabel.Text = "The value is " & value
End If
```

The parentheses around the condition value = 0 are necessary because the logical negation operator (`Not`) has a higher precedence than the equality operator. Figure 5.16 provides a truth table for the logical negation operator.

In most cases, you can avoid using logical negation by expressing the condition differently with relational or equality operators. This flexibility helps you express conditions more naturally. For example, the preceding statement can be written as follows:

```
If value <> 0 Then
    resultLabel.Text = "The value is " & value
End If
```

expression	Not expression
False	True
True	False

Fig. 5.16 | Truth table for operator Not (logical negation).

5.11 Application: Dental Payment Calculator

To demonstrate some of the logical operators, let's consider the following problem:

> *A dentist's office administrator wishes to create an application that employees can use to bill patients. The application must allow users to enter the patient's name and specify which services were performed during the visit. The application will then calculate the total charges. If a user attempts to calculate a bill before any services are specified, or before the patient's name is entered, an error message will be displayed informing the user that necessary input is missing.*

GUI for the Dental Payment Calculator Application

In the **Dental Payment Calculator** application, you'll use two new GUI controls—CheckBoxes and a message dialog—to assist the user in entering data. The CheckBoxes allow the user to select which dental services were performed. Programs often use **message dialogs** to display important messages to the user.

A **CheckBox** is a small square that either is blank or contains a check mark. A CheckBox is known as a **state button** because it can be in the "on" state or the "off" state. When a CheckBox is selected, a check mark appears in the box. Any number of CheckBoxes can be selected at a time, including none at all. The text that appears alongside a CheckBox is called the **CheckBox label**. If the CheckBox is "on" (checked), its **Checked property** has the Boolean value True; otherwise, it's False ("off"). The application's GUI is shown in Fig. 5.17 and the code is shown in Fig. 5.18.

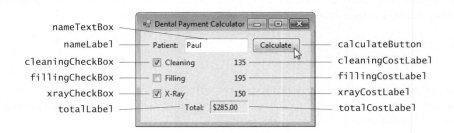

Fig. 5.17 | GUI for **Dental Payment Calculator** application.

```vb
 1    ' Fig. 5.18: DentalPayment.vb
 2    ' Dental Payment Calculator displays bill amount for a dental visit.
 3    Public Class DentalPayment
 4       ' calculate the bill amount
 5       Private Sub calculateButtonClick(ByVal sender As System.Object,
 6          ByVal e As System.EventArgs) Handles calculateButton.Click
 7
 8          ' if no name entered or no CheckBoxes checked, display message
 9          If (nameTextBox.Text = String.Emtpy) OrElse
10             (Not cleaningCheckBox.Checked AndAlso
11              Not xrayCheckBox.Checked AndAlso
12              Not fillingCheckBox.Checked) Then
13
14             totalCostLabel.Text = String.Empty ' clear totalCostLabel
15
16             ' display an error message in a dialog
17             MessageBox.Show(
18                "Please enter a name and check at least one item",
19                "Missing Information", MessageBoxButtons.OK,
20                MessageBoxIcon.Error)
21          Else ' add prices
22             ' total contains amount to bill patient
23             Dim total As Decimal = 0
24
25             ' if patient had a cleaning
26             If cleaningCheckBox.Checked Then
27                total += Val(cleaningCostLabel.Text)
28             End If
29
30             ' if patient had a cavity filled
31             If fillingCheckBox.Checked Then
32                total += Val(fillingCostLabel.Text)
33             End If
34
35             ' if patient had an X-Ray taken
36             If xrayCheckBox.Checked Then
37                total += Val(xrayCostLabel.Text)
38             End If
39
40             ' display the total
41             totalCostLabel.Text = String.Format("{0:C}", total)
42          End If
43       End Sub ' calculateButtonClick
44    End Class ' DentalPayment
```

Fig. 5.18 | Dental Payment Calculator displays bill amount for a dental visit. (Part 1 of 2.)

Message dialog displayed when the user clicks **Calculate**
before entering a name or selecting any **CheckBox**es

Fig. 5.18 | **Dental Payment Calculator** displays bill amount for a dental visit. (Part 2 of 2.)

Using Logical Operators

Recall from the problem statement that an error message should be displayed if the user does not enter a name or select at least one CheckBox. When the user presses the **Calculate** Button, lines 9–12 test these possibilities using logical operators Not, OrElse and AndAlso. The compound condition is split into two parts. If the condition in line 9 is True, the user did not enter a name, so an error message should be displayed. Short-circuit evaluation occurs with the OrElse operator, so the rest of the condition (lines 10–12) is ignored. If the user entered a name, then lines 10–12 check all three CheckBoxes. The expression

```
Not cleaningCheckBox.Checked
```

is True if the cleaningCheckBox is not checked—the Checked property has the value False and the Not operator returns True. If all three CheckBoxes are unchecked, the compound condition in lines 10–12 is True, so an error message should be displayed.

Calculating the Total of the Selected Services

If the user entered a name and selected at least one CheckBox, lines 21–42 calculate the total of the selected dental services. Each condition in lines 26, 31 and 36 uses the value of one of the CheckBox's Checked properties as the condition. If a given CheckBox's Checked property is True, the body statement gets the value from the corresponding price Label, converts it to a number and adds it to the total. Then, line 41 displays the result in the totalCostLabel.

Displaying an Error Message Dialog

Class **MessageBox** creates message dialogs. We use a message dialog in lines 17–20 to display an error message to the user if the condition in lines 9–12 is True. MessageBox method **Show** displays the dialog. This method takes four arguments. The first is the String that's displayed in the message dialog. The second is the String that's displayed in the message dialog's title bar. The third and fourth are predefined constants that specify the Button(s) and the icon to show on the dialog, respectively.

Figure 5.19 shows the message box displayed by lines 17–20. It includes an **OK** button that allows the user to dismiss (that is, close) the message dialog by clicking the button. The program *waits* for the dialog to be closed before executing the next line of code—this type of dialog is known as a **modal dialog**. You can also dismiss the message dialog by clicking the dialog's close box—the button with an **X** in the dialog's upper-right corner.

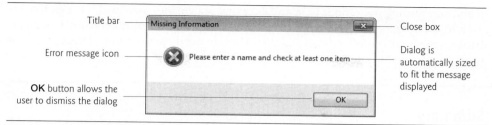

Title bar

Error message icon

OK button allows the
user to dismiss the dialog

Close box

Dialog is
automatically sized
to fit the message
displayed

Fig. 5.19 | Message dialog displayed by calling `MessageBox.Show`.

Summary of Operator Precedence

Figure 5.20 displays the precedence of the operators introduced so far. The operators are shown from top to bottom in decreasing order of precedence.

Operators	Type
^	exponentiation
+ -	unary plus and minus
* /	multiplicative operators
\	integer division
Mod	modulus
+ -	additive operators
&	concatenation
< <= > >= = <>	relational and equality
Not	logical NOT
And AndAlso	logical AND
Or OrElse	logical inclusive OR
Xor	logical exclusive OR
= += -= *= /= \= ^= &=	assignment

Fig. 5.20 | Precedence of the operators discussed so far.

5.12 Wrap-Up

In this chapter, we completed our introduction to the control statements that enable you to control the flow of execution. We demonstrated the `For...Next`, `Select...Case`, `Do...Loop While` and `Do...Loop Until` statements. Any algorithm can be developed using combinations of the sequence structure (that is, statements listed in the order in which they are to execute), the three types of selection statements—`If...Then`, `If...Then...Else` and `Select...Case`—and the seven types of repetition statements—`While...End While`, `Do While...Loop`, `Do Until...Loop`, `Do...Loop While`, `Do...Loop Until`, `For...Next` and `For Each...Next` (which we discuss in Chapter 7). We discussed how you can combine these building blocks using proven program-construction and problem-solving techniques. We showed how to use nested `For...Next` statements. We showed how to alter the flow of program control using the various Exit and Continue statements. You used the logical operators to form more complex conditional expressions in control statements. Chapter 6 discusses methods in greater depth and shows how to use them to organize larger programs as small, manageable pieces.

Summary

Section 5.2 For...Next Repetition Statement
- Counter-controlled repetition requires the name of a control variable, the initial value of the control variable, the increment (or decrement) by which the control variable is modified each time through the loop and the condition that tests for the final value of the control variable.
- The For...Next repetition statement specifies counter-controlled repetition details in a single line of code. In general, counter-controlled repetition should be implemented with For...Next.
- When the For...Next statement is reached, its control variable is declared and initialized. Next, the *implied* loop-continuation condition is tested.
- The To keyword is required and is followed by the control variable's final value.
- The optional Step keyword specifies the increment. If Step and the value following it are omitted, the increment defaults to 1.
- If the loop-continuation condition is initially false, the For...Next's body is not performed.
- When Next is reached, the control variable is incremented by the Step value, and the implied loop-continuation test is performed again.
- The first line of the For...Next statement sometimes is called the For...Next header.
- The general form of the For...Next statement is

  ```
  For initialization To finalValue Step increment
      statement
  Next
  ```

  where the *initialization* expression initializes the loop's control variable, *finalValue* determines whether the loop should continue executing and *increment* specifies the amount the control variable should be incremented each time through the loop.
- When the *initialization* expression in the For...Next statement header declares the control variable, the control variable can be used only in the body of the For...Next statement.
- A variable's scope specifies where the variable can be used in a program.
- The starting value, ending value and increment portions of a For...Next statement can contain arithmetic expressions. t.
- Local type inference determines a local variable's type based on its initializer value.
- You can also use local type inference with the control variable of a For...Next statement.
- The literal type character D (123.45D) indicates that a literal numeric value is of type Decimal. Other common literal type characters include C for Char ("T"C), F for Single (123.45F), S for Short (123S) and L for Long (123L).

Section 5.4 Application: Interest Calculator
- The NumericUpDown control limits a user's choices to a range of values specified by its Minimum and Maximum properties. The Value property specifies the current value displayed in the control and can be used to obtain the current value. The Increment property specifies by how much the current number in the control changes when the user clicks the control's up or down arrow.

- When the user changes the value in a `NumericUpDown` control, a `ValueChanged` event occurs.

- Type `Decimal` should be used for monetary calculations.

- The built-in `Val` function obtains a value from a `String` of characters. The value returned is guaranteed to be a number. `Val` ignores whitespace. `Val` recognizes the decimal point as well as plus and minus signs that indicate whether a number is positive or negative. If `Val` receives **an** argument that cannot be converted to a number, it returns 0.

- The `C` ("currency") format specifier indicates that its corresponding value should be displayed in monetary format—with a dollar sign to the left and commas in the proper locations. This may differ based on your locale throughout the world.

- Other commonly used format specifiers include `F` for floating-point numbers (sets the number of decimal places to two), `N` for numbers (separates every three digits with a comma and sets the number of decimal places to two) and `D` for integers.

Section 5.6 *Select...Case Multiple-Selection Statement*

- A variable that is declared in the class, but outside all of the class's methods is called an instance variable. Such variables are special because they can be used by all of the class's methods.

- The `Select...Case` multiple-selection statement tests a variable or expression for each value that the variable or expression might assume, then takes different actions based on those values.

- The expression following the keywords `Select Case` is called the controlling expression. It is compared in order with each `Case`. If a matching `Case` is found, its code executes, then program control proceeds to the first statement after the `Select...Case` statement.

- `Cases` may contain single values, multiple values or ranges of values. Keyword `To` specifies a range.

- If no match occurs between the controlling expression's value and a `Case`, the optional `Case Else` executes. If there is not a `Case Else`, program control simply continues with the first statement after the `Select...Case`. When used, the `Case Else` must be the last `Case`.

- The required `End Select` keywords terminate the `Select...Case` statement.

- `Case` statements can use relational operators to determine whether the controlling expression satisfies a condition. `Case Is < 0` tests for values less than 0.

- Multiple values can be tested in a `Case` statement by separating the values with commas.

Section 5.7 *Do...Loop While and Do...Loop Until Repetition Statements*

- The `Do...Loop While` repetition statement tests the loop-continuation condition after the loop body is performed—the loop body is always executed at least once.

- The `Do...Loop Until` repetition statement test the loop-termination condition after the loop body is performed—the loop body executes at least once.

Section 5.8 *Using Exit to Terminate Repetition Statements*

- When the `Exit Do` statement executes in a `Do While...Loop`, `Do...Loop While`, `Do Until...Loop` or `Do...Loop Until` statement, that repetition statement terminates and the program continues execution with the first statement after the repetition statement. `Exit For` and `Exit While` cause immediate exit from `For...Next` and `While...End While` loops, respectively.

Section 5.9 *Using Continue in Repetition Statements*

- A `Continue` statement terminates only the current iteration of a repetition statement and continues execution with the next iteration of the loop. `Continue Do` statement can be executed in a `Do While...Loop`, `Do...Loop While`, `Do Until...Loop` or `Do...Loop Until` statement. `Continue For` and `Continue While` can be used in `For...Next` and `While...End While` statements, respectively.

- `Continue For` causes a `For...Next` statement to increment the control variable, then evaluate the loop-continuation test. When `Continue` is used other repetition statements, the program evaluates the loop-continuation (or loop-termination) test immediately.
- `Exit` and `Continue` also can be used in nested control statements.

Section 5.10 Logical Operators
- A condition is an expression that results in a `Boolean` value—`True` or `False`.
- The logical operators can be used to form complex conditions.
- Operator `And` evaluates a complex condition to true if and only if both of its operands are true.
- Operator `Or` evaluates a complex condition to true unless both of its operands are false.
- Operator `And` has a higher precedence than the `Or` operator.
- The operators `AndAlso` and `OrElse` are similar to the `And` and `Or` operators, but an expression containing `AndAlso` or `OrElse` uses short-circuit evaluation.
- A condition containing the logical exclusive OR (`Xor`) operator is true if and only if one of its operands results in a true value and the other results in a false value. If both operands are true or both are false, the entire condition is false.
- The `Not` operator enables you to "reverse" the meaning of a condition.

Section 5.11 Application: Dental Payment Calculator
- A `CheckBox` is known as a state button because it can be in the "on" state or the "off" state.
- When a `CheckBox` is selected, a check mark appears in the box. Any number of `CheckBoxes` can be selected at a time.
- The text that appears alongside a `CheckBox` is called the `CheckBox` label.
- If a `CheckBox` is "on" (checked), its `Checked` property is `True`; otherwise, it's `False` ("off").
- `MessageBox` method `Show` displays a message dialog, which is typically used to display an important message to the user. The method's four arguments are the message `String`, the `String` that's displayed in the dialog's title bar and predefined constants that specify the `Button`(s) and the icon to show on the dialog, respectively.
- A program waits for a message dialog to be closed before executing the next line of code—this type of dialog is known as a modal dialog.

Terminology

Self-Review Exercises

5.1   State whether each of the following is *true* or *false*. If *false*, explain why.

a) The Case Else is required in the Select...Case selection statement.

b) The expression x > y And a < b is true if either x > y is true or a < b is true.

c) An expression containing the Or operator is true if either or both of its operands are true.

d) The expression x <= y AndAlso y > 4 is true if x is less than or equal to y and y is greater than 4.

e) Logical operator Or performs short-circuit evaluation.

f) The Exit Do, Exit For and Exit While statements, when executed in a repetition statement, cause immediate exit from only the current iteration of the repetition statement.

g) The Do...Loop While statement tests the loop-continuation condition *before* the loop body is performed.

h) The Or operator has a *higher* precedence than the And operator.

5.2   Answer each of the following questions.

a) Which property specifies whether a CheckBox is selected?

   1. Selected   2. Checked
   3. Clicked   4. Check

b) Call the _____ method of class MessageBox to display a message dialog.

   1. Display   2. Message
   3. Open   4. Show

c) A unary operator _____.

   1. requires exactly one operand   2. requires two operands
   3. must use the AndAlso keyword   4. can have no operands

d) The _____ operator is used to ensure that two conditions are both true.

   1. Xor   2. AndAlso
   3. Also   4. OrElse

e) The Do...Loop While statement body repeats when the loop-continuation condition _____.

   1. is False after the body executes   2. is False before the body executes
   3. is True after the body executes   4. is True before the body executes

f) An infinite loop occurs when the loop-continuation condition in a `Do While...Loop` or `Do...Loop While` statement _____.

    1. never becomes `True`   2. never becomes `False`

    3. is `False`   4. is tested repeatedly

g) The `Do...Loop Until` statement checks the loop-termination condition _____.

    1. for `False` after the body executes   2. for `False` before the body executes

    3. for `True` after the body executes   4. for `True` before the body executes

h) Counter-controlled repetition _____ the control variable after each iteration.

    1. increments   2. initializes

    3. decrements   4. Either answer 1 or 3

i) What aspect of the control variable determines whether looping should continue?

    1. name   2. initial value

    3. type   4. final value

j) If the `Step` is omitted, the increment of a `For...Next` statement defaults to _____.

    1. `1`   2. `-1`

    3. `0`   4. Either answer 1 or 2

k) The value before the `To` keyword in a `For...Next` statement specifies the _____.

    1. initial value of the counter variable   2. final value of the counter variable

    3. increment   4. number of times the statement iterates

l) Which of the following is the appropriate `For...Next` header for varying the control variable over the following sequence of values: 25, 20, 15, 10, 5?

    1. `For i As Integer = 5 To 25 Step 5`   2. `For i As Integer = 25 To 5 Step -5`

    3. `For i As Integer = 5 To 25 Step -5`   4. `For i As Integer = 25 To 5 Step 5`

m) Which of the following statements describes the `For...Next` header

    `For i As Integer = 81 To 102`

    1. Vary the control variable from 81 to 102 in increments of 1.

    2. Vary the control variable from 81 to 102 in increments of 0.

    3. Vary the control variable from 102 to 81 in increments of -1.

    4. Vary the control variable from 81 to 102 in increments of 2.

n) `Select Case` is a _____-selection statement.

    1. multiple   2. double

    3. single   4. None of the above

o) When does the `Case Else` body execute?

    1. Every time a `Select Case` statement executes.

    2. When more than one `Case` matches the controlling expression.

    3. When the controlling expression does not match any other cases.

    4. None of the above.

p) A `Case` that handles all values larger than a specified value must precede the > operator with keyword _____.

    1. `Select`   2. `Is`

    3. `Case`   4. `All`

q) Use a(n) _____ to separate multiple conditions in a `Case` statement.

    1. period   2. asterisk

    3. comma   4. colon

r) The _____ property determines by how much the current number in a `NumericUp-Down` control changes when the user clicks the up arrow or the down arrow.
   1. `Amount`
   2. `Step`
   3. `Increment`
   4. `Next`

s) Which `For...Next` header alters the control variable from 0 to 50 in increments of 5?
   1. `For i = 0 To 50 Step 50`
   2. `For 0 To 50 Step 5`
   3. `For i = 0 To 50 Step = 5`
   4. `For i = 0 To 50 Step 5`

5.3 Write a statement or a set of statements to accomplish each of the following:
   a) Sum the odd integers between 1 and 99 using a `For...Next` statement. Assume that the `Integer` variables `sum` and `count` have been declared.
   b) Write a statement that exits a `Do While...Loop` statement.
   c) Display in `outputTextBox` the integers from 1 to 20, using a `Do...Loop While` loop and the counter variable `counter`. Display only five integers per line. [*Hint:* Use the expression `counter Mod 5` to determine when five values have been displayed. When the value of this expression is 0, move to the next line; otherwise, display a tab character.]
   d) Repeat part c, using a `For...Next` statement.

Answers to Self-Review Exercises

5.1 a) False. The `Case Else` is optional. b) False. *Both* of the simple conditions must be true for the entire expression to be true. c) True. d) True. e) False. Logical operator `Or` always evaluates both of its operands. f) False. The `Exit Do`, `Exit For` and `Exit While` statements, when executed in a repetition statement, cause immediate exit from the repetition statement. The `Continue Do`, `Continue For` and `Continue While` statements, when executed in a repetition statement, cause immediate exit from the current iteration of the repetition statement. g) False. The `Do...Loop While` statement tests the loop-continuation condition *after* the loop body is performed. h) False. The `And` operator has higher precedence than the `Or` operator.

5.2 a) 2. b) 4. c) 1. d) 2. e) 3. f) 2. g) 3. h) 4. i) 4. j) 4. k) 1. l) 2. m) 1. n) 1. o) 3. p) 2. q) 3. r) 3. s) 4.

5.3 a)
```
        sum = 0
        For count = 1 To 99 Step 2
           sum += count
        Next
```
   b)
```
        Exit Do
```
   c)
```
        Dim counter As Integer = 1

        Do
           outputTextBox.AppendText(counter)

           If counter Mod 5 = 0 Then
              outputTextBox.AppendText(vbCrLf)
           Else
              outputTextBox.AppendText(vbTab)
           End If

           counter += 1
        Loop While counter <= 20
```

d)
```
For counter = 1 To 20
    outputTextBox.AppendText(counter)

    If counter Mod 5 = 0 Then
        outputTextBox.AppendText(vbCrLf)
    Else
        outputTextBox.AppendText(vbTab)
    End If
Next
```

Quick Quiz

5.4 Answer each of the following questions.

a) How many CheckBoxes in a GUI can be selected at once?

1. 0   2. 1
3. 4   4. any number

b) The first argument passed to method MessageBox.Show is _____.

1. the text displayed in the dialog's title bar
2. a constant representing the Buttons displayed in the dialog
3. the text displayed inside the dialog
4. a constant representing the icon that appears in the dialog

c) _____ are used to create complex conditions.

1. Assignment operators   2. Activity diagrams
3. Logical operators   4. Formatting codes

d) Operator AndAlso _____.

1. performs short-circuit evaluation   2. is not a keyword
3. is a comparison operator   4. None of the above.

e) A CheckBox is selected when its Checked property is set to _____.

1. On   2. True
3. Selected   4. Checked

f) The condition *expression1* AndAlso *expression2* evaluates to True if _____.

1. *expression1* is True and *expression2* is False
2. *expression1* is False and *expression2* is True
3. both *expression1* and *expression2* are True
4. both *expression1* and *expression2* are False

g) The condition *expression1* OrElse *expression2* evaluates to False if _____.

1. *expression1* is True and *expression2* is False
2. *expression1* is False and *expression2* is True
3. both *expression1* and *expression2* are True
4. both *expression1* and *expression2* are False

h) The condition *expression1* Xor *expression2* evaluates to True if _____.

1. *expression1* is True and *expression2* is False
2. *expression1* is False and *expression2* is True
3. both *expression1* and *expression2* are True
4. Both answers 1 and 2

i) The condition Not(*expression1* AndAlso *expression2*) evaluates to True if _____.

1. *expression1* is True and *expression2* is False
2. *expression1* is False and *expression2* is True

3. both *expression1* and *expression2* are `False`

4. All of the above.

j) A(n) _____ occurs when a loop-continuation condition in a `Do...Loop While` never becomes `False`.

    1. infinite loop

    3. control statement

    2. counter-controlled loop

    4. nested control statement

k) The _____ statement executes at least once and continues executing until its loop-termination condition becomes `True`.

    1. `Do While...Loop`

    3. `Do...Loop While`

    2. `Do...Loop Until`

    4. `Do Until...Loop`

l) The _____ statement executes at least once and continues executing until its loop-continuation condition becomes `False`.

    1. `Do...Loop Until`

    3. `Do While...Loop`

    2. `Do Until...Loop`

    4. `Do...Loop While`

m) A `Do...Loop Until` repetition statement's loop-termination condition is evaluated _____.

    1. only the first time the body executes

    3. after the body executes

    2. before the body executes

    4. None of the above

n) If its continuation condition is initially `False`, a `Do...Loop While` repetition statement _____.

    1. never executes

    3. executes only once

    2. executes while the condition is `False`

    4. None of the above.

o) The `For...Next` header specifies _____.

    1. control variable and initial value

    3. loop-continuation condition

    2. increment or decrement

    4. All of the above.

p) The _____ is optional in a `For...Next` when the control variable's increment is 1.

    1. keyword `To`

    3. keyword `Step`

    2. initial value of the control variable

    4. final value of the control variable

q) The _____ is used to determine whether a `For...Next` loop continues to iterate.

    1. initial value of the control variable

    3. keyword `Step`

    2. keyword `For`

    4. final value of the control variable

r) In a `For...Next`, the control variable is incremented (or decremented) _____.

    1. when keyword `Next` is reached

    3. before the loop body executes

    2. when keyword `To` is reached

    4. None of the above.

s) `NumericUpDown` properties _____ and _____ specify the range of values that users can select.

    1. `Maximum, Minimum`

    3. `High, Low`

    2. `Top, Bottom`

    4. `Max, Min`

t) The `For...Next` header _____ can be used to vary the control variable over the odd numbers in the range 1–9.

    1. `For i = 1 To 9 Step 1`

    3. `For i = 1 To 9 Step -1`

    2. `For i = 1 To 9 Step 2`

    4. `For i = 1 To 9 Step -2`

u) Which of the following is a syntax error?

    1. Having duplicate `Case` statements in the same `Select Case` statement.

    2. Having a `Case` statement in which the value to the left of a `To` keyword is larger than the value to the right.

3. Preceding a `Case` statement with the `Case Else` statement in a `Select Case` statement.

4. Using keyword `Is` in a `Select Case` statement.

v) Keyword _____ is used to specify a range in a `Case` statement.

1. `Also`   2. `Between`

3. `To`   4. `From`

w) _____ separates multiple values tested in a `Case` statement.

1. A comma   2. An underscore

3. Keyword `Also`   4. A semicolon

x) If the value on the left of the `To` keyword in a `Case` statement is larger than the value on the right, _____.

1. a syntax error occurs

2. the body of the `Case` statement executes

3. the body of the `Case` statement never executes

4. the statement causes a runtime error

y) The expression following the keywords `Select Case` is called a _____.

1. guard condition   2. controlling expression

3. selection expression   4. case expression

Exercises

5.5   *(Retail Sales Calculator Application)* An online retailer sells five products whose retail prices are as follows: Product 1, $2.98; product 2, $4.50; product 3, $9.98; product 4, $4.49 and product 5, $6.87. Write an application that reads a series of pairs of numbers as follows:

a) product number;

b) quantity sold.

Your program should use a `Select...Case` statement to determine the retail price for each product. It should calculate and display the total retail value of all products sold in an output `Label` as shown in Fig. 5.21. Keep the total retail value up to date as the user enters values. [*Hint:* Create instance variables to store the quantity sold of each product so the values are maintained between calls to the event handler.]

Fig. 5.21 | Online Retail Sales GUI.

5.6   *(Table of Decimal, Octal, Hexadecimal and Binary Equivalents)* Write a program that displays in a `TextBox` a table of the binary, octal, and hexadecimal equivalents of the decimal numbers in the range 1–255. If you are not familiar with these number systems, read Appendix C, Number Systems, first. Set the `TextBox`'s `MultiLine` property to `True` and its `ScrollBars` property to `Vertical` so that you can scroll through the results. Figure 5.21 shows the application's GUI.

Fig. 5.22 | Table of Decimal Equivalents GUI.

5.7 *(Triangles of Asterisks)* Write a program that displays the following patterns separately, one below the other in a TextBox. Use For...Next loops to generate the patterns. All asterisks (*) should be displayed one at a time by the statement outputTextBox.AppendText("*") (this causes the asterisks to display side by side). The statement outputTextBox.AppendText(vbCrLf) can be used to position to the next line, and a statement of the form outputTextBox.AppendText(" ") can be used to display spaces for the last two patterns. There should be no other output statements in the program. [*Hint:* The last two patterns require that each line begin with an appropriate number of blanks.] Maximize your use of repetition (with nested For...Next statements) and minimize the number of output statements. Set the TextBox's Font property to Lucida Console, its MultiLine property to True and its ScrollBars property to Vertical so that you can scroll through the results.

```
(a)                (b)                (c)                (d)
*                  **********         **********                  *
**                 *********          *********                  **
***                ********           ********                  ***
****               *******            *******                  ****
*****              ******             ******                  *****
******             *****              *****                  ******
*******            ****               ****                  *******
********           ***                ***                  ********
*********          **                 **                  *********
**********         *                  *                  **********
```

5.8 Assume that nameTextBox is a TextBox and that otherCheckBox is a CheckBox next to which is another TextBox called otherTextBox, in which the user should specify a value. What does this code segment do?

```
1    If (nameTextBox.Text = "" OrElse
2       (otherCheckBox.Checked = True AndAlso
3       otherTextBox.Text = "")) Then
4
5       MessageBox.Show("Please enter a name or value",
6          "Input Error", MessageBoxButtons.OK,
7          MessageBoxIcon.Error)
8
9    End If
```

5.9 *(Using the Debugger: Sibling Survey Application)* This application is located in the Debugging folder with this chapter's examples. The **Sibling Survey** application displays the siblings selected by the user in a dialog. If the user checks either the **Brother(s)** or **Sister(s)** CheckBox and the **No Siblings** CheckBox, the user is asked to verify the selection. Otherwise, the user's selection is displayed in a MessageBox. While testing this application, you noticed that it does not execute properly. Use the debugger to find and correct the logic error(s) in the code. Figure 5.23 shows the correct output for the application. For message dialogs that do not represent errors, this program uses MessageBox-Icon.Information rather than MessageBoxIcon.Error.

Fig. 5.23 | Correct output for the **Sibling Survey** application.

5.10 *(Arithmetic Calculator Application)* Write an application that allows the user to enter a series of numbers and manipulate them. The application should provide users with the option of adding or multiplying the numbers. Users should enter each number in a TextBox. After entering each number, the user clicks an **Enter** Button, and the number is inserted in a ListBox. If the result of a previous calculation is displayed, the **Enter** Button's event handler should clear the result, clear the ListBox and disable the **Add** and **Multiply** Buttons. It should then insert the current number in the **Operands list:** ListBox. When the ListBox contains at least two numbers, the event handler should enable the **Add** and **Multiply** Buttons. The GUI should behave as shown in Figure 5.24.

Fig. 5.24 | Arithmetic Calculator GUI.

5.11   *(What does this code do?)* What is the result of the following code?

```
1   Dim y As Integer
2   Dim x As Integer
3   Dim mysteryValue As Integer
4
5   x = 1
6   mysteryValue = 0
7
8   Do
9       y = x ^ 2
10      displayListBox.Items.Add(y)
11      mysteryValue += 1
12      x += 1
13  Loop While x <= 10
14
15  resultLabel.Text = mysteryValue
```

5.12   *(What's wrong with this code?)* Find the error(s) in the following code. This code should add 10 to the value in y and store it in z. It then should reduce the value of y by one and repeat until y is less than 10. Last, resultLabel should display the final value of z.

```
1   Dim y As Integer = 5
2   Dim z As Integer = 1
3
4   Do
5       z *= y
6   Loop Until y < 1
7
8   y -= 1
9
10  resultLabel.Text = z
```

5.13   *(Using the Debugger: Factorial Application)* This application is located in the Debugging folder with this chapter's examples. The **Factorial** application calculates the factorial of an integer input by the user. The factorial of an integer is the product of the integers from one to that number. For example, the factorial of 3 is 6 ($1 \times 2 \times 3$). While testing the application, you noticed that it did not execute correctly. Use the debugger to find and correct the logic error(s) in the application. Figure 5.25 displays the correct output for the **Factorial** application.

Fig. 5.25 | Correct output for the **Factorial** application.

5.14   *(Present Value Calculator Application)* A bank wants to show its customers how much they would need to invest now (that is, the "present value") to achieve a specified financial goal (that is, the "future value") in 5, 10, 15, 20, 25 or 30 years. Users must provide their financial goal (the amount of money desired after the specified number of years have elapsed), an interest rate and the length of the investment in years. Create an application that calculates and displays the principal (initial amount to invest) needed to achieve the user's financial goal. Your application should allow the user to invest money for 5, 10, 15, 20, 25 or 30 years. For example, a customer who wants to reach the financial goal of $15,000 over a period of 5 years when the interest rate is 6.6% will need to invest $10,896.96, as shown in Fig. 5.26. Use the same GUI for this applicaiton as the one in Fig. 5.5. The formula to calculate the present value is:

$$p = a / (1 + r)^n$$

where

1. p is the amount needed to achieve the future value
2. a is the future-value amount
3. r is the annual interest rate (for example, .05 is equivalent to 5%)
4. n is the number of years the money will be invested.

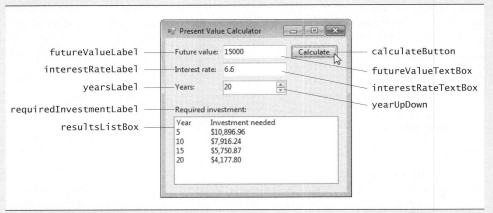

Fig. 5.26 | Future Value Calculator GUI.

5.15   *(What does this code do?)* What is the value of `result` after the following code executes?

```
Dim power As Integer = 5
Dim number As Integer = 10
Dim result As Integer = number

For i As Integer = 1 To (power - 1)
   result *= number
Next
```

5.16   *(Using the Debugger: Savings Calculator Application)* This application is located in the Debugging folder with this chapter's examples. The **Savings Calculator** application calculates the amount that the user will have on deposit after one year. The application gets the initial amount on deposit from the user, and assumes that the user will add $100 to the account every month for the entire year. No interest is added to the account. While testing the application, you noticed that the amount calculated by the application was incorrect. Use the debugger to locate and correct any logic error(s). Figure 5.27 displays the correct output for this application.

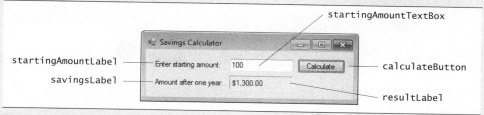

Fig. 5.27 | Correct output for the **Savings Calculator** application.

5.17 *(What does this code do?)* What is output by the following code?

```
 1   Private Sub donationButton_Click(ByVal sender As
 2       System.Object, ByVal e As System.EventArgs) _
 3       Handles donationButton.Click
 4
 5       Select Case Val(donationTextBox.Text)
 6          Case 0
 7             messageLabel.Text = "Please consider donating to our cause."
 8          Case 1 To 100
 9             messageLabel.Text = "Thank you for your donation."
10          Case Is > 100
11             messageLabel.Text = "Thank you very much for your donation!"
12          Case Else
13             messageLabel.Text = "Please enter a valid amount."
14       End Select
15   End Sub
```

5.18 *(What's wrong with this code?)* This Select Case statement should determine whether an Integer is even or odd. Find the error(s) in the following code:

```
 1   Select Case value Mod 2
 2      Case 0
 3         outputLabel.Text = "Odd Integer"
 4      Case 1
 5         outputLabel.Text = "Even Integer"
 6   End Select
```

5.19 *(Using the Debugger: Discount Calculator Application)* This application is located in the Debugging folder with this chapter's examples. The **Discount Calculator** application determines the discount the user receives, based on how much money the user spends. A 15% discount is received for purchases over $200, a 10% discount is received for purchases between $150 and $200, a 5% discount is received for purchases between $100 and $149 and a 2% discount is received for purchases between $50 and $99. While testing your application, you notice that the application is not calculating the discount properly for some values. Use the debugger to find and fix the logic error(s) in the application. Figure 5.28 displays the correct output for the application.

Making a Difference Exercise

5.20 *(Tax Plan Alternatives; The "FairTax")* There are many proposals to make taxation fairer. Check out the FairTax initiative in the United States at

> www.fairtax.org/site/PageServer?pagename=calculator

Fig. 5.28 | Correct output for the **Discount Calculator** application.

Research how the proposed FairTax works. One suggestion is to eliminate income taxes and most other taxes in favor of a 23% consumption tax on all products and services that you buy. Some FairTax opponents question the 23% figure and say that because of the way the tax is calculated, it would be more accurate to say the rate is 30%—check this carefully. Write a program that prompts the user to enter expenses in various expense categories they have (for example, housing, food, clothing, transportation, education, health care, vacations), then displays the estimated Fair-Tax that person would pay. Figure 5.29 shows the application's GUI.

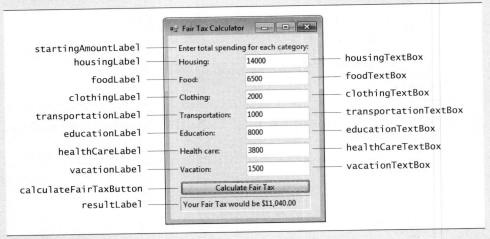

Fig. 5.29 | Fair Tax Calculator GUI.

Methods

6

The greatest invention of the nineteenth century was the invention of the method of invention.
—Alfred North Whitehead

Form ever follows function.
—Louis Henri Sullivan

O! call back yesterday, bid time return.
—William Shakespeare

Answer me in one word.
—William Shakespeare

There is a point at which methods devour themselves.
—Frantz Fanon

Objectives

In this chapter you'll learn:

- To construct programs modularly from methods.

- To create new methods.

- How to pass information between methods.

- Simulation techniques that employ random-number generation.

- How the visibility of identifiers is limited to specific regions of programs.

- To use debugger commands for entering and exiting methods and for continuing program execution.

6.1 Introduction

Experience has shown that the best way to develop and maintain a large program is to construct it from small, simple pieces—a technique known as **divide and conquer**. In this chapter, we formalize our discussion of methods and use them to facilitate the design, implementation, operation and maintenance of larger programs.

We'll take a brief diversion into simulation techniques with random-number generation and develop a version of a popular casino dice game that uses most of the programming techniques you've learned to this point in the book. In addition, we'll introduce two techniques for declaring constants in your programs.

You'll learn that applications can have more than one method with the same name. This technique, called overloading, is used for convenience and clarity when implementing methods that perform similar tasks using different types or numbers of arguments.

6.2 Classes and Methods

Typical programs consist of one or more classes. These classes are composed of smaller pieces called methods, instance variables and (as you'll learn in Chapter 9) properties. You combine new classes with the "prepackaged" classes available in the .NET Framework Class Library and in various other class libraries. The .NET Framework Class Library provides a rich collection of classes and methods for performing:

- common mathematical calculations,
- error checking,
- building sophisticated GUI applications,
- graphics,
- string and character manipulations,
- input/output operations,
- XML processing,
- database manipulations,

- creating applications for the web
- and many other useful operations.

Each of the preceding topics is covered in this book or in its online chapters. Earlier chapters presented various GUI controls, each of which is defined as a class in the .NET Framework Class Library. You can create your own customized classes and methods (beginning in Chapter 9) to meet the unique requirements of a particular application.

Software Engineering Observation 6.1

When possible, use .NET Framework classes and methods instead of writing new classes and methods. This reduces program-development time and can help prevent errors.

You write methods to define specific tasks that a program may use one or more times during its execution. Although the same method can be executed from multiple points in a program, the actual statements that define the method are written only once.

A method is invoked (that is, made to perform its task) by a method call. The method call specifies the method name and provides information (as arguments) that the **callee** (that is, the method being called) requires to do its job. When the method completes its task, it returns control to the caller (that is, the calling method). In some cases, the method also returns a result to the caller.

A common analogy for calling methods and returning results is communication among bosses and workers in a business. A boss (the caller) asks a worker (the callee) to perform a task and return (that is, report) the results when the task is done. The boss does not need to know how the worker performs the designated task. The worker might call other workers—the boss would be unaware of this. This **hiding of implementation details** promotes good software engineering. Figure 6.1 depicts a Boss method communicating with worker methods Worker1, Worker2 and Worker3. In this example Worker1 also acts as a "boss" method to Worker4 and Worker5.

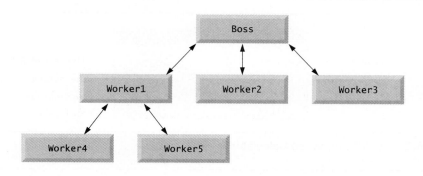

Fig. 6.1 | Boss-method/worker-method relationship.

There are several motivations for dividing code into methods.

- First, the divide-and-conquer approach makes program development more manageable.

- A second motivation is software reusability—the ability to use existing methods as building blocks for new programs. When proper naming and definition conventions are applied, programs can be created from standardized pieces that accomplish specific tasks, to minimize the need for customized code.

- A third motivation is to avoid repeating code in a program—when code is packaged as a method, the code can be executed from various points in a program simply by calling the method.

6.3 Subroutines: Methods That Do Not Return a Value

The programs presented earlier in the book each contain at least one event-handler method that is called in response to an event and performs the program's tasks. An event-handling method is a **subroutine**—a method that performs a task but *does not* return a value. A **function** is a method that performs a task then *does* return a value to the calling method. In Section 6.4, we'll reimplement this section's example by using a function.

To demonstrate a subroutine, we'll create a **Wage Calculator** application. Consider the following problem statement:

> *Employees' weekly salaries are based on the number of hours they worked and their hourly wage. Create an application that accepts this information for one employee then calculates and displays the employee's total (gross) earnings. Assume a standard work week of 40 hours. The wages for 40 or fewer hours are calculated by multiplying the hourly wage by the number of hours worked. Hours over 40 hours are considered "overtime" and earn "time and a half." Salary for time and a half is calculated by multiplying the employee's hourly wage by 1.5 and multiplying the result of that calculation by the number of overtime hours worked. The overtime pay is added to the user's gross earnings for the regular 40 hours of work to calculate the total earnings for that week.*

Figure 6.2 shows a sample output with the labeled control names, and Fig. 6.3 shows the completed code. The program uses the method `DisplayPay` (lines 25–41) to calculate and display an employee's pay based on the hours worked and the hourly wage.

Fig. 6.2 | GUI for the **Wage Calculator** application.

```
 1    ' Fig. 6.3: WageCalculator.vb
 2    ' Calculating and displaying an employee's pay using a method.
 3    Public Class WageCalculator
 4       Const HOURS_IN_A_WEEK As Integer = 168 ' total hours in one week
 5       Const HOUR_LIMIT As Integer = 40 ' maximum hours before overtime
```

Fig. 6.3 | Calculating and displaying an employee's pay using a method. (Part 1 of 2.)

```vb
 6
 7     ' calculate and display the employee's pay
 8     Private Sub calculateButton_Click(ByVal sender As System.Object,
 9        ByVal e As System.EventArgs) Handles calculateButton.Click
10
11        ' get hours worked and hourly wage
12        Dim hoursWorked As Double = Val(hoursTextBox.Text)
13        Dim hourlyWage As Decimal = Val(wageTextBox.Text)
14
15        ' determine whether hoursWorked is less than or equal to 168
16        If hoursWorked <= HOURS_IN_A_WEEK Then
17           DisplayPay(hoursWorked, hourlyWage) ' calls DisplayPay
18        Else
19           MessageBox.Show("Hours worked must be less than or equal to 168",
20              "Invalid Value", MessageBoxButtons.OK, MessageBoxIcon.Error)
21        End If
22     End Sub ' calculateButton_Click
23
24     ' calculate and display wages
25     Sub DisplayPay(ByVal hours As Double, ByVal wages As Decimal)
26        Dim earnings As Decimal ' stores the total earnings
27
28        ' determine wage amount
29        If hours <= HOUR_LIMIT Then
30           ' earnings for regular wages
31           earnings = hours * wages
32        Else
33           ' regular wages for first HOUR_LIMIT hours
34           earnings = HOUR_LIMIT * wages
35
36           ' time and a half for overtime
37           earnings += ((hours - HOUR_LIMIT) * (1.5 * wages))
38        End If
39
40        resultLabel.Text = String.Format("{0:C}", earnings)
41     End Sub ' DisplayPay
42
43     ' clear resultLabel when user enters new hourly wage
44     Private Sub wageTextBox_TextChanged(ByVal sender As System.Object,
45        ByVal e As System.EventArgs) Handles wageTextBox.TextChanged
46        resultLabel.Text = String.Empty ' clear the Label
47     End Sub ' wageTextBox_TextChanged
48
49     ' clear resultLabel when user enters new hours worked
50     Private Sub hoursTextBox_TextChanged(ByVal sender As System.Object,
51        ByVal e As System.EventArgs) Handles hoursTextBox.TextChanged
52        resultLabel.Text = String.Empty ' clear the Label
53     End Sub ' hoursTextBox_TextChanged
54  End Class ' WageCalculator
```

Fig. 6.3 | Calculating and displaying an employee's pay using a method. (Part 2 of 2.)

The program contains four method declarations. Lines 8–22 define the event-handler method calculateButton_Click, the method that executes when the user clicks the Calculate Button. Lines 25–41 define method DisplayPay, a subroutine that executes when it's called from line 17 of method calculateButton_Click. Lines 44–53 define methods wageTextBox_TextChanged and hoursTextBox_TextChanged, which each clear the resultLabel when the user enters a new value in the corresponding TextBox.

Declaring Constants for Values That Do Not Change

Keyword **Const** (lines 4–5) declares a **constant**—a value that cannot be changed after it's initialized. Constants enhance program readability by providing descriptive identifiers for values that do not change. In this program, we want to ensure that the user does not enter a number of hours greater than the total number of hours in a week (that is, 168). This value never changes, so we declare HOURS_IN_A_WEEK as a Const. Similarly, recall from the problem statement that overtime pay is calculated for hours worked over 40 hours. This "hour limit" does not change during the program's execution, so we also declared HOUR_LIMIT as a Const. Using constants eliminates so-called **magic numbers**. For example, repeatedly mentioning the hour limit 40 gives the number 40 an artificial significance and can be confusing when the program includes other 40s that have nothing to do with the hour limit.

Good Programming Practice 6.1

Microsoft recommends using all uppercase letters in the identifier for a constant and placing underscore (_) between each pair of words in the identifier.

Method DisplayPay

When the user clicks the **Calculate** Button, lines 12–13 get the values entered by the user. Line 16 ensures that the hoursWorked is less than or equal to HOURS_IN_A_WEEK. If so, line 17 calls subroutine DisplayPay (lines 25–41), which causes it to execute.

When DisplayPay is called, the program makes a copy of the value of each argument—hoursWorked and hourlyWage—and program control transfers to the method's first line. The method receives the copied values and stores them in the parameters hours and wages. Then lines 29–38 calculate the earnings (accounting for overtime, if necessary) and store the result in Decimal variable earnings. Finally, line 40 displays earnings, using the currency format. When the End Sub statement (line 41) is encountered, program control returns to the next statement in the calling method, calculateButton_Click. In this case, the end of the event handler is reached and the program now waits for the next user interaction.

The first line of method DisplayPay (line 25) shows that DisplayPay declares a Double parameter hours and a Decimal parameter wages. These parameters hold the values passed to DisplayPay so that they can be accessed within this method. The entire declaration of method DisplayPay appears within the body of class WageCalculator.

Subroutine Declarations

The format of a subroutine declaration is

```
Sub method-name(parameter-list)
    declarations and statements
End Sub
```

Keyword Sub indicates that this method will perform a task but will *not* return (that is, give back) any information to its **calling method** when it completes its task. You've already used methods that return information—for example, you used String method Format to create formatted representations of various String and numeric data. When Format completes its task, it returns a formatted String for use in the program.

Method Naming

The *method-name* follows keyword Sub. By convention, method names begin with an uppercase letter and all subsequent words in the name begin with a capital letter.

Parameters and the Parameter List

The parentheses after the method name are used to indicate any **parameters**—additional information that is required by the method to perform its task. An empty set of parentheses indicates that a method does not require any additional information and does not need any parameters. If there are parameters, they are placed in a **parameter-list**—specified by the set of parentheses following the method's name. A method can specify multiple parameters by separating each from the next with a comma—this is known as a comma-separated list. Each parameter has a variable name and a type. We refer to the part of the method that contains the keyword Sub, the method name and the parameter list as the **method header**.

Arguments in Method Calls

There must be one argument in the method call for each parameter in the method declaration. (We'll see an exception to this when we study Optional parameters in Section 6.12.) The type of each argument must be consistent with its corresponding parameter's type; that is, the compiler must be able to implicitly convert the value of the argument to a value of the parameter's type. For example, a parameter of type Double could receive an argument value of 7.35, 22 or –0.03546, but not "hello", because a Double variable cannot contain a String. If a method does not receive any values, the parameter list is empty (that is, the method name is followed by an empty set of parentheses).

Body of a Method

The *declarations and statements* (for example, lines 28–40 of Fig. 6.3) in the method declaration form the method body, which contains code that performs actions, generally by manipulating or processing the method's parameters and by calling other methods. After the statements execute, the method has completed its task. The body of a method declared with Sub must be terminated with keywords End Sub. Control returns to the next statement in the caller when execution reaches the End Sub statement in the called method. The method body is also referred to as a **block**—a group of declarations and executable statements. The bodies of control statements are also blocks. For an If...Else...End If statement, the If part and the Else part are each separate blocks. For a Select...Case statement, each Case is a block. The bodies of repetition statements are also blocks.

Common Programming Error 6.1

Declaring a variable in the method's body with the same name as one of the method's parameters is a compilation error.

Software Engineering Observation 6.2

Method names tend to be verbs because methods typically perform actions. By convention, method names begin with an uppercase first letter. For example, a method that sends an e-mail message might be named SendMail. *An exception to this is an event handler's name, which typically starts with the variable name of the control that generates the event.*

6.4 Functions: Methods That Return a Value

As mentioned in Section 6.3, a function is a method that **returns a value** to the caller. Figure 6.4 reimplements the **Wage Calculator** application of Fig. 6.3 using the function CalculatePay (lines 27–45) to calculate and return an employee's pay based on the hours worked and hourly wage.

```vb
 1   ' Fig. 6.4: WageCalculator.vb
 2   ' Calculating an employee's pay using a function that returns a value.
 3   Public Class WageCalculator
 4      Const HOURS_IN_A_WEEK As Integer = 168 ' total hours in one week
 5      Const HOUR_LIMIT As Integer = 40 ' maximum hours before overtime
 6
 7      ' calculate and display the employee's pay
 8      Private Sub calculateButton_Click(ByVal sender As System.Object, _
 9         ByVal e As System.EventArgs) Handles calculateButton.Click
10
11         ' get hours worked and hourly wage
12         Dim hoursWorked As Double = Val(hoursTextBox.Text)
13         Dim hourlyWage As Decimal = Val(wageTextBox.Text)
14
15         ' determine whether hoursWorked is less than or equal to 168
16         If hoursWorked <= HOURS_IN_A_WEEK Then
17            ' call CalculatePay Function
18            Dim totalPay As Decimal = CalculatePay(hoursWorked, hourlyWage)
19            resultLabel.Text = String.Format("{0:C}", totalPay)
20         Else
21            MessageBox.Show("Hours worked must be less than or equal to 168", _
22               "Invalid Value", MessageBoxButtons.OK, MessageBoxIcon.Error)
23         End If
24      End Sub ' calculateButton_Click
25
26      ' calculate employee's wages
27      Function CalculatePay(ByVal hours As Double, ByVal wages As Decimal) _
28         As Decimal
29
30         Dim earnings As Decimal ' stores the total earnings
31
32         ' determine wage amount
33         If hours <= HOUR_LIMIT Then
34            ' earnings for regular wages
35            earnings = hours * wages
```

Fig. 6.4 | Calculating an employee's pay using a function that returns a value. (Part 1 of 2.)

```
36              Else
37                  ' regular wages for first HOUR_LIMIT hours
38                  earnings = HOUR_LIMIT * wages
39
40                  ' time and a half for overtime
41                  earnings += ((hours - HOUR_LIMIT) * (1.5 * wages))
42              End If
43
44              Return earnings ' returns the total earnings back to the caller
45          End Function ' CalculatePay
46
47          ' clear resultLabel when user enters new hourly wage
48          Private Sub wageTextBox_TextChanged(ByVal sender As System.Object,
49              ByVal e As System.EventArgs) Handles wageTextBox.TextChanged
50              resultLabel.Text = String.Empty ' clear the Label
51          End Sub ' wageTextBox_TextChanged
52
53          ' clear resultLabel when user enters new hours worked
54          Private Sub hoursTextBox_TextChanged(ByVal sender As System.Object,
55              ByVal e As System.EventArgs) Handles hoursTextBox.TextChanged
56              resultLabel.Text = String.Empty ' clear the Label
57          End Sub ' hoursTextBox_TextChanged
58      End Class ' WageCalculator
```

Fig. 6.4 | Calculating an employee's pay using a function that returns a value. (Part 2 of 2.)

When the user clicks the **Calculate** Button, lines 12–13 get the entered values. Line 16 ensures that the hoursWorked is less than or equal to the total number of hours in a week. If so, line 18 calls CalculatePay, which causes it to execute. At this point, the program copies the values of each argument—hoursWorked and hourlyWage—and program control transfers to CalculatePay's first line. The method receives the copied values and stores them in the parameters hours and wages. Then lines 33–42 calculate the earnings and store the result in the Decimal variable earnings. The **Return statement** (line 44) terminates the method and gives the value of earnings to the calling method. The result is returned to the point in line 18 where CalculatePay was called, where it's assigned to variable totalPay. Then line 19 displays totalPay's value.

Function Declarations
The format of a function declaration is

```
Function method-name(parameter-list) As return-type
    declarations and statements
End Function
```

The *method-name*, *parameter-list*, and *declarations and statements* in a function declaration behave like the corresponding elements in a subroutine declaration. In the function header, the *return-type* indicates the type of the value returned from the function to its caller. The statement

> **Return** *expression*

can occur anywhere in a function body and returns the value of *expression* to the caller. When a Return statement executes, control returns immediately to the point at which that function was invoked.

Common Programming Error 6.2

Failure to return a value from a function (for example, by forgetting to provide a Return statement) causes the function to return the default value for the return-type, possibly producing incorrect output.

6.5 Implicit Argument Conversions

An important feature of argument passing is implicit **argument conversion**—converting an argument's value to the type that the method expects to receive in its corresponding parameter. Widening and narrowing conversions are supported. A **widening conversion** occurs when an argument is converted to a parameter of another type that can hold *more* data, whereas a **narrowing conversion** occurs when there is potential for *data loss* during the conversion (that is, a conversion to a parameter of a type that holds a *smaller* amount of data). Figure 6.5 lists the widening conversions that occur between primitive types.

Type	Conversion types
Boolean	No possible widening conversions to other primitive types
Byte	UShort, Short, UInteger, Integer, ULong, Long, Decimal, Single or Double
Char	String
Date	No possible widening conversions to other primitive types
Decimal	Single or Double
Double	No possible widening conversions to other primitive types
Integer	Long, Decimal, Single or Double
Long	Decimal, Single or Double
SByte	Short, Integer, Long, Decimal, Single or Double
Short	Integer, Long, Decimal, Single or Double
Single	Double
String	No possible widening conversions to other primitive types
UInteger	ULong, Long, Decimal, Single or Double
ULong	Decimal, Single or Double
UShort	UInteger, Integer, ULong, Long, Decimal, Single or Double

Fig. 6.5 | Widening conversions between primitive types.

For example, the Math class's Sqrt method (which returns the square root of it's argument) can be called with an Integer argument, even though the method is defined with a Double parameter. The statement

```
resultLabel.Text = Math.Sqrt(4)
```

correctly evaluates Math.Sqrt(4) and displays the value 2. The Integer argument 4 is implicitly converted to the Double value 4.0 before the argument is passed to Math.Sqrt. In this case, the argument does not precisely correspond to the parameter type in the method declaration, so an implicit widening conversion changes the value to the proper type before the method is called. Narrowing conversions can also be performed on arguments passed to methods. For example, if a Double variable containing the value 4.0 were passed to a method expecting an Integer variable, the value would be converted to 4. Some implicit narrowing conversions can cause runtime errors. In the next section, we discuss measures you can take to avoid such errors. In Chapter 7, we introduce exception handling, which can be used to handle the errors caused by failed narrowing conversions.

Conversions also occur for expressions containing values of two or more types. In such expressions, the values' original types are maintained, while *temporary* copies of the values are converted for use in the expression. Each value is converted to the "widest" type in the expression (that is, widening conversions are made until the values are of the same type as the "widest" type). For example, if doubleValue is of type Double and integerValue is of type Integer, when the expression

```
doubleValue + integerValue
```

is evaluated, the value of integerValue is converted to type Double (the widest type in the expression), then added to doubleValue, producing a Double result.

6.6 Option Strict and Data-Type Conversions

Several options are provided for controlling the way the compiler handles types. These options can help you eliminate errors such as those caused by narrowing conversions.

Option Explicit

Option Explicit—which is set to **On** by default and has been enabled in the programs we created in Chapters 2–5—requires you to declare all variables before they're used in a program. This eliminates various errors. For example, when **Option Explicit** is set to **Off**, the compiler interprets misspelled variable names as new variables and implicitly declares them to be of type Object. (Class **Object** is the base type of all types. We'll discuss class Object in more detail in Chapter 10.) This creates subtle errors that can be difficult to debug. It's recommended that you leave this option set to **On**.

Option Strict

A second option, which defaults to **Off**, is **Option Strict**. This option increases program clarity and reduces debugging time. When set to **On**, **Option Strict** causes the compiler to check all conversions and requires you to perform explicit conversions—that is, using a cast operator or a method to force a conversion to occur—for all narrowing conversions or conversions that might cause program termination (for example, conversion of a String, such as "hello", to type Integer).

Option Infer

Option Infer, which defaults to **On**, enables the compiler to infer a variable's type based on its intializer value. For example, in the statement

```
Dim x = 7 ' compiler infers that x is an Integer
```

the compiler infers that x is an `Integer` because the initializer value is an `Integer` literal.

Setting Option Explicit, Option Strict and Option Infer

You can set **Option Explicit**, **Option Strict** and **Option Infer** for all future projects as follows.

  1. Select **Tools > Options...** to display the **Options** dialog (Fig. 6.6).

VB Defaults

ComboBox to set
Option Infer

ComboBox to set
Option Strict

ComboBox to set
Option Explicit

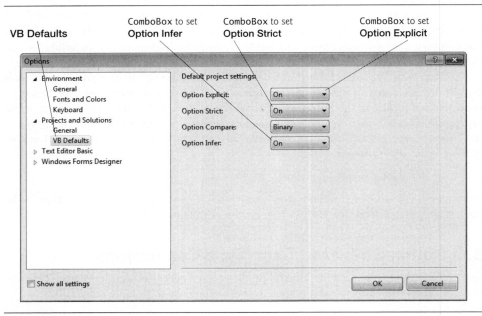

Fig. 6.6 | Modifying **Option Strict**, **Option Infer** and **Option Explicit**.

  2. Under **Projects and Solutions**, select **VB Defaults** and choose the appropriate value in each option's ComboBox.

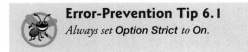

Error-Prevention Tip 6.1

Always set **Option Strict** *to* **On**.

Class **Convert**

Class **Convert**'s methods explicitly convert data from one primitive type to another. The name of each conversion method is the word To, typically followed by the name of the type to which the method converts its argument. For instance, to convert the `String` stored in `numberTextBox.Text` to type `Double`, we use the statement

```
Dim number As Double = Convert.ToDouble(numberTextBox.Text)
```

If `numberTextBox` does not contain a `String` that can be converted to a `Double` value, a `FormatExcepton` will occur. For now we assume that the user enters valid values that can be properly converted. In Chapter 7, you'll learn how to process exceptions when they occur. Some other commonly used `Convert` methods include **ToInt32** (to convert to an Integer), **ToDecimal** (to convert to a `Decimal`) and **ToString** (to convert to a `String`). Each method can receive arguments of any of the primitive types.

Many of the primitive types have a `Parse` method that you can use to convert a `String` to a value of that primitive type. For instance, method **Double.Parse** also converts a `String` representation of a number to a value of type `Double`.

Common Programming Error 6.3

With **Option Strict** *set to* **On,** `Strings` *cannot be assigned directly to numeric variables and numeric values cannot be assigned to* `Strings`. *Doing so causes a compilation error.*

Type-Conversion Functions
Visual Basic also provides **type-conversion functions** for converting between built-in types. Some common type-conversion functions include **CChar** (convert to Char), **CDec** (convert to `Decimal`), **CInt** (convert to Integer), **CDbl** (convert to `Double`) and **CStr** (convert to `String`).

Implicit Type Conversions
When **Option Strict** is **Off** (as it has been for all the code examples so far in this book), type conversions are performed implicitly, and thus you may not realize that a dangerous narrowing conversion has occurred. If the data being converted is incompatible with the new type, a runtime error occurs. **Option Strict** draws your attention to narrowing conversions at compile time so that they can be eliminated or handled properly.

6.7 Passing Arguments: Pass-by-Value vs. Pass-by-Reference

Arguments are passed in one of two ways—**pass-by-value** or **pass-by-reference**. When an argument is passed by value, the program makes a *copy* of the argument's value and passes the copy to the called method. With pass-by-value, changes to the called method's copy *do not* affect the original variable's value in the caller. In contrast, when an argument is passed by reference, the called method *can* access and modify the caller's original data directly. Figure 6.7 demonstrates passing value-type arguments by value and by reference. The program passes the values of variables, `number1`, `number2` and `number3`, in different ways to methods `SquareByValue` (lines 45–53) and `SquareByReference` (lines 56–64). For the purpose of the following discussion, we assume that the user enters the value 2 in the TextBox then presses the **Square** Button.

Keyword ByVal and Method SquareByValue
Keyword `ByVal` in the method header of `SquareByValue` (line 45) indicates that the argument should be passed by value. A parameter declared with keyword `ByVal` is known as a **value parameter**. When `number1` is passed to `SquareByValue` (line 15), a copy of the value stored in `number1` (that is, 2) is passed to the method. Therefore, the value of `number1` in the calling method, `squareButton_Click`, is not modified when parameter `number` is

squared in method `SquareByValue` (line 49)—only the local copy stored in the method's `number` parameter gets modified. `ByVal` is the default for method parameters and it's not required in the parameter declarations.

```vb
1   ' Fig. 6.7: ValueAndReferencePassing.vb
2   ' Passing arguments by value and by reference.
3   Public Class ValueAndReferencePassing
4       ' call methods SquareByValue and SquareByReference
5       Private Sub squareButton_Click(ByVal sender As System.Object,
6           ByVal e As System.EventArgs) Handles squareButton.Click
7           ' get user input and convert it to an Integer value
8           Dim number1 As Integer = Convert.ToInt32(squareTextBox.Text)
9
10          outputTextBox.AppendText(
11              "Passing a value-type argument by value:" & vbCrLf)
12          outputTextBox.AppendText(String.Format(
13              "Before calling SquareByValue, number1 is {0}{1}",
14              number1, vbCrLf))
15          SquareByValue(number1)  ' passes number1 by value
16          outputTextBox.AppendText(String.Format(
17              "After returning from SquareByValue, number1 is {0}{1}{1}",
18              number1, vbCrLf))
19
20          Dim number2 As Integer = Convert.ToInt32(squareTextBox.Text)
21
22          outputTextBox.AppendText(
23              "Passing a value-type argument by reference:" & vbCrLf)
24          outputTextBox.AppendText(String.Format(
25              "Before calling SquareByReference, number2 is {0}{1}",
26              number2, vbCrLf))
27          SquareByReference(number2)  ' passes number2 by reference
28          outputTextBox.AppendText(String.Format(
29              "After returning from SquareByReference, number2 is {0}{1}{1}",
30              number2, vbCrLf))
31
32          Dim number3 As Integer = Convert.ToInt32(squareTextBox.Text)
33
34          outputTextBox.AppendText("Passing a value-type argument" &
35              " by reference, but in parentheses:" & vbCrLf)
36          outputTextBox.AppendText(String.Format("Before calling " &
37              "SquareByReference using parentheses, number3 is {0}{1}",
38              number3, vbCrLf))
39          SquareByReference((number3))  ' passes number3 by value
40          outputTextBox.AppendText(String.Format("After returning from " &
41              "SquareByReference, number3 is {0}", number3))
42      End Sub ' squareButton_Click
43
44      ' squares number by value (note ByVal keyword)
45      Sub SquareByValue(ByVal number As Integer)
46          outputTextBox.AppendText(String.Format(
47              "After entering SquareByValue, number is {0}{1}",
48              number, vbCrLf))
```

Fig. 6.7 | `ByVal` and `ByRef` used to pass value-type arguments. (Part 1 of 2.)

```
49        number *= number
50        outputTextBox.AppendText(String.Format(
51          "Before exiting SquareByValue, number is {0}{1}",
52          number, vbCrLf))
53     End Sub ' SquareByValue
54
55     ' squares number by reference (note ByRef keyword)
56     Sub SquareByReference(ByRef number As Integer)
57        outputTextBox.AppendText(String.Format(
58          "After entering SquareByReference, number is {0}{1}",
59          number, vbCrLf))
60        number *= number
61        outputTextBox.AppendText(String.Format(
62          "Before exiting SquareByReference, number is {0}{1}",
63          number, vbCrLf))
64     End Sub ' SquareByReference
65
66     ' clear the outputTextBox when squareTextBox's value changes
67     Private Sub squareTextBox_TextChanged(ByVal sender As System.Object,
68        ByVal e As System.EventArgs) Handles squareTextBox.TextChanged
69        outputTextBox.Text = String.Empty
70     End Sub ' squareTextBox_TextChanged
71  End Class ' ValueAndReferencePassing
```

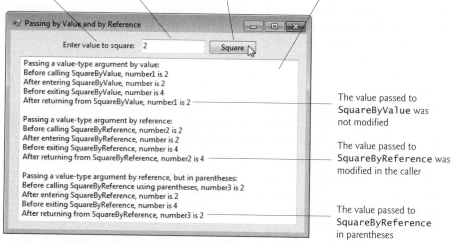

Fig. 6.7 | ByVal and ByRef used to pass value-type arguments. (Part 2 of 2.)

Keyword **ByRef** *and Method* **SquareByReference**

Method SquareByReference uses keyword **ByRef** (line 56) to receive its parameter by reference. A parameter declared with keyword ByRef is known as a **reference parameter**. When squareButton_Click calls SquareByReference (line 27), a reference to the variable number2 is passed, which gives SquareByReference direct access to the original variable in the caller. Any changes that SquareByReference makes to its parameter actually modify the original variable's value. Thus, the value stored in `number2` after `SquareByReference` finishes executing is the same as the final value of the method's `number` parameter.

Preventing a Reference Parameter from Being Modified in the Caller
When an argument is enclosed in an additional set of parentheses, as in line 39, the expression within the parentheses is evaluated and the result of that expression is passed to the method. In line 39, the inner set of parentheses evaluates `number3`, returns its value (that is, 2) and passes this *value* to the method, *even* if the method header includes keyword `ByRef`. Thus, the value of `number3` does not change after it's passed to `SquareByReference` (line 39) enclosed in an additional set of parentheses.

Reusing Values in String Method Format
In lines 17 and 29, we use the format specifier `"{0}{1}{1}"` as part of the format `String`. The values inside the braces indicate which arguments after the format `String` should replace each placeholder. Using `{1}` twice indicates that the second argument after the format `String` (that is, `vbCrLf`) should be inserted into the formatted `String` twice. This allows us to skip a line in the output.

6.8 Scope of Declarations

You've seen declarations of various entities, such as classes, methods, variables and parameters. Declarations introduce names that are used to refer to such entities. A declaration's **scope** is the portion of the program that can refer to the declared entity by its name without qualification—that is, without preceding the entity with a variable name or class name and a dot (`.`) separator. Such an entity is said to be "in scope" for that portion of the program. This section introduces several important scope issues. The Visual Basic language specification does not use formal names to describe scopes. We've chosen our own descriptive names for clarity.

The basic scopes are:

1. **Block scope**—The scope of a variable declared in a block is from the point of the declaration to the end of the block (for example, a variable declared in a control statement's body is in scope only until the end of that control statement).

2. **Method scope**—The scope of a method's local-variable declaration or parameter is from the point at which the declaration appears to the end of that method. This is similar to block scope. Variables with method scope do not retain their values between method calls and are reinitialized each time the method in which they are declared is invoked.

3. **Class scope**—The scope of a member that is declared in the class's body, but outside the bodies of the class's methods is the entire body of the class. This enables a class's methods to use all of the class's members. (You'll learn in Chapter 9 that `Shared` methods of a class can access only the class's `Shared` members.)

Lifetime of a Variable
Although a variable may not be in scope, it may still exist. A variable's **lifetime** is the period during which the variable exists in memory. Some variables exist briefly, some are created and destroyed repeatedly, and others are maintained through the program's execution.

Variables normally exist as long as the construct in which they are declared exists—for instance, a local variable of a method will exist as the call to that method is still executing.

Fund Raiser Application

To demonstrate scoping issues, let's create a **Fund Raiser** application. Consider the following problem statement:

> *An organization is hosting a fund raiser to collect donations. A portion of each donation is used to cover the operating expenses of the organization—the rest of the donation goes to the charity. Create an application that allows the organization to keep track of the total amount of money raised. The application should deduct 17% of each donation to cover operating expenses—the remaining 83% is given to the charity. The application should display the amount of each donation after the 17% for operating expenses is deducted—it also should display the total amount raised for the charity (that is, the total amount donated less operating expenses) for all donations so far.*

The user inputs the amount of a donation into a TextBox and clicks the **Donate** Button to calculate the net amount of the donation that the charity receives after operating expenses have been deducted. In addition, the total amount of money raised for the charity is updated and displayed. Figure 6.8 shows the application's GUI and the code in Fig. 6.9 demonstrates scoping issues.

Fig. 6.8 | GUI for the **Fund Raiser** application.

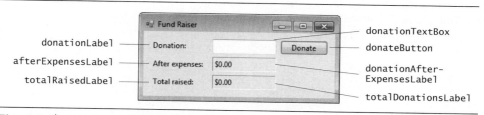

```
 1    ' Fig. 6.9: FundRaiser.vb
 2    ' Calculate total donations after operating expenses.
 3    Public Class FundRaiser
 4       ' stores total of all donations after expenses
 5       Dim totalRaised As Decimal = 0
 6
 7       ' calculate and display donation amount and total donations
 8       Private Sub donateButton_Click(ByVal sender As System.Object,
 9          ByVal e As System.EventArgs) Handles donateButton.Click
10
11          ' get donation amount
12          Dim donation As Decimal =
13             Convert.ToDecimal(Val(donationTextBox.Text))
14
15          ' obtain donation amount after operating costs deduction
16          Dim afterCosts As Decimal = CalculateDonation(donation)
17
```

Fig. 6.9 | Scoping rules in a class. (Part 1 of 2.)

```
18          ' display amount of donation after costs
19          donationAfterExpensesLabel.Text = String.Format("{0:C}", afterCosts)
20
21          ' update total amount of donations received
22          totalRaised += afterCosts
23
24          ' display total amount collected for charity
25          totalDonationsLabel.Text = String.Format("{0:C}", totalRaised)
26      End Sub ' donateButton_Click
27
28      ' calculates donation amount after operating expenses
29      Function CalculateDonation(ByVal donatedAmount As Decimal) As Decimal
30          ' 17% of donation is used to cover operating costs
31          Const COSTS As Decimal = 0.17D
32
33          ' calculate amount of donation after operating expenses
34          Return donatedAmount * (1D - COSTS)
35      End Function ' CalculateDonation
36
37      ' clear donationAfterExpensesLabel when user enters new donation amount
38      Private Sub donationTextBox_TextChanged(ByVal sender As System.Object,
39          ByVal e As System.EventArgs) Handles donationTextBox.TextChanged
40          donationAfterExpensesLabel.Text = String.Empty
41      End Sub ' donationTextBox_TextChanged
42  End Class ' FundRaiser
```

Fig. 6.9 | Scoping rules in a class. (Part 2 of 2.)

Instance Variable totalRaised

Line 5 declares instance variable totalRaised to store the total amount of money raised for charity. This variable is initialized when the Form first loads and retain its value while the application executes (that is, it's not created each time a method is invoked). Instance variables have class scope, so all methods in class FundRaiser have access to this variable and can modify its value.

Method donateButton_Click and Local Variables

Lines 12–13 in the event-handler method donateButton_Click declare and initialize variable donation, which stores the current donation amount. Identifiers, such as donation, that are declared inside a method (but outside a control statement) have method scope. This scope begins at the identifier's declaration and ends at the last statement of the method. Identifiers with method scope cannot be referenced outside of the method in which they are declared. A method's parameters also have method scope.

Identifiers declared inside control statements (such as inside an If...Then statement) have block scope, which begins at the identifier's declaration and ends at the enclosing block's final statement (for example, Else or End If).

Variables with method or block scope are called **local variables**—they cannot be referenced outside the method or block in which they are declared. If a local variable has the same name as a variable with class scope, the local variable hides the class-scope variable (for example, an instance variable) in the block or method. Any expression containing the variable name uses the local variable's value and not the class-scope variable's value.

Line 16 calls method CalculateDonation with the amount of the donation (donation). The result of this call—the net amount that goes to charity after the deduction for operating costs—is assigned to local variable afterCosts. The donation amount after operating costs is formatted as currency and displayed (line 19).

Line 22 updates instance variable totalRaised, which stores the total amount given to the charity after the operating costs have been deducted. Even though totalRaised is not declared in this event handler, the variable is in scope because it's an instance variable of class FundRaiser. Line 25 displays the total amount raised for charity so far.

Method CalculateDonation

Method CalculateDonation (lines 29–35) subtracts the operating cost from the donation amount (donatedAmount) then returns the Decimal result (line 34). Let's consider the limits of method scope. In line 34, temporarily replace donatedAmount with the variable donation, which is declared as a local variable in method donateButton_Click (line 12). The jagged line under donation indicates an error. Variables with method scope can be accessed and modified only in the method in which they're declared. The error message displayed when you rest the mouse pointer on the jagged line indicates that donation is not declared—its "local" to method donateButton_Click, so CalculateDonation cannot "see" donation's declaration. Be sure to replace donation with donatedAmount in line 34.

GUI Controls are Instance Variables

You might be wondering why we've been able to use the GUI controls in all the methods of our classes. When you create a GUI control in the designer, the IDE automatically declares an instance variable with the name you choose for the control. This declaration is placed in a separate file—*YourClassName*.Designer.vb—that is automatically compiled together with *YourClassName*.vb. All of the instance variables in your class's Designer.vb file can be used by your Form class's methods to interact with the GUI. You can view the Designer.vb file by clicking the **Show all files** Button in the **Solution Explorer**, then expanding the node for *YourClassName*.vb.

6.9 Case Study: Random-Number Generation

We now take a brief and hopefully entertaining diversion into a popular programming application—simulation and game playing. In this and the next section, we develop a game-playing program with multiple methods. The program employs many of the control statements presented thus far in the book and introduces several new concepts. The element of chance can be introduced through class **Random**.

Using Keyword *New* to Create a *Random* Object

To this point, you've actually been interacting with many objects. Each control you drag onto the **Form** using the Windows **Forms** Designer is an object of that control's class—for example, in Fig. 6.3, **hoursTextBox** is an object of class **TextBox**. Each of these objects is created for you by the Windows **Forms** Designer in the **Desinger.vb** file that is associated with the class in a Windows **Forms** application. When you want to use objects of most non-GUI classes, you need to create those objects yourself. In the statement

```
Dim randomObject As New Random()
```

Variable **randomObject** is initialized with the result of the **object-creation expression** New Random(). **New** creates a new object of the class specified to its right (that is, Random). The variable **randomObject** now said to "refer to an object of class Random."

The class name is followed by a set of parentheses. As you'll learn in Chapter 9, those parentheses in combination with a class name represent a call to a **constructor**—a special method that is used to initialize an object's data when the object is created. You'll see that arguments can be placed in the parentheses to specify initial values for the object's data. In the preceding statement, we simply leave the parentheses empty. When there are no arguments to be placed in the parentheses, the parentheses can be omitted.

Class *Random* and Method *Next*

We can now use variable **randomObject** to call methods of class Random. The statement

```
Dim randomNumber As Integer = randomObject.Next()
```

declares Integer variable **randomNumber** and assigns to it the value returned by calling Random method **Next**. To interact with an object of a class, you use the variable name that refers to the object followed by a dot separator (.) and the method or property name, just as you've done many times with GUI controls.

Method **Next** generates a positive Integer value greater than or equal to zero and less than the constant **Int32.MaxValue** (2,147,483,647). If Next truly produces values at random, every value in this range has an equal chance (or probability) of being chosen when Next is called. The values returned by Next are actually **pseudorandom numbers**, or a sequence of values produced by a complex mathematical calculation. This calculation requires a **seed value** to begin the chain of calculations. If the seed value is different each time the program is run, the series of values will be different as well (so that the generated numbers are indeed random). When we create a Random object, the seed is based on the current time. Alternatively, we can pass a seed value as an argument in the parentheses after New Random. Using the current time of day as the seed value is effective because the time is likely to change for each Random object we create.

The range of values produced by Next is often different from what is needed in a particular application. For example, a program that simulates coin tossing might require only 0 for "heads" and 1 for "tails." A program that simulates the rolling of a six-sided die would require random integers in the range 1–6. Similarly, a program that randomly predicts the next type of spaceship (out of four possibilities) that flies across the horizon in a video game might require random integers from 1 to 4.

6.9.1 Scaling and Shifting of Random Numbers

By passing an argument to method Next as follows

```
value = 1 + randomObject.Next(6)
```

we can produce integers in the range 1–6. When a single argument is passed to Next, the values returned by Next will be in the range from 0 to (but not including) the value of that argument. This is called **scaling**. The number 6 is the **scaling factor**. We **shift** the range of numbers produced by adding 1 to our previous result, so that the return values are between 1 and 6 rather than 0 and 5.

To simplify the process of specifying a range of random numbers, you can pass two arguments to Next. For example, the preceding statement also could be written as

```
value = randomObject.Next(1, 7)
```

We must use 7 as the second argument to produce integers in the range from 1–6. The first argument indicates the *minimum value* in our desired range, whereas the second is equal to *1 + the maximum value desired*. Figure 6.10 demonstrates the use of class Random and method Next by simulating 20 rolls of a six-sided die and showing the value of each roll. All the values are in the range from 1 to 6, inclusive.

```vb
 1   ' Fig. 6.10: RandomIntegers.vb
 2   ' Random integers from 1 to 6 created by calling Random method Next.
 3   Public Class RandomIntegers
 4      ' display 20 random integers
 5      Private Sub RandomIntegers_Load(ByVal sender As System.Object,
 6         ByVal e As System.EventArgs) Handles MyBase.Load
 7
 8         Dim randomObject As New Random() ' create Random object
 9         Dim randomNumber As Integer
10
11         ' generate 20 random numbers between 1 and 6
12         For i = 1 To 20
13            randomNumber = randomObject.Next(1, 7)
14            outputTextBox.AppendText(randomNumber & "   ")
15
16            If i Mod 5 = 0 Then ' is i a multiple of 5?
17               outputTextBox.AppendText(vbCrLf) ' move to next line of output
18            End If
19         Next
20      End Sub ' RandomIntegers_Load
21   End Class ' RandomIntegers
```

Fig. 6.10 | Random integers from 1 to 6 created by calling Random method Next.

6.9.2 Randomly Selecting Images

The program in Fig. 6.11 uses class `Random` to simulate rolling four six-sided dice and displays in `PictureBox` controls corresponding images for each die value. We use some of the functionality from this program in another example (Fig. 6.14) to demonstrate that the numbers generated by `Next` indeed occur with approximately equal likelihood.

```vb
 1    ' Fig. 6.11: RollDice.vb
 2    ' Rolling four dice and displaying corresponding images.
 3    Public Class RollDice
 4       Dim randomObject As New Random() ' create Random object
 5
 6       ' display results of four rolls
 7       Private Sub rollButton_Click(ByVal sender As System.Object, _
 8          ByVal e As System.EventArgs) Handles rollButton.Click
 9          ' method randomly assigns a face to each die
10          DisplayDie(die1PictureBox)
11          DisplayDie(die2PictureBox)
12          DisplayDie(die3PictureBox)
13          DisplayDie(die4PictureBox)
14       End Sub ' rollButton_Click
15
16       ' get a random die image
17       Sub DisplayDie(ByVal diePictureBox As PictureBox)
18          ' generate random integer in range 1 to 6
19          Dim face As Integer = randomObject.Next(1, 7)
20
21          ' retrieve specific die image from resources
22          Dim pictureResource = My.Resources.ResourceManager.GetObject( _
23             String.Format("die{0}", face))
24
25          ' convert pictureResource to type Image and display in PictureBox
26          diePictureBox.Image = CType(pictureResource, Image)
27       End Sub ' DisplayDie
28    End Class ' RollDice
```

Fig. 6.11 | Rolling four dice and displaying corresponding images.

Displaying Random Images in a PictureBox

The event handler `rollButton_Click` (lines 7–14) calls method `DisplayDie` four times (lines 10–13), once for each `PictureBox` on the `Form`. Calling `DisplayDie` causes four dice to appear as if they were being rolled each time **Roll** is clicked. The images do not appear until the user clicks **Roll** the first time.

Method `DisplayDie` (lines 17–27) specifies the correct image for the face value calculated by method `Next` (line 19). We declare `randomObject` as an instance variable (line 4) of class `RollDice`. This allows the same `Random` object to be used each time `DisplayDie` executes. The code in lines 22–26 sets the `Image` property (line 26) of the `PictureBox` that is passed as an argument.

Embedding Image as Resources in a Project

In this example, we embedded the images into the project as **resources**. This causes the compiler to include the images in the application's executable file and enables the application to access the images through the **My namespace**, which provides many capabilities that make common programming tasks easier. Namespaces organize classes into groups by functionality. For example, namespace `System.Windows.Forms` in the Framework Class Library contains the controls you've been using in your GUIs. Embedded images make it easy to move an application to another location or computer. The images used in this example are located with this chapter's examples in the `Images` folder. To add images to the project as resources:

1. After creating your project, double click **My Project** in the **Solution Explorer** to display the project's properties.

2. Click the **Resources** tab.

3. At the top of the **Resources** tab click the down arrow next to the **Add Resource** button and select **Add Existing File...** (Fig. 6.12) to display the **Add** existing file to resources dialog.

Fig. 6.12 | Preparing to add images to the project as resources.

4. Locate the image files you wish to add as resources and click the **Open** button. The image file names for this example are `die1.png`, `die2.png`, `die3.png`, `die4.png`, `die5.png` and `die6.png`.

5. Save your project.

The files now appear in a folder named **Resources** in the **Solution Explorer**. We'll use this technique in most examples that display images. For more details on the `My` namespace visit `msdn.microsoft.com/en-us/vbasic/ms789188.aspx`.

Using Embedded Images

To use an image (or any other resource) in the project's resources, you use the method **My.Resources.ResourceManager.GetObject**, which takes as an argument the resource name as it appears in the **Resources** tab (for example, "die1") and returns the resource as an Object. Lines 22–23 invoke GetObject with the result of the expression

```
String.Format("die{0}", face)
```

which builds the name of the resource by placing the random number face at the end of the word "die". You must convert this Object to type Image to assign it to the Picture-Box's Image property. Line 26 uses the **CType** function to perform the conversion. CType converts its first argument to the type specified in its second argument. A conversion performed with the CType function is also known as a **cast operation** or more simply as **cast**.

The My namespace also provides direct access to the resources you define with expressions of the form My.Resources.*resourceName*, where *resourceName* is the name you provided to the resource when you created it. When using such an expression, the resource returned already has the appropriate type. For example, My.Resources.die1 is an Image object representing the die1.png image.

6.9.3 Rolling Dice Repeatedly and Displaying Statistics

The next application allows you to repeatedly roll 12 dice to show that the numbers generated by class Random occur with approximately equal frequencies. The program displays the cumulative frequencies of each face, and each roll's faces are displayed using Picture-Boxes. The GUI is shown in Fig. 6.13 and the application code is shown in Fig. 6.14.

Fig. 6.13 | GUI for **Dice Rolling Statistics** application.

```
1   ' Fig. 6.14: DiceStatistics.vb
2   ' Rolling 12 dice with frequency chart.
3   Public Class DiceStatistics
4      Dim randomObject As New Random() ' generate random number
5      Dim ones As Integer = 0 ' count of die face 1
6      Dim twos As Integer = 0 ' count of die face 2
```

Fig. 6.14 | Rolling 12 dice with frequency chart. (Part 1 of 3.)

```vb
 7      Dim threes As Integer = 0 ' count of die face 3
 8      Dim fours As Integer = 0 ' count of die face 4
 9      Dim fives As Integer = 0 ' count of die face 5
10      Dim sixes As Integer = 0 ' count of die face 6
11
12      ' display result of twelve rolls
13      Private Sub rollButton_Click(ByVal sender As System.Object,
14          ByVal e As System.EventArgs) Handles rollButton.Click
15
16          ' display 12 randomly selected die faces
17          DisplayDie(die1PictureBox)
18          DisplayDie(die2PictureBox)
19          DisplayDie(die3PictureBox)
20          DisplayDie(die4PictureBox)
21          DisplayDie(die5PictureBox)
22          DisplayDie(die6PictureBox)
23          DisplayDie(die7PictureBox)
24          DisplayDie(die8PictureBox)
25          DisplayDie(die9PictureBox)
26          DisplayDie(die10PictureBox)
27          DisplayDie(die11PictureBox)
28          DisplayDie(die12PictureBox)
29
30          Dim total As Integer = ones + twos + threes + fours + fives + sixes
31
32          ' display frequencies of faces
33          displayTextBox.Text =
34              "Face" & vbTab & "Frequency" & vbTab & "Percent" & vbCrLf &
35              "1" & vbTab & ones & vbTab & vbTab &
36              String.Format("{0:P2}", ones / total) & vbCrLf &
37              "2" & vbTab & twos & vbTab & vbTab &
38              String.Format("{0:P2}", twos / total) & vbCrLf &
39              "3" & vbTab & threes & vbTab & vbTab &
40              String.Format("{0:P2}", threes / total) & vbCrLf &
41              "4" & vbTab & fours & vbTab & vbTab &
42              String.Format("{0:P2}", fours / total) & vbCrLf &
43              "5" & vbTab & fives & vbTab & vbTab &
44              String.Format("{0:P2}", fives / total) & vbCrLf &
45              "6" & vbTab & sixes & vbTab & vbTab &
46              String.Format("{0:P2}", sixes / total)
47      End Sub ' rollButton_Click
48
49      ' display a single die image
50      Sub DisplayDie(ByVal diePictureBox As PictureBox)
51          Dim face As Integer = randomObject.Next(1, 7)
52
53          ' retrieve specific die image from resources
54          Dim pictureResource = My.Resources.ResourceManager.GetObject(
55              String.Format("die{0}", face))
56
57          ' convert pictureResource to image type and load into PictureBox
58          diePictureBox.Image = CType(pictureResource, Image)
59
```

Fig. 6.14 | Rolling 12 dice with frequency chart. (Part 2 of 3.)

```
60                ' maintain count of die faces
61            Select Case face
62                Case 1 ' die face 1
63                    ones += 1
64                Case 2 ' die face 2
65                    twos += 1
66                Case 3 ' die face 3
67                    threes += 1
68                Case 4 ' die face 4
69                    fours += 1
70                Case 5 ' die face 5
71                    fives += 1
72                Case 6 ' die face 6
73                    sixes += 1
74            End Select
75        End Sub ' DisplayDie
76    End Class ' DiceStatistics
```

Fig. 6.14 | Rolling 12 dice with frequency chart. (Part 3 of 3.)

Figure 6.13 shows the program after the user has clicked **Roll** 100 times. If the values produced by method Next are indeed random, the frequencies of the face values (1–6) should be approximately the same (as the figure illustrates).

To show that the faces occur with approximately equal likelihood, the program maintains statistics. We declare as instance variables counters for each face value in lines 5–10. Lines 33–46 display the frequency of each face as percentages using the **P format specifier**. P2 displays percentages with two digits to the right of the decimal point. The more you roll the dice, the closer each percentage should get to 16.66%.

As the program output demonstrates, method Next can be used to effectively simulate the rolling of a six-sided die. Over the course of many die rolls, each of the possible faces in the range 1–6 appears with equal likelihood, or approximately one-sixth of the time. *No* Case Else is provided in the Select...Case statement (lines 61–74), because we know that the values generated are in the range 1–6. In Chapter 7, we show how to replace the entire Select...Case statement in this program with a single line of code.

Click the **Roll Button** several times and observe the results. A different sequence of random numbers is obtained each time the program is executed, causing the resulting frequencies to vary. When the Button has the focus, you can hold down the *Enter* key to rapidly "press" the button and roll the dice.

6.10 Case Study: A Game of Chance

A popular game of chance is the dice game "craps." The rules of the game are as follows:

> *A player rolls two dice. Each die has six faces. Each face contains 1, 2, 3, 4, 5 or 6 spots. After the dice have come to rest, the sum of the spots on the two upward faces is calculated. If the sum is 7 or 11 on the first throw, the player wins. If the sum is 2, 3 or 12 on the first throw (called "craps"), the player loses (that is, the "house" wins). If the sum is 4, 5, 6, 8, 9 or 10 on the first throw, that sum becomes the player's "point." To win, players must continue rolling the dice until they "make their point" (that is, roll their point value). The player loses by rolling a 7 before making the point.*

Craps GUI

Figure 6.15 shows the GUI for the **Craps** application. This program introduces the **Group-Box** control and uses it to display the user's point. A GroupBox is used to group related controls. Within the GroupBox pointGroupBox, we add two PictureBoxes, which are controls that display images. You can drag and drop a GroupBox onto the Form the same way you would any other control. When adding other controls to a GroupBox (such as the two PictureBoxes in this example), drag and drop the controls within the bounds of the GroupBox on the Form. We set the GroupBox's **Text** property to **Point**. This is the text that displays in the upper-left corner of the GroupBox. We'll modify this text programmatically to display the user's point value. If you leave the Text property blank, the GroupBox displays as a simple border without any text. The statusLabel control is attached to the bottom of the Form. This is known as "docking" the control. When a control is docked to the bottom of a Form, the control becomes as wide as the Form and always remains at the bottom, even if the Form is resized. You can dock a control to the Top, Bottom, Left, Right or Center of a Form by selecting the appropriate value for the control's **Dock** property in the **Properties** window. The application in Fig. 6.16 simulates the game of craps.

Fig. 6.15 | GUI for the **Craps** application.

```
 1    ' Fig. 6.16: Craps.vb
 2    ' Craps game using class Random.
 3    Public Class Craps
 4        ' die-roll constants
 5        Enum DiceNames
 6            SNAKE_EYES = 2
 7            TREY = 3
 8            LUCKY_SEVEN = 7
 9            CRAPS = 7
10            YO_LEVEN = 11
11            BOX_CARS = 12
12        End Enum
13
14        Dim myPoint As Integer ' total point if not 2, 3, 12, 7 or 11
15        Dim myDie1 As Integer ' die1 face
16        Dim myDie2 As Integer ' die2 face
17        Dim randomObject As New Random() ' generate random number
```

Fig. 6.16 | Craps game using class Random. (Part 1 of 4.)

```
18
19      ' begins new game and determines point
20      Private Sub playButton_Click(ByVal sender As System.Object, _
21         ByVal e As System.EventArgs) Handles playButton.Click
22
23         ' initialize variables for new game
24         myPoint = 0
25         pointGroupBox.Text = "Point"
26         statusLabel.Text = String.Empty
27
28         ' remove point-die images
29         pointDie1PictureBox.Image = Nothing
30         pointDie2PictureBox.Image = Nothing
31
32         Dim sum As Integer = RollDice() ' roll dice and calculate sum
33
34         ' check die roll
35         Select Case sum
36            Case DiceNames.LUCKY_SEVEN, DiceNames.YO_LEVEN
37               rollButton.Enabled = False ' disable Roll button
38               statusLabel.Text = "You Win!!!"
39            Case DiceNames.SNAKE_EYES, DiceNames.TREY, DiceNames.BOX_CARS
40               rollButton.Enabled = False ' disable Roll button
41               statusLabel.Text = "Sorry. You Lose."
42            Case Else
43               myPoint = sum ' store the point value
44               pointGroupBox.Text = "Point is " & sum
45               statusLabel.Text = "Roll Again!"
46               DisplayDie(pointDie1PictureBox, myDie1)
47               DisplayDie(pointDie2PictureBox, myDie2)
48               playButton.Enabled = False ' disable Play button
49               rollButton.Enabled = True ' enable Roll button
50         End Select
51      End Sub ' playButton_Click
52
53      ' determines outcome of next roll
54      Private Sub rollButton_Click(ByVal sender As System.Object, _
55         ByVal e As System.EventArgs) Handles rollButton.Click
56
57         Dim sum As Integer = RollDice() ' roll dice and calculate sum
58
59         ' check outcome of roll
60         If sum = myPoint Then ' win
61            statusLabel.Text = "You Win!!!"
62            rollButton.Enabled = False ' disable Roll button
63            playButton.Enabled = True ' enable Play button
64         ElseIf sum = DiceNames.CRAPS Then ' lose
65            statusLabel.Text = "Sorry. You Lose."
66            rollButton.Enabled = False ' disable Roll button
67            playButton.Enabled = True ' enable Play button
68         End If
69      End Sub ' rollButton_Click
70
```

Fig. 6.16 | Craps game using class Random. (Part 2 of 4.)

```
71      ' display die image
72      Sub DisplayDie(ByVal diePictureBox As PictureBox, _
73         ByVal face As Integer)
74
75         ' retrieve specific die image from resources
76         Dim pictureResource = My.Resources.ResourceManager.GetObject( _
77            String.Format("die{0}", face))
78
79         ' convert pictureResource to image type and load into PictureBox
80         diePictureBox.Image = CType(pictureResource, Image)
81      End Sub ' DisplayDie
82
83      ' generate random die rolls
84      Function RollDice() As Integer
85         ' determine random integer
86         myDie1 = randomObject.Next(1, 7) ' choose value from 1 to 6
87         myDie2 = randomObject.Next(1, 7) ' choose value from 1 to 6
88
89         ' display rolls
90         DisplayDie(die1PictureBox, myDie1) ' display first die
91         DisplayDie(die2PictureBox, myDie2) ' display second die
92
93         Return myDie1 + myDie2 ' return sum
94      End Function ' RollDice
95   End Class ' Craps
```

a)

b)

c)

d)

Fig. 6.16 | Craps game using class Random. (Part 3 of 4.)

Fig. 6.16 | Craps game using class `Random`. (Part 4 of 4.)

Game Play

Click the **Play** Button to play the game. You roll two dice on the first and all subsequent rolls. If you do not win or lose on the first roll, the **Play** Button is disabled and the **Roll** Button is enabled. You can then click the **Roll** Button to continue playing the game until you win or lose. At this point, the **Roll** Button is disabled and the **Play** Button is enabled.

The screen captures depict several sample games. Figure 6.16(a) displays the Form before the game has begun. The remaining outputs show several games:

- Figure 6.16(b) shows a game in which the user rolled a 3 and lost on the first roll.
- Figure 6.16(c) shows a game in which the user rolled an 11 and won on the first roll.
- Figure 6.16(d) and (e) show a game in which the user rolled a 5 on the first roll, then lost on the second roll by rolling a 7.
- Finally, Fig. 6.16(f)–(h) show a game in which the user rolled a 6 on the first roll, rolled a 10 on the second roll, then won on the third roll by rolling a 6 again.

Enumerations and Constants

The program includes our first **enumeration**—declared with **Enum...End Enum** in lines 5–12. Enumerations enhance program readability by providing descriptive identifiers for groups of related constant numbers or `String`s. Enumerations help you ensure that values are consistent throughout a program. (Recall that keyword `Const` creates a single constant identifier and that such an identifier must be initialized in its declaration.) In this case, we create an `Enum` of descriptive names for the various dice combinations in craps (that is, SNAKE_EYES, TREY, LUCKY_SEVEN, CRAPS, YO_LEVEN and BOX_CARS). Multiple enumeration members can have the same value—in this example, LUCKY_SEVEN and CRAPS both have the value 7. We use two identifiers for program clarity; on the first roll, a seven causes the player to win (LUCKY_SEVEN), and on subsequent rolls, a seven causes the player to lose (CRAPS). You are not required to provide initializer values for the constants in an Enum. If you do not, the initial value of the first constant will be zero and all others will be initialized to one higher than the preceding constant in the list.

Method playButton_Click

After the declarations for several instance variables (lines 14–17), lines 20–51 declare method playButton_Click to handle playButton's Click event. When the user clicks the **Play** button, method playButton_Click sets up a new game by initializing several values (lines 24–26). Line 26 clears the status Label's Text property.

Setting the Image property of pointDie1PictureBox and pointDie2PictureBox to Nothing (lines 29–30) causes the PictureBoxes to appear blank. Method playButton_Click executes the game's first roll by calling RollDice (line 32). Function RollDice (lines 84–94) generates two random numbers and calls method DisplayDie (lines 72–81) to display the corresponding die images in the PictureBoxes that represent the current roll of the dice.

The Select...Case statement (lines 35–50) analyzes the roll returned by RollDice to determine how play should continue (that is, by terminating the game with a win or loss, or by enabling subsequent rolls). If the user does not win or lose on the first roll, the GroupBox's text is set to display the point value (line 44) and the proper images are displayed in the GroupBox's PictureBoxes (lines 46–47). Depending on the value of the roll, Buttons **Roll** and **Play** become either enabled or disabled (lines 37, 40 and 48–49). Disabling a Button means that no action will be performed when the Button is clicked. Recall that a control can be enabled and disabled by setting its Enabled property to True or False, respectively.

Method rollButton_Click

If the button **Roll** is enabled, clicking it invokes method rollButton_Click (lines 54–69), which executes an additional roll of the dice. Method rollButton_Click then analyzes the roll, letting users know whether they've won or lost.

6.11 Method Overloading

There are several ways to declare methods with variable-length sets of parameters. **Method overloading** allows you to create methods with the *same* name but *different* **signatures**—that is, there are different numbers and/or types of parameters, or they're listed in a different order (by type). A method's signature *does not* include its return type. When you call an overloaded method, the compiler selects the proper method by examining the number, types and order (by type) of the arguments. Often, method overloading is used to create several methods with the same name that perform *similar* tasks on *different* types of data.

Figure 6.17 uses overloaded method Square to calculate the square of both an Integer and a Double. If the compiler looked only at method names during compilation, the code in Fig. 6.17 would be ambiguous—the compiler would not know how to differentiate between the two Square methods. The compiler uses a process known as **overload resolution** to determine which method to call. This process first searches for all methods that *could* be used on the basis of the number and type of arguments that are present. Although it might seem that only one method would match, it's important to remember that values are converted as necessary when they're passed as arguments. Once all matching methods are found, the compiler then selects the closest match.

```
1   ' Fig. 6.17: MethodOverloading.vb
2   ' Using overloaded methods.
3   Public Class MethodOverloading
4      ' call overloaded functions
5      Private Sub MethodOverloading_Load(ByVal sender As System.Object,
6         ByVal e As System.EventArgs) Handles MyBase.Load
7
8         ' call the overloaded Square methods and display the results
9         outputLabel.Text =
10           "The square of Integer 7 is " & Square(7) & vbCrLf &
11           "The square of Double 7.5 is " & Square(7.5)
12     End Sub ' MethodOverloading_Load
13
14     ' method Square takes an Integer and returns an Integer
15     Function Square(ByVal value As Integer) As Integer
16        Return Convert.ToInt32(value ^ 2)
17     End Function ' Square
18
19     ' method Square takes a Double and returns a Double
20     Function Square(ByVal value As Double) As Double
21        Return value ^ 2
22     End Function ' Square
23  End Class ' MethodOverloading
```

outputLabel ⎯⎯⎯

Method Overloading
The square of Integer 7 is 49
The square of Double 7.5 is 56.25

Fig. 6.17 | Using overloaded methods.

Line 10 calls method Square with the argument 7. The compiler treats whole-number literals as Integers by default. So line 10 calls the version of method Square that has an Integer parameter (lines 15–17). Similarly, line 11 calls method Square with the argument 7.5. The compiler treats floating-point literals as Double values by default, line 11 calls the version of method Square that has a Double parameter (lines 20–22).

The call to method Convert.ToInt32 in line 16 *explicitly* converts its argument to type Integer. This is required to prevent compilation errors. The exponent (^) operator expects operands of type Double and *implicitly* converts its operands to that type. Recall that we're now using **Option Strict**, so *implicit* conversions from Double (the result type of the ^ operator) to Integer (the return type of the method) are no longer allowed.

Notes on Method Overloading

Overloaded methods need not have the same number of parameters. The *order* of the parameters (by type) is important to the compiler. For example, if the declaration of method AddMixedTypes begins with

```
Function AddMixedTypes(ByVal a As Integer,
   ByVal b As Double) As Integer
```

and an overloaded version of the method begins with

```
Function AddMixedTypes(ByVal a As Double,
   ByVal b As Integer) As Integer
```

the compiler considers these two AddMixedTypes methods to be distinct.

Also, methods cannot be distinguished only by their return types. For example, if you modify method Square in line 20 of Fig. 6.17 so that its parameter is of type Integer rather than type Double, you'll receive the following compilation error:

```
Public Function Square(value As Integer) As Integer' and
   'Public Function Square(value As Integer) As Double' cannot
      overload each other because they differ only by return types.
```

6.12 Optional Parameters

Methods can have **optional parameters**. Declaring a parameter as **Optional** allows the calling method to vary the number of arguments to pass. An Optional parameter specifies a default value that is assigned to the parameter if the optional argument is omitted.

You can create methods with one or more Optional parameters. All Optional parameters *must* be placed to the right of the method's non-Optional parameters—that is, at the end of the parameter list.

Common Programming Error 6.4

Declaring a non-Optional parameter to the right of an Optional parameter is a compilation error.

When a parameter is declared as Optional, the caller has the *option* of passing that particular argument. For example, the method header

```
Function Power(ByVal base As Integer,
   Optional ByVal exponent As Integer = 2) As Integer
```

specifies the last parameter as Optional. Any call to Power must pass at least an argument for the parameter base, or a compilation error occurs. Optionally, a second argument (for the exponent parameter) can be passed to Power. Consider the following calls to Power:

```
Power()
Power(10)
Power(10, 3)
```

The first call generates a syntax error because a minimum of one argument is required for this method. The second call is valid because one argument (10) is being passed—the Optional exponent is not specified in the method call. The last call is also valid—10 is passed as the one required argument and 3 is passed as the Optional argument.

In the call that passes only one argument (10), parameter exponent defaults to 2, which is the value specified in the method header. Optional parameters must specify a **default value** by using an equal (=) sign followed by the value. For example, the header for Power sets 2 as the default value for exponent. Default values can be used only with parameters declared as Optional.

Figure 6.19 demonstrates an optional parameter. The program calculates the result of raising a base value to an exponent. Method Power (lines 23–33) specifies that its second parameter is Optional. If the user does not specify an exponent, the Optional argument is omitted, and the default parameter value, 2, is used.

Fig. 6.18 | GUI for the **Power** application.

```
1   ' Fig. 6.19: Power.vb
2   ' Optional argument demonstration with method Power.
3   Public Class Power
4      ' reads input and displays result
5      Private Sub calculatePowerButton_Click(ByVal sender As System.Object,
6         ByVal e As System.EventArgs) Handles calculatePowerButton.Click
7
8         Dim value As Integer ' stores the result
9
10        ' call version of Power depending on power input
11        If exponentTextBox.Text <> String.Empty Then
12           value = Power(Convert.ToInt32(baseTextBox.Text),
13              Convert.ToInt32(exponentTextBox.Text))
14        Else
15           value = Power(Convert.ToInt32(baseTextBox.Text))
16           exponentTextBox.Text = Convert.ToString(2)
17        End If
18
19        outputLabel.Text = Convert.ToString(value)
20     End Sub ' calculatePowerButton_Click
21
22     ' use iteration to calculate power
23     Function Power(ByVal base As Integer,
24        Optional ByVal exponent As Integer = 2) As Integer
25
26        Dim result As Integer = 1 ' initialize total
27
28        For i = 1 To exponent ' calculate power
29           result *= base
30        Next
31
32        Return result ' return result
33     End Function ' Power
34
```

Fig. 6.19 | Optional argument demonstration with method Power. (Part 1 of 2.)

```
35    ' clear outputLabel when user changes the base value
36    Private Sub baseTextBox_TextChanged(ByVal sender As System.Object,
37       ByVal e As System.EventArgs) Handles baseTextBox.TextChanged
38       outputLabel.Text = String.Empty
39    End Sub ' baseTextBox_TextChanged
40
41    ' clear outputLabel when user changes the exponent value
42    Private Sub exponentTextBox_TextChanged(ByVal sender As System.Object,
43       ByVal e As System.EventArgs) Handles exponentTextBox.TextChanged
44       outputLabel.Text = String.Empty
45    End Sub ' exponentTextBox_TextChanged
46 End Class ' Power
```

Fig. 6.19 | Optional argument demonstration with method Power. (Part 2 of 2.)

In this example, we use TextBoxes to input data from the user. When the user clicks the **Calculate Power** Button, line 11 determines whether exponentTextBox contains a value. If the condition is true (as in Fig. 6.19(a)), the values in the TextBoxes are converted to Integers using method Convert.ToInt32 then passed to Power (lines 12–13). Otherwise, baseTextBox's value is converted to an Integer and passed as the required argument to Power in line 15. An example of this is shown in Fig. 6.19(b), where we clicked the **Calculate Power** Button without entering an exponent value. The second argument, 2, is provided by the compiler (using the default value of the Optional argument) and is not visible to you in the call. Line 16 displays the default exponent value (2) in exponentTextBox, for clarity (Fig. 6.19(c)).

6.13 Using the Debugger: Debugging Commands

We now present additional debugging commands from the **Standard** toolbar (Fig. 6.20) that provide convenient access to commands in the **Debug** menu. If the **Standard** toolbar isn't visible in the IDE, select **View > Toolbars > Standard**.

Now that you've learned more about methods, we'll demonstrate the **Step Into** and **Step Out** commands that can be used to view the code for a called method as it executes and returns from the method to the caller, respectively. In addition, we'll show how to continue program execution from a breakpoint.

Fig. 6.20 | Debugging controls on Visual Basic 2010 Express's **Standard** toolbar.

To begin, open the **Wage Calculator** application from Fig. 6.3. Next, set a breakpoint at the call to method DisplayPay (line 17) by clicking in the margin indicator bar (Fig. 6.21). Start the debugger to begin executing the **Wage Calculator** application. Enter the value 7.50 in the **Wage per hour:** TextBox, and enter 35 in the **Hours worked:** TextBox, then click the **Calculate** Button. The debugger enters break mode at line 17, indicating that method DisplayPay will execute next.

```
WageCalculator.vb  ×  WageCalculator.vb [Design]

 calculateButton                                   Click

   13          Dim hourlyWage As Decimal = Val(wageTextBox.Text)
   14
   15          ' determine whether hoursWorked is less than or equal to 168
   16          If hoursWorked <= HOURS_IN_A_WEEK Then
   17              DisplayPay(hoursWorked, hourlyWage) ' calls DisplayPay Function
   18          Else
```

Fig. 6.21 | Setting a breakpoint at line 17.

Using the Step Into Command

When the debugger is in break mode and the next statement to execute represents a method call, you can use the **Step Into** command ( ) to transfer control to the called method, so that you can use other debugging commands to step through the method's statements and confirm that the method is executing correctly. If the next statement to execute is not a method call, then the **Step Into** command has the same effect as the **Step Over** command—that is, the debugger executes the current statement and pauses at the next statement to execute. Click the **Step Into** command now to transfer control to method DisplayPay (Fig. 6.22).

Executing the Statements in Method DisplayPay

As you learned in Section 4.12, you can use the **Step Over** command to execute statements one at a time. If you wish to execute several statements without repeatedly clicking the **Step Over** command, you'll want to tell the debugger to continue to a later point in a method's (or the program's) execution. There are two ways to do this. One is to simply

Fig. 6.22 | IDE showing that `DisplayPay` is about to execute.

right click the statement where you'd like to continue step-by-step execution, then select **Run to Cursor** from the menu that appears. The debugger will execute the statements up to, but not including, that statement. When an application is running in the debugger, the **Start Debugging** (▶) command becomes the **Continue** command. If you set another breakpoint then click **Continue**, the debugger will execute statements until it reaches the next breakpoint. If there aren't any breakpoints, the program will simply execute until it completes or until the event handler that you're debugging finishes executing—at which point the program waits for the next user interaction.

Set a breakpoint now at line 40 in method `DisplayPay` by clicking in the margin indicator bar, then click **Continue** to execute the code in method `DisplayPay` up to, but not including, line 40. The next executable statement is now line 40. Click **Continue** again to complete the call to `DisplayPay` and complete the execution of the event handler `calcualteButton_Click`. At this point, the program waits for the next user interaction.

Using the **Step Out** *Command*
Often, in lengthy methods, you'll want to look at a few key lines of code and then continue debugging the caller's code. The **Step Out** command (⇑≣) is useful for such situations, where you do not want to continue stepping through the entire method line by line.

To demonstrate this feature, first remove the breakpoint at line 40. Then, enter new values in the **Wage per hour:** and **Hours worked:** TextBoxes and click the **Calculate** Button. When the debugger enters break mode at line 17, **Step Into** the `DisplayPay` method. At this point you can step through some of the code in method `DisplayPay`. Before you reach the end of the method, click the **Step Out** command to execute the remaining statements in the method and return control to line 17, where the method was called. Click the **Stop Debugging** command to end the debugging session.

6.14 Wrap-Up

In this chapter, you studied methods in greater depth. You learned the difference between subroutines and functions, and when to use each. You learned how to declare named constants using both enumerations and with the `Const` keyword. You learned about how arguments can be implicitly converted to the type of their corresponding parameters. We demonstrated **Option Strict**, which causes the compiler to check all conversions and requires you to perform an explicit conversion for all narrowing conversions that could cause data loss or program termination. You saw how to use class `Random` to generate random numbers that can be used for simulations and game playing. You also learned about the scope of instance variables and local variables in classes and methods, respectively. You learned that multiple methods in one class can be overloaded by providing methods with the same name and different signatures. Such methods can be used to perform the same or similar tasks using different types or different numbers of parameters. You learned how to specify Optional parameters with default values that are passed to a method if a corresponding argument is not provided in a method call. Finally, we demonstrated the **Step Into**, **Continue** and **Step Out** debugging commands, which help you follow the flow of control through the various methods in your programs.

In Chapter 7, you'll learn how to maintain lists and tables of data in arrays. You'll also see a more elegant implementation of the dice-rolling application of Fig. 6.14.

Summary

Section 6.1 Introduction
- Experience has shown that the best way to develop and maintain a large program is to construct it from small, simple pieces—a technique known as divide and conquer.

Section 6.2 Classes and Methods
- Typical programs consist of one or more classes. You combine new classes with "prepackaged" classes available in the .NET Framework Class Library and in various other class libraries.
- You can create your own customized classes and methods to meet the unique requirements of a particular application.
- Methods define specific tasks that a program may use one or more times during its execution.
- Although the same method can be executed from multiple points in a program, the actual statements that define the method are written only once.
- Hiding implementation details promotes good software engineering.
- A method is invoked by a method call. The method call specifies the method name and provides arguments that the method requires to do its job.
- When a method completes its task, it returns control to the calling method. In some cases, the method also returns a result to the caller.

Section 6.3 Subroutines: Methods That Do Not Return a Value
- A subroutine is a method that performs a task but does not return a value. It is declared with the keywords Sub...End Sub.
- A function is a method that performs a task then returns a value to the calling method.
- Keyword Const declares a constant—a value that cannot change after it's initialized. Constants enhance program readability by providing descriptive identifiers for values that do not change.
- When a method is called, the program makes a copy of the value of each argument (if any) and program control transfers to the method's first line. The method receives the copied values and stores them in its parameters.
- When the End Sub statement is encountered, program control returns to the next statement in the calling method.
- Keyword Sub indicates that a method will perform a task but will not return any information to its calling method when it completes its task.
- By convention, method names begin with an uppercase letter and all subsequent words in the name begin with a capital letter.

- In a method declaration, the parentheses after the name indicate any parameters required by the method to perform its task. Empty parentheses indicate that a method does not have parameters.
- A method can specify multiple parameters by separating each from the next with a comma.
- Each parameter has a variable name and a type.
- There must be one argument in the method call for each parameter in the method declaration.
- The type of each argument must be consistent with its corresponding parameter's type.
- The declarations and statements in the method declaration form the method body.
- The method body is also referred to as a block. The bodies of control statements are also blocks.

Section 6.4 Functions: Methods That Return a Value
- A function is declared with the keywords `Function...End Function`.
- A `Return` statement terminates a function and gives a value back to the calling method.
- In a `Function`'s header, the return type indicates the type of the value returned from the function.

Section 6.5 Implicit Argument Conversions
- Implicit argument conversion converts an argument's value to the type that a method expects to receive in its corresponding parameter.
- A widening conversion occurs when an argument is converted to a parameter of another type that can hold more data, whereas a narrowing conversion occurs when there is potential for data loss during the conversion.
- Implicit conversions also occur for expressions containing values of two or more types.

Section 6.6 Option Strict and Data-Type Conversions
- **Option Explicit**, which defaults to **On**, requires you to declare all variables before they're used in a program.
- **Option Strict**, which defaults to **Off**, increases program clarity and reduces debugging time. When set to **On**, **Option Strict** causes the compiler to check all conversions and requires you to perform explicit conversions for all narrowing conversions or conversions that might cause program termination.
- **Option Infer**, which defaults to **On**, enables the compiler to infer a variable's type based on its intializer value.
- Class `Convert`'s methods explicitly convert data from one primitive type to another.
- Many of the primitive types have a `Parse` method that you can use to convert a `String` to a value of that primitive type.
- Visual Basic also provides type-conversion functions for converting between built-in types.

Section 6.7 Passing Arguments: Pass-by-Value vs. Pass-by-Reference
- Arguments are passed in one of two ways—pass-by-value or pass-by-reference.
- When an argument is passed by value, the program makes a copy of the argument's value and passes the copy to the called method. Changes to the called method's copy do not affect the original variable's value in the caller.
- When an argument is passed by reference, the called method can access and modify the caller's original data directly.
- Keyword `ByVal` in a method header indicates that the argument is be passed by value.
- Keyword `ByRef` indicates that the argument is passed by reference.

Section 6.8 Scope of Declarations

- A declaration's scope is the portion of the program that can refer to the declared entity by its name without qualification.
- The scope of a variable declared in a block is from the declaration point to the end of the block.
- The scope of a method's local-variable declaration or parameter is from the point at which the declaration appears to the end of that method.
- Variables with method scope do not retain their values between method calls and are reinitialized each time the method in which they are declared is invoked.
- The scope of a class's members is the entire body of the class. This enables methods of a class to use all of the class's members.
- A variable's lifetime is the period during which the variable exists in memory.
- Variables with method or block scope are called local variables, because they cannot be referenced outside the method or block in which they are declared.
- If a local variable has the same name as a variable with class scope, the local variable hides the module-scope variable in the block or method.

Section 6.9 Case Study: Random-Number Generation

- A Random variable is initialized with the result of an object-creation expression. New creates a new object of the class specified to the right of the New keyword.
- Random method Next generates a positive Integer value greater than or equal to zero and less than the constant Int32.MaxValue (2,147,483,647).
- The values returned by Next are actually pseudorandom numbers.

Section 6.9.1 Scaling and Shifting of Random Numbers

- By passing an argument to method Next you can produce integers in the range 0 up to, but not including, the argument value. The argument is the scaling factor. You can also shift the range of numbers produced by adding a value to the result.
- You can pass two arguments to Next to produce values from the first argument up to, but not including, the second argument.

Section 6.9.2 Randomly Selecting Images

- You can embed images into a project as resources. This causes the compiler to embed the images in the application's executable file and enables the application to access the images through the My namespace.
- To use an image in the project's resources, you use the method My.Resources.ResourceManager.GetObject, which takes as an argument the resource name as it appears in the **Resources** tab and returns the resource as an Object. Then, convert this Object to type Image using the CType function.

Section 6.10 Case Study: A Game of Chance

- A GroupBox is used to group related controls. When adding other controls to a GroupBox, drag and drop the controls within the bounds of the GroupBox.
- A GroupBox's Text property displays in the upper-left corner of the GroupBox.
- You can dock a control to the Top, Bottom, Left, Right or Center of a Form by selecting the appropriate value for the control's Dock property in the **Properties** window.
- An enumeration—declared with Enum...End Enum—enhances program readability by providing descriptive identifiers for groups of related constant numbers or Strings.

Section 6.11 Method Overloading

- Method overloading allows you to create multiple methods with the same name but different signatures—that is, the parameters have different numbers and/or types, or they are listed in a different order (by type). A method's signature does not include its return type.

- When an overloaded method is called, the compiler selects the proper method by examining the number, types and order (by type) of the arguments.

Section 6.12 `Optional` Parameters

- Declaring a parameter as `Optional` allows the calling method to vary the number of arguments to pass. An `Optional` parameter specifies a default value that is assigned to the parameter if the optional argument is omitted.

- All `Optional` parameters must be placed to the right of the method's nonoptional parameters.

Section 6.13 Using the Debugger: Debugging Commands

- The **Step Into** and **Step Out** debugger commands can be used to view the code for a called method as it executes and return from the method to the caller, respectively.

- If the next statement to execute is not a method call, then the **Step Into** command has the same effect as the **Step Over** command.

- If you wish to execute several statements without repeatedly clicking the **Step Over** command, you can right click the statement where you'd like to continue step-by-step execution, then select **Run to Cursor** from the menu that appears. The debugger will execute the statements up to, but not including, that statement.

- When an application is running in the debugger, the **Start Debugging** (▶) command becomes the **Continue** command. If you click **Continue** while in break mode, the debugger will execute statements until it reaches the next breakpoint. If there aren't any, the program will simply execute until it completes or until the event handler that you're debugging finishes executing.

Terminology

Self-Review Exercises

6.1 Answer each of the following questions.

a) Programmers normally use _____.

1. programmer-defined methods
2. preexisting methods
3. both programmer-defined and preexisting methods
4. neither programmer-defined nor preexisting methods

b) The _____ statement in a Function sends a value back to the calling method.

1. Return
2. Back
3. End
4. None of the above

c) Arguments passed to a method can be _____.

1. constants
2. expressions
3. variables
4. All of the above

d) The _____ is a comma-separated list of declarations in a method header.

1. argument list
2. parameter list
3. value list
4. variable list

e) During debugging, the _____ command executes the remaining statements in the current method and returns program control to the place where the method was called.

1. **Step Into**
2. **Step Out**
3. **Step Over**
4. **Steps**

f) The debugger command _____ behaves like the **Step Over** command when the next statement to execute does not contain a method call.

1. **Step Into**
2. **Step Out**
3. **Step Over**
4. **Steps**

g) Instance variables have _____ scope.
    1. block
    2. method
    3. class
    4. None of the above

h) Variables with either method scope or block scope are called _____.
    1. instance variables
    2. local variables
    3. class variables
    4. hidden variables

i) When **Option Strict** is set to On, you must explicitly perform _____.
    1. narrowing conversions
    2. widening conversions
    3. all type conversions
    4. no conversions

j) The methods in class _____ are used to perform explicit conversions.
    1. `Strict`
    2. `Change`
    3. `Convert`
    4. `Conversion`

k) The statement _____ returns a number in the range from 8 to 300.
    1. `randomObject.Next(8, 300)`
    2. `randomObject.Next(8, 301)`
    3. `1 + randomObject.Next(8, 300)`
    4. None of the above

l) The statement _____ returns a number in the range 15 to 35.
    1. `randomObject.Next(15, 36)`
    2. `randomObject.Next(15, 35)`
    3. `10 + randomObject.Next(5, 26)`
    4. Both a and c

m) Use keyword _____ to define groups of related constants.
    1. `ReadOnly`
    2. `Enum`
    3. `Constants`
    4. `Enumeration`

n) The constants defined in an `Enum` _____.
    1. may use repeated values
    2. can be accessed using the `Enum`'s name followed by the member access operator
    3. are not required to declare a value
    4. All of the above

o) To clear the image in a `PictureBox`, set its `Image` property to _____.
    1. "" (double quotes)
    2. `Nothing`
    3. `None`
    4. `Empty`

6.2   State whether each of the following is *true* or *false*. If *false*, explain why.
a) Conversion of a data item from type `Single` to type `Double` is an example of a widening conversion.
b) Variables of type `Char` cannot be converted to type `Integer`.
c) **Option Explicit** causes the compiler to check all conversions and requires you to perform an explicit conversion for all narrowing conversions that could cause data loss or program termination.
d) When an argument is passed by value, the program makes a copy of the argument's value and passes the copy to the called method.

6.3   Give the method header for each of the following:
a) Method `Hypotenuse`, which takes two double-precision, floating-point arguments, `side1` and `side2`, and returns a double-precision, floating-point result.
b) Method `Smallest`, which takes three integers, `x`, `y` and `z`, and returns an integer.
c) Method `Instructions`, which does not take any arguments and does not return a value.
d) Method `IntegerToSingle`, which takes an integer argument, `number`, and returns a floating-point result.

6.4   Find the error in each of the following program segments and explain how the error can be corrected:

```
a) Function Sum(ByVal x As Integer, ByVal y As Integer) As Integer
       Dim result As Integer
       result = x + y
   End Function ' Sum
b) Sub Display(ByVal value As Double)
       Dim value As Double
       resultLabel.Text = Convert.ToString(value)
   End Sub ' Display
c) Sub Product()
       Dim a As Integer = 6
       Dim b As Integer = 5
       Dim result As Integer = a * b
       resultLabel.Text = "Result is " & result
       Return result
   End Sub ' Product
```

Answers to Self-Review Exercises

6.1   a) 3. b) 1. c) 4. d) 2. e) 2. f) 1. g) 3. h) 2. i) 1. j) 3. k) 2. l) 4. m) 2. n) 4. o) 2.

6.2   a True. b) False. Type Char variables can be converted to type Integer with a narrowing conversion. c) False. **Option Strict** causes the compiler to check all conversions and requires you to perform an explicit conversion for all narrowing conversions that could cause data loss or program termination. **Option Explicit** forces you to explicitly declare all variables before they're used in a program. d) True.

6.3
```
a) Function Hypotenuse(ByVal side1 As Double, _
       ByVal side2 As Double) As Double
b) Function Smallest(ByVal x As Integer, _
       ByVal y As Integer, ByVal z As Integer) As Integer
c) Sub Instructions()
d) Function IntegerToSingle(ByVal number As Integer) As Single
```

6.4
a) Error: The method is supposed to return an Integer, but does not.
   Correction: Replace the statement result = x + y with
   ```
   Return x + y
   ```
   or add the following statement at the end of the method body:
   ```
   Return result
   ```
b) Error: Parameter value is redefined in the method declaration.
   Correction: Delete the declaration **Dim value As Double**.
c) Error: The method returns a value, but is declared as a subroutine.
   Correction: Change the method to a function with return type Integer.

Quick Quiz

6.5   Answer each of the following questions.
a) A method defined with keyword Sub _____.
   1. must specify a return type   2. does not accept arguments
   3. returns a value   4. does not return a value
b) The technique of developing large applications from small, manageable pieces is known as _____.
   1. divide and conquer   2. returning a value
   3. click and mortar   4. a building-block algorithm

c) What is the difference between `Sub` and `Function` methods?

   1. `Sub` methods return values, `Function` methods do not.

   2. `Function` methods return values, `Sub` methods do not.

   3. `Sub` methods accept parameters, `Function` methods do not.

   4. `Function` methods accept parameters, `Sub` methods do not.

d) What occurs after a method call is made?

   1. Control is given to the called method. After the method is run, the application continues execution at the point where the method call was made.

   2. Control is given to the called method. After the method is run, the application continues execution with the statement after the called method's definition.

   3. The statement before the method call is executed.

   4. The application terminates.

e) `Functions` can return _____ value(s).

   1. zero   2. exactly one

   3. one or more   4. any number of

f) Which of the following must be true when making a method call?

   1. The number of arguments in the method call must match the number of parameters in the method header.

   2. The argument types must be compatible with their corresponding parameter types.

   3. Both a and b   4. None of the above

g) Which of the following statements correctly returns the variable `value` from a `Function`?

   1. `Return Dim value`   2. `Return value As Integer`

   3. `value Return`   4. `Return value`

h) The debugging command _____ executes the next statement in the application. If the next statement to execute contains a method call, the called method executes in its entirety.

   1. **Step Into**   2. **Step Out**

   3. **Step Over**   4. **Steps**

i) The first line of a method (including the keyword `Sub` or `Function`, the method name, the parameter list and possibly a return type) is known as the method _____.

   1. body   2. title

   3. caller   4. header

j) When **Option Strict** is set to `On`, variables _____.

   1. are passed by value   2. are passed by reference

   3. might need to be converted explicitly to a different type to avoid errors   4. are used only within the block in which they are declared

k) A variable declared inside a class, but outside a method, is called a(n) _____.

   1. local variable   2. hidden variable

   3. instance variable   4. constant variable

l) When **Option Strict** is _____, the implicit conversion from a `Decimal` to an `Integer` results in an error.

   1. `On`   2. `True`

   3. `Off`   4. `False`

m) Keyword _____ indicates pass-by-reference.

   1. `ByReference`   2. `ByRef`

   3. `Ref`   4. `Reference`

n) With _____, changes made to a parameter variable's value do not affect the value of the variable in the calling method.

1. **Option Strict**
2. pass-by-value
3. pass-by-reference
4. None of the above

o) Instance variables _____.

1. can be accessed by a method in the same class
2. have class scope
3. Neither of the above
4. Both of the above

p) Assigning a "smaller" type to a "larger" type is a _____ conversion.

1. narrowing
2. shortening
3. widening
4. lengthening

q) A Single value can be implicitly converted to _____ when **Option Strict** is On.

1. Integer
2. Double
3. Neither of the above
4. Both of the above

r) A Random object can generate pseudorandom numbers of type _____.

1. Integer
2. Single
3. Char
4. Both 1 and 3

s) Constant identifiers within enumerations _____ be assigned the same numeric value.

1. cannot
2. can
3. must
4. should

t) The Next method of class Random can be called using _____.

1. one argument
2. no arguments
3. two arguments
4. All of the above

u) The statement _____ assigns value a random number in the range 5–20.

1. value = randomObject.Next(5, 21)
2. value = randomObject.Next(4, 20)
3. value = randomObject.Next(5, 20)
4. value = randomObject.Next(4, 21)

v) The values returned by the methods of class Random are _____ numbers.

1. pseudorandom
2. completely random
3. ordered
4. None of the above

w) The second argument passed to class Random's Next method is _____.

1. equal to the maximum value you wish to be generated
2. equal to one more than the maximum value you wish to be generated
3. equal to one less than the maximum value you wish to be generated
4. equal to the minimum value you wish to be generated

Exercises

6.6 *(Find the Smallest and Largest Values)* Write an application that allows the user to enter three Double values, then determines and displays the smallest and largest values. Provide methods Minimum and Maximum that each receive three Double values and return a Double result.

6.7 *(Find the Smallest and Largest Values)* Class Math provides methods Min and Max to determine the smaller or larger of two values, respectively. Reimplement your methods Minimum and Maximum from Exercise 6.6 so that they use Math.Min and Math.Max, respectively.

6.8 *(Gas Pump)* A gas pump calculates the cost of gas at a local gas station. The station charges $2.69 per gallon for regular grade gas, $2.79 per gallon for special grade gas and $2.89 per gallon for super grade gas. Create an application that simulates the functionality of the gas pump. The user enters the number of gallons to purchase and clicks the desired grade (each grade is represented by a Button whose Text properties are set to **Regular**, **Special** and **Super**). Each Button's Click event handler calls a method to compute the total cost from the number of gallons entered and the selected grade. [*Note:* Use the `Text` property of each `Button` to pass the selected grade to your method.]

6.9 *(Lottery Number Generator)* A lottery commission offers four different lottery games to play: Three-number, Four-number, Five-number and Five-number + 1 lotteries. Each game has independent numbers. Develop an application that randomly picks numbers for all four games and displays the generated numbers in a GUI. Declare a method that generates a random number based on a range given, and returns the random number as a `String`. The games are played as follows:

  a) Three-number lotteries require players to choose three numbers in the range 0–9.
  b) Four-number lotteries require players to choose four numbers in the range 0–9.
  c) Five-number lotteries require players to choose five numbers in the range 1–39.
  d) Five-number + 1 lotteries require players to choose five numbers in the range 1–49 and an additional number in the range 1–42.

6.10 *(Sales Commissions)* Develop an application that calculates a salesperson's commission from the number of items sold. Assume that all items have a fixed price of $10 per unit. Use a `Select...Case` statement to implement the following sales-commission schedule:

  a) Up to 50 items sold = 6% commission
  b) Between 51 and 100 items sold = 7% commission
  c) Between 101 and 150 items sold = 8% commission
  d) More than 150 items sold = 9% commission

Create an application that inputs the number of items sold and contains a **Calculate** `Button`. When this `Button` is clicked, three methods should be called—one to calculate gross sales, one to calculate the commission percentage based on the commission schedule above and one to calculate the salesperson's earnings. Earnings are defined as gross sales multiplied by commission percentage, divided by 100 (because we're working with a percentage value). The data returned by these three methods should be displayed in the GUI.

6.11 *(Parking Charges)* A parking garage charges a $2.00 minimum fee to park for up to three hours. The garage charges an additional $0.50 per hour for each hour *or part thereof* in excess of three hours. The maximum charge for any given 24-hour period is $10.00. Assume that no car parks for longer than 24 hours at a time. Write a program that calculates and displays the parking charges for each customer who parked a car in this garage yesterday. You should enter in a `TextBox` the hours parked for each customer. The program should display the charge for the current customer. The program should use the method `CalculateCharges` to determine the charge for each customer. Use the techniques described in the chapter to read the `Double` value from a `TextBox`. [*Note:* You may need to use methods `Convert.ToDouble` and `Convert.ToDecimal` when doing calculations with the number of hours and charges, respectively.]

6.12 *(Coin Tossing)* Write an application that simulates coin tossing. Let the program toss the coin each time the user presses the **Toss** button. Count the number of times each side of the coin appears. Display the results. The program should call a separate method `Flip`, which takes no arguments and returns `False` for tails and `True` for heads. Use the head and tail images provided in the `Images` folder with this chapter's examples. [*Note:* If the program simulates the coin tossing realistically, each side of the coin should appear approximately half the time.]

6.13 *(Temperature Converter Application)* Write an application that performs temperature conversions. The application should perform two types of conversions: degrees Fahrenheit to degrees Celsius, and degrees Celsius to degrees Fahrenheit. To convert degrees Fahrenheit to degrees Celsius, use this formula:

```
celsius = (5 / 9) * (fahrenheit - 32)
```

To convert degrees Celsius to degrees Fahrenheit, use this formula:

```
fahrenheit = (9 / 5) * celsius + 32
```

Create Functions to perform each conversion, using the formulas above. The user should provide the temperature to convert. Allow the user to enter a number. Provide separate Buttons that allow the use to convert the number entered into Fahrenheit and Celsius, respectively.

6.14   *(What Does This Code Do?)* What does the following code do? Assume that this method is invoked by using Mystery(70, 80).

```
 1    Sub Mystery(ByVal number1 As Integer, ByVal number2 As Integer)
 2        Dim x As Integer
 3        Dim y As Double
 4
 5        x = number1 + number2
 6        y = x / 2
 7
 8        If y <= 60 Then
 9            resultLabel.Text = "<= 60"
10        Else
11            resultLabel.Text = "Result is " & y
12        End If
13    End Sub ' Mystery
```

6.15   *(What's Wrong With This Code?)* Find the error(s) in the following code, which should take an Integer value as a parameter and return the value of the parameter multiplied by two.

```
 1    Function TimesTwo(ByVal number As Integer) As Integer
 2        Dim result As Integer
 3
 4        result = number * 2
 5    End Function ' TimesTwo
```

6.16   *(Quiz Average Application)* Develop an application that computes a student's average quiz score for all of the quiz scores entered. The user enters each grade and presses a Button to submit it. Use instance variables to keep track of the sum of all the quiz scores entered and the number of quiz scores entered. After the user enters each grade, display the number of quizzes taken and the average for all grades entered so far.

6.17   *(What Does This Code Do?)* What is displayed in displayLabel when the user clicks the enterButton?

```
 1    Public Class ScopeTest
 2        Dim value2 As Integer = 5
 3
 4        Private Sub enterButton_Click(ByVal sender As System.Object, _
 5            ByVal e As System.EventArgs) Handles enterButton.Click
 6
 7            Dim value1 As Integer = 10
 8            Dim value2 As Integer = 3
 9
10            Test(value1)
11            displayLabel.Text = value1.ToString()
12        End Sub ' enterButton_Click
13
14        Sub Test(ByRef value1 As Integer)
15            value1 *= value2
16        End Sub ' Test
17    End Class ' ScopeTest
```

6.18   *(What's Wrong With This Code?)* Find the error(s) in the following code (the method should assign the value 14 to variable `result`). Assume that **Option Strict** is set to On.

```
I   Sub Sum()
2       Dim numberWords As String = "4"
3       Dim number As Integer = 10
4       Dim result As Integer
5
6       result = numberWords + number
7   End Sub ' Sum
```

6.19   *(Guess the Number Application)* Develop an application that generates a random number and prompts the user to guess the number. When the user clicks the **New Game** Button, the application chooses a number in the range 1 to 100 at random. The user enters guesses into the **Guess:** TextBox and clicks the **Enter** Button. If the guess is correct, the game ends, and the user can start a new game. If the guess is not correct, the application should indicate whether the guess is higher or lower than the correct number. Use instance variables for a Random object and to store the randomly generated number in the range of 1 to 100. If a guess is correct, display **Correct!** in the output Label, then disable the **Enter** Button and enable the **New Game** Button. If a guess is higher than the correct answer, display **Too high...** in the output Label. If a guess is lower than the correct answer, display **Too low...** in the output Label. For the user's convenience, give the **Guess:** TextBox the focus after each guess is processed.

Making a Difference Exercises

As computer costs decline, it becomes feasible for every student, regardless of economic circumstance, to have a computer and use it in school. This creates exciting possibilities for improving the educational experience of all students worldwide as suggested by the next two exercises. [*Note:* Check out initiatives such as the One Laptop Per Child Project (www.laptop.org). Also, research "green" laptops—and note the key "going green" characteristics of these devices. Look into the Electronic Product Environmental Assessment Tool (www.epeat.net) which can help you assess the "greenness" of desktops, notebooks and monitors to help you decide which products to purchase.]

6.20   *(Computer-Assisted Instruction)* The use of computers in education is referred to as *computer-assisted instruction* (*CAI*). Write a program that will help an elementary school student learn multiplication. Use a Random object to produce two positive one-digit integers. The program should then prompt the user with a question, such as

```
How much is 6 times 7?
```

The student then inputs the answer. Next, the program checks the student's answer. If it's correct, display the message "Very good!" and ask another multiplication question. If the answer is wrong, display the message "No. Please try again." and let the student try the same question repeatedly until the student finally gets it right. A separate function should be used to generate each new question. This function should be called once when the application begins execution and each time the user answers the question correctly.

6.21   *(Computer-Assisted Instruction: Reducing Student Fatigue)* One problem in CAI environments is student fatigue. This can be reduced by varying the computer's responses to hold the student's attention. Modify the program of Exercise 6.20 so that various comments are displayed for each answer as follows:

Possible responses to a correct answer:

```
Very good!
Excellent!
```

```
Nice work!
Keep up the good work!
```

Possible responses to an incorrect answer:

```
No. Please try again.
Wrong. Try once more.
Don't give up!
No. Keep trying.
```

Use random-number generation to choose a number from 1 to 4 that will be used to select one of the four appropriate responses to each correct or incorrect answer. Use a Select...Case statement to issue the responses.

Arrays

7

Objectives

In this chapter you'll learn:

- How arrays are used to store, sort and search lists and tables of values.

- To declare, initialize and refer to elements of arrays.

- To pass arrays to methods.

- To use the **For Each**...**Next** statement to iterate through all the elements of an array.

- To use the elements of arrays as counters.

- To declare and manipulate rectangular arrays.

7.1 Introduction

This chapter introduces basic concepts of *data structures*—collections of related data items. Arrays are simple data structures consisting only of data items of the *same* type. Arrays normally are "static" entities, in that they typically remain the same size once they're created, although they can be resized (as we show in Section 7.16. We discuss arrays that can represent lists and tables of values. We begin by creating and accessing arrays. We then perform more complex array manipulations, including summing the elements of an array, using arrays to summarize survey results, searching arrays for specific values and sorting arrays so their elements are in ascending order. We also introduce For Each...Next repetition statement and use it to process the elements of an array.

7.2 Arrays

An array is a group of variables (called **elements**) containing values that all have the *same* type. To refer to a particular element in an array, we specify the name of the array and the position number of the element to which we refer.

Figure 7.1 shows a logical representation of an integer array called c. This array contains 12 elements, any one of which can be referred to by giving the name of the array followed by the position number of the element in parentheses (). The first element in every array is the **zeroth element**. Thus, the names of array c's elements are c(0), c(1), c(2) and so on. The highest position number in array c is 11 (also called the array's **upper bound**), which is 1 less than the number of elements in the array (12).

Accessing Array Elements
The position number in parentheses more formally is called an **index** or "subscript." An index must be a nonnegative integer or integer expression. If a program uses an expression

Fig. 7.1 | Array consisting of 12 elements.

as an index, the expression is evaluated first to determine the index. For example, if variable `value1` is equal to 5, and variable `value2` is equal to 6, then the statement

```
c(value1 + value2) += 2
```

adds 2 to array element `c(11)`. The name of an array element can be used on the left side of an assignment statement to place a new value into an array element.

Let's examine array `c` (Fig. 7.1) more closely. The array's name is `c`. Its 12 elements are referred to as `c(0)` through `c(11)`—pronounced as "c sub zero" through "c sub 11," where "sub" derives from "subscript." The value of `c(0)` is –45, the value of `c(1)` is 6, the value of `c(7)` is 62 and the value of `c(11)` is 78. Values stored in arrays can be used in calculations. For example, to determine the total of the values contained in the first three elements of array `c` and then store the result in variable `sum`, we would write

```
sum = c(0) + c(1) + c(2)
```

To divide the value of `c(6)` by 2 using `Integer` division and assign the result to the variable `result`, we'd write

```
result = c(6) \ 2
```

Array Length

Every array "knows" its own length (that is, number of elements), which is determined by the array's `Length` property, as in:

```
c.Length
```

All arrays have the methods and properties of class `System.Array`.

7.3 Declaring and Allocating Arrays

The following statement can be used to declare the array in Fig. 7.1:

```
Dim c(11) As Integer
```

The parentheses that follow the variable name indicate that c is an array. Arrays can be declared to contain elements of *any* type; *every* element of the array is of that type. For example, every element of an Integer array contains an Integer value.

The number in parentheses in the array declaration helps the compiler allocate memory for the array c. In the preceding declarations, the number 11 defines the array's upper bound. Array **bounds** determine what indices can be used to access an element in the array. Here the array bounds are 0 and 11. The bound 0 is implicit in the preceding statement and is *always* the lower bound of every array. An index outside these bounds cannot be used to access elements in the array c. The actual size of the array is one larger (12) than the specified upper bound. We also can explicitly specify the array bounds, as in

```
Dim c(0 To 11) As Integer
```

The *explicit array bounds* specified in the preceding statement indicate that the lower bound of the array is 0 and the upper bound is 11. The *size* of the array is still 12. Because the lower bound *must always be 0*, we do not include "0 To" when declaring an array's bounds in this book.

Initializer Lists

You can follow an array declaration with an equal sign and an initializer list in braces ({ and }) to specify the initial values of the array's elements. For instance,

```
Dim numbers() As Integer = {1, 2, 3, 6}
```

declares and allocates an array containing *four* Integer values. The compiler determines the array bounds from the number of elements in the initializer list—you cannot specify the upper bound of the array when an initializer list is present. Visual Basic 2010 can also use local type inference to determine the type of an array with an initializer list. So, the preceding declaration can be written as:

```
Dim numbers = {1, 2, 3, 6}
```

Default Initialization

When you do not provide an initializer list, the elements in the array are initialized to the default value for the array's type—0 for numeric primitive data-type variables, False for Boolean variables and Nothing for String and other class types.

7.4 Initializing the Values in an Array

Figure 7.2 creates two five-element integer arrays and sets their element values, using an initializer list and a For...Next statement that calculates the element values, respectively. The arrays are displayed in tabular format in the outputTextBox.

Line 10 combines the declaration and initialization of array1 into one statement. The compiler implicitly allocates the array based on the number of values in the initializer list. Line 13 declares and allocates array2, whose size is determined by the expression array1.GetUpperBound(0). Array method **GetUpperBound** returns the index of the last element in the array. The value returned by method GetUpperBound is one less than the value of the array's Length property. For arrays that represent lists of values, the argument passed to GetUpperBound is 0. In this example, array1.GetUpperBound(0) returns 4, which is then used to specify the upper bound of array2, so array1 and array2 have the same upper bound (4) and the same length (5). This makes it easy to display the arrays' contents side-by-side.

```vb
1   ' Fig. 7.2: InitializeArrays.vb
2   ' Initializing array elements with an array initializer and a For...Next
3   Public Class InitalizeArrays
4      ' initialize and display two arrays' contents
5      Private Sub InitalizeArrays_Load(ByVal sender As System.Object,
6         ByVal e As System.EventArgs) Handles MyBase.Load
7
8         ' initializer list specifies the number of elements
9         ' and the value of each element
10        Dim array1() As Integer = {32, 27, 64, 18, 95}
11
12        ' allocate array2 based on length of array1
13        Dim array2(array1.GetUpperBound(0)) As Integer
14
15        ' set values in array2 by a calculation
16        For i = 0 To array2.GetUpperBound(0)
17           array2(i) = 2 + 2 * i ' generate 2, 4, 6, ..., 10
18        Next
19
20        outputTextBox.AppendText(
21           "Index " & vbTab & "Array1" & vbTab & "Array2" & vbCrLf)
22
23        ' display values for both arrays side by side
24        For i = 0 To array1.GetUpperBound(0)
25           outputTextBox.AppendText(
26              i & vbTab & array1(i) & vbTab & array2(i) & vbCrLf)
27        Next
28     End Sub ' InitalizeArrays_Load
29  End Class ' InitalizeArrays
```

outputTextBox ———

Index	Array1	Array2
0	32	2
1	27	4
2	64	6
3	18	8
4	95	10

Fig. 7.2 | Initializing array elements with an array initializer and a For...Next statement.

The For statement in lines 16–18 initializes the elements in array2 to the even integers 2, 4, 6, 8 and 10. These numbers are generated by multiplying each successive value of the loop counter by 2 and adding 2 to the product. The For statement in lines 24–27 displays the values from the two arrays side-by-side in a TextBox.

7.5 Summing the Elements of an Array

Often, the elements of an array represent a series of related values that are used in a calculation. For example, if the elements of an array represent students' exam grades, the instructor might wish to total the elements of the array, then calculate the class average for the exam. Figure 7.3 sums the values contained in a 10-element integer array named `values` and displays the result in `sumLabel`.

```
1   ' Fig. 7.3: SumArray.vb
2   ' Computing the sum of the elements in an array.
3   Public Class SumArray
4       ' use a loop to sum the elements in an array
5       Private Sub SumArray_Load(ByVal sender As System.Object,
6           ByVal e As System.EventArgs) Handles MyBase.Load
7
8           Dim values() As Integer = {85, 77, 91, 44, 65, 72, 99, 84, 95, 100}
9           Dim total As Integer = 0
10
11          ' sum the array element values
12          For i = 0 To values.GetUpperBound(0)
13              total += values(i)
14          Next
15
16          sumLabel.Text = Convert.ToString(total)
17      End Sub ' SumArray_Load
18  End Class ' SumArray
```

totalLabel —— Total of exam grades: 812 —— sumLabel

Fig. 7.3 | Computing the sum of the elements in an array.

Line 8 declares, allocates and initializes the 10-element array `values`. Line 13, in the body of the `For` statement, performs the addition. Alternatively, the values supplied as initializers for `array` could have been read into the program. For example, the user could enter the values through a `TextBox`, or the values could be read from a file on disk. Information about reading values from a file can be found in Chapter 8, Files.

7.6 Using Arrays to Analyze Survey Results

Our next example uses arrays to summarize data collected in a survey. Consider the following problem statement:

> *Twenty students were asked to rate on a scale of 1 to 5 the quality of the food in the student cafeteria, with 1 being "awful" and 5 being "excellent." Place the 20 responses in an integer array and determine the frequency of each rating.*

This is a typical array-processing application (Fig. 7.4). We wish to summarize the number of responses of each type (that is, 1–5). Array `responses` (lines 9–10) is a 20-element integer array containing the students' survey responses. The last value in the array is intentionally an incorrect response (14). When a Visual Basic program executes, array element indices are checked for validity—all indices must be greater than or equal to 0 and less than the length of the array. Any attempt to access an element outside that range of indices results in a runtime error that is known as an `IndexOutOfRangeException`. At the end of this section, we'll discuss the invalid response value, demonstrate array bounds checking and introduce Visual Basic's exception-handling mechanism, which can be used to detect and handle an IndexOutOfRangeException.

```vb
 1  ' Fig. 7.4: StudentPoll.vb
 2  ' Using arrays to summarize poll results.
 3  Public Class StudentPoll
 4     ' summarize and display poll results
 5     Private Sub StudentPoll_Load(ByVal sender As System.Object,
 6        ByVal e As System.EventArgs) Handles MyBase.Load
 7
 8        ' student response array (more typically, input at run time)
 9        Dim responses() As Integer =
10           {1, 2, 5, 4, 3, 5, 2, 1, 3, 3, 1, 4, 3, 3, 3, 2, 3, 3, 2, 14}
11
12        ' response frequency array (indices 0 through 5)
13        Dim frequency(5) As Integer
14
15        ' count frequencies
16        For answer = 0 To responses.GetUpperBound(0)
17           Try
18              frequency(responses(answer)) += 1
19           Catch ex As IndexOutOfRangeException
20              MessageBox.Show(String.Format("{0}{1}responses({2}) = {3}",
21                 ex.Message, vbCrLf, answer, responses(answer)),
22                 "IndexOutOfRangeException",
23                 MessageBoxButtons.OK, MessageBoxIcon.Error)
24           End Try
25        Next
26
27        outputTextBox.AppendText("Rating" & vbTab & "Frequency" & vbCrLf)
28
29        ' display output, ignore element 0 of frequency
30        For rating = 1 To frequency.GetUpperBound(0)
31           outputTextBox.AppendText(
32              rating & vbTab & frequency(rating) & vbCrLf)
33        Next
34     End Sub ' StudentPoll_Load
35  End Class ' StudentPoll
```

a) The MessageBox that's displayed by lines 20–23 when the application processes the responses array's last element, which causes an attempt to access a non-existent element in array frequency

b) The results of the **Student Poll** application summarize only 19 of the 20 values in the responses array, because the invalid value **14** was ignored

Fig. 7.4 | Using arrays to summarize poll results.

The *frequency* Array

We use the *six-element* array frequency (line 13) to count the number of occurrences of each response. Each element is used as a counter for one of the possible types of survey responses—frequency(1) counts the number of students who rated the food as 1, frequency(2) counts the number of students who rated the food as 2, and so on. The results are displayed in outputTextBox.

Summarizing the Results

The For statement (lines 16–25) reads the responses from the array responses one at a time and increments one of the five counters in the frequency array (frequency(1) to frequency(5); we ignore frequency(0) because the survey responses are limited to the range 1–5). The key statement in the loop appears in line 18. This statement increments the appropriate frequency counter as determined by the value of responses(answer).

Let's step through the first few iterations of the For statement:

- When the counter answer is 0, responses(answer) is the value of responses(0) (that is, 1—see line 10). In this case, frequency(responses(answer)) is interpreted as frequency(1), and the counter frequency(1) is incremented by one. To evaluate the expression, we begin with the value in the *innermost* set of parentheses (answer, currently 0). The value of answer is plugged into the expression, and the next set of parentheses (responses(answer)) is evaluated. That value is used as the index for the frequency array to determine which counter to increment (in this case, frequency(1)).

- The next time through the loop answer is 1, responses(answer) is the value of responses(1) (that is, 2—see line 10), so frequency(responses(answer)) is interpreted as frequency(2), causing frequency(2) to be incremented.

- When answer is 2, responses(answer) is the value of responses(2) (that is, 5—see line 10), so frequency(responses(answer)) is interpreted as frequency(5), causing frequency(5) to be incremented, and so on.

Regardless of the number of responses processed in the survey, only a six-element array (in which we ignore element zero) is required to summarize the results, because all the correct response values are between 1 and 5, and the index values for a six-element array are 0–5. In the output in Fig. 7.4, the frequency column summarizes only 19 of the 20 values in the responses array—the last element of the array responses contains an incorrect response that was not counted.

Exception Handling: Processing the Incorrect Response

An exception indicates a problem that occurs while a program executes. The name "exception" suggests that the problem occurs infrequently—if the "rule" is that a statement normally executes correctly, then the problem represents the "exception to the rule." Exception handling enables you to create fault-tolerant programs that can resolve (or handle) exceptions. In many cases, this allows a program to continue executing as if no problems were encountered. For example, the **Student Poll** application still displays results (Fig. 7.4(b)), even though one of the responses was out of range. More severe problems might prevent a program from continuing normal execution, instead requiring the program to notify the user of the problem, then terminate. When the runtime or a method detects a problem, such as an invalid array index or an invalid method argument, it throws an exception—that is, an exception occurs.

The Try Statement

To handle an exception, place any code that might throw an exception in a Try statement (lines 17–24). The Try block (lines 17–18) contains the code that might *throw* an exception, and the Catch block (lines 19–23) contains the code that *handles* the exception if one occurs. You can have many Catch blocks to handle different types of exceptions that might be thrown in the corresponding Try block. When line 18 correctly increments an element of the frequency array, lines 19–23 are ignored. The End Try keywords terminate a Try statement.

Executing the Catch Block

When the program encounters the value 14 in the responses array, it attempts to add 1 to frequency(14), which does not exist—the frequency array has only six elements. Because array bounds checking is performed at execution time, line 18 throws an IndexOutOfRangeException to notify the program of this problem. At this point the Try block terminates and the Catch block begins executing—if you declared any variables in the Try block, they're now out of scope and are not accessible in the Catch block.

The Catch block declares an exception parameter (ex) and a type (IndexOutOfRange-Exception)—the Catch block can handle exceptions of the specified type. Inside the Catch block, you can use the parameter's identifier to interact with a caught exception object.

Entering a Try Statement in the Code Editor

When you create a Try statement in your own code, you begin by typing Try and pressing *Enter*. The IDE then generates the following code:

```
Try

Catch ex As Exception

End Try
```

which can catch *any* type of exception thrown in the Try block. We changed Exception to IndexOutOfRangeException—the type of exception that might occur in line 18.

Message Property of the Exception Parameter

When lines 19–23 *catch* the exception, the program displays a MessageBox indicating the problem that occurred. Line 21 uses the exception object's Message property to get the error message that is stored in the exception object and display it in the MessageBox. Once the user dismisses the MessageBox, the exception is considered handled and the program continues with the next statement after the End Try keywords. In this example, Next (line 25) causes the program to continue with line 16. Chapter 16 includes a detailed treatment of exception handling.

7.7 Die-Rolling Program with an Array of Counters

In Chapter 6, we used a series of counters in our die-rolling program to track the number of occurrences of each face on a six-sided die. We indicated that we can do what we did in

Fig. 6.14 in a more elegant way than using a `Select...Case` statement to write the dice-rolling program. An array version of this application is shown in Fig. 7.5. This new version uses the same GUI as the application in Fig. 6.14.

```vb
 1   ' Fig. 7.5: DiceStatistics.vb
 2   ' Rolling 12 dice with frequency chart.
 3   Public Class DiceStatistics
 4      Dim randomObject As New Random() ' generates random numbers
 5      Dim frequency(6) As Integer ' create 7-element array
 6
 7      ' display result of twelve rolls
 8      Private Sub rollButton_Click(ByVal sender As System.Object,
 9         ByVal e As System.EventArgs) Handles rollButton.Click
10
11         ' display 12 randomly selected die faces
12         DisplayDie(die1PictureBox)
13         DisplayDie(die2PictureBox)
14         DisplayDie(die3PictureBox)
15         DisplayDie(die4PictureBox)
16         DisplayDie(die5PictureBox)
17         DisplayDie(die6PictureBox)
18         DisplayDie(die7PictureBox)
19         DisplayDie(die8PictureBox)
20         DisplayDie(die9PictureBox)
21         DisplayDie(die10PictureBox)
22         DisplayDie(die11PictureBox)
23         DisplayDie(die12PictureBox)
24
25         Dim total As Double = 0
26
27         ' total the die faces (used in percentage calculations)
28         For i = 1 To frequency.GetUpperBound(0)
29            total += frequency(i)
30         Next
31
32         ' display frequencies of faces
33         displayTextBox.Text =
34            "Face" & vbTab & "Frequency" & vbTab & "Percent" & vbCrLf
35
36         ' output frequency values--ignore element 0
37         For i = 1 To frequency.GetUpperBound(0)
38            displayTextBox.Text &= i & vbTab & frequency(i) &
39               vbTab & vbTab & String.Format("{0:P2}",
40               frequency(i) / total) & vbCrLf
41         Next
42      End Sub ' rollButton_Click
43
44      ' display a single die image
45      Sub DisplayDie(ByVal diePictureBox As PictureBox)
46         Dim face As Integer = randomObject.Next(1, 7)
47
```

Fig. 7.5 | Rolling 12 dice with frequency chart. (Part 1 of 2.)

```
48          ' retrieve specific die image from resources
49          Dim pictureResource = My.Resources.ResourceManager.GetObject(
50              String.Format("die{0}", face))
51
52          ' convert pictureResource to image type and load into PictureBox
53          diePictureBox.Image = CType(pictureResource, Image)
54
55          frequency(face) += 1 ' increment appropriate frequency counter
56      End Sub ' DisplayDie
57  End Class ' DiceStatistics
```

Fig. 7.5 | Rolling 12 dice with frequency chart. (Part 2 of 2.)

Lines 61–74 of Fig. 6.14 are replaced by line 55 of Fig. 7.5, which uses face's value as the index for array frequency to determine which element should be incremented during each iteration of the loop. The random number calculation at line 46 produces numbers from 1 to 6 (the values for a six-sided die); thus, the frequency array must have seven elements so we can use the index values 1–6. We ignore frequency element 0. Lines 37–41 replace lines 35–46 from Fig. 6.14. We can loop through array frequency; therefore, we do not have to enumerate each line of text to display in the TextBox, as we did in Fig. 6.14. Recall from Section 6.9 that the more you roll the dice, the closer each percentage should get to 16.66%, as shown in Fig. 7.5(b).

7.8 Case Study: Flag Quiz

Let's create an application that tests a student's knowledge of the flags of various countries. Consider the following problem statement:

A geography instructor would like to quiz students on their knowledge of the flags of various countries. The instructor has asked you to write an application that displays a flag and allows the student to select the corresponding country from a list. The application should inform the user of whether the answer is correct and display the next flag. The application should display a flag randomly chosen from those of Australia, Brazil, China, Italy, Russia, South Africa, Spain and the United States. When the application executes, a given flag should be displayed only once.

The application uses arrays to store information. One array stores the country names. Another stores Boolean values that help us determine whether a particular country's flag has already been displayed, so that no flag is displayed more than once during a quiz.

Flag Quiz GUI

Figure 7.6 shows the application's GUI. The flag images should be added to the project as image resources—you learned how to do this in Section 6.9. The images are located in the Images folder with this chapter's examples. This application introduces the **ComboBox** control, which presents options in a drop-down list that opens when you click the down arrow at the right side of the control. A ComboBox combines features of a TextBox and a ListBox. You can click the down arrow to display a list of predefined items. If you choose an item from this list, that item is displayed in the ComboBox. If the list contains more items than the drop-down list can display at one time, a vertical scrollbar appears. You may also type into the ComboBox control to locate an item. In this application, the user selects an answer from the ComboBox, then clicks the **Submit** Button to check if the selected country name is correct for the currently displayed flag.

Fig. 7.6 | GUI for the **Flag Quiz** application.

ComboBox property **DropDownStyle** determines the ComboBox's appearance. Value **DropDownList** specifies that the ComboBox is *not editable* (you cannot type text in its TextBox). In this ComboBox style, if you press the key that corresponds to the first letter of an item in the ComboBox, that item is selected and displayed in the ComboBox. If multiple items start with the same letter, pressing the key repeatedly cycles through the corresponding items. Set the ComboBox's DropDownStyle property to DropDownList. Then, set the ComboBox's **MaxDropDownItems** property to 4, so that the drop-down list displays a maximum of four items at one time. We do this to demonstrate that a vertical scrollbar is added to the drop-down list to allow users to scroll through the remaining items. We show how to programmatically add items to the ComboBox shortly. Figure 7.7 shows the application's code.

```vb
 1  ' Fig. 7.7: FlagQuiz.vb
 2  ' Using an array of Strings to represent quiz answers.
 3  Public Class FlagQuiz
 4      ' String array stores country names
 5      Dim countries() As String = {"Australia", "Brazil", "China", "Italy",
 6          "Russia", "South Africa", "Spain", "United States"}
 7      Dim randomObject As New Random()
 8
 9      ' Boolean array tracks which flags have been displayed
10      Dim used(countries.GetUpperBound(0)) As Boolean ' all False by default
11
12      Dim count As Integer = 1 ' number of flags shown
13      Dim country As String ' current flag's country
```

Fig. 7.7 | Using an array of Strings to represent quiz answers. (Part 1 of 3.)

```vbnet
14
15        ' handles Flag Quiz Form's Load event
16        Private Sub FlagQuizForm_Load(ByVal sender As System.Object,
17           ByVal e As System.EventArgs) Handles MyBase.Load
18
19           ' display country names in ComboBox
20           countriesComboBox.DataSource = countries
21
22           DisplayFlag() ' display first flag in PictureBox
23        End Sub ' FlagQuizForm_Load
24
25        ' handles Submit Button's Click event
26        Private Sub submitButton_Click(ByVal sender As System.Object,
27           ByVal e As System.EventArgs) Handles submitButton.Click
28
29           ' verify user's answer
30           If countriesComboBox.Text = country Then
31              MessageBox.Show("Correct!", "Correct Answer")
32           Else
33              MessageBox.Show("The correct answer is " & country,
34                 "Incorrect Answer")
35           End If
36
37           ' inform user if quiz is over
38           If count >= countries.Length Then ' quiz is over
39              countriesComboBox.Enabled = False
40              submitButton.Enabled = False
41           Else ' quiz is not over
42              DisplayFlag() ' display next flag
43              countriesComboBox.SelectedIndex = 0 ' select first ComboBox entry
44              count += 1 ' update number of flags shown
45           End If
46        End Sub ' submitButton_Click
47
48        ' return an unused random number
49        Function GetUniqueRandomNumber() As Integer
50           Dim randomNumber As Integer
51
52           Do ' generate random numbers until unused flag is found
53              randomNumber = randomObject.Next(0, used.Length)
54           Loop Until used(randomNumber) = False
55
56           used(randomNumber) = True ' indicate that flag has been used
57           Return randomNumber ' return index for new flag
58        End Function ' GetUniqueRandomNumber
59
60        ' display random flag in PictureBox
61        Sub DisplayFlag()
62           ' unique index ensures that a flag is used no more than once
63           Dim randomNumber As Integer = GetUniqueRandomNumber()
64
65           country = countries(randomNumber) ' get country name
66
```

Fig. 7.7 | Using an array of Strings to represent quiz answers. (Part 2 of 3.)

```
67          ' get image resource--remove spaces from country name
68          Dim pictureResource = My.Resources.ResourceManager.GetObject(
69             country.Replace(" ", ""))
70          flagPictureBox.Image = CType(pictureResource, Image) ' display flag
71       End Sub ' DisplayFlag
72    End Class ' FlagQuiz
```

a) Selecting the correct answer   b) Submitting the answer   c) Confiming correct response

d) Submitting an incorrect answer   e) Showing correct answer   f) Quiz over; controls disabled.

Fig. 7.7 | Using an array of `Strings` to represent quiz answers. (Part 3 of 3.)

Instance Variables

Lines 5–6 create and initialize the array of `Strings` called `countries`. Each element is a `String` containing the name of a country. The compiler determines the size of the array (in this case, eight elements) based on the number of items in the initializer list. Line 7 creates the `Random` object that is used in method `GetUniqueRandomNumber` (lines 49–58). Line 10 creates the `Boolean` array `used`, which helps us determine which of the countries have already been displayed in the quiz. We specify the upper bound of the array `used` by getting the upper bound of the array `countries`. By default, each of array `used`'s elements is set to `False`. Variable `count` (line 12) keeps track of the number of flags displayed so far, and variable `country` (line 13) stores the name of the country that corresponds to the currently displayed flag.

Method `FlagQuiz_Load`

When the application loads, method `FlagQuiz_Load` executes. `ComboBox` property **DataSource** (line 20) specifies the source of the items displayed in the `ComboBox`. In this case, the source is array `countries`. Line 22 calls method `DisplayFlag` (declared in lines 61–71) to display the first flag.

Method `submitButton_Click`

When you click the **Submit** Button, method `submitButton_Click` (lines 26–46) determines whether the selected answer is correct and displays an appropriate message (lines 30–35). If all the flags have been displayed, line 38 indicates that the quiz is over and lines 39–

40 disable the ComboBox and Button. Otherwise, the quiz continues. Line 42 calls method DisplayFlag to display the next flag. Line 43 uses ComboBox property **SelectedIndex** to select the item at index 0 in the ComboBox—ComboBoxes are indexed from 0 like arrays.

Method *GetUniqueRandomNumber*
Method GetUniqueRandomNumber (lines 49–58) uses a Do...Loop Until statement to choose a random number in the bounds of the used array. The loop performs this task until the value at used(randomNumber) is False, indicating that the corresponding country's flag has not yet been displayed. Line 56 marks the flag as used. Line 57 returns the random number.

Method *DisplayFlag*
Method DisplayFlag (lines 61–71) calls method GetUniqueRandomNumber (line 63) to determine which flag to display. Line 65 uses that value as the index into the countries array and stores the current country's name in the variable country. This variable is used in method submitButton_Click to determine whether the selected answer is correct. Lines 68–70 get the corresponding flag's image resource and display it in the flagPictureBox. Some of the country names in the countries array contain spaces. However, the image resource names do not. To use a country name to load the appropriate image resource, we remove any spaces in the country name by calling String method **Replace** on country. The first argument to this method is the substring that should be replaced throughout the original String and the second argument is the replacement substring. In this case, we're replacing each space with the empty String ("").

7.9 Passing an Array to a Method
To pass an array argument to a method, specify the name of the array without using parentheses. For example, if array hourlyTemperatures has been declared as

```
Dim hourlyTemperatures(24) As Integer
```

the method call

```
DisplayDayData(hourlyTemperatures)
```

passes array hourlyTemperatures to method DisplayDayData.

Every array object "knows" its own upper bound (that is, the value returned by the method GetUpperBound), so when you pass an array object to a method, you do not need to pass the upper bound of the array as a separate argument.

For a method to receive an array through a method call, the method's parameter list must specify that an array will be received. For example, the method header for Display-DayData might be written as

```
Sub DisplayDayData(ByVal temperatureData() As Integer)
```

indicating that DisplayDayData expects to receive an Integer array in parameter temperatureData. Arrays *always* are passed by reference, so when you pass an array to method DisplayDayData, it can change the original array's element values.

Although entire arrays are always passed by reference, individual array elements can be passed by value or by reference like simple variables of that type. For instance, array element values of primitive types, such as `Integer`, can be passed either by value or by reference, depending on the method definition. To pass an array element to a method, use the indexed name of the array element as an argument in the method call. Figure 7.8 demonstrates the difference between passing an entire array and passing an array element. The results are displayed in `outputTextBox`.

```
1   ' Fig. 7.8: PassArray.vb
2   ' Passing arrays and individual array elements to methods.
3   Public Class PassArray
4      ' invoke methods to demonstrate passing arrays
5      ' and array elements to methods
6      Private Sub PassArray_Load(ByVal sender As System.Object,
7         ByVal e As System.EventArgs) Handles MyBase.Load
8
9         Dim array1() As Integer = {1, 2, 3, 4, 5}
10
11        outputTextBox.AppendText(
12           "EFFECTS OF PASSING AN ENTIRE ARRAY BY REFERENCE:" & vbCrLf &
13           vbCrLf & "The values of the original array are:" & vbCrLf)
14
15        ' display original elements of array1
16        For i = 0 To array1.GetUpperBound(0)
17           outputTextBox.AppendText(vbTab & array1(i))
18        Next
19
20        ModifyArray(array1) ' array is passed by reference
21        outputTextBox.AppendText(vbCrLf &
22           "The values of the modified array are:" & vbCrLf)
23
24        ' display modified elements of array1
25        For i = 0 To array1.GetUpperBound(0)
26           outputTextBox.AppendText(vbTab & array1(i))
27        Next
28
29        outputTextBox.AppendText(vbCrLf & vbCrLf &
30           "EFFECTS OF PASSING AN ARRAY ELEMENT BY VALUE:" & vbCrLf &
31           vbCrLf & "array1(3) before ModifyElementByVal: " &
32           array1(3) & vbCrLf)
33
34        ModifyElementByVal(array1(3)) ' array element passed by value
35        outputTextBox.AppendText("array1(3) after ModifyElementByVal: " &
36           array1(3) & vbCrLf)
37        outputTextBox.AppendText(vbCrLf & "EFFECTS OF PASSING AN " &
38           "ARRAY ELEMENT BY REFERENCE: " & vbCrLf & vbCrLf &
39           "array1(3) before ModifyElementByRef: " & array1(3) & vbCrLf)
40
41        ModifyElementByRef(array1(3)) ' array element passed by reference
42        outputTextBox.AppendText("array1(3) after ModifyElementByRef: " &
43           array1(3))
44     End Sub ' PassArray_Load
45
```

Fig. 7.8 | Passing arrays and individual array elements to methods. (Part 1 of 2.)

```
46     ' method modifies array it receives (note ByVal)
47     Sub ModifyArray(ByVal arrayParameter() As Integer)
48        For j = 0 To arrayParameter.GetUpperBound(0)
49           arrayParameter(j) *= 2 ' double the array element
50        Next
51     End Sub ' ModifyArray
52
53     ' method modifies integer passed to it
54     ' original is not modified (note ByVal)
55     Sub ModifyElementByVal(ByVal element As Integer)
56        outputTextBox.AppendText(
57           "Value received in ModifyElementByVal: " & element & vbCrLf)
58        element *= 2 ' double the array element
59        outputTextBox.AppendText(
60           "Value calculated in ModifyElementByVal: " & element & vbCrLf)
61     End Sub ' ModifyElementByVal
62
63     ' method modifies integer passed to it
64     ' original is modified (note ByRef)
65     Sub ModifyElementByRef(ByRef element As Integer)
66        outputTextBox.AppendText(
67           "Value received in ModifyElementByRef: " & element & vbCrLf)
68        element *= 2 ' double the array element
69        outputTextBox.AppendText(
70           "Value calculated in ModifyElementByRef: " & element & vbCrLf)
71     End Sub ' ModifyElementByRef
72  End Class ' PassArray
```

outputTextBox ——

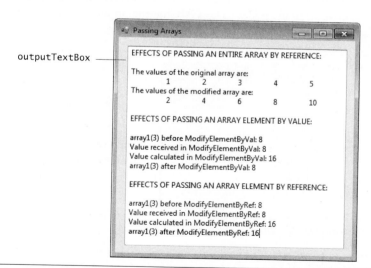

Fig. 7.8 | Passing arrays and individual array elements to methods. (Part 2 of 2.)

The For...Next statement in lines 16–18 displays the five elements of integer array array1 (line 9). Line 20 passes array1 to method ModifyArray (lines 47–51), which then multiplies each element by 2 (line 49). To illustrate that array1's elements were modified in the called method (that is, as enabled by passing by reference), the For...Next statement in lines 25–27 displays the five elements of array1. As the output indicates, the elements of array1 are indeed modified by ModifyArray.

Lines 29–32 display the value of array1(3) before the call to ModifyElementByVal. Line 34 invokes method ModifyElementByVal (lines 55–61) and passes array1(3). When array1(3) is passed by value, the Integer value in position 3 of array array1 (now an 8) is copied and is passed to method ModifyElementByVal, where it becomes the value of parameter element. Method ModifyElementByVal then multiplies element by 2 (line 58). The parameter element of ModifyElementByVal is a local variable that is destroyed when the method terminates. Thus, when control is returned to Main, the unmodified value of array1(3) is displayed.

Lines 37–43 demonstrate the effects of method ModifyElementByRef (lines 65–71). This method performs the same calculation as ModifyElementByVal, multiplying element by 2. In this case, array1(3) is passed by reference, meaning that the value of array1(3) displayed (lines 42–43) is the same as the value calculated in the method (that is, the original value in the caller is modified by the called method).

7.10 For Each...Next Repetition Statement

The **For Each...Next** repetition statement iterates through the values in a data structure, such as an array, without using a loop counter. For Each...Next behaves like a For...Next statement that iterates through the range of indices from 0 to the value returned by Get-UpperBound(0). Instead of a counter, For Each...Next uses a variable to represent the value of each element.

In this example, we'll use the For Each...Next statement to determine the minimum value in a one-dimensional array of grades. The GUI for the application is shown in Fig. 7.9 and the code is shown in Fig. 7.10.

Fig. 7.9 | GUI for the **Find the Smallest** application.

```
1   ' Fig. 7.10: FindTheSmallest.vb
2   ' Using a For Each...Next loop to find the smallest value in an array.
3   Public Class FindTheSmallest
4       Dim gradesArray(9) As Integer ' create 10-element array
5       Dim randomNumber As New Random()
6
```

Fig. 7.10 | Using a For Each...Next loop to find the smallest value in an array. (Part 1 of 2.)

```
 7      ' creates random generated numbers
 8     Private Sub createGradesButton_Click(ByVal sender As System.Object,
 9        ByVal e As System.EventArgs) Handles createGradesButton.Click
10
11        gradesListBox.Items.Clear() ' clear gradesListBox
12        smallestGradeResultLabel.Text = String.Empty ' clear Label
13
14        ' create 10 random numbers and append to output
15        For i = 0 To gradesArray.GetUpperBound(0)
16           gradesArray(i) = randomNumber.Next(100)
17           gradesListBox.Items.Add(gradesArray(i))
18        Next
19
20        findSmallestButton.Enabled = True ' enable Find Smallest button
21     End Sub ' createGradesButton_Click
22
23     ' sorts randomly generated numbers
24     Private Sub findSmallestButton_Click(ByVal sender As System.Object,
25        ByVal e As System.EventArgs) Handles findSmallestButton.Click
26
27        Dim lowGrade As Integer = 100 ' start with the maximum grade value
28
29        ' use For Each...Next to find the minimum grade
30        For Each grade In gradesArray
31           If grade < lowGrade Then
32              lowGrade = grade ' current grade is the lowest one so far
33           End If
34        Next
35
36        smallestGradeResultLabel.Text = Convert.ToString(lowGrade)
37        findSmallestButton.Enabled = False ' disable Find Smallest button
38     End Sub ' findSmallestButton_Click
39  End Class ' FindTheSmallest
```

Fig. 7.10 | Using a For Each...Next loop to find the smallest value in an array. (Part 2 of 2.)

When the user clicks the **Create Grades** Button, method createGradesButton_Click (lines 8–21) creates 10 random grade values in the range 0–99 and places them in the gradesListBox. When the user clicks the **Find Smallest** Button, method findSmallestButton_Click (lines 24–38) uses a For Each...Next statement to find the lowest grade.

The header of the For Each repetition statement (line 30) specifies an Integer variable (grade) and an array (gradesArray). The type of variable grade is determined from the type of the elements in gradesArray, though you can also declare the variable's type explicitly as in

> **For Each** grade **As Integer In** gradesArray

The For Each statement iterates through all the elements in gradesArray, sequentially assigning each value to variable grade. The values are compared to variable lowGrade (line 31), which stores the lowest grade in the array.

The repetition of the For Each...Next statement begins with the element whose index is zero, iterating through all the elements. In this case, grade takes on the successive values that are stored in gradesArray and displayed in the gradesListBox. When all the grades have been processed, lowGrade is displayed (line 36). Although many array calculations are handled best with a counter, For Each is useful when you wish to process *all* of an array's elements and do not need to access the index values in the loop's body.

7.11 Sorting an Array with Method Sort of Class Array

Sorting data (that is, arranging the data in ascending or descending order) is one of the most popular computing applications. For example, a bank sorts all checks by account number, so that it can prepare individual bank statements at the end of each month. Telephone companies sort their lists of accounts by last name and, within last-name listings, by first name, to make it easy to find phone numbers.

Arrays have the methods and properties of class Array in namespace System. Class Array provides methods for creating, modifying, sorting and searching arrays. By default, Array method **Sort** sorts an array's elements into *ascending* order. The next application (GUI in Fig. 7.11 and code in Fig. 7.12) demonstrates method Sort by sorting an array of 10 randomly generated elements (which may contain duplicates).

Fig. 7.11 | GUI for the **Sort Array** application.

```
1    ' Fig. 7.12: SortArray.vb
2    ' Sorting an array with method Array.Sort.
3    Public Class SortArray
```

Fig. 7.12 | Sorting an array with method Array.Sort. (Part 1 of 2.)

```
 4      Dim integerArray(9) As Integer ' create 10-element array
 5      Dim randomNumber As New Random()
 6
 7      ' creates random generated numbers
 8      Private Sub createDataButton_Click(ByVal sender As System.Object,
 9         ByVal e As System.EventArgs) Handles createDataButton.Click
10
11         originalValuesListBox.Items.Clear() ' clear originalValuesListBox
12         sortedValuesListBox.Items.Clear() ' clear sortedValuesListBox
13
14         ' create 10 random numbers and append to output
15         For i = 0 To integerArray.GetUpperBound(0)
16            integerArray(i) = randomNumber.Next(100)
17            originalValuesListBox.Items.Add(integerArray(i))
18         Next
19
20         sortButton.Enabled = True ' enable Sort button
21      End Sub ' createDataButton_Click
22
23      ' sorts randomly generated numbers
24      Private Sub sortButton_Click(ByVal sender As System.Object,
25         ByVal e As System.EventArgs) Handles sortButton.Click
26
27         Array.Sort(integerArray) ' sort array integerArray
28
29         ' creates string with sorted numbers
30         For i = 0 To integerArray.GetUpperBound(0)
31            sortedValuesListBox.Items.Add(integerArray(i))
32         Next
33
34         sortButton.Enabled = False ' disable Sort button
35      End Sub ' sortButton_Click
36   End Class ' SortArray
```

Fig. 7.12 | Sorting an array with method Array.Sort. (Part 2 of 2.)

Method createDataButton_Click (lines 8–21) assigns 10 random values to the elements of integerArray and displays the contents of the array in the originalValuesTextBox. Method sortButton_Click (lines 24–35) sorts integerArray by calling Array.Sort, which takes an array as its argument and sorts the elements in the array in ascending order.

Sorting in Descending Order

To sort an array in descending order, first call method Sort to sort the array, then call Array.**Reverse** with the array as an argument to reverse the order of the elements in the array. Exercise 7.14 asks you to modify this program to display an array's values in both ascending and descending order.

7.12 Searching an Array with Linear Search

Often it's necessary to determine whether an array contains a value that matches a certain **key value**. The process of locating a particular element value in an array is called **searching**. In this section and the next, we use two searching techniques—the simple **linear search** and the more efficient (but more complex) **binary search**.

Our next program (Fig. 7.14) demonstrates a linear search—implemented at lines 39–48—to search a 20-element array that is filled with random values created when the user clicks the **Create Data** Button. The loop at lines 43–48 compares each element of an array with a **search key** (stored in variable searchKey). The user types the search key in the **Enter integer search key:** TextBox and clicks the **Search** Button to start the search. If the search key is found, the index of the matching element is stored in variable index (line 45) and the loop terminates (line 46). If the search key is not found, index will still be –1 (its initial value). The value –1 is a good choice to indicate that the search key is not found because –1 not a valid index number. If the elements of the array being searched are unordered, it's just as likely that the value will be found in the front half of the array as in the back half, so on average the method will have to compare the search key with half the elements of the array. The GUI for this application is shown in Fig. 7.13 and the code is shown in Fig. 7.14.

Other Array Methods for Searching Arrays

Class Array provides a method IndexOf that performs the same operation as the linear search in Fig. 7.14. Class Array also provides methods such as Find and FindAll, which search the array for element(s) that meet certain criteria. The criteria can be more general than simply searching for an element. For instance, the FindAll method allows you to search for all elements in an Integer array that have values in a specified range.

Fig. 7.13 | GUI for the **Linear Search Test** application.

```vb
 1    ' Fig. 7.14: LinearSearchTest.vb
 2    ' Linear search of an array.
 3    Public Class LinearSearchTest
 4       Dim searchData(19) As Integer ' create 20-element array
 5       Dim randomNumber As New Random()
 6
 7       ' create random data and display it
 8       Private Sub createDataButton_Click(ByVal sender As System.Object,
 9          ByVal e As System.EventArgs) Handles createDataButton.Click
10
11          ' create random array elements
12          For i = 0 To searchData.GetUpperBound(0)
13             searchData(i) = randomNumber.Next(1000)
14          Next
15
16          ' display array elements
17          dataListBox.Items.Add("Index" & vbTab & "Value")
18
19          For i = 0 To searchData.GetUpperBound(0)
20             dataListBox.Items.Add(i & vbTab & searchData(i))
21          Next
22
23          searchKeyTextBox.Clear() ' clear search key text box
24          searchButton.Enabled = True ' enable search button
25       End Sub ' createDataButton_Click
26
27       ' search array for search key
28       Private Sub searchButton_Click(ByVal sender As System.Object,
29          ByVal e As System.EventArgs) Handles searchButton.Click
30
31          ' if search key text box is empty, display
32          ' message and exit method
33          If searchKeyTextBox.Text = String.Empty Then
34             MessageBox.Show("You must enter a search key.", "Error",
35                MessageBoxButtons.OK, MessageBoxIcon.Error)
36             Exit Sub ' terminates the method call immediately
37          End If
38
39          Dim searchKey As Integer = Convert.ToInt32(searchKeyTextBox.Text)
40          Dim index As Integer = -1 ' stores index of found value (or -1)
41
42          ' statement iterates linearly through array
43          For i = 0 To searchData.GetUpperBound(0)
44             If searchData(i) = searchKey Then
45                index = i
46                Exit For ' terminate loop because value was found
47             End If
48          Next
49
50          If index >= 0 Then
51             resultLabel.Text = "Found Value in index " & index
52          Else
```

Fig. 7.14 | Linear search of an array. (Part 1 of 2.)

```
53              resultLabel.Text = "Value Not Found"
54          End If
55      End Sub ' searchButton_Click
56  End Class ' LinearSearchTest
```

Fig. 7.14 | Linear search of an array. (Part 2 of 2.)

7.13 Searching a Sorted Array with Array Method BinarySearch

Linear searches work well for small or unsorted arrays, but, for large unsorted arrays, linear searching is inefficient. If the array is *sorted*, the high-speed binary search technique can be used with class Array's **BinarySearch method**. Our program that demonstrates method BinarySearch is nearly identical to the one in Fig. 7.14, so we show only the differences here. The complete code is located in the Fig07_15 folder with this chapter's examples. The sample outputs are shown in Fig. 7.15. The GUI for this application is identical to the one in Fig. 7.13.

As in Fig. 7.14, the user clicks the **Create Data** Button to generate random values. For method BinarySearch to perform correctly, the array must have been sorted. Method createDataButton_Click uses the following call to Array method Sort before displaying the values in the dataListBox:

```
Array.Sort(searchData) ' sort array to enable binary searching
```

In method searchButton_Click, we replaced lines 40–48 of Fig. 7.14 with

```
Dim index As Integer = Array.BinarySearch(searchData, searchKey)
```

which uses Array method BinarySearch to perform a binary search for a key value. The method receives two arguments—the *sorted* integer array searchData (the array to search) and integer `searchKey` (the search key). If the value is found, method `BinarySearch` returns the index of the search key; otherwise, it returns a negative number.

Fig. 7.15 | Binary search of an array.

7.14 Rectangular Arrays

The arrays we've studied so far are **one-dimensional** arrays—they contain a list of values and use only *one* index to access each element. In this section, we introduce **multidimensional** arrays, which require two or more indices to identify particular elements. We concentrate on **two-dimensional** arrays—also known as **rectangular arrays**—which are often used to represent **tables** of values consisting of data arranged in **rows** and **columns** (Fig. 7.16). Each row is the same size, and each column is the same size (hence the term

Fig. 7.16 | Two-dimensional array with three rows and four columns.

"rectangular"). To identify a particular table element, we specify two indices—by convention, the first identifies the element's row, the second the element's column. Figure 7.16 illustrates a rectangular array, a, containing three rows and four columns. A rectangular array with *m* rows and *n* columns is called an ***m*-by-*n* array**; the array in Fig. 7.16 is a 3-by-4 array.

Every element in array a is identified in Fig. 7.16 by an element name of the form a(i, j), where a is the name of the array and i and j are the indices that uniquely identify the row and column, respectively, of each element in array a. Array indices are zero based, so the names of the elements in row 0 all have a *first* index of 0; the names of the elements in column 3 all have a *second* index of 3.

Declaring and Initializing Rectangular Arrays

A two-dimensional rectangular array numbers with two rows and two columns can be declared and initialized with

```
Dim numbers(1, 1) As Integer ' numbers in a 2 by 2 array
numbers(0, 0) = 1 ' leftmost element in row 0
numbers(0, 1) = 2 ' rightmost element in row 0
numbers(1, 0) = 3 ' leftmost element in row 1
numbers(1, 1) = 4 ' rightmost element in row 1
```

Alternatively, the initialization can be written on one line, as shown with and without local type inference below:

```
Dim numbers = {{1, 2}, {3, 4}}
Dim numbers(,) As Integer = {{1, 2}, {3, 4}}
```

The values are grouped by row in braces, with 1 and 2 initializing numbers(0, 0) and numbers(0, 1), respectively, and 3 and 4 initializing numbers(1, 0) and numbers(1, 1), respectively. The compiler determines the number of rows by counting the number of subinitializer lists (represented by the sets of data in curly braces) in the main initializer list. Then the compiler determines the number of columns in each row by counting the number of initializer values in the subinitializer list for that row. The subinitializer lists must have the same number of elements for each row.

Manipulating a Rectangular Array

The program in Fig. 7.17 initializes rectangular array values and uses nested For...Next loops to traverse the array (that is, to manipulate every array element). The contents of the array are displayed in outputTextBox.

```
1   ' Fig. 7.17: RectangularArray.vb
2   ' Initializing and displaying a rectangular array.
3   Public Class RectangularArray
4      ' display the contents of a rectangular array
5      Private Sub RectangularArray_Load(ByVal sender As System.Object, _
6         ByVal e As System.EventArgs) Handles MyBase.Load
7
8         Dim values(,) As Integer = {{1, 2, 3}, {4, 5, 6}}
9
```

Fig. 7.17 | Initializing a rectangular array (Part I of 2.).

```
10              ' output elements of the values array
11              For row = 0 To values.GetUpperBound(0)
12                 For column = 0 To values.GetUpperBound(1)
13                    outputTextBox.AppendText(values(row, column) & vbTab)
14                 Next column
15
16                 outputTextBox.AppendText(vbCrLf)
17              Next row
18           End Sub ' RectangularArray_Load
19        End Class ' RectangularArray
```

Fig. 7.17 | Initializing a rectangular array (Part 2 of 2.).

The program declares rectangular array values (line 8) and uses an initializer list to determine the number of rows, number of columns and initial values of the array's elements. The initializer list contains two sublists. The number of sublists determines the number of rows in the array. The compiler uses the number of elements in the first sublist to determine the number of columns in each row. All subsequent sublists *must* have the same number of initializers as the first sublist; otherwise, a compilation error occurs. The first sublist initializes row 0 of the array to the values 1, 2 and 3; the second sublist initializes row 1 of the array to the values 4, 5 and 6.

The nested For...Next statements in lines 11–17 display the elements of rectangular array values. The outer For...Next statement traverses the rows; the inner For...Next statement traverses the columns within a row. Each For...Next statement calls method GetUpperBound to obtain the upper bound of the dimension it traverses. GetUpperBound with the argument 0 (line 11) returns the number of rows. GetUpperBound with the argument 1 (line 12) returns the number of columns in each row.

7.15 Case Study: Maintaining Grades Using a Rectangular Array

We now present a substantial case study using rectangular arrays. Consider the following problem statement:

An instructor gives three tests to a class of 10 students. The grades on these tests are integers in the range from 0 to 100. The instructor has asked you to develop an application to keep track of each student's average and the class average. The instructor has also asked that there be a choice to view the grades as either numbers or letters. Letter grades should be calculated according to the following grading system:

90–100	*A*
80–89	*B*
70–79	*C*
60–69	*D*
Below 60	*F*

The application should allow a user to input each student's three test grades, then compute each student's average and the class average for all grades entered so far. The application should display numeric grades by default. It should also display a grade distribution chart showing how many of the numeric grades fall into the ranges 0–9, 10–19, … 90–99 and 100.

We'll use a rectangular array with 10 rows and three columns to store the student grades. This application uses most of the programming concepts you've learned up to now in this book. Figure 7.19 shows sample outputs for the **Grade Report** application.

a) **Grade Report** window after the user has entered the first student'a grades and is about to submit them.

b) **Grade Report** window after five students' grades have been entered.

Fig. 7.18 | Sample outputs for the **Grade Report** application. (Part 1 of 2.)

c) **Grade Report** window after the user has entered all 10 students' grades.

d) **Grade Report** window after the user has entered all 10 students' grades and clicked the **Letter** RadioButton to display letter grades.

Fig. 7.18 | Sample outputs for the **Grade Report** application. (Part 2 of 2.)

GUI for the Grade Report Application

Figure 7.19 presents the GUI for the **Grade Report** application. In this application, we introduce RadioButton controls to allow the user to select between displaying grades in numeric or letter format. A **RadioButton** is a small white circle that either is blank or contains a small dot. When a RadioButton is selected, a dot appears in the circle. A RadioButton is known as a state button because it can be in only the "on" (True) state or the "off" (False) state. You've previously used the CheckBox state buttons (introduced in Chapter 5).

RadioButtons are similar to CheckBoxes, but RadioButtons normally appear as a group—only one RadioButton in the group can be selected at a time. Like car radio preset buttons, which can select *only one* station at a time, RadioButtons represent a set of options in which only one option can be selected at a time—also known as **mutually exclusive options**. By default, all RadioButtons become part of the same group. To separate them into several groups, each group must be in a different container (typically a GroupBox).

A RadioButton's Boolean **Checked** property indicates whether the RadioButton is checked (contains a small dot) or unchecked (blank). If the RadioButton is checked, the Checked property returns True; otherwise, it returns False.

A RadioButton also generates an event when its checked state changes. Event **CheckedChanged** occurs when a RadioButton is either selected or deselected. We use this event to switch between the numeric grade and letter grade views in the gradesListBox.

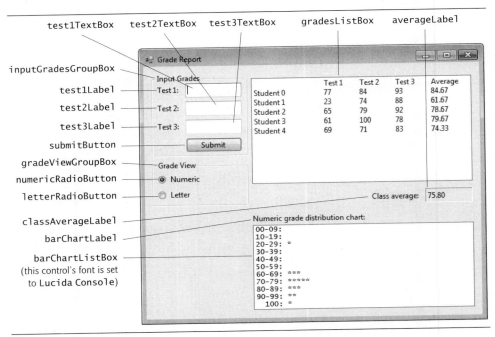

Fig. 7.19 | GUI for the **Grade Report** application

Grade Report Application

Over the next several figures we'll discuss the **Grade Report** application's code. Due to the size of this application, we've split the source code into several small figures.

Figure 7.20 declares class GradeReport's instance variables and Load event handler. The rectangular array grades (line 4) has 10 rows and 3 columns to store the grades for 10 students and three exams per student. Variable studentCount (line 5) keeps track of the number of students processed so far. After 10 students are processed, the program disables the input TextBoxes and **Submit** Button. The GradeReport_Load event handler (lines 8–13) displays the column heads in the gradesListBox.

```
 1  ' Fig. 7.20: GradeReport.vb
 2  ' Grade report using a rectangular array.
 3  Public Class GradeReport
 4     Dim grades(9, 2) As Integer ' stores 10 students' grades on 3 tests
 5     Dim studentCount As Integer = 0 ' number of students entered
 6
 7     ' display heading in gradeListBox
 8     Private Sub GradeReport_Load(ByVal sender As System.Object,
 9        ByVal e As System.EventArgs) Handles MyBase.Load
10        ' headings row for gradesListBox
11        gradesListBox.Items.Add(vbTab & vbTab & "Test 1" & vbTab &
12           "Test 2" & vbTab & "Test 3" & vbTab & "Average")
13     End Sub
14
```

Fig. 7.20 | **Grade Report** application: Instance variables and method GradeReport_Load.

Method submitButton_Click

When the user enters three grades, then presses the **Submit Button**, method submitButton_Click (Fig. 7.21) processes the three grades and displays the current class average and a bar chart showing the grade distribution for all grades entered so far. Lines 20–22 get the three grades from the TextBoxes and assign them to the elements of the grades array in row studentCount. Lines 25–37 build a String representing the current student's grades and average. Lines 28–37 loop through the current row of the grades array and append either a letter grade or numeric grade, based on whether the letterRadioButton's Checked property is True. If so, line 32 calls method LetterGrade to get the letter representation of the numeric grade. Otherwise, line 35 appends the numeric grade. Line 40 calls method CalculateStudentAverage to obtain the current student's average for the three exams.

```
15        ' process one student's grades
16        Private Sub submitButton_Click(ByVal sender As System.Object,
17           ByVal e As System.EventArgs) Handles submitButton.Click
18
19           ' retrieve the student's grades
20           grades(studentCount, 0) = Convert.ToInt32(test1TextBox.Text)
21           grades(studentCount, 1) = Convert.ToInt32(test2TextBox.Text)
22           grades(studentCount, 2) = Convert.ToInt32(test3TextBox.Text)
23
24           ' begin creating String containing the student's grades and average
25           Dim output As String = "Student " & studentCount & vbTab
```

Fig. 7.21 | **Grade Report** application: Method submitButton_Click. (Part 1 of 2.)

```
26
27          ' append each test grade to the output
28          For column = 0 To grades.GetUpperBound(1)
29              ' if the Letter RadioButton is checked
30              If letterRadioButton.Checked = True Then
31                  ' append letter grade to the output
32                  output &= vbTab & LetterGrade(grades(studentCount, column))
33              Else
34                  ' append number grade to the output
35                  output &= vbTab & grades(studentCount, column)
36              End If
37          Next
38
39          ' append the student's test average to the output
40          output &= vbTab & CalculateStudentAverage(studentCount)
41
42          gradesListBox.Items.Add(output) ' add output to the ListBox
43          studentCount += 1 ' update number of students entered
44          averageLabel.Text = CalculateClassAverage() ' display class average
45          DisplayBarChart() ' display the current grade distribution
46
47          ' clear the input TextBoxes and set focus to first TextBox
48          test1TextBox.Clear()
49          test2TextBox.Clear()
50          test3TextBox.Clear()
51          test1TextBox.Focus()
52
53          ' limit number of students
54          If studentCount = grades.GetUpperBound(0) + 1 Then
55              inputGroupBox.Enabled = False ' disable GroupBox's controls
56          End If
57      End Sub ' submitButton_Click
58
```

Fig. 7.21 | **Grade Report** application: Method `submitButton_Click`. (Part 2 of 2.)

Line 42 displays the information for the current student. Line 43 updates the student count. Line 44 and 45 call the methods `CalculateClassAverage` and `DisplayBarChart` to determine the current class average and to display a grade distribution chart based on the grades that have been entered so far. Lines 48–51 prepare the user interface to receive the next student's grades by clearing the TextBoxes and giving the focus to the test1-TextBox. Finally, lines 54–56 check whether grades have been entered for 10 students. If so, line 55 sets the `inputGradeGroupBox`'s `Enabled` property to `False`, which disables all the controls in the GroupBox, preventing the user from entering more grades.

Method *RadioButton_CheckChanged: Handling Multiple Events with One Event Handler*

At any time, the user can select the **Numeric** or **Letter** RadioButton to change how the grades are displayed in the gradesListBox. When the selected RadioButton changes, method RadioButton_CheckChanged (Fig. 7.22) is called. In this example, we handle both RadioButton's CheckChanged events with the same event handler. To do this, double click the **Numeric** RadioButton, then rename the event handler to RadioButton_CheckChanged.

Next, add `letterRadioButton.CheckChanged` to the `Handles` clause of the event handler (lines 62–63). Now this method is called when the `CheckChanged` event occurs for either `RadioButton`. In this case, as long as at least one student has been processed, line 67 calls method `DisplayGrades` to update the presentation of the grades in `gradesListBox`.

```
59      ' handles Numeric and Letter RadioButtons' CheckChanged events
60      Private Sub RadioButton_CheckedChanged(ByVal sender As System.Object,
61         ByVal e As System.EventArgs) _
62         Handles numericRadioButton.CheckedChanged,
63            letterRadioButton.CheckedChanged
64
65         ' if there are grades to display, call DisplayClassGrades
66         If studentCount > 0 Then
67            DisplayClassGrades()
68         End If
69      End Sub ' RadioButton_CheckedChanged
70
```

Fig. 7.22 | Grade Report application: Method `RadioButton_CheckChanged`.

Method CalculateStudentAverage

Method `CalculateStudentAverage` (Fig. 7.23) processes one row of the `grades` array to determine the corresponding student's average. The method returns a `String` containing either the letter grade for that student's average or the numeric value, depending on whether the `letterRadioButton`'s `Checked` property is `True`.

```
71      ' calculates a student's test average
72      Function CalculateStudentAverage(ByVal row As Integer) As String
73         Dim gradeTotal As Integer = 0 ' student's total grade
74
75         ' sum the grades for the student
76         For column = 0 To grades.GetUpperBound(1)
77            gradeTotal += grades(row, column)
78         Next
79
80         Dim studentAverage As String = String.Empty ' output string
81
82         ' calculate the student's test average
83         If letterRadioButton.Checked = True Then
84            studentAverage =
85               LetterGrade(gradeTotal / (grades.GetUpperBound(1) + 1))
86         Else
87            studentAverage = String.Format("{0:F}",
88               (gradeTotal / (grades.GetUpperBound(1) + 1)))
89         End If
90
91         Return studentAverage ' return the student's average
92      End Function ' CalculateStudentAverage
93
```

Fig. 7.23 | Grade Report application: Method `CalculateStudentAverage`.

Method CalculateClassAverage

Method CalculateClassAverage (Fig. 7.24) processes the grades array to determine the class average for all the grades entered so far. The method returns a String containing either the letter grade for the class average or the numeric value, depending on whether the letterRadioButton's Checked property is True.

```
 94     ' calculates the class average
 95     Function CalculateClassAverage() As String
 96        Dim classTotal As Integer = 0 ' class's total grade
 97
 98        ' loop through all rows that currently contain grades
 99        For row = 0 To studentCount - 1
100           ' loop through all columns
101           For column = 0 To grades.GetUpperBound(1)
102              classTotal += grades(row, column) ' add grade to total
103           Next column
104        Next row
105
106        Dim classAverage As String = String.Empty ' output string
107
108        ' if the Letter RadioButton is checked, return letter grade
109        If letterRadioButton.Checked = True Then
110           classAverage = LetterGrade(classTotal /
111              (studentCount * (grades.GetUpperBound(1) + 1)))
112        Else ' return numeric grade
113           classAverage = String.Format("{0:F}", (classTotal /
114              (studentCount * (grades.GetUpperBound(1) + 1))))
115        End If
116
117        Return classAverage ' return the class average
118     End Function ' CalculateClassAverage
119
```

Fig. 7.24 | Grade Report application: Method CalculateClassAverage.

Method LetterGrade

Method LetterGrade (Fig. 7.25) receives a numeric grade and returns the corresponding letter grade as a String.

```
120     ' determines a letter grade corresponding to a numeric grade
121     Function LetterGrade(ByVal grade As Double) As String
122        Dim output As String ' the letter grade to return
123
124        ' determine the correct letter grade
125        Select Case grade
126           Case Is >= 90
127              output = "A"
128           Case Is >= 80
129              output = "B"
```

Fig. 7.25 | Grade Report application: Method LetterGrade. (Part 1 of 2.)

```
130         Case Is >= 70
131            output = "C"
132         Case Is >= 60
133            output = "D"
134         Case Else
135            output = "F"
136      End Select
137
138      Return output ' return the letter grade
139   End Function ' LetterGrade
140
```

Fig. 7.25 | Grade Report application: Method LetterGrade. (Part 2 of 2.)

Method *DisplayClassGrades*

Method DisplayClassGrades (Fig. 7.26) displays the student grades and averages in the gradesListBox. Line 143 clears the ListBox's current contents and lines 146–147 display the column heads in the ListBox. Lines 150–169 processes the grades array to display all the grades entered so far, displaying letter grades if letterRadioButton's Checked property is True. Line 172 updates the class average and displays the result in averageLabel.

```
141   ' display the grades for all students entered
142   Sub DisplayClassGrades()
143      gradesListBox.Items.Clear() ' clear the ListBox
144
145      ' add the header to the ListBox
146      gradesListBox.Items.Add(vbTab & vbTab & "Test 1" & vbTab &
147         "Test 2" & vbTab & "Test 3" & vbTab & "Average")
148
149      ' loop through all the rows
150      For row = 0 To studentCount - 1
151         Dim output As String = "Student " & row & vbTab
152
153         ' loop through all the columns
154         For column = 0 To grades.GetUpperBound(1)
155            If letterRadioButton.Checked = True Then
156               ' add letter grade to output string
157               output &= vbTab & LetterGrade(grades(row, column))
158            Else
159               ' add number grade to output string
160               output &= vbTab & (grades(row, column))
161            End If
162         Next column
163
164         ' add the student's average to the output
165         output &= vbTab & CalculateStudentAverage(row)
166
167         ' add the output to the ListBox
168         gradesListBox.Items.Add(output)
169      Next row
```

Fig. 7.26 | Grade Report application: Method DisplayClassGrades. (Part 1 of 2.)

```
170
171          ' update the class average
172          averageLabel.Text = CalculateClassAverage()
173       End Sub ' DisplayClassGrades
174
```

Fig. 7.26 | **Grade Report** application: Method `DisplayClassGrades`. (Part 2 of 2.)

Method `DisplayBarChart`

Many programs present data to users in a visual or graphical format. For example, numeric values are often displayed as bars in a bar chart. In such a chart, longer bars represent proportionally larger numeric values (see Fig. 7.18). Method `DisplayBarChart` (Fig. 7.27) displays a graphical summary of the grade distribution by creating a bar chart that shows how many numeric grades fall into each of the ranges 0–9, 10–19, … 90–99 and 100.

```
175       ' display a bar chart of the grade distribution
176       Sub DisplayBarChart()
177          barChartListBox.Items.Clear() ' remove current items
178
179          ' stores frequency of grades in each range of 10 grades
180          Dim frequency(10) As Integer
181
182          ' for each grade, increment the appropriate frequency
183          For row = 0 To studentCount - 1
184             For column = 0 To grades.GetUpperBound(1)
185                frequency(grades(row, column) \ 10) += 1
186             Next column
187          Next row
188
189          ' for each grade frequency, display bar of asterisks
190          For count = 0 To frequency.GetUpperBound(0)
191             Dim bar As String ' stores the label and bar
192
193             ' create bar label ( "00-09: ", ..., "90-99: ", "100: " )
194             If count = 10 Then
195                bar = String.Format("{0, 5:D}: ", 100)
196             Else
197                bar = String.Format("{0, 2:D2}-{1, 2:D2}: ",
198                   count * 10, count * 10 + 9)
199             End If
200
201             ' append bar of asterisks
202             For stars = 1 To frequency(count)
203                bar &= ("*")
204             Next
205
206             barChartListBox.Items.Add(bar) ' display bar
207          Next count
208       End Sub ' DisplayBarChart
209    End Class ' GradeReport
```

Fig. 7.27 | **Grade Report** application: Method `DisplayBarChart`.

Lines 180–187 summarize the number of grades in each range using the elements of the 11-element array frequency. Next, lines 190–207 build a String containing the range of values represented by the current bar (lines 194–199) and a bar of asterisks representing the number of grades that fall into that range (lines 202–204). Line 206 then displays this String in the barCharListBox. The format Strings in lines 195 and 197 use field widths to control the number of characters in which each value is output. The format specifier {0, 5:D} (line 195) indicates that an integer value will be displayed in a field of 5 characters right justified by default. So, if the number contains fewer than 5 characters, it will be preceded by an appropriate number of spaces. The format specifier {0, 2:D2} (line 195) indicates that an integer will be displayed in a field of 2 characters. The D2 forces the number to use two character positions—single digit numbers are preceded by a leading 0.

7.16 Resizing an Array with the ReDim Statement

An array's size cannot be changed, so a new array must be created if you need to change the size of an existing array. The **ReDim** statement "resizes" an array at execution time by creating a *new* array and assigning it to the specified array variable. Figure 7.28 demonstrates the ReDim statement.

```vb
1   ' Fig. 7.28: ReDimTest.vb
2   ' Resize an array using the ReDim statement.
3   Public Class ReDimTest
4       ' demonstrate ReDim
5       Private Sub ReDimTest_Load(ByVal sender As System.Object,
6           ByVal e As System.EventArgs) Handles MyBase.Load
7
8           ' create and initialize a 5-element array
9           Dim values1() As Integer = {1, 2, 3, 4, 5}
10          Dim values2() As Integer = {1, 2, 3, 4, 5}
11
12          ' display array length and the elements in array
13          outputTextBox.AppendText(
14              "The original array has " & values1.Length & " elements: ")
15          DisplayArray(values1)
16
17          ' change the size of the array without the Preserve keyword
18          ReDim values1(6)
19
20          ' display new array length and the elements in array
21          outputTextBox.AppendText("New array (without Preserve) has " &
22              values1.Length & " elements: ")
23          DisplayArray(values1)
24
25          ' change the size of the array with the Preserve keyword
26          ReDim Preserve values2(6)
27          values2(6) = 7 ' assign 7 to array element 6
28
29          ' display new array length and the elements in array
30          outputTextBox.AppendText("New array (with Preserve) has " &
31              values2.Length & " elements: ")
```

Fig. 7.28 | Using ReDim statements to change the array size. (Part 1 of 2.)

```
32              DisplayArray(values2)
33       End Sub
34
35       ' display array elements
36       Sub DisplayArray(ByVal array() As Integer)
37          For Each number In array
38             outputTextBox.AppendText(number & "   ")
39          Next
40
41          outputTextBox.AppendText(vbCrLf)
42       End Sub ' DisplayArray
43    End Class ' ReDimTest
```

```
ReDim Test
The original array has 5 elements: 1 2 3 4 5
New array (without Preserve) has 7 elements: 0 0 0 0 0 0 0
New array (with Preserve) has 7 elements: 1 2 3 4 5 0 7
```

Fig. 7.28 | Using ReDim statements to change the array size. (Part 2 of 2.)

Line 9 creates and initializes a five-element array values1. Line 10 creates a second array named values2 containing the same data. Lines 13–15 display the size and elements of values1. Line 18 uses a ReDim statement to change the upper bound of values1 to 6, so that the array now contains seven elements. The ReDim statement contains keyword ReDim, followed by the name of the array to be "resized" and the new upper bound in parentheses. Lines 21–23 then display the size and elements of values1 again. The output of Fig. 7.28 shows that after the ReDim statement executes, the size of values1 is changed to 7 and the value of each element is reinitialized to the default value of the type of the array element (that is, 0 for Integers). To save the original data stored in an array, follow the ReDim keyword with the optional **Preserve** keyword. Line 26 uses Preserve in the ReDim statement to indicate that the existing array elements are to be *preserved* in the now larger array after the array is resized. If the new array is *smaller* than the original array, the existing elements that are outside the bounds of the new array are *discarded*. If the new array is *larger* than the original array, all the existing elements are preserved in the now larger array, and the *extra elements are initialized to the default value* of the type of the array element. For example, after line 26 executes, the value of values2(5) is 0. Line 27 assigns the value 7 to values2(6), so that the now larger array values2 contains elements 1, 2, 3, 4, 5, 0 and 7. Lines 30–32 display the size and elements of values2.

7.17 Wrap-Up

This chapter began our discussion of data structures, using arrays to store data in and retrieve data from lists and tables of values. We demonstrated how to declare an array, initialize an array and refer to individual elements of an array. We showed how to pass arrays to methods. We discussed how to use the For Each...Next statement to iterate through the values in an array without using an index. We used method Sort of class Array to sort an array and method BinarySearch of class Array to search a sorted array efficiently for a specific value. We explained how to declare and manipulate rectangular arrays. Finally, we demonstrated how to use the ReDim statement to dynamically change an array's size. In the next chapter, you'll learn how to write data to and read data from files.

Summary

Section 7.2 Arrays

- An array is a group of variables (called elements) containing values that all have the same type.
- To refer to a particular element in an array, specify the name of the array and the position number of the element.
- The first element in every array is the zeroth element.
- The highest position number in a array is alwas 1 less than the number of elements in the array.
- The position number in parentheses more formally is called an index or "subscript." An index must be a nonnegative integer or integer expression.
- The name of an array element can be used on the left side of an assignment statement to place a new value into an array element.
- Every array "knows" its own length via its Length property.
- All arrays have the methods and properties of class System.Array.

Section 7.3 Declaring and Allocating Arrays

- In an array declaration, the parentheses that follow the variable name indicate the variable represents an array.
- Arrays can be declared to contain elements of any type; every element of the array is of that type.
- The number in parentheses in the array declaration represents the array's upper bound and helps the compiler allocate memory for the array.
- You can follow an array declaration with an equal sign and an initializer list in braces ({ and }) to specify the initial values of the array's elements. The compiler determines the array bounds from the number of elements in the initializer list.
- When you do not provide an initializer list, the elements in the array are initialized to the default value for the array's type—0 for numeric primitive data-type variables, False for Boolean variables and Nothing for String and other class types.

Section 7.4 Initializing the Values in an Array

- Array method GetUpperBound returns the index of the last element in an array. The value returned by method GetUpperBound is one less than the value of the array's Length property.

Section 7.5 Summing the Elements of an Array

- Often, the elements of an array represent a series of related values that are used in a calculation.

Section 7.6 Using Arrays to Analyze Survey Results

- Arrays can be used as sets of counters.
- When an expression contains nested parentheses, its evaluation begins with the value in the innermost set of parentheses.
- When a program is executed, array element indices are checked for validity—all indices must be greater than or equal to 0 and less than the length of the array. If an attempt is made to use an invalid index to access an element, an IndexOutOfRangeException exception occurs.

Section 7.8 Case Study: Flag Quiz

- The ComboBox control presents options in a drop-down list that opens when you click the down arrow at the right side of the control. A ComboBox combines features of a TextBox and a ListBox.

- A ComboBox usually appears as a TextBox with a down arrow to its right. You can click the down arrow to display a list of predefined items. If you choose an item from this list, that item is displayed in the ComboBox.

- You may also type into the ComboBox control to locate an item.

- ComboBox property DropDownStyle determines the ComboBox's appearance. Value DropDownList specifies that the ComboBox is not editable. In this ComboBox style, if you press the key that corresponds to the first letter of an item in the ComboBox, that item is selected and displayed in the ComboBox.

- ComboBox property MaxDropDownItems specifies the maximum number of items to display at one time. A vertical scrollbar is added to the drop-down list to allow users to scroll through the remaining items.

- ComboBox property DataSource specifies the source of the items displayed in the ComboBox.

- String method Replace receives two arguments—the substring that should be replaced throughout the original String and the the replacement substring.

Section 7.9 Passing an Array to a Method

- To pass an array argument to a method, specify the name of the array without using parentheses.

- Every array object "knows" its own upper bound, so when you pass an array object to a method, you do not need to pass the upper bound of the array as a separate argument.

- For a method to receive an array through a method call, the method's parameter list must specify that an array will be received.

- Entire arrays always are passed by reference, so when you pass an array to a method, it can change the original array's element values.

- To pass an array element to a method, use the indexed name of the array element as an argument in the method call. An individual element can be passed by value or by reference.

Section 7.10 For Each...Next Repetition Statement

- The For Each...Next repetition statement iterates through the values in a data structure, such as an array, without using a loop counter.

- When used with one-dimensional arrays, For Each...Next behaves like a For...Next statement that iterates through the range of indices from 0 to the value returned by GetUpperBound(0).

- Instead of a counter, For Each...Next uses a variable to represent the value of each element.

- The header of a For Each repetition statement specifies a variable and an array. The type of variable is determined from the type of the elements in the array.

- The For Each statement iterates through all the elements in the array, sequentially assigning each value to the variable specified in the header.

Section 7.11 Sorting an Array with Method **Sort** of Class **Array**

- Sorting data (that is, arranging the data in ascending or descending order) is one of the most popular computing applications.

- Class Array provides methods for creating, modifying, sorting and searching arrays.

- Array method Sort sorts an array's elements into ascending order.

- To sort an array in descending order, first call method Sort to sort the array, then call Array.Reverse with the array as an argument to reverse the order of the elements in the array.

Section 7.12 Searching an Array with Linear Search

- The process of locating a particular element value in an array is called searching.

- A linear search iterates through all the elements of an array, comparing each element with a search key. If the elements of the array being searched are unordered, it's just as likely that the value will be found in the front half of the array as in the back half, so on average the method will have to compare the search key with half the elements of the array.

- Class Array provides a method IndexOf that performs a linear search. Class Array also provides methods such as Find and FindAll, which search the array for element(s) that meet certain criteria. The criteria can be more general than simply searching for an element.

Section 7.13 Searching a Sorted Array with **Array** Method **BinarySearch**

- Linear searches work well for small or unsorted arrays.

- The high-speed binary search technique is better for sorted arrays.

- Array method BinarySearch performs a binary search for a key value. The method receives a sorted array and a search key. If the value is found, method BinarySearch returns the index of the search key; otherwise, it returns a negative number.

Section 7.14 Rectangular Arrays

- One-dimensional arrays are arrays that contain a list of values.

- Multidimensional arrays require two or more indices to identify particular elements.

- Two-dimensional arrays—also known as rectangular arrays—are often used to represent tables of values consisting of data arranged in rows and columns. Each row is the same size, and each column is the same size (hence the term "rectangular").

- To identify a particular table element, we specify two indices—by convention, the first identifies the element's row, the second the element's column.

- Every element in a rectangular array is identified by an element name of the form a(i, j), where a is the name of the array and i and j are the indices that uniquely identify the row and column, respectively, of each element in array a.

- A rectangular array is declared by placing two bounds separated by a comma in the parentheses that follow the variable name.

- If an initializer list is used, then the parentheses must contain only the comma. The initializer list must have sublists to represent each row and all sublists must have the same number of columns. The compiler determines the number of columns in each row by counting the number of initializer values in the subinitializer list for that row.

- Rectangular arrays are often manipulated with nested For...Next loops.

- For a rectangular array, method GetUpperBound with the argument 0 returns the number of rows. GetUpperBound with the argument 1 returns the number of columns in each row.

Section 7.15 Case Study: Maintaining Grades Using a Rectangular Array

- A RadioButton is a small white circle that either is blank or contains a small dot. When a RadioButton is selected, a dot appears in the circle. A RadioButton is known as a state button because it can be in only the "on" (True) state or the "off" (False) state.

- RadioButtons are similar to CheckBoxes, but RadioButtons normally appear as a group—only one RadioButton in the group can be selected at a time—also known as mutually exclusive options.

- To separate RadioButtons into several groups, each group must be in a different container (typically a GroupBox).

- A RadioButton's Boolean Checked property indicates whether the RadioButton is checked (contains a small dot) or unchecked (blank). If the RadioButton is checked, the Checked property returns True; otherwise, it returns False.

- A CheckedChanged event occurs when a RadioButton is either selected or deselected.

- Many programs present data to users in a visual or graphical format. For example, numeric values are often displayed as bars in a bar chart. In such a chart, longer bars represent proportionally larger numeric values.

Section 7.16 Resizing an Array with the *ReDim* Statement

- The ReDim statement enables you to dynamically change an array's size. It "resizes" an array by creating a new array and assigning it to the specified variable.

- A ReDim statement contains keyword ReDim, followed by the name of the array to be "resized" and the new upper bound in parentheses. The value of each element is reinitialized to the default value of the type of the array element.

- To save the original data stored in an array, follow the ReDim keyword with the optional Preserve keyword. If the new array is smaller than the original array, the existing elements that are outside the bounds of the new array are discarded. If the new array is larger than the original array, all the existing elements are preserved in the now larger array, and the extra elements are initialized to the default value of the type of the array element.

Terminology

array 242
array bounds 244
Array class 243
binary search 262
BinarySearch method of class Array 264
bounds checking 247
Catch block 249
Checked property of the RadioButton
    control 270
CheckedChanged event of the RadioButton
    control 270
column in a rectangular array 265
ComboBox control 252
DataSource property of a ComboBox 254
DropDownList value of property
    DropDownStyle 252
DropDownStyle property of ComboBox 252
element of an array 242
exception 248
exception handling 248
fault-tolerant program 248
For Each...Next statement 258
GetUpperBound method of class Array 244
index of an array 242
initializer list 244
key value 262
length of an array 243
Length property of class Array 243

linear search 262
m-by-*n* array 266
MaxDropDownItems property of ComboBox
    control 252
Message property of an exception 249
multidimensional array 265
mutually exclusive options and
    RadioButtons 270
one-dimensional array 265
Preserve keyword 278
RadioButton control 270
rectangular array 265
ReDim statement 277
Replace method of class String 255
Reverse method of class Array 262
row in a rectangular array 265
search key 262
searching 262
SelectedIndex property of a ComboBox 255
sorting 260
Sort method of class Array 260
table of values 265
two-dimensional array 265
throw an exception 249
Try block 249
Try statement 249
upper bound 242
zeroth element 242

Self-Review Exercises

7.1 Answer each of the following questions:

a) The number that refers to a particular element of an array is called its _____.
   1. value
   2. size
   3. indexed array name
   4. index (or subscript)

b) The indexed array name of one-dimensional array `units`'s element 2 is _____.
   1. `units{2}`
   2. `units(2)`
   3. `units[0,2]`
   4. `units[2]`

c) An array's length is _____.
   1. one more than the array's last index
   2. one less than the array's last index
   3. the same as the array's last index
   4. returned by method `GetUpperBound`

d) Property _____ specifies the source of the data displayed in a `ComboBox`.
   1. `ComboData`
   2. `Source`
   3. `DataList`
   4. `DataSource`

e) `ComboBox` property _____ is 0 when the first `ComboBox` item is selected.
   1. `SelectedIndex`
   2. `SelectedValue`
   3. `Index`
   4. `SelectedNumber`

f) The process of ordering the elements of an array is called _____ the array.
   1. allocating
   2. sorting
   3. declaring
   4. initializing

g) Which of the following sorts array `averageRainfall`?
   1. `Array(averageRainfall).Sort()`
   2. `Sort.Array(averageRainfall)`
   3. `Sort(averageRainfall)`
   4. `Array.Sort(averageRainfall)`

h) Arrays that use two indices are referred to as _____ arrays.
   1. single-subscripted
   2. two-dimensional
   3. double
   4. one-dimensional

i) The expression _____ creates an `Integer` array of two rows and five columns.
   1. `Dim a(2, 5) As Integer`
   2. `Dim a(1, 5) As Integer`
   3. `Dim a(1, 4) As Integer`
   4. `Dim a(2, 4) As Integer`

j) The _____ property determines whether a `RadioButton` is selected.
   1. `Selected`
   2. `Clicked`
   3. `Checked`
   4. `Enabled`

k) The _____ event is raised when a `RadioButton` is either selected or deselected.
   1. `CheckedChanged`
   2. `Changed`
   3. `SelectedChanged`
   4. None of the above

l) When one `RadioButton` in a container is selected, _____.
   1. others can be selected at the same time
   2. a logic error will occur
   3. all others will be deselected
   4. Both 1 and 2

m) Typically, _____ statements are used to iterate over each element in a two-dimensional array.
   1. `Do While...Loop`
   2. nested `For...Next`
   3. `Do...Loop Until`
   4. nested `Do...Loop While`

7.2 State whether each of the following is *true* or *false*. If *false*, explain why.

a) An array can store many different types of values.

b) An array index normally should be of type `Double`.

c) Method `GetUpperBound` returns the highest numbered index in an array.

d) To determine the number of elements in an array, use the `NumberOfElements` property.

e) The linear search works well for unsorted arrays.

Answers to Self-Review Exercises

7.1   a) 4. b) 2. c) 1. d) 4. e) 1. f) 2. g) 4. h) 2. i) 3. j) 3. k) 1. l) 3. m) 2.

7.2   a) False. An array can store only values of the same type. b) False. An array index must be a nonnegative integer or integer expression. c) True. d) False. To determine the number of elements in an array, we can use the `Length` property. e) True.

Quick Quiz

7.3   Answer each of the following questions:

a) Arrays can be declared to hold values of _____.
   1. type `Double`   2. type `Integer`
   3. type `String`   4. any data type

b) An array's elements are related by the fact that they have the same name and _____.
   1. constant value   2. subscript
   3. type   4. value

c) Method _____ returns an array's highest index.
   1. `GetUpperBound`   2. `GetUpperLimit`
   3. `GetHighestIndex`   4. `GetUpperSubscript`

d) The first element in every array is the _____.
   1. subscript   2. zeroth element
   3. length of the array   4. smallest value in the array

e) The initializer list can _____.
   1. be used to determine the size of the array
   2. contain a comma-separated list of initial values for the array elements
   3. be empty
   4. All of the above

f) Which method call sorts array words in ascending order?
   1. `Array.Sort(words)`   2. `words.SortArray()`
   3. `Array.Sort(words, 1)`   4. `Sort(words)`

g) The `ComboBox` control combines a `TextBox` control with a _____ control.
   1. `DateTimePicker`   2. `ListBox`
   3. `NumericUpDown`   4. `Label`

h) Property _____ contains the size of an array.
   1. `Elements`   2. `ArraySize`
   3. `Length`   4. `Size`

i) When declaring an array, a(n) _____ is required inside parentheses in order to indicate that the array is two-dimensional.
   1. comma   2. asterisk
   3. period   4. apostrophe

j) In a _____ array each row contains the same number of columns.
   1. data   2. rectangular
   3. tabular   4. All of the above

k) In an *m*-by-*n* array, the *m* stands for _____.
   1. the number of columns in the array
   2. the total number of array elements
   3. the number of rows in the array
   4. the number of elements in each row

l) Which of the following creates an `Integer` array of five rows and three columns?
   1. `Dim values(5, 3) As Integer`
   2. `Dim values(4, 2 ) As Integer`
   3. `Dim values(4, 3) As Integer`
   4. `Dim values(5, 2) As Integer`

m) Use a _____ to group `RadioButtons` on a `Form`.
   1. `GroupBox` control
   2. `ComboBox` control
   3. `ListBox` control
   4. None of the above

n) The _____ event handler is invoked when the user selects a `RadioButton`.
   1. `Selected`
   2. `CheckedChanged`
   3. `ButtonChanged`
   4. `CheckSelected`

o) The _____ property is set to `True` when a `RadioButton` is selected.
   1. `Selected`
   2. `Chosen`
   3. `On`
   4. `Checked`

p) Two-dimensional arrays are often used to represent _____.
   1. a pie chart
   2. distances
   3. lines
   4. tables

q) Which of the following statements creates `Integer` array `values` with three rows and three columns?
   1. ```
Dim array()() As Integer =
      {{1, 2, 3}, {4, 5, 6}, {7, 8, 9}}
```
   2. ```
Dim array() As Integer =
      {{1, 2, 3}, {4, 5, 6}, {7, 8, 9}}
```
   3. ```
Dim array(,) As Integer =
      {{1, 2, 3}, {4, 5, 6}, {7, 8, 9}}
```
   4. All of the above

# Exercises

**7.4**  Write statements to accomplish each of the following tasks:
   a) Display the value of element 6 of array `numbers`.
   b) Using a `For...Next` statement, assign the value 8 to each of the five elements of one-dimensional `Integer` array `values`.
   c) Total the 100 elements of floating-point array `results`.
   d) Copy 11-element array `source` into the first portion of 34-element array `sourceCopy`.
   e) Determine the smallest and largest values in 99-element floating-point array `data`.

**7.5**  *(Salary Survey Application)* Use a one-dimensional array to solve the following problem: A company pays its salespeople on a commission basis. The salespeople receive $200 per week, plus 9% of their gross sales for that week. For example, a salesperson who grosses $5,000 in sales in a week receives $200 plus 9% of $5,000, a total of $650. Write an application (using an array of counters) that determines how many of the salespeople earned salaries in each of the following ranges (assuming that each salesperson's salary is truncated to an integer amount): $200–299, $300–399, $400–499, $500–599, $600–699, $700–799, $800–899, $900–999 and over $999.

Allow the user to enter the sales for each employee in a TextBox. The user clicks the **Calculate** Button to calculate the salesperson's salary. When the user is done entering this information, clicking the **Show Totals** Button displays how many of the salespeople earned salaries in each of the above ranges.
```

7.6 *(Cafeteria Survey Application)* Twenty students were asked to rate, on a scale from 1 to 10, the quality of the food in the student cafeteria, with 1 being "awful" and 10 being "excellent." Allow the user input to be entered using a ComboBox. Use an Integer array to store the frequency of each rating. Display the frequencies as a bar chart in a ListBox.

7.7 *(What Does This Code Do?)* This function declares numbers as its parameter. What does it return?

```
1   Function Mystery(ByVal numbers() As Integer) As Integer()
2      Dim length As Integer = numbers.Length - 1
3      Dim tempArray(length) As Integer
4
5      For i As Integer = length To 0 Step -1
6         tempArray(length - i) = numbers(i)
7      Next
8
9      Return tempArray
10   End Function ' Mystery
```

7.8 *(What's Wrong with This Code?)* The code that follows uses a For...Next loop to sum the elements in an array. Find the error(s) in the following code:

```
1   Sub SumArray()
2      Dim sum As Integer
3      Dim numbers() As Integer = {1, 2, 3, 4, 5, 6, 7, 8}
4
5      For counter As Integer = 0 To numbers.Length
6         sum += numbers(counter)
7      Next
8   End Sub ' SumArray
```

7.9 *(Road Sign Test Application)* Write an application that tests the user's knowledge of road signs. Your application should display a random sign image and ask the user to select the sign name from a ComboBox. [*Hint:* The application is similar to the **Flag Quiz** application.] You can find the images in the Images folder with this chapter's examples.

7.10 *(Enhanced Cafeteria Survey Application)* A school cafeteria is giving an electronic survey to its students to improve their lunch menu. Create an application that uses a rectangular array to store votes for the survey. The application should display four food items in a ComboBox. Provide **Like** and **Dislike** RadioButtons to allow students to indicate whether they like or dislike a particular food. The user selects an item from the ComboBox, clicks the appropriate RadioButton and presses the **Submit** Button to submit the vote. Display a report that is updated as each new set of responses is entered. Use a rectangular Integer array named votes, with four rows and two columns to summarize the results. Each row corresponds to a food item in the ComboBox. The columns store the number of "like" and "dislike" votes, respectively.

7.11 *(What Does This Code Do?)* What is returned by the following code? Assume that GetStockPrices is a Function that returns a 2-by-31 array, with the first row containing the stock price at the beginning of the day and the last row containing the stock price at the end of the day, for each day of the month.

```
1   Function Mystery() As Integer()
2      Dim prices(1, 31) As Integer
3
4      prices = GetStockPrices()
```

```
5
6        Dim result(30) As Integer
7
8        For i As Integer = 0 To 30
9           result(i) = prices(1, i) - prices(0, i)
10       Next
11
12       Return result
13    End Function ' Mystery
```

7.12   *(What's Wrong with This Code?)* Find the error(s) in the following code. The TwoDArrays procedure should create a two-dimensional array and initialize all its values to one.

```
1    Sub TwoDArrays()
2       Dim array(3, 3) As Integer
3
4       ' assign 1 to all cell values
5       For i As Integer = 0 To 3
6          array(i, i) = 1
7       Next
8    End Sub ' TwoDArrays
```

7.13   *(Duplicate Elimination)* Use a one-dimensional array to solve the following problem: Read in 20 numbers, each of which is between 10 and 100, inclusive. As each number is read, display it in numbersEnteredListBox and, if it's not a duplicate of a number already read, display it in uniqueValuesListBox. Provide for the "worst case" (in which all 20 numbers are different). Use the smallest possible array to solve this problem.

7.14   *(Sorting in Ascending and Descending Order)* Modify the sorting example of Fig. 7.12 so that it displays the "Original values," "Values sorted in ascending order" and "Values sorted in descending order"; your program should display in the last two columns the values sorted in ascending and descending order, respectively.

7.15   *(Telephone-Number Word Generator)* Standard telephone keypads contain the digits zero through nine. The numbers two through nine each have three letters associated with them (Fig. 7.29). Many people find it difficult to memorize phone numbers, so they use the correspondence between digits and letters to develop seven-letter words that correspond to their phone numbers. For example, a person whose telephone number is 686-2377 might use the correspondence indicated in Fig. 7.29 to develop the seven-letter word "NUMBERS." Every seven-letter word corresponds to exactly one seven-digit telephone number. A restaurant wishing to increase its takeout business could surely do so with the number 825-3688 (that is, "TAKEOUT").

Digit	Letters	Digit	Letters
2	A B C	6	M N O
3	D E F	7	P R S
4	G H I	8	T U V
5	J K L	9	W X Y

Fig. 7.29 | Telephone keypad digits and letters.

Every seven-letter phone number corresponds to many different seven-letter combinations. Unfortunately, most of these represent unrecognizable juxtapositions of letters. It's possible, however, that the owner of a barbershop would be pleased to know that the shop's telephone number, 424-7288, corresponds to "HAIRCUT." A veterinarian with the phone number 738-2273 would be pleased to know that the number corresponds to the letters "PETCARE." An automotive dealership would be pleased to know that the dealership number, 639-2277, corresponds to "NEW-CARS."

Write an application that allows the user to enter a seven-digit number in a TextBox, and displays every possible seven-letter word combination corresponding to that number in a multiple line scrollable TextBox when the user clicks the **Generate Words** button. There are 2,187 (3^7) such combinations. Avoid phone numbers with the digits 0 and 1.

7.16 *(Airline Reservations System)* A small airline has just purchased a computer for its new automated reservations system. You've been asked to develop the new system. You are to write an application to assign seats on each flight of the airline's only plane (capacity: 10 seats).

Your application should display RadioButtons that allow the user to choose **First Class** or **Economy**. If the user selects **First Class**, your application should assign a seat in the first-class section (seats 1–5). If the user types **Economy**, your application should assign a seat in the economy section (seats 6–10). Your application should then display a boarding pass indicating the person's seat number and whether it's in the first-class or economy section of the plane.

Use a one-dimensional array of type Boolean to represent the plane's seating chart. All the elements of the array are initially False to indicate that the seats are empty. As each seat is assigned, set the corresponding elements of the array to True to indicate that the seat is no longer available.

Your application should never assign a seat that has already been assigned. When the economy section is full, your application should ask the person if it's acceptable to be placed in the first-class section (and vice versa). If yes, make the appropriate seat assignment. If no, display the message "Next flight leaves in 3 hours."

Making a Difference Exercise

7.17 *(Polling)* The Internet and the web are enabling more people to network, join a cause, voice opinions, and so on. The presidential candidates in 2008 used the Internet intensively to get out their messages and raise money for their campaigns. In this exercise, you'll write a simple polling program that allows users to rate five social-consciousness issues from 1 (least important) to 10 (most important). Pick five causes that are important to you (for example, political issues, global environmental issues). Use a one-dimensional array topics (of type String) to store the five causes. To summarize the survey responses, use a 5-row, 10-column two-dimensional array responses (of type Integer), each row corresponding to an element in the topics array. When the program runs, it should ask the user to rate each issue. Have your friends and family respond to the survey. Then have the program display a summary of the results, including:

a) A tabular report with the five topics down the left side and the 10 ratings across the top, listing in each column the number of ratings received for each topic.
b) To the right of each row, show the average of the ratings for that issue.
c) Which issue received the highest point total? Display both the issue and the point total.
d) Which issue received the lowest point total? Display both the issue and the point total.

Files

Consciousness ... does not appear to itself chopped up in bits. ... A "river" or a "stream" are the metaphors by which it is most naturally described.
—William James

I read part of it all the way through.
—Samuel Goldwyn

I can only assume that a "Do Not File" document is filed in a "Do Not File" file.
—Senator Frank Church,
Senate Intelligence Subcommittee
Hearing, 1975

Objectives

In this chapter you'll learn:

- To use file processing to implement a business application.

- To create, write to and read from files.

- To become familiar with sequential-access file processing.

- To use classes **StreamWriter** and **StreamReader** to write text to and read text from files.

- To organize GUI commands in menus.

- To manage resources with **Using** statements and the Finally block of a **Try** statement.

8.1 Introduction

Variables and arrays offer only temporary storage of data in memory—the data is lost, for example, when a local variable "goes out of scope" or when the program terminates. By contrast, files (and databases, which we cover in Chapter 12) are used for long-term retention of large (and often *vast*) amounts of data, even after the program that created the data terminates, so data maintained in files is often called **persistent data**. Computers store files on **secondary storage devices**, such as magnetic disks, optical disks (like CDs, DVDs and Blu-ray Discs™), USB flash drives and magnetic tapes. In this chapter, we explain how to create, write to and read from data files. We continue our treatment of GUIs, explaining how to organize commands in menus, and showing how to use the Windows Forms Designer to rapidly create menus. We also discuss resource management. As programs execute, they often acquire resources, such as memory and files, that need to be returned to the system so they can be reused at a later point. We show how to ensure that resources are properly returned to the system when they're no longer needed.

8.2 Data Hierarchy

Ultimately, all data items that computers process are reduced to combinations of 0s and 1s. This occurs because it's simple and economical to build electronic devices that can assume two stable states—one represents 0 and the other represents 1. It's remarkable that the impressive functions performed by computers involve only the most fundamental manipulations of 0s and 1s!

Bits

The smallest data item that computers support is called a **bit**, short for "**binary digit**"—a digit that can assume either the value 0 or the value 1. Computer circuitry performs various simple bit manipulations, such as examining the value of a bit, setting the value of a bit and reversing a bit (from 1 to 0 or from 0 to 1). For more information on the binary number system, see Appendix C, Number Systems.

Characters

Programming with data in the low-level form of bits is cumbersome. It's preferable to program with data in forms such as decimal digits (that is, 0, 1, 2, 3, 4, 5, 6, 7, 8 and 9), letters (that is, the uppercase letters A–Z and the lowercase letters a–z) and special symbols (that is, $, @, %, &, *, (,), -, +, ", :, ?, / and many others). Digits, letters and special symbols are referred to as characters. The set of all characters used to write programs and represent data items on a particular computer is called that computer's character set. Because computers can process only 0s and 1s, every character in a computer's character set is represented as a pattern of 0s and 1s. Bytes are composed of eight bits. Visual Basic uses the Unicode character set, in which each character is composed of *two* bytes (and hence 16 bits). You create programs and data items with characters; computers manipulate and process these characters as patterns of bits.

Fields

Just as characters are composed of bits, fields are composed of characters. A field is a group of characters that conveys meaning. For example, a field consisting of uppercase and lowercase letters can represent a person's name.

Data Hierarchy

Data items processed by computers form a data hierarchy (Fig. 8.1), in which data items become larger and more complex in structure as we progress up the hierarchy from bits to characters to fields to larger data aggregates.

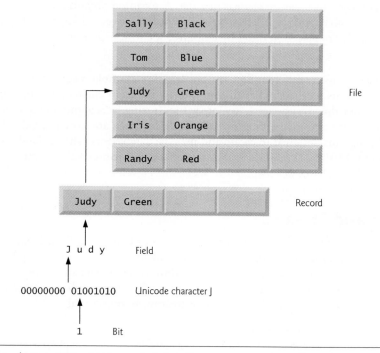

Fig. 8.1 | Data hierarchy (assuming that files are organized into records).

Records

Typically, a **record** is composed of several related fields. In a payroll system, for example, a record for a particular employee might include the following fields:

1. Employee identification number
2. Name
3. Address
4. Hourly pay rate
5. Number of exemptions claimed
6. Year-to-date earnings
7. Amount of taxes withheld

In the preceding example, each field is associated with the same employee. A data file can be implemented as a group of related records.[1] A company's payroll file normally contains one record for each employee. Companies typically have many files, some containing millions, billions or even trillions of characters of information.

To facilitate the retrieval of specific records from a file, at least one field in each record can be chosen as a **record key**, which identifies a record as belonging to a particular person or entity and distinguishes that record from all others. For example, in a payroll record, the employee identification number normally would be the record key.

Sequential Files

There are many ways to organize records in a file. A common organization is called a **sequential file** in which records typically are stored in order by a record-key field. In a payroll file, records usually are placed in order by employee identification number.

Databases

Most businesses use many different files to store data. For example, a company might have payroll files, accounts receivable files (listing money due from clients), accounts payable files (listing money due to suppliers), inventory files (listing facts about all the items handled by the business) and many other files. Related files often are stored in a **database**. A collection of programs designed to create and manage databases is called a **database management system (DBMS)**. You'll learn about databases in Chapter 12 and you'll do additional work with databases in Chapter 13, Web App Development with ASP.NET, and the online Web Services chapter.

8.3 Files and Streams

Visual Basic views a file simply as a sequential **stream** of bytes (Fig. 8.2). Depending on the operating system, each file ends either with an **end-of-file marker** or at a specific byte number that's recorded in a system-maintained administrative data structure for the file. For example, the Windows operating system keeps track of the number of bytes in a file. You open a file from a Visual Basic program by creating an object that enables communi-

---

1. In some operating systems, a file is viewed as nothing more than a collection of bytes, and any organization of the bytes in a file (such as organizing the data into records) is a view created by the application programmer.

cation between a program and a particular file, such as an object of class `StreamWriter` to write text to a file or an object of class `StreamReader` to read text from a file.

Fig. 8.2 | Visual Basic's view of an *n*-byte file.

8.4 Test-Driving the Credit Inquiry Application

A credit manager would like you to implement a **Credit Inquiry** application that enables the credit manager to separately search for and display account information for customers with

- debit balances—customers who owe the company money for previously received goods and services

- zero balances—customers who do not owe the company money

- credit balances—customers to whom the company owes money

The application reads records from a text file then displays the contents of each record that matches the type selected by the credit manager, whom we shall refer to from this point forward simply as "the user."

Opening the File
When the user initially executes the **Credit Inquiry** application, the `Buttons` at the bottom of the window are disabled (Fig. 8.3(a))—the user cannot interact with them until a file has been selected. The company could have several files containing account data, so to begin processing a file of accounts, the user selects **Open...** from the application's custom **File** menu (Fig. 8.3(b)), which you'll create in Section 8.6. This displays an **Open** dialog (Fig. 8.3(c)) that allows the user to specify the name and location of the file from which the records will be read. In our case, we stored the file in the folder `C:\DataFiles` and named the file `Accounts.txt`. The left side of the dialog allows the user to locate the file on disk. The user can then select the file in the right side of the dialog and click the **Open** `Button` to submit the file name to the application. The **File** menu also provides an **Exit** menu item that allows the user to terminate the application.

a) Initial GUI with `Buttons` disabled until the user selects a file from which to read records

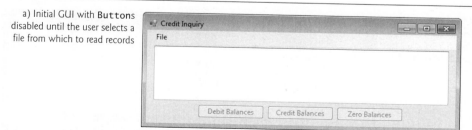

Fig. 8.3 | GUI for the **Credit Inquiry** application. (Part I of 2.)

b) Selecting the **Open...** menu item from the **File** menu displays the **Open** dialog in part (c)

c) The **Open** dialog allows the user to specify the location and name of the file

Fig. 8.3 | GUI for the **Credit Inquiry** application. (Part 2 of 2.)

Displaying Accounts with Credit, Debit and Zero Balances

After selecting a file name, the user can click one of the Buttons at the bottom of the window to display the records that match the specified account type. Figure 8.4(a) shows the accounts with debit balances. Figure 8.4(b) shows the accounts with credit balances. Figure 8.4(c) shows the accounts with zero balances.

a) Clicking the **Debit Balances** Button displays the accounts with *positive* balances (that is, the people who owe the company money)

Fig. 8.4 | GUI for **Credit Inquiry** application. (Part 1 of 2.)

b) Clicking the **Credit Balances** Button displays the accounts with *negative* balances (that is, the people to whom the company owes money)

Negative currency values are displayed in parentheses by default

c) Clicking the **Zero Balances** Button displays the accounts with zero balances (that is, the people who do not have a balance because they've already paid or have not had any recent transactions)

Fig. 8.4 | GUI for **Credit Inquiry** application. (Part 2 of 2.)

8.5 Writing Data Sequentially to a Text File

Before we can implement the **Credit Inquiry** application, we must create the file from which that application will read records. Our first program builds the sequential file containing the account information for the company's clients. For each client, the program obtains through its GUI the client's account number, first name, last name and balance—the amount of money that the client owes to the company for previously purchased goods and services. The data obtained for each client constitutes a "record" for that client. In this application, the account number is used as the record key—files are often maintained in order by their record keys. For simplicity, this program assumes that the user enters records in account number order.

GUI for the Create Accounts Application

The GUI for the **Create Accounts** application is shown in Fig. 8.5. This application introduces the **MenuStrip control** which enables you to place a menu bar in your window. It also introduces **ToolStripMenuItem controls** which are used to create menus and menu items. We show how use the IDE to build the menu and menu items in Section 8.6. There you'll see that the menu and menu item variable names are generated by the IDE and begin with capital letters. Like other controls, you can change the variable names in the **Properties** window by modifying the **(Name)** property.

FileToolStripMenuItem
NewToolStripMenuItem
CloseToolStripMenuItem
ExitToolStripMenuItem

applicationMenuStrip
(on the screen this control has a
slightly lighter color than the
Form's background)

These controls are disabled until
the user specifies a file using the
New... option in the **File** menu

accountNumberLabel — accountNumberTextBox
firstNameLabel — firstNameTextBox
lastNameLabel — lastNameTextBox
balanceLabel — balanceTextBox
addAccountButton

Fig. 8.5 | GUI for the **Create Accounts** application.

Interacting with the Create Accounts Application
When the user initially executes this application, the **Close** menu item, the TextBoxes and the **Add Account** Button are disabled (Fig. 8.6(a))—the user can interact with these controls only after specifying the file into which the records will be saved. To begin creating a file of accounts, the user selects **File > New...** (Fig. 8.6(b)), which displays a **Save As** dialog (Fig. 8.6(c)) that allows the user to specify the name and location of the file into which the records will be placed. The **File** menu provides two other menu items—**Close** to close the file so the user can create another file and **Exit** to terminate the application. After the user specifies a file name, the application opens the file and enables the controls, so the user can begin entering account information. Figure 8.6(d)–(h) shows the sample data being entered for five accounts. The program does not depict how the records are stored in the file. This is a text file, so after you close the program, you can open the file in any text editor to see its contents. Figure 8.6(j) shows the file's contents in **Notepad**.

Fig. 8.6 | User creating a text file of account information. (Part 1 of 3.)

c) **Save As** dialog displayed when user selects **New...** from the **File** menu. In this case, the user is naming the file `Accounts.txt` and placing the file in the `C:\DataFiles` folder.

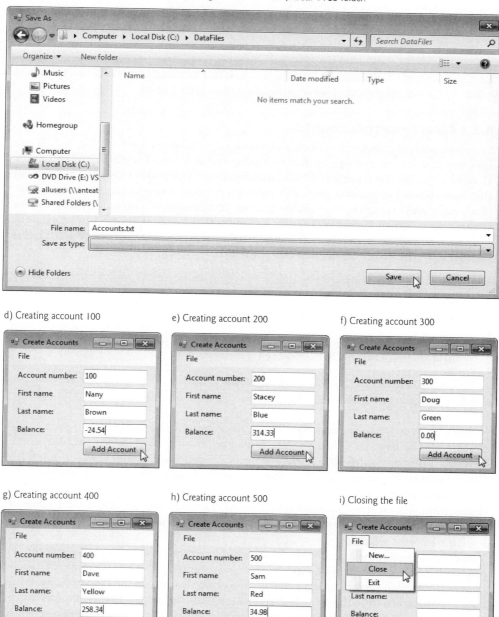

d) Creating account 100   e) Creating account 200   f) Creating account 300

g) Creating account 400   h) Creating account 500   i) Closing the file

Fig. 8.6 | User creating a text file of account information. (Part 2 of 3.)

j) The `Accounts.txt` file
open in **Notepad** to show
how the records were
written to the file. Note the
comma separators between
the data items

Fig. 8.6 | User creating a text file of account information. (Part 3 of 3.)

8.5.1 Class CreateAccounts

Let's now study the declaration of class `CreateAccounts`, which begins in Fig. 8.7. We've split this class into several figures that we analyze one at a time. Framework Class Library classes are grouped by functionality into **namespaces**, which make it easier for you to find the classes needed to perform particular tasks. Line 3 is an **Imports statement**, which indicates that we're using classes from the **System.IO namespace**. This namespace contains stream classes such as **StreamWriter** (for text output) and **StreamReader** (for text input). Line 6 declares `fileWriter` as an instance variable of type `StreamWriter`. We'll use this variable to interact with the file that the user selects.

```
1   ' Fig. 8.7: CreateAccounts.vb
2   ' Program that creates a text file of account information.
3   Imports System.IO ' using classes from this namespace
4
5   Public Class CreateAccounts
6      Dim fileWriter As StreamWriter ' writes data to text file
7
```

Fig. 8.7 | Program that creates a text file of account information.

You must import `StreamWriter` before you can use it. In fact, *all namespaces except System must be imported into a program to use the classes in those namespaces. Namespace System is imported by default into every program.* Classes like `String`, `Convert` and `Math` that we've used frequently in earlier examples are declared in the `System` namespace. So far, we have *not* used `Imports` statements in any of our programs, but we *have* used many classes from namespaces that *must* be imported. For example, all of the GUI controls you've used so far are classes in the `System.Windows.Forms` namespace.

So why were we able to compile those programs? When you create a project, each Visual Basic project type automatically imports several namespaces that are commonly used with that project type. You can see the namespaces (Fig. 8.8) that were automatically imported into your project by right clicking the project's name in the **Properties** window, selecting **Properties** from the menu and clicking the **References** tab. The list appears under **Imported namespaces:**—each namespace with a checkmark is automatically imported into the project. This application is a Windows Forms application. The `System.IO` namespace is not imported by default. To import a namespace, you can either use an `Imports` statement (as in line 3 of Fig. 8.7) or you can scroll through the list in Fig. 8.8 and check the checkbox for the namespace you wish to import.

Fig. 8.8 | Viewing the namespaces that are pre-`Imported` into a Windows Forms application.

8.5.2 Opening the File

When the user selects **File > New...**, method `NewToolStripMenuItem_Click` (Fig. 8.9) is called to handle the **New...** menu item's `Click` event. This method opens the file. First, line 12 calls method `CloseFile` (Fig. 8.11, lines 102–111) in case the user previously opened another file during the current execution of the application. `CloseFile` closes the file associated with this application's `StreamWriter`.

```vb
 8    ' create a new file in which accounts can be stored
 9    Private Sub NewToolStripMenuItem_Click(ByVal sender As System.Object,
10       ByVal e As System.EventArgs) Handles NewToolStripMenuItem.Click
11
12       CloseFile() ' ensure that any prior file is closed
13       Dim result As DialogResult ' stores result of Save dialog
14       Dim fileName As String ' name of file to save data
15
16       ' display dialog so user can choose the name of the file to save
17       Using fileChooser As New SaveFileDialog()
18          result = fileChooser.ShowDialog()
19          fileName = fileChooser.FileName ' get specified file name
20       End Using ' automatic call to fileChooser.Dispose() occurs here
21
22       ' if user did not click Cancel
23       If result <> Windows.Forms.DialogResult.Cancel Then
24          Try
25             ' open or create file for writing
26             fileWriter = New StreamWriter(fileName, True)
27
28             ' enable controls
29             CloseToolStripMenuItem.Enabled = True
30             addAccountButton.Enabled = True
31             accountNumberTextBox.Enabled = True
32             firstNameTextBox.Enabled = True
```

Fig. 8.9 | Using the `SaveFileDialog` to allow the user to select the file into which records will be written. (Part 1 of 2.)

```
33                    lastNameTextBox.Enabled = True
34                    balanceTextBox.Enabled = True
35               Catch ex As IOException
36                  MessageBox.Show("Error Opening File", "Error",
37                     MessageBoxButtons.OK, MessageBoxIcon.Error)
38               End Try
39            End If
40      End Sub ' NewToolStripMenuItem_Click
41
```

Fig. 8.9 | Using the SaveFileDialog to allow the user to select the file into which records will be written. (Part 2 of 2.)

Next, lines 17–20 display the **Save As** dialog and get the file name specified by the user. First, line 17 creates the **SaveFileDialog** object (namespace System.Windows.Forms) named fileChooser. Line 18 calls its **ShowDialog** method to display the SaveFileDialog (Fig. 8.6(c)). This dialog prevents the user from interacting with any other window in the program until the user closes it by clicking either **Save** or **Cancel**, so it's a *modal dialog*. The user selects the location where the file should be stored and specifies the file name, then clicks **Save**. Method ShowDialog returns a **DialogResult** enumeration constant specifying which button (**Save** or **Cancel**) the user clicked to close the dialog. This is assigned to the DialogResult variable result (line 18). Line 19 uses SaveFileDialog property **FileName** to obtain the location and name of the file.

8.5.3 Managing Resources with the Using Statement

Lines 17–20 introduce the **Using statement**, which simplifies writing code in which you obtain, use and release a resource. In this case, the resource is a SaveFileDialog. Windows and dialogs are limited system resources that occupy *memory* and should be returned to the system (to free up that memory) as soon as they're no longer needed. In all our previous applications, this happens when the program terminates. In a long running program, if resources are not returned to the system when they're no longer needed, then a **resource leak** occurs and the resources are not available for use in this or other programs. Objects that represent such resources typically provide a Dispose method that *must* be called to return the resources to the system. The Using statement in lines 17–20 creates a SaveFileDialog object, uses it in lines 18–19, then automatically calls its Dispose method to release the object's resources as soon as End Using is reached, thus guaranteeing that the resources are returned to the system and the memory they occupy is freed up.

Line 23 tests whether the user clicked **Cancel** by comparing result to the constant Windows.Forms.DialogResult.Cancel. If not, line 26 creates a StreamWriter object that we'll use to write data to the file. The two arguments are a String representing the location and name of the file, and a Boolean indicating what to do if the file already exists. If the file doesn't exist, this statement creates the file. If the file does exist, the second argument (True) indicates that new data written to the file should be appended at the end of the file's current contents. If the second argument is False and the file already exists, *the file's contents will be discarded* and new data will be written starting at the *beginning* of the file. Lines 29–34 enable the **Close** menu item and the TextBoxes and Button that are used to enter records into the program. Lines 35–37 catch an **IOException** if there is a problem opening the file. If so, the program displays an error message. If no exception occurs, the file is opened for writing. Most file-processing operations have the potential to throw exceptions, so such operations are typically placed in Try statements.

8.5.4 Adding an Account to the File

After typing information in each TextBox, the user clicks the **Add Account** Button, which calls method addAccountButton_Click (Fig. 8.10) to save the data into the file. If the user entered a valid account number (that is, an integer greater than zero), lines 56–59 write the record to the file by invoking the StreamWriter's WriteLine method, which writes a sequence of characters to the file and positions the output cursor to the beginning of the next line in the file. We separate each field in the record with a comma in this example (this is known as a **comma-delimited text file**), and we place each record on its own line in the file. If an IOException occurs when attempting to write the record to the file, lines 64–66 Catch the exception and display an appropriate message to the user. Similarly, if the user entered invalid data in the accountNumberTextBox or balanceTextBox lines 67–69 catch the **FormatExceptions** thrown by class Convert's methods and display an appropriate error message. Lines 73–77 clear the TextBoxes and return the focus to the account-NumberTextBox so the user can enter the next record.

```vbnet
42      ' add an account to the file
43      Private Sub addAccountButton_Click(ByVal sender As System.Object,
44          ByVal e As System.EventArgs) Handles addAccountButton.Click
45
46          ' determine whether TextBox account field is empty
47          If accountNumberTextBox.Text <> String.Empty Then
48              ' try to store record to file
49              Try
50                  ' get account number
51                  Dim accountNumber As Integer =
52                      Convert.ToInt32(accountNumberTextBox.Text)
53
54                  If accountNumber > 0 Then ' valid account number?
55                      ' write record data to file separating fields by commas
56                      fileWriter.WriteLine(accountNumber & "," &
57                          firstNameTextBox.Text & "," &
58                          lastNameTextBox.Text & "," &
59                          Convert.ToDecimal(balanceTextBox.Text))
60                  Else
61                      MessageBox.Show("Invalid Account Number", "Error",
62                          MessageBoxButtons.OK, MessageBoxIcon.Error)
63                  End If
64              Catch ex As IOException
65                  MessageBox.Show("Error Writing to File", "Error",
66                      MessageBoxButtons.OK, MessageBoxIcon.Error)
67              Catch ex As FormatException
68                  MessageBox.Show("Invalid account number or balance",
69                      "Format Error", MessageBoxButtons.OK, MessageBoxIcon.Error)
70              End Try
71          End If
```

Fig. 8.10 | Writing an account record to the file. (Part 1 of 2.)

```
72
73        accountNumberTextBox.Clear()
74        firstNameTextBox.Clear()
75        lastNameTextBox.Clear()
76        balanceTextBox.Clear()
77        accountNumberTextBox.Focus()
78     End Sub ' addAccountButton_Click
79
```

Fig. 8.10 | Writing an account record to the file. (Part 2 of 2.)

8.5.5 Closing the File and Terminating the Application

When the user selects **File > Close**, method CloseToolStripMenuItem_Click (Fig. 8.11, lines 81–91) calls method CloseFile (lines 102–111) to close the file. Then lines 85–90 disable the controls that should not be available when a file is not open.

```
80     ' close the currently open file and disable controls
81     Private Sub CloseToolStripMenuItem_Click(ByVal sender As System.Object,
82        ByVal e As System.EventArgs) Handles CloseToolStripMenuItem.Click
83
84        CloseFile() ' close currently open file
85        CloseToolStripMenuItem.Enabled = False
86        addAccountButton.Enabled = False
87        accountNumberTextBox.Enabled = False
88        firstNameTextBox.Enabled = False
89        lastNameTextBox.Enabled = False
90        balanceTextBox.Enabled = False
91     End Sub ' CloseToolStripMenuItem_Click
92
93     ' exit the application
94     Private Sub ExitToolStripMenuItem_Click(ByVal sender As System.Object,
95        ByVal e As System.EventArgs) Handles ExitToolStripMenuItem.Click
96
97        CloseFile() ' close the file before terminating application
98        Application.Exit() ' terminate the application
99     End Sub ' ExitToolStripMenuItem_Click
100
101    ' close the file
102    Sub CloseFile()
103       If fileWriter IsNot Nothing Then
104          Try
105             fileWriter.Close() ' close StreamWriter
106          Catch ex As IOException
107             MessageBox.Show("Error closing file", "Error",
108                MessageBoxButtons.OK, MessageBoxIcon.Error)
109          End Try
110       End If
111    End Sub ' CloseFile
112 End Class ' CreateAccounts
```

Fig. 8.11 | Closing the file and terminating the application.

When the user clicks the **Exit** menu item, method `ExitToolStripMenuItem_Click` (lines 94–99) responds to the menu item's `Click` event by exiting the application. Line 97 closes the `StreamWriter` and the associated file, then line 98 terminates the program. The call to method `Close` (line 105) is located in a `Try` block. Method **`Close`** throws an `IOException` if the file cannot be closed properly. In this case, it's important to notify the user that the information in the file or stream might be corrupted.

8.6 Building Menus with the Windows Forms Designer

In the test-drive of the **Credit Inquiry** application (Section 8.4) and in the overview of the **Create Accounts** application (Section 8.5), we demonstrated how menus provide a convenient way to organize the commands that you use to interact with an application without "cluttering" its user interface. Menus contain groups of related commands. When a command is selected, the application performs a specific action (for example, select a file to open, exit the application, etc.).

Menus make it simple and straightforward to locate an application's commands. They can also make it easier for users to use applications. For example, many applications provide a **File** menu that contains an **Exit** menu item to terminate the application. If this menu item is always placed in the **File** menu, then users become accustomed to going to the **File** menu to terminate an application. When they use a new application and it has a **File** menu, they'll already be familiar with the location of the **Exit** command.

The menu that contains a menu item is that menu item's **parent menu**. In the **Create Accounts** application, **File** is the parent menu that contains three menu items—**New...**, **Close** and **Exit**.

Adding a *MenuStrip* to the *Form*

Before you can place a menu on your application, you must provide a **MenuStrip** to organize and manage the application's menus. Double click the `MenuStrip` control in the **Toolbox**. This creates a menu bar (the `MenuStrip`) across the top of the `Form` (below the title bar; Fig. 8.12) and places a `MenuStrip` icon in the **component tray** (the gray area) at the bottom of the designer. You can access the `MenuStrip`'s properties in the **Properties** window by clicking the `MenuStrip` icon in the component tray. We set the `MenuStrip`'s **(Name)** property to `applicationMenuStrip`.

Adding a *ToolStripMenuItem* to *MenuStrip*

You can now use **Design** mode to create and edit menus for your application. To add a menu, click the **Type Here** TextBox (Fig. 8.12) in the menu bar and type the menu's name. For the **File** menu, type `&File` (we'll explain the & in a moment) then press *Enter*. This creates a `ToolStripMenuItem` that the IDE automatically names `FileToolStripMenuItem`. Additional **Type Here** TextBoxes appear, allowing you to add menu items to the menu or add more menus to the menu bar (Fig. 8.13). Most menus and menu items provide **access shortcuts** (or **keyboard shortcuts**) that allow users to open a menu or select a menu item by using the keyboard. For example, most applications allow you to open the **File** menu by typing *Alt + F*. The letter that's used as the shortcut is underlined in the GUI when you press the *Alt* key. To specify the shortcut key, type an ampersand (&) before the character to be underlined—so `&File` underlines the **F** in **File**.

Type menu name in **TextBox**

MenuStrip

MenuStrip icon in component tray

Fig. 8.12 | Editing menus in Visual Studio.

Place the & character before a letter to underline it in the menu, so that the letter can be used as an access shortcut

TextBox for adding another top-level menu

TextBox for adding a menu item to the existing top-level menu

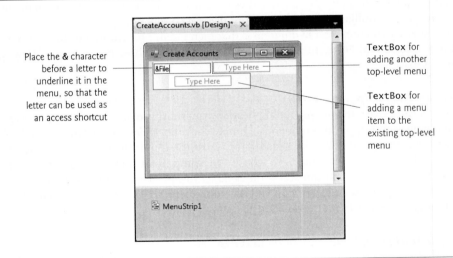

Fig. 8.13 | Adding `ToolStripMenuItems` to a `MenuStrip`.

Adding Menu Items to the File Menu

To add the **New…**, **Close** and **Exit** menu items to the **File** menu, type &New..., &Close and E&xit (one at a time) into the TextBox that appears below the **File** menu. When you press *Enter* after each, a new TextBox appears below that item so you can add another menu item. Placing the & before the x in Exit makes the x the access key—x is commonly used as the access key for the **Exit** menu item. The menu editor automatically names the ToolStripMenuItems for the **New…**, **Close** and **Exit** menu items as NewToolStripMenuItem, CloseToolStripMenuItem and ExitToolStripMenuItem, respectively.

Look-and-Feel Observation 8.1

*By convention, place an ellipsis (...) after the name of a menu item that, when selected, displays a dialog (e.g. **New...**).*

Creating Event Handlers for the Menu Items

Like Buttons, menu items have Click events that notify the program when an item is selected. To create the event handler for a menu item so the application can respond when the menu item is selected, double click the menu item in the Windows Forms Designer then insert your event handling code in the new method's body. In fact, the same event handler method can be used for Buttons and menu items that perform the same task.

8.7 Credit Inquiry Application: Reading Data Sequentially from a Text File

Now that we've presented the code for creating the file of accounts, let's develop the code for the **Credit Inquiry** application which reads that file. Much of the code in this example is similar to the **Create Accounts** application, so we'll discuss only the unique aspects of the application.

8.7.1 Implementing the Credit Inquiry Application

The declaration of class CreditInquiry begins in Fig. 8.14. Line 4 imports the System.IO namespace, which contains the StreamReader class that we'll use to read from the text file in this example. Line 7 declares the instance variable fileName in which we store the file name selected by the user (that is, credit manager) in the **Open** dialog (Fig. 8.3(c)). Lines 9–13 declare the enumeration AccountType, which creates constants that represent the types of accounts that can be displayed.

```
1   ' Fig. 8.14: CreditInquiry.vb
2   ' Read a file sequentially and display contents based on
3   ' account type specified by user (credit, debit or zero balances).
4   Imports System.IO ' using classes from this namespace
5
6   Public Class CreditInquiry
7      Private fileName As String ' name of file containing account data
8
9      Enum AccountType ' constants representing account types
10         CREDIT
11         DEBIT
12         ZERO
13      End Enum ' AccountType
14
```

Fig. 8.14 | Declaring the fileName instance variable and creating the AccountType enumeration that's used to specify the type of account to display.

8.7.2 Selecting the File to Process

When the user selects **File > Open...**, the event handler OpenToolStripMenuItem_Click (Fig. 8.15, lines 16–33) executes. Line 22 creates an **OpenFileDialog**, and line 23 calls its

ShowDialog method to display the **Open** dialog, in which the user selects the file to open. Line 24 stores the selected file name in fileName.

```
15      ' opens a file in which accounts are stored
16      Private Sub OpenToolStripMenuItem_Click(ByVal sender As System.Object,
17         ByVal e As System.EventArgs) Handles OpenToolStripMenuItem.Click
18
19         Dim result As DialogResult ' stores result of Open dialog
20
21         ' create dialog box enabling user to open file
22         Using fileChooser As New OpenFileDialog()
23            result = fileChooser.ShowDialog()
24            fileName = fileChooser.FileName ' get specified file name
25         End Using ' automatic call to fileChooser.Dispose() occurs here
26
27         ' if user did not click Cancel, enable Buttons
28         If result <> Windows.Forms.DialogResult.Cancel Then
29            creditBalancesButton.Enabled = True
30            debitBalancesButton.Enabled = True
31            zeroBalancesButton.Enabled = True
32         End If
33      End Sub ' OpenToolStripMenuItem_Click
34
35      ' exit the application
36      Private Sub ExitToolStripMenuItem_Click(ByVal sender As System.Object,
37         ByVal e As System.EventArgs) Handles ExitToolStripMenuItem.Click
38
39         Application.Exit() ' terminate the application
40      End Sub ' ExitToolStripMenuItem_Click
41
```

Fig. 8.15 | Event handlers for the **Open...** and **Exit** menu items.

8.7.3 Specifying the Type of Records to Display

When the user clicks the **Credit Balances**, **Debit Balances** or **Zero Balances** Button, the program invokes the corresponding event-handler method—creditBalances-Button_Click (Fig. 8.16, lines 43–47), debitBalancesButton_Click (lines 50–54) or zeroBalancesButton_Click (lines 57–61). Each of these methods calls method Display-Accounts (Fig. 8.17), passing a constant from the AccountType enumeration as an argument. Method DisplayAccounts then displays the matching accounts.

```
42      ' display accounts with credit balances
43      Private Sub creditBalancesButton_Click(ByVal sender As System.Object,
44         ByVal e As System.EventArgs) Handles creditBalancesButton.Click
45
46         DisplayAccounts(AccountType.CREDIT) ' displays credit balances
47      End Sub ' creditBalancesButton_Click
48
```

Fig. 8.16 | Each Button event handler calls method DisplayAccounts and passes the appropriate AccountType as an argument to specify which accounts to display. (Part 1 of 2.)

```
49      ' display accounts with debit balances
50      Private Sub debitBalancesButton_Click(ByVal sender As System.Object,
51         ByVal e As System.EventArgs) Handles debitBalancesButton.Click
52
53         DisplayAccounts(AccountType.DEBIT) ' displays debit balances
54      End Sub ' debitBalancesButton_Click
55
56      ' display accounts with zero balances
57      Private Sub zeroBalancesButton_Click(ByVal sender As System.Object,
58         ByVal e As System.EventArgs) Handles zeroBalancesButton.Click
59
60         DisplayAccounts(AccountType.ZERO) ' displays zero balances
61      End Sub ' zeroBalancesButton_Click
62
```

Fig. 8.16 | Each Button event handler calls method DisplayAccounts and passes the appropriate AccountType as an argument to specify which accounts to display. (Part 2 of 2.)

8.7.4 Displaying the Records

Method DisplayAccounts (Fig. 8.17, lines 64–104) receives as an argument an Account-Type constant specifying the type of accounts to display. The method reads the entire file one record at a time until the end of the file is reached, displaying a record only if its balance matches the type of accounts specified by the user.

Opening the File
Line 65 declares the StreamReader variable fileReader that will be used to interact with the file. Line 72 opens the file by passing the fileName instance variable to the Stream-Reader constructor.

```
63      ' display accounts of specified type
64      Sub DisplayAccounts(ByVal accountType As AccountType)
65         Dim fileReader As StreamReader = Nothing
66
67         ' read and display file information
68         Try
69            accountsTextBox.Text = "The accounts are:" & vbCrLf
70
71            ' open file for reading
72            fileReader = New StreamReader(fileName)
73
74            ' read file and display lines that match the balance type
75            Do While Not fileReader.EndOfStream ' while not end of file
76               Dim line As String = fileReader.ReadLine() ' read line
77               Dim fields() As String = line.Split(","c) ' split into fields
78
```

Fig. 8.17 | Method DisplayAccounts opens the file, reads one record at a time, displays the record if it matches the selected AccountType and closes the file when all records have been processed. (Part 1 of 2.)

```
79                      ' get data from fields array
80                      Dim accountNumber As Integer = Convert.ToInt32(fields(0))
81                      Dim firstName As String = fields(1)
82                      Dim lastName As String = fields(2)
83                      Dim balance As Decimal = Convert.ToDecimal(fields(3))
84
85                      If ShouldDisplay(balance, accountType) Then
86                         accountsTextBox.AppendText(accountNumber & vbTab &
87                            firstName & vbTab & lastName & vbTab &
88                            String.Format("{0:C}", balance) & vbCrLf)
89                      End If
90                   Loop
91                Catch ex As IOException
92                   MessageBox.Show("Cannot Read File", "Error",
93                      MessageBoxButtons.OK, MessageBoxIcon.Error)
94                Finally ' ensure that file gets closed
95                   If fileReader IsNot Nothing Then
96                      Try
97                         fileReader.Close() ' close StreamReader
98                      Catch ex As IOException
99                         MessageBox.Show("Error closing file", "Error",
100                           MessageBoxButtons.OK, MessageBoxIcon.Error)
101                     End Try
102                  End If
103               End Try
104            End Sub ' DisplayAccounts
105
106            ' determine whether to display given account based on the balance
107            Function ShouldDisplay(ByVal balance As Double,
108               ByVal type As AccountType) As Boolean
109
110               If balance < 0 AndAlso type = AccountType.CREDIT Then
111                  Return True ' record should be displayed
112               ElseIf balance > 0 AndAlso type = AccountType.DEBIT Then
113                  Return True ' record should be displayed
114               ElseIf balance = 0 AndAlso type = AccountType.ZERO Then
115                  Return True ' record should be displayed
116               End If
117
118               Return False ' record should not be displayed
119            End Function ' ShouldDisplay
120        End Class ' Credit Inquiry
```

Fig. 8.17 | Method `DisplayAccounts` opens the file, reads one record at a time, displays the record if it matches the selected `AccountType` and closes the file when all records have been processed. (Part 2 of 2.)

Reading and Processing Records

The company could have many separate files containing account information. So this application does not know in advance how many records will be processed. In file processing, we receive an indication that the end of the file has been reached when we've read the entire contents of a file. For a `StreamReader`, this is when its **EndOfStream** property returns True (line 75).

As long as the end of the file has not been reached, line 76 uses the StreamReader's **ReadLine method** (which returns a String) to read one line of text from the file. Recall from Section 8.5 that a each line of text in the file represents one "record" and that the record's fields are delimited by commas. To access the record's data, we need to break the String into its separate fields. This is known as **tokenizing** the String. Line 77 breaks the line of text into fields using String method **Split**, which receives a delimiter as an argument. In this case, the delimiter is the character literal ","c—indicating that the delimiter is a comma. A character literal looks like a String literal that contains one character and is followed immediately by the letter c. Method Split returns an array of Strings representing the tokens, which we assign to array variable fields.

Preparing to Display the Record

Lines 80–83 assign the tokens to the local variables accountNumber, firstName, lastName and balance. Line 85 calls method ShouldDisplay (lines 107–119) to determine whether the current record should be displayed. If so, lines 86–88 display the record. If the balance is negative, the currency format specifier (C) formats the value in parentheses (Fig. 8.4(b)). Method ShouldDisplay receives the balance and the AccountType as arguments. If the balance represents the specified AccountType, the method returns True and the record will be displayed by method DisplayAccounts; otherwise, it returns False and the record will not be displayed.

Ensuring that the File is Closed Properly

When performing file processing, exceptions can occur. In this example, if the program is unable to open the file or unable to read from the file, IOExceptions will occur. For this reason, file-processing code normally appears in a Try block. Regardless of whether a program experiences exceptions while processing a file, the program should close the file when it's no longer needed. Suppose we put the statement that closes the StreamReader after the Do While...Loop at line 91. If no exceptions occur, the Try block executes normally and the file is closed. However, if an exception occurs, the Try block terminates immediately—*before* the StreamReader can be closed. We could duplicate the statement that closes the StreamReader in the Catch block, but this would make the code more difficult to modify and maintain. We could also place the statement that closes the StreamReader after the Try statement; however, if the Try block terminated due to a Return statement, code following the Try statement would never execute.

To address these problems, Visual Basic's exception-handling mechanism provides the optional **Finally block**, which—if present—is *guaranteed to execute* regardless of whether the Try block executes successfully or an exception occurs. This makes the Finally block an ideal location in which to place resource release code for resources that are acquired and manipulated in the corresponding Try block (such as files). By placing the statement that closes the StreamReader in a Finally block, we ensure that the file will always be closed properly.

Local variables in a Try block cannot be accessed in the corresponding Finally block. For this reason, variables that must be accessed in both a Try block and its corresponding Finally block should be declared before the Try block, as we did with the StreamReader variable (line 65).

Relationship Between the Using and Try Statements

In Section 8.5.3, we discussed how a Using statement manages resources. The Using statement is actually a shorthand notation for a Try statement with a Finally block. For example, the Using statement in Fig. 8.15 (lines 22–25) is equivalent to the following code

```
Dim fileChooser As New OpenFileDialog()

Try
    result = fileChooser.ShowDialog()
    fileName = fileChooser.FileName ' get specified file name
Finally
    fileChooser.Dispose()
End Try
```

8.8 Wrap-Up

In this chapter, you learned how to use file processing to create and manipulate persistent data. You learned that data is stored as 0s and 1s, and that combinations of these values are used to form bytes, fields, records and eventually files. Next, you learned how to use sequential-access file processing to manipulate records in text files. We began by creating a text-file of accounts using a StreamWriter. We then used a StreamReader to read the contents of the file into a separate application for processing.

In Chapter 9, we show you how to create your own classes and how to use those classes to create objects in your programs. In particular, we present an Account class that could represent a bank account, Card and DeckOfCards classes that could be used to implement a card game, and a Time class that represents the time in 24-hour clock format.

Summary

Section 8.1 Introduction
- Variables and arrays offer only temporary storage of data—the data is lost, for example, when a local variable "goes out of scope" or when the program terminates.
- Files and databases are used for long-term retention of large (and often *vast*) amounts of data, even after the program that created the data terminates.
- Data maintained in files is often called persistent data.
- Computers store files on secondary storage devices.

Section 8.2 Data Hierarchy
- All data items that computers process are reduced to combinations of 0s and 1s.
- The smallest data item that computers support is called a bit and has the value 0 or 1.
- Digits, letters and special symbols are referred to as characters. The set of all characters used to write programs and represent data items on a particular computer is called that computer's character set. Every character in a computer's character set is represented as a pattern of 0s and 1s.
- A byte is composed of eight bits.
- Characters in Visual Basic are Unicode characters composed of two bytes each.
- A field is a group of characters that conveys meaning.
- A record is composed of related fields.

- A data file can be implemented as a group of related records
- Typically, at least one field in each record is chosen as a record key, which uniquely identifies a record as belonging to a particular person or entity and distinguishes that record from all others.
- The most common type of file organization is a sequential file, in which records typically are stored in order by record-key field.
- Related files often are stored in a database. A collection of programs designed to create and manage databases is called a database management system (DBMS).

Section 8.3 Files and Streams
- Visual Basic views a file as a sequential stream of bytes.
- Visual Basic imposes no structure on files. You must structure files to meet the requirements of your applications.

Section 8.5 Writing Data Sequentially to a Text File
- The MenuStrip control enables you to place a menu bar in your window.
- ToolStripMenuItem controls are used to create menus and menu items.

Section 8.5.1 Class CreateAccounts
- Framework Class Library classes are grouped by functionality into namespaces.
- An Imports statement indicates that you're using classes from a particular namespace.
- The System.IO namespace contains stream classes such as StreamWriter and StreamReader.
- All namespaces except System must be imported into a program to use the classes in those namespaces. Namespace System is imported by default into every program.
- Each Visual Basic project type imports several commonly used namespaces.

Section 8.5.2 Opening the File
- A SaveFileDialog object's ShowDialog method displays a modal dialog that allows the user to specify the location and name of a file. The method returns a DialogResult enumeration constant specifying which button (**Save** or **Cancel**) the user clicked to close the dialog.
- SaveFileDialog property FileName returns the location and name of the selected file.

Section 8.5.3 Managing Resources with the Using Statement
- The Using statement simplifies writing code in which you obtain, use and release a resource.
- Objects which represent resources that should be returned to the system typically provide a Dispose method that must be called to return the resources.
- When End Using is reached, the Using statement automatically calls the Dispose method of the object created in the statement's first line.
- The StreamWriter constructor receives two arguments—a String representing the location and name of the file, and a Boolean indicating what to do if the file already exists. If the file doesn't exist, it's created. If the file does exist, a second argument of True indicates that new data written to the file should be appended to the end of the file's current contents. If the second argument is False and the file already exists, the file's contents will be discarded and new data will be written starting at the beginning of the file.
- Most file processing operations have the potential to throw IOExceptions, so such operations are typically placed in Try statements.

Section 8.5.4 Adding an Account to the File

- StreamWriter method WriteLine writes a sequence of characters to a file and positions the output cursor to the beginning of the next line in the file.

Section 8.5.5 Closing the File and Terminating the Application

- StreamWriter method Close closes the stream and the corresponding file.

Section 8.6 Building Menus with the Windows Forms Designer

- Menus contain groups of related commands that, when selected, cause the application to perform specific actions.

- A MenuStrip organizes an application's menus. You can access the MenuStrip's properties in the **Properties** window by clicking the MenuStrip icon in the component tray.

- You can use **Design** mode to create and edit menus for your application.

- To specify the shortcut key for a menu or menu item, type an ampersand (&) before the character to be underlined in the menu or menu item's name.

- Like Buttons, menu items have Click events that notify the program when an item is selected.

Section 8.7 Credit Inquiry Application: Reading Data Sequentially from a Text File

- OpenFileDialog method ShowDialog display an **Open** dialog, in which the user can select the file to open. The method returns a DialogResult enumeration constant specifying which button (**Open** or **Cancel**) the user clicked to close the dialog.

- OpenFileDialog property FileName returns the location and name of the selected file.

- A StreamReader reads text from the file specified as the argument to the object's constructor.

- StreamReader property EndOfStream returns True if the end of the file has been reached.

- StreamReader method ReadLine returns one line of text from a file as a String.

- String method Split receives a delimiter as an argument and tokenizes a String, using the delimiter to separate the tokens. Method Split returns an array of Strings representing the tokens.

- Visual Basic's exception-handling mechanism provides the optional Finally block, which—if present—is guaranteed to execute regardless of whether the Try block executes successfully or an exception occurs. The Finally block is an ideal location in which to place resource release code for resources such as files that are acquired and manipulated in the corresponding Try block.

- Local variables in a Try block cannot be accessed in the corresponding Finally block.

- The Using statement is a shorthand notation for a Try statement with a Finally block.

Terminology

Self-Review Exercises

8.1 Answer each of the following questions:

a) The smallest data item a computer can process is called a _____.
   1. database
   2. byte
   3. file
   4. bit

b) A group of related records is stored in a _____.
   1. file
   2. field
   3. bit
   4. byte

c) Data maintained in a file is called _____.
   1. persistent data
   2. bits
   3. secondary data
   4. databases

d) Methods from the _____ class can be used to write data to a file.
   1. StreamReader
   2. WriteFile
   3. StreamWriter
   4. None of the above

e) Namespace _____ provides the classes and methods you need to perform file processing.
   1. System.IO
   2. System.Files
   3. System.Stream
   4. System.Windows.Forms

f) Sometimes a group of related files is called a _____.
   1. field
   2. database
   3. collection
   4. byte

g) A(n) _____ allows the user to select a file to open.
   1. CreateFileDialog
   2. OpenFileDialog
   3. MessageBox
   4. None of the above

h) Digits, letters and special symbols are referred to as _____.
   1. constants
   2. Integers
   3. characters
   4. None of the above

i) StreamReader method _____ reads a line from a file.
   1. ReadLine
   2. Read
   3. ReadAll
   4. ReadToNewline

j) A _____ contains information that is read in the order it was written.
   1. sequential-access file
   2. StreamWriter
   3. StreamReader
   4. None of the above

k) Methods from class _____ can be used to read data from a file.
   1. StreamWriter
   2. FileReader
   3. StreamReader
   4. None of the above.

Answers to Self-Review Exercises

8.1 a) 4. b) 1. c) 1. d) 3. e) 1. f) 2. g) 2. h) 3. i) 1. j) 1. k) 3.

Exercises

8.2 *(Enhanced Class Average Application)* The class average application of Fig. 4.12 allowed the user to enter a set of grades then calculate and display the total of the grades and the class average. Create an application that enables the user to select a file in which to store grades. The application should allow the user to write any number of grades into that file and it should write one grade per line. Next, modify the application of Fig. 4.12 to allow the user to specify the location and name of a file containing grades. The application should read the grades from the file, then display the total of the grades and the class average.

8.3 *(Enhanced Student Poll Application)* Figure 7.4 contains an array of survey responses that is hard-coded into the program. Suppose we wish to process survey results that are stored in a file. First, create an application that enables the user to write survey responses to a file. Use a Stream-Writer to create a file called SurveyResponses.txt and write each response on a separate line. Modify the code in Fig. 7.4 to read the survey responses from SurveyResponses.txt by using a StreamReader. The program should continue to read responses until it reaches the end of file. The results should be output to the TextBox.

8.4 *(Telephone-Number Word Generator)* Modify the telephone-number word generator that you created in Exercise 7.15 to write to a file every possible seven-letter word combination corresponding to a telephone number.

8.5 *(Writing a Grade Report to a File)* Modify the Grade Report application in Section 7.15 to provide an option that allows the user to write the entire grade report to a file. The report should include all of the information in the gradesListBox, the class average and the grade distribution chart from the barChartListBox. To get the data from the ListBoxes, use each ListBox's Items collection. For example, to output the first line in the gradesListBox, you'd write the value of the expression gradesListBox.Items(0).ToString() to the file.

8.6 *(Reading Grades into a Two-Dimensional Array)* Modify your solution to Exercise 8.5 to allow the user to read the grades from a text file, rather than entering them via the GUI. Assume that the file contains 10 lines of text and that each line contains three grades.

Object-Oriented Programming: Classes and Objects

9

Nothing can have value without being an object of utility.
—Karl Marx

Your public servants serve you right.
—Adlai E. Stevenson

You will see something new. Two things. And I call them Thing One and Thing Two.
—Dr. Theodor Seuss Geisel

Objectives

In this chapter you'll learn:

- How to declare a class and use it to create an object.
- How to implement a class's behaviors as methods.
- How to implement a class's attributes as instance variables and properties.
- How to use a constructor to ensure that an object's attributes are initialized.
- How to use properties to ensure that only valid data is placed in attributes.
- How composition enables you to construct classes by reusing other classes.
- To implement classwide information with **Shared** class variables.
- To use the **Object Browser** to discover the capabilities of the classes in the .NET Framework Class Library.

9.1 Introduction

We introduced the basic terminology and concepts of object-oriented programming in Section 1.14. Many applications consist of one or more classes, each containing one or more methods. If you become part of a development team in industry, you may work on applications that contain hundreds, or even thousands, of classes. In this chapter, we motivate the notion of classes with real-world examples and use complete working applications to demonstrate creating your own classes and manipulating objects of those classes.

9.2 Classes, Objects, Methods and Instance Variables

We begin with a real-world analogy to help you understand classes and their contents. Suppose you want to drive a car and make it go faster by pressing down on its accelerator pedal. What must happen before you can do this? Well, before you can drive a car, someone has to design it. A car typically begins as engineering drawings, similar to the blueprints used to design a house. These engineering drawings include the design for an accelerator pedal to make the car go faster. The accelerator pedal "hides" the complex mechanisms that actually make the car go faster, just as the brake pedal "hides" the mechanisms that slow the car and the steering wheel "hides" the mechanisms that turn the car. This "hiding" enables people with little or no knowledge of how automotive hardware works to easily drive a car.

Unfortunately, you cannot drive a car's engineering drawings. Before you can drive a car, the car must be built from the engineering drawings that describe it. A completed car has an *actual* accelerator pedal to make it go faster, but even that's not enough—the car will not accelerate on its own, so the driver must *press* the accelerator pedal.

Now let's use our car example to introduce some key programming concepts. Performing a task in a program requires a method. The method describes the mechanisms that actually perform its tasks. The method hides these mechanisms from its user, just as the accelerator pedal of a car hides from the driver the mechanisms that make the car go faster. We begin by creating a program unit called a *class* to house a method, just as a car's engineering drawings house the design of an accelerator pedal. In a class, you provide one or more methods that are designed to perform the class's tasks. For example, the class in the next section represents a bank account and contains methods to deposit money in the account, withdraw money from the account and inquire what the current balance is.

Just as you cannot drive an engineering drawing of a car, you cannot "drive" a class. Just as someone has to build a car from its engineering drawings before you can actually drive it, *you must build an object of a class before you can get a program to perform the tasks the class describes how to do.*

When you drive a car, pressing its gas pedal sends a message to the car to perform a task—that is, to go faster. Similarly, you send **messages** to an object—each message is a method call that tells one of the object's methods to perform its task. Any program code that interacts with any objects of a particular class (from outside those objects) is known as a **client** of that class—objects provide services to the class's clients.

We've used the car analogy to introduce classes, objects and methods. In addition to the capabilities a car provides, it also has many *attributes*, such as its color, the number of doors, the amount of gas in its tank, its current speed and its odometer reading. Like the car's capabilities, its attributes are represented as part of a car's design in its engineering diagrams. As you drive a car, these attributes are always associated with the car. For example, each car *knows* how much gas is in its own gas tank, but *not* how much is in the tanks of *other* cars. Similarly, an object has attributes that are carried with it as it's used in a program. These attributes are specified in the object's class. For example, a bank account object has a balance attribute that represents the amount of money in the account. Each bank account object knows the balance in the account it represents, but *not* the balances of *other* accounts. Attributes are specified by a class's instance variables.

9.3 Account Class

We begin with a business example that consists of classes `Account` and `AccountTest`. The `Account` class (declared in file `Account.vb` of Fig. 9.2) represents a bank account that has a balance—an actual bank account class would include other information, such as name, address, telephone number and account number. The `AccountTest` class (Fig. 9.3) creates and uses an object of class `Account`. The classes are placed in separate files for clarity, but it's possible to place them in the same file. The GUI for the `AccountTest` application is shown in Fig. 9.1. When the program initially executes, it creates an `Account` object and displays its initial balance in the `accountBalanceValueLabel`. The user can enter a deposit or withdrawal amount in the `inputTextBox`, then press the **Deposit** `Button` to make a deposit or the **Withdraw** `Button` to make a withdrawal. After each operation, the `accountBalanceValueLabel` is updated with the new balance.

Fig. 9.1 | GUI for the application that tests class `Account`.

Adding a Class to a Project

For each example in this chapter, you'll add a class to your project. To do this, right click the project name in the **Solution Explorer** and select **Add > Class...** from the menu that appears. In the **Add New Item** dialog that appears, enter the name of your new file—in this case Account.vb—then click the **Add** Button. A new file will be added to your project with an empty Account class. Add the code from Fig. 9.2 to this file.

Account Class Declaration

The Account class declaration (Fig. 9.2) begins at line 3. The keyword **Public** is an access modifier. Only **Public** classes can be reused in other projects. Every class declaration contains keyword **Class** followed immediately by the class's name. Every class's body ends with the keywords **End Class**, as in line 49.

```vb
1   ' Fig. 9.2: Account.vb
2   ' Account class for maintaining a bank account balance.
3   Public Class Account
4       Private balanceValue As Decimal ' instance variable stores the balance
5
6       ' constructor initializes balanceValue
7       Public Sub New(Optional ByVal initialBalance As Decimal = 0D)
8           ' if initialBalance is less than 0, throw an exception
9           If initialBalance < 0D Then
10              Throw New ArgumentOutOfRangeException(
11                  "Initial balance must be greater than or equal to 0.")
12          End If
13
14          balanceValue = initialBalance ' initialize balanceValue
15      End Sub ' New
16
17      ' deposit money to the account
18      Public Sub Deposit(ByVal depositAmount As Decimal)
19          ' if depositAmount is less than or equal to 0, throw an exception
20          If depositAmount <= 0D Then
21              Throw New ArgumentOutOfRangeException(
22                  "Deposit amount must be positive.")
23          End If
24
25          balanceValue += depositAmount ' add depositAmount to balanceValue
26      End Sub ' Deposit
27
28      ' withdraw money from the account
29      Public Sub Withdraw(ByVal withdrawalAmount As Decimal)
30          ' if withdrawalAmount is greater than Balance, throw an exception
31          If withdrawalAmount > Balance Then  ' invokes lines 45-47
32              Throw New ArgumentOutOfRangeException(
33                  "Withdrawal amount must be less than or equal to balance.")
34          ElseIf withdrawalAmount <= 0D Then
35              Throw New ArgumentOutOfRangeException(
36                  "Withrawal amount must be positive.")
37          End If
38
```

Fig. 9.2 | Account class for maintaining a bank account balance. (Part 1 of 2.)

```
39              ' subtract withdrawalAmount from balanceValue
40              balanceValue -= withdrawalAmount
41          End Sub ' Withdraw
42
43          ' return the current balance
44          Public ReadOnly Property Balance As Decimal
45              Get
46                  Return balanceValue
47              End Get
48          End Property ' Balance
49      End Class ' Account
```

Fig. 9.2 | Account class for maintaining a bank account balance. (Part 2 of 2.)

Account Class Instance Variables

Class Account contains one Decimal instance variable—balanceValue (line 4)—that represents the Account's balance. In earlier examples, we declared instance variables with the keyword Dim. Here, we use the **Private** member-access modifier. Class members declared with member access modifier Private are accessible *only* within the class, which gives the class complete control over how those members are used. This is known as encapsulating the data in the class. Class members declared with member-access modifier Public are accessible wherever the program has a reference to an Account object.

Instance variables declared with Dim default to Private access. For clarity, every instance variable and method definition should be preceded by a member access modifier. We'll explicitly use Private rather than Dim to indicate that our instance variables are Private.

Account Class Constructor and Throwing Exceptions

When you create an object of a class, the class's **constructor** is called to initialize the object. *A constructor call is required for every object that's created.* By default, the compiler provides a **default constructor** with no parameters in any class that does not explicitly include a constructor. Alternatively, you can provide a **parameterless constructor** that contains code and takes no parameters, or that takes only Optional parameters so you can call it with no arguments. If you provide *any* constructors for a class, the compiler will *not* provide a default constructor for that class.

Constructors must be named New and are generally declared Public—Private constructors are beyond the scope of the book. Constructors are implemented as Sub procedures, *because they cannot return values.* Like methods, they can be overloaded.

Class Account defines a constructor (lines 7–15). It declares one Optional parameter with a default value of 0D (line 7) that represents the Account's initial balance. Because the *only* parameter is Optional, this constructor also serves as the class's parameterless constructor—it can be called with no arguments. Lines 9–12 validate the initialBalance parameter's value. If it's greater than or equal to 0, line 14 assigns initialBalance to the balanceValue instance variable. We assume that an Account cannot have a negative initial balance, so if initialBalance is negative, the constructor throws an exception of type **ArgumentOutOfRangeException** (lines 10–11), which notifies the client code that an invalid argument was passed to the constructor. As you learned in Chapter 7, you can use Try...Catch to catch exceptions and attempt to recover from them, which we'll do in Fig. 9.3. The **Throw statement** (lines 10–11) creates a new object of type ArgumentOutOf-

RangeException. The parentheses following the class name indicate a call to the constructor, which receives an error message String as its argument. After the exception object is created, the Throw statement immediately terminates the constructor (line 14 is *not* executed) and the exception is returned to the code that attempted to create the Account object.

Method Deposit

Method Deposit (lines 18–26) receives a deposit amount as an argument and attempts to add that amount to the balance. A deposit amount must be positive, so lines 20–23 check whether depositAmount is less than or equal to 0 and, if so, throw an ArgumentOutOfRangeException with an appropriate error message. This terminates the Deposit method (line 25 is *not* executed) and returns the exception to the caller. If depositAmount is greater than 0, line 25 adds it to the balanceValue.

Method Withdraw

Method Withdraw (lines 29–41) receives a withdrawal amount as an argument and attempts to subtract that amount from the balance. A withdrawal amount must be a positive number that is less than or equal to the Account's balance. If the withdrawalAmount is not valid, lines 32–33 or 35–36 throw an ArgumentOutOfRangeException with an appropriate error message. If withdrawalAmount is valid, line 40 subtracts it from balanceValue.

Property Balance

A class's methods *can* manipulate the class's Private instance variables, but *clients cannot*. Classes often provide Public properties that allow clients to assign values to (*set*) or obtain the values of (*get*) Private instance variables. Each property contains a Set accessor (to modify the variable's value) and/or a Get accessor (to retrieve the variable's value).

For the Account class, we'd like the client code to be able to get the Account's balance, but *not* modify it—all modifications should be performed by methods Deposit and Withdraw. A property is defined with the Property...End Property keywords. A property that can be used *only to get* a value is declared as a ReadOnly property and provides *only* a Get accessor.

Lines 44–48 define class Account's Public ReadOnly property named Balance. Client code can use this property to obtain the current account balance. We also use the property inside the class at line 31 in method Withdraw when we check whether the withdrawalAmount is greater than the current balance. When the compiler sees Balance used in a way that needs a value, it invokes the property's Get accessor (lines 45–47). When you type the first line of this property then press *Enter*, the IDE will automatically insert an empty Get accessor (Get...End Get) and the End Property keywords. You can then type the Return statement at line 46 to complete the Get accessor's declaration. Later in this chapter, we'll declare properties with *both* Get and Set accessors. If you type the first line of a property without the ReadOnly keyword, then the IDE will generate empty Get *and* Set accessors for you.

Class AccountTest

The AccountTest class declaration (Fig. 9.3) creates the Account object account as an instance variable (line 4). The variable's type is Account—the class we declared in Fig. 9.2. Each new class you create becomes a new type that can be used to declare variables and create objects. You can declare new class types as needed; this is one reason why Visual Basic is known as an **extensible language**.

```vb
 1    ' Fig. 9.3: AccountTest.vb
 2    ' Create and manipulate an Account object.
 3    Public Class AccountTest
 4       Private account As New Account() ' create an Account object
 5
 6       ' display the initial account balance when program executes
 7       Private Sub AccountTest_Load(ByVal sender As System.Object,
 8          ByVal e As System.EventArgs) Handles MyBase.Load
 9
10          accountBalanceValueLabel.Text =
11             String.Format("{0:C}", account.Balance)
12       End Sub ' AccountTest_Load
13
14       ' process a deposit
15       Private Sub depositButton_Click(ByVal sender As System.Object,
16          ByVal e As System.EventArgs) Handles depositButton.Click
17
18          Try
19             ' get deposit amount
20             Dim depositAmount As Decimal =
21                Convert.ToDecimal(inputTextBox.Text)
22             account.Deposit(depositAmount) ' make the deposit
23             accountBalanceValueLabel.Text =
24                String.Format("{0:C}", account.Balance)
25          Catch ex As ArgumentOutOfRangeException
26             MessageBox.Show("Deposit amount must be positive.",
27                "Error", MessageBoxButtons.OK, MessageBoxIcon.Error)
28          End Try
29
30          inputTextBox.Clear() ' clear the inputTextBox
31          inputTextBox.Focus() ' allow user to type in the inputTextBox
32       End Sub ' depositButton_Click
33
34       ' process a withdrawal
35       Private Sub withdrawButton_Click(ByVal sender As System.Object,
36          ByVal e As System.EventArgs) Handles withdrawButton.Click
37
38          Try
39             ' get withdrawal amount
40             Dim withdrawalAmount As Decimal =
41                Convert.ToDecimal(inputTextBox.Text)
42             account.Withdraw(withdrawalAmount) ' make the withdrawal
43             accountBalanceValueLabel.Text =
44                String.Format("{0:C}", account.Balance)
45          Catch ex As ArgumentOutOfRangeException
46             MessageBox.Show("Withdrawal amount must be greater than 0 " &
47                "and less than or equal to the account balance.",
48                "Error", MessageBoxButtons.OK, MessageBoxIcon.Error)
49          End Try
```

Fig. 9.3 | Creating and manipulate an Account object. (Part 1 of 2.)

```
50          inputTextBox.Clear() ' clear the inputTextBox
51          inputTextBox.Focus() ' allow user to type in the inputTextBox
52       End Sub ' withdrawButton_Click
53    End Class ' AccountTest
54
```

a) Specifying a deposit amount

b) Showing the new account balance

c) Specifying a withdrawal amount

d) Showing the new account balance

e) Specifying an invalid deposit amount

f) MessageBox displayed after an invalid deposit

Fig. 9.3 | Creating and manipulate an Account object. (Part 2 of 2.)

Object-Creation Expressions

Variable account is initialized (line 4) with the result of the **object-creation expression** New Account(). New creates a new object of the class specified to the right of the New keyword (that is, Account). The class name is followed by parentheses, which together with the class name represent a call to class's constructor. In this example, we left the parentheses empty. Because we don't pass an argument, the default value 0D is used for the Account's initial balance (because of the Optional parameter in line 7 of Fig. 9.2). When there are no arguments, the parentheses can be omitted, though we include them for clarity. Although Visual Basic is *not* case sensitive, it *does* allow you to create objects (for example, account) with the "same" name as their class (e.g. Account)—we do this throughout the book.

Method AccountTest_Load

Method AccountTest_Load (lines 7–12) displays the account object's initial balance in the accountBalanceValueLabel by using the expression account.Balance to access the account object's Balance property. The property returns the current value of the account object's instance variable balanceValue.

Method depositButton_Click

Method depositButton_Click (lines 15–32) attempts to make a deposit and display the new account balance. These operations are performed in a Try...Catch in case the call to the account object's Deposit method throws an ArgumentOutOfRangeException. Lines 20–21 get the user input. Line 22 passes that value to the account object's Deposit method. Lines 23–24 display the new balance by accessing the account object's Balance property. If the Deposit method throws an ArgumentOutOfRangeException, lines 25–27 catch it and display a MessageBox. Lines 30–31 clear the inputTextBox and give it the focus so the user can enter the next deposit or withdrawal amount.

Method withdrawButton_Click

Method withdrawButton_Click (lines 35–53) attempts to make a withdrawal and display the new account balance. Again, these operations are performed in a Try...Catch in case the call to the account object's Withdraw method throws an ArgumentOutOfRangeException. Lines 40–41 get the user input. Line 42 passes that value to the account object's Withdraw method. Lines 43–44 display the new balance by accessing the account object's Balance property. If the Withdrawal method throws an ArgumentOutOfRangeException, lines 45–48 catch it and display a MessageBox. Lines 51–52 clear the inputTextBox and give it the focus so the user can enter the next deposit or withdrawal amount.

IntelliSense for Class Account

When you create this application and type "account." in the IDE, *IntelliSense* displays the list of items that can appear to the right of the dot—such as the methods Deposit and Withdraw and the property Balance—just as it does for classes from the .NET framework.

9.4 Value Types and Reference Types

Data types are divided into two categories—**value types** and **reference types**. A variable of a value type (such as Integer) contains a single *value* of that type. For example, Fig. 9.4 shows an Integer variable named count that contains the value 7.

```
Dim count As Integer = 7
```

count

| 7 |

A variable (count) of a value type (Integer)
contains a value (7) of that type

Fig. 9.4 | Value type variable and its value.

By contrast, a variable of a reference type (sometimes called a **reference**) contains the *address* where an object is stored in memory. Such a variable is said to **refer to an object**. The actual object to which the variable refers can contain many individual pieces of data (that is, its instance variables). Line 4 of Fig. 9.3 created an Account object in memory and stored the object's location in reference variable account of type Account. Figure 9.5 shows the relationship between the variable account and the Account object. The Account object is shown with its balanceValue instance variable.

Fig. 9.5 | Reference type variable.

Reference Type Variables Initialized to *Nothing*

A reference type variable is initialized by default to the value Nothing if you do not initialize it in its declaration to refer to an object. When you attempt to use a variable that contains Nothing to interact with an object, you'll receive a NullReferenceException.

Most Primitive Types are Value Types

Visual Basic's primitive types are value types, except for the reference type String (which actually represents the String class in the .NET framework). The primitive value types include the **integral types** (Byte, SByte, Short, UShort, Integer, UInteger, Long and ULong), the **floating-point types** (Single and Double) and types Boolean, Date, Decimal and Char. Appendix B lists the primitive types with their sizes and ranges of values.

9.5 Case Study: Card Shuffling and Dealing Simulation

Next, we show how to create and manipulate an array of objects. The elements of an array can be of either value types or reference types. This section uses random number generation and an array of references to objects representing playing cards, to develop a class that simulates card shuffling and dealing. You can then use this class to implement applications that play specific card games. First, we develop class Card (Fig. 9.7), which represents a playing card that has a face (for example, "Ace", "Two", "Three", ..., "Jack", "Queen", "King") and a suit (for example, "Hearts", "Diamonds", "Clubs", "Spades"). Next, we develop the DeckOfCards class (Fig. 9.8), which creates a deck of 52 playing cards in which each element is a Card object. We then build a test application DeckOfCardsTest (Fig. 9.9) that demonstrates class DeckOfCards's card shuffling and dealing capabilities.

GUI for the Card Shuffling and Dealing Simulation

Figure 9.6 shows the application's GUI. At any time, the user can click the **Shuffle** Button to shuffle the deck of cards. Each time the user clicks the **Deal** Button, five cards are dealt and displayed as images in PictureBoxes. When only two cards remain in the deck, the last three PictureBoxes are left empty.

Class *Card*

Class Card (Fig. 9.7) contains two String instance variables—face and suit—that store references to the face name and suit name for a specific Card. The constructor for the class (lines 8–11) receives two Strings that it uses to initialize face and suit. Method ToString (lines 14–16) creates a String consisting of the face of the card, the String " of " and the suit of the card.

Fig. 9.6 | GUI for the card shuffling and dealing simulation.

```
 1    ' Fig. 9.7: Card.vb
 2    ' Card class represents a playing card.
 3    Public Class Card
 4       Private face As String ' face of card ("Ace", "Two", ...)
 5       Private suit As String ' suit of card ("Hearts", "Diamonds", ...)
 6
 7       ' two-argument constructor initializes card's face and suit
 8       Public Sub New(ByVal cardFace As String, ByVal cardSuit As String)
 9          face = cardFace ' initialize face of card
10          suit = cardSuit ' initialize suit of card
11       End Sub ' New
12
13       ' return String representation of Card, Overrides defined in Ch 10
14       Public Overrides Function ToString() As String
15          Return face & " of " & suit
16       End Function ' ToString
17    End Class ' Card
```

Fig. 9.7 | Card class represents a playing card.

Composition

A class can have references to objects of other classes as members. This is called composition and is sometimes referred to as a *has-a* relationship. In this example, an object of class Card needs to know the face and suit of the Card, so a Card object has two references to String objects.

Method ToString

Method ToString (lines 14–16) takes no arguments and returns a String representation of a Card. Method ToString must be declared as shown in line 14 and is the standard method used to create a String representation of *any* object. For most classes, you should declare method ToString to return information that matches the unique requirements of your class. We discuss the keyword Overrides in detail in Chapter 10.

Class DeckOfCards

Class DeckOfCards (Fig. 9.8) creates an instance variable array named deck, which consists of 52 Card objects (line 5). This is another example of composition—a DeckOfCards *has an* array of 52 Cards. Like primitive-type array declarations, the declaration of an array of objects includes the name of the array variable (deck) and its upper bound in parentheses, followed by the keyword As and the type of the array elements. Class DeckOfCards also declares an Integer instance variable currentCard (line 6) representing the next Card to be dealt from the deck array.

```vb
1   ' Fig. 9.8: DeckOfCards.vb
2   ' DeckOfCards class represents a deck of playing cards.
3   Public Class DeckOfCards
4       Private Const NUMBER_OF_CARDS As Integer = 52 ' number of cards
5       Private deck(NUMBER_OF_CARDS - 1) As Card ' array of Card objects
6       Private currentCard As Integer ' index of next Card to be dealt
7       Private Shared randomNumbers As New Random() ' random number generator
8
9       ' constructor fills deck of Cards
10      Public Sub New()
11          Static faces() As String = {"Ace", "Two", "Three", "Four", "Five",
12              "Six", "Seven", "Eight", "Nine", "Ten", "Jack", "Queen", "King"}
13          Static suits() As String = {"Hearts", "Diamonds", "Clubs", "Spades"}
14          currentCard = 0 ' set currentCard so first Card dealt is deck(0)
15
16          ' populate deck array with Card objects
17          For count = 0 To deck.GetUpperBound(0)
18              deck(count) = New Card(faces(count Mod 13), suits(count \ 13))
19          Next
20      End Sub ' New
21
22      ' shuffle deck of Cards with simple one-pass algorithm
23      Public Sub Shuffle()
24          ' after shuffling, dealing should start at deck(0) again
25          currentCard = 0 ' reinitialize currentCard
26
27          ' for each Card, pick another random Card and swap them
28          For first = 0 To deck.GetUpperBound(0)
29              ' select a random number between 0 and 51
30              Dim second As Integer = randomNumbers.Next(NUMBER_OF_CARDS)
31
32              ' swap current Card with randomly selected Card
33              Dim temp As Card = deck(first) ' store copy of deck(first)
34              deck(first) = deck(second) ' move deck(second) to deck(first)
35              deck(second) = temp ' move original deck(first) to deck(second)
36          Next
37      End Sub ' Shuffle
38
39      ' deal one Card
40      Public Function DealCard() As Card
41          ' determine whether Cards remain to be dealt
42          If currentCard <= deck.GetUpperBound(0) Then
43              Dim lastCard As Integer = currentCard ' store current card number
44              currentCard += 1 ' increment current card number
45              Return deck(lastCard)
```

Fig. 9.8 | DeckOfCards class represents a deck of playing cards. (Part 1 of 2.)

```
46            Else
47                  Return Nothing ' no more cards to deal
48            End If
49        End Function ' DealCard
50    End Class ' DeckOfCards
```

Fig. 9.8 | DeckOfCards class represents a deck of playing cards. (Part 2 of 2.)

The parameterless constructor (lines 10–20) initializes the deck of cards. When first created, the deck array's elements are Nothing by default, so the constructor uses a For statement (lines 17–19) to fill the deck array with Cards. This statement initializes control variable count to 0 and loops while count is less than or equal to deck.GetUpperBound(0), causing count to take on each integer value from 0 to 51 (the deck array's indices). Each Card is initialized with two Strings—one from array faces (which contains the Strings "Ace" through "King") and one from array suits (which contains the Strings "Hearts", "Diamonds", "Clubs" and "Spades"). The calculation count Mod 13 always results in a value from 0 to 12 (the 13 indices of the faces array in lines 11–12), and the calculation count \ 13 always results in a value from 0 to 3 (the four indices of the suits array in line 13). When the deck array is initialized, it contains the Cards with faces "Ace" through "King" in order for each suit—Hearts then Diamonds then Clubs then Spades.

Static Local Variables

The arrays faces (line 11–12) and suits (line 13) are declared with the keyword Static. A **Static local variable** is initialized *only* the first time you call the method or constructor in which the variable is declared. It retains its value when the method or constructor finishes executing. The next time you call the method or constructor, the Static local variable contains the value it had when the function last exited. We declared arrays faces and suits as Static so they're created and initialized *only* the first time the DeckOfCards constructor is called—regardless of the number of DeckOfCards objects you create. This improves performance.

Method Shuffle

Method Shuffle (lines 23–37) shuffles the Cards in the deck. The method loops through all 52 Cards (array indices 0 to 51). For each Card, a number between 0 and 51 is picked randomly to select another Card (line 30). Next, the current Card object and the randomly selected Card object are swapped in the array (lines 33–35). The extra variable temp temporarily stores one of the two Card objects being swapped. The swap cannot be performed with only the two statements

```
deck(first) = deck(second)
deck(second) = deck(first)
```

For example, if deck(first) is the "Ace" of "Spades" and deck(second) is the "Queen" of "Hearts", after the first assignment, *both* array elements contain the "Queen" of "Hearts" and the "Ace" of "Spades" is *lost*—hence, the extra variable temp is needed. After the For loop terminates, the Card objects are randomly ordered. Only 52 swaps are made in a single pass of the entire array, and the array of Card objects is shuffled!

[*Note:* It's recommended that you use a so-called unbiased shuffling algorithm for real card games. Such an algorithm ensures that all possible shuffled card sequences are equally likely to occur. A popular unbiased shuffling algorithm is the Fisher-Yates algorithm— en.wikipedia.org/wiki/Fisher%E2%80%93Yates_shuffle. This page also shows how to implement the algorithm in several programming languages, including Visual Basic.]

Method *DealCard*

Method DealCard (lines 40–49) deals one Card in the array. Recall that currentCard indicates the index of the next Card to be dealt (that is, the Card at the top of the deck). Thus, line 42 compares currentCard to the upper bound (51) of the deck array. If the deck is not empty (that is, currentCard is less than or equal to 51), line 43 assigns currentCard (the index of the card that will be returned) to temporary variable lastCard, line 44 increments currentCard to prepare for the next call to DealCard and line 45 returns deck(lastCard), which represents the top card of the deck for this call to DealCard. Otherwise, DealCard returns Nothing to indicate that all the cards have been dealt.

Shuffling and Dealing Cards

Figure 9.9 demonstrates the card shuffling and dealing capabilities of class DeckOfCards (Fig. 9.8). The images used in this example are located in the CardImages folder with this chapter's examples and were added to the project as resources. Line 4 creates a DeckOfCards object named deck.

```vb
 1  ' Fig. 9.9: DeckOfCardsTest.vb
 2  ' Card shuffling and dealing application.
 3  Public Class DeckOfCardsTest
 4     Private deck As New DeckOfCards() ' create the deck of cards
 5
 6     ' shuffle the deck when user clicks the Shuffle Button
 7     Private Sub shuffleButton_Click(ByVal sender As System.Object,
 8        ByVal e As System.EventArgs) Handles shuffleButton.Click
 9
10        deck.Shuffle() ' shuffles the deck
11        card1PictureBox.Image = Nothing ' clear image
12        card2PictureBox.Image = Nothing ' clear image
13        card3PictureBox.Image = Nothing ' clear image
14        card4PictureBox.Image = Nothing ' clear image
15        card5PictureBox.Image = Nothing ' clear image
16        dealButton.Enabled = True ' allow user to click the Deal Button
17        MessageBox.Show("Deck is shuffled")
18     End Sub ' shuffleButton_Click
19
20     ' deal five cards
21     Private Sub dealButton_Click(ByVal sender As System.Object,
22        ByVal e As System.EventArgs) Handles dealButton.Click
23
24        card1PictureBox.Image = GetCardImage(deck.DealCard())
25        card2PictureBox.Image = GetCardImage(deck.DealCard())
26        card3PictureBox.Image = GetCardImage(deck.DealCard())
27        card4PictureBox.Image = GetCardImage(deck.DealCard())
28        card5PictureBox.Image = GetCardImage(deck.DealCard())
29     End Sub ' dealButton_Click
30
```

Fig. 9.9 | Card shuffling and dealing application. (Part 1 of 2.)

```
31        ' return an image for the Card argument
32        Private Function GetCardImage(ByVal card As Card) As Image
33           If card IsNot Nothing Then
34              ' retrieve specific card image from resources
35              Dim pictureResource = My.Resources.ResourceManager.GetObject(
36                 card.ToString().Replace(" ", ""))
37              Return CType(pictureResource, Image) ' return Image
38           Else
39              dealButton.Enabled = False ' disable the Deal Button
40              Return Nothing ' no more cards
41           End If
42        End Function ' GetCardImage
43     End Class ' DeckOfCardsTest
```

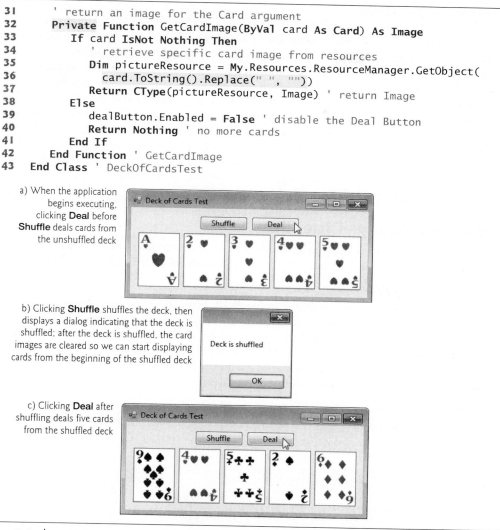

a) When the application begins executing, clicking **Deal** before **Shuffle** deals cards from the unshuffled deck

b) Clicking **Shuffle** shuffles the deck, then displays a dialog indicating that the deck is shuffled; after the deck is shuffled, the card images are cleared so we can start displaying cards from the beginning of the shuffled deck

c) Clicking **Deal** after shuffling deals five cards from the shuffled deck

Fig. 9.9 | Card shuffling and dealing application. (Part 2 of 2.)

Method shuffleButton_Click

Recall that the DeckOfCards constructor creates the 52 Card objects in order by suit and then by face within each suit. When you click the **Shuffle** Button, line 10 invokes deck's Shuffle method to randomly rearrange the Card objects. Then, lines 11–15 clear the card images, line 16 enables the **Deal** Button and line 17 displays a MessageBox indicating that the deck is shuffled.

Method dealButton_Click

Each time you click the **Deal** Button, lines 24–28 call the deck's DealCard method repeatedly to deal five Cards. Each Card is passed to method GetCardImage, which returns the corresponding image for that Card.

Method *GetCardImage*

The Private method GetCardImage (lines 32–42) receives a Card as an argument. Private methods are called **utility methods**, or **helper methods**, because they can be called only by other methods of the class to support their operation. If the card parameter's value is not Nothing (line 33), the method uses the Card's String representation to locate the corresponding Image resource. Line 36 calls the Card's ToString method to get the String representation of the face and suit. This String contains spaces (for example, "Ace of Spades"); however, the names of the image resources do not. So line 36 also calls the String method Replace to replace all spaces in the String returned by ToString with the empty String. Thus, if the Card's ToString method returned "Ace of Spades", then the name of the image resource would be "AceofSpades". Line 37 returns the Image for the card. If the card parameter is Nothing, then line 39 disables the **Deal** Button and line 40 returns Nothing to indicate that there is no Image to display.

9.6 Case Study: Time Class

We now discuss a Time class with three Integer instance variables—hourValue, minuteValue and secondValue—representing the time in universal-time (24-hour clock) format.

GUI for Testing Class *Time's Properties*

The GUI for this application is shown in Fig. 9.10. You can set the hour, minute and second using the three TextBoxes. If you specify an invalid value, an exception occurs. The program catches the exception and displays an appropriate message in a MessageBox. You can also press the **Increment Second** Button to add one second to the time. When you update the time, the program displays the new values of the hour, minute and second in the output1Label and displays the standard and universal times in the output2Label.

Fig. 9.10 | GUI for testing class Time's properties.

Time Class Declaration

The application consists of classes Time (Fig. 9.11) and TimeTest (Fig. 9.12). Class Time declares properties Hour (lines 29–41), Minute (lines 44–56) and Second (lines 59–71) to control access to instance variables hourValue, minuteValue and secondValue, respectively. Each of these properties contains a Get accessor and a Set accessor. The Set accessors perform validation to ensure that the corresponding instance variables are set to valid values; otherwise, they throw an exception and the corresponding instance variable is *not* modified. Each Get accessor returns the appropriate instance variable's value.

```vb
1    ' Fig. 9.11: Time.vb
2    ' Time class with Hour, Minute and Second properties.
3    Public Class Time
4       ' declare Integer instance variables for the hour, minute and second
5       Private hourValue As Integer ' 0 - 23
6       Private minuteValue As Integer ' 0 - 59
7       Private secondValue As Integer ' 0 - 59
8
9       ' Time constructor with hour, minute and second as optional parameters
10      Public Sub New(Optional ByVal h As Integer = 12,
11         Optional ByVal m As Integer = 0, Optional ByVal s As Integer = 0)
12         SetTime(h, m, s) ' call SetTime with three arguments
13      End Sub ' New
14
15      ' Time constructor: another Time object supplied
16      Public Sub New(ByVal t As Time)
17         SetTime(t.hourValue, t.minuteValue, t.secondValue)
18      End Sub ' New
19
20      ' set a new time value using universal time, check validity of the data
21      Public Sub SetTime(ByVal h As Integer, ByVal m As Integer,
22         ByVal s As Integer)
23         Hour = h ' Set accessor validates the hour
24         Minute = m ' Set accessor validates the minute
25         Second = s ' Set accessor validates the second
26      End Sub ' SetTime
27
28      ' property Hour
29      Public Property Hour() As Integer
30         Get ' return hourValue
31            Return hourValue
32         End Get
33
34         Set(ByVal value As Integer) ' set hourValue
35            If (value >= 0 AndAlso value < 24) Then ' in range 0-23?
36               hourValue = value ' value is valid
37            Else ' invalid hour
38               Throw New ArgumentOutOfRangeException("hour must be 0-23")
39            End If
40         End Set
41      End Property ' Hour
42
43      ' property Minute
44      Public Property Minute() As Integer
45         Get ' return minuteValue
46            Return minuteValue
47         End Get
```

Fig. 9.11 | Time class with Hour, Minute and Second properties. (Part 1 of 2.)

```vbnet
48      Set(ByVal value As Integer) ' set minuteValue
49          If (value >= 0 AndAlso value < 60) Then ' in range 0-59?
50              minuteValue = value ' value is valid
51          Else ' invalid minute
52              Throw New ArgumentOutOfRangeException("minute must be 0-59")
53          End If
54      End Set
55   End Property ' Minute
56
57   ' property Second
58   Public Property Second() As Integer
59      Get ' return secondValue
60          Return secondValue
61      End Get
62
63      Set(ByVal value As Integer) ' set secondValue
64          If (value >= 0 AndAlso value < 60) Then ' in range 0-59?
65              secondValue = value ' value is valid
66          Else   ' invalid second
67              Throw New ArgumentOutOfRangeException("second must be 0-59")
68          End If
69      End Set
70   End Property ' Second
71
72   ' return Time as a String in universal-time (24-hour clock) format
73   Public Function ToUniversalString() As String
74      Return String.Format("{0}:{1:D2}:{2:D2}", Hour, Minute, Second)
75   End Function ' ToUniversalString
76
77   ' return Time as a String in standard-time (12-hour clock) format
78   Public Overrides Function ToString() As String
79      Dim suffix As String ' AM or PM suffix
80      Dim standardHour As Integer ' a standard hour in the range 1-12
81
82      ' determine whether the 12-hour clock suffix should be AM or PM
83      If Hour < 12 Then
84          suffix = "AM"
85      Else
86          suffix = "PM"
87      End If
88
89      ' convert hour from universal-time format to standard-time format
90      If (Hour = 12 OrElse Hour = 0) Then
91          standardHour = 12 ' noon or midnight
92      Else
93          standardHour = Hour Mod 12 ' 1 through 11, AM or PM
94      End If
95
96      Return String.Format("{0}:{1:D2}:{2:D2} {3}",
97          standardHour, Minute, Second, suffix)
98   End Function ' ToString
99 End Class ' Time
```

Fig. 9.11 | Time class with Hour, Minute and Second properties. (Part 2 of 2.)

Time Class Constructors

Like methods, constructors of a class can be overloaded. To do so, you provide a separate constructor declaration with the same name (New) for each version but different numbers, types and/or orders of parameters (that is, different signatures). Class Time of Fig. 9.11 includes two overloaded constructors (lines 10–18) that provide various ways to initialize Time objects. Each constructor calls method SetTime to set the hour, minute and second values. In line 17, notice that we access the argument Time object's Private instance variables directly with the expressions t.hourValue, t.minuteValue and t.secondValue. *When one object of a class has a reference to another object of the same class, the first object can access all of the second object's data, methods and properties (including those that are Private).*

The compiler invokes the appropriate constructor by matching the number, types and order of the arguments specified in the constructor call with the number, types and order of the parameters specified in each constructor method declaration. The following statements demonstrate how these overloaded constructors can be used:

```
Dim time1 As New Time() ' use default hour, minute and second
Dim time2 As New Time(2) ' use default minute and second
Dim time3 As New Time(21, 34) ' use default second
Dim time4 As New Time(12, 25, 42) ' all arguments supplied
Dim time5 As New Time(time4) ' copy another Time object
```

The first four statements call the constructor in lines 10–13 using varying numbers of arguments. The last statement calls the constructor in lines 16–18.

Common Programming Error 9.1

A constructor can call other class methods that use instance variables not yet initialized. Using instance variables before they've been initialized can lead to logic errors.

Method SetTime

Method SetTime (lines 21–26) receives three parameters representing the hour, minute and second. Rather than validating the hour, minute and second values in both method SetTime *and* in the properties, method SetTime simply assigns its arguments to the corresponding properties (lines 23–25). Assigning a value to a property invokes the property's Set accessor, which, in turn, validates the value. Coding SetTime this way ensures that we do not duplicate the validation code. Only the properties in this class actually modify the instance variables, so if one is set incorrectly, we can focus on debugging its corresponding property to correct the problem.

Properties Hour, Minute and Second

Properties Hour, Minute and Second are read-write properties—they include both Get and Set accessors. These enable clients of class Time to get the values of the class's instance variables and modify them in a controlled manner, respectively. Because we want client code to be able to both get and set the hour, minute and second, we could have declared the instance variables Public. However, using Public instance variables in a class is dangerous—other parts of the program could accidentally or maliciously set Public instance variables to invalid values, producing potentially disastrous results. Public access to instance variables should be accomplished through properties. The properties also can be used throughout class Time as well.

Software Engineering Observation 9.1

Access all of your class's instance variables through their corresponding properties, even inside the class definition. This makes your class easier to maintain, modify and debug.

Method *ToUniversalString*

Method ToUniversalString (lines 74–76) takes no arguments and returns a String in universal-time format, consisting of the Hour property value, two digits for the Minute property value and two digits for the Second property value. For example, if the time were 1:30:07 PM, method ToUniversalString would return the String "13:30:07". Format specifier D2 formats a single-digit integer value with a leading 0.

Method *ToString*

Method ToString (lines 79–99) takes no arguments and returns a String in standard-time format, consisting of the Hour, Minute and Second property values separated by colons and followed by AM or PM (for example, 1:27:06 PM). Lines 84–88 determine the proper AM or PM suffix. Lines 91–95 determine the proper formatting for the hour—hours from 0 to 11 display with AM, hours from 12 to 23 display with PM, hour 0 displays as 12 (midnight), hours 1–12 display as is and hours 13–23 display as 1–11 (PM).

Using the *Time* Class

Class TimeTest (Fig. 9.12) provides a GUI for testing class Time. The GUI contains three text boxes in which the user can enter values for the Time object's Hour, Minute and Second properties, respectively. Class TimeTest creates an object of class Time (line 4) using default arguments and assigns its reference to variable time.

```
1    ' Fig. 9.12: TimeTest.vb
2    ' Accessing data via properties.
3    Public Class TimeTest
4       Dim time As New Time() ' construct Time with zero arguments
5
6       ' invoked when user clicks the Add 1 to Second button
7       Private Sub addSecondButton_Click(ByVal sender As System.Object,
8          ByVal e As System.EventArgs) Handles incrementSecondButton.Click
9
10         time.Second = (time.Second + 1) Mod 60 ' add 1 to Second
11
12         ' add one minute if 60 seconds have passed
13         If time.Second = 0 Then
14            time.Minute = (time.Minute + 1) Mod 60 ' add 1 to Minute
15
16            ' add one hour if 60 minutes have passed
17            If time.Minute = 0 Then
18               time.Hour = (time.Hour + 1) Mod 24 ' add 1 to Hour
19            End If
20         End If
21
22         UpdateDisplay() ' update the TextBoxes and output Labels
23      End Sub ' addSecondButton_Click
```

Fig. 9.12 | Accessing data via properties. (Part 1 of 3.)

```
24
25      ' set time based on TextBox values
26      Private Sub setTimeButton_Click(ByVal sender As System.Object,
27          ByVal e As System.EventArgs) Handles setTimeButton.Click
28
29          ' ensure that hour, minute and second are in range
30          Try
31              If setHourTextBox.Text <> String.Empty Then
32                  time.Hour = Convert.ToInt32(setHourTextBox.Text)
33              End If
34
35              If setMinuteTextBox.Text <> String.Empty Then
36                  time.Minute = Convert.ToInt32(setMinuteTextBox.Text)
37              End If
38
39              If setSecondTextBox.Text <> String.Empty Then
40                  time.Second = Convert.ToInt32(setSecondTextBox.Text)
41              End If
42          Catch ex As ArgumentOutOfRangeException
43              MessageBox.Show("The hour, minute or second was out of range",
44                  "Out of Range", MessageBoxButtons.OK, MessageBoxIcon.Error)
45          End Try
46
47          UpdateDisplay() ' update the TextBoxes and output Labels
48      End Sub ' setTimeButton_Click
49
50      ' update time display
51      Private Sub UpdateDisplay()
52          setHourTextBox.Text = Convert.ToString(time.Hour)
53          setMinuteTextBox.Text = Convert.ToString(time.Minute)
54          setSecondTextBox.Text = Convert.ToString(time.Second)
55          output1Label.Text = ("Hour: " & time.Hour & "; Minute: " &
56              time.Minute & "; Second: " & time.Second)
57          output2Label.Text = ("Standard time is: " & time.ToString() &
58              "; Universal Time is: " & time.ToUniversalString())
59      End Sub ' UpdateDisplay
60  End Class ' TimeTest
```

a) Setting the time to 11:59:58 AM

Fig. 9.12 | Accessing data via properties. (Part 2 of 3.)

b) Incrementing the time to 11:59:59 AM

c) Incrementing the time to 12:00:00 PM

d) Attempting to set an invalid hour causes an `ArgumentOutOfRangeException`

Fig. 9.12 | Accessing data via properties. (Part 3 of 3.)

Method *addSecondButton_Click*

The GUI contains an **Increment Second** Button that enables the user to increment the Second property value by 1 without having to use the corresponding text box. Method addSecondButton_Click (lines 7–23) uses properties to determine and set the new time, ensuring that the values for the hour, minute and second are updated properly. For example, 23:59:59 becomes 00:00:00 when the user presses **Increment Second**. Line 22 calls method UpdateDisplay (lines 51–59) to update the TextBoxes and the output Labels with the new time.

Method *setTimeButton_Click*

Method setTimeButton_Click (lines 26–48) checks each TextBox to ensure that it's not empty. For each TextBox that's not empty, the method sets the corresponding property of the Time object to the value in the TextBox. If any of the Time object's properties throws an exception, lines 43–44 display a MessageBox indicating that one of the values was out of range.

Method UpdateDisplay

Method UpdateDisplay (lines 51–59) updates the TextBoxes with the current values of the Time object's Hour, Minute and Second properties. Then, lines 57–58 display the time in standard-time format (by invoking Time method ToString) and universal-time format (by invoking Time method ToUniversalString).

Notes on Set and Get Accessors

Although providing Set and Get accessors appears to be the same as making the instance variables Public, this is *not* the case. This is another of Visual Basic's subtleties that makes the language so attractive from a software-engineering standpoint. If an instance variable is Public, it can be read or written by *any* method in the program. If an instance variable is Private, a Public Get accessor seems to allow other methods to read the data at will. However, the Get accessor can control the formatting and display of the data. A Public Set accessor can scrutinize attempts to modify the instance variable's value, thus ensuring that the new value is appropriate for that instance variable. For example, an attempt to set the day of the month to 37 would be rejected, and an attempt to set a person's weight to a negative value would be rejected. Therefore, although Set and Get accessors provide access to Private data, the implementation of these methods can restrict access to that data.

The declaration of instance variables as Private does not guarantee data integrity. You must provide validity checking—Visual Basic provides only the framework with which you can design better programs.

Using the With Statement

The With statement allows you to make multiple references to the same object in a concise manner. For example, we can replace lines 52–58 of Fig. 9.12 (which all reference the same object, time) with

```
With time
    setHourTextBox.Text = Convert.ToString(.Hour)
    setMinuteTextBox.Text = Convert.ToString(.Minute)
    setSecondTextBox.Text = Convert.ToString(.Second)
    output1Label.Text = ("Hour: " & .Hour & "; Minute: " &
        .Minute & "; Second: " & .Second)
    output2Label.Text = ("Standard time is: " & .ToString() &
        "; Universal Time is: " & .ToUniversalString())
End With
```

These lines of code are collectively known as a **With statement block**. At the beginning of the block, we specify the object (time) that we'll be using in the block. The With statement allows you to access an object's members in the block without having to specify the name of the object before the dot separator—for example, .Hour() instead of time.Hour.

9.7 Class Scope

A class's instance variables and methods have **class scope**. Within this scope, a class's members are accessible to all of the class's other members and can be referenced simply by name. Outside a class's scope, class members cannot be referenced directly by name. Those class members that are visible (such as Public members) can be accessed through a variable that refers to an object of the class (for example, `time.Hour`). In Section 9.12, you'll see that `Public Shared` members are accessed through the class name.

9.8 Object Initializers

Object initializers use the `With` keyword to allow you to create an object and initialize its properties in the same statement. This is useful when a class does not provide an appropriate constructor to meet your needs. For example, the `Time` class used in this section (from Fig. 9.11) does not provide constructors that can receive only the minute and second, or only the second, as arguments. To use object initializers, you follow the object creation expression with the `With` keyword and an **object initializer list**—a comma-separated list in curly braces ({ }) of properties and their values as in the following statements:

```
Dim timeObject1 As New Time() With {.Minute = 33, .Second = 12}
Dim timeObject2 As New Time() With {.Minute = 45}
```

The `With` keyword indicates that the new object is used to access the properties specified in the object-initializer list. Each property name must be preceded by the dot separator (.) and can appear only once in the object-initializer list. The object-initializer list cannot be empty and cannot contain properties that are declared as `Shared` (Section 9.12), `Const` (Section 9.13) or `ReadOnly` (Section 9.13).

The first of the preceding statements creates a `Time` object (`timeObject1`) and initializes it with class `Time`'s parameterless constructor. The object initializer then executes the property initializers in the order in which they appear. In this case, the time is set to `12:33:12`. Recall that an object intializer first calls the class's constructor. The parameterless `Time` constructor initializes the time to noon (`12:00:00`). The object initializer then sets each specified property to the supplied value. In this case, the `Minute` property is set to `33` and the `Second` property is set to `12`. The `Hour` property retains its default value. Of course, the `Set` accessors of the properties still validate the values in the object-initializer list.

The second of the preceding statements uses an object intializer to create a new `Time` object (`timeObject2`) and set only its `Minute` property. The time is set to `12:45:00`. First, the `Time` constructor initializes the time to noon (`12:00:00`). Then, the object initializer sets the `Minute` property to `45`. The `Hour` and `Second` properties retain their default values.

9.9 Auto-Implemented Properties

The properties we declared in class `Time` each perform validation to ensure that the hour, minute and second always contain valid values. For properties that do not have any additional logic in their `Set` and `Get` accessors, there is a new feature in Visual Basic 2010—called **auto-implemented properties**—that allows you to write one line of code and have the compiler to generate the property's code for you. For example, if the `Time` class's `Hour` property did not require validation in Fig. 9.11, we could have replaced line 5 and lines 29–41 with

```
Public Property Hour As Integer
```

The compiler would then generate a `Private` instance variable of type `Integer` named `_Hour` and the following property code

```
    Public Property Hour As Integer
        Get
            Return _Hour
        End Get

        Set(ByVal value As Integer)
            _Hour = value
        End Set
    End Property
```

You can also assign an initial value to an auto-implemented property in its declaration, just as you can for a class's instance variables.

Auto-implemented properties are provided as a convenience feature for "simple" properties like the one described above. In general, however, you should perform validation in a property's Set accessor. Doing so requires *you* to define the property *and* its corresponding instance variable.

9.10 Using Me to Access the Current Object

Every object of a class shares *one copy* of the class's method declarations. We've seen that an object's methods can manipulate the object's data. But how do methods know *which* object's instance variables to manipulate? Every object can *access itself* through its **Me** reference. On every call to a non-Shared method, the compiler passes an object's Me reference as an *implicit* argument. The Me reference can then be used to access a particular object's members implicitly (by the compiler) or explicitly (which is rarely needed). (Section 9.12 introduces Shared class members and explains why the Me reference is *not* implicitly passed to Shared methods.)

Accessing Shadowed Instance Variables with Me
When a method has a parameter or local variable with the same name as one of the class's instance variables, the instance variable is "hidden" until the method terminates execution—this is called **shadowing**. You can use the Me reference to access the shadowed instance variable. Assume that we have a Time class with hour, minute and second instance variables. The following Time class constructor's parameters shadow (have the same name as) the class's instance variables, so we use Me to access each shadowed instance variable:

```
    Public Sub New(ByVal hour As Integer,
        ByVal minute As Integer, ByVal second As Integer)

        Me.hour = hour ' initializes instance variable hour
        Me.minute = minute ' initializes instance variable minute
        Me.second = second ' initializes instance variable second
    End Sub ' New
```

The identifiers qualified with "Me." represent the instance variables. The unqualified identifiers represent the constructor's parameters.

9.11 Garbage Collection

Every object you create uses various system resources, including the memory that holds the object itself. These resources must be returned to the system when they're no longer needed to avoid **resource leaks**. The Common Language Runtime (CLR) performs automatic **garbage collection** to reclaim the memory occupied by objects that are no longer in use. When there are no more references to an object, it's **marked for garbage collection** by the CLR. The memory for such an object can be reclaimed when the CLR executes its **garbage collector**, which is responsible for retrieving the memory of objects that are no longer used, so that the memory can be used for other objects. Resources like memory that are allocated and reclaimed by the CLR are known as **managed resources**.

Other types of resource leaks can occur. For example, an application may open a file on disk to modify the file's contents. If the application does not close the file, other applications may not be allowed to use the file until the application that opened the file finishes. An application that no longer needs a file should close it immediately so that other programs can access it. Resources like files that *you* must manage are known as **unmanaged resources** (because they're not managed by the CLR). Such resources are typically scarce and should be released as soon as they're no longer needed by a program.

The `Using` statement (which you learned about in Chapter 8) specifies a list of resources and disposes of them at the end of the `Using` statement, indicated by the `End Using` keywords. This statement ensures the disposal of its resources regardless of how the code in the `Using` statement terminates.

9.12 Shared Class Members

Each object has its *own* copy of the instance variables of its class. In certain cases, all objects of a class should share *only one* copy of a particular variable. A **Shared class variable** represents **classwide information**—all objects of the class share the same variable, no matter how many objects of the class have been instantiated. Together, a class's instance variables and `Shared` variables are know as the class's **fields**.

*Motivation for **Shared** Variables*
Let's use a video game example to explain the need for `Shared` classwide data. Suppose we have a video game in which `Martians` attack other space creatures. A `Martian` tends to be brave and willing to attack when it's aware that at least four other `Martians` are present. If fewer than five `Martians` are present, all `Martians` become cowardly. For this reason, each `Martian` must know the `martianCount`. We could endow class `Martian` with a `martianCount` instance variable. If we were to do this, then every `Martian` would have a separate *copy* of the instance variable, and every time we create a `Martian`, we would have to update the instance variable `martianCount` in *every* `Martian`. The redundant copies waste space, and updating those copies is time consuming. Worse yet, while we're updating the individual copies of `martianCount`, there will be periods of time during which some of these copies have not yet been updated, so we could have inconsistent bravery behavior among the `Martians`. Instead, we declare `martianCount` to be `Shared` so that it is classwide data. Each `Martian` can then see the `martianCount` as if it were instance data of that `Martian`, but Visual Basic maintains only *one* copy of the `Shared martianCount` to save space. We also save time, in that the `Martian` constructor increments only the `Shared martianCount`—there is only one copy, so we do not have to increment separate copies of `martianCount` for each `Martian` object. This also prevents inconsistent bravery behavior among the `Martians`.

*Class **Employee** with **Shared** Variables*

Our next example uses class Employee (Fig. 9.13) to demonstrate a Private Shared class variable and a Public Shared Property to access that value. The Shared class variable countValue is initialized to zero by default (line 6). It maintains a count of the number of Employee objects that have been created.

```vb
1    ' Fig. 9.13: Employee.vb
2    ' Class Employee uses Shared variable.
3    Public Class Employee
4       Private firstNameValue As String ' employee first name
5       Private lastNameValue As String ' employee last name
6       Private Shared countValue As Integer ' Employee objects in memory
7
8       ' Employee constructor
9       Public Sub New(ByVal first As String, ByVal last As String)
10          firstNameValue = first
11          lastNameValue = last
12          countValue += 1 ' increment shared count of employees
13       End Sub ' New
14
15       ' return first name
16       Public ReadOnly Property FirstName() As String
17          Get
18             Return firstNameValue
19          End Get
20       End Property ' FirstName
21
22       ' return last name
23       Public ReadOnly Property LastName() As String
24          Get
25             Return lastNameValue
26          End Get
27       End Property ' LastName
28
29       ' property Count
30       Public Shared ReadOnly Property Count() As Integer
31          Get
32             Return countValue
33          End Get
34       End Property ' Count
35    End Class ' Employee
```

Fig. 9.13 | Class Employee uses Shared variable.

When Employee objects exist, Shared member countValue can be used in any Employee method or property—in this example, the constructor increments countValue (line 12). If no objects of class Employee exist, member countValue can be referenced through the Shared ReadOnly Property Count (lines 30–34)—you do *not* have to create an Employee object to call the Get method of a Shared Property. We declared property Count as ReadOnly so that client code cannot modify countValue.

Scope of *Shared* Members

Shared class members have class scope. A class's Public Shared members can be accessed via the class name using the dot separator (for example, *ClassName.sharedMemberName*), as in lines 8, 13 and 18 of Fig. 9.14. A class's Private Shared members can be accessed by clients only indirectly through the class's non-Private methods and properties. Shared class members are available as soon as the class is loaded into memory at execution time; they exist for the duration of program execution, *even when no objects of that class exist*. To allow clients to access a Private Shared class member when no objects of the class exist, you must provide a non-Private Shared method or property, like Count (Fig. 9.13).

Testing *Shared* Variables

Class SharedTest (Fig. 9.14) demonstrates the Shared members of Fig. 9.13. Lines 7–8 use class Employee's ReadOnly Shared Property Count to obtain the current value of countValue. No Employee objects exist yet, so countValue is 0. We access Count using the expression Employee.Count. Line 10 then creates an Employee object, causing countValue to be incremented by 1. Lines 11–13 output the Employee's name and use ReadOnly Shared Property Count to display the updated countValue (now 1). Line 15 creates a second Employee object, then lines 16–19 output the Employee's name and use ReadOnly Shared Property Count to display the updated countValue (now 2). Lines 22–23 set the Employee objects' references to Nothing, so that employee1 and employee2 no longer refer to the Employee objects. This "marks" the objects for garbage collection, because there are no more references to these objects in the program. The garbage collector *can* now reclaim the objects' memory, but it's *not guaranteed when (or if)* this will occur. *When a program terminates, all memory used by that program is returned to the system.*

```vb
1   ' Fig. 9.14: SharedTest.vb
2   ' Demonstrate Shared members.
3   Public Class SharedTest
4      Private Sub SharedTest_Load(ByVal sender As System.Object,
5         ByVal e As System.EventArgs) Handles MyBase.Load
6
7         outputTextBox.AppendText("Employees before instantiation: " &
8            Employee.Count & vbCrLf) ' Count is a Shared property
9
10        Dim employee1 As New Employee("Susan", "Baker") ' call constructor
11        outputTextBox.AppendText(vbCrLf & "Created employee: " &
12           employee1.FirstName & " " & employee1.LastName & vbCrLf &
13           "Current number of Employees is: " & Employee.Count & vbCrLf)
14
15        Dim employee2 As New Employee("Bob", "Blue") ' call constructor
16        outputTextBox.AppendText(vbCrLf & "Created employee: " &
17           employee2.FirstName & " " & employee2.LastName & vbCrLf &
18           "Current number of Employees is: " & Employee.Count &
19           vbCrLf & vbCrLf)
20
21        outputTextBox.AppendText("Marking employees for garbage collection")
22        employee1 = Nothing ' mark employee1 for garbage collection
```

Fig. 9.14 | Demonstrate Shared members. (Part 1 of 2.)

```
23          employee2 = Nothing ' mark employee2 for garbage collection
24      End Sub ' SharedTest_Load
25  End Class ' SharedTest
```

a) Showing the number
of Employees before
and after Employee
objects are created

Employees before instantiation: 0

Created employee: Susan Baker
Current number of Employees is: 1

Created employee: Bob Blue
Current number of Employees is: 2

Marking employees for garbage collection

Fig. 9.14 | Demonstrate Shared members. (Part 2 of 2.)

Shared Members and the Me Reference

Shared methods and properties do not have access to the Me reference, which can be used to directly access only non-Shared class members. Shared class members exist independently of any class objects and even when there are no objects of that class. Like other methods and properties, Shared methods and properties *can* use a reference to an object to access that object's non-Shared members.

Shared Constructors

Shared variables are often initialized to their default values or to other values in their declarations. When a Shared variable requires initialization that cannot be accomplished in its declaration (such as complex calculations or constructor arguments), you can perform the initialization in a **Shared constructor**. Such a constructor is preceded by the Shared modifier and can be used to initialize only the class's Shared variables. A Shared constructor is implicitly Public, must be declared with no parameters and is guaranteed to execute before a program creates any objects of the class or accesses any Shared class members. A class can have both a Shared constructor and a non-Shared parameterless constructor.

9.13 Const and ReadOnly Fields

Some data needs to be modifiable and some does not. Constants are fields whose values cannot change during program execution. To create a constant in a class, declare an identifier as either Const or ReadOnly. Neither type of constant can be modified once initialized—the compiler will flag as an error any attempt to do so.

Const

A **Const** identifier *must be initialized at compile time in its declaration and can be initialized only to constant values,* such as integers, floating-point numbers, string literals, characters and other Const values. For example, in Fig. 9.8, we used the following Const declaration:

```
Private Const NUMBER_OF_CARDS As Integer = 52 ' number of cards
```

to create a constant representing the number of cards in a deck of playing cards.

ReadOnly

In some cases, a constant's value is not known until *execution time*—either because the constant is initialized with a non-constant value (such as a variable), or because the constant must be initialized with a (possibly) different value on a per-object basis. For example, in a large company, each employee typically has a unique employee ID that does not change. Such a value would be initialized by a constructor at the time you create each Employee object. An identifier declared as `ReadOnly` can be initialized *either* in its declaration *or* in the class's constructor(s). The following declaration creates an `employeeID` constant that might be part of an `Employee` class:

```
Private ReadOnly employeeID As Integer  ' unique employee ID
```

To initialize the constant employee-by-employee, you can use the constructor:

```
Public Sub New(ByVal ID As Integer)
    employeeID = ID ' initialize constant with constructor argument
End Sub
```

Accessing **Public** *Constants from Client Code*

`Const`s are implicitly `Shared`. If you have a `Public Const` value, client code can access it with the class name followed by the dot separator and the `Const`'s name. Each object of a class with a `ReadOnly` constant has a *separate copy* of the constant, unless you explicitly declare the constant as `Shared`. If you have a `Public ReadOnly` constant in your class, client code can access it via a reference to an object of that class.

9.14 Shared Methods and Class `Math`

Class `Math` provides a collection of `Shared` methods that enable you to perform common mathematical calculations. For example, you can calculate the square root of 900.0 with the `Shared` method call

```
Math.Sqrt(900.0)
```

which evaluates to and returns 30.0. Method `Sqrt` takes an argument of type `Double` and returns a result of type `Double`. We do not create a `Math` object before calling method `Sqrt`. All `Math` class methods are `Shared` and are therefore called by preceding the name of the method with the class name `Math` and a dot (.) separator. Figure 9.15 summarizes several `Math` class methods. In the figure, x and y are of type `Double`. Methods `Min` and `Max` have overloaded versions for several types.

Method	Description	Example
Abs(x)	returns the absolute value of x	Abs(23.7) is 23.7 Abs(0) is 0 Abs(-23.7) is 23.7
Ceiling(x)	rounds x to the smallest integer not less than x	Ceiling(9.2) is 10.0 Ceiling(-9.8) is -9.0

Fig. 9.15 | Common `Math` class methods. (Part I of 2.)

Method	Description	Example
Floor(x)	rounds x to the largest integer not greater than x	Floor(9.2) is 9.0 Floor(-9.8) is -10.0
Max(x, y)	returns the larger value of x and y (overloaded for each of the primitive numeric types)	Max(2.3, 12.7) is 12.7 Max(-2.3, -12.7) is -2.3
Min(x, y)	returns the smaller value of x and y (overloaded for each of the primitive numeric types)	Min(2.3, 12.7) is 2.3 Min(-2.3, -12.7) is -12.7
Pow(x, y)	calculates x raised to the power y (x^y)	Pow(2.0, 7.0) is 128.0 Pow(9.0, .5) is 3.0
Sqrt(x)	returns the square root of x	Sqrt(9.0) is 3.0 Sqrt(2.0) is 1.4142135623731

Fig. 9.15 | Common Math class methods. (Part 2 of 2.)

Math Class Constants PI and E

Class Math also declares two commonly used mathematical constants: Math.PI and Math.E. These values are declared in class Math with the modifiers Public and Const. The constant Math.PI represents π (3.14159265358979323846)—the ratio of a circle's circumference to its diameter. The constant Math.E (2.7182818284590452354) is the base value for natural logarithms (calculated with Shared Math method Log).

9.15 Object Browser

Visual Studio's **Object Browser** lists all the class libraries that are available to the application, including the Framework Class Library classes and programmer-defined classes. You use the **Object Browser** to learn about the functionality provided by specific classes. To open the **Object Browser**, right click any class, method or property in the code editor and select **Go To Definition**. If the source code for the selected type is available (for example, it's another class in the same project), the source code opens rather than the **Object Browser**.

Figure 9.16 shows the **Object Browser** after right clicking the class Random in line 7 of Fig. 9.8 and selecting **Go To Definition**. Figure 9.17 shows the **Object Browser** after the user selects method Next of class Random in Fig. 9.16. The **Object Browser** lists all non-Private members provided by class Random in the upper-right portion of the window, which offers you instant access to information regarding the services of the selected class. This is an excellent way to learn more about the classes you're using.

9.16 Wrap-Up

This chapter investigated the object-oriented programming concepts of classes, objects, methods, instance variables and Shared class members. We presented several complete class declarations consisting of Private data, overloaded constructors for initialization flexibility, properties for manipulating the class's data, and methods that performed the services provided by each class.

Classes available to the application are listed here   Selected class's non-`Private` members are listed here   Details of a particular member are listed here (or a summary of the class if a specific member is not selected)

Fig. 9.16 | **Object Browser** when user selects class Random from the code editor.

Fig. 9.17 | **Object Browser** for class Random's Next method.

You learned how to initialize the properties of an object with an object-initializer list. You saw that a class can have references to objects of other classes as members—a concept known as composition. We discussed how garbage collection reclaims the memory of objects that are no longer needed. We motivated Shared class members, and demonstrated how to declare and use Shared variables and methods in your own classes. You learned how to declare and initialize Const and ReadOnly members. We also showed how to use the **Object Browser** to learn the functionality provided by the classes of the Framework Class Library.

In the next chapter, we continue our discussion of classes by introducing a form of software reuse called inheritance. We'll see that classes often share common attributes and behaviors. In such cases, it's possible to define those attributes and behaviors in a common "base" class and "inherit" those capabilities into new class declarations.

Summary

Section 9.2 Classes, Objects, Methods and Instance Variables
- Performing a task in a program requires a method.
- In a class, you provide one or more methods that are designed to perform the class's tasks.
- You must build an object of a class before a program can perform the class's tasks.
- Each message sent to an object is a method call that tells a method to perform its task.
- Any code that interacts with any object of a particular class is known as a client of that class—objects provide services to the class's clients.
- An object has attributes that are carried with it as it's used in a program. These attributes are specified in the object's class.
- Attributes are specified by the class's instance variables.

Section 9.3 Account Class
- To add a class to a project, right click the project name in the **Solution Explorer** and select **Add > Class...**.
- The keyword Public is an access modifier.
- Only Public classes can be reused in other projects.
- Every class declaration contains keyword Class followed immediately by the class's name. Every class's body ends with the keywords End Class.
- Private class members are accessible only within the class in which they are declared.
- Public class members are accessible wherever the program has a reference to an object of the class.
- Instance variables declared with Dim default to Private access.
- A constructor call is required for every object that is created.
- The compiler provides a default constructor with no parameters in any class that does not explicitly declare a constructor. If you provide any constructors for a class, the compiler will not provide a default one.
- You can provide a parameterless constructor that contains code and takes no parameters, or that takes only Optional parameters so you can call it with no arguments.
- Constructors must be named New and be implemented as Sub procedures.
- Constructors can be overloaded.
- A Throw statement immediately returns its exception argument to the caller.

- Classes often provide `Public` properties that allow clients to assign values to (set) or obtain the values of (get) `Private` instance variables. Each property typically contains a `Set` accessor (to modify the variable's value) and a `Get` accessor (to retrieve the variable's value).

- A property is defined with the `Property...End Property` keywords.

- A `ReadOnly` property provides only a `Get` accessor.

- Each class you create becomes a new type that can be used to declare variables and create objects.

- An object-creation expression creates a new object of the class specified to the right of `New` and calls the object's constructor.

Section 9.4 Value Types and Reference Types

- A variable of a value type (such as `Integer`) contains a single value of that type.

- A variable of a reference type (sometimes called a reference) contains the location where an object is stored in memory. Such a variable is said to refer to an object.

- A reference-type variable is initialized by default to the value `Nothing` if you do not initialize it to refer to an object.

- Except for the reference type `String`, Visual Basic's primitive types are value types.

Section 9.5 Case Study: Card Shuffling and Dealing Simulation

- The elements of an array can be of either value types or reference types.

- A class can have references to objects of other classes as members. This is called composition and is sometimes referred to as the *has-a* relationship.

- `Private` methods are called utility methods, or helper methods, because they can be called only by other methods of the class to support their operation.

- Method `ToString` takes no arguments and returns a `String` representation of an object.

- `String` method `Replace` replaces substrings in a `String`. All occurrences of the method's first `String` argument are replaced with its second `String` argument.

Section 9.6 Case Study: Time Class

- Constructors can be overloaded. The compiler invokes the appropriate constructor by matching the number, types and order of the arguments in the constructor call with the number, types and order of the parameters specified in each constructor's declaration.

- When one object of a class has a reference to another object of the same class, the first object can access all of the second object's data, methods and properties (including those that are `Private`).

- Assigning a value to a property invokes the property's `Set` accessor.

- `Private` instance variables do not guarantee data integrity. You must provide validity checking.

- The `With` statement allows you to access an object's members inside the statement without having to specify the name of the object before the dot separator.

Section 9.7 Class Scope

- A class's instance variables and methods have class scope. Within this scope, a class's members are accessible to all of the class's members and can be referenced simply by name.

Section 9.8 Object Initializers

- Object initializers use the `With` keyword to allow you to create an object and initialize its properties in the same statement. To use an object initializer, follow the object creation expression with the `With` keyword and an object initializer list in curly braces (`{ }`) containing the properties to initialize and their values.

- Each property name must be preceded by the dot separator (.) and can appear only once in the object-initializer list.

- An object-initializer list cannot be empty and cannot contain properties that are declared Shared, Const or ReadOnly.

Section 9.9 Auto-Implemented Properties
- For properties that do not have any additional logic in their Set and Get accessors, auto-implemented properties allow you to write one line of code and have the compiler to generate the property's instance variable and accessors.

Section 9.10 Using Me to Access the Current Object
- Every object can access itself through the Me reference. On every method call, the compiler passes an object's Me reference as an implicit argument to each of the object's non-Shared methods.

- When a method has a parameter or local variable with the same name as one of the class's instance variables, the instance variable is shadowed until the method terminates execution.

- Shadowed class members can be accessed via the Me reference.

Section 9.11 Garbage Collection
- Every object you create uses various system resources, such as memory. These resources must be returned to the system when they're no longer needed to avoid resource leaks.

- The Common Language Runtime (CLR) performs automatic garbage collection to reclaim the memory occupied by objects that are no longer in use.

Section 9.12 Shared Class Members
- A Shared class variable represents classwide information—all objects of the class share the same variable. Together, a class's instance variables and Shared variables are know as the class's fields.

- Shared class members have class scope.

- A class's Public Shared members can be accessed by clients via the class name and a dot separator.

- A class's Private Shared class members can be accessed by clients only indirectly through the class's non-Private methods and properties.

- Shared class members are available as soon as the class is loaded into memory at execution time; they exist for the duration of program execution, even when no objects of that class exist.

- Shared methods and properties do not have access to the Me reference.

- A Shared constructor is implicitly Public, must be declared with no parameters, can initialize only the class's Shared variables and is guaranteed to execute before a program creates any objects of the class or accesses any Shared class members.

Section 9.13 Const and ReadOnly Members
- Constants are values that cannot change during program execution.

- An identifier declared as Const must be initialized in its declaration. Const fields can be initialized only to constant values.

- An identifier declared as ReadOnly can be initialized either in its declaration *or* in the class's constructor(s). Constant fields with values that cannot be determined at compile time must be declared ReadOnly.

Section 9.14 Shared Methods and Class Math
- Class Math provides a collection of Shared methods that enable you to perform common mathematical calculations.

- Class `Math` also declares two commonly used mathematical constants: `Math.PI` and `Math.E`. These values are declared in class `Math` with the modifiers `Public` and `Const`.

Section 9.15 Object Browser
- Visual Studio's **Object Browser** lists all the libraries that are available to an application, including the Framework Class Library classes and programmer-defined classes. You use the **Object Browser** to learn about the functionality provided by specific classes. To open the **Object Browser**, right click any class, method or property in the code editor and select **Go To Definition**.

Terminology

access modifier 318
`ArgumentOutOfRangeException` class 319
auto-implemented property 338
`Class...End Class` keywords 318
class scope 337
classwide information 340
client of a class 317
composition 325
`Const` keyword 343
constructor 319
default constructor 319
encapsulation 319
extensible language 321
field of a class 340
floating-point type 324
garbage collector 340
`Get` accessor of a `Property` 320
`Get...End Get` keywords 320
has-a relationship 325
helper method 330
integral type 324
managed resource 340
marked for garbage collection 340
`Math.E` 345
`Math.PI` 345
`Me` reference 339
message (send to an object) 317
Object Browser 345

object-creation expression 322
object initializer 338
object initializer list 338
parameterless constructor 319
`Private` member-access modifier 319
`Property...End Property` keywords 320
`Public` keyword 318
`Public` property 320
`ReadOnly` keyword 344
`ReadOnly` property 320
refer to an object 323
reference 323
reference type 323
resource leak 340
`Set` accessor of a `Property` 320
shadowing an instance variable 339
`Shared` class variable 340
`Shared` constructor 343
`Static` local variable 327
`String` class 324
throw an exception 319
`Throw` statement 319
`ToString` method 325
unmanaged resource 340
utility method 330
value type 323
`With` statement 337
`With` statement block 337

Self-Review Exercises

9.1 Answer each of the following questions:
  a) Properties can contain both _____ accessors.

    1. `Return` and `Value`   2. `Get` and `Value`
    3. `Get` and `Set`   4. `Return` and `Set`

  b) Instance variable declarations should be preceded by which of the following keywords.
    1. `Dim`   2. `Private`
    3. `Public`   4. Any of the above

c) Instance variables are considered _____ by default.
    1. `Private`
    3. `Dimensional`
    2. `Public`
    4. None of the above

9.2 Fill in the blanks in each of the following:
a) A(n) _____ variable represents classwide information.
b) The keyword _____ specifies that an object or variable is not modifiable after it's initialized at runtime.
c) A method declared `Shared` cannot access _____ class members.

9.3 State whether each of the following is *true* or *false*. If *false*, explain why.
a) The `Me` reference allows an object to access its own non-`Shared` members.
b) A `Shared` member of a class can be referenced when no object of that type exists.
c) `ReadOnly` variables must be initialized in a declaration.
d) An object initializer first calls the class's constructor, then assigns the specified property values.

9.4 Write a code to accomplish following: Suppose class `Book` defines properties `Title`, `Author` and `Year`. Use an object initializer to create an object of class `Book` and initialize its properties.

Answers to Self-Review Exercises

9.1 a) 3. b) 2. c) 1.

9.2 a) `Shared`. b) `ReadOnly`. c) non-`Shared`.

9.3 a) True. b) True. c) False. They can also be initialized in the class's constructors. d) True.

9.4 `New Book() With {.Title = "Visual Basic 2010 How to Program",`
    `.Author = "Deitel", .Year = 2010}`

Quick Quiz

9.5 Answer each of the following questions:
a) Keyword _____ introduces a class definition.
    1. `NewClass`
    3. `VBClass`
    2. `ClassDef`
    4. `Class`
b) Keyword _____ is used to create an object.
    1. `CreateObject`
    3. `Create`
    2. `Instantiate`
    4. `New`
c) The _____ is used to retrieve the value of an instance variable.
    1. Get accessor of a property
    3. `Client` method of a class
    2. `Retrieve` method of a class
    4. Set accessor of a property
d) An important difference between constructors and other methods is that _____.
    1. constructors cannot specify a return data type
    2. constructors cannot specify any parameters
    3. other methods are implemented as `Sub` procedures
    4. constructors can assign values to instance variables
e) A class can yield many _____, just as a primitive data type can yield many values.
    1. names
    3. values
    2. objects (instances)
    4. types

f) Instance variables declared `Private` are not accessible _____.

1. outside the class
2. by other methods of the same class
3. inside the same class
4. All of the above.

g) A class definition ends with the keyword(s) _____.

1. `Class End`
2. `End Class`
3. `EndClass`
4. `End`

h) A(n) _____ language is one that can be "extended" with new data types.

1. data
2. extensible
3. typeable
4. None of the above.

i) Variables can be initialized _____.

1. when they are declared
2. to their default values
3. in a constructor
4. All of the above

j) A(n) _____ can ensure that a value is appropriate for a data member before the data member is assigned that value.

1. `Get` accessor
2. `Access` accessor
3. `Modify` accessor
4. `Set` accessor

Exercises

9.6   *(Invoice Class)* Create a class called `Invoice` that a hardware store might use to represent an invoice for an item sold at the store. An `Invoice` should include four pieces of information as instance variables—a part number (type `String`), a part description (type `String`), a quantity of the item being purchased (type `Integer`) and a price per item (type `Integer`). Your class should have a constructor that initializes the four instance variables. Provide a property for each instance variable. If the quantity is not positive, it should be set to 0. If the price per item is not positive, it should be set to 0. Use validation in the properties for these instance variables to ensure that they remain positive. In addition, provide a method named `DisplayInvoiceAmount` that calculates and displays the invoice amount (that is, multiplies the quantity by the price per item). Write an application that demonstrates class `Invoice`'s capabilities.

9.7   *(Employee Class)* Create a class called `Employee` that includes three pieces of information as instance variables—a first name (type `String`), a last name (type `String`) and a monthly salary (type `Integer`). Your class should have a constructor that initializes the three instance variables. Provide a property for each instance variable. The property for the monthly salary should ensure that its value remains positive—if an attempt is made to assign a negative value, throw an exception. Write an application that demonstrates class `Employee`'s capabilities. Create two `Employee` objects and display each object's *yearly* salary. Then give each `Employee` a 10% raise and display each `Employee`'s yearly salary again.

9.8   *(DateInformation Class)* Create a class called `DateInformation` that includes three pieces of information as instance variables—a month (type `Integer`), a day (type `Integer`) and a year (type `Integer`). Your class should provide properties that enable a client of the class to `Get` and `Set` the month, day and year values. The `Set` accessors should perform validation and throw exceptions for invalid values. Your class should have a constructor that initializes the three instance variables and uses the class's properties to set each instance variable's value. Provide a method `ToString` that returns the month, day and year separated by forward slashes (/). Write an application that demonstrates class `DateInformation`'s capabilities.

9.9   *(Savings Account Class)* Create class `SavingsAccount`. Use a `Shared` class variable to store the `annualInterestRate` for all `SavingsAccounts`. Each object of the class contains a `Private` instance variable `savingsBalance` indicating the amount the saver currently has on deposit. Provide the CalculateMonthlyInterest method to calculate the monthly interest by multiplying the savingsBalance by the annualInterestRate divided by 12; this interest should be added to savingsBalance and returned to the method caller. Provide a Shared method ModifyInterestRate that sets the annualInterestRate to a new value. Write an application to test class SavingsAccount. Instantiate two SavingsAccount objects, saver1 and saver2, with balances of $2000.00 and $3000.00, respectively. Set annualInterestRate to 4%, then calculate the monthly interest and display the amounts of interest earned and the new balances for each of the savers. Then set the annualInterestRate to 5% and calculate the next month's interest and display the amounts of interest earned and the new balances for each of the savers.

9.10 *(Square Class)* Write a class that implements a Square shape. Class Square should contain a Side property for accessing Private data. Provide a constructor that takes a side length as a value. Also provide the following ReadOnly properties:

    a) Perimeter returns 4 × Side.
    b) Area returns Side × Side.
    c) Diagonal returns the square root of the expression $(2 \times Side^2)$.

The Perimeter, Area and Diagonal properties should not have corresponding instance variables; rather, their Get accessors should use the Side property's value in calculations that return the desired values. Write an application to test your new Square class.

9.11 *(Enhancing Class Time)* Write a GUI application that is similar to Fig. 9.12, but with two more buttons—**Add 1 to Minute** and **Add 1 to Hour**. Modify class Time of Fig. 9.11 to provide a Tick method that increments the time by one second. Also provide methods IncrementMinute to increment the minute and method IncrementHour to increment the hour. The Tick method, the IncrementMinute method and the IncrementHour method should be called when you click the **Add 1 to Second** button, the **Add 1 to Minute** button and the **Add 1 to Hour** button, respectively. Be sure to test the following cases:

    a) incrementing into the next minute.
    b) incrementing into the next hour.
    c) incrementing into the next day (that is, 11:59:59 PM to 12:00:00 AM).

9.12 *(Modifying the Internal Data Representation of a Class)* It would be perfectly reasonable for the Time class of Fig. 9.11 to represent the time internally as the number of seconds since midnight rather than the three integer values hourValue, minuteValue and secondValue. Clients could use the same Public methods and properties and get the same results. Modify the Time class of Fig. 9.11 to implement the Time as the number of seconds since midnight and show that no change is visible to the clients of the class by using the modified Time class with the TimeTest class of Fig. 9.12.

9.13 *(Account Information Application)* A bank wants you to create a GUI application that will allow bank employees to view the clients' information. The application interface should have four Labels and four TextBoxes, which are used to display first name, last name, account number and account balance, respectively. The interface should also have two Buttons, **Previous** and **Next**, which allow the bank manager to search through each client's information backward and forward, respectively. Create a Customer class to represent the client with first name, last name, account number and account balance. When the GUI application is loaded, create an array of Customer objects, then display the first client's information to the manager. [*Hint:* Use object initializers in the array's initializer list to create each Customer object.] If the current client is the first in the array, the last client in the array is displayed when the manager clicks the **Previous** button. If the current client is the last in the array, the first client in the array is displayed when the manager clicks the **Next** button.

9.14 *(Project: Evaluating Poker Hands)* The card shuffling and dealing application in Section 9.5 can be used as the foundation for a Poker-game program. Study the different types of Poker hands at en.wikipedia.org/wiki/List_of_poker_hands. Create a class called PokerHand that can hold five Cards and provides appopriate properties and methods to help evaluate a hand. You might also need to modify class Card with ReadOnly properties that return the Face and Suit of a Card. Modify the card shuffling and dealing program to evaluate the dealt hand and display the type of hand. [*Instructor Note:* No solution is provided for this exercise.]

Making a Difference Exercises

9.15   *(Target-Heart-Rate Calculator)* While exercising, you can use a heart-rate monitor to see that your heart rate stays within a safe range suggested by your trainers and doctors. According to the American Heart Association (AHA) (www.americanheart.org/presenter.jhtml?identifier=4736), the formula for calculating your *maximum heart rate* in beats per minute is 220 minus your age in years. Your *target heart rate* is a range that is 50–85% of your maximum heart rate. [*Note:* These formulas are estimates provided by the AHA. Maximum and target heart rates may vary based on the health, fitness and gender of the individual. Always consult a physician or qualified health care professional before beginning or modifying an exercise program.] Create a class called HeartRates. The class's instance variables should include the person's first name, last name and date of birth (consisting of separate attributes for the month, day and year of birth). Your class should have a constructor that receives this data as parameters. For each instance variable provide a property with a Get and a Set accessor. The class also should include a method that calculates and returns the person's age (in years), a method that calculates and returns the person's maximum heart rate and a method that calculates and returns the person's target heart rate. Write an application that prompts for the person's information, instantiates an object of class HeartRates and displays the information from that object—including the person's first name, last name and date of birth—then calculates and displays the person's age in (years), maximum heart rate and target-heart-rate range.

9.16   *(Computerization of Health Records)* A health care issue that has been in the news lately is the computerization of health records. This possibility is being approached cautiously because of sensitive privacy and security concerns, among others. Computerizing health records could make it easier for patients to share their health profiles and histories among their various health care professionals. This could improve the quality of health care, help avoid drug conflicts and erroneous drug prescriptions, reduce costs and in emergencies, could save lives. In this exercise, you'll design a "starter" HealthProfile class for a person. The class attributes should include the person's first name, last name, gender, date of birth (consisting of separate attributes for the month, day and year of birth), height (in inches) and weight (in pounds). Your class should have a constructor that receives this data. For each instance variable provide a property with a Get and Set accessor. The class also should include methods that calculate and return the user's age in years, maximum heart rate and target-heart-rate range (see Exercise 9.15), and body mass index (BMI; see Exercise 3.16). Write an application that prompts for the person's information, instantiates an object of class HealthProfile for that person and displays the information from that object—including the person's first name, last name, gender, date of birth, height and weight—then calculates and displays the person's age in years, BMI, maximum heart rate and target-heart-rate range. It should also display the "BMI values" chart from Exercise 3.16.

Object-Oriented Programming: Inheritance and Polymorphism

10

Say not you know another entirely, till you have divided an inheritance with him.
—Johann Kasper Lavater

This method is to define as the number of a class the class of all classes similar to the given class.
—Bertrand Russell

A philosopher of imposing stature doesn't think in a vacuum. Even his most abstract ideas are, to some extent, conditioned by what is or is not known in the time when he lives.
—Alfred North Whitehead

Objectives

In this chapter you'll learn:

- What inheritance is and how it promotes software reuse.
- To use keyword **Inherits** to create a derived class that inherits attributes and behaviors from a base class.
- To use access modifier **Protected** to give derived-class methods access to base-class members.
- How constructors are used in inheritance hierarchies.
- What polymorphism is and how it makes systems extensible and maintainable.
- To distinguish between abstract and concrete classes.

10.1 Introduction

This chapter continues our discussion of object-oriented programming by introducing **inheritance**, a form of software reuse in which a new class is created quickly and easily by absorbing an existing class's members and customizing them with new or modified capabilities. With inheritance, you can save time during program development and build better software by *reusing* proven, high-quality classes. Enormous numbers of these classes are available in **class libraries** provided by Microsoft and independent software vendors.

When creating a class, rather than declaring completely new members, you can designate that the new class *inherits* the members of an existing class. The existing class is called the **base class**, and the new class is the **derived class**.

A derived class can add its own instance variables, Shared variables, properties and methods, and it can customize methods and properties it inherits. Therefore, a derived class is *more specific* than its base class and represents a more *specialized group of objects*.

We explain and demonstrate **polymorphism**, which enables you to conveniently program "in the general" rather than "in the specific." As we send method calls in this general way, the specific objects "do the right thing." You'll see that polymorphism simplifies programming with classes and makes it easy to extend systems with new capabilities.

10.2 Base Classes and Derived Classes

Inheritance enables an *is-a* **relationship**. In an *is-a* relationship, an object of a derived class also can be treated as an object of its base class. For example, a car *is a* vehicle. Figure 10.1 lists several simple examples of base classes and derived classes—base classes tend to be *more general* and derived classes tend to be *more specific*. Base-class objects *cannot* be treated as objects of their derived classes—although all cars are vehicles, *not* all vehicles are cars (the other vehicles could be trucks, planes or bicycles, for example).

Base class	Derived classes
Student	A GraduateStudent is a Student An UndergraduateStudent is a Student
Shape	A Circle is a Shape A Triangle is a Shape
Loan	A CarLoan is a Loan A HomeImprovementLoan is a Loan
BankAccount	A CheckingAccount is a BankAccount A SavingsAccount is a BankAccount

Fig. 10.1 | Inheritance examples.

Because every derived-class object *is an* object of its base class, and one base class can have *many* derived classes, the set of objects represented by a base class is typically larger than the set of objects represented by any of its derived classes. For example, the *base class* Vehicle represents *all* vehicles, including cars, trucks, boats, bicycles and so on. By contrast, *derived class* Car represents a smaller, more specific subset of vehicles.

CommunityMember *Inheritance Hierarchy*
Figure 10.2 shows a sample UML class diagram of an **inheritance hierarchy**. A college community has thousands of community members, including employees, students and alumni. Employees are either faculty members or staff members. Faculty members are either administrators (such as deans and department chairpersons) or teachers. The hierarchy could contain many other classes. For example, students can be graduate or undergraduate students. Undergraduate students can be freshmen, sophomores, juniors or seniors.

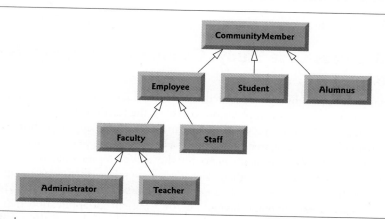

Fig. 10.2 | Inheritance hierarchy for university CommunityMembers.

Each arrow in the inheritance hierarchy represents an *is-a* relationship. As we follow the arrows *upward* in this class hierarchy, we can state, for instance, that "an Employee *is a* CommunityMember" and "a Teacher *is a* Faculty member." A **direct base class** is the class from which a derived class explicitly inherits. An **indirect base class** is inherited from two or more levels up in the class hierarchy. So, class `CommunityMember` is the direct base class of `Employee`, `Student` and `Alumnus`, and is an indirect base class of all the other classes in the diagram. Starting from the bottom of the diagram, you can follow the arrows and apply the *is-a* relationship up to the topmost base class. For example, an `Administrator` *is a* `Faculty` member, *is an* `Employee` and *is a* `CommunityMember`.

Shape Inheritance Hierarchy

Now consider the `Shape` inheritance hierarchy in Fig. 10.3. It begins with base class `Shape`, which is inherited by derived classes `TwoDimensionalShape` and `ThreeDimensional-Shape`—Shapes are either `TwoDimensionalShapes` or `ThreeDimensionalShapes`. The third level of the hierarchy contains more specific types of `TwoDimensionalShapes` and `Three-DimensionalShapes`. As in Fig. 10.2, we can follow the arrows from the derived classes at the bottom of the diagram to the topmost base class in this class hierarchy to identify several *is-a* relationships. For example, a `Triangle` *is a* `TwoDimensionalShape` and *is a* `Shape`, while a `Sphere` *is a* `ThreeDimensionalShape` and *is a* `Shape`. `Shape` is a *direct base class* of classes `TwoDimensionalShape` and `ThreeDimensionalShape`, and is an *indirect base class* of all the classes on the third level.

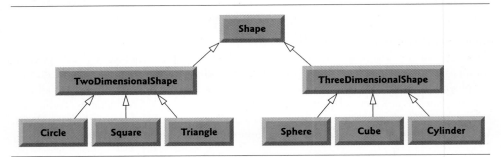

Fig. 10.3 | Inheritance hierarchy for `Shapes`.

10.3 Business Case Study: Commission Employees Class Hierarchy

In this section, we use a business-oriented inheritance hierarchy containing types of employees in a company's payroll application to discuss the relationship between a base class and its derived class. All employees of the company have a lot in common, but *Commission employees* (who will be represented as objects of a base class) are paid a percentage of their sales, while *base-salaried commission employees* (who will be represented as objects of a derived class) receive a percentage of their sales *plus* a base salary. First, we present *base class* `CommissionEmployee`. Next, we create a *derived class* `BasePlusCommissionEmployee` that inherits from class `CommissionEmployee`. Then we present an application that creates a `BasePlusCommissionEmployee` object and demonstrates that it has all the capabilities of the base class *and* the derived class, but calculates its earnings differently.

10.3.1 Creating Base Class `CommissionEmployee`

Consider class `CommissionEmployee` (Fig. 10.4). The `Public` services of class `CommissionEmployee` include:

- a constructor (lines 11–20)

- properties FirstName (line 4), LastName (line 5), SocialSecurityNumber (line 6), GrossSales (lines 23–36) and CommissionRate (lines 39–52)

- methods CalculateEarnings (lines 55–57) and ToString (lines 60–66).

The class also declares Private instance variables grossSalesValue and commissionRate-Value (lines 7–8) to represent the employee's gross sales and commission rate. Recall that the compiler automatically generates a Private instance variable for each auto-implemented property, so a CommissionEmployee actually has *five* Private instance variables.

The Set accessors of properties GrossSales and CommissionRate validate their arguments before assigning the values to instance variables grossSalesValue and commission-RateValue, respectively. Properties FirstName, LastName and SocialSecurityNumber are *auto-implemented* in this example, because we're not providing any validation code in their Set accessors. We could validate the first and last names—perhaps by ensuring that they're of a reasonable length. The social security number could be validated to ensure that it contains nine digits, with or without dashes (for example, 123-45-6789 or 123456789).

```vb
1    ' Fig. 10.4: CommmissionEmployee.vb
2    ' CommissionEmployee base class.
3    Public Class CommissionEmployee
4       Public Property FirstName() As String ' auto-implemented
5       Public Property LastName() As String ' auto-implemented
6       Public Property SocialSecurityNumber() As String ' auto-implemented
7       Private grossSalesValue As Decimal ' gross weekly sales
8       Private commissionRateValue As Double ' commission percentage
9
10      ' five-argument constructor
11      Public Sub New(ByVal first As String, ByVal last As String,
12         ByVal ssn As String, ByVal sales As Decimal, ByVal rate As Double)
13
14         ' implicit call to class Object's constructor occurs here
15         FirstName = first
16         LastName = last
17         SocialSecurityNumber = ssn
18         GrossSales = sales ' validate and store gross sales
19         CommissionRate = rate ' validate and store commission rate
20      End Sub ' New
21
22      ' property GrossSales
23      Public Property GrossSales() As Decimal
24         Get
25            Return grossSalesValue
26         End Get
27
28         Set(ByVal sales As Decimal)
29            If sales >= 0D Then ' validate gross sales
30               grossSalesValue = sales ' valid
31            Else
```

Fig. 10.4 | CommissionEmployee base class. (Part 1 of 2.)

```
32              Throw New ArgumentOutOfRangeException(
33                  "Gross sales must be greater than or equal to 0")
34          End If
35        End Set
36      End Property ' GrossSales
37
38      ' property CommissionRate
39      Public Property CommissionRate() As Double
40        Get
41            Return commissionRateValue
42        End Get
43
44        Set(ByVal rate As Double)
45            If rate > 0.0 AndAlso rate < 1.0 Then ' validate rate
46                commissionRateValue = rate ' valid
47            Else
48                Throw New ArgumentOutOfRangeException(
49                    "Interest rate must be greater than 0 and less than 1")
50            End If
51        End Set
52      End Property ' CommissionRate
53
54      ' calculate earnings
55      Public Overridable Function CalculateEarnings() As Decimal
56          Return Convert.ToDecimal(CommissionRate) * GrossSales
57      End Function ' CalculateEarnings
58
59      ' return String representation of CommissionEmployee object
60      Public Overrides Function ToString() As String
61          Return "commission employee: " & FirstName & " " & LastName &
62              vbCrLf & "social security number: " & SocialSecurityNumber &
63              vbCrLf & "gross sales: " & String.Format("{0:C}", GrossSales) &
64              vbCrLf & "commission rate: " &
65              String.Format("{0:F}", CommissionRate)
66      End Function ' ToString
67   End Class ' CommissionEmployee
```

Fig. 10.4 | CommissionEmployee base class. (Part 2 of 2.)

All Classes Inherit Directly or Indirectly from *Object* (from Namespace *System*)

You use inheritance to create new classes from existing classes. In fact, every class except Object inherits from an existing class. When you do not explicitly specify the base class in a new class declaration, the compiler implicitly assumes that the class **Inherits** from Object. The class hierarchy begins with class Object (in namespace System), which *every* class directly or indirectly extends (or "inherits from"). So, the beginning of class CommissionEmployee could have been written as

```
Public Class CommissionEmployee
    Inherits Object
```

You typically do not include "Inherits Object" in your code, since it's implied. Class CommissionEmployee inherits the methods of class Object—class Object does not have any fields. One of the methods inherited from class Object is ToString, so every class has a ToString method that returns a String representation of the object on which it's called. We discuss the default behavior of method ToString momentarily.

CommissionEmployee *Constructor*

Constructors are *not* inherited, so class CommissionEmployee does not inherit class Object's constructor. However, class CommissionEmployee's constructor (lines 11–20) calls Object's constructor implicitly. In fact, the first task of *any* derived-class constructor is to call its *direct* base class's constructor, either explicitly or implicitly (if no constructor call is specified), to ensure that the instance variables declared in the base class are initialized properly. The syntax for calling a base-class constructor *explicitly* is discussed in Section 10.3.2. If the code does not include an explicit call to the base-class constructor, Visual Basic implicitly calls the base class's default or parameterless constructor. The comment in line 14 of Fig. 10.4 indicates where the implicit call to the base class Object's default constructor occurs (you do not need to write the code for this call). Object's default constructor does nothing. Even if a class does not have constructors, the default constructor that the compiler implicitly creates for the class will call the base class's default or parameterless constructor. After the implicit call to Object's constructor occurs, lines 15–19 assign values to the class's properties.

Method CalculateEarnings *and Declaring Methods* Overridable

Method CalculateEarnings (lines 55–57) calculates a CommissionEmployee's earnings. Line 56 multiplies the CommissionRate by the GrossSales and returns the result. A base-class method must be declared Overridable if a derived class should be allowed to override the method with a version more appropriate for that class. When we create class BasePlusCommissionEmployee, we'll want to override (redefine) CommissionEmployee's CalculateEarnings method to *customize* the earnings calculation for a BasePlusCommissionEmployee. For this reason, we declared CalculateEarnings as Overridable in line 55. In BasePlusCommissionEmployee, we'll declare method CalculateEarnings with the keyword Overrides.

Method ToString *and Overriding Base Class Methods*

Method ToString (lines 60–66) returns a String containing information about the CommissionEmployee. The keyword Overrides (line 60) indicates that this method overrides (redefines) the version of ToString that was inherited from CommissionEmployee's base class (that is, Object). In class Object, method ToString is declared as:

```
Public Overridable Function ToString() As String
```

so that ToString can be overridden in any derived class.

If you do not override ToString in class CommissionEmployee, the default implementation inherited from class Object would return only "*ProjectName*.CommissionEmployee"—for this example, we named the project InheritanceTest.

10.3.2 Creating Derived Class BasePlusCommissionEmployee

Most of a BasePlusCommissionEmployee's capabilities are similar, if not identical, to the those of class CommissionEmployee (Fig. 10.4). Both classes require instance variables for the first name, last name, social security number, gross sales and commission rate, and properties and methods to manipulate that data. To create class BasePlusCommissionEmployee *without* using inheritance, we probably would have *copied* the code from class CommissionEmployee and *pasted* it into class BasePlusCommissionEmployee, then modified the new class to include a base salary instance variable, and the methods and properties that manipulate the base salary, including a new CalculateEarnings method. This *copy-and-paste approach* is often error prone and time consuming. Worse yet, it can spread many physical copies of the same code (including errors) throughout a system, creating a code-maintenance nightmare. Is there a way to "absorb" the instance variables and methods of one class in a way that makes them part of another class without duplicating code? Indeed there is—using the elegant object-oriented programming technique of inheritance.

Software Engineering Observation 10.1

With inheritance, the common instance variables and methods of all the classes in the hierarchy are declared only in a base class. When changes are required for these common features, you need to make the changes only in the base class—derived classes then inherit the changes. Without inheritance, the changes would need to be made to all the source-code files that contain copies of the code in question.

Declaring Class *BasePlusCommissionEmployee*

We now discuss the second part of our introduction to inheritance by declaring the derived class BasePlusCommissionEmployee (Fig. 10.5), which *inherits* most of its capabilities from class CommissionEmployee (line 4). A BasePlusCommissionEmployee *is a* CommissionEmployee (because inheritance passes on the capabilities of class CommissionEmployee), but class BasePlusCommissionEmployee also has

- instance variable baseSalaryValue (line 6)
- property BaseSalary (lines 19–32).

Also, BasePlusCommissionEmployee provides

- a constructor (lines 9–16)
- a customized version of method CalculateEarnings (lines 35–37)
- a customized version of method ToString (lines 40–43).

```
1   ' Fig. 10.5: BasePlusCommissionEmployee.vb
2   ' BasePlusCommissionEmployee inherits from class CommissionEmployee.
3   Public Class BasePlusCommissionEmployee
4      Inherits CommissionEmployee
5
6      Private baseSalaryValue As Decimal ' base salary per week
7
8      ' six-argument constructor
9      Public Sub New(ByVal first As String, ByVal last As String,
10        ByVal ssn As String, ByVal sales As Decimal,
11        ByVal rate As Double, ByVal salary As Decimal)
12
13        ' use MyBase reference to call CommissionEmployee constructor
14        MyBase.New(first, last, ssn, sales, rate)
```

Fig. 10.5 | BasePlusCommissionEmployee class inherits from class CommissionEmployee. (Part 1 of 2.)

```
15          BaseSalary = salary ' validate and store base salary
16       End Sub ' New
17
18       ' property BaseSalary
19       Public Property BaseSalary() As Decimal
20          Get
21             Return baseSalaryValue
22          End Get
23
24          Set(ByVal salary As Decimal)
25             If salary >= 0D Then ' validate base salary
26                baseSalaryValue = salary ' valid
27             Else
28                Throw New ArgumentOutOfRangeException(
29                   "Base salary must be greater than or equal to 0")
30             End If
31          End Set
32       End Property ' BaseSalary
33
34       ' calculate earnings
35       Public Overrides Function CalculateEarnings() As Decimal
36          Return BaseSalary + MyBase.CalculateEarnings()
37       End Function ' CalculateEarnings
38
39       ' return String representation of BasePlusCommissionEmployee object
40       Public Overrides Function ToString() As String
41          Return "base-plus-" & MyBase.ToString() & vbCrLf &
42             "base salary: " & String.Format("{0:C}", BaseSalary)
43       End Function ' ToString
44    End Class ' BasePlusCommissionEmployee
```

Fig. 10.5 | BasePlusCommissionEmployee class inherits from class CommissionEmployee. (Part 2 of 2.)

Inheriting from Class CommissionEmployee

Keyword Inherits in line 4 of the class declaration indicates that class BasePlusCommissionEmployee inherits *all* of the Public members (*and*, as we'll soon see, Protected members if there were any) of class CommissionEmployee. We do not redeclare the base class's Private instance variables—these are nevertheless present (but hidden) in derived class objects. Even though they're present, they're declared Private in the base class, so as we'll see in a moment, we'll have to make special provision to access this base-class information from the derived class. The CommissionEmployee constructor is *not* inherited. Thus, the Public services of BasePlusCommissionEmployee include its

- constructor (lines 9–16)
- the Public methods and properties inherited from class CommissionEmployee
- property BaseSalary (lines 19–32), which *cannot* be auto-implemented because it performs validation in its Set accessor
- method CalculateEarnings (lines 35–37)
- method ToString (lines 40–43).

BasePlusCommissionEmployee Constructor

Each derived-class constructor must implicitly or explicitly call its base-class constructor to ensure that the instance variables inherited from the base class are properly initialized. BasePlusCommissionEmployee's *six-argument constructor* (lines 9–16) explicitly calls class CommissionEmployee's *five-argument constructor* (line 14) to initialize the base class portion of a BasePlusCommissionEmployee object (that is, the five instance variables from class CommissionEmployee). Line 14 uses the **base-class constructor call syntax**—keyword **MyBase**, followed by the dot (.) separator, followed by New and a set of parentheses containing the arguments to the base-class constructor—first, last, ssn, sales and rate. Then, line 15 initializes the BasePlusCommissionEmployee's base salary.

If the BasePlusCommissionEmployee constructor did not include line 14, Visual Basic would attempt to invoke class CommissionEmployee's parameterless or default constructor, which does not exist, so a compilation error would occur. The explicit base-class constructor call (line 14) must be the *first* statement in the derived-class constructor's body.

Overriding Method CalculateEarnings

Class BasePlusCommissionEmployee's CalculateEarnings method (lines 35–37) overrides class CommissionEmployee's CalculateEarnings method (Fig. 10.4, lines 55–57) to calculate the earnings of a base-salaried commission employee. The new version obtains the portion of the employee's earnings based on *commission alone* by calling CommissionEmployee's CalculateEarnings method with the expression MyBase.CalculateEarnings() (line 36). BasePlusCommissionEmployee's CalculateEarnings method then adds the BaseSalary to this value to calculate the total earnings of the derived-class employee. Note the syntax used to invoke an overridden base-class method from a derived class—place the keyword MyBase and a dot (.) separator before the base-class method name. By having BasePlusCommissionEmployee's CalculateEarnings method invoke CommissionEmployee's CalculateEarnings method to calculate part of a BasePlusCommissionEmployee object's earnings, we *avoid duplicating the code and reduce code-maintenance problems.*

Overriding Method ToString

BasePlusCommissionEmployee's ToString method (lines 40–43) overrides class CommissionEmployee's ToString method (Fig. 10.4, lines 60–66) to return a String representation that's appropriate for a BasePlusCommissionEmployee. The derived class creates part of a BasePlusCommissionEmployee object's String representation by concatenating "base-plus-" with the String returned by calling CommissionEmployee's ToString method via the expression MyBase.ToString() (line 41). BasePlusCommissionEmployee's ToString method then concatenates the remainder of a BasePlusCommissionEmployee object's String representation (that is, the value of class BasePlusCommissionEmployee's base salary) before returning the String.

10.3.3 Testing Class BasePlusCommissionEmployee

Figure 10.6 tests class BasePlusCommissionEmployee. Lines 9–10 create a BasePlusCommissionEmployee object and pass "Bob", "Lewis", "333-33-3333", 5000, 0.04 and 300 to the constructor as the first name, last name, social security number, gross sales, commission rate and base salary, respectively. Lines 13–22 use BasePlusCommissionEmployee's properties to output the object's data. Notice that we're able to access *all* of the Public properties of classes CommissionEmployee *and* BasePlusCommissionEmployee here. Lines

25–26 calculate and display the BasePlusCommissionEmployee's earnings by calling its CaculateEarnings method. Because this method is called on a BasePlusCommission-Employee object, the derived-class version of the method executes. Next, lines 29–31 modify the GrossSales, CommissionRate and BaseSalary properties. Lines 34–36 output the updated data—this time by calling the BasePlusCommissionEmployee's ToString method. Again, because this method is called on a BasePlusCommissionEmployee object, the derived class version of the method executes. Finally, lines 39–40 calculate and display the BasePlusCommissionEmployee's updated earnings.

```vb
1    ' Fig. 10.6: InheritanceTest.vb
2    ' Testing derived class BasePlusCommissionEmployee.
3    Public Class InheritanceTest
4       ' demonstrate class BasePlusCommissionEmployee
5       Private Sub InheritanceTest_Load(ByVal sender As System.Object,
6          ByVal e As System.EventArgs) Handles MyBase.Load
7
8          ' instantiate BasePlusCommissionEmployee object
9          Dim employee As New BasePlusCommissionEmployee(
10            "Bob", "Lewis", "333-33-3333", 5000D, 0.04, 300D)
11
12         ' get base-salaried commission employee data
13         outputTextBox.AppendText(
14            "Employee information obtained by properties:" & vbCrLf &
15            "First name is " & employee.FirstName & vbCrLf &
16            "Last name is " & employee.LastName & vbCrLf &
17            "Social Security Number is " & employee.SocialSecurityNumber &
18            vbCrLf & "Gross sales is " &
19            String.Format("{0:C}", employee.GrossSales) & vbCrLf &
20            "Commission rate is " &
21            String.Format("{0:F}", employee.CommissionRate) & vbCrLf &
22            "Base salary is " & String.Format("{0:C}", employee.BaseSalary))
23
24         ' display the employee's earnings
25         outputTextBox.AppendText(vbCrLf & vbCrLf & "Earnings: " &
26            String.Format("{0:C}", employee.CalculateEarnings()))
27
28         ' modify properties
29         employee.GrossSales = 10000D ' set gross sales
30         employee.CommissionRate = 0.05 ' set commission rate
31         employee.BaseSalary = 1000D ' set base salary
32
33         ' get new employee information
34         outputTextBox.AppendText(vbCrLf & vbCrLf &
35            "Updated employee information returned by ToString: " &
36            vbCrLf & employee.ToString())
37
38         ' display the employee's earnings
39         outputTextBox.AppendText(vbCrLf & vbCrLf & "Earnings: " &
40            String.Format("{0:C}", employee.CalculateEarnings()))
41      End Sub ' InheritanceTest_Load
42   End Class ' InheritanceTest
```

Fig. 10.6 | Testing derived class BasePlusCommissionEmployee. (Part 1 of 2.)

Fig. 10.6 | Testing derived class `BasePlusCommissionEmployee`. (Part 2 of 2.)

10.4 Constructors in Derived Classes

Creating a derived-class object begins a *chain of constructor calls* in which the derived-class constructor, *before* performing its own tasks, invokes its direct base class's constructor either explicitly (via the `MyBase` reference) or implicitly (calling the base class's default or parameterless constructor). Similarly, if the base class is derived from another class (as is *every* class except `Object`), the base-class constructor invokes the constructor of the next class up the hierarchy, and so on. The last constructor called in the chain is *always* the constructor for class `Object`. The original derived-class constructor's body finishes executing *last*.

Each base class's constructor manipulates the base-class instance variables that are part of the derived-class object. For example, let's reconsider the `CommissionEmployee`–`BasePlusCommissionEmployee` hierarchy from Figs. 10.4 and 10.5. When a program creates a `BasePlusCommissionEmployee` object (Fig. 10.6, lines 9–10), the `BasePlusCommissionEmployee` constructor is called. That constructor, before executing its full body code, immediately calls `CommissionEmployee`'s constructor (Fig. 10.5, line 14), which in turn calls `Object`'s constructor. Class `Object`'s constructor has an empty body, so it immediately returns control to the `CommissionEmployee`'s constructor, which then initializes the `Private` instance variables of `CommissionEmployee` (Fig. 10.4, lines 15–19) that are part of the `BasePlusCommissionEmployee` object. When the `CommissionEmployee`'s constructor completes execution, it returns control to the `BasePlusCommissionEmployee`'s constructor, which initializes the `BasePlusCommissionEmployee` object's baseSalary-Value (via property `BaseSalary`; Fig. 10.5, line 15).

10.5 Protected Members

This section introduces the access modifier `Protected`. A base class's `Protected` members can be accessed *only* by members of that base class and by members of its derived classes.

In inheritance, `Public` members of the base class become `Public` members of the derived class, and `Protected` members of the base class become `Protected` members of the derived class. A base class's `Private` members are *not* inherited by its derived classes.

Derived-class methods can refer to Public and Protected members inherited from the base class simply by using the member names.

Derived-class methods cannot directly access Private members of their base class. A derived class can change the state of Private base-class instance variables only through Public *and* Protected methods provided in the base class and inherited by the derived class.

In most cases, it's better to use Private instance variables to encourage proper software engineering. Your code will be easier to maintain, modify and debug.

Using Protected instance variables creates several potential problems. First, the derived-class object can set an inherited variable's value directly without using a Set accessor. Therefore, a derived-class object can assign an *invalid* value to the variable.

Another problem with using Protected instance variables is that derived-class methods are more likely to be written so that they depend on the base class's data implementation. *In practice, derived classes should depend only on the base-class services (that is, non-Private methods and properties) and not on the base-class data implementation.* With Protected instance variables in the base class, all the derived classes of the base class may need to be modified if the base-class implementation changes. In such a case, the software is said to be **brittle**, because a small change in the base class can "break" derived-class implementations. You should be able to change the base-class implementation while still providing the same services to the derived classes. Of course, if the base-class services change, you must reimplement the derived classes.

Software Engineering Observation 10.2

Use the Protected access modifier on a method when a base class is to provide the method to its derived classes but not to other clients.

Software Engineering Observation 10.3

Declaring base-class instance variables Private (as opposed to Protected) enables the base-class implementation of these instance variables to change without affecting derived-class implementations.

10.6 Introduction to Polymorphism: Polymorphic Video Game

Suppose we design a video game that manipulates objects of many different types, including objects of classes Martian, Venutian, Plutonian, SpaceShip and LaserBeam. Imagine that each class inherits from the common base class called SpaceObject, which contains method Draw. Each derived class implements this method in a manner appropriate to that class. A screen-manager program maintains a collection (for example, a SpaceObject array) of references to objects of the various classes. To refresh the screen, the screen manager periodically sends each object the same message, Draw. However, each object responds in a unique way. For example, a Martian object might *draw itself* in red with the appropriate number of antennae. A SpaceShip object might *draw itself* as a bright silver flying saucer. A LaserBeam object might *draw itself* as a bright red beam across the screen. The same message (in this case, Draw) sent to a variety of objects has *many forms* of results, hence the term polymorphism.

A screen manager might use polymorphism to make the system **extensible** and facilitate adding new classes to a system with minimal modifications to the system's code. Suppose that we want to add Mercurian objects to our video game. To do so, we must build a class Mercurian that inherits from SpaceObject and provides its own Draw method implementation. When objects of class Mercurian appear in the SpaceObject collection, the screen-manager code invokes method Draw, exactly as it does for the other objects in the collection, regardless of their types. So the new Mercurian class simply *plugs right in* without any modification of the screen-manager code by the programmer. Thus, without modifying the system (other than to build new classes and modify the code that creates new objects), programmers can use polymorphism to include types that were not envisioned when the system was created.

10.7 Abstract Classes and Methods

When we think of a class type, we assume that programs will create objects of that type. In some cases, however, it's useful to declare classes for which you *never* intend to instantiate objects. Such classes are called **abstract classes**. Because they're used only as base classes in inheritance hierarchies, we refer to them as **abstract base classes**. These classes cannot be used to instantiate objects, because, as you'll soon see, abstract classes are *incomplete*. We demonstrate abstract classes in Section 10.8.

The purpose of an abstract class is primarily to provide an appropriate base class from which other classes can inherit and thus share a common design. In the Shape hierarchy of Fig. 10.3, for example, derived classes inherit the notion of what it means to be a Shape—possibly including common properties such as Location, Color and Border-Thickness, and behaviors such as Draw, Move, Resize and ChangeColor. Classes that *can* be used to instantiate objects are called **concrete classes**. Such classes provide implementations of *every* method they declare (some of the implementations can be inherited). For example, we could derive concrete classes Circle, Square and Triangle from abstract base class TwoDimensionalShape. Similarly, we could derive concrete classes Sphere, Cube and Tetrahedron from abstract base class ThreeDimensionalShape. Abstract base classes are *too general* to create real objects—they specify only what is common among derived classes. We need to be more specific before we can create objects. For example, if you send the Draw message to abstract class TwoDimensionalShape, it knows that two-dimensional shapes should be *drawable*, but it does not know *what specific shape to draw*, so it cannot implement a real Draw method. Concrete classes provide the *specifics* that make it reasonable to instantiate objects.

Declaring Abstract Classes and Abstract Methods

You make a class abstract by declaring it with keyword **MustInherit**. An abstract class normally contains one or more **abstract methods**. An abstract method is declared with keyword **MustOverride**, as in

```
Public MustOverride Sub Draw() ' abstract method
```

MustOverride methods do not provide implementations. A class that contains *any* MustOverride methods must be declared as a MustInherit class even if it contains *some* concrete methods. Each concrete derived class of a MustInherit base class must provide concrete implementations of *all* the base class's MustOverride methods. Constructors and Shared methods cannot be overridden, so they cannot be declared MustOverride.

Common Programming Error 10.1

Attempting to instantiate an object of an abstract class is a compilation error.

Common Programming Error 10.2

Failure to implement a base class's abstract methods in a derived class is a compilation error unless the derived class is also declared MustInherit.

10.8 Case Study: Payroll System Class Hierarchy Using Polymorphism

Let's reexamine the CommissionEmployee–BasePlusCommissionEmployee hierarchy that we explored in Section 10.3. Now we use an abstract method and polymorphism to perform payroll calculations based on the type of employee. We create an enhanced employee hierarchy to solve the following problem:

> *A company pays its employees on a weekly basis. The employees are of three types: Salaried employees are paid a fixed weekly salary regardless of the number of hours worked, commission employees are paid a percentage of their sales, and base-plus-commission employees receive a base salary plus a percentage of their sales. The company wants to implement an application that performs its payroll calculations polymorphically.*

We use abstract (that is, MustInherit) class Employee to represent the *general concept* of an employee. The classes that inherit from Employee are SalariedEmployee and CommissionEmployee. Class BasePlusCommissionEmployee inherits from CommissionEmployee. The UML class diagram in Fig. 10.7 shows our polymorphic employee inheritance hierarchy. Abstract class name Employee is italicized, as per UML convention; concrete class names are not italicized.

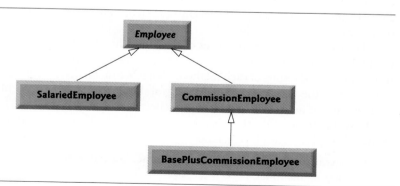

Fig. 10.7 | Employee hierarchy UML class diagram.

The following five sections implement the Employee class hierarchy. The first four sections show the abstract base class Employee and the concrete derived classes Salaried-Employee, CommissionEmployee, and the indirectly derived concrete class BasePlusCommissionEmployee. The last section shows a test program that builds objects of these classes and processes them polymorphically.

10.8.1 Abstract Base Class Employee

Abstract base class Employee declares the set of methods that a program can invoke on all employees. Each employee, regardless of the way his or her earnings are calculated, has a first name, a last name and a social security number. So Public properties FirstName, LastName and SocialSecurityNumber will appear in abstract base class Employee.

Class Employee also provides methods CalculateEarnings and ToString. Method CalculateEarnings certainly applies to all employees, but each *specific* earnings calculation depends on the employee's class. So we declare the method as MustOverride in base class Employee because a default implementation does not make sense for that method—there is not enough information to determine what amount CalculateEarnings should return for a *general* Employee. Each derived class Overrides CalculateEarnings with an appropriate *specific* implementation. In the test program, we'll maintain an array of Employee variables, each holding a reference to an Employee object. Of course, *there cannot be Employee objects because Employee is an abstract class*—thanks to inheritance, however, all objects of all derived classes of Employee may be thought of as Employee objects.

Although we cannot instantiate objects of abstract base classes, we *can* use abstract base class variables to refer to objects of any concrete classes derived from those abstract classes. Programs typically use such variables to manipulate derived-class objects polymorphically. The program we build in Fig. 10.13 iterates through an array of Employee variables and calls CalculateEarnings for each Employee object. These method calls are processed polymorphically. Including the abstract method CalculateEarnings in class Employee forces every directly derived concrete class of Employee to override Calculate-Earnings.

Method ToString in class Employee returns a String containing the first name, last name and social security number of the employee. Each derived class of Employee will override method ToString to create a String representation of an object of that class that contains the employee's type (for example, "salaried employee:") followed by the rest of the employee's information.

Fig. 10.8 shows the four classes of the hierarchy of Fig. 10.7 down the left side and methods CalculateEarnings and ToString across the top. For each class, the diagram shows the desired results of each method. [*Note:* We do not list base class Employee's properties because they're not overridden in any of the derived classes—each of these properties is inherited and used "as is" by each of the derived classes.]

Class Employee (Fig. 10.9) is a MustInherit class, meaning it can be used *only* as an abstract base class. The class includes

- a constructor that takes the first name, last name and social security number as arguments (lines 9–14)

- properties for the first name, last name and social security number (lines 4–6)

- method ToString (lines 17–20), which returns the String representation of an Employee

- MustOverride (abstract) method CalculateEarnings (line 23), which *must* be implemented by concrete derived classes.

	CalculateEarnings	ToString
Employee	`MustOverride`	*FirstName LastName* social security number: *SSN*
Salaried-Employee	*WeeklySalary*	salaried employee: *FirstName LastName* social security number: *SSN* weekly salary: *WeeklySalary*
Commission-Employee	*CommissionRate * GrossSales*	commission employee: *FirstName LastName* social security number: *SSN* gross sales: *GrossSales*; commission rate: *CommissionRate*
BasePlus-Commission-Employee	*(CommissionRate * GrossSales) + BaseSalary*	base-salaried commission employee: *FirstName LastName* social security number: *SSN* gross sales: *GrossSales*; commission rate: *CommissionRate*; base salary: *BaseSalary*

Fig. 10.8 | Polymorphic interface for the `Employee` hierarchy classes.

```
1    ' Fig. 10.9: Employee.vb
2    ' Employee abstract base class.
3    Public MustInherit Class Employee
4       Public Property FirstName() As String  ' auto-implemented
5       Public Property LastName() As String   ' auto-implemented
6       Public Property SocialSecurityNumber() As String ' auto-implemented
7
8       ' three-argument constructor
9       Public Sub New(ByVal first As String, ByVal last As String,
10         ByVal ssn As String)
11         FirstName = first ' invoke auto-implemented property
12         LastName = last ' invoke auto-implemented property
13         SocialSecurityNumber = ssn ' invoke auto-implemented property
14      End Sub ' New
15
16      ' return String representation of Employee object
17      Public Overrides Function ToString() As String
18         Return String.Format("{0} {1}{2}{3} {4}", FirstName, LastName,
19            vbCrLf, "social security number:", SocialSecurityNumber)
20      End Function ' ToString
21
22      ' abstract method overridden by derived classes
23      Public MustOverride Function CalculateEarnings() As Decimal
24   End Class ' Employee
```

Fig. 10.9 | Employee abstract base class.

Why did we decide to declare `CalculateEarnings` as a `MustOverride` method? It simply does not make sense to provide an implementation of this method in class

Employee. We cannot calculate the earnings for a *general* Employee—we first must know the *specific* Employee type to determine the appropriate earnings calculation. By declaring this method MustOverride, we indicate that *every* concrete derived class *must* provide an appropriate CalculateEarnings implementation that Overrides the base class method, and that a program will be able to use base-class Employee variables to invoke method CalculateEarnings polymorphically for *every* type of Employee.

10.8.2 Concrete Derived Class SalariedEmployee

Class SalariedEmployee (Fig. 10.10) inherits from class Employee (line 4) and overrides CalculateEarnings (lines 33–35), which makes SalariedEmployee a concrete class. The class includes

- a constructor (lines 9–14) that takes a first name, a last name, a social security number and a weekly salary as arguments

- a WeeklySalary property that has a Get accessor (lines 18–20) to return weeklySalaryValue's value and a Set accessor (lines 22–29) to assign a new nonnegative value to instance variable weeklySalaryValue

- a method CalculateEarnings (lines 33–35) to calculate a SalariedEmployee's earnings

- a method ToString (lines 38–42) that returns a String including the employee's type, namely, "salaried employee:", followed by employee-specific information produced by base class Employee's ToString method, and the value of SalariedEmployee's WeeklySalary property.

```vb
1    ' Fig. 10.10: SalariedEmployee.vb
2    ' SalariedEmployee class inherits Employee
3    Public Class SalariedEmployee
4       Inherits Employee
5
6       Private weeklySalaryValue As Decimal ' employee's weekly salary
7
8       ' four-argument constructor
9       Public Sub New(ByVal first As String, ByVal last As String,
10         ByVal ssn As String, ByVal salary As Decimal)
11
12         MyBase.New(first, last, ssn) ' pass to Employee constructor
13         WeeklySalary = salary ' validate and store salary
14      End Sub ' New
15
16      ' property WeeklySalary
17      Public Property WeeklySalary() As Decimal
18         Get
19            Return weeklySalaryValue
20         End Get
21
22         Set(ByVal salary As Decimal)
23            If salary >= 0D Then ' validate salary
24               weeklySalaryValue = salary ' valid
```

Fig. 10.10 | SalariedEmployee class derived from class Employee. (Part 1 of 2.)

```vbnet
25              Else
26                 Throw New ArgumentOutOfRangeException(
27                    "Salary must be greater than or equal to 0")
28              End If
29          End Set
30      End Property ' WeeklySalary
31
32      ' calculate earnings; override abstract method CalculateEarnings
33      Public Overrides Function CalculateEarnings() As Decimal
34          Return WeeklySalary
35      End Function ' CalculateEarnings
36
37      ' return String representation of SalariedEmployee object
38      Public Overrides Function ToString() As String
39          Return String.Format(
40             "salaried employee: {0}{1}weekly salary: {2:C}",
41             MyBase.ToString(), vbCrLf, WeeklySalary)
42      End Function ' ToString
43   End Class ' SalariedEmployee
```

Fig. 10.10 | SalariedEmployee class derived from class Employee. (Part 2 of 2.)

Class SalariedEmployee's constructor passes the first name, last name and social security number to base class Employee's constructor (line 12). Method CalculateEarnings overrides abstract method CalculateEarnings of Employee with a concrete implementation that returns the SalariedEmployee's weekly salary.

SalariedEmployee's ToString method (lines 38–42) overrides Employee method ToString. If class SalariedEmployee did not override ToString, the class would have inherited Employee's ToString method. In that case, SalariedEmployee's ToString method would simply return the employee's full name and social security number, which does not fully represent a SalariedEmployee. To produce a complete String representation of a SalariedEmployee, the derived class's ToString method returns "salaried employee:" followed by the base-class Employee-specific information (that is, first name, last name and social security number) obtained by invoking the base class's ToString method (line 41)—a nice example of code reuse. The String representation of a Salaried-Employee also contains the employee's weekly salary obtained from the WeeklySalary property.

10.8.3 Concrete Derived Class CommissionEmployee

Class CommissionEmployee (Fig. 10.11) inherits from class Employee (line 4); therefore, CommissionEmployee no longer declares the properties that are declared in base class Employee. The class includes

- a constructor (lines 10–16) that takes a first name, a last name, a social security number, a sales amount and a commission rate

- Get accessors (lines 20–22 and 36–38) that retrieve the values of instance variables grossSalesValue and commissionRateValue, respectively

- Set accessors (lines 24–31 and 40–47) that assign validated new values to these instance variables

- method CalculateEarnings (lines 51–53) to calculate a CommissionEmployee's earnings
- method ToString (lines 56–60), which returns the employee's type, namely, "commission employee:" and employee-specific information, including the full name and social security number, and the values of properties GrossSales and CommissionRate.

The CommissionEmployee's constructor passes the first name, last name and social security number to the Employee constructor (line 13) to initialize Employee's Private instance variables. Method ToString calls base-class method ToString (line 59) to obtain the Employee-specific information (that is, first name, last name and social security number).

```vb
1    ' Fig. 10.11: CommmissionEmployee.vb
2    ' CommissionEmployee class represents a commission employee.
3    Public Class CommissionEmployee
4       Inherits Employee
5
6       Private grossSalesValue As Decimal ' gross weekly sales
7       Private commissionRateValue As Double ' commission percentage
8
9       ' five-argument constructor
10      Public Sub New(ByVal first As String, ByVal last As String,
11         ByVal ssn As String, ByVal sales As Decimal, ByVal rate As Double)
12
13         MyBase.New(first, last, ssn) ' pass to Employee constructor
14         GrossSales = sales ' validate and store gross sales
15         CommissionRate = rate ' validate and store commission rate
16      End Sub ' New
17
18      ' property GrossSales
19      Public Property GrossSales() As Decimal
20         Get
21            Return grossSalesValue
22         End Get
23
24         Set(ByVal sales As Decimal)
25            If sales >= 0D Then ' validate gross sales
26               grossSalesValue = sales ' valid
27            Else
28               Throw New ArgumentOutOfRangeException(
29                  "Gross sales must be greater than or equal to 0")
30            End If
31         End Set
32      End Property ' GrossSales
33
34      ' property CommissionRate
35      Public Property CommissionRate() As Double
36         Get
37            Return commissionRateValue
38         End Get
39
```

Fig. 10.11 | CommissionEmployee class derived from Employee. (Part 1 of 2.)

```
40          Set(ByVal rate As Double)
41             If rate > 0.0 AndAlso rate < 1.0 Then ' validate rate
42                commissionRateValue = rate ' valid
43             Else
44                Throw New ArgumentOutOfRangeException(
45                   "Interest rate must be greater than 0 and less than 1")
46             End If
47          End Set
48       End Property ' CommissionRate
49
50       ' calculate earnings
51       Public Overrides Function CalculateEarnings() As Decimal
52          Return Convert.ToDecimal(CommissionRate) * GrossSales
53       End Function ' CalculateEarnings
54
55       ' return String representation of CommissionEmployee object
56       Public Overrides Function ToString() As String
57          Return String.Format("commission employee: {0}{1}" &
58             "gross sales: {2:C}{1}commission rate: {3:F}",
59             MyBase.ToString(), vbCrLf, GrossSales, CommissionRate)
60       End Function ' ToString
61    End Class ' CommissionEmployee
```

Fig. 10.11 | CommissionEmployee class derived from Employee. (Part 2 of 2.)

10.8.4 Indirect Concrete Derived Class BasePlusCommissionEmployee

Class BasePlusCommissionEmployee (Fig. 10.12) inherits class CommissionEmployee (line 4) and therefore is an *indirect* derived class of class Employee. Class BasePlusCommission-Employee has

- a constructor (lines 9–16) that takes as arguments a first name, a last name, a social security number, a sales amount, a commission rate *and* a base salary—the first five are passed to the CommissionEmployee constructor (line 14) to initialize the inherited members

- a property BaseSalary whose Set accessor (lines 24–31) assigns a validated new value to instance variable baseSalaryValue, and whose Get accessor (lines 20–22) returns baseSalaryValue

- method CalculateEarnings (lines 35–37) which calculates a BasePlusCommis-sionEmployee's earnings—line 36 calls base-class CommissionEmployee's CalculateEarnings method to calculate the *commission-based portion* of the employee's earnings (another nice example of code reuse)

- method ToString (lines 40–43) which creates a String representation of a Base-PlusCommissionEmployee that contains "base-plus-", followed by the String obtained by invoking base-class CommissionEmployee's ToString method (another nice example of code reuse), then the base salary.

Recall that CommissionEmployee's ToString method calls Employee's ToString method, so BasePlusCommissionEmployee's ToString initiates a chain of method calls that spans all three levels of the Employee hierarchy.

```vb
1   ' Fig. 10.12: BasePlusCommissionEmployee.vb
2   ' BasePlusCommissionEmployee inherits from class CommissionEmployee.
3   Public Class BasePlusCommissionEmployee
4      Inherits CommissionEmployee
5
6      Private baseSalaryValue As Decimal ' base salary per week
7
8      ' six-argument constructor
9      Public Sub New(ByVal first As String, ByVal last As String,
10        ByVal ssn As String, ByVal sales As Decimal,
11        ByVal rate As Double, ByVal salary As Decimal)
12
13        ' call CommissionEmployee constructor
14        MyBase.New(first, last, ssn, sales, rate)
15        BaseSalary = salary ' validate and store base salary
16     End Sub ' New
17
18     ' property BaseSalary
19     Public Property BaseSalary() As Decimal
20        Get
21           Return baseSalaryValue
22        End Get
23
24        Set(ByVal salary As Decimal)
25           If salary >= 0D Then ' validate base salary
26              baseSalaryValue = salary ' valid
27           Else
28              Throw New ArgumentOutOfRangeException(
29                 "Base salary must be greater than or equal to 0")
30           End If
31        End Set
32     End Property ' BaseSalary
33
34     ' calculate earnings
35     Public Overrides Function CalculateEarnings() As Decimal
36        Return BaseSalary + MyBase.CalculateEarnings()
37     End Function ' CalculateEarnings
38
39     ' return String representation of BasePlusCommissionEmployee object
40     Public Overrides Function ToString() As String
41        Return String.Format("base-plus-{0}{1}base salary: {2:C}",
42           MyBase.ToString(), vbCrLf, BaseSalary)
43     End Function ' ToString
44  End Class ' BasePlusCommissionEmployee
```

Fig. 10.12 | BasePlusCommissionEmployee derived from CommissionEmployee.

10.8.5 Demonstrating Polymorphic Processing

To test our Employee hierarchy, the program in Fig. 10.13 creates an object of each of the three concrete classes SalariedEmployee, CommissionEmployee and BasePlusCommissionEmployee. The program manipulates these objects, first via variables of each object's own type, then polymorphically, using an array of Employee variables. Lines 8–13 create an object of each of the three concrete Employee derived classes. Lines 16–26 display (nonpolymorphically) the String representation and earnings of each of these objects in outputTextBox1.

Creating an Array of Abstract Base Class *Employee* Variables

Lines 29–30 create and initialize array employees with three Employees. This statement is valid because, through inheritance, a SalariedEmployee *is an* Employee, a CommissionEmployee *is an* Employee and a BasePlusCommissionEmployee *is an* Employee. Therefore, we can assign the references of SalariedEmployee, CommissionEmployee and BasePlusCommissionEmployee objects to base-class Employee variables, even though Employee is a MustInherit (abstract) class.

Polymorphically Processing *Employees*

Lines 36–41 iterate through array employees and invoke methods ToString (line 39) and CalculateEarnings (line 40) with Employee variable currentEmployee, which is assigned the reference to a different Employee in the array during each iteration. The output

```vb
1    ' Fig. 10.13: PolymorphismTest.vb
2    ' Employee hierarchy test program.
3    Public Class PolymorphismTest
4       Private Sub PolymorphismTest_Load(ByVal sender As System.Object,
5          ByVal e As System.EventArgs) Handles MyBase.Load
6
7          ' create derived-class objects
8          Dim salariedEmployee As New SalariedEmployee(
9             "John", "Smith", "111-11-1111", 800D)
10         Dim commissionEmployee As New CommissionEmployee(
11            "Sue", "Jones", "333-33-3333", 10000D, 0.06)
12         Dim basePlusCommissionEmployee As New BasePlusCommissionEmployee(
13            "Bob", "Lewis", "444-44-4444", 5000D, 0.04, 300D)
14
15         ' display each employee's info nonpolymorphically
16         outputTextBox1.AppendText(
17            "Employees processed individually:" & vbCrLf & vbCrLf &
18            String.Format("{0}{1}earned: {2:C}{1}{1}",
19               salariedEmployee.ToString(), vbCrLf,
20               salariedEmployee.CalculateEarnings()) &
21            String.Format("{0}{1}earned: {2:C}{1}{1}",
22               commissionEmployee.ToString(), vbCrLf,
23               commissionEmployee.CalculateEarnings()) &
24            String.Format("{0}{1}earned: {2:C}",
25               basePlusCommissionEmployee.ToString(), vbCrLf,
26               basePlusCommissionEmployee.CalculateEarnings()))
27
28         ' create three-element Employee array
29         Dim employees() As Employee = {salariedEmployee,
30            commissionEmployee, basePlusCommissionEmployee}
31
32         outputTextBox2.AppendText(
33            "Employees processed polymorphically:" & vbCrLf & vbCrLf)
34
```

Fig. 10.13 | Employee class hierarchy test program. (Part 1 of 2.)

```
35          ' polymorphically process each element in array employees
36          For Each currentEmployee In employees
37              outputTextBox2.AppendText(
38                  String.Format("{0}{1}earned {2:C}{1}{1}",
39                      currentEmployee.ToString(), vbCrLf,
40                      currentEmployee.CalculateEarnings()))
41          Next
42      End Sub ' PolymorphismTest_Load
43  End Class ' PolymorphismTest
```

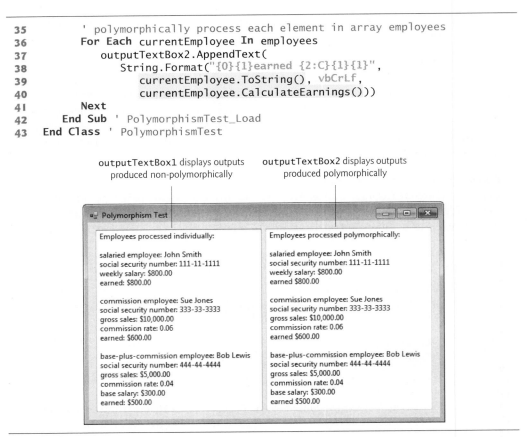

outputTextBox1 displays outputs produced non-polymorphically

outputTextBox2 displays outputs produced polymorphically

Fig. 10.13 | Employee class hierarchy test program. (Part 2 of 2.)

displayed in outputTextBox2 illustrates that the appropriate methods for each class are indeed invoked—you can compare the results in outputTextBox2 with the non-polymorphic results in outputTextBox1 to see that they're identical. All calls to methods ToString and CalculateEarnings are resolved *polymorphically* at execution time, based on the type of the object to which currentEmployee refers. This process is known as late binding. For example, line 39 explicitly invokes method ToString of the object to which currentEmployee refers. As a result of late binding, the proper ToString method to call is decided at execution time rather than at compile time.

10.9 Online Case Study: Interfaces

The book's Companion Website (www.pearsonhighered.com/deitel) provides an introduction to interfaces. An interface describes a set of methods that can be called on an object but it does not provide concrete implementations for the methods. Programmers can declare classes that implement (that is, declare the methods of) one or more interfaces. Each interface method must be declared in all the classes that implement the interface. Once a class implements an interface, all objects of that class have an *is-a* relationship with the interface type, and all objects of the class are guaranteed to provide the functionality described by the interface. This is true of all derived classes of that class as well.

Interfaces are particularly useful for assigning *common functionality to possibly unrelated classes*. This allows objects of unrelated classes to be processed polymorphically—objects of classes that implement the *same interface* can respond to the *same method calls*. To demonstrate creating and using interfaces, we modify our payroll application to create a general accounts payable application that can calculate payments due not only for company employees, but also for invoice amounts to be billed for purchased goods.

10.10 Wrap-Up

This chapter introduced inheritance—the ability to create a class by absorbing an existing class's members, customizing them as appropriate and adding new capabilities. You learned how to use the keyword Inherits to create a derived class using inheritance and how to override base-class methods to provide versions that are more appropriate for derived-class objects.

We discussed the access modifier Protected—derived-class methods can access Protected base-class members. We demonstrated the order in which constructors are called for objects of classes that are part of an inheritance hierarchy.

We introduced polymorphism—an object-oriented concept that enables you to write programs that handle, in a general manner, objects of a wide variety of classes related by inheritance.

Polymorphism makes programs more extensible. We began with an example of how polymorphism would allow a screen manager to display several "space" objects. We then discussed MustOverride methods (abstract methods that do not provide an implementation) and MustInherit classes (abstract classes that typically have one or more MustOverride methods). You learned that abstract classes cannot be used to instantiate objects, whereas concrete classes can. We showed how abstract classes are used at the top of an inheritance hierarchy. We introduced late binding, which enables the proper methods to be called when objects at various levels of an inheritance hierarchy are referenced at execution time via base class variables.

You're now familiar with classes, objects, encapsulation, inheritance and polymorphism—the essential aspects of object-oriented programming. In the next chapter, we introduce one of Microsoft's more recent technologies, LINQ (Language Integrated Query), which enables you to write expressions that can retrieve information from a wide variety of data sources such as arrays, files, collections and databases. You'll see how to search, sort and "filter" data using LINQ.

Summary

Section 10.1 Introduction

- Inheritance is a form of software reuse in which a new class is created by absorbing an existing class's members and customizing them with new or modified capabilities.

- When creating a class, you can designate that the new class inherits the members of an existing class. The existing class is called the base class and the new class is the derived class.

- A direct base class is the specific base class from which a derived class inherits.

- An indirect base class is inherited from two or more levels up in the class hierarchy.

- A derived class is more specific than its base class and normally represents a more specialized group of objects.

- The class hierarchy begins with class Object (in namespace System), from which every class directly or indirectly inherits.

Section 10.2 Base Classes and Derived Classes

- An *is-a* relationship represents inheritance. In an *is-a* relationship, an object of a derived class also can be treated as an object of its base class, but not vice versa.

- Base classes tend to be more general and derived classes tend to be more specific.

- The set of objects represented by a base class is typically larger than the set of objects represented by any of its derived classes.

- The common aspects of a base class and its derived classes are expressed in the base class.

- A derived class can override (redefine) a base-class method with a customized implementation appropriate for the derived class.

Section 10.3.1 Creating Base Class CommissionEmployee

- A class that does not explicitly specify its base class inherits from Object.

- Class Object does not have any fields. One of the methods inherited from class Object is ToString, so every class has a ToString method. Method ToString is typically overridden to return a String representation of the contents of an object.

- The first task of any derived-class constructor is to call its direct base class's constructor, either explicitly or implicitly, to ensure that the base class instance variables are initialized properly.

- If a derived class constructor does not explicitly call the base class's constructor, the base class's default or parameterless constructor is called.

- If a class does not have constructors, the default constructor for the class will call the base class's default or parameterless constructor.

- A base-class method must be declared Overridable if a derived class should be allowed to override the method with a version more appropriate for that class.

- Keyword Overrides indicates that a method overrides an Overridable base class method.

Section 10.3.2 Creating Derived Class BasePlusCommissionEmployee

- Keyword Inherits indicates that a class inherits all of the Public members (and Protected members if there are any) of the specified base class.

- Though not inherited, the base class's Private instance variables are nevertheless present (but hidden) in derived class objects.

- To call a base class constructor explicitly, use the base-class constructor call syntax—keyword MyBase, followed by the dot (.) separator, followed by New and a set of parentheses containing the arguments to the base-class constructor. An explicit base-class constructor call must be the first statement in the derived-class constructor's body.

- To invoke an overridden base-class method from a derived class, place the keyword MyBase and a dot (.) separator before the base-class method name.

Section 10.3.3 Testing Class BasePlusCommissionEmployee

- When you call an Overridable base class method on a derived class object, the derived class version of the method executes. This is the basis of polymorphism.

Section 10.4 Constructors in Derived Classes

- Creating a derived-class object begins a chain of constructor calls in which the derived-class constructor, before performing its own tasks, invokes its direct base class's constructor. This process continues until class Object's constructor is reached.

Section 10.5 **Protected** Members

- A base class's Protected members can be accessed only by that base class and its derived classes.

- In inheritance, Public members of the base class become Public members of the derived class, and Protected members of the base class become Protected members of the derived class. A base class's Private members are not inherited by its derived classes.

- It's better to use Private instance variables (rather than Protected ones) to encourage proper software engineering.

Section 10.6 Introduction to Polymorphism: Polymorphic Video Game

- The same message sent to a variety of objects has many forms of results, hence the term polymorphism.

- Polymorphism helps makes systems extensible. Without modifying a system (other than to build new classes and modify the code that creates new objects), you can use polymorphism to include types that were not envisioned when the system was created.

Section 10.7 Abstract Classes and Methods

- An abstract class is a base class from which other classes can inherit a common design. Abstract classes cannot be used to instantiate objects.

- Classes that can be used to instantiate objects are called concrete classes. Such classes provide implementations of every method they declare (some of the implementations can be inherited).

- A method with a parameter of an abstract base-class type can be passed an object of any concrete class that directly or indirectly inherits the base class specified as the parameter's type.

- You make a class abstract by declaring it with keyword MustInherit. An abstract class normally contains one or more abstract methods.

- A MustOverride method is an abstract method and does not provide an implementation.

- A class that contains any MustOverride methods must be declared as MustInherit.

- Each concrete derived class of a MustInherit base class must provide concrete implementations of all the base class's MustOverride methods.

- Constructors and Shared methods cannot be overridden, so they cannot be declared MustOverride.

Section 10.8 Case Study: Payroll System Class Hierarchy Using Polymorphism

- An abstract base class declares the "interface" to the hierarchy—that is, the set of methods and properties that a program can invoke on all objects of the abstract base class's derived classes.

- Although you cannot instantiate objects of an abstract class, you can use an abstract class to declare variables that can refer to objects of any concrete classes derived from the abstract class. Programs typically use such variables to manipulate derived-class objects polymorphically.

- MustOverride methods enable a class hierarchy designer to require that each derived concrete class provide concrete implementations of those methods.

- Polymorphic method calls are resolved at execution time via a process known as late binding.

- A base-class variable can be used to invoke only methods declared in the base class.

Terminology

abstract base class 368
abstract class 368
abstract method 368
base class 356
base-class constructor call syntax 364
brittle software 367
class hierarchy 358
class library 356
concrete class 368
derived class 356
direct base class 357
extensible 368
implement an interface 378
indirect base class 357

inheritance 356
inheritance hierarchy 357
Inherits keyword 360
interface 378
is-a relationship 356
late binding 378
MustInherit keyword 368
MustOverride keyword 368
MyBase keyword 364
Overridable keyword 361
override a base class method 361
Overrides keyword 361
polymorphism 356
Protected access modifier 366

Self-Review Exercises

10.1 Fill in the blanks in each of the following statements:

a) _____ is a form of software reusability in which new classes acquire the members of existing classes and enhance those classes with new capabilities.

b) A base class's _____ members can be accessed only in the base-class declaration and in derived-class declarations.

c) In a(n) _____ relationship, an object of a derived class can also be treated as an object of its base class.

d) A base class's _____ members are accessible anywhere that the application has a reference to an object of that base class or to an object of any of its derived classes.

e) When an object of a derived class is instantiated, a base class _____ is called implicitly or explicitly.

f) Derived-class constructors can call base-class constructors via the _____ keyword.

g) If a class contains at least one abstract method, the class must be declared _____.

h) Classes from which objects can be instantiated are called _____ classes.

i) With _____, you use base-class variables to invoke methods on base-class and derived-class objects and those objects "do the right thing."

j) Methods of a class that do not provide implementations must be declared using keyword _____.

10.2 State whether each of the following is *true* or *false*. If a statement is *false*, explain why.

a) Base-class constructors are not inherited by derived classes.

b) A Car class has *is-a* relationships with the SteeringWheel and Brakes classes.

c) When a derived class redefines a base-class method by using the same signature and return type, the derived class is said to overload that base-class method.

d) It's possible to treat base-class objects and derived-class objects similarly.

e) All methods in an abstract class must explicitly be declared as MustOverride methods.

f) It's a compilation error to invoke a derived-class-only method through a base-class variable.

g) If a base class declares a MustOverride method, a derived class must implement that method.

h) An object of a class that implements an interface may be thought of as an object of that interface type.

Answers to Self-Review Exercises

10.1   a) Inheritance. b) `Protected`. c) *is-a* or inheritance. d) `Public`. e) constructor. f) `MyBase`. g) `MustInherit`. h) concrete. i) polymorphism. j) `MustOverride`.

10.2   a) True. b) False. These are examples of *has-a* relationships. Class `Car` has an *is-a* relationship with class `Vehicle`. c) False. This is known as overriding, not overloading. d) True. e) False. An abstract class can include methods with implementations and `MustOverride` methods. f) True. g) False. Only a concrete derived class must implement the method. Not implementing the method in a derived class causes that class to be abstract (and it must explicitly be declared `MustInherit`). h) True.

Exercises

Discussion Exercises

10.3   *(Inheritance Advantages)* Discuss the ways in which inheritance promotes software reuse, saves time during application development and helps prevent errors.

10.4   *(Polymorphism Advantages)* How does polymorphism enable you to program "in the general" rather than "in the specific?" Discuss the key advantages of programming "in the general."

10.5   *(Abstract Methods)* What are abstract methods? Describe the circumstances in which an abstract method would be appropriate.

10.6   *(Polymorphism and Extensibility)* How does polymorphism promote extensibility?

10.7   *(Student Inheritance Hierarchy)* Draw a UML class diagram for an inheritance hierarchy for college students similar to the hierarchy shown in Fig. 10.2. Use `Student` as the base class of the hierarchy, then extend `Student` with classes `UndergraduateStudent` and `GraduateStudent`. Continue to extend the hierarchy as deeply (that is, as many levels) as possible. For example, `Freshman`, `Sophomore`, `Junior` and `Senior` might extend `UndergraduateStudent`, and `DoctoralStudent` and `MastersStudent` might be derived classes of `GraduateStudent`. After drawing the hierarchy, discuss the relationships that exist between the classes. You do not need to write any code for this exercise.

10.8   *(Protected vs. Private Access)* Some programmers prefer not to use `Protected` access, because they believe it breaks the encapsulation of the base class. Discuss the relative merits of using `Protected` access vs. using `Private` access in base classes.

Programming Exercises

10.9   *(Account Inheritance Hierarchy)* Create an inheritance hierarchy that a bank might use to represent customer bank accounts. All customers at this bank can deposit (that is, credit) money into their accounts and withdraw (that is, debit) money from their accounts. More specific types of accounts also exist. Savings accounts, for instance, earn interest on the money they hold. Checking accounts, on the other hand, don't earn interest and charge a fee per transaction.

Create base class `Account` and derived classes `SavingsAccount` and `CheckingAccount` that inherit from class `Account`. Base class `Account` should include a `Private` instance variable of type `Decimal` to represent the account balance. The class should provide a constructor that receives an initial balance and uses it to initialize the instance variable with a `Public` property. The property should validate the initial balance to ensure that it's greater than or equal to `0.0`. If not, the balance should be set to `0.0`, and the `Set` accessor should throw an exception, indicating that the initial balance was invalid. The class should provide two `Public` methods. Method `Credit` should add an amount to the current balance. Method `Debit` should withdraw money from the `Account` and ensure that the debit amount does not exceed the `Account`'s balance. If it does, the balance should be left unchanged, and the method should throw an exception indicating that the debit amount exceeded the account balance. The class should also provide a Get accessor in property Balance that returns the current balance.

Derived class SavingsAccount should inherit the functionality of an Account, but also include a Double instance variable indicating the interest rate (percentage) assigned to the Account. Class SavingsAccount's constructor should receive the initial balance, as well as an initial value for the interest rate. SavingsAccount should provide Public method CalculateInterest that returns a Decimal indicating the amount of interest earned by an account. Method CalculateInterest should determine this amount by multiplying the interest rate by the account balance. [*Note:* SavingsAccount should inherit methods Credit and Debit without redefining them.]

Derived class CheckingAccount should inherit from base class Account and include a Decimal instance variable that represents the fee charged per transaction. CheckingAccount's constructor should receive the initial balance, as well as a parameter indicating a fee amount. Class CheckingAccount should redefine methods Credit and Debit so that they subtract the fee from the account balance whenever either transaction is performed successfully. CheckingAccount's versions of these methods should invoke the base-class Account version to perform the updates to an account balance. CheckingAccount's Debit method should charge a fee only if money is actually withdrawn (that is, the debit amount does not exceed the account balance).

After defining the classes in this hierarchy, write an application that creates objects of each class and tests their methods. Add interest to the SavingsAccount object by first invoking its CalculateInterest method, then passing the returned interest amount to the object's Credit method.

10.10 *(Payroll System Modification)* Modify the payroll system of Figs. 10.9–10.13 to include two additional Employee derived classes—class PieceWorker represents an employee who is paid based on the number of pieces of merchandise produced and class HourlyWorker who is paid by the hour and receives overtime pay (1.5 times the regular hourly wage) for hours worked in excess of 40 hours. Class PieceWorker should contain Private instance variables wageValue (to store the employee's wage per piece) and piecesValue (to store the number of pieces produced). Class HourlyWorker should contain Private instance variables hoursValue (to store the employee's hours worked) and wageValue (to store wage per hour). In each class, provide a concrete implementation of method CalculateEarnings. In class PieceWorker, the method should calculate the employee's earnings by multiplying the number of pieces produced by the wage per piece. In class HourlyWorker, the method should calculate the employee's earnings by multiplying the wages times the hours worked for 40 or fewer hours. For any hours worked over 40, an HourlyWorker should receive 1.5 times the regular hourly wage. Create objects of each of the new classes and place them in the array of Employee variables. For each Employee, polymorphically display its String representation and earnings.

10.11 *(Shape Hierarchy)* Implement a portion of the Shape hierarchy shown in Fig. 10.3. You should implement the two-dimensional shapes Circle and Square and the three-dimensional shapes Sphere and Cube). Each TwoDimensionalShape should contain method GetArea to calculate the area of the two-dimensional shape. Each ThreeDimensionalShape should have methods GetArea and GetVolume to calculate the surface area and volume, respectively, of the three-dimensional shape. Use the following formulas for the area and volume of the various shapes:

a) Area of a Square: Side * Side
b) Area of a Circle: Math.PI * Radius * Radius, where Radius is the radius of the Circle
c) Area of a Sphere: 4 * Math.PI * Radius * Radius where Radius is the radius of the Sphere
d) Volume of a Sphere: (4 / 3) * Math.PI * Radius * Radius * Radius
e) Area of a Cube: 6 * Side * Side
f) Volume of a Cube: Side * Side * Side

Create a program that uses an array of Shape references to objects of each concrete class in the hierarchy. The program should display a String representation of each object. Each object's ToString method should display all of that object's data, its area and, for ThreeDimensionalShapes, its volume.

10.12 *(Package Inheritance Hierarchy)* Package-delivery services, such as FedEx®, DHL® and UPS®, offer many shipping options, each with specific costs associated. Create an inheritance hierarchy to represent various types of packages. Use Package as the base class of the hierarchy, then include classes TwoDayPackage and OvernightPackage that derive from Package. Base class Package should include Private instance variables representing the name, address, city, state and ZIP code for the package's sender and recipient, and instance variables that store the weight (in ounces) and cost per ounce to ship the package. Package's constructor should initialize these Private instance variables with Public properties. Ensure that the weight and cost per ounce contain positive values; otherwise, throw exceptions. Package should provide a Public method CalculateCost that returns a Decimal indicating the cost associated with shipping the package. Package's CalculateCost method should determine the cost by multiplying the weight by the cost per ounce. Derived class TwoDayPackage should inherit the functionality of base class Package, but also include an instance variable that represents a flat fee that the shipping company charges for two-day delivery service. TwoDayPackage's constructor should receive a value to initialize this instance variable. TwoDayPackage should redefine method CalculateCost so that it computes the shipping cost by adding the flat fee to the weight-based cost calculated by base class Package's CalculateCost method. Class OvernightPackage should inherit directly from class Package and contain an instance variable representing an additional fee per ounce charged for overnight-delivery service. OvernightPackage should redefine method CalculateCost so that it adds the additional fee per ounce to the standard cost per ounce before calculating the shipping cost. Write an application that creates objects of each type of Package and polymorphically calculates the cost of shipping each package.

11

Introduction to LINQ

*You shall listen to all sides and
filter them from your self.*
—Walt Whitman

*The portraitist can select one
tiny aspect of everything shown
at a moment to incorporate into
the final painting.*
—Robert Nozick

Objectives

In this chapter you'll learn:

- Basic LINQ concepts.

- How to query an array using LINQ.

- How to sort an array in ascending or descending order using LINQ.

- How to perform transformations on the results of a LINQ query.

- How to select a portion of the properties for each object in a query result.

- How to create new objects as the result of a LINQ query.

- How a LINQ query executes only when you iterate over the results—a concept called deferred execution.

11.1 Introduction

Large amounts of data are often stored in a database—an organized collection of data. (We discuss databases in detail in Chapter 12, Databases and LINQ.) A database management system (DBMS) provides mechanisms for storing, organizing, retrieving and modifying data contained in the database. Today's most popular database systems are relational databases. A language called Structured Query Language (SQL)—pronounced "sequel"—is an international standard used with relational databases to perform queries (that is, to request information that satisfies given criteria) and to manipulate data. For years, programs that accessed a relational database passed SQL queries as Strings to the database management system then processed the results.

A logical extension of querying and manipulating data in databases is to perform similar operations on any sources of data, such as arrays, collections (like the Items collection of a ListBox) and files. Microsoft developed LINQ (Language Integrated Query) to enable you to write query expressions similar to SQL queries that retrieve information from a wide variety of data sources—not just relational databases—using a *common syntax* that is *built into* Visual Basic. This enables you to take advantage of the IDE's *IntelliSense* feature when writing LINQ queries—*IntelliSense* is *not* provided for SQL queries.

We use LINQ to Objects in this chapter to query the contents of arrays, selecting elements that satisfy a set of conditions—this is known as filtering. We also use LINQ to Objects to perform common array manipulations such as sorting an array. Figure 11.1 shows the types of LINQ queries we cover in this book and how we use them.

Types of LINQ and How We Use Them in This Book

LINQ to Objects

- Retrieve information from arrays (Chapter 11, Introduction to LINQ)
- Select GUI controls from a collection of controls in a Windows Forms application (Chapter 17, Strings and Characters)
- Query .NET collections using LINQ to Objects (Chapter 25, Data Structures and Generic Collections)

LINQ to SQL

- Retrieve information from a database and insert data into a database (Chapter 12, Databases and LINQ)

Fig. 11.1 | LINQ usage throughout the book. (Part 1 of 2.)

Types of LINQ and How We Use Them in This Book

- Retrieve information from a database to be used in a web-based application (Chapter 13, Web App Development with ASP.NET)
- Query and update a database (Chapter 23, Web Services)

LINQ to XML

- Query an XML document using LINQ to XML (Chapter 21, XML and LINQ to XML)
- Process XML returned by WCF services (Chapter 23, Web Services)
- Process XML returned by web services to a Silverlight application (Chapter 24, Silverlight, Rich Internet Applications and Multimedia)

Fig. 11.1 | LINQ usage throughout the book. (Part 2 of 2.)

11.2 Querying an Array of Primitive-Type Elements Using LINQ

LINQ allows you to look at collections of data, extract information and manipulate data. In a LINQ query, you might want to locate all Employees whose salaries are in a specific range (Section 11.3). To respond to that query, LINQ has to *iterate* over the data, looking at each item to see if the Employee's salary is in range and, if so, selecting that item. You might also manipulate the data—for example, for each Employee in the result of the preceding query, you could increase the Employee's base salary by 4%.

You were introduced to interfaces in Section 10.9. LINQ to Objects works with objects that implement the IEnumerable interface, which enables a program to iterate over a collection of data. In fact, the For Each...Next statement is specifically used to iterate over IEnumerable objects, such as arrays—arrays implement the IEnumerable interface. Any object of a class that implements the IEnumerable interface has an *is-a* relationship with IEnumerable—this is true of collections like the Items collection in a ListBox and other collections that we introduce in the online Chapter 25.

Figure 11.2 demonstrates querying the array of Integers named values (declared in line 9) in various ways using LINQ. Repetition statements that filter arrays focus on the process of getting the results—iterating through the elements and checking whether they satisfy the desired criteria. In contrast, LINQ specifies the *conditions* that selected elements must satisfy, not the *steps* necessary to get the results. The query in lines 20–22 specifies that the results should consist of all the Integers in the values array that are greater than 4. It does not specify *how* those results are obtained—nevertheless, the compiler generates all the necessary code.

```
1    ' Fig. 11.2: LINQWithArrayOfIntegers.vb
2    ' LINQ to Objects using an Integer array.
3    Public Class LINQWithArrayOfIntegers
```

Fig. 11.2 | LINQ to Objects using an Integer array. (Part 1 of 3.)

```vb
 4      ' test several LINQ queries
 5      Private Sub LINQWithArrayOfIntegers_Load(ByVal sender As System.Object,
 6         ByVal e As System.EventArgs) Handles MyBase.Load
 7
 8         ' create an integer array
 9         Dim values() As Integer = {2, 9, 5, 0, 3, 7, 1, 4, 8, 6}
10
11         ' display each element, separated by spaces
12         outputTextBox.AppendText(String.Format(
13            "Original array:{0}", vbCrLf))
14         For Each element In values
15            outputTextBox.AppendText("   " & element)
16         Next
17
18         ' LINQ query that obtains values greater than 4 from the array
19         Dim filtered =
20            From value In values
21            Where (value > 4)
22            Select value
23
24         ' display filtered results
25         outputTextBox.AppendText(String.Format(
26            "{0}{0}Array values greater than 4:{0}", vbCrLf))
27         For Each element In filtered
28            outputTextBox.AppendText("   " & element)
29         Next
30
31         ' use Order By clause to sort original array in ascending order
32         Dim sorted =
33            From value In values
34            Order By value
35            Select value
36
37         ' display sorted results
38         outputTextBox.AppendText(String.Format(
39            "{0}{0}Original array, sorted:{0}", vbCrLf))
40         For Each element In sorted
41            outputTextBox.AppendText("   " & element)
42         Next
43
44         ' sort the filtered results into descending order
45         Dim sortFilteredResults =
46            From value In filtered
47            Order By value Descending
48            Select value
49
50         ' display the sorted results
51         outputTextBox.AppendText(String.Format(
52            "{0}{0}Values greater than 4, descending order (chained):{0}",
53            vbCrLf))
54         For Each element In sortFilteredResults
55            outputTextBox.AppendText("   " & element)
56         Next
```

Fig. 11.2 | LINQ to Objects using an Integer array. (Part 2 of 3.)

```
57
58          ' filter original array and sort in descending order
59          Dim sortAndFilter =
60              From value In values
61              Where value > 4
62              Order By value Descending
63              Select value
64
65          ' display the filtered and sorted results
66          outputTextBox.AppendText(String.Format(
67              "{0}{0}Values greater than 4, descending order (one query):{0}",
68              vbCrLf))
69          For Each element In sortAndFilter
70              outputTextBox.AppendText("    " & element)
71          Next
72      End Sub ' LINQWithArrayOfIntegers_Load
73  End Class ' LINQWithArrayOfIntegers
```

Fig. 11.2 | LINQ to Objects using an `Integer` array. (Part 3 of 3.)

Filtering the Elements of an Array

Our first LINQ query begins with a `From` clause (line 20), which specifies a range variable (`value`) and the data source to query (the array `values`). The range variable represents each item in the data source, much like the control variable in a `For Each...Next` statement. Introducing the range variable in the `From` clause at the beginning of the query allows the IDE to provide *IntelliSense* while you write the rest of the query—the IDE knows the type of the range variable (via local type inference), so it can display the methods and properties of the object.

If the condition in the `Where` clause (line 21) evaluates to `True`, the element is selected—that is, it's included in the collection of `Integer`s that represents the query results. Here, the `Integer`s in the array are included only if they're greater than 4.

For each item in the data source, the `Select` clause (line 22) determines what value appears in the results. In this case, it's the `Integer` that the range variable currently represents. The `Select` clause is usually placed at the end of the query for clarity, though it may be placed after the `From` clause and before other clauses, or omitted. If omitted, the range variable is implicitly selected. Later, you'll see that the Select clause can *transform* the selected items—for example, Select value * 2 in this example would have multiplied each selected value in the result by 2.

Displaying the Results of a LINQ Query

Lines 27–29 display the query results using a For Each...Next statement. A LINQ query returns an IEnumerable object. Therefore, you can use a For Each...Next statement to iterate over the results of any LINQ query.

Sorting LINQ Query Results

The LINQ query in lines 33–35 selects the elements of the array values and returns an IEnumerable object containing a sorted copy of the elements. The **Order By clause** (line 34) sorts the query results in *ascending* order. The LINQ queries in lines 46–48 and 60–63 use the **Descending** modifier in the Order By clause to sort query results in *descending* order. An **Ascending** modifier also exists but is rarely used, because it's the default.

You can use the Order By clause only for values that can be compared to one another to determine their sorting order. In particular, the Order By clause supports values of any type that implements the interface IComparable, such as the primitive numeric types and String. Such types provide a CompareTo method that returns a negative, zero or positive value indicating whether one value is less than, equal to or greater than another value, respectively.

Chaining LINQ Queries

The query in lines 46–48 shows that you can *chain LINQ queries* by having one query operate on the results of another. In this case, the query sorts filtered (the result of the query in lines 20–22) in descending order.

Combining the **Where** and **Order By** Clauses in a LINQ Query

The query in lines 60–63 uses the Where and Order By clauses to filter the elements of array values, looking for all values greater than 4, and sorts the results in descending order.

11.3 Querying an Array of Reference-Type Elements Using LINQ

LINQ is not limited to querying arrays of primitive types. It can be used with most data types. It cannot be used when a query does not have a defined meaning—for example, you cannot use Order By on objects that cannot be compared to one another to determine sorting order. Figure 11.3 presents class Employee and Fig. 11.4 uses LINQ to perform the following operations on an array of Employee objects:

- Select *all* Employees with salaries in the range $4000–6000.
- Sort Employees by LastName *then* by FirstName for Employees that have the same LastName.
- Obtain the *first* Employee in the sorted collection of Employees.
- Select the *unique* LastNames.
- Select *just* the FirstName and LastName from each Employee object.

```vb
1   ' Fig. 11.3: Employee.vb
2   ' Employee class with FirstName, LastName and MonthlySalary properties.
3   Public Class Employee
4      Public Property LastName As String   ' employee's last name
5      Public Property FirstName As String  ' employee's first name
6      Private monthlySalaryValue As Decimal ' monthly salary of employee
7
8      ' constructor initializes first name, last name and monthly salary
9      Public Sub New(ByVal first As String, ByVal last As String,
10        ByVal salary As Decimal)
11
12        FirstName = first ' calls FirstName property's Set accessor
13        LastName = last ' calls LastName property's Set accessor
14        MonthlySalary = salary ' calls MonthlySalary property's Set accessor
15     End Sub ' New
16
17     ' property that gets and sets the employee's monthly salary
18     Public Property MonthlySalary() As Decimal
19        Get
20           Return monthlySalaryValue
21        End Get
22
23        Set(ByVal value As Decimal)
24           If value >= 0 Then ' if salary is non-negative
25              monthlySalaryValue = value
26           Else
27              Throw New ArgumentOutOfRangeException(
28                 "Salary must be greater than or equal to 0")
29           End If
30        End Set
31     End Property ' MonthlySalary
32
33     ' return a String containing the employee's information
34     Public Overrides Function ToString() As String
35        Return String.Format("{0,-10} {1,-10} {2,10:C}",
36           FirstName, LastName, MonthlySalary)
37     End Function ' ToString
38  End Class ' Employee
```

Fig. 11.3 | Employee class with FirstName, LastName and MonthlySalary properties.

```vb
1   ' Fig. 11.4: LINQWithEmployeeArray.vb
2   ' LINQ to Objects using an array of Employee objects.
3   Public Class LINQWithEmployeeArray
4      Private Sub LINQWithEmployeeArray_Load(ByVal sender As System.Object,
5         ByVal e As System.EventArgs) Handles MyBase.Load
6
7         ' initialize array of employees
8         Dim employees() As Employee = {
9            New Employee("Jason", "Red", 5000D),
10           New Employee("Ashley", "Green", 7600D),
```

Fig. 11.4 | LINQ to Objects using an array of Employee objects. (Part 1 of 3.)

```
11              New Employee("Matthew", "Indigo", 3587.5D),
12              New Employee("James", "Indigo", 4700.77D),
13              New Employee("Luke", "Indigo", 6200D),
14              New Employee("Jason", "Blue", 3200D),
15              New Employee("Wendy", "Brown", 4236.4D)} ' end initializer list
16
17          ' display all employees
18          outputTextBox.AppendText(String.Format(
19              "Original array:{0}", vbCrLf))
20          For Each element In employees
21              outputTextBox.AppendText(
22                  String.Format("   {0}{1}", element, vbCrLf))
23          Next
24
25          ' filter a range of salaries using AndAlso in a LINQ query
26          Dim between4K6K =
27              From employee In employees
28              Where (employee.MonthlySalary >= 4000D AndAlso
29                  employee.MonthlySalary <= 6000D)
30              Select employee
31
32          ' display employees making between 4000 and 6000 per month
33          outputTextBox.AppendText(String.Format(
34              "{0}Employees earning in the range {1:C}-{2:C} per month:{0}",
35              vbCrLf, 4000, 6000))
36          For Each element In between4K6K
37              outputTextBox.AppendText(
38                  String.Format("   {0}{1}", element, vbCrLf))
39          Next
40
41          ' order the employees by last name, then first name with LINQ
42          Dim nameSorted =
43              From employee In employees
44              Order By employee.LastName, employee.FirstName
45              Select employee
46
47          ' attempt to display the first result of the above LINQ query
48          outputTextBox.AppendText(String.Format(
49              "{0}First employee when sorted by name:{0}", vbCrLf))
50
51          If nameSorted.Count() > 0 Then
52              outputTextBox.AppendText(nameSorted.First().ToString() & vbCrLf)
53          Else
54              outputTextBox.AppendText("not found" & vbCrLf)
55          End If
56
57          ' use LINQ's Distinct clause to select unique last names
58          Dim lastNames =
59              From employee In employees
60              Select employee.LastName
61              Distinct
62
```

Fig. 11.4 | LINQ to Objects using an array of Employee objects. (Part 2 of 3.)

```
63          ' display unique last names
64          outputTextBox.AppendText(String.Format(
65              "{0}Unique employee last names:{0}", vbCrLf))
66          For Each element In lastNames
67              outputTextBox.AppendText(
68                  String.Format("   {0}{1}", element, vbCrLf))
69          Next
70
71          ' use LINQ to select first and last names
72          Dim names =
73              From employee In employees
74              Select employee.FirstName, employee.LastName
75
76          ' display first and last names
77          outputTextBox.AppendText(String.Format(
78              "{0}Names only:{0}", vbCrLf))
79          For Each element In names
80              outputTextBox.AppendText(
81                  String.Format("   {0}{1}", element, vbCrLf))
82          Next
83      End Sub ' LINQWithEmployeeArray_Load
84  End Class ' LINQWithEmployeeArray
```

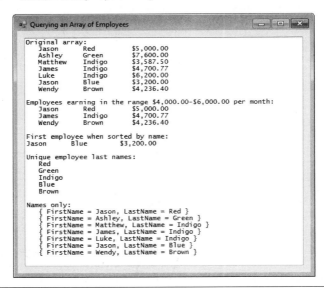

Fig. 11.4 | LINQ to Objects using an array of Employee objects. (Part 3 of 3.)

Filtering Employees Based on MonthlySalary

Lines 28–29 of Fig. 11.4 shows a Where clause that accesses the properties of the range variable employee. In this example, the compiler *infers* that the range variable is of type Employee because employees was declared as an array of Employees (lines 8–15). Any Boolean expression can be used in a Where clause. Lines 28–29 use AndAlso to combine conditions. Here, only employees that have a salary between $4,000 and $6,000 per month, inclusive, are included in the query result. Lines 36–39 display the query results.

Each element in the result is an Employee object, so when each element is *implicitly* converted to a String (line 38), Employee's ToString method is called implicitly.

Sorting Employees by LastName and FirstName

Line 44 uses an Order By clause to sort the Employees in the result according to *multiple* properties specified in a comma-separated list. In this query, the employees are sorted alphabetically by last name. Each group of Employees that have the same last name is then sorted within the group by first name.

Using the Count and First Extension Methods

As we've mentioned, LINQ operates on IEnumerable objects. The IEnumerable interface contains the overloaded method GetEnumerator, which returns an object that can be used to iterate over a collection of data. Though IEnumerable declares only the overloaded GetEnumerator method, you can actually call *many* other methods on an IEnumerable object. In the IDE, when you type the name of an IEnumerable object (such as an array or the result of a LINQ query) then type the dot (.) separator, *IntelliSense* shows you a list of the methods and properties that can be used with that object. In the list, some of the method names are preceded by the icon 🔹. These are so-called extension methods. *Extension methods allow you to enhance the functionality of an existing class or interface without modifying the class's or interface's source code.* In fact, Microsoft has defined most LINQ capabilities as extension methods for the IEnumerable interface and you can call these directly on any IEnumerable object. For example, if you have an array of Doubles called numbers and you want to calculate the average of its values, you can simply call the Average extension method, as in numbers.Average(). You can also create your own extension methods, which is beyond the scope of this book; so, we show how to do this at www.deitel.com/books/vb2010htp/. Some of IEnumerable's 45 extension methods are shown in Fig. 11.5.

IEnumerable Extension Method	Description
Any	Determines if the IEnumerable object contains any elements.
Average	Calculates the average of the numbers in an IEnumerable object.
Cast	Converts the elements of an IEnumerable object to the specified type.
Contains	Determines if the IEnumerable object contains the specified value.
Count	Counts the number of elements in an IEnumerable object.
Distinct	Returns the unique items in an IEnumerable object.
ElementAt	Returns the element at the specified index in an IEnumerable object.
First	Returns the first element in an IEnumerable object.
Last	Returns the last element in an IEnumerable object.
Max	Finds the maximum element in an IEnumerable object.
Min	Finds the minimum element in an IEnumerable object.
Reverse	Reverses the elements in an IEnumerable object.
Sum	Calculates the sum of the numbers in an IEnumerable object.

Fig. 11.5 | Some common IEnumerable extension methods.

Line 51 introduces the **Count** extension method, which returns the number of elements in the result of the query at lines 43–45. The **First** extension method (line 52) returns the first element in the result—an Employee object in this example. If the result does not contain any elements, method First throws an InvalidOperationException. For this reason, we use extension method Count to ensure that the query result contains at least one item (line 51) before calling First.

You might wonder why Microsoft chose to use extension methods rather than simply including these methods directly in the IEnumerable interface. There are 45 extension methods for interface IEnumerable, so it would be costly to implement the interface for every class that wants to be an IEnumerable when you only need a few of the methods for your class. Separately, the extension methods for IEnumerable are implemented in such a manner that they are defined once and can be used on any IEnumerable object, so you do not need to customize these methods for your own classes.

Selecting Specific Properties of an Object

Line 60 uses the **Select** clause in a new way. Rather than selecting the range variable, we select each Employee's LastName property. In this case, the query result is a collection of only of the last names—which are String objects, rather than complete Employee objects. The **Distinct** clause (line 61) prevents duplicate values from appearing in the query results. In this case, it eliminates duplicate last names—*this occurs because the clauses in a LINQ query are applied in the order in which they appear, each using the results of the previous clause in the query.*

Creating Objects of Anonymous Types

The last LINQ query in the example (lines 73–74) selects only the properties FirstName and LastName from each Employee object. You can select *portions* of matching objects by specifying the properties to select in a comma-separated list. *Only* the selected properties can be accessed when iterating over the query results.

When you select a portion of an object's properties, the compiler *creates a new class* containing those properties—FirstName and LastName in this example—*and* the methods that are inherited by all classes from class Object. The new class does not have a name and cannot be used by you to create new objects—such classes are called **anonymous types**. In the anonymous type, the compiler overrides the inherited ToString method to return a String representation of the object in the form:

```
{ propertyName1 = value1, propertyName2 = value2, ... }
```

Local type inference allows you to use the anonymous type—the compiler can infer the anonymous type from the query in lines 73–74. In addition, the IDE provides *IntelliSense* support for the compiler-generated anonymous types. In the loop at lines 79–82, the compiler infers that the control variable's type is the anonymous type containing the FirstName and LastName properties and the methods inherited from class Object. If you type a dot (.) separator after the control variable's name (element) in line 81, the IDE displays the *IntelliSense* window (Fig. 11.6) showing the anonymous type's properties and methods.

When you execute this program, line 81 implicitly calls the anonymous type's ToString method to get the String representation of each element. You can see in the program's output that the ToString method of an anonymous type returns the property names and their values, enclosed in braces.

Fig. 11.6 | *IntelliSense* window for the anonymous type produced by the query in lines 73–74 of Fig. 11.4.

You can create your own anonymous types, which is beyond the scope of this book; so we show how to do this at www.deitel.com/books/vb2010htp/.

11.4 Deferred Execution and Transforming Query Results

LINQ uses a technique called deferred execution—*a query executes only when you iterate over the results, not when the query is defined.* This allows you to create a query once and execute it many times. This is similar to how methods are used. If you make any changes to the data in a LINQ query's data source, the next time you iterate over the query's results, the query will process the current data in the data source.

Figure 11.7 filters an array of Strings by searching for those that begin with "r". Initially the array (lines 8–9) contains two such Strings. Later in the program we modify the array then reexecute the LINQ query to demonstrate deferred execution. This example also demonstrates how to *transform* the items that match the Where clause—in this case, each matching String is converted to uppercase in the query result.

```
1   ' Fig. 11.7: DeferredExecution.vb
2   ' Demonstrating deferred execution and transforming objects.
3   Public Class DeferredExecution
4      Private Sub DeferredExecution_Load(ByVal sender As System.Object,
5         ByVal e As System.EventArgs) Handles MyBase.Load
6
7         ' create an array of Strings
8         Dim colors() As String =
9            {"aqua", "rust", "yellow", "red", "blue", "orange"}
10
11        ' select Strings starting with "r" and convert them to uppercase
12        Dim startsWithR =
13           From color In colors
14           Where (color.StartsWith("r"))
15           Order By color
16           Select color.ToUpper()
17
18        ' display query results
19        For Each item In startsWithR
20           outputTextBox.AppendText(item & "      ")
21        Next
```

Fig. 11.7 | LINQ to Objects using an array of Strings. (Part 1 of 2.)

```
22
23              outputTextBox.AppendText(vbCrLf)
24
25              ' modify array elements to help demonstrate deferred execution
26              colors(4) = "ruby" ' change "blue" to "ruby"
27              colors(5) = "rose" ' change "orange" to "rose"
28
29              ' reexecute the query and display updated query results
30              For Each item In startsWithR
31                  outputTextBox.AppendText(item & "     ")
32              Next
33          End Sub ' DeferredExecution_Load
34      End Class ' DeferredExecution
```

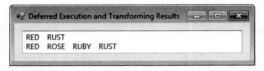

Fig. 11.7 | LINQ to Objects using an array of `Strings`. (Part 2 of 2.)

Calling a Method of an Object in a LINQ Query's **Where** Clause

The query in lines 13–16 filters the `colors` array by using `String` method `StartsWith` in the `Where` clause (line 14) to determine whether each item in the array starts with the letter "r". Method `StartsWith` uses a case sensitive comparison to determine whether a `String` starts with the `String` in the method's argument. If the `String` starts with "r", the `StartsWith` method returns `True` and the element is included in the query results.

Transforming the Results

In Section 11.2, we mentioned that the `Select` clause can transform the selected items. The `Select` clause (line 16) transforms the `Strings` in the result by converting each `String` to uppercase using `String` method `ToUpper`.

Modifying the Array's Contents and Reexecuting the Query

We created the query only once (lines 13–16), yet iterating over the results (lines 19–21 and 30–32) gives two different lists of colors. This demonstrates LINQ's *deferred execution*. The first line of output (produced by lines 19–21) shows the two `Strings` that begin with "r" in the original array. Lines 26–27 replaced the `Strings` "blue" and "orange" in the original array with the `Strings` "ruby" and "rose". Notice that the second line of output (produced by lines 30–32) shows four matching `Strings` rather than two—*the changes to the data source were included when we reexecuted the query.*

11.5 LINQ Resource Center

This chapter introduced LINQ's basic capabilities and syntax. We use more advanced features of LINQ in later chapters. We've created an extensive LINQ Resource Center that contains many links to additional information, including blogs by Microsoft LINQ team members, sample chapters, tutorials, videos, FAQs, resource sites and webcasts. Browse the LINQ Resource Center (www.deitel.com/LINQ/) to learn about this exciting technology.

11.6 Wrap-Up

This chapter used LINQ (Language Integrated Query) to query and manipulate data. We showed how to filter an array or collection using LINQ's Where clause, and how to sort the query results using the Order By clause. You used the Select clause to select specific properties of an object. We showed how to filter Strings starting with a specified character or series of characters by using String method StartsWith. We used the LINQ's Distinct clause to remove duplicates from the results of a LINQ query. You also learned about several extension methods for IEnumerable objects.

In Chapter 12, we begin our discussion of databases, which organize data so that it can be retained for long periods, yet selected and updated quickly. We introduce LINQ to SQL, which allows you to write LINQ queries that extract data from databases. You can then interact with the objects in the query results to insert data in, update data in and delete data from databases.

Summary

Section 11.1 Introduction

- Large amounts of data are often stored in a database—an organized collection of data.
- A database management system (DBMS) provides mechanisms for storing, organizing, retrieving and modifying data contained in the database.
- SQL is an international standard used with relational databases to perform queries and to manipulate data.
- Microsoft developed LINQ to enable you to write queries, similar to SQL, that retrieve information from a wide variety of data sources using a common syntax that is built into Visual Basic.
- The IDE provides *IntelliSense* support for LINQ queries.
- Selecting elements that satisfy a set of conditions is known as filtering.

Section 11.2 Querying an Array of Primitive-Type Elements Using LINQ

- LINQ to Objects works with objects that implement the IEnumerable interface, which enables a program to iterate over a collection of data.
- The For Each...Next statement is used to iterate over IEnumerable objects.
- Arrays implement the IEnumerable interface.
- In a LINQ query, the From clause specifies a range variable and the data source to query. The range variable represents each item in the data source.
- Introducing the range variable in the From clause at the beginning of the query allows the IDE to provide *IntelliSense* while you write the rest of the query.
- If the condition in the Where clause evaluates to True, the element is selected (included in the query results).
- For each item in the data source, the Select clause determines what value appears in the results.
- A LINQ query returns an IEnumerable object.
- The Order By clause sorts the query results in ascending order by default. The Descending modifier can be used in the Order By clause to sort query results in descending order. An Ascending modifier also exists but is rarely used, because it's the default.
- The Order By clause supports values of any type that implements the interface IComparable, such as the primitive numeric types and String. Such types provide a CompareTo method that returns

a negative, zero or positive value indicating whether one value is less than, equal to or greater than another value, respectively.

- You can chain LINQ queries by having one query operate on the results of another.

Section 11.3 Querying an Array of Reference-Type Elements Using LINQ

- LINQ infers the type of a range variable based on the query's data source.
- Any Boolean expression can be used in a Where clause.
- An Order By clause can sort objects in the result according to multiple properties specified in a comma-separated list.
- Most LINQ capabilities are defined as extension methods for the IEnumerable interface. You can call these on any IEnumerable object.
- The Count extension method returns the number of elements in an IEnumerable object.
- The First extension method returns the first element in an IEnumerable object. If the result does not contain any elements, method First throws an InvalidOperationException.
- The Distinct clause prevents duplicate values from appearing in the query results.
- You can select portions of matching objects by specifying the properties to select in a comma-separated list. Only the selected properties can be accessed when iterating over the query results.
- When you select a portion of an object's properties, the compiler creates a new class containing only those properties and the methods that are inherited by all classes from class Object. The new class does not have a name and cannot be used by you to create new objects—such classes are called anonymous types. In the anonymous type, the compiler overrides the inherited ToString method to return a String representation of the object.
- Local type inference allows you to use an anonymous type.
- The IDE provides full *IntelliSense* support for the anonymous types generated by the compiler.

Section 11.4 Deferred Execution and Transforming Query Results

- LINQ uses a technique called deferred execution—a query executes only when you iterate over the results, not when the query is defined. This allows you to create a query once and execute it many times.
- If you make any changes to the data in a LINQ query's data source, the next time you iterate over the query's results, the query will process the current data in the data source.
- The Select clause can be used to transform the values in a query result.
- String method StartsWith determines whether a String starts with the String in the method's argument. Method StartsWith uses a case-sensitive comparison.
- String method ToUpper returns a String with uppercase letters.

Terminology

Self-Review Exercises

11.1 Fill in the blanks in each of the following statements:
   a) Microsoft developed _____ to enable you to write queries, similar to SQL, that retrieve information from a wide variety of data sources using a common syntax that is built into Visual Basic.
   b) Use the _____ extension method to determine the number of elements in the result of a LINQ query.
   c) The LINQ _____ clause is used for filtering.
   d) To get only unique results from a LINQ query, use the _____ clause.
   e) To sort the elements of a LINQ query, use the _____ clause.
   f) Selecting elements that satisfy a set of conditions is known as _____.
   g) In a LINQ query, the From clause specifies a(n) _____ and the data source to query.
   h) LINQ uses a technique called _____—a query executes only when you iterate over the results, not when the query is defined.

11.2 State whether each of the following is *true* or *false*. If *false*, explain why.
   a) The Select clause in a LINQ query is optional.
   b) LINQ to Objects queries can be used on any IEnumerable object.
   c) A key advantage of SQL queries over LINQ queries is that the SQL syntax is built into Visual Basic and the IDE provides *IntelliSense* for SQL.
   d) When you write a LINQ query, it immediately determines the results.
   e) LINQ specifies the conditions that selected elements must satisfy, not the steps necessary to get the results.
   f) The Order By clause of a LINQ query by default sorts the array in descending order.
   g) LINQ can query arrays of only primitive types.
   h) Most LINQ capabilities are methods of the IEnumerable interface.
   i) The results of a LINQ query are the same regardless of the order in which the clauses appear.

Answers to Self-Review Exercises

11.1 a) LINQ. b) Count. c) Where. d) Distinct. e) Order By. f) filtering. g) range variable. h) deferred execution.

11.2 a) True. b) True. c) False. LINQ's syntax is built into Visual Basic and the IDE provides *IntelliSense* for LINQ, but not for SQL. d) False. The LINQ query executes when you iterate over the query's result. e) True. f) False. The default order is ascending. g) False. You can query arrays of any type with LINQ. h) False. Most LINQ capabilities are implemented as extension methods for the IEnumerable interface. i) False. The order does matter—the clauses in a LINQ query are applied in the order in which they appear and this can affect the result.

Exercises

Short Answer Exercises

11.3 Why did Microsoft choose to use extension methods for LINQ rather than simply including these methods in the IEnumerable interface?

11.4 Write a LINQ query that squares all the elements of an array that contains the even integers from 2 to 20.

11.5 Write a LINQ query that selects all the 7s in an array that contains 7, 2, 7, 5, 5, 7, 9, 1, 4, 3, 7, 7, 1, 2, 6. Then determine how many elements are in the result.

11.6 Write a LINQ query that selects all the Employees from the array in Fig. 11.4 with salaries greater than $4000. Then determine how many Employees are in the result and calculate the average of those salaries.

Programming Exercises

11.7 *(Querying an Array of Invoice Objects)* Use the class Invoice provided in the ex11_03 folder with this chapter's examples to create an array of Invoice objects. Use the sample data shown in Fig. 11.8. Class Invoice includes four properties—a PartNumber (type Integer), a PartDescription (type String), a Quantity of the item being purchased (type Integer) and a Price (type Decimal). Write an application that performs the following LINQ queries on the array of Invoice objects and displays the results:

  a) Sort the Invoice objects by PartDescription.
  b) Sort the Invoice objects by Price.
  c) Select the PartDescription and Quantity and sort the results by Quantity.
  d) Select from each Invoice the PartDescription and the value of the Invoice (that is, Quantity * Price). Order the results by the value of the invoice. Name the calculated column InvoiceTotal by using the expression

```
InvoiceTotal = item.Quantity * item.Price
```

  where item is the name of the range variable in the LINQ query.
  e) Using the results of the LINQ query in part (d), select the InvoiceTotals in the range $200 to $500.

Part number	Part description	Quantity	Price
83	Electric sander	7	57.98
24	Power saw	18	99.99
7	Sledge hammer	11	21.50
77	Hammer	76	11.99
39	Lawn mower	3	79.50
68	Screwdriver	106	6.99
56	Jig saw	21	11.00
3	Wrench	34	7.50

Fig. 11.8 | Sample data for Exercise 11.7.

11.8 *(Array Sorting Application)* Modify the sorting example of Fig. 7.12 so that it lists three columns of data headed "Original values," "Values sorted in ascending order" and "Values sorted in descending order"; your program should display in the last two columns the values sorted in ascending and descending order, respectively. Use LINQ to sort the values.

11.9 *(Duplicate Word Removal)* Write an application that inputs a sentence from the user (assume no punctuation), then determines and displays the non-duplicate words in alphabetical order. Treat uppercase and lowercase letters the same. [*Hint:* You can use String method Split with no arguments, as in sentence.Split(), to break a sentence into an array of Strings containing the individual words. By default, Split uses spaces as delimiters. Use String method ToLower in the Select and Order By clauses of your LINQ query to obtain the lowercase version of each word.]

Databases and LINQ

Now go, write it before them in a table, and note it in a book, that it may be for the time to come for ever and ever.
—Isaiah 30:8

It is a capital mistake to theorize before one has data.
—Arthur Conan Doyle

Objectives

In this chapter you'll learn:

- The relational database model.

- To use LINQ to retrieve and manipulate data from a database.

- To add data sources to projects.

- To use the Object Relational Designer to create LINQ to SQL classes.

- To use the IDE's drag-and-drop capabilities to display database tables in applications.

- To use data binding to move data seamlessly between GUI controls and databases.

- To create Master/Detail views that enable you to select a record and display its details.

12.1 Introduction

A database is an organized collection of data. A database management system (DBMS) provides mechanisms for storing, organizing, retrieving and modifying data. Today's most popular DBMSs manage relational databases, which organize data simply as tables with *rows* and *columns*.

Some popular proprietary DBMSs are Microsoft SQL Server, Oracle, Sybase and IBM DB2. PostgreSQL and MySQL are popular *open-source* DBMSs that can be downloaded and used *freely* by anyone. In this chapter, we use Microsoft's free SQL Server Express, which is installed with Visual Basic Express and Visual Studio. It can also be downloaded separately from Microsoft (www.microsoft.com/express/sql).

SQL Server Express provides most of the features of Microsoft's full (fee-based) SQL Server product, but has some limitations, such as a maximum database size of four gigabytes and allowing only one application at a time to interact with a database. A SQL Server Express database can be easily migrated to a full version of SQL Server—we did this with our deitel.com website once our database became too large for SQL Server Express.

Chapter 11 introduced LINQ to Objects and used it to to manipulate data stored in arrays. LINQ to SQL allows you to manipulate data stored in a *SQL Server* or *SQL Server Express* relational database. The SQL in LINQ to SQL stands for *SQL Server, not SQL*. As with LINQ to Objects, the IDE provides *IntelliSense* for your LINQ to SQL queries.

This chapter introduces general concepts of relational databases, then explores LINQ to SQL and the IDE's tools for working with databases. In later chapters, you'll see other practical database and LINQ to SQL applications, such as a web-based bookstore and a web based airline reservation service. Databases are at the heart of almost all "industrial strength" applications.

12.2 Relational Databases

A relational database organizes data simply in tables. Figure 12.1 illustrates a sample Employees table that might be used in a personnel system. The table stores the attributes of employees. Tables are composed of rows (also called records) and columns (also called fields) in which values are stored. This table consists of six rows (one per employee) and five columns (one per attribute). The attributes are the employee's ID, name, department, salary and location. The ID column of each row is the table's primary key—a column (or group of columns) requiring a *unique* value that cannot be duplicated in other rows. This guarantees that each primary key value can be used to identify *one* row. A primary key composed of two or more columns is known as a composite key. Good examples of primary-key columns in other applications are a book's ISBN number in a book information system or a part number in an inventory system—values in each of these columns must be unique. LINQ to SQL *requires every table to have a primary key* to support updating the data in tables. The rows in Fig. 12.1 are displayed in ascending order by primary key. But they could be listed in decreasing (descending) order or in no particular order at all.

Table **Employees**

	ID	Name	Department	Salary	Location
	23603	Jones	413	1100	Trenton
	24568	Kerwin	413	2000	Trenton
Row	34589	Larson	642	1800	Los Angeles
	35761	Myers	611	1400	Orlando
	47132	Neumann	413	9000	Trenton
	78321	Stephens	611	8500	Orlando

Primary key   Column

Fig. 12.1 | Employees table sample data.

Each *column* represents a different data *attribute*. Some column values may be duplicated between rows. For example, three different rows in the Employees table's Department column contain the number 413, indicating that these employees work in the same department.

You can use LINQ to SQL to define queries that select subsets of the data from a table. For example, a program might select data from the Employees table to create a query result that shows where each department is located, in increasing order by Department number (Fig. 12.2).

Department	Location
413	Trenton
611	Orlando
642	Los Angeles

Fig. 12.2 | Distinct Department and Location data from the Employees table.

12.3 A Books Database

We now consider a simple Books database that stores information about some Deitel publications. First, we overview the database's tables. A database's tables, their fields and the relationships among them are collectively known as a database schema. LINQ to SQL uses a database's schema to define classes that enable you to interact with the database. Next, we show how to use LINQ to SQL to retrieve information from the Books database. The database file—Books.mdf—is provided with this chapter's examples. SQL Server database files have the .mdf ("master data file") file-name extension.

Authors *Table of the* Books *Database*

The database consists of three tables: Authors, Titles and AuthorISBN. The Authors table (described in Fig. 12.3) consists of three columns that maintain each author's unique ID number, first name and last name, respectively. Figure 12.4 contains the data from the Authors table.

Column	Description
AuthorID	Author's ID number in the database. In the Books database, this integer column is defined as an identity column, also known as an autoincremented column—for each row inserted in the table, the AuthorID value is increased by 1 automatically to ensure that each row has a unique AuthorID. This is the *primary key.*
FirstName	Author's first name (a string).
LastName	Author's last name (a string).

Fig. 12.3 | Authors table of the Books database.

AuthorID	FirstName	LastName
1	Harvey	Deitel
2	Paul	Deitel
3	Greg	Ayer
4	Dan	Quirk

Fig. 12.4 | Data from the Authors table of the Books database.

Titles *Table of the* Books *Database*

The Titles table (described in Fig. 12.5) consists of four columns that maintain information about each book in the database, including its ISBN, title, edition number and copyright year. Figure 12.6 contains the data from the Titles table.

Column	Description
ISBN	ISBN of the book (a string). The table's primary key. ISBN is an abbreviation for "International Standard Book Number"—a numbering scheme that publishers worldwide use to give every book a *unique* identification number.
Title	Title of the book (a string).
EditionNumber	Edition number of the book (an integer).
Copyright	Copyright year of the book (a string).

Fig. 12.5 | Titles table of the Books database.

ISBN	Title	Edition-Number	Copy-right
0131752421	Internet & World Wide Web How to Program	4	2008
0132222205	Java How to Program	7	2007
0132404168	C How to Program	5	2007
0136053033	Simply Visual Basic 2008	3	2009
013605305X	Visual Basic 2008 How to Program	4	2009
013605322X	Visual C# 2008 How to Program	3	2009
0136151574	Visual C++ 2008 How to Program	2	2008
0136152503	C++ How to Program	6	2008

Fig. 12.6 | Data from the Titles table of the Books database.

AuthorISBN *Table of the* Books *Database*

The AuthorISBN table (described in Fig. 12.7) consists of two columns that maintain ISBNs for each book and their corresponding authors' ID numbers. This table associates authors with their books. The AuthorID column is a **foreign key**—a column in this table that matches the primary-key column in another table (that is, AuthorID in the Authors table). The ISBN column is also a foreign key—it matches the primary-key column (that is, ISBN) in the Titles table. Together the AuthorID and ISBN columns in this table form a *composite primary key*. Every row in this table uniquely matches one author to one book's ISBN. Figure 12.8 contains the data from the AuthorISBN table of the Books database.

Column	Description
AuthorID	The author's ID number, a foreign key to the Authors table.
ISBN	The ISBN for a book, a foreign key to the Titles table.

Fig. 12.7 | AuthorISBN table of the Books database.

AuthorID	ISBN	AuthorID	ISBN
1	0131752421	*(continued)*	
1	0132222205	2	0132222205
1	0132404168	2	0132404168
1	0136053033	2	0136053033
1	013605305X	2	013605305X
1	013605322X	2	013605322X
1	0136151574	2	0136151574
1	0136152503	2	0136152503
2	0131752421	3	0136053033
(continued)		4	0136151574

Fig. 12.8 | Data from the AuthorISBN table of the Books database.

Foreign Keys

A database might consist of many tables. A goal when designing a database is to minimize the amount of duplicated data among the database's tables. Foreign keys, which are specified when a database table is created, link the data in multiple tables.

Every foreign-key value must appear as another table's primary-key value so the DBMS can ensure that the foreign key value is valid. For example, the DBMS ensures that the AuthorID value for a particular row of the AuthorISBN table (Fig. 12.8) is valid by checking that there is a row in the Authors table with that AuthorID as the primary key.

Foreign keys also allow related data in multiple tables to be selected from those tables—this is known as joining the data. There is a one-to-many relationship between a primary key and a corresponding foreign key (for example, one author can write many books and one book can be written by many authors). This means that a foreign key can appear *many* times in its own table but only *once* (as the primary key) in another table. For example, the ISBN 0131450913 can appear in several rows of AuthorISBN (because this book has several authors) but only once in Titles, where ISBN is the primary key.

Entity-Relationship Diagram for the Books Database

Figure 12.9 is an entity-relationship (ER) diagram for the Books database. This diagram shows the tables in the database and the relationships among them. The first compartment in each box contains the table's name. The names in italic font are primary keys—AuthorID in the Authors table, AuthorID and ISBN in the AuthorISBN table, and ISBN in the Titles table. Every row *must* have a value in the primary-key column, and the value of the key must be *unique* in the table; otherwise, the DBMS will report an error. The names AuthorID and ISBN in the AuthorISBN table are *both* italic—together these form a *composite primary key* for the AuthorISBN table.

The lines connecting the tables in Fig. 12.9 represent the relationships among the tables. Consider the line between the Authors and AuthorISBN tables. On the Authors end of the line, there's a 1, and on the AuthorISBN end, an infinity symbol (∞). This indicates a one-to-many relationship—for *each* author in the Authors table, there can be an *arbi-*

trary number of ISBNs for books written by that author in the `AuthorISBN` table (that is, an author can write any number of books). Note that the relationship line links the `AuthorID` column in the `Authors` table (where `AuthorID` is the primary key) to the `AuthorID` column in the `AuthorISBN` table (where `AuthorID` is a foreign key)—the line between the tables links the primary key to the matching foreign key.

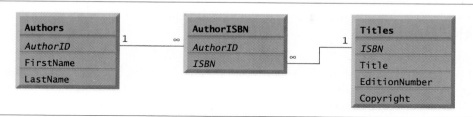

Fig. 12.9 | Entity-relationship diagram for the `Books` database.

The line between the `Titles` and `AuthorISBN` tables illustrates a one-to-many relationship—one book can be written by many authors. Note that the line between the tables links the primary key `ISBN` in table `Titles` to the corresponding foreign key in table `AuthorISBN`. The relationships in Fig. 12.9 illustrate that the sole purpose of the `AuthorISBN` table is to provide a many-to-many relationship between the `Authors` and `Titles` tables—an author can write *many* books, and a book can have *many* authors.

12.4 LINQ to SQL

LINQ to SQL enables you to access data in *SQL Server databases* using the same LINQ syntax introduced in Chapter 11. You interact with the database via classes that are automatically generated from the database schema by the IDE's **LINQ to SQL Designer**. For each table in the database, the IDE creates two classes:

- A class that represents a row of the table: This class contains properties for each column in the table. LINQ to SQL creates objects of this class—called **row objects**—to store the data from individual rows of the table.

- A class that represents the table: LINQ to SQL creates an object of this class to store a collection of row objects that correspond to all of the rows in the table.

Relationships between tables are also taken into account in the generated classes:

- In the class for a row object, an additional property is created for each foreign key. This property returns the row object of the corresponding primary key in another table. For example, the LINQ to SQL class that represents the rows of the `Books` database's `AuthorISBN` table also contains an `Author` property and a `Title` property—from any `AuthorISBN` row object, you can access the full author and title information.

- In the class for a row object, an additional property is created for the collection of row objects with foreign-keys that reference the row object's primary key. For example, the LINQ to SQL class that represents the rows of the `Books` database's `Authors` table contains an `AuthorISBNs` property that you can use to get all of the

ISBNs for books written by that author. The IDE automatically adds the "s" to "AuthorISBN" to indicate that this property represents a collection of AuthorISBN objects. Similarly, the LINQ to SQL class that represents the rows of the Titles table also contains an AuthorISBNs property that you can use to get all of the AuthorIDs for the co-authors of a particular title.

Once generated, the LINQ to SQL classes have full *IntelliSense* support in the IDE. Section 12.7 demonstrates queries that use the relationships among the Books database's tables to join data.

IQueryable Interface

LINQ to SQL works through the **IQueryable** interface, which inherits from the IEnumerable interface introduced in Chapter 11. When a LINQ to SQL query on an IQueryable object executes against the database, the results are loaded into objects of the corresponding LINQ to SQL classes for convenient access in your code.

DataContext Class

All LINQ to SQL queries occur via a **DataContext** class, which controls the flow of data between the program and the database. A specific DataContext derived class, which inherits from the class System.Data.Linq.DataContext, is created when the LINQ to SQL classes representing each row of the table are generated by the IDE. This derived class has properties for each table in the database, which can be used as data sources in LINQ queries. Any changes made to the DataContext can be saved back to the database using the DataContext's **SubmitChanges** method, so with LINQ to SQL you can modify the database's contents.

12.5 Querying a Database with LINQ

In this section, we demonstrate how to *connect* to a database, *query* it and *display* the results of the query. There is little code in this section—the IDE provides *visual programming* tools and *wizards* that simplify accessing data in applications. These tools establish database connections and create the objects necessary to view and manipulate the data through Windows Forms GUI controls—a technique known as **data binding**.

Our first example performs a simple query on the Books database from Section 12.3. We retrieve the entire Authors table and use data binding to display its data in a **DataGridView**—a control from namespace System.Windows.Forms that can display data from a data source in tabular format. The basic steps we'll perform are:

- Connect to the Books database.
- Create the LINQ to SQL classes required to use the database.
- Add the Authors table as a data source.
- Drag the Authors table data source onto the **Design** view to create a GUI for displaying the table's data.
- Add a few statements to the program to allow it to interact with the database.

The GUI for the program is shown in Fig. 12.10. All of the controls in this GUI are automatically generated when we drag a data source that represents the Authors table onto the Form in **Design** view. The BindingNavigator at the top of the window is a collection of controls that allow you to navigate through the records in the DataGridView that fills the rest of the window. The BindingNavigator controls also allow you to add records, delete records and save your changes to the database. If you add a new record, note that empty (NULL) values are not allowed in the Books database, so attempting to save a new record without specifying a value for each field will cause an error.

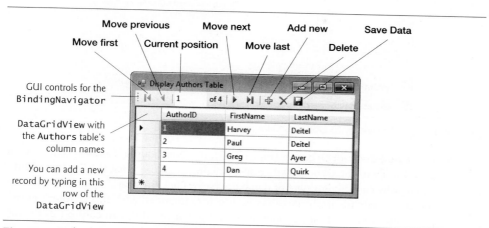

Fig. 12.10 | GUI for the **Display Authors Table** application.

12.5.1 Creating LINQ to SQL Classes

This section presents the steps required to create LINQ to SQL classes for a database.

Step 1: Creating the Project
Create a new **Windows Forms Application** named DisplayTable. Change the name of the source file to DisplayAuthorsTable.vb. The IDE updates the Form's class name to match the source file. Set the Form's **Text** property to Display Authors Table.

Step 2: Adding a Database to the Project and Connecting to the Database
To interact with a database, you must create a connection to the database. This will also give you the option of copying the database file to your project.

1. In Visual Basic 2010 Express, select **View > Other Windows > Database Explorer** to display the **Database Explorer** window. By default, it appears on the left side of the IDE. If you're using a full version of Visual Studio, select **View > Server Explorer** to display the **Server Explorer**. From this point forward, we'll refer to the **Database Explorer**. If you have a full version of Visual Studio, substitute **Server Explorer** for **Database Explorer** in the steps.

2. Click the **Connect to Database** icon ( ) at the top of the **Database Explorer**. If the **Choose Data Source** dialog appears (Fig. 12.11), select **Microsoft SQL Server Database File** from the **Data source:** list. If you check the **Always use this selection** CheckBox, the IDE will use this type of database file by default when you connect to databases in the future. Click **Continue** to display the **Add Connection** dialog.

Fig. 12.11 | **Choose Data Source** dialog.

3. In the **Add Connection** dialog (Fig. 12.12), the **Data source:** TextBox reflects your selection from the **Choose Data Source** dialog. You can click the **Change...** Button to select a different type of database. Next, click **Browse...** to locate and select the Books.mdf file in the Databases directory included with this chapter's examples. You can click **Test Connection** to verify that the IDE can connect to the database through SQL Server Express. Click **OK** to create the connection.

 Error-Prevention Tip 12.1

SQL Server Express allows only one application at a time to access a database file. Ensure that no other program is using the database file before you attempt to add it to the project.

Fig. 12.12 | **Add Connection** dialog.

Step 3: Generating the LINQ to SQL classes

After the database has been added, you must select the database from which the LINQ to SQL classes will be created. LINQ to SQL uses the database's schema to help define the classes.

1. Right click the project name in the **Solution Explorer** and select **Add > New Item...** to display the **Add New Item** dialog. Select the **LINQ to SQL Classes** template, name the new item Books.dbml and click the **Add** button. The **Object Relational Designer** window will appear (Fig. 12.13). You can also double click the Books.dbml file in the **Solution Explorer** to open the **Object Relational Designer**.

Fig. 12.13 | Object Relational Designer window.

2. Expand the Books.mdf database node in the **Database Explorer**, then expand the **Tables** node. Drag the Authors, Titles and AuthorISBN tables onto the **Object Relational Designer**. The IDE prompts whether you want to copy the database to the project directory. Select **Yes**. The **Object Relational Designer** will display the tables that you dragged from the **Database Explorer** (Fig. 12.14). Notice that the **Object Relational Designer** named the class that represents items from the Authors table as Author, and named the class that represents the Titles table as Title. This is because one object of the Author class represents one author—a single row from the Authors table. Similarly, one object of the Title class represents one book—a single row from the Titles table.

3. Save the Books.dbml file.

Fig. 12.14 | Object Relational Designer window showing the selected tables from the Books database and their relationships.

When you save Books.dbml, the IDE generates the LINQ to SQL classes that you can use to interact with the database. These include a class for each table you selected from the database and a derived class of DataContext named BooksDataContext that enables you to programmatically interact with the database.

Error-Prevention Tip 12.2

Be sure to save the file in the Object Relational Designer before trying to use the LINQ to SQL classes in code. The IDE does not generate the classes until you save the file.

12.5.2 Data Bindings Between Controls and the LINQ to SQL Classes

The IDE's automatic data binding capabilities simplify creating applications that can view and modify the data in a database. You must write a small amount of code to enable the autogenerated data-binding classes to interact with the autogenerated LINQ to SQL classes. You'll now perform the steps to display the contents of the Authors table in a GUI.

Step 1: Adding the Author LINQ to SQL Class as a Data Source

To use the LINQ to SQL classes for data binding, you must first add them as a data source.

1. Select **Data > Add New Data Source...** to display the **Data Source Configuration Wizard**.

2. The LINQ to SQL classes are used to create objects representing the tables in the database, so we'll use an **Object** data source. In the dialog, select **Object** and click **Next >**. Expand the tree view as shown in Fig. 12.15 and ensure that **Author** is checked. An object of this class will be used as the data source.

3. Click **Finish**.

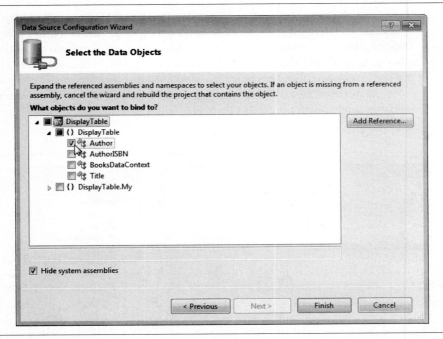

Fig. 12.15 | Selecting the Author LINQ to SQL class as the data source.

The Authors table in the database is now a data source that can be used by the bindings. Open the **Data Sources** window (Fig. 12.16) by selecting **Data > Show Data Sources**. You can see the Author class that you added in the previous step. The columns of the database's Authors table should appear below it, as well as an AuthorISBNs entry representing the relationship between the database's Authors and AuthorISBN tables.

Fig. 12.16 | **Data Sources** window showing the Author class as a data source.

Step 2: Creating GUI Elements
Next, you'll use the **Design** view to create a GUI control that can display the Authors table's data.

1. Switch to **Design** view for the DisplayAuthorsTable class.

2. Click the **Author** node in the **Data Sources** window—it should change to a drop-down list. Open the drop-down by clicking the down arrow and ensure that the DataGridView option is selected—this is the GUI control that will be used to display and interact with the data.

3. Drag the **Author** node from the **Data Sources** window onto the Form in **Design** view.

The IDE creates a DataGridView (Fig. 12.17) with the correct column names and a **BindingNavigator** (AuthorBindingNavigator) that contains Buttons for moving between entries, adding entries, deleting entries and saving changes to the database. The IDE also generates a **BindingSource** (AuthorBindingSource), which handles the transfer of data between the data source and the data-bound controls on the Form. Nonvisual components such as the BindingSource and the non-visual aspects of the BindingNavigator appear in the component tray—the gray region below the Form in **Design** view. We use the default names for automatically generated components throughout this chapter to show exactly what the IDE creates. To make the **DataGridView** occupy the entire window, select the DataGridView, then use the **Properties** window to set the Dock property to Fill.

Step 3: Connecting the BooksDataContext to the AuthorBindingSource
The final step is to connect the BooksDataContext (created with the LINQ to SQL classes in Section 12.5.1) to the AuthorBindingSource (created with in Section 12.5.2), so that the application can interact with the database. Figure 12.18 shows the small amount of code needed to obtain data from the database and to save any changes that the user makes to the data back into the database.

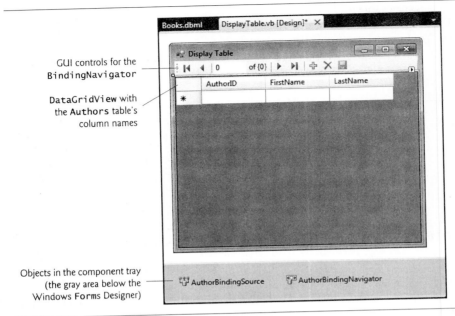

GUI controls for the
BindingNavigator

DataGridView with
the **Authors** table's
column names

Objects in the component tray
(the gray area below the
Windows **Forms** Designer)

Fig. 12.17 | Component tray holds nonvisual components in **Design** view.

```vb
 1    ' Fig. 12.18: DisplayTable.vb
 2    ' Displaying data from a database table in a DataGridView.
 3    Public Class DisplayTable
 4       Private database As New BooksDataContext() ' LINQ to SQL data context
 5
 6       ' load data from database into DataGridView
 7       Private Sub DisplayTable_Load(ByVal sender As System.Object,
 8          ByVal e As System.EventArgs) Handles MyBase.Load
 9
10          ' use LINQ to order the data for display
11          AuthorBindingSource.DataSource =
12             From author In database.Authors
13             Order By author.AuthorID
14             Select author
15       End Sub ' DisplayTable_Load
16
17       ' save the changes into the database
18       Private Sub AuthorBindingNavigatorSaveItem_Click(
19          ByVal sender As System.Object, ByVal e As System.EventArgs) _
20          Handles AuthorBindingNavigatorSaveItem.Click
21
22          Validate() ' validate input fields
23          AuthorBindingSource.EndEdit() ' indicate edits are complete
24          database.SubmitChanges() ' write changes to database file
25       End Sub ' AuthorBindingNavigatorSaveItem_Click
26    End Class ' DisplayTable
```

Fig. 12.18 | Displaying data from a database table in a DataGridView. (Part 1 of 2.)

Fig. 12.18 | Displaying data from a database table in a `DataGridView`. (Part 2 of 2.)

As mentioned in Section 12.4, a `DataContext` object is used to interact with the database. The `BooksDataContext` class was automatically generated by the IDE when you created the LINQ to SQL classes to allow access to the `Books` database. Line 4 creates an object of this class named `database`.

Create the `Form`'s `Load` handler by double clicking the `Form`'s title bar in **Design** view. We allow data to move between the `DataContext` and the `BindingSource` by creating a LINQ query that extracts data from the `BooksDataContext`'s `Authors` property (lines 12–14), which corresponds to the `Authors` table in the database. The `AuthorBindingSource`'s **`DataSource`** property (line 11) is set to the results of this query. The `AuthorBinding-Source` uses the `DataSource` to extract data from the database and to populate the `DataGridView`.

Step 4: Saving Modifications Back to the Database

If the user modifies the data in the `DataGridView`, we'd also like to save the modifications in the database. By default, the `BindingNavigator`'s **Save Data** Button (🖫) is disabled. To enable it, right click this `Button`'s icon and select **Enabled**. Then, double click the icon to create its `Click` event handler.

Saving the data entered into the `DataGridView` back to the database is a three-step process (lines 22–24). First, all controls on the form are validated (line 22)—if any of the controls have event handlers for the `Validating` event, those execute. You typically handle this event to determine whether a control's contents are valid. Second, line 23 calls `EndEdit` on the `AuthorBindingSource`, which forces it to save any pending changes in the `BooksDataContext`. Finally, line 24 calls **`SubmitChanges`** on the `BooksDataContext` to store the changes in the database. For efficiency, LINQ to SQL saves only data that has changed.

Step 5: Configuring the Database File to Persist Changes

By default, when you run the program in debug mode, the database file is overwritten with the original database file each time you execute the program. This allows you to test your program with the original content until it works correctly. When you run the program in release mode (*Ctrl* +), any changes you make to the database persist automatically. You can persist changes between program executions in debug mode by selecting the database in the **Solution Explorer** and setting the **Copy to Output Directory** property in the **Properties** window to **Copy if newer**.

12.6 Dynamically Binding Query Results

Now that you've seen how to display an entire database table in a `DataGridView`, we show how to perform several different queries and display the results in a `DataGridView`. The **Display Query Results** application (Fig. 12.19) allows the user to select a query from the `ComboBox` at the bottom of the window, then displays the results of the query.

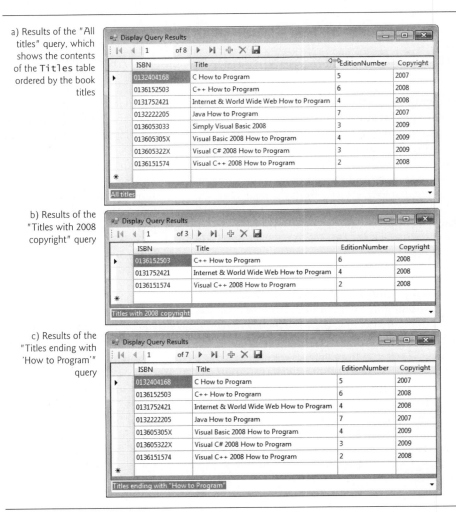

a) Results of the "All titles" query, which shows the contents of the `Titles` table ordered by the book titles

b) Results of the "Titles with 2008 copyright" query

c) Results of the "Titles ending with 'How to Program'" query

Fig. 12.19 | Sample execution of the Display Query Results application.

12.6.1 Creating the Display Query Results GUI

Perform the following steps to build the **Display Query Results** application's GUI.

Step 1: Creating the Project

First, create a new **Windows Forms Application** named `DisplayQueryResult`. Rename the source file to `TitleQueries.vb`. Set the Form's **Text** property to `Display Query Results`.

Step 2: Creating the LINQ to SQL Classes
Follow the steps in Section 12.5.1 to add the Books database to the project and generate the LINQ to SQL classes.

Step 3: Creating a DataGridView to Display the Titles Table
Follow *Steps 1* and *2* in Section 12.5.2 to create the data source and the DataGridView. In this example, select the Title class (rather than the Author class) as the data source, and drag the **Title** node from the **Data Sources** window onto the form.

Step 4: Adding a ComboBox to the Form
In **Design** view, add a ComboBox named queriesComboBox below the DataGridView on the Form. Users will select which query to execute from this control. Set the ComboBox's Dock property to Bottom and the DataGridView's Dock property to Fill.

Next, you'll add the names of the queries to the ComboBox. Open the ComboBox's **String Collection Editor** by right clicking the ComboBox and selecting **Edit Items**. You can also access the **String Collection Editor** from the ComboBox's smart tag menu. A smart tag menu provides you with quick access to common properties you might set for a control (such as the Multiline property of a TextBox), so you can set these properties directly in **Design** view, rather than in the **Properties** window. You can open a control's smart tag menu by clicking the small arrowhead (▶) that appears in the control's upper-right corner in **Design** view. In the **String Collection Editor**, add the following three items to queriesComboBox— one for each of the queries we'll create:

1. All titles

2. Titles with 2008 copyright

3. Titles ending with "How to Program"

12.6.2 Coding the Display Query Results Application
Next you must write code that executes the appropriate query each time the user chooses a different item from queriesComboBox. Double click queriesComboBox in **Design** view to generate a queriesComboBox_SelectedIndexChanged event handler (Fig. 12.20, lines 7–37) in the TitleQueries.vb file. In the event handler, add a Select Case statement (lines 12–34) to change the TitleBindingSource's DataSource property to a LINQ query that returns the correct set of data. The data bindings created by the IDE *automatically* update the TitleDataGridView *each time* we change its DataSource. The **MoveFirst** method of the BindingSource (line 36) moves to the first row of the result each time a query executes. The results of the queries in lines 16–18, 22–25 and 30–33 are shown in Fig. 12.19(a), (b) and (c), respectively.

```
1   ' Fig. 12.20: TitleQueries.vb
2   ' Displaying the result of a user-selected query in a DataGridView.
3   Public Class TitleQueries
4      Private database As New BooksDataContext() ' LINQ to SQL data context
5
```

Fig. 12.20 | Displaying the result of a user-selected query in a DataGridView. (Part 1 of 3.)

```vbnet
 6      ' loads data into TitleBindingSource based on user-selected query
 7      Private Sub queriesComboBox_SelectedIndexChanged(
 8         ByVal sender As System.Object, ByVal e As System.EventArgs) _
 9         Handles queriesComboBox.SelectedIndexChanged
10
11         ' set the data displayed according to what is selected
12         Select Case queriesComboBox.SelectedIndex
13            Case 0 ' all titles
14               ' use LINQ to order the books by title
15               TitleBindingSource.DataSource =
16                  From book In database.Titles
17                  Order By book.Title
18                  Select book
19            Case 1 ' titles with 2008 copyright
20               ' use LINQ to get titles with 2008 copyright and sort them
21               TitleBindingSource.DataSource =
22                  From book In database.Titles
23                  Where book.Copyright = "2008"
24                  Order By book.Title
25                  Select book
26            Case 2 ' titles ending with "How to Program"
27               ' use LINQ to get titles ending with
28               ' "How to Program" and sort them
29               TitleBindingSource.DataSource =
30                  From book In database.Titles
31                  Where book.Title.EndsWith("How to Program")
32                  Order By book.Title
33                  Select book
34         End Select
35
36         TitleBindingSource.MoveFirst() ' move to first entry
37      End Sub ' queriesComboBox_SelectedIndexChanged
38
39      ' display results of all titles query when Form loads
40      Private Sub TitleQueries_Load(ByVal sender As System.Object,
41         ByVal e As System.EventArgs) Handles MyBase.Load
42
43         ' set the ComboBox to show the default query that
44         ' selects all books from the Titles table and causes the
45         ' queriesComboBox's SelectedIndexChanged event handler to execute
46         queriesComboBox.SelectedIndex = 0
47      End Sub ' TitleQueries_Load
48
49      ' save changes from the BooksDataContext into the database
50      Private Sub TitleBindingNavigatorSaveItem_Click(
51         ByVal sender As System.Object, ByVal e As System.EventArgs) _
52         Handles TitleBindingNavigatorSaveItem.Click
53
54         Validate() ' validate input fields
55         TitleBindingSource.EndEdit() ' indicate edits are complete
56         database.SubmitChanges() ' write changes to database file
57
```

Fig. 12.20 | Displaying the result of a user-selected query in a DataGridView. (Part 2 of 3.)

```
58          ' after saving, display the results of the "all titles" query
59             queriesComboBox.SelectedIndex = 0
60       End Sub ' TitleBindingNavigatorSaveItem_Click
61    End Class ' TitleQueries
```

Fig. 12.20 | Displaying the result of a user-selected query in a `DataGridView`. (Part 3 of 3.)

Customizing the Form's Load Event Handler
Create the `TitleQueries_Load` event handler (lines 40–47) by double clicking the title bar in **Design** view. When the `Form` loads, it should display the complete list of books from the `Titles` table, sorted by title. Rather than defining the same LINQ query as in lines 15–18, we can programmatically cause the `queriesComboBox_SelectedIndexChanged` event handler to execute simply by setting the `queriesComboBox`'s `SelectedIndex` to 0 (line 46).

Saving Changes
Follow the instructions in the previous example to add a handler for the `BindingNavigator`'s **Save Data** `Button` (lines 50–60). Note that, except for changes to the names, the three lines are identical. The last statement (line 59) displays the results of the `All titles` query in the `DataGridView`. Recall that the changes to the database will persist between program executions if you execute the program in release mode (*Ctrl + F5*).

12.7 Retrieving Data from Multiple Tables with LINQ

In this section, we concentrate on LINQ to SQL features that simplify querying and combining data from multiple tables. The **Joining Tables with LINQ** application (Fig. 12.21) uses LINQ to SQL to combine and organize data from multiple tables, and shows the results of queries that perform the following tasks:

- Get a list of all the authors and the ISBNs of the books they've authored, sorted by last name then first name (Fig. 12.21(a)).

- Get a list of all the authors and the titles of the books they've authored, sorted by last name then first; for each author sort the titles alphabetically (Fig. 12.21(b)).

- Get a list of all the book titles grouped by author, sorted by last name then first; for a given author sort the titles alphabetically (Fig. 12.21(c)).

a) List of authors and the ISBNs of the books they've authored; sort the authors by last name then first name

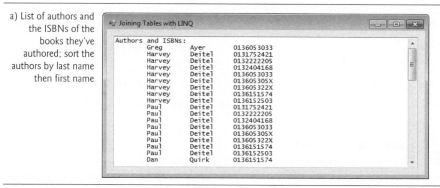

Fig. 12.21 | Outputs from the **Joining Tables with LINQ** application. (Part 1 of 2.)

b) List of authors and the titles of the book's they've authored; sort the authors by last name then first name; for a given author, sort the titles alphabetically

c) List of titles grouped by author; sort the authors by last name then first name; for a given author, sort the titles alphabetically

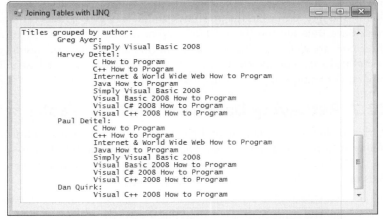

Fig. 12.21 | Outputs from the **Joining Tables with LINQ** application. (Part 2 of 2.)

GUI for the Joining Tables with LINQ Application

For this example (Fig. 12.22–Fig. 12.25), create a Windows Forms application named JoinQueries and rename the Form.vb file as JoiningTableData.vb. We set the following properties for the outputTextBox:

- Font property: Set to Lucida Console to display the output in a fixed-width font.

- Anchor property: Set to Top, Bottom, Left, Right so that you can resize the window and the outputTextBox will resize accordingly.

- Scrollbars property: Set to Vertical, so that you can scroll through the output.

Follow the steps from previous sections to set up the connection to the database and the LINQ to SQL classes.

Creating the BooksDataContext

The code combines data from the three tables in the Books database and displays the relationships between the book titles and authors in three different ways. It uses LINQ to SQL classes that have been created using the same steps as the first two examples. As in previous examples, the `BooksDataContext` object (Fig. 12.22, line 7) allows the program to interact with the database.

```vb
 1    ' Fig. 12.22: JoiningTableData.vb
 2    ' Using LINQ to perform aggregate data from several tables.
 3    Public Class JoiningTableData
 4       Private Sub JoiningTableData_Load(ByVal sender As System.Object,
 5          ByVal e As System.EventArgs) Handles MyBase.Load
 6
 7          Dim database As New BooksDataContext() ' LINQ to SQL data context
 8
```

Fig. 12.22 | Creating the `BooksDataContext` for querying the `Books` database.

Combining Author Names with the ISBNs of the Books They've Written
The first query (Fig. 12.23, lines 11–14) joins data from two tables and returns a list of author names and the ISBNs representing the books they've written, sorted by `LastName` then `FirstName`. The query takes advantage of the properties that LINQ to SQL creates based on foreign-key relationships between the database's tables. These properties enable you to easily combine data from related rows in multiple tables.

```vb
 9        ' get authors and ISBNs of each book they co-authored
10        Dim authorsAndISBNs =
11           From author In database.Authors
12           From book In author.AuthorISBNs
13           Order By author.LastName, author.FirstName
14           Select author.FirstName, author.LastName, book.ISBN
15
16        outputTextBox.AppendText("Authors and ISBNs:")
17
18        ' display authors and ISBNs in tabular format
19        For Each element In authorsAndISBNs
20           outputTextBox.AppendText(
21              String.Format("{0}{1}{2,-10} {3,-10} {4,-10}", vbCrLf, vbTab,
22                 element.FirstName, element.LastName, element.ISBN))
23        Next
24
```

Fig. 12.23 | Getting a list of authors and the ISBNs of the books they've authored.

The first `From` clause (line 11) gets one `author` from the `Authors` table. The second `From` clause (line 12) uses the generated `AuthorISBNs` property of the `Author` class to get only the rows in the `AuthorISBN` table that link to the current `author`—that is, the ones that have the same `AuthorID` as the current `author`. The combined result of the two `From` clauses is a collection of all the authors and the ISBNs of the books they've authored. The two `From` clauses introduce two range variables into the scope of this query—other clauses can access both range variables to combine data from multiple tables. Line 14 combines the `FirstName` and `LastName` of an author from the `Authors` table with a corresponding ISBN from the `AuthorISBNs` table.

Combining Author Names with the Titles of the Books They've Written
The second query (Fig. 12.24, lines 27–31) gives similar output, but uses the foreign-key relationships to go one step further and get the actual title of each book that an author wrote. The first From clause (line 27) gets one title from the Titles table. The second From clause (line 28) uses the generated AuthorISBNs property of the Title class to get only the rows in the AuthorISBN table that link to the current title—that is, the ones that have the same ISBN as the current title. Each of those book objects contains an Author property that represents the foreign-key relationship between the AuthorISBNs table and the Authors table. This Author property gives us access to the names of the authors for the current book.

```
25          ' get authors and titles of each book they co-authored
26          Dim authorsAndTitles =
27              From title In database.Titles
28              From book In title.AuthorISBNs
29              Let author = book.Author
30              Order By author.LastName, author.FirstName, title.Title
31              Select author.FirstName, author.LastName, title.Title
32
33          outputTextBox.AppendText(vbCrLf & vbCrLf & "Authors and titles:")
34
35          ' display authors and titles in tabular format
36          For Each element In authorsAndTitles
37              outputTextBox.AppendText(
38                  String.Format("{0}{1}{2,-10} {3,-10} {4}", vbCrLf, vbTab,
39                  element.FirstName, element.LastName, element.Title))
40          Next
41
```

Fig. 12.24 | Getting a list of authors and the titles of the books they've authored.

Line 29 introduces the **Let query operator**, which allows you to declare a new variable in a LINQ query—usually to create a shorter name for an expression. The variable can be accessed in later statements just like a range variable. The author variable created in the Let clause refers to book.Author. The Select clause (line 31) uses the author and title variables introduced earlier in the query to get the FirstName and LastName of each author from the Authors table and the Title of each book from the Titles table.

Organizing Book Titles by Author
Most queries return results with data arranged in a relational-style table of rows and columns. The last query (Fig. 12.25, lines 45–51) returns hierarchical results. Each element in the results contains the name of an Author and a list of Titles that the author wrote. The LINQ query does this by using a nested query in the Select clause. The outer query iterates over the authors in the database. The inner query takes a specific author and retrieves all titles that the author worked on. The Select clause (lines 47–51) creates an anonymous type with two properties:

- The property Name (line 47) combines each author's name, separating the first and last names by a space.

- The property `Titles` (line 48) receives the result of the nested query, which returns the `Title` of each book written by the current `author`.

The nested `For Each...Next` statements (lines 57–67) use the properties of the anonymous type created by the query to output the hierarchical results. The outer loop displays the author's name and the inner loop displays the titles of all the books written by that author.

```
42          ' get authors and titles of each book
43          ' they co-authored; group by author
44          Dim titlesByAuthor =
45             From author In database.Authors
46             Order By author.LastName, author.FirstName
47             Select Name = author.FirstName & " " & author.LastName,
48                Titles =
49                   From book In author.AuthorISBNs
50                   Order By book.Title.Title
51                   Select book.Title.Title
52
53          outputTextBox.AppendText(
54             vbCrLf & vbCrLf & "Titles grouped by author:")
55
56          ' display titles written by each author, grouped by author
57          For Each author In titlesByAuthor
58             ' display authors
59             outputTextBox.AppendText(
60                String.Format("{0}{1}{2}:", vbCrLf, vbTab, author.Name))
61
62             ' display titles written by that author
63             For Each title In author.Titles
64                outputTextBox.AppendText(
65                   String.Format("{0}{1}{1}{2}", vbCrLf, vbTab, title))
66             Next title
67          Next author
68       End Sub ' JoningTableData_Load
69    End Class ' JoiningTableData
```

Fig. 12.25 | Getting a list of titles grouped by authors.

Notice the duplicate `Title` identifier in the expression `book.Title.Title` used in the inner `Order By` and `Select` clauses (lines 50–51). This is due to the database having a `Title` column in the `Titles` table, and is another example of following foreign-key relationships. The range variable `book` iterates over the rows of the `AuthorISBN` for the current author's books. Each book's `Title` property contains the corresponding row from the `Titles` table for that book. The second `Title` in the expression returns the `Title` column (the title of the book) from that row of the `Titles`.

12.8 Creating a Master/Detail View Application

Figure 12.26 demonstrates a so-called **master/detail view**—one part of the GUI (the master) allows you to select an entry, and another part (the details) displays detailed information about that entry. In this example, if you select an author from the **Author:** ComboBox, the application displays the details of the books written by that author (Fig. 12.26(b)). If you select a book title from the **Title:** ComboBox, the application displays the co-authors of that book (Fig. 12.26(c)).

a) **Master/Detail** application when it begins execution before an author or title is selected; no results are displayed in the DataGridView until the user makes a selection from one of the ComboBoxes

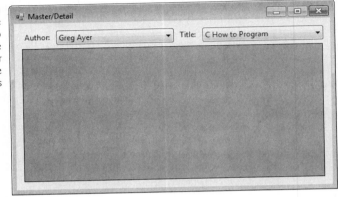

b) Select **Harvey Deitel** from the **Author:** drop-down list to view books he's co-authored

c) Select **C++ How to Program** from the **Title:** drop-down to view the authors who wrote that book

Fig. 12.26 | **Master/Detail** application.

12.8.1 Creating the Master/Detail GUI

You've seen that the IDE can automatically generate the `BindingSource`, `BindingNavi-gator` and GUI elements when you drag a data source onto the `Form`. While this works for simple applications, those with more complex operations involve writing more substantial amounts of code. Before explaining the code, we list the steps required to create the GUI.

Step 1: Creating the Project
Create a new **Windows Forms Application** called `MasterDetail`. Name the source file `Details.vb` and set the `Form`'s `Text` property to **Master/Detail**.

Step 2: Creating LINQ to SQL Classes
Follow the instructions in Section 12.5.1 to add the `Books` database and create the LINQ to SQL classes to interact with the database.

Step 3: Creating GUI Elements
Add two `Label`s and two `ComboBox`es to the top of the `Form`. Position them as shown in Fig. 12.27. The `Label` and `ComboBox` on the left should be named `authorLabel` and `authorComboBox`, respectively. The `Label` and `ComboBox` on the right should be named `titleLabel` and `titleComboBox`. Set the `Text` properties of the `Label`s to `Author:` and `Title:`, respectively. Also change the `DropDownStyle` properties of the `ComboBox`es from `DropDown` to `DropDownList`—this prevents the user from being able to type in the control.

Fig. 12.27 | Finished design of **Master/Detail** application.

Next, create a `DataGridView` called `booksDataGridView` to hold the details that are displayed. Unlike previous examples, do not automatically create it by dragging a data source from the **Data Sources** window—this example sets the data source programmatically. Instead, drag the `DataGridView` from the **Toolbox**. Resize the `DataGridView` so that it fills the remainder of the Form. Because this control is only for *viewing* data, set its Read-Only property to True using the **Properties** window.

Finally, we need to add two `BindingSources` from the **Data** section of the **Toolbox**, one for information from the `Titles` table and one for information from the `Authors` table. Name these `titleBindingSource` and `authorBindingSource`, respectively. As in the previous examples, these appear in the component tray. These `BindingSources` are used as data sources for the `DataGridView`—the data source switches between them, depending on whether we want to view a list of `Titles` or a list of `Authors`. With the GUI creation complete, we can now write the code to provide the master/detail functionality.

12.8.2 Coding the Master/Detail Application

Nested Class `AuthorBinding`

As you saw in Fig. 12.26, the **Author:** ComboBox displays each author's full name. This example uses data binding to display the names in the ComboBox. When you bind a collection of objects to a ComboBox's DataSource property, the ComboBox normally displays the result of calling ToString on each object in the collection. If the String representation is not appropriate, you can specify *one* property of each object in the collection that should be displayed. In this example, we want to display each author's first and last name.

Recall that the author's name is stored as *two* separate fields in the database, so the auto-generated Author class does not have single property that returns the full name. For this reason, we use a class called AuthorBinding (Fig. 12.28, lines 8–11) to help display the author's full name. Class AuthorBinding's Name property stores an author's full name, and the Author property stores the Author object that contains the author's information from the database. Class AuthorBinding is intended for use only in this example, so we defined it inside class Details—it's a so-called **nested class**. Class definitions may be nested inside other classes when they're intended to be used only by their enclosing classes—that is, they're not meant for use by other programs.

```
 1    ' Fig. 12.28: Details.vb
 2    ' Using a DataGridView to display details based on a selection.
 3    Public Class Details
 4        Private database As New BooksDataContext() ' connection to database
 5
 6        ' this class helps us display each author's first
 7        ' and last name in the authors drop-down list
 8        Private Class AuthorBinding
 9            Public Property Author As Author ' contained Author object
10            Public Property Name As String ' author's full name
11        End Class ' AuthorBinding
12
```

Fig. 12.28 | Nested class AuthorBinding in class Details.

Configuring the Data Sources

The ComboBox's **DisplayMember** property is set to the String "Name" (Fig. 12.29, line 17), which tells the ComboBox to use the Name property of the objects in its DataSource to determine what text to display for each item. The `DataSource` in this case is the result of the LINQ query in lines 21–27, which creates an `AuthorBinding` object for each author. The `authorComboBox` will contain the `Name` of each author in the query result. Recall from Section 9.8 that object initializers (like lines 23–27) can initialize an object without explicitly calling a constructor.

```
13        ' initialize data sources when the Form is loaded
14        Private Sub Details_Load(ByVal sender As System.Object,
15           ByVal e As System.EventArgs) Handles MyBase.Load
16
17           authorComboBox.DisplayMember = "Name" ' display AuthorBinding.Name
18
19           ' set the authorComboBox's DataSource to the list of authors
20           authorComboBox.DataSource =
21              From author In database.Authors
22              Order By author.LastName, author.FirstName
23              Select New AuthorBinding With
24              {
25                 .Author = author,
26                 .Name = author.FirstName & " " & author.LastName
27              }
28
29           titleComboBox.DisplayMember = "Title" ' display Title.Title
30
31           ' set the titleComboBox's DataSource to the list of titles
32           titleComboBox.DataSource =
33              From title In database.Titles
34              Order By title.Title
35              Select title
36
37           booksDataGridView.DataSource = Nothing ' initially, display no data
38        End Sub ' Details_Load
39
```

Fig. 12.29 | Configuring the `ComboBox`es' and `DataGridView`'s data sources.

For the `titleComboBox`, we specify that each book's `Title` should be displayed (line 29). The LINQ query in lines 33–35 returns a sorted list of `Title` objects and assigns it to the `titleComboBox`'s `DataSource`.

Initially, we don't want to display any data in the `DataGridView`. However, when you set a `ComboBox`'s `DataSource`, the control's `SelectedIndexChanged` event handler is called. To prevent this when the program first loads, we explicitly set the `DataGridView`'s `DataSource` property to `Nothing` (line 37).

The BindingSource of a DataGridView
Simple GUI elements like `ComboBox`es can work directly from a data source, such as the result of a LINQ to SQL query. However, a `DataGridView` requires a `BindingSource` as its `DataSource`. While building the GUI, you created two `BindingSource` objects—one for displaying a list of `Authors` and one for displaying a list of `Titles`. You can change the columns and data displayed in the `DataGridView` merely by changing its `DataSource` be-

tween the two BindingSource objects. The DataGridView automatically determines the column names it needs to display from its BindingSource and refreshes itself when the BindingSource changes.

Method *authorComboBox_SelectedIndexChanged*

The authorComboBox_SelectedIndexChanged event handler (Fig. 12.30, 41–57) performs three distinct operations. First, it retrieves the selected Author (lines 46–47) from the authorComboBox. The ComboBox's SelectedItem property returns an Object, so we convert the SelectedItem property's value to the type AuthorBinding—recall that the ComboBox's DataSource was set to a collection of AuthorBinding objects. Then, the event handler accesses the AuthorBinding's Author property to retrieve the wrapped Author object.

```vb
40      ' display titles that were co-authored by the selected author
41      Private Sub authorComboBox_SelectedIndexChanged(
42         ByVal sender As System.Object, ByVal e As System.EventArgs) _
43         Handles authorComboBox.SelectedIndexChanged
44
45         ' get the selected Author object from the ComboBox
46         Dim currentAuthor =
47            CType(authorComboBox.SelectedItem, AuthorBinding).Author
48
49         ' set the titleBindingSource's DataSource to the
50         ' list of titles written by the selected author
51         titleBindingSource.DataSource =
52            From book In currentAuthor.AuthorISBNs
53            Select book.Title
54
55         ' display the titles in the DataGridView
56         booksDataGridView.DataSource = titleBindingSource
57      End Sub ' authorComboBox_SelectedIndexChanged
58
```

Fig. 12.30 | Displaying the books for the selected author.

Next, the event handler uses LINQ to retrieve the Title objects representing books that the currentAuthor worked on (lines 52–53). The results of the LINQ query are assigned to the DataSource property of titleBindingSource (line 51). The event handler sets the titleBindingSource because we want to display Title objects associated with the currentAuthor. Finally, the DataGridView's DataSource is assigned titleBindingSource to display the books this author wrote (line 56).

Method *titleComboBox_SelectedIndexChanged*

The titleComboBox_SelectedIndexChanged event handler (60–75) is nearly identical to authorComboBox_SelectedIndexChanged. Line 65 gets the selected Title from the ComboBox. Lines 69–71 set the authorsBindingSource's DataSource to the list of Authors for the current book. Finally, the DataGridView's DataSource is assigned authorBindingSource to display the authors who wrote this book (line 74).

```
59        ' display the authors of the selected title
60        Private Sub titleComboBox_SelectedIndexChanged(
61           ByVal sender As System.Object, ByVal e As System.EventArgs) _
62           Handles titleComboBox.SelectedIndexChanged
63
64           ' get the selected Title object from the ComboBox
65           Dim currentTitle = CType(titleComboBox.SelectedItem, Title)
66
67           ' set the authorBindingSource's DataSource to the
68           ' list of authors for the selected title
69           authorBindingSource.DataSource =
70              From book In currentTitle.AuthorISBNs
71              Select book.Author
72
73           ' display the authors in the DataGridView
74           booksDataGridView.DataSource = authorBindingSource
75        End Sub ' titleComboBox_SelectedIndexChanged
76     End Class ' Details
```

Fig. 12.31 | Displaying the authors of the selected book.

12.9 Address Book Case Study

Our next example (Fig. 12.32) implements a simple AddressBook application that enables users to perform the following tasks on the database AddressBook.mdf (which is included in the directory with this chapter's examples):

- Insert new contacts
- Find contacts whose last names begin with the specified letters
- Update existing contacts
- Delete contacts

We populated the database with six fictional contacts.

a) Use the BindingNavigator's controls at the top of the window to navigate through the contacts in the database; initially there are six contacts in the database

Fig. 12.32 | Manipulating an address book. (Part 1 of 2.)

b) Type a search `String` in the **Last Name:** TextBox then press **Find** to locate contacts whose last names begin with that `String`; only two names start with "Br" so the BindingNavigator indicates two matching records

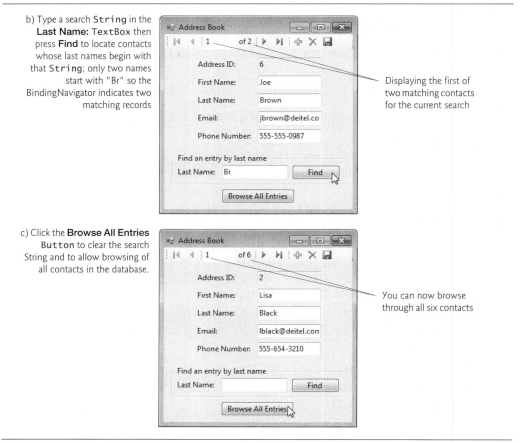

Displaying the first of two matching contacts for the current search

c) Click the **Browse All Entries** Button to clear the search String and to allow browsing of all contacts in the database.

You can now browse through all six contacts

Fig. 12.32 | Manipulating an address book. (Part 2 of 2.)

Rather than displaying a database table in a `DataGridView`, this application presents the details of one contact at a time in several `TextBox`es. The `BindingNavigator` at the top of the window allows you to control which *row* of the table is displayed at any given time. The `BindingNavigator` also allows you to add a contact, delete a contact and save changes to a contact. When you run the application, experiment with the `BindingNavigator`'s controls. The CD- or DVD-like buttons of the `BindingNavigator` allow you to change the currently displayed row. Adding a row clears the `TextBox`es and sets the `TextBox` to the right of **Address ID** to zero. When you save a new entry, the **Address ID** field is automatically changed from zero to a unique number by the database.

Recall from Section 12.5 that to allow changes to the database to *persist* between executions of the application, you can run the program in release mode (*Ctrl + F5*).

12.9.1 Creating the Address Book Application's GUI

We discuss the application's code momentarily. First we show the steps to create this application.

Step 1: Creating the Project

Create a new **Windows Forms Application** named AddressBook. Rename the Form AddressBook and its source file Contacts.vb, then set the Form's **Text** property to Address Book.

Step 2: Creating LINQ to SQL Classes and Data Source

Follow the instructions in Section 12.5.1 to add a database to the project and generate the LINQ to SQL classes. For this example, add the AddressBook database and name the file AddressBook.dbml. You must also add the Addresses table as a data source, as we did with the Authors table in *Step 1* of Section 12.5.2.

Step 3: Displaying the Details of Each Row

In the earlier sections, you dragged an object from the **Data Sources** window to the Form to create a DataGridView that was bound to the data in that object. The IDE allows you to specify the type of control(s) that it will create when you drag and drop an object from the **Data Sources** window onto a Form. In **Design** view, click the Addresses node in the **Data Sources** window. Note that this becomes a drop-down list when you select it. Click the down arrow to view the items in the list. The item to the left of **DataGridView** is initially highlighted in blue, because the default control that's bound to a table is a DataGridView. Select the **Details** option (Fig. 12.33) in the drop-down list to indicate that the IDE should create a set of Label/TextBox pairs for each column-name/column-value pair when you drag and drop Address onto the Form.

Fig. 12.33 | Specifying that an Address should be displayed as a set of Labels and TextBoxes.

Step 4: Dragging the **Address** Data-Source Node to the **Form**

Drag the Address node from the **Data Sources** window to the Form. This automatically creates a BindingNavigator and the Labels and TextBoxes corresponding to the columns of the database table. The fields may be placed out of order, with the Email at the top. Reorder the components, using **Design** view, so they're in the proper order shown in Fig. 12.32.

Step 5: Making the **AddressID TextBox ReadOnly**

The AddressID column of the Addresses table is an autoincremented identity column, so users should not be allowed to edit the values in this column. Select the TextBox for the AddressID and set its ReadOnly property to True using the **Properties** window.

Step 6: Adding Controls to Allow Users to Specify a Last Name to Locate

While the BindingNavigator allows you to browse the address book, it would be more convenient to be able to find a specific entry by last name. To add this functionality to the application, we must create controls to allow the user to enter a last name and provide event handlers to perform the search.

Add a Label named findLabel, a TextBox named findTextBox, and a Button named findButton. Place these controls in a GroupBox named findGroupBox, then set its Text property to **Find an entry by last name**. Set the Text property of the Label to Last Name: and set the Text property of the Button to Find.

Step 7: Allowing the User to Return to Browsing All Rows of the Database

To allow users to return to browsing all the contacts after searching for contacts with a specific last name, add a Button named browseAllButton below the findGroupBox. Set the Text property of browseAllButton to **Browse All Entries**.

12.9.2 Coding the Address Book Application

Method RefreshContacts

As we showed in previous examples, we must connect the AddressBindingSource that controls the GUI with the AddressBookDataContext that interacts with the database. In this example, we do this in the RefreshContacts method (Fig. 12.34, lines 8–17), which is called from several other methods in the application. Method RefreshContacts sets the AddressBindingSource's DataSource property to the result of a LINQ query on the Addresses table. We created a Private method in this example, because there are three locations in the program where we need to update the AddressBindingSource's DataSource property.

```
 1   ' Fig. 12.34: Contacts.vb
 2   ' Manipulating an address book.
 3   Public Class Contacts
 4       ' LINQ to SQL data context
 5       Private database As New AddressBookDataContext()
 6
 7       ' fill the AddressBindingSource with all rows, ordered by name
 8       Private Sub RefreshContacts()
 9           ' use LINQ to create a data source from the database
10           AddressBindingSource.DataSource =
11               From address In database.Addresses
12               Order By address.LastName, address.FirstName
13               Select address
14
15           AddressBindingSource.MoveFirst() ' go to the first result
16           findTextBox.Clear() ' clear the Find TextBox
17       End Sub ' RefreshContacts
18
```

Fig. 12.34 | Creating the BooksDataContext and defining method RefreshContacts for use in other methods.

Method Contacts_Load

Method Contacts_Load (Fig. 12.35) calls RefreshContacts (line 23) so that the first record is displayed when the application starts. As before, you create the Load event handler by double clicking the Form's title bar.

```
19      ' when the form loads, fill it with data from the database
20      Private Sub Contacts_Load(ByVal sender As System.Object,
21         ByVal e As System.EventArgs) Handles MyBase.Load
22
23         RefreshContacts() ' fill binding with data from database
24      End Sub ' Contacts_Load
25
```

Fig. 12.35 | Calling RefreshContacts to fill the DataGridView when the application loads.

Method *AddressBindingNavigatorSaveItem_Click*

Method AddressBindingNavigatorSaveItem_Click (Fig. 12.36) saves the changes to the database when the BindingNavigator's save Button is clicked. We call RefreshContacts after saving to re-sort the data and move back to the first element.

```
26      ' save the changes made to the data
27      Private Sub AddressBindingNavigatorSaveItem_Click(
28         ByVal sender As System.Object, ByVal e As System.EventArgs) _
29         Handles AddressBindingNavigatorSaveItem.Click
30
31         Validate() ' validate input fields
32         AddressBindingSource.EndEdit() ' indicate edits are complete
33         database.SubmitChanges() ' write changes to database file
34
35         RefreshContacts() ' change back to initial unfiltered data on save
36      End Sub ' AddressBindingNavigatorSaveItem_Click
37
```

Fig. 12.36 | Saving changes to the database when the user clicks the **Save Data** Button.

The AddressBook database is configured to require values for the first name, last name, phone number or e-mail. We have not checked for errors to simplify the code—if any of the fields are empty when you attempt to save, a SqlException exception (namespace System.Data.SqlClient) will be thrown.

Method *findButton_Click*

Method findButton_Click (Fig. 12.37) uses LINQ to select only people whose last names start with the characters entered in the findTextBox. The query sorts the results by last name then first name (lines 45–48). When you enter a last name and click **Find**, the BindingNavigator allows the user to browse only the rows containing the matching last names. This is because the data source bound to the Form's controls (the result of the LINQ query) has changed and now contains only a limited number of rows.

```
38      ' load data for the rows with the specified
39      ' last name into the AddressBindingSource
40      Private Sub findButton_Click(ByVal sender As System.Object,
41         ByVal e As System.EventArgs) Handles findButton.Click
```

Fig. 12.37 | Finding the contacts whose last names begin with a specified String. (Part 1 of 2.)

```
42
43            ' use LINQ to find people with the specified last name
44            AddressBindingSource.DataSource =
45                From address In database.Addresses
46                Where address.LastName.StartsWith(findTextBox.Text)
47                Order By address.LastName, address.FirstName
48                Select address
49
50            AddressBindingSource.MoveFirst() ' go to first result
51        End Sub ' findButton_Click
52
```

Fig. 12.37 | Finding the contacts whose last names begin with a specified `String`. (Part 2 of 2.)

Method browseAllButton_Click

Method `browseAllButton_Click` (Fig. 12.38) allows users to return to browsing all the rows after searching for specific rows. Double click `browseAllButton` to create a `Click` event handler. Have the event handler call `RefreshContacts` (line 57) to restore the data source to the full list of people and clear the `findTextBox`.

```
53        ' reload AddressBindingSource with all rows
54        Private Sub browseAllButton_Click(ByVal sender As System.Object,
55            ByVal e As System.EventArgs) Handles browseAllButton.Click
56
57            RefreshContacts() ' change back to initial unfiltered data
58        End Sub ' browseAllButton_Click
59    End Class ' Contacts
```

Fig. 12.38 | Allowing the user to browse all contacts.

12.10 Tools and Web Resources

Our extensive LINQ Resource Center at `www.deitel.com/LINQ` contains many links to additional information, including blogs by Microsoft LINQ team members, sample chapters, tutorials, videos, downloads, FAQs, forums, webcasts and other resource sites.

A useful tool for learning LINQ is LINQPad (`www.linqpad.net`), which allows you to execute and view the results of any Visual Basic or C# expression, including LINQ queries. It also supports connecting to a SQL Server database and querying it using SQL and LINQ to SQL.

12.11 Wrap-Up

This chapter introduced the relational database model, LINQ to SQL and the IDE's visual programming tools for working with databases. You examined the contents of a simple `Books` database and learned about the relationships among the tables in the database. You used LINQ and the LINQ to SQL classes generated by the IDE to retrieve data from, add new data to, delete data from and update data in a SQL Server Express database.

We discussed the LINQ to SQL classes automatically generated by the IDE, such as the `DataContext` class that controls interactions with the database. You learned how to use the IDE's tools to connect to databases and to generate LINQ to SQL classes based on a database's schema. You then used the IDE's drag-and-drop capabilities to automatically generate GUIs for displaying and manipulating database data.

In the next chapter, we demonstrate how to build web applications using Microsoft's ASP.NET technology. We introduce the concept of a three-tier application, which is divided into three pieces that can reside on the same computer or be distributed among separate computers across a network such as the Internet. One of these tiers—the information tier—typically stores data in a database.

Summary

Section 12.1 Introduction

- A database is an organized collection of data.
- A database management system (DBMS) provides mechanisms for storing, organizing, retrieving and modifying data.
- SQL Server Express provides most of the features of Microsoft's full (fee-based) SQL Server product, but has some limitations, such as a maximum database size of 4 gigabytes and allowing only one application at a time to interact with a database.
- A SQL Server Express database can be easily migrated to a full version of SQL Server.
- LINQ to SQL allows you to manipulate relational data stored in a SQL Server or SQL Server Express database.

Section 12.2 Relational Databases

- A relational database organizes data simply in tables.
- Tables are composed of rows and columns (also called fields) in which values are stored.
- A column (or group of columns) of each row is the table's primary key—a column (or group of columns) requiring a unique value that cannot be duplicated in other rows. This guarantees that a primary key value can be used to uniquely identify a row.
- A primary key composed of two or more columns is known as a composite key.
- Each column represents a different data attribute.
- Rows are unique (by primary key) within a table, but some column values may be duplicated between rows.

Section 12.3 A Books Database

- A database's tables, their fields and the relationships between them are collectively known as a database schema.
- LINQ to SQL uses a database's schema to define classes that enable you to interact with the database.
- A foreign key is a column in one table that matches the primary-key column in another table.
- Foreign keys, which are specified when a database table is created, link the data in multiple tables.
- Every foreign-key value must appear as another table's primary-key value so the DBMS can ensure that the foreign-key value is valid.
- Foreign keys also allow related data in multiple tables to be selected from those tables—this is known as joining the data.

- There's a one-to-many relationship between a primary key and a corresponding foreign key—a foreign key can appear many times in its own table but only once (as the primary key) in another table.
- An entity-relationship (ER) diagram shows the tables in a database and their relationships.
- Every row must have a value in the primary-key column, and the value of the key must be unique in the table.

Section 12.4 LINQ to SQL

- LINQ to SQL enables you to access data in SQL Server databases using LINQ syntax.
- You interact with LINQ to SQL via classes that are automatically generated by the IDE's LINQ to SQL Designer based on the database schema.
- LINQ to SQL requires every table to have a primary key to support modifying the data in the tables.
- The IDE creates a class for each table. Objects of these classes represent the collections of rows in the corresponding tables.
- The IDE also creates a class for a row of each table with a property for each column in the table. Objects of these classes (row objects) hold the data from individual rows in the database's tables.
- In the class for a row object, an additional property is created for each foreign key. This property returns the row object of the corresponding primary key in another table.
- In the class for a row object, an additional property is created for the collection of row objects with foreign-keys that reference the row object's primary key.
- Once generated, the LINQ to SQL classes have full *IntelliSense* support in the IDE.

Section 12.5 Querying a Database with LINQ

- The IDE provides visual programming tools and wizards that simplify accessing data in your projects. These tools establish database connections and create the objects necessary to view and manipulate the data through the GUI—a technique known as data binding.
- A DataGridView (namespace System.Windows.Forms) displays data from a data source in tabular format.
- A BindingNavigator is a collection of controls that allow you to navigate through the records displayed in a GUI. The BindingNavigator controls also allow you to add records, delete records and save your changes to the database.

Section 12.5.1 Creating LINQ to SQL Classes

- To interact with a database, you must create a connection to the database.
- In Visual Basic 2010 Express, use the **Database Explorer** window to connect to the database. In full versions of Visual Studio 2010, use the **Server Explorer** window.
- After connecting to the database, you can generate the LINQ to SQL classes by adding a new **LINQ to SQL Classes** item to your project, then dragging the tables you wish to use from the **Database Explorer** onto the **Object Relational Designer**. When you save the .dbml file, the IDE generates the LINQ to SQL classes.

Section 12.5.2 Data Bindings Between Controls and the LINQ to SQL Classes

- To use the LINQ to SQL classes for data binding, you must first add them as a data source.
- Select **Data > Add New Data Source...** to display the **Data Source Configuration Wizard**. Use an **Object** data source. Select the LINQ to SQL object that you wish to use as a data source. You can

now drag that data source from the **Data Sources** window onto the Form to create a GUI control that can display the table's data.

- By default, the IDE creates a DataGridView with the correct column names and a BindingNavigator that contains Buttons for moving between entries, adding entries, deleting entries and saving changes to the database.

- The IDE also generates a BindingSource, which handles the transfer of data between the data source and the data-bound controls on the Form.

- The result of a LINQ query on the DataContext can be assigned to the BindingSource's DataSource property. The BindingSource uses the DataSource to extract data from the database and to populate the DataGridView.

- To save the user's changes to the data in the DataGridView, enable the BindingNavigator's **Save Data** Button (🖫). Then, double click the icon to create its Click event handler. In the event handler, you must validate the data, call EndEdit on the BindingSource to save pending changes in the DataContext, and call SubmitChanges on the DataContext to store the changes in the database. For efficiency, LINQ to SQL saves only data that has changed.

Section 12.6 Dynamically Binding Query Results
- The IDE displays smart tag menus for many GUI controls to provide you with quick access to common properties you might set for a control, so you can set these properties directly in **Design** view. You can open a control's smart tag menu by clicking the small arrowhead (▶) that appears in the control's upper-right corner in **Design** view.

- The MoveFirst method of the BindingSource moves to the first row of the result.

Section 12.7 Retrieving Data from Multiple Tables with LINQ
- To join data from multiple tables you use the properties that LINQ to SQL creates based on foreign-key relationships between the database's tables. These properties enable you to easily access related rows in other tables.

- The Let query operator allows you to declare a new variable in a query—usually to create a shorter name for an expression. The variable can be accessed in later clauses just like a range variable.

- Most queries return result with data arranged in relational-style rows and columns. With LINQ to SQL you can create queries that return hierarchical results in which each item in the result contains a collection of other items.

Section 12.8 Creating a Master/Detail View Application
- In a master/detail view, one part of the GUI (the master) allows you to select an entry, and another part (the details) displays detailed information about that entry.

- Class definitions may be nested inside other classes.

- A ComboBox's DisplayMember property indicates which property to display in the ComboBox from each object in its DataSource.

- You can change the columns and data displayed in a DataGridView by changing its DataSource. The DataGridView automatically determines the column names it needs to display from the BindingSource.

Section 12.9 Address Book Case Study
- The IDE allows you to specify the type of control(s) that it creates when you drag and drop a data-source member onto a Form. The **Details** option indicates that the IDE should create a set of Label/TextBox pairs for each column-name/column-value pair in the data source.

Terminology

Add Connection dialog 411
autoincremented database column 406
BindingNavigator class 415
BindingSource class 415
Choose Data Source dialog 411
column of a database table 405
connection to a database 411
composite key 405
data binding 410
Data Source Configuration Wizard 414
Data Sources window 415
database 404
Database Explorer window 411
database management system (DBMS) 404
database schema 406
DataContext class 410
DataGridView class 410
DataSource property of class
    BindingSource 417
DisplayMember property of the ComboBox
    control 428
EndEdit method of class BindingSource 417
entity-relationship (ER) diagram 408

field in a database table 405
foreign key 407
identity column in a database table 406
IQueryable interface 410
joining database tables 408
Let query operator (LINQ) 424
LINQ to SQL 404
LINQ to SQL Designer 409
many-to-many relationship 409
master/detail view 425
Microsoft SQL Server Express 404
MoveFirst method of class BindingSource 419
nested class 428
Object data source 414
Object Relational Designer window 413
one-to-many relationship 408
primary key 405
relational database 405
row object 409
row of a database table 405
smart tag menu 419
SubmitChanges method of a DataContext 417
table in a database 405

Self-Review Exercises

12.1 Fill in the blanks in each of the following statements:
a) A table in a relational database consists of _____ and _____ in which values are stored.
b) The _____ uniquely identifies each row in a relational database table.
c) A relational database can be manipulated in LINQ to SQL via a(n) _____ object, which contains properties for accessing each table in the database.
d) The _____ control (presented in this chapter) displays data in rows and columns that correspond to the rows and columns of a data source.
e) Merging data from multiple relational database tables is called _____ the data.
f) A(n) _____ is a column (or group of columns) in a relational database table that matches the primary-key column (or group of columns) in another table.
g) A(n) _____ object serves as an intermediary between a data source and its corresponding data-bound GUI control.
h) The _____ property of a control specifies where it gets the data it displays.
i) The _____ clause declares a new temporary variable within a LINQ query.

12.2 State whether each of the following is *true* or *false*. If *false*, explain why.
a) Providing the same value for a foreign key in multiple rows causes the DBMS to report an error.
b) Providing a foreign-key value that does not appear as a primary-key value in another table is an error.
c) The result of a query can be sorted in ascending or descending order.
d) A BindingNavigator object can extract data from a database.
e) LINQ to SQL automatically saves changes made back to the database.

Answers to Self-Review Exercises

12.1 a) rows, columns. b) primary key. c) `DataContext`. d) `DataGridView`. e) joining. f) foreign key. g) `BindingSource`. h) `DataSource`. i) `Let`.

12.2 a) False. Multiple rows can have the same value for a foreign key. Providing the same value for the primary key in multiple rows causes the DBMS to report an error, because duplicate primary keys would prevent each row from being identified uniquely. b) True. c) True. d) False. A `BindingNavigator` allows users to browse and manipulate data displayed by another GUI control. A `DataContext` can extract data from a database. e) False. You must call the `SubmitChanges` method of the `DataContext` to save the changes made back to the database.

Exercises

12.3 *(Display Authors Table Application Modification)* Modify the **DisplayTable** application in Section 12.5 to contain a `TextBox` and a `Button` that allow the user to search for specific authors by last name. Include a `Label` to identify the `TextBox`. Using the techniques presented in Section 12.9, create a LINQ query that changes the `DataSource` property of `AuthorBindingSource` to contain only the specified authors.

12.4 *(Display Query Results Application Modification)* Modify the **Display Query Results** application in Section 12.6 to contain a `TextBox` and a `Button` that allow the user to perform a search of the book titles in the `Titles` table of the `Books` database. Use a `Label` to identify the `TextBox`. When the user clicks the `Button`, the application should execute and display the result of a query that selects all the rows in which the search term entered by the user in the `TextBox` appears anywhere in the `Title` column. For example, if the user enters the search term "Visual," the `DataGridView` should display the rows for *Simply Visual Basic 2008*, *Visual Basic 2008 How to Program*, *Visual C# 2008 How to Program* and *Visual C++ 2008 How to Program*. If the user enters "Simply," the `DataGridView` should display only the row for *Simply Visual Basic 2008*. [*Hint:* Use the `Contains` method of the `String` class.]

12.5 *(Baseball Database Application)* Build an application that executes a query against the `Players` table of the `Baseball` database included in the `Databases` folder with this chapter's examples. Display the table in a `DataGridView`, and add a `TextBox` and `Button` to allow the user to search for a specific player by last name. Use a `Label` to identify the `TextBox`. Clicking the `Button` should execute the appropriate query.

12.6 *(Baseball Database Application Modification)* Modify Exercise 12.5 to allow the user to locate players with batting averages in a specific range. Add a `minimumTextBox` for the minimum batting average (0.000 by default) and a `maximumTextBox` for the maximum batting average (1.000 by default). Use a `Label` to identify each `TextBox`. Add a `Button` for executing a query that selects rows from the `Players` table in which the `BattingAverage` column is greater than or equal to the specified minimum value and less than or equal to the specified maximum value.

12.7 *(Project: AdventureWorks Sample Database)* In this exercise, use Microsoft's sample `AdventureWorks` database. There are several versions available, depending on what version of SQL Server you're using and your operating system. We used the `AdventureWorks` LT version of the database—a smaller version with fewer tables and less data than the full version. The files for SQL Server 2008 can be downloaded from

`msftdbprodsamples.codeplex.com/Release/ProjectReleases.aspx?ReleaseId=24854`

The installer allows you to select which version of the database to install.

Use the `AdventureWorks` database in an application that runs multiple queries on the database and displays the results. First, it should list customers and their addresses. As this is a large list, limit the number of results to ten. [*Hint:* Use LINQ's `Take` clause at the end of the query to return a limited number of results. The `Take` clause consists of the `Take` operator, then an `Integer` specifying how many rows to take.] Second, if a category has subcategories, the output should show the category with its subcategories indented below it. The queries described here require the `Adventure-Works` tables `Address`, `Customer`, `CustomerAddress` and `ProductCategory`.

12.8 *(Project: AdventureWorks Master/Detail view)* Use the Microsoft `AdventureWorks` database from Exercise 12.7 to create a master/detail view. One master list should be customers, and the other should be products—these should show the details of products the customers purchased, and customers who purchased those products, respectively. Note that there are many customers in the database who did not order any products, and many products that no one ordered. Restrict the drop-down lists so that only customers that have submitted at least one order and products that have been included in at least one order are displayed. The queries in this exercise require the `Customer`, `Product`, `SalesOrderHeader` and `SalesOrderDetail` tables.

Web App Development with ASP.NET

13

… the challenges are for the designers of these applications: to forget what we think we know about the limitations of the Web, and begin to imagine a wider, richer range of possibilities. It's going to be fun.
—Jesse James Garrett

If any man will draw up his case, and put his name at the foot of the first page, I will give him an immediate reply. Where he compels me to turn over the sheet, he must wait my leisure.
—Lord Sandwich

Objectives

In this chapter you'll learn:

- Web application development using ASP.NET.
- To handle the events from a Web Form's controls.
- To use validation controls to ensure that data is in the correct format before it's sent from a client to the server.
- To maintain user-specific information.
- To create a data-driven web application using ASP.NET and LINQ to SQL.

13.1 Introduction

In this chapter, we introduce **web-application development** with Microsoft's **ASP.NET** technology. Web-based applications create web content for web-browser clients.

We present several examples that demonstrate web-application development using **Web Forms, web controls** (also called **ASP.NET server controls**) and Visual Basic programming. Web Form files have the file-name extension **.aspx** and contain the web page's GUI. You customize Web Forms by adding web controls including labels, textboxes, images, buttons and other GUI components. The Web Form file represents the web page that is sent to the client browser. We often refer to Web Form files as **ASPX files**.

An ASPX file created in Visual Studio has a corresponding class written in a .NET language—we use Visual Basic in this book. This class contains event handlers, initialization code, utility methods and other supporting code. The file that contains this class is called the **code-behind file** and provides the ASPX file's programmatic implementation.

To develop the code and GUIs in this chapter, we used Microsoft's **Visual Web Developer 2010 Express**—a free IDE designed for developing ASP.NET web applications. The full version of Visual Studio 2010 includes the functionality of Visual Web Developer, so the instructions we present for Visual Web Developer also apply to Visual Studio 2010. The database example (Section 13.8) also requires SQL Server 2008 Express. See the *Before You Begin* section of the book for additional information on this software.

In the online chapter, Web App Development: A Deeper Look, we present several additional web-application development topics, including:

- master pages to maintain a uniform look-and-feel across the Web Forms in a web application

- creating password-protected websites with registration and login capabilities

- using the **Web Site Administration Tool** to specify which parts of a website are password protected

- using ASP.NET AJAX to quickly and easily improve the user experience for your web applications, giving them responsiveness comparable to that of desktop applications.

13.2 Web Basics

In this section, we discuss what occurs when a user requests a web page in a browser. In its simplest form, a *web page* is nothing more than an *HTML (HyperText Markup Language) document* (with the extension .html or .htm) that describes to a web browser the document's content and how to format it.

HTML documents normally contain *hyperlinks* that link to different pages or to other parts of the same page. When the user clicks a hyperlink, a web server locates the requested web page and sends it to the user's web browser. Similarly, the user can type the *address of a web page* into the browser's *address field* and press *Enter* to view the specified page.

Web development tools like Visual Web Developer typically use a "stricter" version of HTML called *XHTML (Extensible HyperText Markup Language)*. ASP.NET produces web pages as XHTML documents.

URIs and URLs

URIs (Uniform Resource Identifiers) identify resources on the Internet. URIs that start with http:// are called *URLs (Uniform Resource Locators)*. Common URLs refer to files, directories or server-side code that performs tasks such as database lookups, Internet searches and business application processing. If you know the URL of a publicly available resource anywhere on the web, you can enter that URL into a web browser's address field and the browser can access that resource.

Parts of a URL

A URL contains information that directs a browser to the resource that the user wishes to access. Web servers make such resources available to web clients. Popular web servers include Microsoft's Internet Information Services (IIS) and Apache's HTTP Server.

Let's examine the components of the URL

```
http://www.deitel.com/books/downloads.html
```

The http:// indicates that the HyperText Transfer Protocol (HTTP) should be used to obtain the resource. HTTP is the web protocol that enables clients and servers to communicate. Next in the URL is the server's fully qualified hostname (www.deitel.com)—the name of the web server computer on which the resource resides. This computer is referred to as the host, because it houses and maintains resources. The hostname www.deitel.com is translated into an IP (Internet Protocol) address—a numerical value that uniquely identifies the server on the Internet. A Domain Name System (DNS) server maintains a database of hostnames and their corresponding IP addresses, and performs the translations automatically.

The remainder of the URL (/books/downloads.html) specifies the resource's location (/books) and name (downloads.html) on the web server. The location could represent an actual directory on the web server's file system. For *security* reasons, however, the location is typically a *virtual directory*. The web server translates the virtual directory into a real location on the server, thus hiding the resource's true location.

Making a Request and Receiving a Response
When given a URL, a web browser uses HTTP to retrieve and display the web page found at that address. Figure 13.1 shows a web browser sending a request to a web server. Figure 13.2 shows the web server responding to that request.

Fig. 13.1 | Client requesting a resource from a web server.

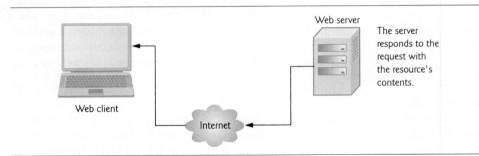

Fig. 13.2 | Client receiving a response from the web server.

13.3 Multitier Application Architecture

Web-based applications are multitier applications (sometimes referred to as *n*-tier applications). Multitier applications divide functionality into separate tiers (that is, logical groupings of functionality). Although tiers can be located on the *same* computer, the tiers of web-based applications commonly reside on *separate* computers for security and scalability. Figure 13.3 presents the basic architecture of a three-tier web-based application.

Information Tier
The information tier (also called the bottom tier) maintains the application's data. This tier typically stores data in a relational database management system. For example, a retail store might have a database for storing product information, such as descriptions, prices and quantities in stock. The same database also might contain customer information, such as user names, billing addresses and credit card numbers. This tier can contain multiple databases, which together comprise the data needed for an application.

Top tier
(Client tier)   Browser   User interface

XHTML

Middle tier
(Business logic tier)   Web server   Business logic
implemented in
ASP.NET

LINQ

Bottom tier
(Information tier)   DBMS   Database

Fig. 13.3 | Three-tier architecture.

Business Logic

The **middle tier** implements business logic, controller logic and presentation logic to control interactions between the application's clients and its data. The middle tier acts as an intermediary between data in the information tier and the application's clients. The middle-tier controller logic processes client requests (such as requests to view a product catalog) and retrieves data from the database. The middle-tier presentation logic then processes data from the information tier and presents the content to the client. Web applications typically present data to clients as web pages.

Business logic in the middle tier enforces *business rules* and ensures that data is reliable before the server application updates the database or presents the data to users. Business rules dictate how clients can and cannot access application data, and how applications process data. For example, a business rule in the middle tier of a retail store's web-based application might ensure that all product quantities remain positive. A client request to set a negative quantity in the bottom tier's product information database would be rejected by the middle tier's business logic.

Client Tier

The **client tier**, or **top tier**, is the application's user interface, which gathers input and displays output. Users interact directly with the application through the user interface (typically viewed in a web browser), keyboard and mouse. In response to user actions (for example, clicking a hyperlink), the client tier interacts with the middle tier to make requests and to retrieve data from the information tier. The client tier then displays to the user the data retrieved from the middle tier. The client tier never directly interacts with the information tier.

13.4 Your First Web Application

Our first example displays the web server's time of day in a browser window (Fig. 13.4). When this application executes—that is, a web browser requests the application's web page—the web server executes the application's code, which gets the current time and displays it in a Label. The web server then returns the result to the web browser that made the request, and the web browser renders the web page containing the time. We executed this application in both the Internet Explorer and Firefox web browsers to show you that the web page renders identically in each.

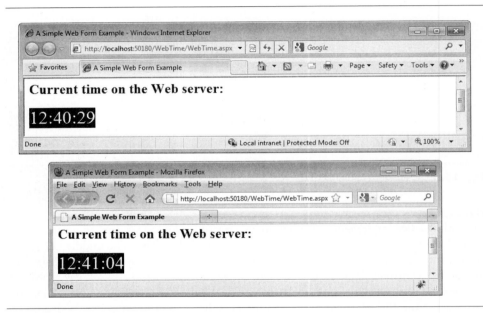

Fig. 13.4 | WebTime web application running in both Internet Explorer and Firefox.

Testing the Application in Your Default Web Browser
To test this application in your default web browser, perform the following steps:

1. Open Visual Web Developer.

2. Select **Open Web Site...** from the **File** menu.

3. In the **Open Web Site** dialog (Fig. 13.5), ensure that **File System** is selected, then navigate to this chapter's examples, select the WebTime folder and click the **Open Button**.

4. Select WebTime.aspx in the **Solution Explorer**, then type *Ctrl* + *F5* to execute the web application.

Testing the Application in a Selected Web Browser
If you wish to execute the application in another web browser, you can copy the web page's address from your default browser's address field and paste it into another browser's address field, or you can perform the following steps:

Fig. 13.5 | Open Web Site dialog.

1. In the **Solution Explorer**, right click WebTime.aspx and select **Browse With...** to display the **Browse With** dialog (Fig. 13.6).

Fig. 13.6 | Selecting another web browser to execute the web application.

2. From the **Browsers** list, select the browser in which you'd like to test the web application and click the **Browse** Button.

If the browser you wish to use is not listed, you can use the **Browse With** dialog to add items to or remove items from the list of web browsers.

13.4.1 Building the WebTime Application

Now that you've tested the application, let's create it in Visual Web Developer.

Step 1: Creating the Web Site Project

Select **File > New Web Site...** to display the **New Web Site** dialog (Fig. 13.7). In the left column of this dialog, ensure that **Visual Basic** is selected, then select **Empty Web Site** in the middle column. At the bottom of the dialog you can specify the location and name of the web application.

Fig. 13.7 | Creating an **ASP.NET Web Site** in Visual Web Developer.

The **Web location:** ComboBox provides the following options:

- **File System:** Creates a new website for testing on your local computer. Such websites execute in Visual Web Developer's built-in ASP.NET Development Server and can be accessed only by web browsers running on the same computer. You can later "publish" your website to a production web server for access via a local network or the Internet. Each example in this chapter uses the **File System** option, so select it now.

- **HTTP:** Creates a new website on an IIS web server and uses HTTP to allow you to put your website's files on the server. IIS is Microsoft's software that is used to run production websites. If you own a website and have your own web server, you might use this to build a new website directly on that server computer. You must be an Administrator on the computer running IIS to use this option.

- **FTP**: Uses File Transfer Protocol (FTP) to allow you to put your website's files on the server. The server administrator must first create the website on the server for you. FTP is commonly used by so-called "hosting providers" to allow website owners to share a server computer that runs many websites.

Change the name of the web application from WebSite1 to WebTime, then click the **OK** Button to create the website.

Step 2: Adding a Web Form to the Website and Examining the Solution Explorer

A **Web Form** represents one page in a web application—we'll often use the terms "page" and "Web Form" interchangeably. A Web Form contains a web application's GUI. To create the WebTime.aspx Web Form:

1. Right click the project name in the **Solution Explorer** and select **Add New Item...** to display the **Add New Item** dialog (Fig. 13.8).

Fig. 13.8 | Adding a new **Web Form** to the website with the **Add New Item** dialog.

2. In the left column, ensure that **Visual Basic** is selected, then select **Web Form** in the middle column.

3. In the **Name:** TextBox, change the file name to WebTime.aspx, then click the **Add** Button.

After you add the Web Form, the IDE opens it in **Source** view by default (Fig. 13.9). This view displays the markup for the Web Form. As you become more familiar with ASP.NET and building web sites in general, you might use **Source** view to perform high precision adjustments to your design or to program in the JavaScript language that executes in web browsers. For the purposes of this chapter, we'll keep things simple by working exclusively in **Design** mode. To switch to **Design** mode, you can click the **Design** Button at the bottom of the code editor window.

Source mode shows only the Web Form's markup

Split mode allows you to view the Web Form's markup and design at the same time

Design mode allows you to build a Web Form using similar techniques to building a Windows Form

Fig. 13.9 | Web Form in **Source** view.

The Solution Explorer

The **Solution Explorer** (Fig. 13.10) shows the contents of the website. We expanded the node for WebTime.aspx to show you its code-behind file WebTime.aspx.vb. Visual Web Developer's **Solution Explorer** contains several buttons that differ from Visual Basic Express. The **View Designer** button allows you to open the Web Form in **Design** mode. The **Copy Web Site** button opens a dialog that allows you to move the files in this project to another location, such as a remote web server. This is useful if you're developing the application on your local computer but want to make it available to the public from a different location. Finally, the **ASP.NET Configuration** button takes you to a web page called the **Web Site Administration Tool**, where you can manipulate various settings and security options for your application.

View Code View Designer
Nest Related Files Copy Web Site
Refresh
Properties ASP.NET Configuration
Code-behind file that contains the application's business logic ASPX page represents the application's user interface

Fig. 13.10 | **Solution Explorer** window for an **Empty Web Site** project.

If the ASPX file is not open in the IDE, you can open it in **Design** mode three ways:

- double click it in the **Solution Explorer**
- select it in the **Solution Explorer** and click the **View Designer** (🖼) `Button`
- right click it in the **Solution Explorer** and select **View Designer**

To open the code-behind file in the code editor, you can

- double click it in the **Solution Explorer**
- select the ASPX file in the **Solution Explorer**, then click the **View Code** (🖼) `Button`
- right click the code-behind file in the **Solution Explorer** and select **Open**

The Toolbox

Figure 13.11 shows the **Toolbox** displayed in the IDE when the project loads. Part (a) displays the beginning of the **Standard** list of web controls, and part (b) displays the remaining web controls and the list of other control groups. We discuss specific controls listed in Fig. 13.11 as they're used throughout the chapter. Many of the controls have similar or identical names to Windows `Forms` controls presented earlier in the book.

Fig. 13.11 | Toolbox in Visual Web Developer.

The Web Forms Designer

Figure 13.12 shows the initial Web Form in **Design** mode. You can drag and drop controls from the **Toolbox** onto the Web Form. You can also type at the current cursor location to add so-called static text to the web page. In response to such actions, the IDE generates the appropriate markup in the ASPX file.

Cursor appears here by default   Cursor's current location in the document

Fig. 13.12 | **Design** mode of the Web Forms Designer.

Step 3: Changing the Title of the Page

Before designing the Web Form's content, you'll change its title to A Simple Web Form Example. This title will be displayed in the web browser's title bar (see Fig. 13.4). It's typically also used by search engines like Google and Bing when they index real websites for searching. Every page should have a title. To change the title:

1. Ensure that the ASPX file is open in **Design** view.

2. View the Web Form's properties by selecting **DOCUMENT**, which represents the Web Form, from the drop-down list in the **Properties** window.

3. Modify the **Title** property in the **Properties** window by setting it to A Simple Web Form Example.

Designing a Page

Designing a Web Form is similar to designing a Windows Form. To add controls to the page, drag-and-drop them from the **Toolbox** onto the Web Form in **Design** view. The Web Form and each control are objects that have properties, methods and events. You can set these properties visually using the **Properties** window or programmatically in the code-behind file. You can also type text directly on a Web Form at the cursor location.

   Controls and other elements are placed sequentially on a Web Form one after another in the order in which you drag-and-drop them onto the Web Form. The cursor indicates the insertion point in the page. If you want to position a control between existing text or controls, you can drop the control at a specific position between existing page elements. You can also rearrange controls with drag-and-drop actions in **Design** view. The positions of controls and other elements are relative to the Web Form's upper-left corner. This type of layout is known as relative positioning and it allows the browser to move elements and resize them based on the size of the browser window. Relative positioning is the default, and we'll use it throughout this chapter.

   For precise control over the location and size of elements, you can use absolute positioning in which controls are located exactly where you drop them on the Web Form. If you wish to use absolute positioning:

1. Select **Tools > Options....**, to display the **Options** dialog.

2. If it isn't checked already, check the **Show all settings** checkbox.

3. Next, expand the **HTML Designer > CSS Styling** node and ensure that the checkbox labeled **Change positioning to absolute for controls added using Toolbox, paste or drag and drop** is selected.

Step 4: Adding Text and a Label

You'll now add some text and a Label to the Web Form. Perform the following steps to add the text:

1. Ensure that the Web Form is open in **Design** mode.

2. Type the following text at the current cursor location:

```
Current time on the Web server:
```

3. Select the text you just typed, then select **Heading 2** from the **Block Format** Combo-Box (Fig. 13.13) to format this text as a heading that will appear in a larger bold font. In more complex pages, headings help you specify the relative importance of parts of that content—like sections in a book chapter.

Block Format ComboBox

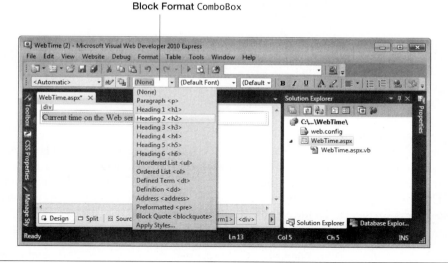

Fig. 13.13 | Changing the text to **Heading 2** heading.

4. Click to the right of the text you just typed and press the *Enter* key to start a new paragraph in the page. The Web Form should now appear as in Fig. 13.14.

5. Next, drag a Label control from the **Toolbox** into the new paragraph or double click the Label control in the **Toolbox** to insert the Label at the current cursor position.

6. Using the **Properties** window, set the Label's (ID) property to timeLabel. This specifies the variable name that will be used to programmatically change the Label's Text.

The cursor is positioned here after inserting a new paragraph by pressing *Enter*

Fig. 13.14 | WebTime.aspx after inserting text and a new paragraph.

7. Because, the Label's Text will be set programmatically, delete the current value of the Label's Text property. When a Label does not contain text, its name is displayed in square brackets in **Design** view (Fig. 13.15) as a placeholder for design and layout purposes. This text is not displayed at execution time.

Label control

Fig. 13.15 | WebTime.aspx after adding a Label.

Step 5: Formatting the Label
Formatting in a web page is performed with CSS (Cascading Style Sheets). The details of CSS are beyond the scope of this book. However, it's easy to use CSS to format text and elements in a Web Form via the tools built into Visual Web Developer. In this example, we'd like to change the Label's background color to black, its foreground color yellow and make its text size larger. To format the Label, perform the following steps:

1. Click the Label in **Design** view to ensure that it's selected.

2. Select **View > Other Windows > CSS Properties** to display the **CSS Properties** window at the left side of the IDE (Fig. 13.16).

3. Right click in the **Applied Rules** box and select **New Style...** to display the **New Style** dialog (Fig. 13.17).

4. Type the new style's name—.timeStyle—in the **Selector:** ComboBox. Styles that apply to specific elements must be named with a dot (.) preceding the name. Such a style is called a CSS class.

5. Each item you can set in the **New Style** dialog is known as a CSS attribute. To change timeLabel's foreground color, select the **Font** category from the **Category** list, then select the yellow color swatch for the **color** attribute.

6. Next, change the **font-size** attribute to xx-large.

Fig. 13.16 | CSS Properties window.

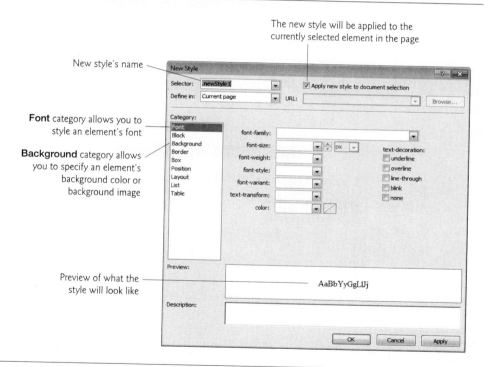

Fig. 13.17 | New Style dialog.

7. To change `timeLabel`'s background color, select the **Background** category, then select the black color swatch for the **background-color** attribute.

The **New Style** dialog should now appear as shown in (Fig. 13.18). Click the **OK Button** to apply the style to the `timeLabel` so that it appears as shown in Fig. 13.19. Also, notice that the Label's `CssClass` property is now set to `timeStyle` in the **Properties** window.

Fig. 13.18 | **New Style** dialog after changing the Label's font size, foreground color and background color.

Fig. 13.19 | **Design** view after changing the Label's style.

Step 6: Adding Page Logic

Now that you've designed the GUI, you'll write code in the code-behind file to obtain the server's time and display it on the Label. First, open WebTime.aspx.vb by double clicking its node in the **Solution Explorer**. In this example, you'll add an event handler to the code-behind file to handle the Web Form's **Init** event, which occurs when the page is first requested by a web browser. The event handler for this event—named **Page_Init**—initialize the page. The only initialization required for this example is to set the timeLabel's Text property to the time on the web server computer. To create the Page_Init event handler:

1. Select **(Page Events)** from the left ComboBox at the top of the code editor window.

2. Select **Init** from the right ComboBox at the top of the code editor window.

3. Complete the event handler by inserting the following code in the `Page_Init` event handler:

```
' display the server's current time in timeLabel
timeLabel.Text = DateTime.Now.ToString("hh:mm:ss")
```

Step 7: Setting the Start Page and Running the Program

To ensure that `WebTime.aspx` loads when you execute this application, right click it in the **Solution Explorer** and select **Set As Start Page**. You can now run the program in one of several ways. At the beginning of Fig. 13.4, you learned how to view the Web Form by typing *Ctrl + F5* to run the application. You can also right click an ASPX file in the **Solution Explorer** and select **View in Browser**. Both of these techniques execute the ASP.NET Development Server, open your default web browser and load the page into the browser, thus running the web application. The development server stops when you exit Visual Web Developer.

If problems occur when running your application, you can run it in debug mode by selecting **Debug > Start Debugging**, by clicking the **Start Debugging** Button ([▶]) or by typing *F5* to view the web page in a web browser with debugging enabled. You cannot debug a web application unless debugging is explicitly enabled in the application's `Web.config` file—a file that is generated when you create an ASP.NET web application. This file stores the application's configuration settings. You'll rarely need to manually modify `Web.config`. The first time you select **Debug > Start Debugging** in a project, a dialog appears and asks whether you want the IDE to modify the `Web.config` file to enable debugging. After you click **OK**, the IDE executes the application. You can stop debugging by selecting **Debug > Stop Debugging**.

Regardless of how you execute the web application, the IDE will compile the project before it executes. In fact, ASP.NET compiles your web page whenever it changes between HTTP requests. For example, suppose you browse the page, then modify the ASPX file or add code to the code-behind file. When you reload the page, ASP.NET recompiles the page on the server before returning the response to the browser. This important behavior ensures that clients always see the latest version of the page. You can manually compile an entire website by selecting **Build Web Site** from the **Debug** menu in Visual Web Developer.

13.4.2 Examining `WebTime.aspx`'s Code-Behind File

Figure 13.20 presents the code-behind file `WebTime.aspx.vb`. Line 3 of Fig. 13.20 begins the declaration of class `WebTime`. In Visual Basic, a class declaration can span multiple source-code files—the separate portions of the class declaration in each file are known as **partial classes**. The **Partial modifier** indicates that the code-behind file is part of a larger class. Like Windows `Forms` applications, the rest of the class's code is generated for you based on your visual interactions to create the application's GUI in **Design** mode. That code is stored in other source code files as partial classes with the same name. The compiler assembles all the partial classes that have the same into a single class declaration.

Line 4 indicates that `WebTime` inherits from class **Page** in namespace **System.Web.UI**. This namespace contains classes and controls for building web-based applications. Class `Page` represents the default capabilities of each page in a web application—all pages inherit directly or indirectly from this class.

```
 1    ' Fig. 13.20: WebTime.aspx.vb
 2    ' Code-behind file for a page that displays the current time.
 3    Partial Class WebTime
 4       Inherits System.Web.UI.Page
 5
 6       ' initializes the contents of the page
 7       Protected Sub Page_Init(ByVal sender As Object, _
 8          ByVal e As System.EventArgs) Handles Me.Init
 9
10          ' display the server's current time in timeLabel
11          timeLabel.Text = DateTime.Now.ToString("hh:mm:ss")
12       End Sub ' Page_Init
13    End Class ' WebTime
```

Fig. 13.20 | Code-behind file for a page that displays the web server's time.

Lines 7–12 define the `Page_Init` event handler, which initializes the page in response to the page's `Init` event. The only initialization required for this page is to set the time-Label's `Text` property to the time on the web server computer. The statement in line 11 retrieves the current time (`DateTime.Now`) and formats it as *hh:mm:ss*. For example, 9 AM is formatted as 09:00:00, and 2:30 PM is formatted as 02:30:00. As you'll see, variable `timeLabel` represents an ASP.NET `Label` control. The ASP.NET controls are defined in namespace `System.Web.UI.WebControls`.

13.5 Standard Web Controls: Designing a Form

This section introduces some of the web controls located in the **Standard** section of the **Toolbox** (Fig. 13.11). Figure 13.21 summarizes the controls used in the next example.

Web control	Description
TextBox	Gathers user input and displays text.
Button	Triggers an event when clicked.
HyperLink	Displays a hyperlink.
DropDownList	Displays a drop-down list of choices from which a user can select an item.
RadioButtonList	Groups radio buttons.
Image	Displays images (for example, PNG, GIF and JPG).

Fig. 13.21 | Commonly used web controls.

A Form Gathering User Input

Figure 13.22 depicts a form for gathering user input. This example does not perform any tasks—that is, no action occurs when the user clicks **Register**. As an exercise, we ask you to provide the functionality. Here we focus on the steps for adding these controls to a Web Form and for setting their properties. Subsequent examples demonstrate how to handle the events of many of these controls. To execute this application:

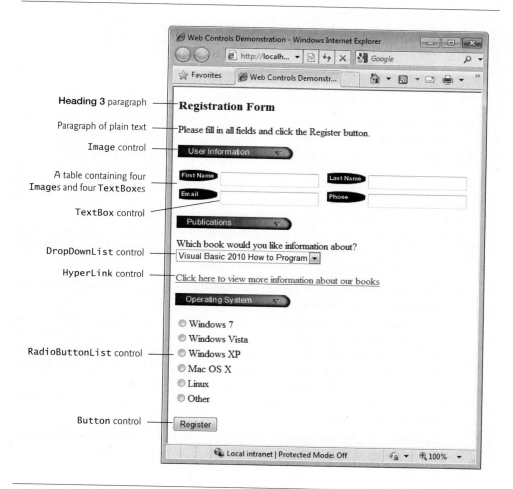

Fig. 13.22 | Web Form that demonstrates web controls.

1. Select **Open Web Site...** from the **File** menu.

2. In the **Open Web Site** dialog, ensure that **File System** is selected, then navigate to this chapter's examples, select the WebControls folder and click the **Open** Button.

3. Select WebControls.aspx in the **Solution Explorer**, then type *Ctrl + F5* to execute the web application in your default web browser.

Create the Web Site
To begin, follow the steps in Section 13.4.1 to create an **Empty Web Site** named WebControls, then add a Web Form named WebControls.aspx to the project. Set the document's Title property to "Web Controls Demonstration". To ensure that WebControls.aspx loads when you execute this application, right click it in the **Solution Explorer** and select **Set As Start Page**.

Adding the Images to the Project

The images used in this example are located in the images folder with this chapter's examples. Before you can display images in the Web Form, they must be added to your project. To add the images folder to your project:

1. Open Windows Explorer.

2. Locate and open this chapter's examples folder (ch13).

3. Drag the images folder from Windows Explorer into Visual Web Developer's **Solution Explorer** window and drop the folder on the name of your project.

The IDE will automatically copy the folder and its contents into your project.

Adding Text and an Image to the Form

Next, you'll begin creating the page. Perform the following steps:

1. First create the page's heading. At the current cursor position on the page, type the text "Registration Form", then use the **Block Format** ComboBox in the IDE's toolbar to change the text to **Heading 3** format.

2. Press *Enter* to start a new paragraph, then type the text "Please fill in all fields and click the Register button".

3. Press *Enter* to start a new paragraph, then double click the **Image** control in the Toolbox. This control inserts an image into a web page, at the current cursor position. Set the Image's (ID) property to userInformationImage. The **ImageUrl** property specifies the location of the image to display. In the **Properties** window, click the ellipsis for the ImageUrl property to display the **Select Image** dialog. Select the images folder under **Project folders:** to display the list of images. Then select the image user.png.

4. Click **OK** to display the image in **Design** view, then click to the right of the Image and press *Enter* to start a new paragraph.

Adding a Table to the Form

Form elements are often placed in tables for layout purposes—like the elements that represent the first name, last name, e-mail and phone information in Fig. 13.22. Next, you'll create a table with two rows and two columns in **Design** mode.

1. Select **Table > Insert Table** to display the **Insert Table** dialog (Fig. 13.23). This dialog allows you to configure the table's options.

2. Under **Size**, ensure that the values of **Rows** and **Columns** are both 2—these are the default values.

3. Click **OK** to close the **Insert Table** dialog and create the table.

By default, the contents of a table cell are aligned vertically in the middle of the cell. We changed the vertical alignment of all cells in the table by setting the valign property to top in the **Properties** window. This causes the content in each table cell to align with the top of the cell. You can set the valign property for each table cell individually or by selecting all the cells in the table at once, then changing the valign property's value.

Fig. 13.23 | Insert Table dialog.

After creating the table, controls and text can be added to particular cells to create a neatly organized layout. Next, add Image and TextBox controls to each the four table cells as follows:

1. Click the table cell in the first row and first column of the table, then double click the Image control in the **Toolbox**. Set its (ID) property to firstNameImage and set its ImageUrl property to the image fname.png.

2. Next, double click the TextBox control in the **Toolbox**. Set its (ID) property to firstNameTextBox. As in Windows Forms, a **TextBox** control allows you to obtain text from the user and display text to the user

3. Repeat this process in the first row and second column, but set the Image's (ID) property to lastNameImage and its ImageUrl property to the image lname.png, and set the TextBox's (ID) property to lastNameTextBox.

4. Repeat *Steps 1* and *2* in the second row and first column, but set the Image's (ID) property to emailImage and its ImageUrl property to the image email.png, and set the TextBox's (ID) property to emailTextBox.

5. Repeat *Steps 1* and *2* in the second row and second column, but set the Image's (ID) property to phoneImage and its ImageUrl property to the image phone.png, and set the TextBox's (ID) property to phoneTextBox.

Creating the Publications Section of the Page
This section contains an Image, some text, a DropDownList control and a HyperLink control. Perform the following steps to create this section:

1. Click below the table, then use the techniques you've already learned in this section to add an Image named publicationsImage that displays the publications.png image.

2. Click to the right of the Image, then press *Enter* and type the text "Which book would you like information about?" in the new paragraph.

3. Hold the *Shift* key and press *Enter* to create a new line in the current paragraph, then double click the **DropDownList** control in the **Toolbox**. Set its (ID) property to booksDropDownList. This control is similar to the Windows Forms ComboBox control, but doesn't allow users to type text. When a user clicks the drop-down list, it expands and displays a list from which the user can make a selection.

4. You can add items to the DropDownList using the **ListItem Collection Editor**, which you can access by clicking the ellipsis next to the DropDownList's Items property in the **Properties** window, or by using the **DropDownList Tasks** smart-tag menu. To open this menu, click the small arrowhead that appears in the upper-right corner of the control in **Design** mode (Fig. 13.24). Visual Web Developer displays smart-tag menus for many ASP.NET controls to facilitate common tasks. Clicking **Edit Items...** in the **DropDownList Tasks** menu opens the **ListItem Collection Editor**, which allows you to add ListItem elements to the DropDownList. Add items for "Visual Basic 2010 How to Program", "Visual C# 2008 How to Program", "Java How to Program" and "C++ How to Program" by clicking the **Add** Button four times. For each item, select it, then set its Text property to one of the four book titles.

Fig. 13.24 | **DropDownList Tasks** smart-tag menu.

5. Click to the right of the DropDownList and press *Enter* to start a new paragraph, then double click the **HyperLink** control in the **Toolbox** to add a hyperlink to the web page. Set its (ID) property to booksHyperLink and its Text property to "Click here to view more information about our books". Set the **NavigateUrl** property to http://www.deitel.com. This specifies the resource or web page that will be requested when the user clicks the HyperLink. Setting the **Target** property to _blank specifies that the requested web page should open in a new browser window. By default, HyperLink controls cause pages to open in the same browser window.

Completing the Page
Next you'll create the **Operating System** section of the page and the **Register** Button. This section contains a **RadioButtonList** control, which provides a series of radio buttons from

which the user can select only one. The **RadioButtonList Tasks** smart-tag menu provides an **Edit Items...** link to open the **ListItem Collection Editor** so that you can create the items in the list. Perform the following steps:

1. Click to the right of the HyperLink control and press *Enter* to create a new paragraph, then add an Image named osImage that displays the os.png image.

2. Click to the right of the Image and press *Enter* to create a new paragraph, then add a RadioButtonList. Set its (ID) property to osRadioButtonList. Use the **ListItem Collection Editor** to add the items shown in Fig. 13.22.

3. Finally, click to the right of the RadioButtonList and press *Enter* to create a new paragraph, then add a **Button**. A Button web control represents a button that triggers an action when clicked. Set its (ID) property to registerButton and its Text property to Register. As stated earlier, clicking the **Register** button in this example does not do anything.

You can now execute the application (*Ctrl + F5*) to see the Web Form in your browser.

13.6 Validation Controls

This section introduces a different type of web control, called a **validation control** or **validator**, which determines whether the data in another web control is in the proper format. For example, validators can determine whether a user has provided information in a required field or whether a zip-code field contains exactly five digits. Validators provide a mechanism for validating user input on the client. When the page is sent to the client, the validator is converted into JavaScript that performs the validation in the client web browser. JavaScript is a scripting language that enhances the functionality of web pages and is typically executed on the client. Unfortunately, some client browsers might not support scripting or the user might disable it. For this reason, you should always perform validation on the server. ASP.NET validation controls can function on the client, on the server or both.

Validating Input in a Web Form

The Web Form in Fig. 13.25 prompts the user to enter a name, e-mail address and phone number. A website could use a form like this to collect contact information from visitors. After the user enters any data, but before the data is sent to the web server, validators ensure that the user *entered a value in each field* and that the e-mail address and phone-number values are in an acceptable format. In this example, (555) 123-4567, 555-123-4567 and 123-4567 are all considered valid phone numbers. Once the data is submitted, the web server responds by displaying a message that repeats the submitted information. A real business application would typically store the submitted data in a database or in a file on the server. We simply send the data back to the client to demonstrate that the server received the data. To execute this application:

1. Select **Open Web Site...** from the **File** menu.

2. In the **Open Web Site** dialog, ensure that **File System** is selected, then navigate to this chapter's examples, select the Validation folder and click the **Open** Button.

3. Select Validation.aspx in the **Solution Explorer**, then type *Ctrl + F5* to execute the web application in your default web browser.

In the sample output:

- Fig. 13.25(a) shows the initial Web Form
- Fig. 13.25(b) shows the result of submitting the form before typing any data in the TextBoxes
- Fig. 13.25(c) shows the results after entering data in each TextBox, but specifying an invalid e-mail address and invalid phone number
- Fig. 13.25(d) shows the results after entering valid values for all three TextBoxes and submitting the form.

a) Initial Web Form

b) Web Form after the user presses the **Submit Button** without having entered any data in the TextBoxes; each TextBox is followed by an error message that was displayed by a validation control

RequiredFieldValidator controls

Fig. 13.25 | Validators in a Web Form that retrieves user contact information. (Part 1 of 2.)

c) Web Form after the user enters a name, an invalid e-mail address and an invalid phone number in the TextBoxes, then presses the **Submit** Button; the validation controls display error messages in response to the invalid e-mail and phone number values

RegularExpressionValidator controls

d) The Web Form after the user enters valid values for all three TextBoxes and presses the **Submit** Button

Fig. 13.25 | Validators in a Web Form that retrieves user contact information. (Part 2 of 2.)

Creating the Web Site

To begin, follow the steps in Section 13.4.1 to create an **Empty Web Site** named Valida-tion, then add a Web Form named Validation.aspx to the project. Set the document's Title property to "Demonstrating Validation Controls". To ensure that Valida-tion.aspx loads when you execute this application, right click it in the **Solution Explorer** and select **Set As Start Page**.

Creating the GUI

To create the page, perform the following steps:

1. Type "Please fill out all the fields in the following form:", then use the **Block Format** ComboBox in the IDE's toolbar to change the text to **Heading 3** format and press *Enter* to create a new paragraph.

2. Insert a three row and two column table. You'll add elements to the table momentarily.

3. Click below the table and add a Button. Set its (ID) property to submitButton and its Text property to Submit. Press *Enter* to create a new paragraph. By default, a Button control in a Web Form sends the contents of the form back to the server for processing.

4. Add a Label. Set its (ID) property to outputLabel and clear its Text property—you'll set it programmatically when the user clicks the submitButton. Set the outputLabel's Visible property to False, so the Label does not appear in the client's browser when the page loads for the first time. You'll programmatically display this Label after the user submits valid data.

Next you'll add text and controls to the table you created in *Step 2* above. Perform the following steps:

1. In the left column, type the text "Name:" in the first row, "E-mail:" in the second row and "Phone:" in the row column.

2. In the right column of the first row, add a TextBox and set its (ID) property to nameTextBox.

3. In the right column of the second row, add a TextBox and set its (ID) property to emailTextBox. Then type the text "e.g., email@domain.com" to the right of the TextBox.

4. In the right column of the third row, add a TextBox and set its (ID) property to phoneTextBox. Then type the text "e.g., (555) 555-1234" to the right of the TextBox.

Using RequiredFieldValidator Controls

We use three RequiredFieldValidator controls (found in the **Validation** section of the **Toolbox**) to ensure that the name, e-mail address and phone number TextBoxes are not empty when the form is submitted. A RequiredFieldValidator makes an input control a required field. If such a field is empty, validation fails. Add a RequiredFieldValidator as follows:

1. Click to the right of the nameTextBox in the table and press *Enter* to move to the next line.

2. Add a RequiredFieldValidator, set its (ID) to nameRequiredFieldValidator and set the ForeColor property to Red.

3. Set the validator's ControlToValidate property to nameTextBox to indicate that this validator verifies the nameTextBox's contents.

4. Set the validator's ErrorMessage property to "Please enter your name". This is displayed on the Web Form only if the validation fails.

5. Set the validator's `Display` property to `Dynamic`, so the validator occupies space on the Web Form only when validation fails. When this occurs, space is allocated dynamically, causing the controls below the validator to shift downward to accommodate the `ErrorMessage`, as seen in Fig. 13.25(a)–(c).

Repeat these steps to add two more `RequiredFieldValidator`s in the second and third rows of the table. Set their (ID) properties to `emailRequiredFieldValidator` and `phoneRequiredFieldValidator`, respectively, and set their `ErrorMessage` properties to "`Please enter your email address`" and "`Please enter your phone number`", respectively.

Using RegularExpressionValidator Controls

This example also uses two `RegularExpressionValidator` controls to ensure that the e-mail address and phone number entered by the user are in a valid format. Regular expressions are beyond the scope of this book; however, Visual Web Developer provides several *predefined* regular expressions that you can simply select to take advantage of this powerful validation control. Add a `RegularExpressionValidator` as follows:

1. Click to the right of the `emailRequiredFieldValidator` in the second row of the table and add a `RegularExpressionValidator`, then set its (ID) to `emailRegularExpressionValidator` and its `ForeColor` property to Red.

2. Set the `ControlToValidate` property to `emailTextBox` to indicate that this validator verifies the `emailTextBox`'s contents.

3. Set the validator's `ErrorMessage` property to "`Please enter an e-mail address in a valid format`".

4. Set the validator's `Display` property to `Dynamic`, so the validator occupies space on the Web Form only when validation fails.

Repeat the preceding steps to add another `RegularExpressionValidator` in the third row of the table. Set its (ID) property to `phoneRequiredFieldValidator` and its `ErrorMessage` property to "`Please enter a phone number in a valid format`", respectively.

A `RegularExpressionValidator`'s `ValidationExpression` property specifies the regular expression that validates the `ControlToValidate`'s contents. Clicking the ellipsis next to property `ValidationExpression` in the **Properties** window displays the **Regular Expression Editor** dialog, which contains a list of **Standard expressions** for phone numbers, zip codes and other formatted information. For the `emailRegularExpressionValidator`, we selected the standard expression **Internet e-mail address**. If the user enters text in the `emailTextBox` that does not have the correct format and either clicks in a different text box or attempts to submit the form, the `ErrorMessage` text is displayed in red.

For the `phoneRegularExpressionValidator`, we selected **U.S. phone number** to ensure that a phone number contains an optional three-digit area code either in parentheses and followed by an optional space or without parentheses and followed by a required hyphen. After an optional area code, a phone number must contain three digits, a hyphen and another four digits. For example, (555) 123-4567, 555-123-4567 and 123-4567 are all valid phone numbers.

Submitting the Web Form's Contents to the Server

If all five validators are successful (that is, each `TextBox` is filled in, and the e-mail address and phone number provided are valid), clicking the **Submit** button sends the form's data to the server. As shown in Fig. 13.25(d), the server then responds by displaying the sub-mitted data in the outputLabel.

Examining the Code-Behind File for a Web Form That Receives User Input

Figure 13.26 shows the code-behind file for this application. Notice that this code-behind file does not contain any implementation related to the validators. We say more about this soon. In this example, we respond to the page's **Load** event to process the data submitted by the user. This event occurs each time the page loads into a web browser—as opposed to the Init event, which executes only the first time the page is requested by the user. The event handler for this event is **Page_Load** (lines 7–30). To create the event handler, open Validation.aspx.vb in the code editor and perform the following steps:

1. Select **(Page Events)** from the left ComboBox at the top of the code editor window.

2. Select **Load** from the right ComboBox at the top of the code editor window.

3. Complete the event handler by inserting the code from Fig. 13.26.

```
1   ' Fig. 13.26: Validation.aspx.vb
2   ' Code-behind file for the form demonstrating validation controls.
3   Partial Class Validation
4      Inherits System.Web.UI.Page
5
6      ' Page_Load event handler executes when the page is loaded
7      Protected Sub Page_Load(ByVal sender As Object,
8         ByVal e As System.EventArgs) Handles Me.Load
9
10        ' if this is not the first time the page is loading
11        ' (i.e., the user has already submitted form data)
12        If IsPostBack Then
13           Validate() ' validate the form
14
15           If IsValid Then
16              ' retrieve the values submitted by the user
17              Dim name As String = nameTextBox.Text
18              Dim email As String = emailTextBox.Text
19              Dim phone As String = phoneTextBox.Text
20
21              ' create a table indicating the submitted values
22              outputLabel.Text = "Thank you for your submission<br/>" &
23                 "We received the following information:<br/>"
24              outputLabel.Text &=
25                 String.Format("Name: {0}{1}E-mail:{2}{1}Phone:{3}",
26                    name, "<br/>", email, phone)
27              outputLabel.Visible = True ' display the output message
28           End If
29        End If
30     End Sub ' Page_Load
31  End Class ' Validation
```

Fig. 13.26 | Code-behind file for a Web Form that obtains a user's contact information.

Differentiating Between the First Request to a Page and a Postback

Web programmers using ASP.NET often design their web pages so that the current page reloads when the user submits the form; this enables the program to receive input, process it as necessary and display the results in the same page when it's loaded the second time. These pages usually contain a form that, when submitted, sends the values of all the controls to the server and causes the current page to be requested again. This event is known as a **postback**. Line 12 uses the `IsPostBack` property of class `Page` to determine whether the page is being loaded due to a postback. The first time that the web page is requested, `IsPostBack` is `False`, and the page displays only the form for user input. When the postback occurs (from the user clicking **Submit**), `IsPostBack` is `True`.

Server-Side Web Form Validation

Server-side Web Form validation must be implemented programmatically. Line 13 calls the current `Page`'s **Validate** method to validate the information in the request. This validates the information as specified by the validation controls in the Web Form. Line 15 uses the `IsValid` property of class `Page` to check whether the validation succeeded. If this property is set to `True` (that is, validation succeeded and the Web Form is valid), then we display the Web Form's information. Otherwise, the web page loads without any changes, except any validator that failed now displays its `ErrorMessage`.

Processing the Data Entered by the User

Lines 17–19 retrieve the values of `nameTextBox`, `emailTextBox` and `phoneTextBox`. When data is posted to the web server, the data that the user entered is accessible to the web application through the web controls' properties. Next, lines 22–27 set `outputLabel`'s `Text` to display a message that includes the name, e-mail and phone information that was submitted to the server. In lines 22, 23 and 26, notice the use of `<br/>` rather than `vbCrLf` to start new lines in the `outputLabel`—`<br/>` is the markup for a line break in a web page. Line 27 sets the `outputLabel`'s `Visible` property to `True`, so the user can see the thank-you message and submitted data when the page reloads in the client web browser.

13.7 Session Tracking

Originally, critics accused the Internet and business of failing to provide the customized service typically experienced in "brick-and-mortar" stores. To address this problem, businesses established mechanisms by which they could *personalize* users' browsing experiences, tailoring content to individual users. Businesses achieve this level of service by tracking each customer's movement through the Internet and combining the collected data with information provided by the consumer, including billing information, personal preferences, interests and hobbies.

Personalization

Personalization makes it possible for businesses to communicate effectively with their customers and also improves users' ability to locate desired products and services. Companies that provide content of particular interest to users can establish relationships with customers and build on those relationships over time. Furthermore, by targeting consumers with personal offers, recommendations, advertisements, promotions and services, businesses create customer loyalty. Websites can use sophisticated technology to allow visitors to customize home pages to suit their individual needs and preferences. Similarly, online shopping sites often store personal information for customers, tailoring notifications and special offers to their interests. Such services encourage customers to visit sites more frequently and make purchases more regularly.

Privacy

A trade-off exists between personalized business service and protection of privacy. Some consumers embrace tailored content, but others fear the possible adverse consequences if the info they provide to businesses is released or collected by tracking technologies. Consumers and privacy advocates ask: What if the business to which we give personal data sells or gives that information to another organization without our knowledge? What if we do not want our actions on the Internet—a supposedly anonymous medium—to be tracked and recorded by unknown parties? What if unauthorized parties gain access to sensitive private data, such as credit-card numbers or medical history? These are questions that must be addressed by programmers, consumers, businesses and lawmakers alike.

Recognizing Clients

To provide personalized services to consumers, businesses must be able to recognize clients when they request information from a site. As we have discussed, the request/response system on which the web operates is facilitated by HTTP. Unfortunately, HTTP is a *stateless protocol*—it *does not* provide information that would enable web servers to maintain state information regarding particular clients. This means that web servers cannot determine whether a request comes from a particular client or whether the same or different clients generate a series of requests.

To circumvent this problem, sites can provide mechanisms by which they identify individual clients. A session represents a unique client on a website. If the client leaves a site and then returns later, the client will still be recognized as the same user. When the user closes the browser, the session ends. To help the server distinguish among clients, each client must identify itself to the server. Tracking individual clients is known as session tracking. One popular session-tracking technique uses cookies (discussed in Section 13.7.1); another uses ASP.NET's `HttpSessionState` object (used in Section 13.7.2). Additional session-tracking techniques are beyond this book's scope.

13.7.1 Cookies

Cookies provide you with a tool for personalizing web pages. A cookie is a piece of data stored by web browsers in a small text file on the user's computer. A cookie maintains information about the client during and between browser sessions. The first time a user visits the website, the user's computer might receive a cookie from the server; this cookie is then reactivated each time the user revisits that site. The collected information is intended to be an anonymous record containing data that is used to personalize the user's future visits to the site. For example, cookies in a shopping application might store unique identifiers for users. When a user adds items to an online shopping cart or performs another task resulting in a request to the web server, the server receives a cookie containing the user's unique identifier. The server then uses the unique identifier to locate the shopping cart and perform any necessary processing.

In addition to identifying users, cookies also can indicate users' shopping preferences. When a Web Form receives a request from a client, the Web Form can examine the cookie(s) it sent to the client during previous communications, identify the user's preferences and immediately display products of interest to the client.

Every HTTP-based interaction between a client and a server includes a header containing information either about the request (when the communication is from the client to the server) or about the response (when the communication is from the server to the client). When a Web Form receives a request, the header includes information such as the request type and any cookies that have been sent previously from the server to be stored on the client machine. When the server formulates its response, the header information contains any cookies the server wants to store on the client computer and other information, such as the MIME type of the response.

The expiration date of a cookie determines how long the cookie remains on the client's computer. If you do not set an expiration date for a cookie, the web browser maintains the cookie for the duration of the browsing session. Otherwise, the web browser maintains the cookie until the expiration date occurs. Cookies are deleted when they expire.

Portability Tip 13.1

Users may disable cookies in their web browsers to help ensure their privacy. Such users will experience difficulty using web applications that depend on cookies to maintain state information.

13.7.2 Session Tracking with `HttpSessionState`

The next web application demonstrates session tracking using the .NET class `Http-SessionState`. When you execute this application, the `Options.aspx` page (Fig. 13.27(a)), which is the application's **Start Page**, allows the user to select a programming language from a group of radio buttons. When the user clicks **Submit**, the selection is sent to the web server for processing. The web server uses an `HttpSessionState` object to store the chosen language and the ISBN number for one of our books on that topic. Each user that visits the site has a unique `HttpSessionState` object, so the selections made by one user are maintained separately from all other users. After storing the selection, the server returns the page to the browser (Fig. 13.27(b)) and displays the user's selection and some information about the user's unique session (which we show just for demonstration purposes). The page also includes links that allow the user to choose between selecting another programming language or viewing the `Recommendations.aspx` page (Fig. 13.27(e)), which lists recommended books pertaining to the programming language(s) that the user selected previously. If the user clicks the link for book recommendations, the information stored in the user's unique `HttpSessionState` object is read and used to form the list of recommendations. To test this application:

1. Select **Open Web Site...** from the **File** menu.

2. In the **Open Web Site** dialog, ensure that **File System** is selected, then navigate to this chapter's examples, select the `Sessions` folder and click the **Open Button**.

3. Select `Options.aspx` in the **Solution Explorer**, then type *Ctrl + F5* to execute the web application in your default web browser.

a) User selects a language from the `Options.aspx` page, then presses **Submit** to send the selection to the server

b) `Options.aspx` page is updated to hide the controls for selecting a language and to display the user's selection; the user clicks the hyperlink to return to the list of languages and make another selection

c) User selects another language from the `Options.aspx` page, then presses **Submit** to send the selection to the server

Fig. 13.27 | ASPX file that presents a list of programming languages. (Part 1 of 2.)

d) Options.aspx page is updated to hide the controls for selecting a language and to display the user's selection; the user clicks the hyperlink to get a list of book recommendations

e) Recommendations.aspx displays the list of recommended books based on the user's selections

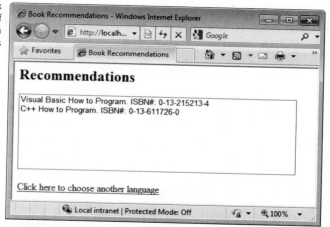

Fig. 13.27 | ASPX file that presents a list of programming languages. (Part 2 of 2.)

Creating the Web Site

To begin, follow the steps in Section 13.4.1 to create an **Empty Web Site** named Sessions, then add two Web Forms named Options.aspx and Recommendations.aspx to the project. Set the Options.aspx document's Title property to "Sessions" and the Recommendations.aspx document's Title property to "Book Recommendations". To ensure that Options.aspx is the first page to load for this application, right click it in the **Solution Explorer** and select **Set As Start Page**.

13.7.3 Options.aspx: Selecting a Programming Language

The Options.aspx page Fig. 13.27(a) contains the following controls arranged vertically:

1. A Label with its (ID) property set to promptLabel and its Text property set to "Select a programming language:". We used the techniques shown in *Step 5* of Section 13.4.1 to create a CSS style for this label named .labelStyle, and set the style's font-size attribute to large and the font-weight attribute to bold.

2. The user selects a programming language by clicking one of the radio buttons in a `RadioButtonList`. Each radio button has a `Text` property and a `Value` property. The `Text` property is displayed next to the radio button and the `Value` property represents a value that is sent to the server when the user selects that radio button and submits the form. In this example, we'll use the `Value` property to represent the ISBN for the recommended book.

   Create a `RadioButtonList` with its (ID) property set to `languageList`. Use the **ListItem Collection Editor** to add five radio buttons with their `Text` properties set to `Visual Basic`, `Visual C#`, `C`, `C++` and `Java`, and their `Value` properties set to 0-13-215213-4, 0-13-605322-X, 0-13-512356-2, 0-13-611726-0 and 0-13-605306-8, respectively

3. A `Button` with its (ID) property set to `submitButton` and its `Text` property set to `Submit`. In this example, we'll handle this `Button`'s `Click` event. You can create its event handler by double clicking the `Button` in **Design** view.

4. A `Label` with its (ID) property set to `responseLabel` and its `Text` property set to `"Welcome to Sessions!"`. This `Label` should be placed immediately to the right of the `Button` so that the `Label` appears at the top of the page when we hide the preceding controls on the page. Reuse the CSS style you created in *Step 1* by setting this `Label`'s `CssClass` property to `labelStyle`.

5. Two more `Label`s with their (ID) properties set to `idLabel` and `timeoutLabel`, respectively. Clear the text in each `Label`'s `Text` property—you'll set these programmatically with information about the current user's session.

6. A `HyperLink` with its (ID) property set to `languageLink` and its `Text` property set to `"Click here to choose another language"`. Set its `NavigateUrl` property by clicking the ellipsis next to the property in the **Properties** window and selecting `Options.aspx` from the **Select URL** dialog.

7. A `HyperLink` with its (ID) property set to `recommendationsLink` and its `Text` property set to `"Click here to get book recommendations"`. Set its `NavigateUrl` property by clicking the ellipsis next to the property in the **Properties** window and selecting `Recommendations.aspx` from the **Select URL** dialog.

8. Initially, the controls in *Steps 4–7* will not be displayed, so set each control's `Visible` property to `False`.

Session Property of a **Page**
Every Web Form includes a user-specific `HttpSessionState` object, which is accessible through property `Session` of class `Page`. Throughout this section, we use this property to manipulate the current user's `HttpSessionState` object. When a page is first requested, a unique `HttpSessionState` object is created by ASP.NET and assigned to the Page's `Session` property.

Code-Behind File for **Options.aspx**
Fig. 13.28 presents the code-behind file for the `Options.aspx` page. When this page is requested, the `Page_Load` event handler (lines 9–40) executes before the response is sent to the client. Since the first request to a page is not a postback, the code in lines 12–39 *does not* execute the first time the page loads.

Postback Processing

When the user presses **Submit**, a postback occurs. The form is submitted to the server and the Page_Load event handler executes. Lines 15–19 display the controls shown in Fig. 13.27(b) and lines 22–24 hide the controls shown in Fig. 13.27(a). Next, lines 27–32 ensure that the user selected a language and, if so, display a message in the response-Label indicating the selection. Otherwise, the message "You did not select a language" is displayed.

```vb
1   ' Fig. 13.28: Options.aspx.vb
2   ' Process user's selection of a programming language by displaying
3   ' links and writing information in an HttpSessionState object.
4   Partial Class Options
5      Inherits System.Web.UI.Page
6
7      ' if postback, hide form and display links to make additional
8      ' selections or view recommendations
9      Protected Sub Page_Load(ByVal sender As Object,
10        ByVal e As System.EventArgs) Handles Me.Load
11
12        If IsPostBack Then
13           ' user has submitted information, so display message
14           ' and appropriate hyperlinks
15           responseLabel.Visible = True
16           idLabel.Visible = True
17           timeoutLabel.Visible = True
18           languageLink.Visible = True
19           recommendationsLink.Visible = True
20
21           ' hide other controls used to make language selection
22           promptLabel.Visible = False
23           languageList.Visible = False
24           submitButton.Visible = False
25
26           ' if the user made a selection, display it in responseLabel
27           If languageList.SelectedItem IsNot Nothing Then
28              responseLabel.Text &= " You selected " &
29                 languageList.SelectedItem.Text
30           Else
31              responseLabel.Text &= "You did not select a language."
32           End If
33
34           ' display session ID
35           idLabel.Text = "Your unique session ID is: " & Session.SessionID
36
37           ' display the timeout
38           timeoutLabel.Text = "Timeout: " & Session.Timeout & " minutes."
39        End If
40     End Sub ' Page_Load
41
```

Fig. 13.28 | Process user's selection of a programming language by displaying links and writing information in an HttpSessionState object. (Part 1 of 2.)

```
42       ' record the user's selection in the Session
43       Protected Sub submitButton_Click(ByVal sender As Object,
44          ByVal e As System.EventArgs) Handles submitButton.Click
45
46          ' if the user made a selection
47          If languageList.SelectedItem IsNot Nothing Then
48             ' add name/value pair to Session
49             Session.Add(languageList.SelectedItem.Text,
50                languageList.SelectedItem.Value)
51          End If
52       End Sub ' submitButton_Click
53    End Class ' Options
```

Fig. 13.28 | Process user's selection of a programming language by displaying links and writing information in an HttpSessionState object. (Part 2 of 2.)

The ASP.NET application contains information about the HttpSessionState object (Session) for the current client. Property SessionID (displayed in line 35) contains the unique session ID—a sequence of random letters and numbers. The first time a client connects to the web server, a unique session ID is created for that client and a temporary cookie is written to the client so the server can identify the client on subsequent requests. When the client makes additional requests, the client's session ID from that temporary cookie is compared with the session IDs stored in the web server's memory to retrieve the client's HttpSessionState object. HttpSessionState property Timeout (displayed in line 38) specifies the maximum amount of time that an HttpSessionState object can be inactive before it's discarded. By default, if the user does not interact with this web application for 20 minutes, the HttpSessionState object is discarded by the server and a new one will be created if the user interacts with the application again. Figure 13.29 lists some common HttpSessionState properties.

Properties	Description
Count	Specifies the number of key/value pairs in the Session object.
IsNewSession	Indicates whether this is a new session (that is, whether the session was created during loading of this page).
Keys	Returns a collection containing the Session object's keys.
SessionID	Returns the session's unique ID.
Timeout	Specifies the maximum number of minutes during which a session can be inactive (that is, no requests are made) before the session expires. By default, this property is set to 20 minutes.

Fig. 13.29 | HttpSessionState properties.

Method submitButton_Click
In this example, we wish to store the user's selection in an HttpSessionState object when the user clicks the **Submit** Button. The submitButton_Click event handler (lines 43–52) adds a key/value pair to the HttpSessionState object for the current user, specifying the

language chosen and the ISBN number for a book on that language. The HttpSession-State object is a dictionary—a data structure that stores key/value pairs. A program uses the key to store and retrieve the associated value in the dictionary. We cover dictionaries in more depth in the online Collections chapter.

The key/value pairs in an HttpSessionState object are often referred to as session items. They're placed in an HttpSessionState object by calling its **Add** method. If the user made a selection (line 47), lines 49–50 get the selection and its corresponding value from the languageList by accessing its SelectedItem's Text and Value properties, respectively, then call HttpSessionState method Add to add this name/value pair as a session item in the HttpSessionState object (Session).

If the application adds a session item that has the same name as an item previously stored in the HttpSessionState object, the session item is replaced—the names in session items *must* be unique. Another common syntax for placing a session item in the HttpSessionState object is Session(*Name*) = *Value*. For example, we could have replaced lines 49–50 with

```
Session(languageList.SelectedItem.Text) =
    languageList.SelectedItem.Value
```

Software Engineering Observation 13.1

A Web Form should not use instance variables to maintain client state information, because each new request or postback is handled by a new instance of the page. Instead, maintain client state information in HttpSessionState objects, because such objects are specific to each client.

Software Engineering Observation 13.2

A benefit of using HttpSessionState objects (rather than cookies) is that HttpSessionState objects can store any type of object (not just Strings) as attribute values. This provides you with increased flexibility in determining the type of state information to maintain for clients.

13.7.4 Recommendations.aspx: Displaying Recommendations Based on Session Values

After the postback of Options.aspx, the user may request book recommendations. The book-recommendations hyperlink forwards the user to the page Recommendations.aspx (Fig. 13.27(e)) to display the recommendations based on the user's language selections. The page contains the following controls arranged vertically:

1. A Label with its (ID) property set to recommendationsLabel and its Text property set to "Recommendations:". We created a CSS style for this label named .labelStyle, and set the font-size attribute to x-large and the font-weight attribute to bold. (See *Step 5* in Section 13.4.1 for information on creating a CSS style.)

2. A ListBox with its (ID) property set to booksListBox. We created a CSS style for this label named .listBoxStyle. In the **Position** category, we set the width attribute to 450px and the height attribute to 125px. The px indicates that the measurement is in pixels.

3. A HyperLink with its (ID) property set to languageLink and its Text property set to "Click here to choose another language". Set its NavigateUrl property by clicking the ellipsis next to the property in the **Properties** window and selecting Options.aspx from the **Select URL** dialog. When the user clicks this link, the Options.aspx page will be reloaded. Requesting the page in this manner *is not* considered a postback, so the original form in Fig. 13.27(a) will be displayed.

Code-Behind File for *Recommendations.aspx*

Figure 13.30 presents the code-behind file for Recommendations.aspx. Event handler Page_Init (lines 7–27) retrieves the session information. If a user has not selected a language in the Options.aspx page, the HttpSessionState object's **Count** property will be 0 (line 11). This property provides the number of session items contained in a HttpSessionState object. If the Count is 0, then we display the text **No Recommendations** (line 20), clear the ListBox and hide it (lines 21–22), and update the Text of the HyperLink back to Options.aspx (line 25).

```
1   ' Fig. 13.30: Recommendations.aspx.vb
2   ' Creates book recommendations based on a Session object.
3   Partial Class Recommendations
4      Inherits System.Web.UI.Page
5
6      ' read Session items and populate ListBox with any book recommendations
7      Protected Sub Page_Init(ByVal sender As Object,
8         ByVal e As System.EventArgs) Handles Me.Init
9
10        ' determine whether Session contains any information
11        If Session.Count <> 0 Then
12           For Each keyName In Session.Keys
13              ' use keyName to display one of Session's name/value pairs
14              booksListBox.Items.Add(keyName &
15                 " How to Program. ISBN#: " & Session(keyName))
16           Next
17        Else
18           ' if there are no session items, no language was chosen, so
19           ' display appropriate message and clear and hide booksListBox
20           recommendationsLabel.Text = "No Recommendations"
21           booksListBox.Items.Clear()
22           booksListBox.Visible = False
23
24           ' modify languageLink because no language was selected
25           languageLink.Text = "Click here to choose a language"
26        End If
27     End Sub ' Page_Init
28  End Class ' Recommendations
```

Fig. 13.30 | Session data used to provide book recommendations to the user.

If the user chose at least one language, the loop in lines 12–16 iterates through the HttpSessionState object's keys (line 12) by accessing the HttpSessionState's **Keys** property, which returns a collection containing all the keys in the session. Lines 14–15 concatenate the keyName, the String " How to Program. ISBN#: " and the key's corresponding value, which is returned by Session(keyName). This String is the recommendation that is added to the ListBox.

13.8 Case Study: Database-Driven ASP.NET Guestbook

Many websites allow users to provide feedback about the website in a guestbook. Typically, users click a link on the website's home page to request the guestbook page. This page usually consists of a form that contains fields for the user's name, e-mail address, message/feedback and so on. Data submitted on the guestbook form is then stored in a database located on the server.

In this section, we create a guestbook Web Form application. The GUI (Fig. 13.31) contains a GridView data control, which displays all the entries in the guestbook in tabular format. This control is located in the **Toolbox**'s **Data** section. We explain how to create and configure this data control shortly. The GridView displays **abc** in **Design** mode to indicate data that will be retrieved from a data source at runtime. You'll learn how to create and configure the GridView shortly.

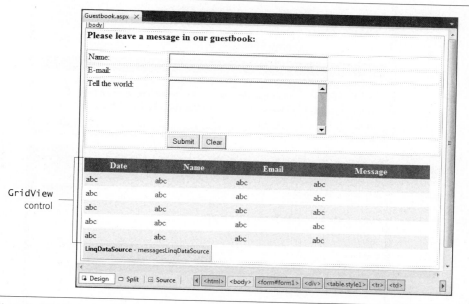

Fig. 13.31 | Guestbook application GUI in **Design** mode.

The Guestbook Database

The application stores the guestbook information in a SQL Server database called Guestbook.mdf located on the web server. (We provide this database in the databases folder with this chapter's examples.) The database contains a single table named Messages.

Testing the Application

To test this application:

1. Select **Open Web Site...** from the **File** menu.

2. In the **Open Web Site** dialog, ensure that **File System** is selected, then navigate to this chapter's examples, select the Guestbook folder and click the **Open** Button.

3. Select Guestbook.aspx in the **Solution Explorer**, then type *Ctrl + F5* to execute the web application in your default web browser.

Figure 13.32(a) shows the user submitting a new entry. Figure 13.32(b) shows the new entry as the last row in the GridView.

a) User enters data for the name, e-mail and message, then presses Submit to send the data to the server

b) Server stores the data in the database, then refreshes the GridView with the updated data

Fig. 13.32 | Sample execution of the **Guestbook** application.

13.8.1 Building a Web Form that Displays Data from a Database

We now explain how to build this GUI and set up the data binding between the `GridView` control and the database. Many of these steps are similar to those performed in Chapter 12 to access and interact with a database in a Windows application. We discuss the code-behind file in Section 13.8.2. To build the guestbook application, perform the following steps:

Step 1: Creating the Web Site

To begin, follow the steps in Section 13.4.1 to create an **Empty Web Site** named `Guestbook` then add a Web Form named `Guestbook.aspx` to the project. Set the document's `Title` property to `"Guestbook"`. To ensure that `Guestobook.aspx` loads when you execute this application, right click it in the **Solution Explorer** and select **Set As Start Page**.

Step 2: Creating the Form for User Input

In **Design** mode, add the text `Please leave a message in our guestbook:`, then use the **Block Format** ComboBox in the IDE's toolbar to change the text to **Heading 3** format. Insert a table with four rows and two columns, configured so that the text in each cell aligns with the top of the cell. Place the appropriate text (see Fig. 13.31) in the top three cells in the table's left column. Then place `TextBox`es named `nameTextBox`, `emailTextBox` and `messageTextBox` in the top three table cells in the right column. Configure the `TextBox`es as follows:

- Set the `nameTextBox`'s width to `300px`.

- Set the `emailTextBox`'s width to `300px`.

- Set the `messageTextBox`'s width to `300px` and height to `100px`. Also set this control's `TextMode` property to `MultiLine` so the user can type a message containing multiple lines of text.

Finally, add `Button`s named `submitButton` and `clearButton` to the bottom-right table cell. Set the buttons' `Text` properties to `Submit` and `Clear`, respectively. We discuss the buttons' event handlers when we present the code-behind file. You can create these event handlers now by double clicking each `Button` in **Design** view.

Step 3: Adding a `GridView` Control to the Web Form

Add a `GridView` named `messagesGridView` that will display the guestbook entries. This control appears in the **Data** section of the **Toolbox**. The colors for the `GridView` are specified through the **Auto Format...** link in the **GridView Tasks** smart-tag menu that opens when you place the `GridView` on the page. Clicking this link displays an **AutoFormat** dialog with several choices. In this example, we chose **Professional**. We show how to set the `GridView`'s data source (that is, where it gets the data to display in its rows and columns) shortly.

Step 4: Adding a Database to an ASP.NET Web Application

To use a SQL Server Express database file in an ASP.NET web application, you must first add the file to the project's `App_Data` folder. For security reasons, this folder can be accessed only by the web application on the server—clients cannot access this folder over a network. The web application interacts with the database on behalf of the client.

The **Empty Web Site** template does not create the `App_Data` folder. To create it, right click the project's name in the **Solution Explorer**, then select **Add ASP.NET Folder >**

App_Data. Next, add the `Guestbook.mdf` file to the `App_Data` folder. You can do this in one of two ways:

- Drag the file from Windows Explorer and drop it on the `App_Data` folder.

- Right click the `App_Data` folder in the **Solution Explorer** and select **Add Existing Item...** to display the **Add Existing Item** dialog, then navigate to the databases folder with this chapter's examples, select the `Guestbook.mdf` file and click **Add**. [*Note:* Ensure that **Data Files** is selected in the ComboBox above or next to the **Add Button** in the dialog; otherwise, the database file will not be displayed in the list of files.]

Step 5: Creating the LINQ to SQL Classes

As in Chapter 12, you'll use LINQ to interact with the database. To create the LINQ to SQL classes for the `Guestbook` database:

1. Right click the project in the **Solution Explorer** and select **Add New Item...** to display the **Add New Item** dialog.

2. In the dialog, select **LINQ to SQL Classes**, enter `Guestbook.dbml` as the **Name**, and click **Add**. A dialog appears asking if you would like to put your new LINQ to SQL classes in the `App_Code` folder; click **Yes**. The IDE will create an `App_Code` folder and place the LINQ to SQL classes information in that folder.

3. In the **Database Explorer** window, drag the `Guestbook` database's `Messages` table from the **Database Explorer** onto the **Object Relational Designer**. Finally, save your project by selecting **File > Save All**.

Step 6: Binding the `GridView` to the `Messages` Table of the `Guestbook` Database

You can now configure the `GridView` to display the database's data.

1. Open the **GridView Tasks** smart-tag menu, then select **<New data source...>** from the **Choose Data Source** ComboBox to display the **Data Source Configuration Wizard** dialog.

2. In this example, we use a **LinqDataSource** control that allows the application to interact with the `Guestbook.mdf` database through LINQ. Select LINQ, then set the ID of the data source to `messagesLinqDataSource` and click **OK** to begin the **Configure Data Source** wizard.

3. In the **Choose a Context Object** screen, ensure that `GuestbookDataContext` is selected in the ComboBox, then click **Next >**.

4. The **Configure Data Selection** screen (Fig. 13.33) allows you to specify which data the `LinqDataSource` should retrieve from the data context. Your choices on this page design a `Select` LINQ query. The **Table** drop-down list identifies a table in the data context. The `Guestbook` data context contains one table named `Messages`, which is selected by default. *If you haven't saved your project* since creating your LINQ to SQL classes (*Step 5*), the list of tables *will not appear*. In the **Select** pane, ensure that the checkbox marked with an asterisk (*) is selected to indicate that you want to retrieve all the columns in the `Messages` table.

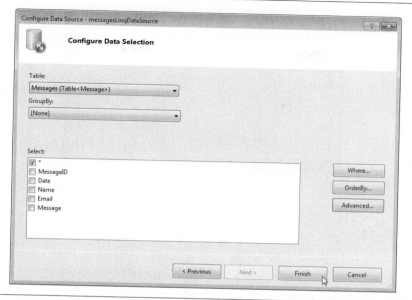

Fig. 13.33 | Configuring the query used by the LinqDataSource to retrieve data.

5. Click the **Advanced...** button, then select the **Enable the LinqDataSource to perform automatic inserts** CheckBox and click **OK**. This configures the LinqDataSource control to automatically insert new data into the database when new data is inserted in the data context. We discuss inserting new guestbook entries based on users' form submissions shortly.

6. Click **Finish** to complete the wizard.

A control named messagesLinqDataSource now appears on the Web Form directly below the GridView (Fig. 13.34). This control is represented in **Design** mode as a gray box containing its type and name. It will *not* appear on the web page—the gray box simply provides a way to manipulate the control visually through **Design** mode—similar to how the objects in the component tray are used in **Design** mode for a Windows Forms application.

The GridView now has column headers that correspond to the columns in the Messages table. The rows each contain either a number (which signifies an autoincremented column) or **abc** (which indicates string data). The actual data from the Guestbook.mdf database file will appear in these rows when you view the ASPX file in a web browser.

Step 7: Modifying the Columns of the Data Source Displayed in the GridView
It's not necessary for site visitors to see the MessageID column when viewing past guestbook entries—this column is merely a unique primary key required by the Messages table within the database. So, let's modify the GridView to prevent this column from displaying on the Web Form.

1. In the **GridView Tasks** smart tag menu, click **Edit Columns** to display the **Fields** dialog (Fig. 13.35).

Fig. 13.34 | **Design** mode displaying `LinqDataSource` control for a `GridView`.

Fig. 13.35 | Removing the `MessageID` column from the `GridView`.

2. Select **MessageID** in the **Selected fields** pane, then click the ⊠ Button. This removes the `MessageID` column from the `GridView`.

3. Click **OK** to return to the main IDE window, then set the `Width` property of the `GridView` to 650px.

The `GridView` should now appear as shown in Fig. 13.31.

13.8.2 Modifying the Code-Behind File for the Guestbook Application

After building the Web Form and configuring the data controls used in this example, double click the **Submit** and **Clear** buttons in **Design** view to create their corresponding `Click` event handlers in the code-behind file (Fig. 13.36). The IDE generates empty event handlers, so we must add the appropriate code to make these buttons work properly. The event handler for `clearButton` (lines 36–41) clears each `TextBox` by setting its `Text` property to an empty string. This resets the form for a new guestbook submission.

```vb
1    ' Fig. 13.36: Guestbook.aspx.vb
2    ' Code-behind file that defines event handlers for the guestbook.
3    Partial Class Guestbook
4       Inherits System.Web.UI.Page
5
6       ' Submit Button adds a new guestbook entry to the database,
7       ' clears the form and displays the updated list of guestbook entries
8       Protected Sub submitButton_Click(ByVal sender As Object, _
9          ByVal e As System.EventArgs) Handles submitButton.Click
10
11          ' create dictionary of parameters for inserting
12          Dim insertParameters As New ListDictionary()
13
14          ' add current date and the user's name, e-mail address and message
15          ' to dictionary of insert parameters
16          insertParameters.Add("Date", Date.Now.ToShortDateString())
17          insertParameters.Add("Name", nameTextBox.Text)
18          insertParameters.Add("Email", emailTextBox.Text)
19          insertParameters.Add("Message", messageTextBox.Text)
20
21          ' execute an INSERT LINQ statement to add a new entry to the
22          ' Messages table in the Guestbook data context that contains the
23          ' current date and the user's name, e-mail address and message
24          messagesLinqDataSource.Insert(insertParameters)
25
26          ' clear the TextBoxes
27          nameTextBox.Text = String.Empty
28          emailTextBox.Text = String.Empty
29          messageTextBox.Text = String.Empty
30
31          ' update the GridView with the new database table contents
32          messagesGridView.DataBind()
33       End Sub ' submitButton_Click
34
35       ' Clear Button clears the Web Form's TextBoxes
36       Protected Sub clearButton_Click(ByVal sender As Object, _
37          ByVal e As System.EventArgs) Handles clearButton.Click
38          nameTextBox.Text = String.Empty
39          emailTextBox.Text = String.Empty
40          messageTextBox.Text = String.Empty
41       End Sub ' clearButton_Click
42    End Class ' Guestbook
```

Fig. 13.36 | Code-behind file for the guestbook application.

Lines 8–33 contain submitButton's event-handling code, which adds the user's information to the Guestbook database's Messages table. To use the values of the TextBoxes on the Web Form as the parameter values inserted into the database, we must create a List-Dictionary of insert parameters that are key/value pairs.

Line 12 creates a ListDictionary object. Lines 16–19 used the ListDictionary's Add method to store key/value pairs that represent each of the four insert parameters—the current date and the user's name, e-mail address, and message. Invoking the LinqData-Source method Insert (line 24) inserts the data in the data context, adding a row to the Messages table and automatically updating the database. We pass the ListDictionary object as an argument to the Insert method to specify the insert parameters. After the data is inserted into the database, lines 27–29 clear the TextBoxes, and line 32 invokes messagesGridView's DataBind method to refresh the data that the GridView displays. This causes messagesLinqDataSource (the GridView's source) to execute its Select command to obtain the Messages table's newly updated data.

13.9 Online Case Study: ASP.NET AJAX

In the online chapter, Web App Development: A Deeper Look, you learn the difference between a traditional web application and an Ajax (Asynchronous JavaScript and XML) web application. You also learn how to use ASP.NET AJAX to quickly and easily improve the user experience for your web applications, giving them responsiveness comparable to that of desktop applications. To demonstrate ASP.NET AJAX capabilities, you enhance the validation example by displaying the submitted form information without reloading the entire page. The only modifications to this web application appear in Validation.aspx file. You use Ajax-enabled controls to add this feature.

13.10 Online Case Study: Password-Protected Books Database Application

In the online chapter, Web App Development: A Deeper Look, we include a web application case study in which a user logs into a password-protected website to view a list of publications by a selected author. The application consists of several pages and provides website registration and login capabilities. You'll learn about ASP.NET master pages, which allow you to specify a common look-and-feel for all the pages in your app. We also introduce the **Web Site Administration Tool** and use it to configure the portions of the application that can be accessed only by users who are logged into the website.

13.11 Wrap-Up

In this chapter, we introduced web-application development using ASP.NET and Visual Web Developer 2010 Express. We began by discussing the simple HTTP transactions that take place when you request and receive a web page through a web browser. You then learned about the three tiers (that is, the client or top tier, the business logic or middle tier and the information or bottom tier) that comprise most web applications.

Next, we explained the role of ASPX files (that is, Web Form files) and code-behind files, and the relationship between them. We discussed how ASP.NET compiles and executes web applications so that they can be displayed in a web browser. You also learned how to build an ASP.NET web application using Visual Web Developer.

The chapter demonstrated several common ASP.NET web controls used for displaying text and images on a Web Form. We also discussed validation controls, which allow you to ensure that user input on a web page satisfies certain requirements.

We discussed the benefits of maintaining a user's state information across multiple pages of a website. We then demonstrated how you can include such functionality in a web application by using session tracking with `HttpSessionState` objects.

Finally, we built a guestbook application that allows users to submit comments about a website. You learned how to save the user input in a SQL Server database and how to display past submissions on the web page. In the next chapter, we present an in-depth treatment of additional Windows Forms GUI controls.

Summary

Section 13.1 Introduction
- ASP.NET technology is Microsoft's technology for web-application development.
- Web Form files have the file-name extension `.aspx` and contain the web page's GUI. A Web Form file represents the web page that is sent to the client browser.
- The file that contains the programming logic of a Web Form is called the code-behind file.

Section 13.2 Web Basics
- URIs (Uniform Resource Identifiers) identify documents on the Internet. URIs that start with `http://` are called URLs (Uniform Resource Locators).
- A URL contains information that directs a browser to the resource that the user wishes to access. Computers that run web server software make such resources available.
- In a URL, the hostname is the name of the server on which the resource resides. This computer usually is referred to as the host, because it houses and maintains resources.
- A hostname is translated into a unique IP address that identifies the server. This translation is performed by a domain-name system (DNS) server.
- The remainder of a URL specifies the location and name of a requested resource. For security reasons, the location is normally a virtual directory. The server translates the virtual directory into a real location on the server.
- When given a URL, a web browser performs uses HTTP to retrieve and display the web page found at that address.

Section 13.3 Multitier Application Architecture
- Multitier applications divide functionality into separate tiers—logical groupings of functionality—that commonly reside on separate computers for security and scalability.
- The information tier (also called the bottom tier) maintains data pertaining to the application. This tier typically stores data in a relational database management system.
- The middle tier implements business logic, controller logic and presentation logic to control interactions between the application's clients and the application's data. The middle tier acts as an intermediary between data in the information tier and the application's clients.
- Business logic in the middle tier enforces business rules and ensures that data is reliable before the server application updates the database or presents the data to users.

- The client tier, or top tier, is the application's user interface, which gathers input and displays output. Users interact directly with the application through the user interface (typically viewed in a web browser), keyboard and mouse. In response to user actions, the client tier interacts with the middle tier to make requests and to retrieve data from the information tier. The client tier then displays to the user the data retrieved from the middle tier.

Section 13.4.1 Building the WebTime Application

- **File System** websites are created and tested on your local computer. Such websites execute in Visual Web Developer's built-in ASP.NET Development Server and can be accessed only by web browsers running on the same computer. You can later "publish" your website to a production web server for access via a local network or the Internet.

- **HTTP** websites are created and tested on an IIS web server and use HTTP to allow you to put your website's files on the server. If you own a website and have your own web server computer, you might use this to build a new website directly on that server computer.

- **FTP** websites use File Transfer Protocol (FTP) to allow you to put your website's files on the server. The server administrator must first create the website on the server for you. FTP is commonly used by so called "hosting providers" to allow website owners to share a server computer that runs many websites.

- A Web Form represents one page in a web application and contains a web application's GUI.

- You can view the Web Form's properties by selecting DOCUMENT in the **Properties** window. The Title property specifies the title that will be displayed in the web browser's title bar when the page is loaded.

- Controls and other elements are placed sequentially on a Web Form one after another in the order in which you drag-and-drop them onto the Web Form. The cursor indicates the insertion point in the page. This type of layout is known as relative positioning. You can also use absolute positioning in which controls are located exactly where you drop them on the Web Form.

- When a Label does not contain text, its name is displayed in square brackets in **Design** view as a placeholder for design and layout purposes. This text is not displayed at execution time.

- Formatting in a web page is performed with Cascading Style Sheets (CSS).

- A Web Form's Init event occurs when the page is first requested by a web browser. The event handler for this event—named Page_Init—initialize the page.

Section 13.4.2 Examining WebTime.aspx's Code-Behind File

- A class declaration can span multiple source-code files—the separate portions of the class declaration in each file are known as partial classes. The Partial modifier indicates that the class in a particular file is part of a larger class.

- Every Web Form class inherits from class Page in namespace System.Web.UI. Class Page represents the default capabilities of each page in a web application.

- The ASP.NET controls are defined in namespace System.Web.UI.WebControls.

Section 13.5 Standard Web Controls: Designing a Form

- An Image control's ImageUrl property specifies the location of the image to display.

- By default, the contents of a table cell are aligned vertically in the middle of the cell. You can change this with the cell's valign property.

- A TextBox control allows you to obtain text from the user and display text to the user.

- A DropDownList control is similar to the Windows Forms ComboBox control, but doesn't allow users to type text. You can add items to the DropDownList using the **ListItem Collection Editor**, which you can access by clicking the ellipsis next to the DropDownList's Items property in the **Properties** window, or by using the **DropDownList Tasks** menu.

- A HyperLink control adds a hyperlink to a Web Form. The NavigateUrl property specifies the resource or web page that will be requested when the user clicks the HyperLink.
- A RadioButtonList control provides a series of radio buttons from which the user can select only one. The **RadioButtonList Tasks** smart-tag menu provides an **Edit Items...** link to open the **ListItem Collection Editor** so that you can create the items in the list.
- A Button control triggers an action when clicked.

Section 13.6 Validation Controls

- A validation control determines whether the data in another web control is in the proper format.
- When the page is sent to the client, the validator is converted into JavaScript that performs the validation in the client web browser.
- Some client browsers might not support scripting or the user might disable it. For this reason, you should always perform validation on the server.
- A RequiredFieldValidator control ensures that its ControlToValidate is not empty when the form is submitted. The validator's ErrorMessage property specifies what to display on the Web Form if the validation fails. When the validator's Display property is set to Dynamic, the validator occupies space on the Web Form only when validation fails.
- A RegularExpressionValidator uses a regular expression to ensure data entered by the user is in a valid format. Visual Web Developer provides several predefined regular expressions that you can simply select to validate e-mail addresses, phone numbers and more. A RegularExpressionValidator's ValidationExpression property specifies the regular expression to use for validation.
- A Web Form's Load event occurs each time the page loads into a web browser. The event handler for this event is Page_Load.
- ASP.NET pages are often designed so that the current page reloads when the user submits the form; this enables the program to receive input, process it as necessary and display the results in the same page when it's loaded the second time.
- Submitting a web form is known as a postback. Class Page's IsPostBack property returns True if the page is being loaded due to a postback.
- Server-side Web Form validation must be implemented programmatically. Class Page's Validate method validates the information in the request as specified by the Web Form's validation controls. Class Page's IsValid property returns True if validation succeeded.

Section 13.7 Session Tracking

- Personalization makes it possible for e-businesses to communicate effectively with their customers and also improves users' ability to locate desired products and services.
- To provide personalized services to consumers, e-businesses must be able to recognize clients when they request information from a site.
- HTTP is a stateless protocol—it does not provide information regarding particular clients.
- Tracking individual clients is known as session tracking.

Section 13.7.1 Cookies

- A cookie is a piece of data stored in a small text file on the user's computer. A cookie maintains information about the client during and between browser sessions.
- The expiration date of a cookie determines how long the cookie remains on the client's computer. If you do not set an expiration date for a cookie, the web browser maintains the cookie for the duration of the browsing session.

Section 13.7.2 Session Tracking with **HttpSessionState**
- Session tracking is implemented with class HttpSessionState.

Section 13.7.3 **Options.aspx:** Selecting a Programming Language
- Each radio button in a RadioButtonList has a Text property and a Value property. The Text property is displayed next to the radio button and the Value property represents a value that is sent to the server when the user selects that radio button and submits the form.
- Every Web Form includes a user-specific HttpSessionState object, which is accessible through property Session of class Page.
- HttpSessionState property SessionID contains a client's unique session ID. The first time a client connects to the web server, a unique session ID is created for that client and a temporary cookie is written to the client so the server can identify the client on subsequent requests. When the client makes additional requests, the client's session ID from that temporary cookie is compared with the session IDs stored in the web server's memory to retrieve the client's HttpSessionState object.
- HttpSessionState property Timeout specifies the maximum amount of time that an HttpSessionState object can be inactive before it's discarded. Twenty minutes is the default.
- The HttpSessionState object is a dictionary—a data structure that stores key/value pairs. A program uses the key to store and retrieve the associated value in the dictionary.
- The key/value pairs in an HttpSessionState object are often referred to as session items. They're placed in an HttpSessionState object by calling its Add method. Another common syntax for placing a session item in the HttpSessionState object is Session(*Name*) = *Value*.
- If an application adds a session item that has the same name as an item previously stored in the HttpSessionState object, the session item is replaced—session items names *must* be unique.

Section 13.7.4 **Recommendations.aspx:** Displaying Recommendations Based on Session Values
- The Count property returns the number of session items stored in an HttpSessionState object.
- HttpSessionState's Keys property returns a collection containing all the keys in the session.

Section 13.8 Case Study: Database-Driven ASP.NET Guestbook
- A GridView data control displays data in tabular format. This control is located in the **Toolbox**'s **Data** section.

Section 13.8.1 Building a Web Form that Displays Data from a Database
- To use a SQL Server Express database file in an ASP.NET web application, you must first add the file to the project's App_Data folder. For security reasons, this folder can be accessed only by the web application on the server—clients cannot access this folder over a network. The web application interacts with the database on behalf of the client.
- A LinqDataSource control allows a web application to interact with a database through LINQ.

Section 13.8.2 Modifying the Code-Behind File for the Guestbook Application
- To insert data into a database using a LinqDataSource, you must create a ListDictionary of insert parameters that are formatted as key/value pairs.
- A ListDictionary's Add method stores key/value pairs that represent each insert parameter.
- A GridView's DataBind method refreshes the data that the GridView displays.

Terminology

Add method of class `HttpSessionState` 479
AJAX (Asynchronous Javascript and XML) 488
ASP.NET 444
ASP.NET AJAX 488
ASP.NET server control 444
ASPX file 444
`.aspx` filename extension 444
bottom tier 446
business logic 447
`Button` control 465
client tier 447
code-behind file 444
controller logic 447
`ControlToValidate` property of a validation control 468
cookie 472
`Count` property of class `HttpSessionState` 480
`DataBind` method of a `GridView` 488
`Display` property of a validation control 469
DNS (domain name system) server 445
`DOCUMENT` property of a Web Form 454
`DropDownList` control 464
`ErrorMessage` property of a validation control 468
expiration date of a cookie 473
`GridView` control 481
host 445
hostname 445
`HttpSessionState` class 473
`HyperLink` control 464
`Image` control 462
`ImageUrl` property of an `Image` web control 462
information tier 446
`Init` event of a Web Form 458
IP (Internet Protocol) address 445
`IsPostBack` property of `Page` class 471
`IsValid` property of `Page` class 471
key/value pair 479
`Keys` property of `HttpSessionState` class 480
`LinqDataSource` control 484
`ListDictionary` class 488
`Load` event of Web Form 470
middle tier 447

multitier application 446
n-tier application 446
`NavigateUrl` property of a `HyperLink` control 464
`Page` class 459
`Page_Init` event handler 458
`Page_Load` event handler 470
partial class 459
`Partial` modifier 459
personalization 471
postback 471
presentation logic 447
`RadioButtonList` control 464
`RegularExpressionValidator` validation control
`RequiredFieldValidator` control 468
session item 479
`Session` property of `Page` class 476
session tracking 472
`SessionID` property of `HttpSessionState` class 478
`System.Web.UI` namespace 459
`Target` property of a `HyperLink` control 464
`TextBox` control 463
tier in a multitier application 446
`Timeout` property of `HttpSessionState` class 478
`Title` property of a Web Form 454
top tier 447
unique session ID of an ASP.NET client 478
`Validate` property of `Page` class 471
validation control 465
`ValidationExpression` property of a `Regular-ExpressionValidator` control 469
validator 465
`Visible` property of an ASP.NET control 468
Visual Web Developer 2010 Express 444
web application development 444
web control 444
Web Form 444
web server 445
`Web.config` ASP.NET configuration file 459

Self-Review Exercises

13.1 State whether each of the following is *true* or *false*. If *false*, explain why.
   a) Web Form file names end in `.aspx`.
   b) `App.config` is a file that stores configuration settings for an ASP.NET web application.

    c) A maximum of one validation control can be placed on a Web Form.

    d) A LinqDataSource control allows a web application to interact with a database.

13.2 Fill in the blanks in each of the following statements:

    a) Web applications contain three basic tiers: _____, _____, and _____.

    b) The _____ web control is similar to the ComboBox Windows control.

    c) A control which ensures that the data in another control is in the correct format is called a(n) _____.

    d) A(n) _____ occurs when a page requests itself.

    e) Every ASP.NET page inherits from class _____.

    f) The _____ file contains the functionality for an ASP.NET page.

Answers to Self-Review Exercises

13.1 a) True. b) False. Web.config is the file that stores configuration settings for an ASP.NET web application. c) False. An unlimited number of validation controls can be placed on a Web Form. d) True.

13.2 a) bottom (information), middle (business logic), top (client). b) DropDownList. c) validator. d) postback. e) Page. f) code-behind.

Exercises

13.3 *(WebTime Modification)* Modify the WebTime example to contain drop-down lists that allow the user to modify such Label properties as BackColor, ForeColor and Font-Size. Configure these drop-down lists so that a postback occurs whenever the user makes a selection. When the page reloads, it should reflect the specified changes to the properties of the Label displaying the time.

13.4 *(Page Hit Counter)* Create an ASP.NET page that uses session tracking to keep track of how many times the client computer has visited the page. Set the HttpSession object's Timeout property to DateTime.Now.AddDays(1) to keep the session in effect for one day into the future. Display the number of page hits every time the page loads.

13.5 *(Guestbook Application Modification)* Add validation to the guestbook application in Section 13.8. Use validation controls to ensure that the user provides a name, a valid e-mail address and a message.

13.6 *(WebControls Modification)* Modify the example of Section 13.5 to add functionality to the **Register** Button. When the user clicks the Button, validate all of the input fields to ensure that the user has filled out the form completely, and entered a valid email address and phone number. If any of the fields are not valid, appropriate messages should be displayed by validation controls. If the fields are all valid, direct the user to another page that displays a message indicating that the registration was successful followed by the registration information that was submitted from the form.

13.7 *(Project: Web-Based Address Book)* Using the techniques you learned in Section 13.8, create a web-based Address book with similar functionality to the **Address Book** application that you created in Section 12.9. Display the address book's contents in a GridView. Allow the user to search for entries with a particular last name.

Windows Forms GUI: A Deeper Look

14

. . .The user should feel in control of the computer; not the other way around. This is achieved in applications that embody three qualities: responsiveness, permissiveness, and consistency.
—Apple Computer, Inc.

. . .the wisest prophets make sure of the event first.
—Horace Walpole

Objectives

In this chapter you'll learn:

- Design principles of graphical user interfaces (GUIs).

- How to process mouse and keyboard events.

- How to create and manipulate `Panel`, `ToolTip`, `MonthCalendar`, `LinkLabel` and `CheckedListBox` controls.

- To create menus, submenus, menu items and checked menu items.

- To create multiple document interface (MDI) programs.

- To use visual inheritance.

- To create an animation by generating events with a `Timer`.

14.1 Introduction

In this chapter, we present additional GUI components that will help you develop richer, more sophisticated GUIs. We begin with an overview of controls, components and common features of Forms. Next, we demonstrate alternate ways to create event handlers via the code editor window and the **Properties** window. Then you'll learn about common features of all controls and the IDE features for positioning, aligning and sizing controls.

We show how to use Panels to group controls and how to display visual hints called tool tips that are displayed when the user hovers the mouse over a control. You'll learn how to process mouse and keyboard events. We provide a more detailed example of menus that includes submenus and checked menu items, and discusses how to maintain a mutually exclusive set of menu items. Next, we introduce the MonthCalendar and DateTimePicker controls for manipulating dates and times in a GUI. We show how LinkLabels can be used to add hyperlinks to an application and demonstrate how to execute another program in response to clicking a hyperlink. We review the ListBox control and introduce the CheckedListBox control for displaying lists of items that can be checked or unchecked.

Next, we demonstrate a multiple document interface (MDI)—a window that can contain other windows. We introduce visual inheritance and show how to use it to maintain a consistent look-and-feel throughout an application. Finally, we demonstrate the Timer component, which is a non-visual component that generates events at fixed time intervals. We use a Timer to control an animation that displays 20 images per second.

14.2 Controls and Components

Figure 14.1 displays the Windows Forms controls and components from the **Toolbox**. The difference between a control and a component is that a component is not visual at execution time. An example of a component is a Timer, which generates events at specified time intervals, but is not actually displayed on the screen. When you drag a component onto the Form in **Design** view, the component is placed in the component tray below the Form. You can select a component from the component tray to access its properties and events in the **Properties** window.

Toolbox Categories

The controls and components are organized into categories by functionality. Selecting the category **All Windows Forms** at the top of the **Toolbox** allows you to view all the controls and components from the other tabs in one list (as shown in Fig. 14.1).

This category displays all controls and components

Categories that organize controls and components by functionality

Fig. 14.1 | Components and controls for Windows Forms.

The Active Window

When there are several windows on the screen, the active window is the *frontmost* one. A window becomes active when the user clicks inside it. The active window is said to "have the focus." For example, in Visual Studio the active window is the **Toolbox** when you're selecting an item from it, or the **Properties** window when you're editing a control's properties.

Auto-Generated Code

As you know, a Form is a container for controls and components. When you drag a control or component from the **Toolbox** onto the Form, Visual Studio generates code that instantiates the object and sets its basic properties to default values. This code is updated when the control or component's properties are modified in the **Properties** window. The generated code is placed by the IDE in a separate file. Although we could write this code ourselves, it's easier to create and modify controls and components using the **Toolbox** and **Properties** windows and let Visual Studio to handle the details.

Common Properties of a Form

Figure 14.2 lists some common Form properties, methods and an event—some of which you've used in earlier chapters.

Form properties, methods and an event	Description
Common Properties	
AcceptButton	Button that is clicked when *Enter* is pressed.
AutoScroll	Boolean value that allows or disallows scrollbars when needed.
CancelButton	Button that is clicked when the *Escape* key is pressed.
FormBorderStyle	Border style for the Form (for example, none, single, three-dimensional).
Font	Font of text displayed on the Form, and the default font for controls added to the Form.
Text	Text in the Form's title bar.
Common Methods	
Close	Closes a Form and releases all resources, such as the memory used for the Form's controls and components. A closed Form cannot be reopened.
Hide	Hides a Form, but does not destroy the Form or release its resources.
Show	Displays a hidden Form.
Common Event	
Load	Occurs before a Form is displayed to the user. The handler for this event is displayed in the Visual Studio editor when you double click the Form in the Visual Studio designer.

Fig. 14.2 | Common Form properties, methods and an event.

14.3 Creating Event Handlers

In all the GUI applications you've created so far, you double clicked a control on the Form to create an event handler for that control. This technique creates an event handler for a control's default event—the event most frequently used with that control. Typically, controls can generate many different types of events, and each type can have its own event handler. For instance, you've already created Click event handlers for Buttons by double clicking a Button in design view (Click is the default event for a Button). However your application can also provide an event handler for a Button's MouseEnter event, which occurs when you move the mouse pointer into the Button. We now discuss how to create an event handler for an event that's not a control's default event.

Creating Event Handlers from the **Code** Editor Window

Visual Basic 2010 Express Edition allows you to create event handlers from the **Code** editor. At the top of the **Code** editor window, you'll find two ComboBoxes. If you select a control in your Form from the left ComboBox (Fig. 14.3(a)), the right ComboBox is populated

with all the events for that control (Fig. 14.3(b)). If you select an event from the right ComboBox, your text cursor will move to its location in the code. If the event handler does not
already exist, it will be created.

a) Selecting a control
in the **Code** editor
window

b) Displaying the list
of events for the
selected control

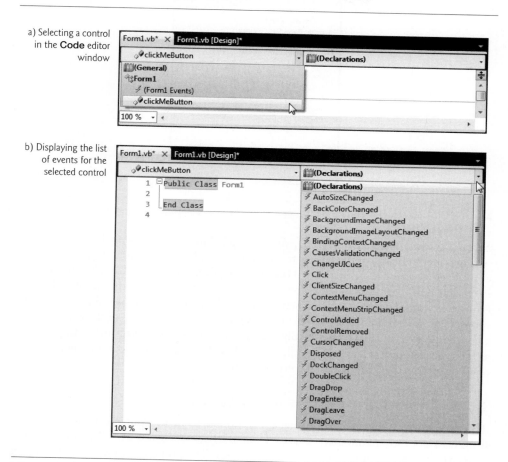

Fig. 14.3 | Viewing the events for a Button in the **Code** editor.

Using the Properties Window to Create Event Handlers

You can also create event handlers through the **Properties** window in **Design** view. If you
select a control on the Form, then click the **Events** icon ( ) in the **Properties** window, all
the events for that control are listed in the window (Fig. 14.4). You can double click an
event's name to display the event handler in the editor. If the event handler does not already exist, it will be created. You can also select an event, then use the drop-down list to
its right to choose an existing method that will be used as the event handler for that event.
The methods that appear in this drop-down list are the class's methods that have the proper signature to be an event handler for the selected event. You can return to viewing the
properties of a control by selecting the **Properties** icon.

Fig. 14.4 | Viewing events for a `Button` control in the **Properties** window.

Specifying the Same Event Handler for Multiple Controls in Design View

A single method can handle events from *many* controls. For example, to create a `Click` event handler that can handle the `Click` events of three `Buttons`, select all three `Buttons` in **Design** view, then double click the event you want to handle in the **Events** tab of the **Properties** window. If you create a new event handler this way, you should rename it appropriately, so that it does not appear to be associated with only one of the controls. You can also select each control individually and use the **Events** tab to select an existing method as the event handler. The event handler's `Handles` clause specifies a comma-separated list of all the events that will invoke the event handler.

14.4 Control Properties and Layout

This section overviews properties that are common to many controls. Controls inherit from class `Control` (namespace `System.Windows.Forms`). Figure 14.5 lists some of class `Control`'s commonly used properties and methods. The properties shown here can be set for many controls. For example, the `Text` property specifies the text that appears on a control. The location of this text varies depending on the control. In a Windows Form, the text appears in the title bar, but the text of a `Button` appears on its face.

TabIndex and TabStop Properties

When you press the *Tab* key in an executing Windows application, controls receive the focus in the order specified by their `TabIndex` property. This property is set by the IDE based on the order in which controls are added to a `Form`, but you can modify this property to change the tabbing order. `TabIndex` is helpful for users who enter information in many controls, such as a set of `TextBoxes` that represent a user's name, address and telephone number. The user can enter information, then quickly select the next control by pressing the *Tab* key. To prevent a control from receiving the focus in this manner, you can set its `TabStop` property to `False`.

Class **Control**'s properties and methods	Description
Common Properties	
BackColor	The control's background color.
BackgroundImage	The control's background image.
Enabled	Specifies whether the user can interact with the control. A disabled control typically appears "grayed out."
Focused	Indicates whether the control has the focus.
Font	The Font used to display the control's text.
ForeColor	The control's foreground color. This usually determines the color of the text in the Text property.
TabIndex	The tab order of the control. When the *Tab* key is pressed, the focus transfers between controls based on the tab order. You can set this order.
TabStop	If True, then a user can give focus to this control via the *Tab* key.
Text	The text associated with the control. The location and appearance of the text vary depending on the type of control.
Visible	Indicates whether the control is visible.
Common Methods	
Focus	Acquires the focus.
Hide	Hides the control (sets the Visible property to False).
Show	Shows the control (sets the Visible property to True).

Fig. 14.5 | Class Control's common properties and methods.

Enabled *and* Visible *Properties*

The Enabled property indicates whether the user can interact with a control to generate an event. If a control is disabled, it's often because an option is unavailable to the user at that time. For example, text editor applications often disable the "paste" command until the user *copies* some text. In most cases, a disabled control's text appears in gray (rather than in black). You can also hide a control from the user without disabling the control by setting the Visible property to False or by calling method Hide. In each case, the control still exists but is not visible on the Form.

Properties That Affect the Layout, Size and Position of Controls

You can use anchoring and docking to specify the layout of controls inside a container (such as a Form). **Anchoring** causes controls to remain at a fixed distance from the sides of the container even when the container is resized. Anchoring enhances the user experience. For example, if the user expects a control to appear in a certain corner of the application, anchoring ensures that the control will always be in that corner—even if the user resizes the Form. Docking attaches a control to a container such that the control stretches across an entire side or fills an entire area. For example, a button docked to the top of a container stretches across the entire top of that container regardless of the container's width.

When parent containers are resized, anchored controls are moved (and possibly resized) so that the distance from the sides to which they're anchored does not vary. By default, most controls are anchored to the *top-left corner* of the Form. To see the effects of anchoring a control, create a simple Windows application that contains two Buttons. Anchor one control to the right and bottom sides by setting the Anchor property as shown in Fig. 14.6. Leave the other control unanchored. Execute the application and widen the Form. The Button anchored to the bottom-right corner is always the same distance from the Form's bottom-right corner (Fig. 14.7), but the other control stays its original distance from the top-left corner of the Form.

Fig. 14.6 | Manipulating the **Anchor** property of a control.

Fig. 14.7 | Anchoring demonstration.

Sometimes, it's desirable for a control to span an entire side of the Form, even when the Form is resized. For example, a control such as a status bar typically should remain at the bottom of the Form. Docking allows a control to span an entire side (left, right, top or bottom) of its parent container or to fill the entire container. When the parent control is resized, the docked control resizes as well. In Fig. 14.8, a Button is docked at the top of the Form (spanning the top portion). When the Form is resized, the Button is resized to the Form's new width. Forms have a **Padding** property that specifies the distance between the docked controls and the Form edges. This property specifies four values (one for each side), and each value is set to 0 by default. Some common control-layout properties are summarized in Fig. 14.9.

Fig. 14.8 | Docking a `Button` to the top of a `Form`.

Control layout properties	Description
Anchor	Causes a control to remain at a fixed distance from the side(s) of the container even when the container is resized.
Dock	Allows a control to span one side of its container or to fill the remaining space in the container.
Padding	Sets the space between a container's edges and docked controls. The default is 0, causing the control to appear flush with the container's sides.
Location	Specifies the location (as a set of coordinates) of the upper-left corner of the control, in relation to its container.
Size	Specifies the size of the control in pixels as a `Size` object, which has properties `Width` and `Height`.
MinimumSize, MaximumSize	Indicate the minimum and maximum sizes of a `Control`, respectively.

Fig. 14.9 | `Control` layout properties.

The Anchor and Dock properties of a `Control` are set with respect to the `Control`'s parent container, which could be a `Form` or another parent container (such as a `Panel`; discussed in Section 14.5). The minimum and maximum `Form` (or other `Control`) sizes can be set via properties `MinimumSize` and `MaximumSize`, respectively. Both are of type `Size`, which has properties `Width` and `Height` to specify the size of the `Form`. Properties `MinimumSize` and `MaximumSize` allow you to design the GUI layout for a given size range. The user cannot make a `Form` smaller than the size specified by property `MinimumSize` and cannot make a `Form` larger than the size specified by property `MaximumSize`. To set a `Form` to a fixed size (where the `Form` cannot be resized by the user), set its minimum and maximum sizes to the same values or set its `FormBorderStyle` property to `FixedSingle`.

Using Visual Studio To Edit a GUI's Layout
Visual Studio provides tools that help you with GUI layout. In Chapter 3, you learned about the blue snap lines that appear to help you position a control with respect to other controls on a `Form` and the `Form`'s edges. These make the control you're dragging appear to "snap into place." Visual Studio also provides the **Format** menu, which contains several options for modifying your GUI's layout. The **Format** menu appears in the IDE only in **Design** view. Some formatting features include:

- Aligning multiple controls
- Making multiple controls have the same size
- Adjusting the horizontal and vertical spacing between controls
- Centering controls on the Form horizontally or vertically

14.5 GroupBoxes and Panels

GroupBoxes (introduced in Chapter 6) and Panels arrange controls on a GUI. They're typically used to group several controls of similar functionality or several controls that are related in a GUI. All of the controls that you drag onto a GroupBox or a Panel *move together* when you move the GroupBox or Panel to a new position the Form in **Design** view.

The primary difference between these two controls is that GroupBoxes can display a text caption and cannot have scrollbars, whereas Panels can display scrollbars but do not have a text caption. GroupBoxes have thin borders by default; Panels can be set so that they also have borders by changing their BorderStyle property. Figures 14.10 and 14.11 list some common properties of GroupBoxes and Panels, respectively.

GroupBox properties	Description
Controls	A collection of the controls that the GroupBox contains.
Text	Specifies the caption text displayed at the top of the GroupBox.

Fig. 14.10 | GroupBox properties.

Panel properties	Description
AutoScroll	Indicates whether scrollbars appear when the Panel is too small to display all of its controls. The default value is False.
BorderStyle	Sets the border of the Panel. The default value is None; other options are Fixed3D and FixedSingle.
Controls	A collection of the controls that the Panel contains.

Fig. 14.11 | Panel properties.

Look-and-Feel Observation 14.1
Panels and GroupBoxes can contain other Panels and GroupBoxes for more complex layouts.

Look-and-Feel Observation 14.2
You can organize a GUI by anchoring and docking controls inside a GroupBox or Panel. The GroupBox or Panel can then be anchored or docked inside a Form. This divides controls into functional "groups" that can be arranged easily.

When you drag new controls from the **Toolbox** into the GroupBox, they're added to the GroupBox's Controls property and become part of the GroupBox. The GroupBox's Text property specifies the caption.

To create a Panel, drag its icon from the **Toolbox** onto the Form. You can then add controls directly to the Panel by dragging them from the **Toolbox** onto the Panel. To enable the scrollbars, set the Panel's AutoScroll property to True. If the Panel is resized and cannot display all of its controls, scrollbars appear (Fig. 14.12). The scrollbars can be used to view all the controls in the Panel—both at design time *and* at execution time. In Fig. 14.12, we placed six Buttons vertically in a scrollable Panel. When you click one of these Buttons, the event handler (lines 5–11) changes the Text on the outputLabel to "You pressed: " followed by the Text of the clicked Button. All six Buttons' Click events are processed by this event handler. We set the Panel's BorderStyle property to FixedSingle, so you can see it on the Form. The sample output shows the results of clicking the first and last Buttons in the Panel.

```vb
1   ' Fig. 14.12: PanelDemo.vb
2   ' Displaying Buttons in a scrollable Panel.
3   Public Class PanelDemo
4       ' display which Button was pressed
5       Private Sub Button_Click(ByVal sender As System.Object,
6           ByVal e As System.EventArgs) Handles Button1.Click, Button2.Click,
7           Button3.Click, Button4.Click, Button5.Click, Button6.Click
8
9           ' display the Button's text in the outputLabel
10          outputLabel.Text = "You pressed: " & CType(sender, Button).Text
11      End Sub ' Button_Click
12  End Class ' PanelDemo
```

Fig. 14.12 | Using GroupBoxes and Panels to arrange Buttons.

14.6 ToolTips

In Chapter 2, we discussed tool tips—the helpful text that appears when the mouse hovers over a GUI control. The tool tips displayed in Visual Studio serve as useful reminders of each toolbar icon's functionality. Many programs use tool tips to remind users of each control's purpose. For example, Microsoft Word has tool tips that help users determine the purpose of the application's icons. This section demonstrates how to use the ToolTip component to add tool tips to your applications. Figure 14.13 describes common properties, a common event, and a common method of class ToolTip.

ToolTip properties, an event, and a method	Description
Common Properties	
AutoPopDelay	The amount of time (in milliseconds) that the tool tip appears while the mouse is over a control.
InitialDelay	The amount of time (in milliseconds) that a mouse must hover over a control before a tool tip appears.
ReshowDelay	The amount of time (in milliseconds) between which two different tool tips appear (when the mouse is moved from one control to another).
Common Event	
Draw	Raised when the tool tip is displayed. This event allows programmers to modify the appearance of the tool tip.
Common Method	
Show	Sets the tool tip's text and displays it.

Fig. 14.13 | ToolTip properties, an event and a method.

When you add a ToolTip component from the **Toolbox**, it appears in the component tray below the Form in **Design** mode. Once a ToolTip is added to a Form, a new property appears in the **Properties** window for each of the Form's other controls. This property appears in the **Properties** window as **ToolTip on**, followed by the name of the ToolTip component. For instance, if our Form's ToolTip were named ToolTip1 (the default name), you would set a control's **ToolTip on ToolTip1** property value to specify the text that will be displayed when the user positions the mouse over that control. Figure 14.14 demonstrates the ToolTip component. For this example, we create a GUI containing a Label, a TextBox and a Button, so that we can demonstrate a different tool tip for each. The ToolTip component automatically handles the event that causes the tool tip to display for each component, so we show only the sample outputs for this program.

Fig. 14.14 | Demonstrating the ToolTip component.

In this example, we used the default name of the ToolTip component—ToolTip1. Figure 14.15 shows the ToolTip component in the component tray. We set the tool tip text for the Label to "Hovering Over the Label". Figure 14.16 demonstrates setting the tool tip text for the first Label.

ToolTip component
in component tray

Fig. 14.15 | ToolTip component in the component tray.

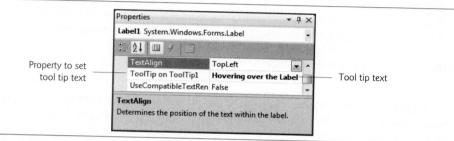

Property to set
tool tip text

Tool tip text

Fig. 14.16 | Setting a control's tool tip text.

14.7 Mouse-Event Handling

This section explains how to handle mouse events, such as clicks, presses and moves, which are generated when the user interacts with a control via the mouse. Mouse events can be handled for any control that derives from class System.Windows.Forms.Control. For most mouse events, information about the event is passed to the event-handling method through an object of class MouseEventArgs.

Class MouseEventArgs contains information related to the mouse event, such as the mouse pointer's *x*- and *y*-coordinates, the mouse button pressed (Right, Left or Middle) and the number of times the mouse was clicked. The *x*- and *y*-coordinates of the Mouse-EventArgs object are relative to the control that generated the event—that is point *(0,0)* represents the upper-left corner of the control where the mouse event occurred. Several common mouse events are described in Fig. 14.17.

Mouse events and event arguments
Mouse Events with Event Argument of Type EventArgs
MouseEnter   Occurs when the mouse cursor enters the control's boundaries.
MouseLeave   Occurs when the mouse cursor leaves the control's boundaries.

Fig. 14.17 | Mouse events and event arguments. (Part 1 of 2.)

Mouse events and event arguments	
Mouse Events with Event Argument of Type `MouseEventArgs`	
`MouseDown`	Occurs when a mouse button is pressed while the mouse cursor is within a control's boundaries.
`MouseHover`	Occurs when the mouse cursor hovers within the control's boundaries.
`MouseMove`	Occurs when the mouse cursor is moved while in the control's boundaries.
`MouseUp`	Occurs when a mouse button is released when the cursor is within the control's boundaries.
Class `MouseEventArgs` *Properties*	
`Button`	Specifies which mouse button was pressed (`Left`, `Right`, `Middle` or `None`).
`Clicks`	The number of times the mouse button was clicked.
`X`	The x-coordinate within the control where the event occurred.
`Y`	The y-coordinate within the control where the event occurred.

Fig. 14.17 | Mouse events and event arguments. (Part 2 of 2.)

Figure 14.18 uses mouse events to draw on a Form. Whenever the user drags the mouse (that is, moves the mouse while a mouse button is pressed), small circles appear on the Form at the position where each mouse event occurs during the drag operation. To create the event handlers in this example, select the Form in **Design** view, click the **Events** icon (⚡) in the **Properties** window then double click the event name—you'll need to do this once each for the MouseDown, MouseUp and MouseMove events.

```
1   ' Fig. 14.18: Painter.vb
2   ' Using the mouse to draw on a Form.
3   Public Class Painter
4      Private shouldPaint As Boolean = False ' determines whether to paint
5
6      ' should paint when mouse button is pressed down
7      Private Sub Painter_MouseDown(ByVal sender As System.Object,
8         ByVal e As MouseEventArgs) Handles MyBase.MouseDown
9         shouldPaint = True
10     End Sub ' Painter_MouseDown
11
12     ' stop painting when mouse button is released
13     Private Sub Painter_MouseUp(ByVal sender As System.Object,
14        ByVal e As MouseEventArgs) Handles MyBase.MouseUp
15        shouldPaint = False
16     End Sub ' Painter_MouseUp
17
18     ' draw circle whenever mouse moves with its button held down
19     Private Sub Painter_MouseMove(ByVal sender As System.Object,
20        ByVal e As MouseEventArgs) Handles MyBase.MouseMove
```

Fig. 14.18 | Using the mouse to draw on a Form. (Part 1 of 2.)

```
21              ' check if mouse button is being pressed
22              If (shouldPaint) Then
23                  ' draw a circle where the mouse pointer is present
24                  Using g As Graphics = CreateGraphics()
25                      g.FillEllipse(
26                          New SolidBrush(Color.BlueViolet), e.X, e.Y, 4, 4)
27                  End Using
28              End If
29          End Sub ' Painter_MouseMove
30      End Class ' Painter
```

Fig. 14.18 | Using the mouse to draw on a Form. (Part 2 of 2.)

Line 4 declares variable shouldPaint, which determines whether to draw on the Form. We want to draw only while the mouse button is pressed (that is, held down). When the user clicks or holds down a mouse button, the system generates a MouseDown event and the event handler Painter_MouseDown (lines 7–10) sets shouldPaint to True. When the user releases the mouse button, the system generates a MouseUp event, shouldPaint is set to False in the Painter_MouseUp event handler (lines 13–16) and the program stops drawing. Unlike MouseMove events, which occur continuously as the user moves the mouse, the system generates a MouseDown event only when a mouse button is first pressed and generates a MouseUp event only when a mouse button is released.

Whenever the mouse moves over a control, the MouseMove event for that control occurs. Inside the Painter_MouseMove event handler (lines 19–29), the program draws only if shouldPaint is True. Line 24 calls inherited Form method CreateGraphics to create a Graphics object that allows the program to draw on the Form. Class Graphics provides methods that draw various shapes. For example, lines 25–26 use method FillEllipse to draw a circle. The first parameter to method FillEllipse in this case is an object of class SolidBrush, which specifies the solid color that will fill the shape. The color is provided as an argument to class SolidBrush's constructor. Type Color contains many predefined color constants—we selected Color.BlueViolet. FillEllipse draws an oval in a bounding rectangle that is specified by the x- and y-coordinates of its upper-left corner, its width and its height—the final four arguments to the method. The x- and y-coordinates represent the location of the mouse event, which the event handler receives in its MouseEventArgs argument (e.X and e.Y). To draw a circle, we set the width and height of the bounding rectangle so that they're equal—in this example, both are 4 pixels.

Like dialog boxes, Graphics objects need to be returned to the system when they are no longer needed. For this reason, we create the Graphics object in a Using statement (lines 24–27). When the program reaches line 27, the Graphics object's Dispose method is called to return the Graphics object's resources back to the system. Classes Graphics, SolidBrush and Color are all part of the System.Drawing namespace.

14.8 Keyboard-Event Handling

Key events occur when keyboard keys are pressed and released. Such events can be handled for any control that inherits from System.Windows.Forms.Control. There are three key events—KeyPress, KeyUp and KeyDown. The KeyPress event occurs when the user presses a key that represents an ASCII character. The specific key can be determined with property KeyChar of the event handler's KeyPressEventArgs argument. ASCII is a 128-character set of alphanumeric symbols, a full listing of which can be found in Appendix D.

The KeyPress event does not indicate whether modifier keys (for example, *Shift*, *Alt* and *Ctrl*) were pressed when a key event occurred. If this information is important, the KeyUp or KeyDown events can be used. The KeyEventArgs argument for each of these events contains information about modifier keys. Often, modifier keys are used in conjunction with the mouse to select or highlight information. Figure 14.19 lists important key-event information. Several properties return values from the Keys enumeration, which provides constants that specify the various keys on a keyboard. The Keys enumeration constants can be combined to indicate multiple keys pressed at the same time.

Keyboard events and event arguments	
Key Events with Event Arguments of Type KeyEventArgs	
KeyDown	Generated when a key is initially pressed.
KeyUp	Generated when a key is released.
Key Event with Event Argument of Type KeyPressEventArgs	
KeyPress	Generated when a key is pressed.
Class KeyPressEventArgs properties	
KeyChar	Returns the ASCII character for the key pressed.
Handled	Indicates whether the KeyPress event was handled.
Class KeyEventArgs properties	
Alt	Indicates whether the *Alt* key was pressed.
Control	Indicates whether the *Ctrl* key was pressed.
Shift	Indicates whether the *Shift* key was pressed.
Handled	Indicates whether the event was handled.
KeyCode	Returns the key code for the key as a value from the Keys enumeration. This does not include modifier-key information. It's used to test for a specific key.

Fig. 14.19 | Keyboard events and event arguments. (Part 1 of 2.)

Keyboard events and event arguments	
KeyData	Returns the key code for a key combined with modifier information as a Keys value. This property contains all the information about the pressed key.
KeyValue	Returns the key code as an int, rather than as a value from the Keys enumeration. This property is used to obtain a numeric representation of the pressed key. The int value is known as a Windows virtual key code.
Modifiers	Returns a Keys value indicating any pressed modifier keys (*Alt*, *Ctrl* and *Shift*). This property is used to determine modifier-key information only.

Fig. 14.19 | Keyboard events and event arguments. (Part 2 of 2.)

Figure 14.20 demonstrates the use of the key-event handlers to display a key pressed by a user. The program is a Form with two Labels that displays the pressed key on one Label and modifier-key information on the other.

```vb
1    ' Fig. 14.20: KeyDemo
2    ' Displaying information about the key the user pressed.
3    Public Class KeyDemo
4       ' display the character pressed using KeyChar
5       Private Sub KeyDemo_KeyPress(ByVal sender As System.Object,
6          ByVal e As KeyPressEventArgs) Handles MyBase.KeyPress
7
8          charLabel.Text = "Key pressed: " & e.KeyChar
9       End Sub ' KeyDemo_KeyPress
10
11      ' display modifier keys, key code, key data and key value
12      Private Sub KeyDemo_KeyDown(ByVal sender As System.Object,
13         ByVal e As KeyEventArgs) Handles MyBase.KeyDown
14
15         If e.Alt Then ' key is Alt
16            keyInfoLabel.Text = "Alt: Yes" & vbCrLf
17         Else ' key is not Alt
18            keyInfoLabel.Text = "Alt: No" & vbCrLf
19         End If
20
21         If e.Shift Then ' key is Shift
22            keyInfoLabel.Text &= "Shift: Yes" & vbCrLf
23         Else ' key is not Shift
24            keyInfoLabel.Text &= "Shift: No" & vbCrLf
25         End If
26
27         If e.Control Then ' key is Control
28            keyInfoLabel.Text &= "Control: Yes" & vbCrLf
29         Else ' key is not Control
30            keyInfoLabel.Text &= "Control: No" & vbCrLf
31         End If
32
```

Fig. 14.20 | Demonstrating keyboard events. (Part 1 of 2.)

```
33            ' diplay key code, key data and key value
34            keyInfoLabel.Text &= "KeyCode: " & e.KeyCode.ToString() &
35              vbCrLf & "KeyData: " & e.KeyData.ToString() & vbCrLf &
36              "KeyValue: " & e.KeyValue.ToString()
37        End Sub ' KeyDemo_KeyDown
38
39        ' clear Labels when keys are released
40        Private Sub KeyDemo_KeyUp(ByVal sender As System.Object,
41          ByVal e As KeyEventArgs) Handles MyBase.KeyUp
42
43            charLabel.Text = String.Empty
44            keyInfoLabel.Text = String.Empty
45        End Sub ' KeyDemo_KeyUp
46    End Class ' KeyDemo
```

a) *H* pressed

b) *F1* pressed

c) *$* pressed

d) *Shift* pressed

Fig. 14.20 | Demonstrating keyboard events. (Part 2 of 2.)

Initially, the two Labels (charLabel and keyInfoLabel) contain "Just press" and "a key...", respectively. When the user presses a key, charLabel displays the key's character value, and keyInfoLabel displays related information. Because the KeyDown and KeyPress events convey different information, the application handles both.

The KeyPress event handler (lines 5–9) accesses the KeyChar property of the Key-PressEventArgs object. This returns the pressed key as a Char, which we then display in charLabel (line 8). If the pressed key is not an ASCII character, then the KeyPress event will not occur, and charLabel will not display any text. ASCII is a common encoding format for letters, numbers, punctuation marks and other characters. It does not support keys such as the function keys (such as *F1*) or the modifier keys (*Alt, Ctrl* and *Shift*).

The KeyDown event handler (lines 12–37) displays information from its KeyEventArgs object. The event handler tests for the *Alt, Shift* and *Ctrl* keys by using the Alt, Shift and Control properties, each of which returns a Boolean value—True if the corresponding key is pressed and False if otherwise. The event handler then displays the KeyCode, KeyData and KeyValue properties.

The KeyCode property returns a Keys enumeration value (line 34). The KeyCode property returns the pressed key, but does not provide any information about modifier keys. Thus, both a capital "A" and a lowercase "a" are represented as the *A* key.

The KeyData property (line 35) also returns a Keys enumeration value, but this property includes data about modifier keys. Thus, if "A" is input, the KeyData shows that both the *A* key and the *Shift* key were pressed. Lastly, KeyValue (line 36) returns the key code of the pressed key as an Integer. This Integer is the key code, which provides an Integer value for a wide range of keys and for mouse buttons. The key code is useful when testing for non-ASCII keys (such as *F12*).

The KeyUp event handler (lines 40–45) clears both Labels when the key is released. As we can see from the output, non-ASCII keys are not displayed in charLabel, because the KeyPress event is not generated. For example, charLabel does not display any text when you press the *F1* or *Shift* keys, as shown in Fig. 14.20(b) and (d). However, the Key-Down event is still generated, and keyInfoLabel displays information about the key that is pressed. The Keys enumeration can be used to test for specific keys by comparing the key pressed to a specific KeyCode.

Software Engineering Observation 14.1

To make a control react when a particular key is pressed (such as Enter*), handle a key event for that control and test for the pressed key. To allow a* Button *to be clicked when the user presses the* Enter *key on a* Form*, set the* Form*'s* AcceptButton *property.*

14.9 Menus

In Section 8.6, you learned how to create basic menus to organize groups of related commands. Although commands vary between applications, some—such as **Open** and **Save**—are common to many applications. Menus organize commands without "cluttering" the application's user interface. In this section, we take a deeper look at menus and the different types of menu items.

In Fig. 14.21, an expanded menu from Visual Basic 2010 Express lists various menu items and submenus (menus within a menu). Menu items are typically displayed down and indented to the right of the top-level menu, but they can be displayed to the left if there is not enough space to the right on the screen. The menu that contains a menu item is called the menu item's parent menu. A menu item that contains a submenu is considered to be the parent of the submenu.

Shortcut Keys

All menu items can have *Alt* key shortcuts (also called access shortcuts or hotkeys), which are accessed by pressing *Alt* and the underlined letter (for example, *Alt F* expands the **File** menu). Menus that are not top-level menus can have shortcut keys as well (combinations of *Ctrl, Shift, Alt, F1, F2*, letter keys, etc.).

To create an access shortcut (or keyboard shortcut), type an ampersand (&) before the character to be underlined. For example, to create the **File** menu item with the letter **F** underlined, type &File. To display an ampersand, type &&. To add other shortcut keys (like those shown in Fig. 14.21) for menu items, set the ShortcutKeys property of the appropriate ToolStripMenuItems. To do this, select the down arrow to the right of this property in the **Properties** window. In the window that appears (Fig. 14.22), use the CheckBoxes and drop-down list to select the shortcut keys. When you're finished, click elsewhere on the screen. You can hide the shortcut keys by setting property Show-ShortcutKeys to False, and you can modify how the control keys are displayed in the menu item by modifying property ShortcutKeyDisplayString.

Menu   Menu items   Shortcut key   Submenu

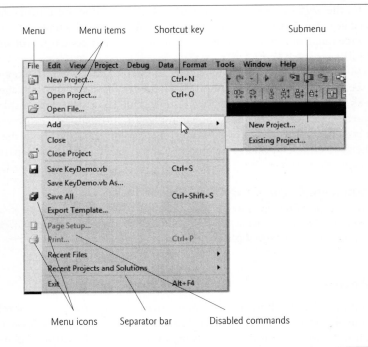

Menu icons   Separator bar   Disabled commands

Fig. 14.21 | Menus, submenus, menu items and menu icons.

Select modifier keys

Select key (modifier and key combination specifies the shortcut key for the menu item)

Fig. 14.22 | Setting a menu item's shortcut keys.

Look-and-Feel Observation 14.3

Buttons can have access shortcuts. Place the & symbol immediately before the desired character in the Button's text. To press the button by using its access key in the running application, press Alt and the underlined character. If the underlines are not visisble at runtime, press the Alt key to display the underlines.

Other Menu Item Types

Menu items can be grouped logically by inserting lines between groups of items—these are called separator bars. You can also add TextBoxes and ComboBoxes as menu items. When adding an item in **Design** mode, you may have noticed that before you click to enter text for a new item, you're provided with a drop-down list. Clicking the down arrow (Fig. 14.23) allows you to select the type of item to add—**MenuItem** (of type ToolStrip-MenuItem, the default), **ComboBox** (of type ToolStripComboBox), **Separator** (of type ToolStripSeparator) and **TextBox** (of type ToolStripTextBox). We focus on Tool-StripMenuItems. [*Note:* If you view this drop-down list for top-level menu items like the **File** menu, the **Separator** option will not display.] Common properties of MenuStrip and ToolStripMenuItem and a common event of a ToolStripMenuItem are summarized in Fig. 14.24.

Fig. 14.23 | Menu item options.

MenuStrip and ToolStripMenuItem properties and an event	Description
MenuStrip Properties	
Items	Contains the top-level menu items for this MenuStrip.
RightToLeft	Causes text to display from right to left. This is useful for languages that are read from right to left.
ToolStripMenuItem Properties	
Checked	Indicates whether a menu item is checked. The default value is False, meaning that the menu item is unchecked.
CheckOnClick	Indicates that a menu item should appear checked or unchecked as the item is clicked.
DropDownItems	Lists the submenu items for a particular menu item.
ShortcutKey-DisplayString	Specifies text that should appear beside a menu item for a shortcut key. If left blank, the key names are displayed.

Fig. 14.24 | MenuStrip and ToolStripMenuItem properties and an event. (Part 1 of 2.)

MenuStrip and ToolStripMenuItem properties and an event	Description
ShortcutKeys	Specifies the shortcut key for the menu item.
ShowShortcutKeys	Indicates whether a shortcut key is shown beside the menu item text. The default is True, which displays the shortcut key.
Text	Specifies the menu item's text. To create an *Alt* access shortcut, precede a character with & (for example, &File to specify a menu named **File** with the letter **F** underlined).
Common ToolStripMenuItem Event	
Click	Generated when an item is clicked or a shortcut key is used to select a menu item.

Fig. 14.24 | MenuStrip and ToolStripMenuItem properties and an event. (Part 2 of 2.)

Using Menus and Menu Items

Class MenuTest (Fig. 14.25) creates a simple menu on a Form. The Form has a top-level **File** menu with menu items **About** (which displays a MessageBox) and **Exit** (which terminates the program). The program also includes a **Format** menu, which contains menu items that change the format of the text on a Label. The **Format** menu has submenus **Color** and **Font**, which change the color and font of the text on a Label.

```
 1    ' Fig. 14.25: MenuTest.vb
 2    ' Using menus to change font colors and styles.
 3    Public Class MenuTest
 4
 5       ' display MessageBox when About menu item is selected
 6       Private Sub aboutToolStripMenuItem_Click(
 7          ByVal sender As System.Object, ByVal e As System.EventArgs) _
 8          Handles aboutToolStripMenuItem.Click
 9
10          MessageBox.Show("This is an example" & vbNewLine &
11             "of using menus.", "About", MessageBoxButtons.OK,
12             MessageBoxIcon.Information)
13       End Sub ' aboutToolStripMenuItem_Click
14
15       ' exit program when Exit menu item is selected
16       Private Sub exitToolStripMenuItem_Click(
17          ByVal sender As System.Object, ByVal e As System.EventArgs) _
18          Handles exitToolStripMenuItem.Click
19
20          Application.Exit()
21       End Sub ' exitToolStripMenuItem_Click
22
```

Fig. 14.25 | Menus for changing text font and color. (Part 1 of 4.)

```vbnet
23        ' reset checkmarks for Color menu items
24        Private Sub ClearColor()
25           ' clear all checkmarks
26           blackToolStripMenuItem.Checked = False
27           blueToolStripMenuItem.Checked = False
28           redToolStripMenuItem.Checked = False
29           greenToolStripMenuItem.Checked = False
30        End Sub ' ClearColor
31
32        ' update Menu state and color displayLabel black
33        Private Sub blackToolStripMenuItem_Click(
34           ByVal sender As System.Object, ByVal e As System.EventArgs) _
35           Handles blackToolStripMenuItem.Click
36
37           ClearColor() ' reset checkmarks for Color menu items
38           displayLabel.ForeColor = Color.Black ' set Color to Black
39           blackToolStripMenuItem.Checked = True
40        End Sub ' blackToolStripMenuItem_Click
41
42        ' update Menu state and color displayLabel blue
43        Private Sub blueToolStripMenuItem_Click(
44           ByVal sender As System.Object, ByVal e As System.EventArgs) _
45           Handles blueToolStripMenuItem.Click
46
47           ClearColor() ' reset checkmarks for Color menu items
48           displayLabel.ForeColor = Color.Blue ' set Color to Blue
49           blueToolStripMenuItem.Checked = True
50        End Sub ' blueToolStripMenuItem_Click
51
52        ' update Menu state and color displayLabel red
53        Private Sub redToolStripMenuItem_Click(
54           ByVal sender As System.Object, ByVal e As System.EventArgs) _
55           Handles redToolStripMenuItem.Click
56
57           ClearColor() ' reset checkmarks for Color menu items
58           displayLabel.ForeColor = Color.Red ' set Color to Red
59           redToolStripMenuItem.Checked = True
60        End Sub ' redToolStripMenuItem_Click
61
62        ' update Menu state and color displayLabel green
63        Private Sub greenToolStripMenuItem_Click(
64           ByVal sender As System.Object, ByVal e As System.EventArgs) _
65           Handles greenToolStripMenuItem.Click
66
67           ClearColor() ' reset checkmarks for Color menu items
68           displayLabel.ForeColor = Color.Green ' set Color to Green
69           greenToolStripMenuItem.Checked = True
70        End Sub ' greenToolStripMenuItem_Click
71
72        ' reset checkmarks for Font menu items
73        Private Sub ClearFont()
74           timesToolStripMenuItem.Checked = False
75           courierToolStripMenuItem.Checked = False
```

Fig. 14.25 | Menus for changing text font and color. (Part 2 of 4.)

```
76          comicToolStripMenuItem.Checked = False
77      End Sub ' ClearFont
78
79      ' update Menu state and set Font to Times New Roman
80      Private Sub timesToolStripMenuItem_Click(
81          ByVal sender As System.Object, ByVal e As System.EventArgs) _
82          Handles timesToolStripMenuItem.Click
83
84          ClearFont() ' reset checkmarks for Font menu items
85          timesToolStripMenuItem.Checked = True
86
87          ' set Times New Roman font
88          displayLabel.Font =
89              New Font("Times New Roman", 14, displayLabel.Font.Style)
90      End Sub ' timesToolStripMenuItem_Click
91
92      ' update Menu state and set Font to Courier New
93      Private Sub courierToolStripMenuItem_Click(
94          ByVal sender As System.Object, ByVal e As System.EventArgs) _
95          Handles courierToolStripMenuItem.Click
96
97          ClearFont() ' reset checkmarks for Font menu items
98          courierToolStripMenuItem.Checked = True
99
100         ' set Courier font
101         displayLabel.Font =
102             New Font("Courier New", 14, displayLabel.Font.Style)
103     End Sub ' courierToolStripMenuItem_Click
104
105     ' update Menu state and set Font to Comic Sans MS
106     Private Sub comicToolStripMenuItem_Click(
107         ByVal sender As System.Object, ByVal e As System.EventArgs) _
108         Handles comicToolStripMenuItem.Click
109
110         ClearFont() ' reset checkmarks for Font menu items
111         comicToolStripMenuItem.Checked = True
112
113         ' set Comic Sans MS font
114         displayLabel.Font =
115             New Font("Comic Sans MS", 14, displayLabel.Font.Style)
116     End Sub ' comicToolStripMenuItem_Click
117
118     ' toggle checkmark and toggle bold style
119     Private Sub boldToolStripMenuItem_Click(
120         ByVal sender As System.Object, ByVal e As System.EventArgs) _
121         Handles boldToolStripMenuItem.Click
122         ' toggle menu item checkmark
123         boldToolStripMenuItem.Checked = Not boldToolStripMenuItem.Checked
124
125         ' use Xor to toggle bold, keep all other styles
126         displayLabel.Font = New Font(displayLabel.Font.FontFamily, 14,
127             displayLabel.Font.Style Xor FontStyle.Bold)
128     End Sub ' boldToolStripMenuItem_Click
```

Fig. 14.25 | Menus for changing text font and color. (Part 3 of 4.)

```
129
130      ' toggle checkmark and toggle italic style
131      Private Sub italicToolStripMenuItem_Click(
132         ByVal sender As System.Object, ByVal e As System.EventArgs) _
133         Handles italicToolStripMenuItem.Click
134         ' toggle menu item checkmark
135         italicToolStripMenuItem.Checked =
136            Not italicToolStripMenuItem.Checked
137
138         ' use Xor to toggle italic, keep all other styles
139         displayLabel.Font = New Font(displayLabel.Font.FontFamily, 14,
140            displayLabel.Font.Style Xor FontStyle.Italic)
141      End Sub ' italicToolStripMenuItem_Click
142   End Class ' MenuTest
```

a) Initial application GUI

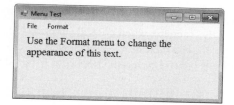

b) **Font** submenu showing **Bold** being slected

c) GUI after **Bold** was selected in part (b)

d) Selecting **Red** from **Color** submenu

e) GUI after **Red** was selected in part (d)

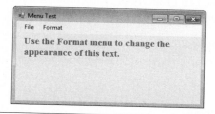

f) **About** dialog displayed by selecting **About** from the **File** menu

Fig. 14.25 | Menus for changing text font and color. (Part 4 of 4.)

Building the GUI

To create this GUI, drag a Label onto the Form and set its AutoSize property to False, its Font property to Times New Roman 14pt and its Text property to "Use the Format menu to change the appearance of this text." To create the menus, begin by dragging the MenuStrip from the **ToolBox** onto the Form. Then use **Design** mode to create the menu structure shown in the sample outputs. The **File** menu (`fileToolStripMenuItem`) has menu items **About** (`aboutToolStripMenuItem`) and **Exit** (`exitToolStripMenuItem`). The **Format** menu (`formatToolStripMenuItem`) has two submenus:

- **Color** (`colorToolStripMenuItem`) contains menu items **Black** (`blackToolStrip-MenuItem`), **Blue** (`blueToolStripMenuItem`), **Red** (`redToolStripMenuItem`) and **Green** (`greenToolStripMenuItem`). Set the **Black** menu item's **Checked** property to `True`, because at the start of the program, the text on the **Form** is black.

- **Font** (`fontToolStripMenuItem`) contains menu items **Times New Roman** (`times-ToolStripMenuItem`), **Courier New** (`courierToolStripMenuItem`), **Comic Sans MS** (`comicToolStripMenuItem`), a separator bar (`dashToolStripMenuItem`), **Bold** (`boldToolStripMenuItem`) and **Italic** (`italicToolStripMenuItem`). Set the **Times New Roman** menu item's **Checked** property to `True`, because this is the original font for the text on the **Form**.

Event Handlers for the *About* and *Exit* Menu Items

The **About** menu item in the **File** menu displays a `MessageBox` when clicked (lines 6–13). The **Exit** menu item closes the application through `Shared` method `Exit` of class **Application** (line 20). Class **Application**'s `Shared` methods control program execution. Method `Exit` causes our application to terminate.

Event Handlers for the *Color Submenu's* Menu Items

We made the items in the **Color** submenu (**Black**, **Blue**, **Red** and **Green**) mutually exclusive—the user can select only one at a time. To indicate that a menu item is selected, we'll set each **Color** menu item's **Checked** property to `True`. This causes a check to appear to the left of a menu item.

Each **Color** menu item has its own `Click` event handler. The event handler for color **Black** is `blackToolStripMenuItem_Click` (lines 33–40). Similarly, the event handlers for colors **Blue**, **Red** and **Green** are `blueToolStripMenuItem_Click` (lines 43–50), `redToolStripMenuItem_Click` (lines 53–60) and `greenToolStripMenuItem_Click` (lines 63–70), respectively. To make the **Color** menu items mutually exclusive, each event handler calls method `ClearColor` (lines 24–30) before setting its corresponding `Checked` property to `True`. Method `ClearColor` sets the `Checked` property of each color `MenuItem` to `False`, effectively preventing more than one menu item from being selected at a time.

Software Engineering Observation 14.2

The mutual exclusion of menu items is not enforced by the `MenuStrip`. You must program this behavior.

Event Handlers for the *Font Submenu's* Menu Items

The **Font** menu contains three menu items for fonts (**Times New Roman**, **Courier New** and **Comic Sans MS**) and two menu items for font styles (**Bold** and **Italic**). We added a separator bar between the font and font-style menu items to indicate that these are separate options. A **Font** object can specify multiple styles at once (for example, a font can be both bold and italic). We discuss how to change the **Font** on the **Label** momentarily. We set the font menu items to display checks. As with the **Color** menu, we enforce mutual exclusion of these items in our event handlers.

The event handlers for menu items **Times New Roman**, **Courier New** and **Comic Sans MS** are `timesToolStripMenuItem_Click` (lines 80–90), `courierToolStripMenuItem_Click` (lines 93–103) and `comicToolStripMenuItem_Click` (lines 106–116), respectively. Each event handler clears the `Checked` properties for all the font menu items by calling method `ClearFont` (lines 73–77), then sets to `True` the `Checked` property of the menu item that raised the event. This makes the font menu items mutually exclusive. The event handlers for the **Bold** and **Italic** menu items (lines 119–128 and 131–141) use the `Xor` operator to combine font styles.

Changing the *Label*'s Font

To change the font style on a `Label`, set its `Font` property to a new **Font object** (for example, lines 88–89). The `Font` constructor used here takes the font name, font size and font style as arguments. When we change the font in lines 88–89, 101–102 and 114–115, we change only the font name. The second and third arguments to the `Font` constructor use the `Label`'s current font size and current font style.

When we change the the font in lines 126–127 and lines 139–140, we change only the font's style. The style is specified with a member of the **FontStyle enumeration**, which contains `Regular`, `Bold`, `Italic`, `Strikeout` and `Underline`. A `Font` object's **Style** property is read-only, so it can be set only when the `Font` object is created.

Styles can be combined via **bitwise operators**—operators that perform manipulations on bits of information. All data is represented in the computer as combinations of 0s and 1s. Each 0 or 1 represents a bit. The `FontStyle` bit values are selected in a way that allows us to combine different `FontStyle` elements to create compound styles, using bitwise operators. These styles are not mutually exclusive, so we can combine different styles and remove them without affecting the combination of previous `FontStyle` elements. We can combine these various font styles using either the `Or` operator or the `Xor` operator. When the `Or` operator is applied to two bits, if at least one bit of the two has the value 1, then the result is 1. Combining styles using the `Or` operator works as follows. Assume that `FontStyle.Bold` is represented by bits 01 and that `FontStyle.Italic` is represented by bits 10. When we use the `Or` operator to combine the styles, we obtain the bits 11.

```
01  =  Bold
10  =  Italic
--
11  =  Bold and Italic
```

The `Or` operator helps create style combinations. However, what happens if we want to undo a style combination?

The `Xor` operator enables us to combine styles and to undo existing style settings. When `Xor` is applied to two bits, if both bits have the same value, then the result is 0. If both bits are different, then the result is 1.

Combining styles using `Xor` works as follows. Assume, again, that `FontStyle.Bold` is represented by bits 01 and that `FontStyle.Italic` is represented by bits 10. When we use `Xor` on both styles, we obtain the bits 11.

```
01  =  Bold
10  =  Italic
--
11  =  Bold and Italic
```

Now suppose that we would like to remove the FontStyle.Bold style from the previous combination of FontStyle.Bold and FontStyle.Italic. The easiest way to do so is to reapply the Xor operator to the compound style and FontStyle.Bold.

```
11  =  Bold and Italic
01  =  Bold
--
10  =  Italic
```

The advantages of using bitwise operators to combine FontStyle values become more evident when we consider that there are five different FontStyle values (Bold, Italic, Regular, Strikeout and Underline), resulting in 16 different FontStyle combinations. Using bitwise operators to combine font styles greatly reduces the amount of code required to check all possible font combinations.

In Fig. 14.25, we need to set the FontStyle so that the text appears in bold if it was not bold originally, and vice versa. Line 127 uses the Xor operator to do this. If displayLabel.Font.Style is bold, then the resulting style is not bold. If the text is originally italic, the resulting style is bold and italic rather than just bold. The same applies for FontStyle.Italic in line 140.

14.10 MonthCalendar Control

Many applications manipulate dates and times. The .NET Framework provides two controls that allow an application to retrieve date and time information—MonthCalendar and DateTimePicker (Section 14.11).

The **MonthCalendar** control (Fig. 14.26) displays a monthly calendar. The user can select a date from the currently displayed month or can use the provided links to navigate to another month. When a date is selected, it's highlighted. A range of dates can be selected by clicking one date on the calendar, then holding the *Shift* key while clicking another date. The default event for this control is **DateChanged**, which occurs when a new date is selected. Properties are provided that allow you to modify the appearance of the calendar, how many dates can be selected at once, and the minimum and maximum dates that may be selected. MonthCalendar properties and a common event are summarized in Fig. 14.27.

Fig. 14.26 | MonthCalendar control.

MonthCalendar properties and an event	Description
MonthCalendar Properties	
FirstDayOfWeek	Sets which day of the week is the first displayed for each week.
MaxDate	The last date that can be selected.
MaxSelectionCount	The maximum number of dates that can be selected at once.
MinDate	The first date that can be selected.
MonthlyBoldedDates	An array of dates that will be displayed in bold in the calendar.
SelectionEnd	The last of the dates selected by the user.
SelectionRange	The dates selected by the user.
SelectionStart	The first of the dates selected by the user.
Common MonthCalendar Event	
DateChanged	Generated when a date is selected in the calendar.

Fig. 14.27 | MonthCalendar properties and an event.

14.11 DateTimePicker Control

The **DateTimePicker** control (see output of Fig. 14.29) is similar to the MonthCalendar control, but displays the calendar when the user clicks the control's down arrow. The Date-TimePicker can be used to retrieve date and time information from the user. The **Value** property stores a **DateTime** (namespace System), which always contains both date and time information. Visual Basic's Date primitive type is actually an alias for type DateTime. You can retrieve the date information alone by using the **Date** property of the DateTime returned by the control's Value property, and the time information alone by using the DateTime's **TimeOfDay** property. By default, this control stores the current date and time.

A DateTimePicker provides more properties than a MonthCalendar to edit the look-and-feel of the drop-down calendar. Property **Format** specifies the user's selection options using the **DateTimePickerFormat** enumeration. The values in this enumeration are **Long** (displays the date in long format, as in **Thursday, July 10 2008**), **Short** (displays the date in short format, as in **7/10/2008**), **Time** (displays a time value, as in **5:31:02 PM**) and **Custom** (indicates that a custom format will be used). If value Custom is used, the display in the DateTimePicker is specified using property **CustomFormat**. The default event for this control is **ValueChanged**, which occurs when the selected value (whether a date or a time) is changed. DateTimePicker properties and a common event are summarized in Fig. 14.28.

DateTimePicker properties and an event	Description
DateTimePicker Properties	
CalendarForeColor	Sets the text color for the calendar.

Fig. 14.28 | DateTimePicker properties and an event. (Part 1 of 2.)

DateTimePicker properties and an event	Description
CalendarMonth-Background	Sets the calendar's background color.
CustomFormat	Sets the custom format string for the user's options.
Format	Sets the format of the date and/or time displayed in the control.
MaxDate	The maximum date and time that can be selected.
MinDate	The minimum date and time that can be selected.
ShowCheckBox	Indicates whether a CheckBox should be displayed to the left of the selected date and time.
ShowUpDown	Used to indicate that the control should have up and down Buttons. This is helpful for instances when the DateTimePicker is used to select a time—the Buttons can be used to increase or decrease hour, minute and second values.
Value	The date and/or time selected by the user.
Common DateTimePicker Event	
ValueChanged	Generated when the Value property changes, including when the user selects a new date or time.

Fig. 14.28 | DateTimePicker properties and an event. (Part 2 of 2.)

Demonstrating a DateTimePicker

Figure 14.29 demonstrates using the DateTimePicker control to select an item's drop-off date. Many companies use such functionality. For instance, several online DVD-rental companies specify the day a movie is sent out, and the estimated time that the movie will arrive at your home. In this application, the user selects a drop-off day, and then an estimated arrival date is displayed. The date is always two days after drop off, three days if a Sunday is reached (mail is not delivered on Sunday).

```vb
1   ' Fig. 14.29: DateTimePickerDemo.vb
2   ' Using a DateTimePicker to select a drop off date.
3   Public Class DateTimePickerDemo
4      ' set DateTimePicker's MinDate and MaxDate properties
5      Private Sub DateTimePickerDemo_Load(ByVal sender As System.Object,
6         ByVal e As System.EventArgs) Handles MyBase.Load
7         ' user cannot select days before today
8         dropOffDateTimePicker.MinDate = DateTime.Today
9
10        ' user can select days up to one year from now
11        dropOffDateTimePicker.MaxDate = DateTime.Today.AddYears(1)
12     End Sub ' DateTimePickerDemo_Load
13
```

Fig. 14.29 | Demonstrating DateTimePicker. (Part 1 of 2.)

```
14        ' display delivery date
15        Private Sub dropOffDateTimePicker_ValueChanged(
16           ByVal sender As System.Object, ByVal e As System.EventArgs) _
17           Handles dropOffDateTimePicker.ValueChanged
18
19           Dim dropOffDate As DateTime = dropOffDateTimePicker.Value
20
21           ' add an extra day when items are dropped off Friday-Sunday
22           If dropOffDate.DayOfWeek = DayOfWeek.Friday Or
23              dropOffDate.DayOfWeek = DayOfWeek.Saturday Or
24              dropOffDate.DayOfWeek = DayOfWeek.Sunday Then
25              ' estimate three days for delivery
26              outputLabel.Text = dropOffDate.AddDays(3).ToLongDateString()
27           Else ' otherwise estimate only two days for delivery
28              outputLabel.Text = dropOffDate.AddDays(2).ToLongDateString()
29           End If
30        End Sub ' dropOffDateTimePicker_ValueChanged
31     End Class ' DateTimePickerDemo
```

a) `DateTimePicker` showing current date

b) Selecting a drop-off date

c) Delivery date based on drop-off date

Fig. 14.29 | Demonstrating DateTimePicker. (Part 2 of 2.)

The DateTimePicker (dropOffDateTimePicker) has its Format property set to Long, so the user can select a date and not a time in this application. When the user selects a date, the ValueChanged event occurs. The event handler for this event (lines 15–30) first retrieves the selected date from the DateTimePicker's Value property (line 19). Lines 22–24 use DateTime's DayOfWeek property to determine the day of the week on which the selected date falls. The day values are represented using the DayOfWeek enumeration. Lines 26 and 28 use DateTime's AddDays method to increase the date by three days or two days, respectively. Then a string representing the delivery date is obtained by calling method ToLongDateString.

In this application, we do not want the user to be able to select a drop-off day before the current day, or one that is more than a year into the future. To enforce this, we set the DateTimePicker's MinDate and MaxDate properties when the Form is loaded (lines 8 and

11). Days from the current month that are prior to the MinDate are not displayed. Date-Time property Today returns the current day, and method AddYears (with an argument of 1) is used to specify a date one year in the future.

Let's take a closer look at the output. This application begins by displaying the current date (Fig. 14.29(a)). In Fig. 14.29(b), we selected the 29th of January as the package drop-off date. In Fig. 14.29(c), the estimated delivery date is displayed as Feburary 1st.

14.12 LinkLabel Control

The LinkLabel control displays links to other resources, such as files or web pages. A LinkLabel appears as underlined text (colored blue by default). When the mouse moves over the link, the pointer changes to a hand, just like a hyperlink in a web browser. The link can change color to indicate whether the link is new, previously visited or active. When clicked, the LinkLabel generates a LinkClicked event. Class LinkLabel is derived from class Label and therefore inherits all of class Label's functionality. Figure 14.30 lists several LinkLabel properties and a common event.

LinkLabel properties and an event	Description
Common Properties	
ActiveLinkColor	Specifies the color of the link when clicked.
LinkArea	Specifies which portion of text in the LinkLabel is part of the link.
LinkBehavior	Specifies the link's behavior, such as how the link appears when the mouse is placed over it.
LinkColor	Specifies the original color of all links before they've been visited. The default color is set by the system, but is usually blue.
LinkVisited	If True, the link appears as though it has been visited (its color is changed to that specified by property VisitedLinkColor). The default value is False.
Text	Specifies the control's text.
UseMnemonic	If True, the & character can be used in the Text property to create a shortcut (similar to the *Alt* shortcut in menus).
VisitedLinkColor	Specifies the color of visited links. The default color is set by the system, but is usually purple.
Common Event (event argument type is LinkLabelLinkClickedEventArgs)	
LinkClicked	Generated when the link is clicked.

Fig. 14.30 | LinkLabel properties and an event.

Class LinkLabelTestForm (Fig. 14.31) uses three LinkLabels to link to the C: drive, the Deitel website (www.deitel.com) and the Notepad application, respectively. The Text properties of the LinkLabel's cDriveLinkLabel, deitelLinkLabel and notepadLinkLabel describe each link's purpose.

```vb
 1  ' Fig. 14.31: LinkLabelTest.vb
 2  ' Using LinkLabels to create hyperlinks.
 3  Public Class LinkLabelTest
 4     ' browse C:\ drive
 5     Private Sub cDriveLinkLabel_LinkClicked(ByVal sender As System.Object,
 6        ByVal e As LinkLabelLinkClickedEventArgs) _
 7        Handles cDriveLinkLabel.LinkClicked
 8
 9        cDriveLinkLabel.LinkVisited = True ' change LinkColor after click
10        Process.Start("C:\")
11     End Sub ' cDriveLinkLabel_LinkClicked
12
13     ' browse www.deitel.com in the default web browser
14     Private Sub deitelLinkLabel_LinkClicked(ByVal sender As System.Object,
15        ByVal e As LinkLabelLinkClickedEventArgs) _
16        Handles deitelLinkLabel.LinkClicked
17
18        deitelLinkLabel.LinkVisited = True ' change LinkColor after click
19        Process.Start("http://www.deitel.com")
20     End Sub ' deitelLinkLabel_LinkClicked
21
22     ' run the Notepad application
23     Private Sub notepadLinkLabel_LinkClicked(ByVal sender As System.Object,
24        ByVal e As LinkLabelLinkClickedEventArgs) _
25        Handles notepadLinkLabel.LinkClicked
26
27        notepadLinkLabel.LinkVisited = True ' change LinkColor after click
28        Process.Start("notepad")
29     End Sub ' notepadLinkLabel_LinkClicked
30  End Class ' LinkLabelTest
```

a) Click the first LinkLabel to look at contents of C: drive

b) Click the second LinkLabel to display the Deitel website in your default web browser

Fig. 14.31 | LinkLabels used to link to a drive, a web page and an application. (Part 1 of 2.)

c) Click the third `LinkLabel` to open Notepad

Fig. 14.31 | `LinkLabel`s used to link to a drive, a web page and an application. (Part 2 of 2.)

The event handlers for the `LinkLabel`s call method **Start** of class **Process** (namespace **System.Diagnostics**), which allows you to execute other programs from an application. Method **Start** can take one argument, the file to open (a **String**), or two arguments, the application to run and its command-line arguments (two **Strings**). Method **Start**'s arguments can be in the same form as if they were provided for input to the Windows **Run** command (**Start > Run...**). For applications that are known to Windows (such as Notepad), full path names are not required, and the .exe extension often can be omitted. To open a file that has a file type that Windows recognizes, simply use the file's full path name. The Windows operating system must be able to use the application associated with the given file's extension to open the file.

The event handler for `cDriveLinkLabel`'s `LinkClicked` event browses the `C:` drive (lines 5–11). Line 9 sets the `LinkVisited` property to `True`, which changes the link's color from blue to purple (the `LinkVisited` colors can be configured through the **Properties** window in Visual Studio). The event handler then passes "`C:\`" to method **Start** (line 10), which opens a **Windows Explorer** window to show the `C:` drive's contents.

The event handler for `deitelLinkLabel`'s `LinkClicked` event (lines 14–20) opens the web page `www.deitel.com` in the user's default Internet browser. We achieve this by passing the web page address as a **String** (line 19), which opens the web page.

The event handler for `notepadLinkLabel`'s `LinkClicked` event (lines 23–29) opens the Notepad application. Line 28 passes the argument "`notepad`" to method **Start**, which runs `notepad.exe`. In line 28, the .exe extension is not required—Windows automatically recognizes the argument given to method **Start** as an executable file.

14.13 ListBox and CheckedListBox Controls

The `ListBox` (introduced in Section 4.10) control allows the user to view and select from multiple items in a list. The **CheckedListBox** control extends a `ListBox` by including CheckBoxes next to each item in the list. This allows users to place checks on multiple items at once, as is possible with CheckBox controls. (Users also can select multiple items from a `ListBox` by setting the `ListBox`'s **SelectionMode** property, which is discussed shortly.) In both controls, scrollbars appear if the number of items exceeds the `ListBox`'s viewable area.

Figure 14.32 lists common `ListBox` properties and methods, and a common event. The `SelectionMode` property determines the number of items that can be selected. This property has the possible values None, One, MultiSimple and MultiExtended (from the SelectionMode enumeration)—the differences among these settings are explained in Fig. 14.32. The SelectedIndexChanged event occurs when the user selects a new item.

ListBox properties, methods and an event	Description
Common Properties	
Items	The collection of items in the ListBox.
MultiColumn	Indicates whether the ListBox can break a list into multiple columns, which eliminates vertical scrollbars from the display.
SelectedIndex	Returns the index of the selected item, or -1 if no items have been selected. If the user selects multiple items, this property returns only one of the selected indices. For this reason, if multiple items are selected, you should use property SelectedIndices.
SelectedIndices	Returns a collection containing the indices of all selected items.
SelectedItem	Returns a reference to the selected item.
SelectedItems	Returns a collection of the selected item(s).
SelectionMode	Determines the number of items that can be selected and the means through which multiple items can be selected. Values None, One, MultiSimple (multiple selection allowed) or MultiExtended (multiple selection allowed using a combination of arrow keys or mouse clicks and *Shift* and *Ctrl* keys).
Sorted	Indicates whether items are sorted alphabetically. Setting this property's value to True sorts the items. The default value is False.
Common Methods	
ClearSelected	Deselects all items in the ListBox.
GetSelected	Takes an index as an argument, and returns True if the corresponding item is selected.
Common Event	
SelectedIndexChanged	Generated when the selected index changes.

Fig. 14.32 | ListBox properties, methods and an event.

Both the ListBox and CheckedListBox have properties Items, SelectedItem and SelectedIndex. Property Items returns all the list items as an ObjectCollection. Many .NET GUI components (for example, ListBoxes) use collections to expose lists of internal objects (for example, items contained within a ListBox). Property SelectedItem returns the ListBox's currently selected item. If the user can select multiple items, use collection SelectedItems to obtain all the selected items as a collection. Property SelectedIndex returns the index of the selected item—if there could be more than one, use property SelectedIndices. If no items are selected, property SelectedIndex returns -1. Method GetSelected takes an index and returns True if the corresponding item is selected.

Adding Items Programmatically

To add items to a ListBox or to a CheckedListBox, we must add objects to its Items collection. This can be accomplished by calling method Add to add a String to the ListBox's or CheckedListBox's Items collection. For example, we could write

```
myListBox.Items.Add( myListItem )
```

to add String *myListItem* to ListBox *myListBox*. To add multiple objects, you can either call method Add multiple times or call method AddRange to add an array of objects. Classes ListBox and CheckedListBox each call the submitted object's ToString method to determine the text for the corresponding object's entry in the list. This allows you to add non-String objects to a ListBox or a CheckedListBox that later can be returned through properties SelectedItem and SelectedItems.

Adding Items Via the String Collection Editor

Alternatively, you can add items to ListBoxes and CheckedListBoxes visually by examining the Items property in the **Properties** window. Clicking the ellipsis (...) button opens the **String Collection Editor**, which contains a text area for adding items; each item appears on a separate line (Fig. 14.33). The IDE then generates the code to add these Strings to the Items collection.

Fig. 14.33 │ String Collection Editor.

CheckedListBox Control

The CheckedListBox control derives from class ListBox and includes a CheckBox next to each item. As in ListBoxes, items can be added via methods Add and AddRange or through the **String Collection Editor**. CheckedListBoxes imply that multiple items can be selected, and the only possible values for the SelectionMode property are None and One. One allows multiple selection, because CheckBoxes imply that there are no logical restrictions on the items—the user can select as many items as required. Thus, the only choice is whether to give the user multiple selection or no selection at all. This keeps the CheckedListBox's behavior consistent with that of CheckBoxes. Figure 14.34 lists some common properties, a common method and a common event of class CheckedListBox.

> **Common Programming Error 14.1**
>
> *The IDE displays an error message if you attempt to set the SelectionMode property to MultiSimple or MultiExtended in the **Properties** window of a CheckedListBox. If this value is set programmatically, a runtime error occurs.*

CheckedListBox properties, a method and an event	Description
Common Properties	*(All the ListBox properties, the method and the event are inherited by CheckedListBox.)*
CheckedItems	Contains the collection of items that are checked. This is distinct from the selected item, which is highlighted (but not necessarily checked). There can be at most one selected item at any given time.
CheckedIndices	Returns a collection of indices for all checked items.
CheckOnClick	If True, clicking an item selects it and checks/unchecks it. By default this property is False—the user must select an item, then click it again to check/uncheck it.
SelectionMode	Determines how many items can be checked. The only possible values are One (allows multiple checks to be placed) or None (does not allow any checks to be placed).
Common Method	
GetItemChecked	Takes an index and returns True if the corresponding item is checked.
Common Event (Event arguments ItemCheckEventArgs)	
ItemCheck	Generated when an item is checked or unchecked.
ItemCheckEventArgs Properties	
CurrentValue	Indicates whether the current item is checked or unchecked. Possible values are Checked, Unchecked and Indeterminate.
Index	Returns the zero-based index of the item that changed.
NewValue	Specifies the new state of the item.

Fig. 14.34 | CheckedListBox properties, a method and an event.

ItemCheck Event of the CheckedListBox Control

Event ItemCheck occurs when a user checks or unchecks a CheckedListBox item. Event argument properties CurrentValue and NewValue return CheckState values for the current and new state of the item, respectively. A comparison of these values allows you to determine whether the CheckedListBox item was checked or unchecked. The Checked-ListBox control inherits the SelectedItems and SelectedIndices properties from class ListBox. It also includes properties CheckedItems and CheckedIndices, which return information about the checked items and indices.

In Fig. 14.35, class CheckedListBoxTestForm uses a CheckedListBox and a ListBox to display a user's book selections. The CheckedListBox allows the user to select multiple titles. In the **String Collection Editor**, we added items for some Deitel books—C, C++, Internet & WWW, Java, VB 2008, Visual C++ 2008, and Visual C# 2008 (the acronym HTP stands for "How to Program"). The ListBox (named displayListBox) displays the user's selections.

```vb
1    ' Fig. 14.35: CheckedListBoxTest.vb
2    ' Using the checked ListBox to add items to a display ListBox
3    Public Class CheckedListBoxTest
4       ' add an item to or remove an item from displayListBox
5       Private Sub itemCheckedListBox_ItemCheck(
6          ByVal sender As System.Object, ByVal e As ItemCheckEventArgs) _
7          Handles itemCheckedListBox.ItemCheck
8
9          ' obtain selected item
10         Dim item As String = itemCheckedListBox.SelectedItem.ToString()
11
12         ' if the selected item is checked add it to displayListBox;
13         ' otherwise, remove it from displayListBox
14         If e.NewValue = CheckState.Checked Then
15            displayListBox.Items.Add(item)
16         Else
17            displayListBox.Items.Remove(item)
18         End If
19      End Sub ' itemCheckedListBox_ItemCheck
20   End Class ' CheckedListBoxTest
```

Fig. 14.35 | CheckedListBox and ListBox used in a program to display a user selection.

When the user checks or unchecks an item in itemCheckedListBox, an ItemCheck event occurs and event handler itemCheckedListBox_ItemCheck (lines 5–19) executes. An If...Else statement (lines 14–18) determines whether the user checked or unchecked an item in the CheckedListBox. Line 14 uses the ItemCheckEventArgs property NewValue to determine whether the item is being checked (CheckState.Checked). If the user checks an item, line 15 adds the checked entry to displayListBox. If the user unchecks an item, line 17 removes the corresponding item from displayListBox. This event handler was created by selecting the CheckedListBox in **Design** mode, viewing the control's events in the **Properties** window and double clicking the ItemCheck event.

14.14 Multiple Document Interface (MDI) Windows

So far, we've built only single document interface (SDI) applications. Such programs can support only one open window or document at a time. To work with multiple documents, the user must execute another instance of the SDI application. Many applications have multiple document interfaces (MDIs), which allow users to work with several documents at once—for example, graphics applications like Corel PaintShop Pro and Adobe Photoshop allow you to edit multiple images at once.

Parent and Child Windows

The main application window of an MDI program is called the parent window, and each window inside the application is referred to as a child window. Although an MDI application can have many child windows, there is only one parent window. Furthermore, only one child window can be active at a time. Child windows cannot be parents themselves and cannot be moved outside their parent. In all other ways (closing, minimizing, resizing, etc.), a child window behaves like any other window. A child window's functionality can be different from the functionality of other child windows of the parent. Figure 14.36 depicts a sample MDI application.

Fig. 14.36 | MDI parent window and MDI child windows.

Specifying that a **Form** is an MDI Container

To create an MDI Form, set the Form's `IsMdiContainer` property to True. The Form changes appearance, as in Fig. 14.37.

Fig. 14.37 | SDI and MDI forms.

Creating a Class for Child **Forms**

Next, create a child Form class to be added to the Form. To do this, right click the project in the **Solution Explorer**, select **Add > Windows Form...** and name the file. Edit the Form as you like. To add the child Form to the parent, we must create a new child Form object, set its `MdiParent` property to the parent `Form` and call the child `Form`'s `Show` method. In general, to add a child `Form` to a parent, you would write

```
Dim childForm As New ChildFormClass()
childForm.MdiParent = parentForm
childForm.Show()
```

In most cases, the parent `Form` creates the child, so the *parentForm* reference is `Me`. The code to create a child usually resides in an event handler, which creates a new window in response to a user action. Menu selections (such as **File > New > Window**) are commonly used to create new child windows.

MDI Container Features

Class `Form` property `MdiChildren` returns an array of child `Form` references. This is useful if the parent window wants to check the status of all its children (for example, ensuring that all are saved before the parent closes). Property `ActiveMdiChild` returns a reference to the active child window; it returns `Nothing` if there are no active child windows. Other features of MDI windows are described in Fig. 14.38.

MDI Form properties, a method and an event	Description
Common MDI Child Properties	
`IsMdiChild`	Indicates whether a `Form` is an MDI child. If `True`, the `Form` is an MDI child (read-only property).
`MdiParent`	Specifies the MDI parent `Form` of the child.
Common MDI Parent Properties	
`ActiveMdiChild`	Returns the `Form` that is the currently active MDI child (returns `Nothing` if no children are active).
`IsMdiContainer`	Indicates whether a `Form` can be an MDI parent. If `True`, the `Form` can be an MDI parent. The default value is `False`.
`MdiChildren`	Returns the MDI children as an array of `Forms`.
Common Method	
`LayoutMdi`	Arranges child forms in an MDI parent `Form`. The method takes as a parameter an `MdiLayout` enumeration constant (`ArrangeIcons`, `Cascade`, `TileHorizontal` or `TileVertical`). Figure 14.41 depicts the effects of these values.
Common Event	
`MdiChildActivate`	Generated when an MDI child is closed or activated.

Fig. 14.38 | MDI Form properties, a method and an event.

Manipulating Child Windows

Child windows can be minimized, maximized and closed independent of the parent window. Figure 14.39 shows two images—one containing two minimized child windows and a second containing a maximized child window. When the parent is minimized or closed, the child windows are minimized or closed as well. The title bar in Fig. 14.39(b) is **Form1 - [Child]**. When a child window is maximized, its title bar text is inserted into the parent window's title bar. When a child window is minimized or maximized, its title bar displays a restore icon, which can be used to return the child window to its previous size (that is, its size before it was minimized or maximized).

Fig. 14.39 | Minimized and maximized child windows.

Tracking Child Windows in Menus

Class `MenuStrip` provides property `MdiWindowListItem` to track which child windows are open in an MDI container. The property specifies which menu, if any, displays a list of open child windows. When a new child window is opened, an entry is added to the list (as in the first screen of Figure 14.40). If more than nine child windows are open, the list includes the option **More Windows...**, which allows the user to select a window from a list in a dialog.

> **Good Programming Practice 14.1**
>
> *When creating MDI applications, include a menu that displays a list of the open child windows. This helps the user select a child window quickly, rather than having to search for it in the parent window.*

Arranging Child Windows

MDI containers allow you to organize child windows by calling method `LayoutMdi` of the parent `Form`. Method `LayoutMdi` receives as its argument one of the `MdiLayout` enumeration constants—`ArrangeIcons`, `Cascade`, `TileHorizontal` and `TileVertical`. Tiled windows completely fill the parent and do not overlap; such windows can be arranged horizontally (value `TileHorizontal`) or vertically (value `TileVertical`). Cascaded windows (value `Cascade`) overlap—each is the same size and displays a visible title bar, if possible. Value `ArrangeIcons` arranges the icons for any minimized child windows. If minimized windows are scattered around the parent window, value `ArrangeIcons` orders them neatly at the bottom-left corner of the parent window. Figure 14.41 illustrates the values of the `MdiLayout` enumeration.

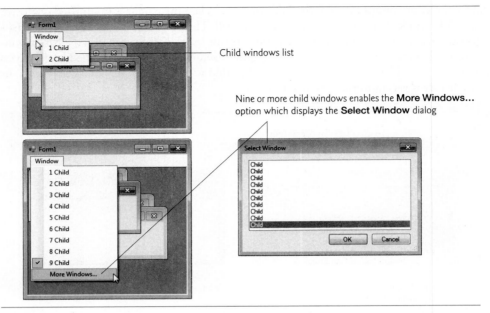

Child windows list

Nine or more child windows enables the **More Windows...** option which displays the **Select Window** dialog

Fig. 14.40 | MenuStrip property MdiWindowListItem example.

Fig. 14.41 | MdiLayout enumeration values.

Demonstrating an MDI

Class `UsingMDI` (Fig. 14.42) demonstrates MDI windows. It creates instances of child `ChildForm` (Fig. 14.43), each containing a `PictureBox` that displays an image. The parent MDI `Form` contains menus that enable users to create and arrange child `Form`s.

```
1   ' Fig. 14.42: UsingMDI.vb
2   ' MDI parent and child windows.
3   Public Class UsingMDI
4      ' create Visual C# image window
5      Private Sub csToolStripMenuItem_Click(ByVal sender As System.Object,
6         ByVal e As System.EventArgs) Handles csToolStripMenuItem.Click
7         ' create new child
8         Dim child As New ChildForm("Visual C# 2008 How to Program",
9            "vcs2008htp")
10        child.MdiParent = Me ' set parent
11        child.Show() ' display child
12     End Sub ' csToolStripMenuItem_Click
13
14     ' create Visual C++ image window
15     Private Sub cppToolStripMenuItem_Click(
16        ByVal sender As System.Object, ByVal e As System.EventArgs) _
17        Handles cppToolStripMenuItem.Click
18        ' create new child
19        Dim child As New ChildForm("Visual C++ 2008 How to Program",
20           "vcpp2008htp")
21        child.MdiParent = Me ' set parent
22        child.Show() ' display child
23     End Sub ' cppToolStripMenuItem_Click
24
25     ' create Visual Basic window
26     Private Sub vbToolStripMenuItem_Click(ByVal sender As System.Object,
27        ByVal e As System.EventArgs) Handles vbToolStripMenuItem.Click
28        ' create new child
29        Dim child As New ChildForm("Visual Basic 2008 How to Program",
30           "vb2008htp")
31        child.MdiParent = Me ' set parent
32        child.Show() ' display child
33     End Sub ' vbToolStripMenuItem_Click
34
35     ' exit application
36     Private Sub exitToolStripMenuItem_Click(
37        ByVal sender As System.Object, ByVal e As System.EventArgs) _
38        Handles exitToolStripMenuItem.Click
39
40        Application.Exit()
41     End Sub ' exitToolStripMenuItem_Click
42
43     ' set Cascade layout
44     Private Sub cascadeToolStripMenuItem_Click(
45        ByVal sender As System.Object, ByVal e As System.EventArgs) _
46        Handles cascadeToolStripMenuItem.Click
```

Fig. 14.42 | MDI parent-window class. (Part 1 of 2.)

```
47
48        Me.LayoutMdi(MdiLayout.Cascade)
49     End Sub ' cascadeToolStripMenuItem_Click
50
51     ' set TileHorizontal layout
52     Private Sub tileHorizontalToolStripMenuItem_Click(
53        ByVal sender As System.Object, ByVal e As System.EventArgs) _
54        Handles tileHorizontalToolStripMenuItem.Click
55
56        Me.LayoutMdi(MdiLayout.TileHorizontal)
57     End Sub ' tileHorizontalToolStripMenuItem_Click
58
59     ' set TileVertical layout
60     Private Sub tileVerticalToolStripMenuItem_Click(
61        ByVal sender As System.Object, ByVal e As System.EventArgs) _
62        Handles tileVerticalToolStripMenuItem.Click
63
64        Me.LayoutMdi(MdiLayout.TileVertical)
65     End Sub ' tileVerticalToolStripMenuItem_Click
66  End Class ' UsingMDI
```

a) Selecting a menu item that displays a child window

b) Child window displayed

c) Cascading child windows

d) Child windows cascaded

Fig. 14.42 | MDI parent-window class. (Part 2 of 2.)

UsingMDI

Class UsingMDI (Fig. 14.42) is the application's MDI parent Form. This Form is created first and contains two top-level menus. The **File** menu (fileToolStripMenuItem) contains both an **Exit** item (exitToolStripMenuItem) and a **New** submenu (newToolStripMenuItem) consisting of items for each child window. The **Window** menu (windowToolStripMenuItem), provides options for laying out the MDI children, plus a list of the active MDI children.

In the **Properties** window, we set the Form's IsMdiContainer property to True, making the Form an MDI parent. In addition, we set the MenuStrip's MdiWindowListItem property to windowToolStripMenuItem so that the **Window** menu can list the open MDI child windows.

The **Cascade** menu item's (cascadeToolStripMenuItem) event handler (lines 44–49) cascades the child windows by calling the parent Form's LayoutMdi method with the argument MdiLayout.Cascade (line 48). The **Tile Horizontal** menu item's (tileHorizontalToolStripMenuItem) event handler (lines 52–57) arranges the child windows horizontally by calling the parent Form's LayoutMdi method with the argument MdiLayout.TileHorizontal (line 56). Finally, the **Tile Vertical** menu item's (tileVerticalToolStripMenuItem) event handler (lines 60–65) arranges the child windows vertically by calling the parent Form's LayoutMdi method with the argument MdiLayout.TileVertical (line 64).

ChildForm

At this point, the application is still incomplete—we must define the MDI child class. To do this, right click the project in the **Solution Explorer** and select **Add > Windows Form....** Name the new class in the dialog as ChildForm (Fig. 14.43). Next, add a PictureBox (displayPictureBox) to ChildForm. When you provide a constructor in a Form class, the fist statement in its body *must* be a call to the base class's InitializeComponent method to ensure that the *Form* is constructed properly. In the constructor, Line 7 sets the title bar text. In lines 10–14, we retrieve the appropriate image file (fileName) as a resource, convert it to an Image, and set displayPictureBox's Image property.

```vb
1   ' Fig. 14.43: ChildForm.vb
2   ' Child window of MDI parent.
3   Public Class ChildForm
4      Public Sub New(ByVal title As String, ByVal fileName As String)
5         ' ensure that Designer generated code executes
6         InitializeComponent()
7         Text = title ' set title text
8
9         ' retrieve specific image from resources
10        Dim pictureResource = My.Resources.ResourceManager.GetObject(
11           fileName)
12
13        ' convert pictureResource to image type and load into PictureBox
14        displayPictureBox.Image = CType(pictureResource, Image)
15     End Sub ' New
16  End Class ' ChildForm
```

Fig. 14.43 | MDI child ChildForm.

The parent MDI Form (Fig. 14.42) creates new child windows using class ChildForm. The event handlers in lines 5–33 of Fig. 14.42 create a new child Form corresponding to the menu item clicked. Lines 8–9, 19–20 and 29–30 create new instances of ChildForm. Lines 10, 21 and 31 set each child's MdiParent property to the parent Form (Me). Lines 11, 22 and 32 call method Show to display each ChildForm.

14.15 Visual Inheritance

Chapter 10 discussed how to create classes by inheriting from other classes. In fact, you've used inheritance in every application so far, because every new Form class you create inherits from class Form. The code that indicates the inheritance relationship appears in the Form's Designer.vb file.

Inheriting from class Form is an example of visual inheritance. The derived Form class contains the functionality of its Form base class, including any base-class properties, methods, variables and controls. The derived class also inherits all visual aspects—such as size, component layout, spacing between GUI components, colors and fonts—from its base class.

Visual inheritance enables you to achieve visual consistency across your applications by giving them a common look-and-feel and makes it easier for users to move between applications. For example, you could define a base Form that contains a product's logo, a specific background color, a predefined menu bar and other elements. You then could use the base Form throughout an application for uniformity and branding.

Class *VisualInheritanceForm*

Class VisualInheritanceForm (Fig. 14.44) derives from Form. Its GUI contains two Labels with the text **Bugs, Bugs, Bugs** and **Copyright 2010 by Deitel & Associates, Inc.**, as well as one Button displaying the text **Learn More**. When a user presses the **Learn More** Button, the event handler learnMoreButton_Click (lines 5–12) displays a MessageBox that provides some informative text.

```
1   ' Fig. 14.44: VisualInheritanceForm.vb
2   ' Base Form for use with visual inheritance.
3   Public Class VisualInheritanceForm
4      ' display MessageBox when Button is clicked
5      Private Sub learnMoreButton_Click(ByVal sender As System.Object,
6         ByVal e As System.EventArgs) Handles learnMoreButton.Click
7
8         MessageBox.Show(
9            "Bugs, Bugs, Bugs is a product of Deitel & Associates, Inc.",
10           "Learn More", MessageBoxButtons.OK,
11           MessageBoxIcon.Information)
12     End Sub ' learnMoreButton_Click
13  End Class ' VisualInheritanceForm
```

Fig. 14.44 | Class VisualInheritanceForm, which inherits from class Form, contains a Button (**Learn More**). (Part 1 of 2.)

Fig. 14.44 | Class `VisualInheritanceForm`, which inherits from class `Form`, contains a Button (**Learn More**). (Part 2 of 2.)

Packaging Class VisualInheritanceForm for Reuse

To allow other `Forms` to inherit from `VisualInheritanceForm`, we must package it as a class library in a `.dll` file. To do so, right click the project name in the **Solution Explorer** and select **Properties**, then choose the **Application** tab. In the **Application type** drop-down list, change **Windows Forms Application** to **Class Library**. Building the project produces the `.dll`. The name of the solution that contains `VisualInheritanceForm` becomes parts of the class's fully qualified name—in this case, `VisualInheritance.VisualInheritance-Form`. [*Note:* A class library cannot be executed as a standalone application. The screenshots in Fig. 14.44 were taken before changing the project to be a class library.]

Visually Inheriting from Class VisualInheritanceForm

To visually inherit from `VisualInheritanceForm`, first create a new Windows Forms application named `VisualInheritanceTest` and name its `.vb` file `VisualInheritance-Test.vb`. Before you can use class `VisualInheritanceForm` in another project, you must reference its `.dll` file (also known as an assembly). This is known as adding a reference. To do so:

1. Select **Project > Add Reference....**

2. In the **Add Reference** dialog, click the **Browse** tab then locate and select the `VisualInheritanceForm.dll` file (located in the `bin\Release` directory of the `VisualInheritance` project we created in Fig. 14.44.

3. Click **OK** to add the reference to the project.

Next, click the **Show All Files** icon (▨) in the **Solution Explorer** and expand node for `VisualInheritanceTest.vb`. Open the `VisualInheritanceTest.Designer.vb` file and modify the line

```
Inherits System.Windows.Forms.Form
```

to indicate that the application's Form should inherit from class `VisualInheritanceForm` instead. The `Inherits` line in the `Designer.vb` file should now appear as follows:

```
Inherits VisualInheritance.VisualInheritanceForm
```

You must either specify `VisualInheritanceForm`'s fully qualified name or use an `Imports` declaration to indicate that the new application uses classes from the namespace `Visual-`

Inheritance. In **Design** view, the new application's Form now displays the inherited controls of the base class `VisualInheritanceForm` (as shown in Fig. 14.45). You can now add more components to the Form.

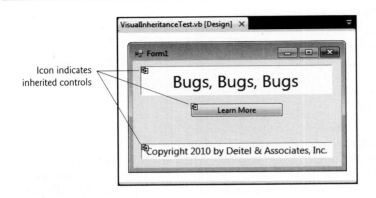

Icon indicates inherited controls

Fig. 14.45 | Form demonstrating visual inheritance.

Class `VisualInheritanceTest`

Class `VisualInheritanceTest` (Fig. 14.46) derives from `VisualInheritanceForm` (Fig. 14.44). The GUI contains the components inherited from `VisualInheritanceForm` and a new Button with the text **About this Program**. When the user presses this Button, the event handler `aboutButton_Click` (lines 5–12) displays another MessageBox providing different informative text.

Figure 14.46 demonstrates that the components, their layouts and the functionality of base-class `VisualInheritanceForm` (Fig. 14.44) are inherited by `VisualInheritance-Test`. If a user clicks the button **Learn More**, the base class event handler `learnMore-Button_Click` displays a MessageBox. The derived class `VisualInheritanceTest` cannot modify the inherited controls.

```vb
1   ' Fig. 14.46: VisualInheritanceTest.vb
2   ' Derived Form using visual inheritance.
3   Public Class VisualInheritanceTest
4      ' display MessageBox when Button is clicked
5      Private Sub aboutButton_Click(ByVal sender As System.Object,
6         ByVal e As System.EventArgs) Handles aboutButton.Click
7
8         MessageBox.Show(
9            "This program was created by Deitel & Associates",
10           "About this Program", MessageBoxButtons.OK,
11           MessageBoxIcon.Information)
12     End Sub ' aboutButton_Click
13  End Class ' VisualInheritanceTest
```

Fig. 14.46 | Class `VisualInheritanceTest`, which inherits from class `VisualInheritanceForm`, contains an additional Button. (Part 1 of 2.)

Derived class cannot modify these controls

Derived class can modify this control

Fig. 14.46 | Class VisualInheritanceTest, which inherits from class VisualInheritanceForm, contains an additional Button. (Part 2 of 2.)

14.16 Animation with the Timer Component

A Timer component generates Tick events at fixed time intervals. The interval is specified in the Timer's Interval property, which defines the number of milliseconds (thousandths of a second) between events. By default, timers are disabled and do not generate events. To allow a Timer to generate events, set its Enabled property to True. The application in Fig. 14.47 animates a series of images by displaying a new image every 50 milliseconds. There are 30 images in the animation (included with this chapter's examples). The images were added to the project as resources that are named "deitel" followed by a number in the range 0–29 indicating the order in which the images are displayed.

```
1   ' Fig. 14.47: AnimationDemo.vb
2   ' Animating images with a Timer component.
3   Public Class AnimationDemo
4      Private currentImage As Integer = 0' current image number
5      Private Const TOTAL_IMAGES = 30 ' total number of images
6
7      ' display next image
8      Private Sub animationTimer_Tick(ByVal sender As System.Object,
9         ByVal e As System.EventArgs) Handles animationTimer.Tick
10
11         ' get the resource representing the image
12         Dim pictureResource =
13            My.Resources.ResourceManager.GetObject("deitel" & currentImage)
14
15         ' convert pictureResource to type Image and load into PictureBox
16         logoPictureBox.Image = CType(pictureResource, Image)
```

Fig. 14.47 | Animating images with a Timer component. (Part 1 of 2.)

```
17
18          ' increment currentImage
19          currentImage = (currentImage + 1) Mod TOTAL_IMAGES
20      End Sub ' animationTimer_Tick
21   End Class ' AnimationDemo
```

Fig. 14.47 | Animating images with a `Timer` component. (Part 2 of 2.)

Line 4 declares variable `currentImage` to represent the index of the image that will be displayed next. Line 5 declares the constant `TOTAL_IMAGES` to represent the total number of images in the animation. When the `Timer`'s `Tick` event occurs, the event handler (lines 8–20) gets the resource for the current image (lines 12–13), changes the `logoPictureBox`'s `Image` property to the new `Image` (line 16) and increments `currentImage` (line 19). When `currentImage` reaches 29, line 19 resets `currentImage` to 0 so the animation continues with the first image.

14.17 Wrap-Up

This chapter introduced additional Windows Forms GUI controls. We discussed how to create event handlers from the code editor window and the **Properties** window. You learned how to use a control's properties and Visual Studio to specify the layout of your GUI. We used `Panel`s to organize other controls. We displayed helpful text on a GUI with `ToolTip` components, and demonstrated how to handle mouse and keyboard events. We presented more detail on creating menus. You learned the `DateTimePicker` and `Month-Calendar` controls, which allow users to input date and time values quickly while minimizing input errors. We used `LinkLabel`s to open applicatons and web pages when the user clicked a hyperlink. We introduced `CheckedListBox`es for presenting lists items that can be checked or unchecked. We then introduced multiple document interfaces. The chapter concluded with demonstrations of visual inheritance and controlling an animaton with a `Timer` Control. Chapter 15 introduces graphics capabilities for drawing on an application, and multimedia capabilities for playing audio and video in applications.

Summary

Section 14.2 Controls and Components

- The difference between a control and a component is that a component is not visual at execution time. When you drag a component onto the `Form` in **Design** view, the component is placed in the component tray below the `Form`.

- The controls and components are organized in the **Toolbox** into categories by functionality.
- When there are several windows on the screen, the active window is the frontmost one. The active window is said to "have the focus."

Section 14.3 Creating Event Handlers

- Double clicking a control on a Form in **Design** view creates the control's default event handler.
- Controls can generate many types of events, and each type can have its own event handler.
- Selecting a control from the left ComboBox at the top of the **Code** editor window, populates the right ComboBox with the control's events. Selecting an event from the right ComboBox moves the cursor to that event's handler in the code or creates the event handler if it does not already exist.
- Selecting a control on the Form in **Design** view then clicking the **Events** icon ( ) in the **Properties** window lists that control's events. You can double click an event's name to display the event handler in the editor or to create the event handler if it does not already exist.
- To create an event handler that can handle an event for several controls, select all the controls in **Design** view, then double click the event you want to handle in the **Events** tab of the **Properties** window. The event handler's Handles clause specifies a comma-separated list of all the events that will invoke the event handler.

Section 14.4 Control Properties and Layout

- Controls derive from class Control (of namespace System.Windows.Forms).
- The Focus method transfers the focus to a control and makes it the active control.
- The Enabled property indicates whether the user can interact with a control to generate an event.
- You can hide a control from the user without disabling the control by setting the Visible property to False or by calling method Hide.
- Anchoring causes controls to remain at a fixed distance from the sides of the container.
- Docking attaches a control to a container such that the control stretches across an entire side.
- A Form's Padding property specifies the distance between the docked controls and the Form edges.
- The Anchor and Dock properties of a Control are set with respect to the Control's parent container, which could be a Form or other parent container (such as a Panel).
- A Control's minimum and maximum sizes are set via properties MinimumSize and MaximumSize.
- Visual Studio's **Format** menu contains several options for modifying your GUI's layout.

Section 14.5 GroupBoxes and Panels

- GroupBoxes and Panels arrange controls on a GUI.
- GroupBoxes and Panels are typically used to group several controls of similar functionality or several controls that are related in a GUI.
- GroupBoxes can display a caption (i.e., text) and do not include scrollbars, whereas Panels can include scrollbars and do not include a caption.
- GroupBoxes have thin borders by default; Panels can be set so that they also have borders, by changing their BorderStyle property.
- The controls of a GroupBox or Panel are added to the container's Controls property.
- To enable a Panel's scrollbars, set the Panel's AutoScroll property to True. If the Panel is resized and cannot display all of its controls, scrollbars appear.

Section 14.6 ToolTips

- The ToolTip component can be used to add tool tips to your application.

- Once a ToolTip is added to a Form, a new property appears in the **Properties** window for the Form's controls. The property's name is **ToolTip on** followed by the name of the ToolTip component. Set this property to specify a control's tool tip text.

Section 14.7 Mouse-Event Handling

- Mouse events, such as clicks, presses and moves, are generated when the mouse interacts with any control that derives from class System.Windows.Forms.Control.

- Class MouseEventArgs contains information related to the mouse event, such as the coordinates of the mouse pointer, the mouse button pressed and the number of times the mouse was clicked.

- Whenever the user clicks or holds down a mouse button, the system generates a MouseDown event.

- When the user releases the mouse button, the system generates a single MouseUp event.

- Moving the mouse over a control causes a MouseMove event for that control.

Section 14.8 Keyboard-Event Handling

- Key events KeyPress, KeyUp and KeyDown occur in response to keyboard interactions.

- KeyPress occurs when the user presses a key that represents an ASCII character. The specific key can be determined with property KeyChar of the event handler's KeyPressEventArgs argument.

- KeyPress does not indicate whether modifier keys (e.g., *Shift*, *Alt* and *Ctrl*) were pressed when a key event occurred. If this information is important, the KeyUp or KeyDown events can be used.

- The KeyEventArgs argument for each Key event contains information about modifier keys. Several properties return values from the Keys enumeration, which provides constants that specify the various keys on a keyboard.

- The KeyEventArgs argument's KeyCode property returns the pressed key, but does not provide any information about modifier keys.

- The KeyEventArgs argument's KeyData property returns a Keys enumeration value, including data about modifier keys.

Section 14.9 Menus

- A menu that contains a menu item is called the menu item's parent menu. A menu item that contains a submenu is considered to be the parent of the submenu.

- All menus and menu items can have shortcut keys.

- Some menu items display check marks, indicating that multiple options on the menu can be selected at once.

- To create an access shortcut, type an ampersand (&) before the character to be underlined.

- To add other shortcut keys, set the ShortcutKeys property of the ToolStripMenuItem.

- You can hide the shortcut keys by setting property ShowShortcutKeys to False.

- A menu item's Checked property is used to display a check to the left of the menu item.

Section 14.10 MonthCalendar Control

- The MonthCalendar control displays a monthly calendar from which the user can select a date.

- A MonthCalendar's DateChanged event occurs when a new date is selected.

Section 14.11 DateTimePicker Control

- The DateTimePicker control can be used to retrieve date and/or time information from the user.

- DateTimePicker property Format specifies the user's selection options by using constants from the DateTimePickerFormat enumeration.

- The DateTimePicker's ValueChanged event occurs when the selected value changes.

*Section 14.12 **LinkLabel** Control*
- The LinkLabel control displays links to other resources, such as files or web pages.
- A LinkLabel appears as underlined text (colored blue by default). When the mouse moves over the link, the pointer changes to a hand—similar to a hyperlink in a web page.
- The link can change color to indicate whether the link is new, previously visited or active.
- When clicked, the LinkLabel generates a LinkClicked event.

*Section 14.13 **ListBox** and **CheckedListBox** Controls*
- ListBox property SelectionMode determines the number of items that can be selected.
- The SelectedIndexChanged event of class ListBox occurs when the user selects a new item.
- Property Items returns all the list items as a collection.
- Property SelectedItem returns the currently selected item.
- To add items to a ListBox, add objects to its Items collection. Call method Add to add an object to the ListBox's Items collection.
- You can add items to ListBoxes and CheckedListBoxes visually by examining the Items property in the **Properties** window.
- The CheckedListBox control extends a ListBox by including CheckBoxes next to each item.
- Items can be added to a CheckedListBox control via methods Add and AddRange or through the **String Collection Editor**.
- CheckedListBoxes imply that multiple items can be selected.
- An ItemCheck event occurs whenever a user checks or unchecks a CheckedListBox item.

Section 14.14 Multiple Document Interface (MDI) Windows
- Multiple document interface (MDI) programs enable users to edit multiple documents at once.
- The application window of an MDI program is called the parent window, and each window inside the application is referred to as a child window.
- Child windows cannot be parents themselves and cannot be moved outside their parent.
- To create an MDI Form, create a new Form and set its IsMdiContainer property to True.
- To add a child Form to the parent, create a new child Form object, set its MdiParent property to the parent Form and call the child Form's Show method.
- Child windows can be minimized, maximized and closed inside the parent window.
- Property MdiWindowListItem of class MenuStrip specifies which menu, if any, displays a list of open child windows.
- The child windows in an MDI application can be arranged by calling method LayoutMdi of the parent Form.

Section 14.15 Visual Inheritance
- Visual inheritance allows you to create a new Form by inheriting from an existing Form. The derived Form class contains the functionality of its base class.
- Visual inheritance enables you to achieve visual consistency across applications by reusing code.

*Section 14.16 Animation with the **Timer** Component*
- A Timer component generates Tick events at set intervals specified by the Timer's Interval property, which defines the number of milliseconds (thousandths of a second) between events.
- A Timer's Enabled property must be set to True before the Timer will generate events.

Terminology

access shortcut 513
active window 497
ActiveMdiChild property of class Form 534
AddDays method of DateTime 525
AddYears method of DateTime 526
anchor a control 501
Application class 520
bitwise operator 521
cascaded windows 535
Checked property of class
    ToolStripMenuItem 520
CheckedListBox class 528
child window in an MDI Form 533
Color 509
Control class 500
Controls property of class GroupBox 505
CreateGraphics method of class Form 509
CustomFormat property of class
    DateTimePicker 523
Date property of type DateTime 523
DateChanged event of class MonthCalendar 522
DateTime 523
DateTimePicker class 523
DateTimePickerFormat enumeration 523
DayOfWeek enumeration 525
DayOfWeek property of DateTime 525
default event of a control 498
dock a control 502
Enabled property of class Control 501
Exit method of class Application 520
FillEllipse method of class Graphics 509
Font class 521
FontStyle enumeration 521
Format property of class DateTimePicker 523
GetSelected method of class ListBox 529
Graphics class 509
hotkey 513
Interval property of class Timer 543
IsMdiContainer property of class Form 533
ItemCheck event of class CheckedListBox 531
Items property of class ListBox 529
key code 513
key event 510
KeyChar property of class
    KeyPressEventArgs 510
KeyDown event of class Control 510
KeyEventArgs class 510
KeyPress event of class Control 510
KeyPressEventArgs class 510

Keys enumeration 510
KeyUp event of class Control 510
LayoutMdi method of class Form 535
LinkClicked event of a LinkLabel 526
LinkLabel class 526
MaxDate property of class DateTimePicker 525
MdiChildren property of class Form 534
MdiLayout enumeration 535
MdiParent property of class Form 534
MdiWindowListItem property of class
    MenuStrip 535
MinDate property of class DateTimePicker 525
modifier key 510
MonthCalendar class 522
mouse click 507
mouse event 507
mouse move 507
mouse press 507
MouseEventArgs class 507
multiple document interface (MDI) 533
ObjectCollection class 529
Padding property of class Form 502
Panel control 504
parent menu 513
parent window in an MDI Form 533
Process class 528
SelectedIndex property of class ListBox 529
SelectedIndexChanged event of class
    ListBox 529
SelectedIndices property of class ListBox 529
SelectedItem property of class ListBox 529
SelectedItems property of class ListBox 529
SelectionMode enumeration 529
SelectionMode property of class ListBox 528
separator bar in a menu 515
ShortcutKeyDisplayString property of class
    ToolStripMenuItem 513
ShortcutKeys property of class
    ToolStripMenuItem 513
ShowShortcutKeys property of class
    ToolStripMenuItem 513
single document interface (SDI) 532
SolidBrush class 509
Start method of class Process 528
Style property of class Font 521
submenu 513
System.Diagnostics namespace 528
TabIndex property of class Control 500
TabStop property of class Control 500

Self-Review Exercises

14.1 State whether each of the following is *true* or *false*. If *false*, explain why.
a) The KeyData property includes data about modifier keys.
b) A Form is a container.
c) All mouse events use the same event arguments class.
d) A control's tool tip text is set with the ToolTip property of class Control.
e) Menus organize groups of related classes.
f) Menu items can display ComboBoxes, checkmarks and access shortcuts.
g) The ListBox control allows only a single selection (like a RadioButton).
h) An MDI child window can have MDI children.
i) MDI child windows can be moved outside the boundaries of their parent window.

14.2 Fill in the blanks in each of the following statements:
a) The active control is said to have the _____.
b) The Form acts as a(n) _____ for the controls that are added.
c) Class _____ and class _____ help arrange controls on a GUI and provide logical groups for radio buttons.
d) Typical mouse events include _____, _____ and _____.
e) _____ events are generated when a key on the keyboard is pressed or released.
f) The modifier keys we discussed in this chapter are _____, _____ and _____.
g) Method _____ of class Process can open files and web pages.
h) The _____ property of class MenuStrip allows a menu to display a list of child windows.
i) The _____ window layout option makes all MDI windows the same size and layers them so that every title bar is visible (if possible).
j) _____ are typically used to display hyperlinks to other resources, files or web pages.

Answers To Self-Review Exercises

14.1 a) True. b) True. c) False. Some mouse events use EventArgs, others use MouseEventArgs. d) False. A control's tool tip text is set using a ToolTip component that must be added to the application. e) False. Menus organize groups of related commands. f) True. g) False. The ListBox control allows single or multiple selection. h) False. Only an MDI parent window can have MDI children. An MDI parent window cannot be an MDI child. i) False. MDI child windows cannot be moved outside their parent window.

14.2 a) focus. b) container. c) GroupBox, Panel. d) mouse clicks, mouse presses, mouse moves. e) Key. f) *Shift, Ctrl, Alt.* g) Start. h) MdiWindowListItem. i) Cascade. j) LinkLabels.

Exercises

14.3 *(Enhanced Drawing Application)* Extend the program of Fig. 14.18 to include options for changing the size and color of the circles drawn. Create a GUI similar to Fig. 14.48. The user should be able to draw on the application's Panel. To retrieve a Graphics object for drawing, call method *panelName*.CreateGraphics(), substituting in the name of your Panel. Remember to call the Graphics object's Dispose method when the object is no longer needed.

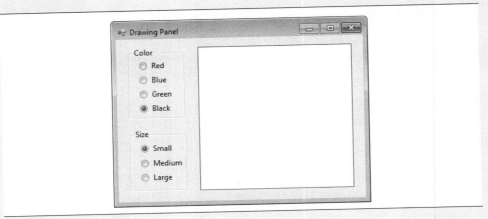

Fig. 14.48 | Drawing Panel GUI.

14.4 *(Guess the Number)* Write a program that plays "guess the number" as follows: Your program chooses the number to be guessed by selecting an Integer at random in the range 1–1000. The program then displays the following text in a label:

```
I have a number between 1 and 1000--can you guess my number?
Please enter your first guess.
```

A TextBox should be used to input the guess. As each guess is input, the background color should change to red or blue. Red indicates that the user is getting "warmer," blue that the user is getting "colder." A Label should display either "Too High" or "Too Low," to help the user zero in on the correct answer. When the user guesses the correct answer, display "Correct!" in a message box, change the Form's background color to green and disable the TextBox. Recall that a TextBox (like other controls) can be disabled by setting the control's Enabled property to False. Provide a Button that allows the user to play the game again. When the Button is clicked, generate a new random number, change the background to the default color and enable the TextBox.

14.5 *(MDI Text Editor)* Create an MDI text editor. Each child window should contain a multiline TextBox. The MDI parent should have a **Format** menu with submenus to control the size, font and color of the text in the active child window. Each submenu should have at least three options. In addition, the parent should have a **File** menu with menu items **New** (create a new child), **Close** (close the active child) and **Exit** (exit the application). The parent should have a **Window** menu to display a list of the open child windows and their layout options.

14.6 *(Enhanced Drawing Application)* Modify your solution to Fig. 14.3 so that it is an MDI application with child windows in which the user can draw. Add menus to the MDI application that allow the user to modify the size and color of the paint brush. When running this application, be aware that a child window will be cleared if one of the windows overlaps another.

Graphics and Multimedia

Objectives

In this chapter you will learn:

- To use graphics contexts and graphics objects.
- To manipulate colors and fonts.
- To understand and use GDI+ `Graphics` methods to draw lines, rectangles, `String`s and images.
- To use class `Image` to manipulate and display images.
- To draw complex shapes from simple shapes with class `GraphicsPath`.
- To use Windows Media Player to play audio and video.
- To print graphics to a printer.

15.1 Introduction

In the previous chapter, you learned more about Windows Forms GUI controls and we presented a simple animation of a spinning logo. In this chapter, we overview the traditional capabilities for incorporating graphics and multimedia into Windows Forms applications. You'll learn techniques for drawing two-dimensional shapes and for controlling colors and fonts. The drawing capabilities are part of namespace System.Drawing and the other namespaces that make up the .NET GDI+. GDI+ is an application programming interface (API) that provides classes for creating two-dimensional graphics, and manipulating fonts and images.

We start with basic drawing capabilities, then present more powerful features, such as changing the styles of the lines used to draw shapes and controlling the colors and patterns of filled shapes. Next, we explore techniques for manipulating images. Then, you'll learn how to add the Windows Media Player control to the **Toolbox** and use it to play audios and videos. The chapter concludes with an introduction to printing in which we demonstrate how to display a print preview and how to print directly to your computer's printer.

We also provide three online chapters that present Microsoft's latest approach to GUI, graphics, animation and multimedia—Windows Presentation Foundation (WPF):

- Windows Presentation Foundation (WPF) GUI
- WPF Graphics and Multimedia
- Silverlight and Rich Internet Applications

Silverlight is a subset of WPF for building web applications with rich GUIs, graphics and multimedia capabilities comparable to those in desktop applications.

15.2 Drawing Classes and the Coordinate System

Namespaces System.Drawing and System.Drawing.Drawing2D contain the most commonly used GDI+ components. Class Graphics contains methods used for drawing Strings, lines, rectangles and other shapes. The drawing methods of class Graphics usually require a Pen or Brush object to render a specified shape. The Pen draws shape outlines; the Brush draws solid objects.

Colors and Fonts

The Color structure contains numerous Shared properties that represent the colors of various graphical components, plus methods that allow users to create new colors. A structure is like a class in that it can have attributes and behaviors, but it's a value type rather than a reference type. Class Font contains properties that define the characteristics of fonts. Class FontFamily contains methods for obtaining font information.

Coordinate System

Let's consider GDI+'s coordinate system (Fig. 15.1), a scheme for identifying every point on the screen. The upper-left corner of a GUI component (such as a Panel or a Form) has the coordinates (0, 0). A coordinate pair has both an *x*-coordinate (the horizontal coordinate) and a *y*-coordinate (the vertical coordinate). The *x*-coordinate is the horizontal distance *to the right* from the upper-left corner. The *y*-coordinate is the vertical distance *downward* from the upper-left corner. The *x*-axis defines every horizontal coordinate, and the *y*-axis defines every vertical coordinate. You position text and shapes on the screen by specifying their (*x*, *y*) coordinates. Coordinate units are measured in pixels ("picture elements"), which are the smallest units of resolution on a display monitor.

> **Portability Tip 15.1**
> *Different display monitors have different resolutions, so the density of pixels varies among monitors. This might cause the sizes of graphics to appear different on different monitors.*

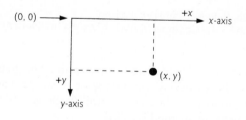

Fig. 15.1 | GDI+ coordinate system. Units are measured in pixels.

Points and Rectangles

The System.Drawing namespace provides several structures that represent sizes and locations in the coordinate system. The Point structure represents the *x-y* coordinates of a point on a two-dimensional plane. The Rectangle structure defines the upper-left *x-y* coordinates, width and height of a rectangular shape. The Size structure represents the width and height of a shape.

15.3 Graphics Contexts and Graphics Objects

A graphics context represents a drawing surface that enables drawing on the screen. A Graphics object manages a graphics context, controlling how information is drawn. Graphics objects contain methods for drawing, font manipulation, color manipulation and other graphics-related actions. Every derived class of System.Windows.Forms.Form inherits an OnPaint method in which most graphics operations are performed. The arguments to the OnPaint method include a **PaintEventArgs** object from which we can obtain a Graphics object for drawing on the Form. We must obtain the Graphics object on each call to the method, because the properties of the graphics context that the graphics object represents could change. Method OnPaint triggers the Control's **Paint** event.

Overriding *OnPaint*

When drawing on a Form, you can override method OnPaint to retrieve a Graphics object from its PaintEventArgs argument. To override the inherited OnPaint method, use the following method header:

```
Protected Overrides Sub OnPaint(PaintEventArgs e)
```

Next, call the base class's OnPaint method to execute any code in the base class's version of the method, as in:

```
MyBase.OnPaint(e)
```

Then extract the incoming Graphics object from the argument, as in:

```
Dim graphicsObject As Graphics = e.Graphics
```

Variable graphicsObject can now be used to draw shapes and Strings on the Form.

Handling the *Paint* Event

Rather than overriding the OnPaint method, you can add an event handler for the Paint event. Visual Studio .NET generates the Paint event handler in this format:

```
Protected Sub MyEventHandler_Paint(
    ByVal sender As Object, ByVal e As PaintEventArgs)
```

Calling *OnPaint*

You seldom call the OnPaint method directly, because drawing graphics is an event-driven process. An event—such as *covering*, *uncovering* or *resizing* a Form—calls the OnPaint method of that Form. Similarly, when any control (such as a TextBox or Label) is displayed, that control's OnPaint method is called.

You can force a call to OnPaint by calling a Control's **Invalidate** method, which refreshes a control and repaints all its graphical components. Class Control has several overloaded Invalidate methods that allow you to update portions of a control.

Getting a Graphics Context for a Control

Controls, such as Labels and Buttons, do not have their own graphics contexts, but you can create them. To draw on a control, first create a graphics object by invoking the control's CreateGraphics method, as in:

```
Dim graphicsObject As Graphics = controlName.CreateGraphics();
```

Now you can use the methods provided in class Graphics to draw on the control.

15.4 Colors

Colors can enhance a program's appearance and help convey meaning, just as a red traffic light indicates stop, yellow indicates caution and green indicates go. Structure Color defines methods and properties used to manipulate colors.

ARGB Values

Every color can be created from a combination of alpha, red, green and blue components (called **ARGB values**). All four ARGB components are `Byte`s that represent integer values in the range 0 to 255. The alpha value determines the opacity of the color. For example, the alpha value 0 represents a transparent color, and the value 255 represents an opaque color. Alpha values between 0 and 255 result in a weighted blending effect of the color's RGB value with that of any background color, causing a semitransparent effect. The first number in the RGB value defines the amount of red in the color, the second defines the amount of green and the third defines the amount of blue. The larger the value, the greater the amount of that color. You can choose from almost 17 million colors. If a particular computer cannot display all these colors, it will display the color closest to the one specified. Figure 15.2 summarizes some predefined `Color` properties (all are `Public`, `Shared` and `ReadOnly`), and Fig. 15.3 describes several `Color` methods and properties.

Constants in structure `Color`	RGB value	Constants in structure `Color`	RGB value
Orange	255, 165, 0	White	255, 255, 255
Pink	255, 192, 203	Gray	128, 128, 128
Cyan	0, 255, 255	DarkGray	169, 169, 169
Magenta	255, 0, 255	Red	255, 0, 0
Yellow	255, 255, 0	Green	0, 255, 0
Black	0, 0, 0	Blue	0, 0, 255

Fig. 15.2 | `Color` structure `Shared ReadOnly` properties and their RGB values.

Color methods and properties	Description
Common Methods	
FromArgb	A `Shared` method that creates a color based on red, green and blue values expressed as `Integer`s from 0 to 255. The overloaded version allows specification of alpha, red, green and blue values.
FromName	A `Shared` method that creates a color from a name, passed as a `String`.
Common Properties	
A	A `Byte` between 0 and 255, representing the alpha component.
R	A `Byte` between 0 and 255, representing the red component.
G	A `Byte` between 0 and 255, representing the green component.
B	A `Byte` between 0 and 255, representing the blue component.

Fig. 15.3 | `Color` structure members.

Figure 15.3 describes two **FromArgb** method calls. One takes three `Integer` arguments, and one takes four `Integer` arguments (all argument values must be between 0 and 255, inclusive). Both take `Integer` arguments specifying the amount of red, green and blue. The other version also allows the user to specify the alpha component; the three-argument version defaults the alpha to 255 (opaque). Both methods return a `Color` object. `Color` properties **A**, **R**, **G** and **B** return `Bytes` that represent `Integer` values from 0 to 255, corresponding to the amounts of alpha, red, green and blue, respectively.

Pens and Brushes

You draw shapes and `Strings` with `Pens` and `Brushes`. A `Pen` is used to draw lines. Most drawing methods require a `Pen` object. The overloaded `Pen` constructors allow you to specify the colors and widths of the lines you wish to draw. Namespace `System.Drawing` also provides predefined `Pens` in class `Pens` and predefined `Brushes` in class `Brushes`. All classes derived from class `Brush` define objects that color the interiors of graphical shapes. For example, the `SolidBrush` constructor takes a `Color` object—the color to draw. In most `Fill` methods of class `Graphics`, `Brushes` fill a space with a color, pattern or image. Figure 15.4 summarizes some `Brushes` and their functions.

Class	Description
HatchBrush	Fills a region with a pattern. The pattern is defined by a member of the **HatchStyle** enumeration, a foreground color (with which the pattern is drawn) and a background color.
LinearGradientBrush	Fills a region with a gradual blend of one color to another—known as a **gradient**. Linear gradients are defined along a line. They can be specified by the two colors, the angle of the gradient (which specifies the direction) and either the width of a rectangle or two points.
SolidBrush	Fills a region with one color that is specified by a `Color` object.
TextureBrush	Fills a region by repeating a specified `Image` across the surface.

Fig. 15.4 | Classes that derive from class `Brush`.

Manipulating Colors

Figure 15.5 demonstrates several of the methods and properties described in Fig. 15.3. It displays two overlapping rectangles, allowing you to experiment with color values, color names and alpha values (for transparency).

When the application begins executing, its `Form` is displayed. This results in a call to method `OnPaint` to paint the `Form`'s contents. Line 13 gets a reference to the `Graphics` object that is received as part of the `PaintEventArgs` parameter and assigns it to `graphicsObject`. Lines 14 and 15 create a black and a white `SolidBrush` for drawing solid shapes on the `Form`. Class **SolidBrush** derives from class `Brush`, so a `SolidBrush` can be passed to any method that expects a `Brush` parameter.

```
1   ' Fig. 15.5: ShowColors.vb
2   ' Color value and alpha demonstration.
3   Public Class ShowColors
4      ' color for back rectangle
5      Private backgroundColor As Color = Color.Wheat
```

Fig. 15.5 | Color value and alpha demonstration. (Part 1 of 3.)

```vb
 6
 7      ' color for front rectangle
 8      Private foregroundColor As Color = Color.FromArgb(100, 0, 0, 255)
 9
10      ' override Form's OnPaint method
11      Protected Overrides Sub OnPaint(ByVal e As PaintEventArgs)
12         MyBase.OnPaint(e) ' call base class's OnPaint
13         Dim graphicsObject As Graphics = e.Graphics ' get graphics object
14         Dim textBrush As New SolidBrush(Color.Black) ' create text brush
15         Dim brush As New SolidBrush(Color.White) ' create solid brush
16
17         ' draw white background
18         graphicsObject.FillRectangle(brush, 4, 4, 275, 180)
19
20         ' display name of backgroundColor
21         graphicsObject.DrawString(
22            backgroundColor.Name, Me.Font, textBrush, 40, 5)
23
24         ' set brush color and display back rectangle
25         brush.Color = backgroundColor
26         graphicsObject.FillRectangle(brush, 45, 20, 150, 120)
27
28         ' display Argb values of front color
29         graphicsObject.DrawString("Alpha: " & foregroundColor.A &
30            " Red: " & foregroundColor.R & " Green: " &
31            foregroundColor.G & " Blue: " & foregroundColor.B, Me.Font,
32            textBrush, 55, 165)
33
34         ' set brush color and display front rectangle
35         brush.Color = foregroundColor
36         graphicsObject.FillRectangle(brush, 65, 35, 170, 130)
37      End Sub ' OnPaint
38
39      ' change back rectangle's color
40      Private Sub setColorNameButton_Click(ByVal sender As System.Object,
41         ByVal e As System.EventArgs) Handles setColorNameButton.Click
42         ' set backColor to color specified in text box
43         backgroundColor = Color.FromName(colorNameTextBox.Text)
44         Invalidate() ' refresh Form
45      End Sub ' setColorNameButton_Click
46
47      ' change front rectangle's color
48      Private Sub setColorValueButton_Click(ByVal sender As System.Object,
49         ByVal e As System.EventArgs) Handles setColorValueButton.Click
50         ' obtain new front color from text boxes
51         foregroundColor = Color.FromArgb(
52            Convert.ToInt32(alphaTextBox.Text),
53            Convert.ToInt32(redTextBox.Text),
54            Convert.ToInt32(greenTextBox.Text),
55            Convert.ToInt32(blueTextBox.Text))
56         Invalidate() ' refresh Form
57      End Sub ' setColorValueButton_Click
58   End Class ' ShowColors
```

Fig. 15.5 | Color value and alpha demonstration. (Part 2 of 3.)

a) Setting the name of the background color

b) Setting the values of the foreground color

Fig. 15.5 | Color value and alpha demonstration. (Part 3 of 3.)

Line 18 uses Graphics method FillRectangle to draw a solid white rectangle using the SolidBrush created in line 15. FillRectangle takes as arguments

- a Brush
- the *x*- and *y*-coordinates of the rectangle's upper-left corner
- the width and height of the rectangle

Lines 21–22 display the Name of the backgroundColor with Graphics method Draw-String. There are several overloaded DrawString methods; the version demonstrated in lines 21–22 takes as arguments

- the String to display
- the display Font (the Form's current Font in this example)
- the Brush to use for drawing
- the *x*- and *y*-coordinates of the location for the String's first character

Lines 25–26 assign the backgroundColor value to brush's Color property and display a rectangle. Lines 29–32 extract and display foregroundColor's ARGB values and draw a String containing those values. Lines 35–36 assign the foregroundColor value to brush's Color property, then draw a filled rectangle in the foregroundColor that overlaps the rectangle drawn at line 26.

Button event handler setColorNameButton_Click (lines 40–45) uses class Color's Shared method **FromName** to create a new Color object from the color name that a user enters in a TextBox. The color names that can be used with this method are defined in the KnowColor enumeration. This Color is assigned to backgroundColor (line 43). Then line 44 invokes the Form's Invalidate method to indicate that the Form should be repainted, which results in a call to OnPaint to update the Form on the screen.

Button event handler setColorValueButton_Click (lines 48–57) uses Color method FromArgb to construct a new Color object from the ARGB values that a user specifies via

TextBoxes, then assigns the newly created Color to foregroundColor. Line 56 invokes the Form's Invalidate method to indicate that the Form should be repainted, which results in a call to OnPaint to update the Form on the screen.

Changing the alpha value of the foregroundColor from 0 to 255, makes the effects of alpha blending apparent. The sample output in Fig. 15.5(a) shows that the red back rectangle blends with the blue front rectangle to create purple where they overlap. Note that you cannot modify an existing Color object. To use a different color, create a new Color object.

Using the *ColorDialog* to Select Colors from a Color Palette

A **ColorDialog** is a built-in dialog box that allows users to select from a palette of available colors or to create custom colors. Figure 15.6 demonstrates the ColorDialog. When a user selects a color and presses **OK**, the application retrieves the user's selection via the Color-Dialog's **Color** property.

```vb
1   ' Fig. 15.6: ColorDialogDemo.vb
2   ' ColorDialog used to change background and text color.
3   Public Class ColorDialogDemo
4      ' create ColorDialog object
5      Private Shared colorChooser As New ColorDialog()
6
7      ' change background color
8      Private Sub setBackgroundColorButton_Click(
9         ByVal sender As System.Object, ByVal e As System.EventArgs) _
10        Handles setBackgroundColorButton.Click
11
12        ' show ColorDialog and get result
13        colorChooser.FullOpen = True
14        Dim result As DialogResult = colorChooser.ShowDialog()
15
16        If result = Windows.Forms.DialogResult.OK Then
17           Me.BackColor = colorChooser.Color ' set background color
18        End If
19     End Sub ' setBackgroundColorButton_Click
20
21     ' change text color
22     Private Sub setTextColorButton_Click(ByVal sender As System.Object,
23        ByVal e As System.EventArgs) Handles setTextColorButton.Click
24
25        ' get chosen color
26        Dim result As DialogResult = colorChooser.ShowDialog()
27
28        If result = Windows.Forms.DialogResult.OK Then
29           setBackgroundColorButton.ForeColor = colorChooser.Color
30           setTextColorButton.ForeColor = colorChooser.Color
31        End If
32     End Sub ' setTextColorButton_Click
33  End Class ' ColorDialogDemo
```

Fig. 15.6 | ColorDialog used to change background and text color. (Part 1 of 2.)

a) Displaying the `ColorDialog`, selecting the cyan color swatch and changing the `Form`'s background color

b) Displaying the `ColorDialog`, selecting the purple color swatch and changing the text color on the `Button`s

Fig. 15.6 | `ColorDialog` used to change background and text color. (Part 2 of 2.)

The GUI for this application contains two `Button`s. The `setBackgroundColorButton` allows the user to change the `Form`'s background color. The `setTextColorButton` allows the user to change the `Button`s' text color. Line 5 creates a `Private Shared ColorDialog` named `colorChooser`, which is used in the event handlers for both `Button`s.

Lines 8–19 define the setBackgroundColorButton_Click event handler. The method sets the ColorDialog's FullOpen property to True (line 13), so the dialog displays all available colors, as shown in the screen capture in Fig. 15.6. When FullOpen is False, the dialog shows only the color swatches. Line 14 invokes colorChooser's ShowDialog method to display the dialog. The dialog's Color property stores the user's selection. If the user clicks **OK**, line 17 modifies the Form's background color by setting its BackColor property to the dialog's Color property.

Lines 22–32 define the setTextColorButton_Click event handler. If the user clicks **OK** in the dialog, lines 29–30 set the text color of both buttons to the selected color.

Users are not restricted to the ColorDialog's 48 color swatches. To create a custom color, users can click anywhere in the ColorDialog's large rectangle, which displays various color shades. Adjust the slider, hue and other features to refine the color. When finished, click the **Add to Custom Colors** Button, which adds the custom color to a square in the **Custom Colors** section of the dialog. Clicking **OK** sets the Color property of the ColorDialog to that color.

15.5 Fonts

This section introduces methods and constants related to font control. The properties of Font objects cannot be modified. If you need a different Font, you must create a new Font object. There are many overloaded versions of the Font constructor for initializing Font objects. Some properties of class Font are summarized in Fig. 15.7.

Property	Description
Bold	Returns True if the font is bold.
FontFamily	Returns the font's FontFamily—a grouping structure to organize fonts and define their similar properties.
Height	Returns the height of the font in pixels.
Italic	Returns True if the font is italic.
Name	Returns the font's name as a String.
Size	Returns a float value indicating the current font size measured in design units (design units are any specified unit of measurement for the font).
SizeInPoints	Returns a float value indicating the current font size measured in points.
Strikeout	Returns True if the font is in strikeout format.
Underline	Returns True if the font is underlined.

Fig. 15.7 | Font class read-only properties.

The Size property returns the font size as measured in design units, whereas SizeInPoints returns the font size as measured in points (the more common measurement). Design units allow the font size to be specified in one of several units of measurement, such as inches or millimeters. Some versions of the Font constructor accept a GraphicsUnit argument. GraphicsUnit is an enumeration that allows you to specify the unit of measurement that describes the font size. Members of the GraphicsUnit enumeration include Point (1/72 inch), Display (1/75 inch for the screen and 1/100 inch for printers),

Document (1/300 inch), Millimeter, Inch and Pixel. If this argument is provided, the Size property contains the size of the font as measured in the specified design unit, and the SizeInPoints property contains the corresponding size of the font in points. For example, if we create a Font having size 1 and specify the unit of measurement as GraphicsUnit.Inch, the Size property will be 1 and the SizeInPoints property will be 72, because there are 72 points to the inch. The default measurement for the font size is GraphicsUnit.Point (thus, the Size and SizeInPoints properties will be equal).

Class Font has several constructors. Most require a font name, which is a String representing a font currently supported by the system. Common fonts include Microsoft SansSerif and Serif. Most Font constructors also require as arguments

- the font size
- the font style

The font style is specified with constants from the **FontStyle** enumeration (Bold, Italic, Regular, Strikeout and Underline). You can combine font styles with the Or operator, as in FontStyle.Italic Or FontStyle.Bold, which makes a font *both* italic and bold. When you draw a string with Graphics method **DrawString**, the method sets the current drawing font—the font in which the text displays—to its Font argument.

Common Programming Error 15.1

Specifying a font that is not available on a system is a logic error. If this occurs, the system's default font is substituted.

Drawing Strings in Different Fonts

Figure 15.8 displays text in different fonts and sizes. The program uses the Font constructor to initialize the Font objects (lines 12, 16, 20 and 24). Each call to the Font constructor passes a font name (e.g., Arial, Times New Roman, Courier New or Tahoma) as a String, a font size (a float) and a FontStyle object (style). Graphics method DrawString sets the font and draws the text at the specified location. Note that line 8 creates a DarkBlue SolidBrush object (brush). All Strings drawn with that brush appear in DarkBlue.

```vb
1   ' Fig. 15.8 FontDemo.vb
2   ' Fonts and FontStyles.
3   Public Class FontDemo
4      ' demonstrate various font and style settings
5      Protected Overrides Sub OnPaint(ByVal e As PaintEventArgs)
6         MyBase.OnPaint(e) ' call base class's OnPaint
7         Dim graphicsObject As Graphics = e.Graphics
8         Dim brush As New SolidBrush(Color.DarkBlue)
9
10        ' arial, 12 pt bold
11        Dim style As FontStyle = FontStyle.Bold
12        Dim arial As New Font("Arial", 12, style)
13
14        ' times new roman, 12 pt regular
15        style = FontStyle.Regular
16        Dim timesNewRoman As New Font("Times New Roman", 12, style)
```

Fig. 15.8 | Fonts and FontStyles. (Part 1 of 2.)

```
17
18          ' courier new, 16 pt bold and italic
19          style = FontStyle.Bold Or FontStyle.Italic
20          Dim courierNew As New Font("Courier New", 16, style)
21
22          ' tahoma, 18 pt strikeout
23          style = FontStyle.Strikeout
24          Dim tahoma As New Font("Tahoma", 18, style)
25
26          graphicsObject.DrawString(arial.Name &
27             " 12 point bold.", arial, brush, 10, 10)
28
29          graphicsObject.DrawString(timesNewRoman.Name &
30             " 12 point plain.", timesNewRoman, brush, 10, 30)
31
32          graphicsObject.DrawString(courierNew.Name &
33             " 16 point bold and italic.", courierNew, brush, 10, 50)
34
35          graphicsObject.DrawString(tahoma.Name &
36             " 18 point strikeout.", tahoma, brush, 10, 70)
37       End Sub ' OnPaint
38    End Class ' FontDemo
```

Fig. 15.8 | Fonts and FontStyles. (Part 2 of 2.)

Font Metrics

You can determine precise information about a font's metrics (or properties), such as height, descent (the amount that characters dip below the baseline), ascent (the amount characters rise above the baseline) and leading (the difference between the ascent of one line and the descent of the previous line). Figure 15.9 illustrates these font metrics.

Fig. 15.9 | Font metrics illustration.

Class `FontFamily` defines characteristics common to a group of related fonts. Class `FontFamily` provides several methods used to determine the font metrics shared by members of a particular family. These methods are summarized in Fig. 15.10.

Method	Description
GetCellAscent	Returns an `Integer` representing the ascent of a font as measured in design units.
GetCellDescent	Returns an `Integer` representing the descent of a font as measured in design units.
GetEmHeight	Returns an `Integer` representing the height of a font as measured in design units.
GetLineSpacing	Returns an `Integer` representing the distance between two consecutive lines (that is, the leading) of text as measured in design units.

Fig. 15.10 | `FontFamily` methods that return font-metric information.

Fig. 15.11 displays the metrics of two fonts. Line 11 creates `Font` object `arial` and sets it to 10-point Arial font. Line 12 uses `Font` property `FontFamily` to obtain object `arial`'s `FontFamily` object. Lines 15–16 output the `String` representation of the font. Lines 18–28 then use methods of class `FontFamily` to obtain the ascent, descent, height and leading of the font and draw strings containing this information. Lines 31–51 repeat the process for font `sansSerif`, which uses the Microsoft Sans Serif `FontFamily`.

```
1   ' Fig. 15.11: FontMetricsDemo.vb
2   ' Displaying font metric information
3   Public Class FontMetricsDemo
4      ' displays font information
5      Protected Overrides Sub OnPaint(ByVal e As PaintEventArgs)
6         MyBase.OnPaint(e) ' call base class's OnPaint
7         Dim graphicsObject As Graphics = e.Graphics
8         Dim brush As New SolidBrush(Color.DarkBlue)
9
10        ' Arial font metrics
11        Dim arial As New Font("Arial", 10)
12        Dim family As FontFamily = arial.FontFamily
13
14        ' display Arial font metrics
15        graphicsObject.DrawString("Current Font: " &
16           arial.ToString(), arial, brush, 10, 10)
17
18        graphicsObject.DrawString("Ascent: " &
19           family.GetCellAscent(FontStyle.Regular), arial, brush, 10, 30)
20
21        graphicsObject.DrawString("Descent: " &
22           family.GetCellDescent(FontStyle.Regular), arial, brush, 10, 50)
23
```

Fig. 15.11 | Displaying font metric information. (Part 1 of 2.)

```
24    graphicsObject.DrawString("Height: " &
25       family.GetEmHeight(FontStyle.Regular), arial, brush, 10, 70)
26
27    graphicsObject.DrawString("Leading: " &
28       family.GetLineSpacing(FontStyle.Regular), arial, brush, 10, 90)
29
30    ' display Sans Serif font metrics
31    Dim sanSerif As New Font("Microsoft Sans Serif",
32       12, FontStyle.Italic)
33    family = sanSerif.FontFamily
34
35    graphicsObject.DrawString("Current Font: " &
36       sanSerif.ToString(), sanSerif, brush, 10, 130)
37
38    graphicsObject.DrawString("Ascent: " &
39       family.GetCellAscent(FontStyle.Regular),
40       sanSerif, brush, 10, 150)
41
42    graphicsObject.DrawString("Descent: " &
43       family.GetCellDescent(FontStyle.Regular),
44       sanSerif, brush, 10, 170)
45
46    graphicsObject.DrawString("Height: " &
47       family.GetEmHeight(FontStyle.Regular), sanSerif, brush, 10, 190)
48
49    graphicsObject.DrawString("Leading: " &
50       family.GetLineSpacing(FontStyle.Regular),
51       sanSerif, brush, 10, 210)
52    End Sub ' OnPaint
53 End Class ' FontMetricsDemo
```

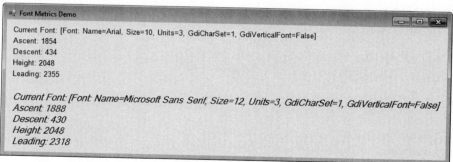

Fig. 15.11 | Displaying font metric information. (Part 2 of 2.)

15.6 Drawing Lines, Rectangles and Ovals

This section presents Graphics methods for drawing lines, rectangles and ovals. Each of the drawing methods has several overloaded versions. Methods that draw hollow shapes typically require as arguments

- a Pen
- four Integers

Methods that draw solid shapes typically require as arguments

- a Brush
- four Integers

The first two Integer arguments are the coordinates of the upper-left corner of the shape (or its enclosing area), and the last two indicate the shape's (or enclosing area's) width and height. Figure 15.12 summarizes several Graphics methods and their parameters.

Graphics Drawing Methods and Descriptions

```
DrawLine(ByVal p As Pen, ByVal x1 As Integer, ByVal y1 As Integer,
    ByVal x2 As Integer, ByVal y2 As Integer)
```
Draws a line from (x1, y1) to (x2, y2). The Pen determines the line's color, style and width.

```
DrawRectangle(ByVal p As Pen, ByVal x As Integer, ByVal y As Integer,
    ByVal width As Integer, ByVal height As Integer)
```
Draws a rectangle of the specified width and height. The top-left corner of the rectangle is at point (x, y). The Pen determines the rectangle's color, style and border width.

```
FillRectangle(ByVal b As Brush, ByVal x As Integer, ByVal y As Integer,
    ByVal width As Integer, ByVal height As Integer)
```
Draws a solid rectangle of the specified width and height. The top-left corner of the rectangle is at point (x, y). The Brush determines the fill pattern inside the rectangle.

```
DrawEllipse(ByVal p As Pen, ByVal x As Integer, ByVal y As Integer,
    ByVal width As Integer, ByVal height As Integer)
```
Draws an ellipse inside a bounding rectangle of the specified width and height. The top-left corner of the bounding rectangle is located at (x, y). The Pen determines the color, style and border width of the ellipse.

```
FillEllipse(ByVal b As Brush, ByVal x As Integer, ByVal y As Integer,
    ByVal width As Integer, ByVal height As Integer)
```
Draws a filled ellipse in a bounding rectangle. The top-left corner of the bounding rectangle is located at (x, y). The Brush determines the pattern inside the ellipse.

Fig. 15.12 | Graphics methods that draw lines, rectangles and ovals.

Figure 15.13 draws lines, rectangles and ellipses. In this application, we also demonstrate methods that draw filled and unfilled shapes.

```
1   ' Fig. 15.13: LinesRectanglesOvals.vb
2   ' Demonstrating lines, rectangles and ovals.
3   Public Class FrmLinesRectanglesOvals
4       ' override Form OnPaint method
5       Protected Overrides Sub OnPaint(ByVal e As PaintEventArgs)
6           MyBase.OnPaint(e) ' call base class's OnPaint
7
8           ' get graphics object
9           Dim g As Graphics = e.Graphics
```

Fig. 15.13 | Demonstration of methods that draw lines, rectangles and ellipses. (Part 1 of 2.)

```vbnet
10        Dim brush As New SolidBrush(Color.Blue)
11        Dim pen As New Pen(Color.Black)
12
13        ' create filled rectangle
14        g.FillRectangle(brush, 90, 30, 150, 90)
15
16        ' draw lines to connect rectangles
17        g.DrawLine(pen, 90, 30, 110, 40)
18        g.DrawLine(pen, 90, 120, 110, 130)
19        g.DrawLine(pen, 240, 30, 260, 40)
20        g.DrawLine(pen, 240, 120, 260, 130)
21
22        ' draw top rectangle
23        g.DrawRectangle(pen, 110, 40, 150, 90)
24
25        ' set brush to red
26        brush.Color = Color.Red
27
28        ' draw base Ellipse
29        g.FillEllipse(brush, 280, 75, 100, 50)
30
31        ' draw connecting lines
32        g.DrawLine(pen, 380, 55, 380, 100)
33        g.DrawLine(pen, 280, 55, 280, 100)
34
35        ' draw Ellipse outline
36        g.DrawEllipse(pen, 280, 30, 100, 50)
37     End Sub ' OnPaint
38  End Class ' LinesRectanglesOvals
```

Fig. 15.13 | Demonstration of methods that draw lines, rectangles and ellipses. (Part 2 of 2.)

Methods **FillRectangle** and **DrawRectangle** (lines 14 and 23) draw rectangles on the screen. For each method, the first argument specifies the drawing object to use. The FillRectangle method uses a Brush object (in this case, an instance of SolidBrush—a class that derives from Brush), whereas the DrawRectangle method uses a Pen object. The next two arguments specify the coordinates of the upper-left corner of the **bounding rectangle**, which represents the area in which the rectangle will be drawn. The fourth and fifth arguments specify the rectangle's width and height. Method DrawLine (lines 17–20) takes as arguments

- a Pen

- two pairs of Integers, specifying the start and end of a line

The method then draws a line, using the Pen object.

Methods `FillEllipse` and `DrawEllipse` (lines 29 and 32) each provide overloaded versions that take five arguments

- the first argument specifies the drawing object to use
- the next two arguments specify the upper-left coordinates of the bounding rectangle representing the area in which the ellipse will be drawn
- the last two arguments specify the bounding rectangle's width and height

Figure 15.14 depicts an ellipse bounded by a rectangle. The ellipse touches the midpoint of each of the four sides of the bounding rectangle. The bounding rectangle is not displayed on the screen.

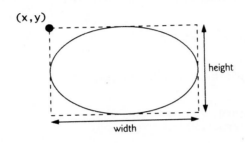

Fig. 15.14 | Ellipse bounded by a rectangle.

15.7 Drawing Arcs

Arcs are portions of ellipses and are measured in degrees, beginning at a starting angle and continuing for a specified number of degrees called the arc angle. An arc is said to sweep (traverse) its arc angle, beginning from its starting angle. Arcs that sweep in a clockwise direction are measured in positive degrees, whereas arcs that sweep in a counterclockwise direction are measured in negative degrees. Figure 15.15 depicts two arcs. Note that the arc at the left of the figure sweeps upward from zero degrees to approximately −110 degrees. Similarly, the arc at the right of the figure sweeps downward from zero degrees to approximately 110 degrees.

Fig. 15.15 | Positive and negative arc angles.

Note the dashed boxes around the arcs in Fig. 15.15. Each arc is drawn as part of an oval (the rest of which is not visible). When drawing an oval, we specify the oval's dimensions in the form of a bounding rectangle that encloses the oval. The boxes in Fig. 15.15 correspond to these bounding rectangles. The `Graphics` methods used to draw arcs—`DrawArc`, `DrawPie` and `FillPie`—are summarized in Fig. 15.16.

Graphics methods and descriptions

`DrawArc(ByVal p As Pen, ByVal x As Integer, ByVal y As Integer,`
   `ByVal width As Integer, ByVal height As Integer,`
   `ByVal startAngle As Integer, ByVal sweepAngle As Integer)`
Draws an arc beginning from angle `startAngle` (in degrees) and sweeping `sweepAngle` degrees. The ellipse is defined by a bounding rectangle of `width`, `height` and upper-left corner (x,y). The `Pen` determines the color, border width and style of the arc.

`DrawPie(ByVal p As Pen, ByVal x As Integer, ByVal y As Integer,`
   `ByVal width As Integer, ByVal height As Integer,`
   `ByVal startAngle As Integer, ByVal sweepAngle As Integer)`
Draws a pie section of an ellipse beginning from angle `startAngle` (in degrees) and sweeping `sweepAngle` degrees. The ellipse is defined by a bounding rectangle of `width`, `height` and upper-left corner (x,y). The `Pen` determines the color, border width and style of the arc.

`FillPie(ByVal b As Brush, ByVal x As Integer, ByVal y As Integer,`
   `ByVal width As Integer, ByVal height As Integer,`
   `ByVal startAngle As Integer, ByVal sweepAngle As Integer)`
Functions similarly to `DrawPie`, except draws a solid arc (i.e., a sector). The `Brush` determines the fill pattern for the solid arc.

Fig. 15.16 | Graphics methods for drawing arcs.

Figure 15.17 draws six images (three arcs and three filled pie slices) to demonstrate some of the arc drawing methods. To illustrate the bounding rectangles that determine the sizes and locations of the arcs, the arcs are displayed inside red rectangles that have the same *x-y* coordinates, width and height arguments as those that define the bounding rectangles for the arcs.

```
 1    ' Fig. 15.17: DrawArcs.vb
 2    ' Drawing various arcs on a Form.
 3    Public Class DrawArcs
 4       ' draw arcs
 5       Private Sub DrawArcs_Paint(ByVal sender As Object,
 6          ByVal e As System.Windows.Forms.PaintEventArgs) Handles Me.Paint
 7          ' get graphics object
 8          Dim graphicsObject As Graphics = e.Graphics
 9          Dim rectangle1 As New Rectangle(15, 35, 80, 80)
10          Dim brush1 As New SolidBrush(Color.Firebrick)
11          Dim pen1 As New Pen(brush1, 1)
```

Fig. 15.17 | Drawing various arcs on a Form. (Part 1 of 2.)

```
12          Dim brush2 As New SolidBrush(Color.DarkBlue)
13          Dim pen2 As New Pen(brush2, 1)
14
15          ' start at 0 and sweep 360 degrees
16          graphicsObject.DrawRectangle(pen1, rectangle1)
17          graphicsObject.DrawArc(pen2, rectangle1, 0, 360)
18
19          ' start at 0 and sweep 110 degrees
20          rectangle1.Location = New Point(100, 35)
21          graphicsObject.DrawRectangle(pen1, rectangle1)
22          graphicsObject.DrawArc(pen2, rectangle1, 0, 110)
23
24          ' start at 0 and sweep -270 degrees
25          rectangle1.Location = New Point(185, 35)
26          graphicsObject.DrawRectangle(pen1, rectangle1)
27          graphicsObject.DrawArc(pen2, rectangle1, 0, -270)
28
29          ' start at 0 and sweep 360 degrees
30          rectangle1.Location = New Point(15, 120)
31          rectangle1.Size = New Size(80, 40)
32          graphicsObject.DrawRectangle(pen1, rectangle1)
33          graphicsObject.FillPie(brush2, rectangle1, 0, 360)
34
35          ' start at 270 and sweep -90 degrees
36          rectangle1.Location = New Point(100, 120)
37          graphicsObject.DrawRectangle(pen1, rectangle1)
38          graphicsObject.FillPie(brush2, rectangle1, 270, -90)
39
40          ' start at 0 and sweep -270 degrees
41          rectangle1.Location = New Point(185, 120)
42          graphicsObject.DrawRectangle(pen1, rectangle1)
43          graphicsObject.FillPie(brush2, rectangle1, 0, -270)
44      End Sub ' DrawArcs_Paint
45  End Class ' DrawArcs
```

Fig. 15.17 | Drawing various arcs on a Form. (Part 2 of 2.)

Lines 8–13 create the objects that we need to draw arcs—a Graphics object, a Rectangle, SolidBrushes and Pens. Lines 16–17 then draw a rectangle and an arc inside the rectangle. The arc sweeps 360 degrees, forming a circle. Line 20 changes the location of the Rectangle by setting its Location property to a new Point. The Point constructor takes as arguments the *x*- and *y*-coordinates of the new Point. The Location property determines the upper-left corner of the Rectangle. After drawing the rectangle, the program draws an arc that starts at 0 degrees and sweeps 110 degrees. Because the angles increase in a clockwise direction, the arc sweeps downward. Lines 25–27 perform similar functions, except that the specified arc sweeps –270 degrees. The Size property of a Rectangle determines the arc's height and width.

Line 31 sets the Size property to a new Size object, which changes the size of the rectangle. The remainder of the program is similar to the portions described above, except that a SolidBrush is used with method FillPie. The resulting arcs, which are filled, can be seen in the bottom half of the sample output (Fig. 15.17).

15.8 Drawing Polygons and Polylines

Polygons are multisided shapes. There are several Graphics methods used to draw polygons—DrawLines draws a series of connected lines, DrawPolygon draws a closed polygon and FillPolygon draws a solid polygon. These methods are described in Fig. 15.18.

Method	Description
DrawLines	Draws a series of connected lines. The coordinates of each point are specified in an array of Point objects. If the last point is different from the first point, the figure is not closed.
DrawPolygon	Draws a polygon. The coordinates of each point are specified in an array of Point objects. If the last point is different from the first point, those two points are connected to close the polygon.
FillPolygon	Draws a solid polygon. The coordinates of each point are specified in an array of Point objects. If the last point is different from the first point, those two points are connected to close the polygon.

Fig. 15.18 | Graphics methods for drawing polygons.

Figure 15.19 draws polygons and connected lines via the methods listed in Fig. 15.18. In the Paint event handler, line 9 gets the Graphics object for drawing on the Form. Lines 11–16 create three arrays of Points that represent the points in a collection of lines, a polygon and a filled polygon. Lines 22–24 call Graphics methods DrawLines, DrawPolygon and FillPolygon. Methods DrawLines and DrawPolygon take a Pen as their first argument. Method FillPolygon takes a Brush as its first argument. All three methods take an array of Points as their second argument. Method DrawLines draws lines from one Point to the next in the array. Methods DrawPolygon and FillPolygon also draw a line from the last point in the array to the first point in the array to close the shape.

```
1    ' Fig. 15.19: DrawPolygons.vb
2    ' Demonstrating polygons.
3    Public Class DrawPolygons
```

Fig. 15.19 | Demonstrating polygons. (Part 1 of 2.)

```
 4      ' draw panel Paint event handler
 5      Private Sub DrawPolygons_Paint(ByVal sender As Object,
 6         ByVal e As System.Windows.Forms.PaintEventArgs) Handles Me.Paint
 7
 8         ' get graphics object for panel
 9         Dim graphicsObject As Graphics = e.Graphics
10
11         Dim points1() As Point = {New Point(20, 20), New Point(10, 150),
12            New Point(100, 100), New Point(50, 75)}
13         Dim points2() As Point = {New Point(120, 20), New Point(110, 150),
14            New Point(200, 100), New Point(150, 75)}
15         Dim points3() As Point = {New Point(220, 20), New Point(210, 150),
16            New Point(300, 100), New Point(250, 75)}
17
18         ' initialize default pen and brush
19         Dim pen As New Pen(Color.DarkBlue)
20         Dim brush As New SolidBrush(Color.DarkBlue)
21
22         graphicsObject.DrawLines(pen, points1)
23         graphicsObject.DrawPolygon(pen, points2)
24         graphicsObject.FillPolygon(brush, points3)
25      End Sub ' DrawPolygons_Paint
26   End Class ' DrawPolygons
```

Fig. 15.19 | Demonstrating polygons. (Part 2 of 2.)

15.9 Additional Brush Types

.NET offers many other graphics capabilities. The Brush hierarchy, for example, also includes **HatchBrush**, **LinearGradientBrush**, **PathGradientBrush** and **TextureBrush**.

Gradients, Line Styles and Fill Patterns

The program in Fig. 15.20 demonstrates several graphics features, such as dashed lines, thick lines and the ability to fill shapes with various patterns. These represent just a few of the additional capabilities of the System.Drawing namespace.

Lines 7–73 define the DrawShapes_Paint event handler. Lines 14–15 create a LinearGradientBrush (namespace System.Drawing.Drawing2D) object named linearBrush to enable users to draw with a color gradient. The LinearGradientBrush used in this example takes four arguments

- a Rectangle

- two Colors
- a constant from the LinearGradientMode enumeration

Linear gradients are defined along a line that determines the gradient endpoints. This line can be specified either by the start and end points or by the diagonal of a rectangle. The first argument, Rectangle drawArea1, represents the endpoints of the linear gradient—the upper-left corner is the starting point, and the bottom-right corner is the ending point. The second and third arguments specify the colors the gradient will use. In this case, the color of the ellipse will gradually change from Color.Blue to Color.Yellow. The last argument, a type from the enumeration **LinearGradientMode**, specifies the linear gradient's direction. In our case, we use LinearGradientMode.ForwardDiagonal, which creates a gradient from the upper-left to the lower-right corner. We then use Graphics method FillEllipse in line 18 to draw an ellipse with linearBrush; the color gradually changes from blue to yellow, as described above.

```vb
1   ' Fig. 15.20: DrawShapes.vb
2   ' Drawing various shapes on a Form.
3   Imports System.Drawing.Drawing2D
4
5   Public Class DrawShapes
6      ' draw various shapes on Form
7      Private Sub DrawShapes_Paint(ByVal sender As Object,
8         ByVal e As System.Windows.Forms.PaintEventArgs) Handles Me.Paint
9
10        Dim graphicsObject As Graphics = e.Graphics
11
12        ' ellipse rectangle and gradient brush
13        Dim drawArea1 As New Rectangle(5, 35, 30, 100)
14        Dim linearBrush As New LinearGradientBrush(drawArea1, Color.Blue,
15           Color.Yellow, LinearGradientMode.ForwardDiagonal)
16
17        ' draw ellipse filled with a blue-yellow gradient
18        graphicsObject.FillEllipse(linearBrush, 5, 30, 65, 100)
19
20        ' pen and location for red outline rectangle
21        Dim thickRedPen As New Pen(Color.Red, 10)
22        Dim drawArea2 As New Rectangle(80, 30, 65, 100)
23
24        ' draw thick rectangle outline in red
25        graphicsObject.DrawRectangle(thickRedPen, drawArea2)
26
27        ' bitmap texture
28        Dim textureBitmap As New Bitmap(10, 10)
29
30        ' get bitmap graphics
31        Dim graphicsObject2 As Graphics = Graphics.FromImage(textureBitmap)
32
33        ' brush and pen used throughout program
34        Dim solidColorBrush As New SolidBrush(Color.Red)
35        Dim coloredPen As New Pen(solidColorBrush)
```

Fig. 15.20 | Drawing various shapes on a Form. (Part 1 of 2.)

```
36
37         ' fill textureBitmap with yellow
38         solidColorBrush.Color = Color.Yellow
39         graphicsObject2.FillRectangle(solidColorBrush, 0, 0, 10, 10)
40
41         ' draw small black rectangle in textureBitmap
42         coloredPen.Color = Color.Black
43         graphicsObject2.DrawRectangle(coloredPen, 1, 1, 6, 6)
44
45         ' draw small blue rectangle in textureBitmap
46         solidColorBrush.Color = Color.Blue
47         graphicsObject2.FillRectangle(solidColorBrush, 1, 1, 3, 3)
48
49         ' draw small red square in textureBitmap
50         solidColorBrush.Color = Color.Red
51         graphicsObject2.FillRectangle(solidColorBrush, 4, 4, 3, 3)
52
53         ' create textured brush and
54         ' display textured rectangle
55         Dim texturedBrush As New TextureBrush(textureBitmap)
56         graphicsObject.FillRectangle(texturedBrush, 155, 30, 75, 100)
57
58         ' draw pie-shaped arc in white
59         coloredPen.Color = Color.White
60         coloredPen.Width = 6
61         graphicsObject.DrawPie(coloredPen, 240, 30, 75, 100, 0, 270)
62
63         ' draw lines in green and yellow
64         coloredPen.Color = Color.Green
65         coloredPen.Width = 5
66         graphicsObject.DrawLine(coloredPen, 395, 30, 320, 150)
67
68         ' draw a rounded, dashed yellow line
69         coloredPen.Color = Color.Yellow
70         coloredPen.DashCap = DashCap.Round
71         coloredPen.DashStyle = DashStyle.Dash
72         graphicsObject.DrawLine(coloredPen, 320, 30, 395, 150)
73     End Sub ' DrawShapes_Paint
74 End Class ' DrawShapes
```

Fig. 15.20 | Drawing various shapes on a Form. (Part 2 of 2.)

In line 21, we create Pen object thickRedPen. We pass to thickRedPen's constructor Color.Red and Integer argument 10, indicating that we want thickRedPen to draw red lines that are 10 pixels wide.

Line 28 creates a new **Bitmap** image, which initially is empty. Class Bitmap can produce images in color and gray scale; this particular Bitmap is 10 pixels wide and 10 pixels tall. Method **FromImage** (line 31) is a Shared member of class Graphics and retrieves the Graphics object associated with an Image, which may be used to draw on an image. Lines 38–51 draw on the Bitmap a pattern consisting of black, blue, red and yellow rectangles and lines. A TextureBrush is a brush that fills the interior of a shape with an image rather than a solid color. In lines 55–56, TextureBrush object textureBrush fills a rectangle with our Bitmap. The TextureBrush constructor used in line 55 takes as an argument an image that defines its texture.

Next, we draw a pie-shaped arc with a thick white line. Lines 59–60 set coloredPen's color to White and modify its width to be 6 pixels. We then draw the pie on the Form by specifying the Pen, the x-coordinate, y-coordinate, the width and height of the bounding rectangle and the start and sweep angles.

Lines 64–66 draw a green line that is five pixels wide. Finally, lines 70–71 use enumerations **DashCap** and **DashStyle** (namespace System.Drawing.Drawing2D) to specify settings for a dashed line. Line 70 sets the DashCap property of coloredPen (not to be confused with the DashCap enumeration) to a member of the DashCap enumeration. The DashCap enumeration specifies the styles for the ends of each dash in a dashed line. In this case, we want both ends of the dashed line to be rounded, so we use DashCap.Round. Line 71 sets the DashStyle property of coloredPen (not to be confused with the DashStyle enumeration) to DashStyle.Dash, indicating that we want our line to consist entirely of dashes.

General Paths

Our next example demonstrates a **general path**. A general path is a shape constructed from straight lines and complex curves. An object of class **GraphicsPath** (namespace System.Drawing.Drawing2D) represents a general path. The GraphicsPath class provides functionality that enables the creation of complex shapes from vector-based primitive graphics objects. A GraphicsPath object consists of figures defined by simple shapes. The start point of each vector-graphics object (such as a line or an arc) added to the path is connected by a straight line to the endpoint of the previous object. When called, the **Close-Figure** method attaches the final vector-graphic object endpoint to the initial starting point for the current figure by a straight line, then starts a new figure. Method **StartFigure** begins a new figure within the path without closing the previous figure.

The program in Fig. 15.21 draws general paths in the shape of five-pointed stars. Lines 15–16 define two Integer arrays, representing the x- and y-coordinates of the points in the star, and line 19 defines GraphicsPath object star. A loop (lines 22–25) then creates lines to connect the points of the star and adds these lines to star. We use GraphicsPath method **AddLine** to append a line to the shape. The arguments of AddLine specify the coordinates for the line's endpoints; each new call to AddLine adds a line from the previous point to the current point. Line 27 uses GraphicsPath method CloseFigure to complete the shape.

Line 30 sets the origin of the Graphics object. The arguments to method Translate-Transform indicate that the origin should be translated to the coordinates (150, 150). The loop in lines 33–40 draws the star 18 times, rotating it around the origin. Line 34 uses Graphics method RotateTransform to move to the next position on the Form; the argument specifies the rotation angle in degrees. Graphics method FillPath (line 39) then draws a filled version of the star with the Brush created in lines 36–37. The application determines the SolidBrush's color randomly, using Random method Next.

```vb
1   ' Fig. 15.21: DrawStars.vb
2   ' Using paths to draw stars on the Form.
3   Imports System.Drawing.Drawing2D
4
5   Public Class DrawStars
6       ' create path and draw stars along it
7       Private Sub DrawStars_Paint(ByVal sender As Object,
8           ByVal e As System.Windows.Forms.PaintEventArgs) Handles Me.Paint
9
10          Dim graphicsObject As Graphics = e.Graphics
11          Dim random As New Random()
12          Dim brush As New SolidBrush(Color.DarkMagenta)
13
14          ' x and y points of the path
15          Dim xPoints() As Integer = {55, 67, 109, 73, 83, 55, 27, 37, 1, 43}
16          Dim yPoints() As Integer = {0, 36, 36, 54, 96, 72, 96, 54, 36, 36}
17
18          ' create graphics path for star
19          Dim star As New GraphicsPath()
20
21          ' create a star from a series of points
22          For i As Integer = 0 To 8 Step 2
23              star.AddLine(xPoints(i), yPoints(i),
24                  xPoints(i + 1), yPoints(i + 1))
25          Next
26
27          star.CloseFigure() ' close the shape
28
29          ' translate the origin to (150, 150)
30          graphicsObject.TranslateTransform(150, 150)
31
32          ' rotate the origin and draw the stars in random colors
33          For i As Integer = 1 To 18
34              graphicsObject.RotateTransform(20)
35
36              brush.Color = Color.FromArgb(random.Next(200, 255),
37                  random.Next(255), random.Next(255), random.Next(255))
38
39              graphicsObject.FillPath(brush, star)
40          Next
41      End Sub ' DrawStars_Paint
42  End Class ' DrawStars
```

Fig. 15.21 | Paths used to draw stars on a Form. (Part 1 of 2.)

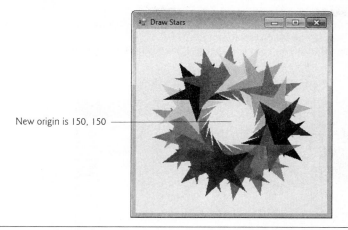

New origin is 150, 150

Fig. 15.21 | Paths used to draw stars on a Form. (Part 2 of 2.)

15.10 Loading, Displaying and Scaling Images

.NET's multimedia capabilities include graphics, images, animations, audio and video. This section presents image manipulation. Figure 15.22 loads an Image (System.Drawing namespace), then allows the user to scale the Image to a specified width and height up to 400 by 400 pixels. The "yellowflowers" image was added to the application as a resource.

```
1  ' Fig. 15.22: ScaleImage.vb
2  ' Displaying and resizing an image
3  Public Class ScaleImage
4     Private imageValue As Image
5     Private graphicsObject As Graphics
6
7     ' load the image and obtain the Graphics object
8     Private Sub ScaleImage_Load(ByVal sender As Object,
9        ByVal e As System.EventArgs) Handles Me.Load
10
11        Dim pictureResource =
12           My.Resources.ResourceManager.GetObject("yellowflowers")
13
14        imageValue = CType(pictureResource, Image)
15        graphicsObject = Me.CreateGraphics()
16     End Sub ' ScaleImage_Load
17
18     ' get NumericUpDown values and use them to size image
19     Private Sub NumericUpDown_ValueChanged(ByVal sender As System.Object,
20        ByVal e As System.EventArgs) _
21        Handles widthNumericUpDown.ValueChanged,
22           heightNumericUpDown.ValueChanged
23
```

Fig. 15.22 | Image resizing. (Part 1 of 2.)

```
24          ' clear the Form then draw the image
25          graphicsObject.Clear(Me.BackColor)
26          graphicsObject.DrawImage(imageValue, 5, 5,
27             widthNumericUpDown.Value, heightNumericUpDown.Value)
28       End Sub ' NumericUpDown_ValueChanged
29    End Class ' ScaleImage
```

a) Scaled image after setting the **Width** and **Heigth** NumericUpDowns to 100

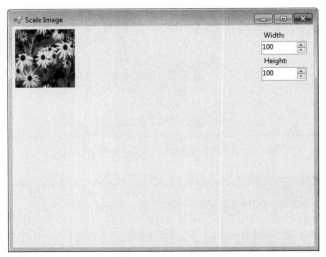

a) Scaled image after setting the **Width** NumericUpDown to 300 and the **Height** NumericUpDown to 400

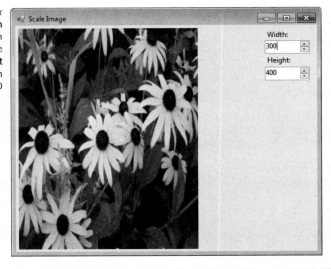

Fig. 15.22 | Image resizing. (Part 2 of 2.)

Line 4 declares Image variable imageValue. Lines 11–14 in the Form's Load event handler load the Image from a resource named "yellowflowers". Line 15 uses the Form's inherited **CreateGraphics** method to create a Graphics object for drawing on the Form. When you change the value in either NumericUpDown control, lines 19–28 scale and redraw the image. Line 25 calls Graphics method **Clear** to paint the entire Form in the current background color. Lines 26–27 call Graphics method **DrawImage**, passing as arguments the image to draw, the x-coordinate of the image's upper-left corner, the y-coordinate of the image's upper-left corner, the width of the image and the height of the image. If the width and height do not correspond to the image's original dimensions, the image is scaled to fit the new width and height.

15.11 Windows Media Player

The Windows Media Player control enables an application to play video and sound in many multimedia formats. These include MPEG (Motion Pictures Experts Group) audio and video, AVI (audio-video interleave) video, WAV (Windows wave-file format) audio and MIDI (Musical Instrument Digital Interface) audio. Users can find pre-existing audio and video on the Internet, or they can create their own files, using available sound and graphics packages.

Figure 15.23 demonstrates the Windows Media Player control. This control is not displayed in the **Toolbox** by default, so you must add it. First right click inside the **Toolbox** and select **Choose Items...** to display the **Choose Toolbox Items** dialog. Click the **COM components** tab, then scroll down and select the option **Windows Media Player**. Click the **OK** button to dismiss the dialog. The Windows Media Player control now appears in the **Toolbox**. Drag the control onto your Form, then set the control's Dock property to Fill. Add a MenuStrip with a **File** menu that contains **Open** and **Exit** menu items. Finally, add an OpenFileDialog named openMediaFileDialog.

The Windows Media Player control provides several Buttons that allow the user to play the current file, pause, stop, play the previous file, rewind, forward and play the next file. The control also includes a volume control and trackbars to select a specific position in the media file.

```
1   ' Fig. 15.23: MediaPlayer.vb
2   ' Windows Media Player control used to play media files.
3   Public Class MediaPlayer
4      ' open new media file in Windows Media Player
5      Private Sub OpenToolStripMenuItem_Click(ByVal sender As System.Object,
6         ByVal e As System.EventArgs) Handles OpenToolStripMenuItem.Click
7
8         openMediaFileDialog.ShowDialog() ' allow user to select file
9
10        ' load and play the media clip
11        AxWindowsMediaPlayer1.URL = openMediaFileDialog.FileName
12     End Sub ' OpenToolStripMenuItem_Click
13
14     ' exit the program when the exit menu item is clicked
15     Private Sub ExitToolStripMenuItem_Click(ByVal sender As System.Object,
16        ByVal e As System.EventArgs) Handles ExitToolStripMenuItem.Click
17        Application.Exit()
18     End Sub ' ExitToolStripMenuItem_Click
19  End Class ' MediaPlayer
```

Fig. 15.23 | Windows Media Player control used to play media files. (Part 1 of 2.)

Fig. 15.23 | Windows Media Player control used to play media files. (Part 2 of 2.)

When a user chooses **Open** from the **File** menu, event handler `OpenToolStripMenu-Item_Click` (lines 5–12) displays the `openMediaFileDialog` (line 8) so the user can choose an audio or video file to play. Line 11 then sets the `URL` property of the Windows Media Player control (named `AxWindowsMediaPlayer1`) to the name of the file chosen by the user. The `URL` property specifies the file that Windows Media Player is currently using. We provided a sample video in the `video` folder with this chapter's examples, but you can select any video to test the program.

15.12 Printing

The next application uses the graphics techniques presented in this chapter to print a paycheck on your printer. The user inputs to a GUI (Fig. 15.24) that resembles a check: the check number, the date, the numeric amount of the check, the employee's name, the amount of the check written in words and the company's address information. Pressing

Fig. 15.24 | GUI for the **Check Writer** application.

the **Preview** Button displays the format of the check in a **Print preview** dialog so the user can see if the format is acceptable. Pressing the **Print** Button prints the check. To implement the printing capabilities, you'll use objects from the **Printing** section of the **Toolbox**.

GUI for the Check Writer Application

The GUI consists of Labels, TextBoxes and a DateTimePicker laid out to resemble a check. The **Preview** and **Print** Buttons enable you to display a **Print preview** dialog containing the check and to print the check, respectively.

In addition to the controls shown in Fig. 15.24, we also dragged a PrintPreview-Dialog and a PrintDocument from the **Printing** section of the **Toolbox** onto the Form and named them printPreviewDialog and printDocument, respectively. A **PrintPreviewDialog** displays a dialog in which the user can view the document that will print before it's sent to the printer. A **PrintDocument** object allows you to specify how to print a specified document. The default event for a PrintDocument is the **PrintPage** event, which occurs when the data required to print the current page is needed—that is, when the document is printed or a print preview is generated. You can create the event handler for this event by double clicking the printDocument object in the component tray in **Design** view. In this event handler, you define what will print by using the Graphics capabilities presented in this chapter.

Coding the Check Writer Application

Figure 15.25 presents the code for the **Check Writer** application. We've already presented the Graphics features used in this example, so this discussion focuses on the printing features. Line 3 Imports the **System.Drawing.Printing namespace** so that the application can access Windows printing services. Lines 7–81 define the PrintPage event handler for the printDocument object that specifies what will print.

Declaring the Variables Used in the PrintPage Event Handler

Line 11 declares a Font variable named fontObject that is used to specify the text font. Lines 14–15 declare Integer variables that represent the *x*- and *y*-coordinates where controls appear on the Form. Lines 18 and 21 declare Integer variables, which specify the coordinates of the left and top margins, respectively, of the page to be printed. These values are determined by using the **MarginBounds.Left** and **MarginBounds.Top** properties of the PrintPageEventArgs object (e from line 8) that is passed when the PrintPage event occurs. The MarginBounds represent the printable area of the page. Line 24 declares the String variable controlText, which stores text from the controls that will be printed.

```
1    ' Fig. 15.25: CheckWriter.vb
2    ' Printing a paycheck.
3    Imports System.Drawing.Printing
4
5    Public Class CheckWriter
6       ' PrintPage event raised for each page to be printed
7       Private Sub printDocument_PrintPage(ByVal sender As System.Object,
8          ByVal e As System.Drawing.Printing.PrintPageEventArgs) _
9          Handles printDocument.PrintPage
```

Fig. 15.25 | Printing a paycheck. (Part 1 of 4.)

```
10
11        Dim fontObject As Font ' variable to store the font
12
13        ' store a control's x- and y-coordinates
14        Dim yPosition As Integer
15        Dim xPosition As Integer
16
17        ' represent the left margin of the page
18        Dim leftMargin As Integer = e.MarginBounds.Left
19
20        ' represent the top margin of the page
21        Dim topMargin As Integer = e.MarginBounds.Top
22
23        ' store a control's text
24        Dim controlText As String = Nothing
25
26        ' iterate over the controls on the Form,
27        ' printing the text displayed in each control
28        For Each controlObject In Me.Controls
29           ' do not print Buttons
30           If Not (TypeOf controlObject Is Button) Then
31              controlText = controlObject.Text
32
33              Select Case controlObject.Name
34                 Case "dateTimePicker" ' underline the date
35                    fontObject = New Font("Segoe UI", 9.0F,
36                       FontStyle.Underline)
37                 Case "amountTextBox" ' draw a box around the amount
38                    e.Graphics.DrawRectangle(Pens.Black,
39                       amountTextBox.Location.X + leftMargin,
40                       amountTextBox.Location.Y + topMargin - 2,
41                       amountTextBox.Width, amountTextBox.Height)
42                    fontObject = controlObject.Font ' default font
43                 Case Else
44                    fontObject = controlObject.Font ' default font
45              End Select
46
47              ' set the string positions relative to the page margins
48              xPosition = leftMargin + controlObject.Location.X
49              yPosition = topMargin + controlObject.Location.Y
50
51              ' draw the text in a graphics object
52              e.Graphics.DrawString(controlText, fontObject,
53                 Brushes.Black, xPosition, yPosition)
54           End If
55        Next controlObject
56
57        ' draw a line for the payee's name
58        e.Graphics.DrawLine(Pens.Black,
59           payeeTextBox.Location.X + leftMargin,
60           payeeTextBox.Location.Y + topMargin + 15,
61           payeeTextBox.Location.X + payeeTextBox.Width + leftMargin,
62           payeeTextBox.Location.Y + topMargin + 15)
```

Fig. 15.25 | Printing a paycheck. (Part 2 of 4.)

```
63
64            ' draw a line for the amount
65          e.Graphics.DrawLine(Pens.Black,
66              dollarsTextBox.Location.X + leftMargin,
67              dollarsTextBox.Location.Y + topMargin + 15,
68              dollarsTextBox.Location.X + dollarsTextBox.Width + leftMargin,
69              dollarsTextBox.Location.Y + topMargin + 15)
70
71            ' draw the memo line
72          e.Graphics.DrawLine(Pens.Black,
73              memoTextBox.Location.X + leftMargin,
74              memoTextBox.Location.Y + topMargin + 15,
75              memoTextBox.Location.X + memoTextBox.Width + leftMargin,
76              memoTextBox.Location.Y + topMargin + 15)
77
78            ' draw a box around the check
79          e.Graphics.DrawRectangle(Pens.Black, leftMargin,
80              topMargin, Me.Width, Me.Height - 60)
81        End Sub ' document_PrintPage
82
83      ' print the document
84      Private Sub printButton_Click(ByVal sender As System.Object,
85        ByVal e As System.EventArgs) Handles printButton.Click
86
87          ' if no printers are installed, display an error message
88          If PrinterSettings.InstalledPrinters.Count = 0 Then
89            ErrorMessage()
90          Else
91            printDocument.Print() ' print the document
92          End If
93      End Sub ' printButton_Click
94
95      ' display the document in a print preview dialog
96      Private Sub previewButton_Click(ByVal sender As System.Object,
97        ByVal e As System.EventArgs) Handles previewButton.Click
98
99          ' if no printers are installed, display an error message
100         If PrinterSettings.InstalledPrinters.Count = 0 Then
101           ErrorMessage()
102         Else
103           printPreviewDialog.Document = printDocument ' specify document
104           printPreviewDialog.ShowDialog() ' show print preview dialog
105         End If
106     End Sub ' previewButton_Click
107
108     ' display an error message to the user
109     Sub ErrorMessage()
110       MessageBox.Show("No printers installed. You must " &
111           "have a printer installed to preview or print the document.",
112           "Print Error", MessageBoxButtons.OK, MessageBoxIcon.Error)
113     End Sub ' ErrorMessage
114 End Class ' CheckWriter
```

Fig. 15.25 | Printing a paycheck. (Part 3 of 4.)

a) GUI after the user fills
in the fields with the
information for the check

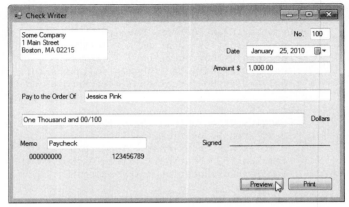

b) **Print preview** dialog that displays when the user clicks the **Preview** Button. We used the zoom button (🔍▾) to set the zoom level to 150% so the check appears as shown here. The user can click the printer icon in the upper-left corner of the dialog to print the check, or can click the **Close** Button, then click **Print** in the main GUI.

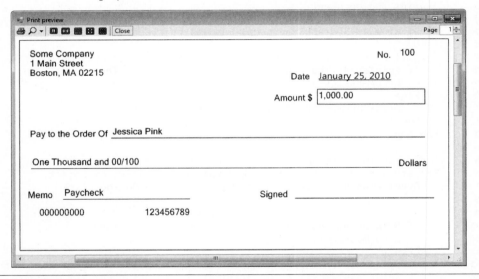

Fig. 15.25 | Printing a paycheck. (Part 4 of 4.)

Iterating Through the Controls on the Form

Lines 28–55 iterate through the controls on the Form to print the check. References to all of the Form's controls are stored in the Form's **Controls** property. The If...Then statement (lines 30–54) determines whether the current control is a Button. The **TypeOf...Is** operator returns True if the variable between TypeOf and Is refers to an object of the type specified to the right of Is. If the current control is not a Button, the body of the If...Then statement executes; otherwise, the loop continues to the next control on the Form. Line 31 stores the value of the current control's Text property—the text displayed to the user or entered by the user.

The Select Case statement (lines 33–45) specifies how each control prints. The first Case (lines 34–36) handles the dateTimePicker control. It sets fontObject to the date's font style.

The second Case (lines 37–42) executes if the control is amountTextBox. This Case draws the box around the check amount. The x- and y-coordinates of the rectangle are specified by adding the TextBox's x-y location on the Form to variables leftMargin and topMargin, respectively. Recall that you begin printing the check at the corner of the top and left margins of the page. Adding the margin values to the Location properties ensures that amountTextBox prints in the same position as it appears on the Form. (Line 40 subtracts two points of space to center the box on the text.) Line 42 sets the font of the text to draw to the same value as the font used to display text in the control.

The third Case (lines 43–44) executes for all the other controls. This Case sets the fontObject to the same value as the font used to display text in the control.

Line 48 sets the xPosition variable to leftMargin + controlObject.Location.X. By adding the x-coordinate of the current control to the left margin of the printed page, you ensure that the check will not be drawn outside the left margin of the printed page. Line 49 perform a similar operation, setting yPosition to the sum of the top margin and y-coordinate of the control's location. Lines 52–53 call the DrawString method on the e.Graphics property to display the current control's text. The fourth and fifth arguments are the x- and y-coordinates where the first character of the String prints. The xPosition and yPosition variables cause the text of each control to print at the correct location on the page.

Drawing Lines for the Payee, Payee Amount and Memo Information
Checks contain lines for payee, payment amount and memo information. Lines 58–76 draw these lines. We added 15 pixels to the y-coordinates for each line because each control's y-coordinate represents the *top* of the control and we want to draw the line at the bottom of the control.

Drawing a Border for the Check
The Form's border is not contained in a control, so we draw a rectangle around the check to be printed (lines 79–80). Method DrawRectangle's second argument specifies the x-coordinate of the upper-left corner of the rectangle. We use the value leftMargin to align the rectangle with the left margin of the printed page. The third argument specifies the y-coordinate of the upper-left corner of the rectangle. We use the value topMargin to align the rectangle with the top margin of the printed page.

The fourth and fifth arguments specify the width and height of the rectangle. The width is set to Me.Width, which returns the width of the Form. The height is set to Me.Height - 60—the height of the Form minus 60 pixels. We subtract 60 because we do not want to print the space for the Buttons at the bottom of the Form. These Buttons were created to allow users to print and preview the checks—they were not intended to be printed on the checks.

Event Handlers for the **Preview** and **Print** Buttons
The event handlers for the **Preview** and **Print** Buttons cause the PrintPage event for the printDocument object. When the user clicks **Preview**, method previewButton_Click (lines 96–106) first checks whether your computer has any printers installed (line 100). If

not, line 101 calls method `ErrorMessage` (lines 109–113) to display an error message. The **Print preview** dialog cannot display a preview unless there is at least one printer installed. If there is, line 103 assigns the `printDocument` object to the `printPreviewDialog`'s **Document** property to specify which document will be previewed. Then line 104 calls the `printPreviewDialog`'s `ShowDialog` method to display the dialog. This causes a `PrintPage` event on the `printDocument` object, which executes the `printDocument_PrintPage` event handler in lines 7–81 to create the graphics for the preview.

Method `printButton_Click` (lines 84–93) works similarly to method `previewButton_Click`. The key difference is line 91, which calls the `printDocument`'s `Print` method to send the document to the printer. This causes a `PrintPage` event on the `printDocument` object, which executes the event handler in lines 7–81 to create the graphics that will be printed.

15.13 Wrap-Up

This chapter began with an introduction to the .NET framework's drawing capabilities. We then presented more powerful drawing capabilities, such as changing the styles of the lines used to draw shapes and controlling the colors and patterns of filled shapes.

You learned techniques for manipulating images. We discussed class `Image`, which can store and manipulate images of various formats. You also learned how to incorporate the Windows Media Player control in an application to play audio or video. Finally, we introduced printing features, showing how to display a print preview and how to print to your computer's printer

This completes the print portion of *Visual Basic 2010 How to Program*. We've provided a dozen online chapters in PDF format at the book's Companion Website:

> www.pearsonhighered.com/deitel/

These chapters extend some of the chapters in the print book and also cover intermediate and advanced Visual Basic material.

Online chapters	
16 Exception Handling: A Deeper Look	23 Web Services
17 Strings and Characters: A Deeper Look	24 Silverlight and Rich Internet Applications
18 Files and Streams: A Deeper Look	25 Collections and Generics
19 Windows Presentation Foundation (WPF) GUI	26 ATM Case Study, Part 1: Object-Oriented Design with the UML
20 WPF Graphics and Multimedia	27 ATM Case Study, Part 2: Implementing an Object-Oriented Design
21 XML and LINQ to XML	
22 Web App Development with ASP.NET: A Deeper Look	

Fig. 15.26 | Online chapters.

Summary

Section 15.1 Introduction
- .NET contains many sophisticated drawing capabilities as part of namespace System.Drawing and the other namespaces that make up the .NET GDI+.
- GDI+ is an API that provides classes for creating two-dimensional vector graphics, and manipulating fonts and images.

Section 15.2 Drawing Classes and the Coordinate System
- Namespaces System.Drawing and System.Drawing.Drawing2D contain the most commonly used GDI+ components.
- Class Graphics contains methods used for drawing Strings, lines, rectangles and other shapes on a Control. These methods usually require a Pen or Brush object to render a shape. A Pen draws shape outlines; a Brush draws solid objects.
- The Color structure contains numerous Shared properties that represent colors of graphical components, plus methods that allow users to create new colors.
- Class Font contains properties that define characteristics of fonts.
- Class FontFamily contains methods for obtaining font information.
- The upper-left corner of a control has the coordinates (0, 0). The *x*-coordinate is the horizontal distance to the right from the upper-left corner. The *y*-coordinate is the vertical distance downward from the upper-left corner.
- You position text and shapes on the screen by specifying their coordinates in pixels.
- The Point structure represents the *x-y* coordinates of a point on a two-dimensional plane.
- The Rectangle structure defines the location, width and height of a rectangular shape.
- The Size structure represents the width and height of a shape.

Section 15.3 Graphics Contexts and Graphics Objects
- A graphics context represents a drawing surface that enables drawing on the screen. A Graphics object manages a graphics context by controlling how information is drawn.
- Every derived class of Form inherits an OnPaint method in which most graphics operations are performed. The OnPaint method triggers the Control's Paint event. Instead of overriding the OnPaint method, you can add an event handler for the Paint event.
- You can force a call to OnPaint by calling a Control's Invalidate method.
- To draw on a control, first create a graphics object by invoking the control's CreateGraphics method, then use the Graphics object's methods to draw on the control.

Section 15.4 Colors
- Structure Color defines methods and constants used to manipulate colors.
- Every color can be created from a combination of alpha, red, green and blue components (called ARGB values). All four ARGB values are integer values in the range 0–255.
- The alpha value determines the opacity of the color—0 represents a transparent color and 255 represents an opaque color. Alpha values between 0 and 255 result in a weighted blending effect of the color's RGB value with that of any background color, causing a semitransparent effect.
- Method FromArgb returns a Color object based on its ARGB or RGB arguments.
- The overloaded Pen constructors allow you to specify the colors and widths of lines.
- The System.Drawing namespace provides a Pens class containing predefined Pens.

- Derived classes of Brush define objects that color the interiors of graphical shapes.
- The SolidBrush constructor takes a Color object representing the color to draw.
- Fill methods use Brushes to fill a space with a color, pattern or image.
- Graphics method FillRectangle draws a filled-in rectangle. FillRectangle takes as parameters a Brush, the *x*- and *y*-coordinates of the rectangle's upper-left corner and its width and height.
- There are several overloaded DrawString methods; one takes as arguments the String to display, the display Font, the Brush to use for drawing and the coordinates of the String's first character.
- Class Color's Shared method FromName creates a new Color object from a String.
- A ColorDialog allows users to select from a palette of available colors or to create custom colors. An application retrieves the user's selection via the ColorDialog's Color property.
- Setting ColorDialog's FullOpen property to True indicates that the dialog should display all available colors. When FullOpen is False, the dialog shows only color swatches.

Section 15.5 Fonts
- A Font's Size property returns the font size as measured in design units, whereas property SizeInPoints returns the font size as measured in points. Design units allow the font size to be specified in one of several units of measurement, such as inches or millimeters.
- Some Font constructors accept a GraphicsUnit enumeration argument that allows you to specify the unit of measurement for the font size. Members of the GraphicsUnit enumeration include Point (1/72 inch), Display (1/75 inch on the screen or 1/100 inch on a printer), Document (1/300 inch), Millimeter, Inch and Pixel.
- Most Font constructors require a font name, the font size and the font style. The font style is specified with a constant from the FontStyle enumeration (Bold, Italic, Regular, Strikeout and Underline, or a combination of these). You can combine font styles with the Or operator.
- You can determine a font's metrics, such as height, descent, ascent and leading.
- Class FontFamily defines characteristics common to a group of related fonts. Class FontFamily provides methods to determine the font metrics shared by members of a particular family.

Section 15.6 Drawing Lines, Rectangles and Ovals
- Methods that draw hollow shapes typically require as arguments a Pen and four Integers. Methods that draw solid shapes typically require as arguments a Brush and four Integers. The Integers represent the bounding box of the shape.
- Methods FillRectangle and DrawRectangle draw rectangles. For each method, the first argument specifies the drawing object to use—for FillRectangle a Brush object and for DrawRectangle method a Pen object. The last four arguments represent the rectangle's bounding box.
- Method DrawLine takes a Pen and two pairs of Integers that specify the start and end of a line. The method then draws a line, using the Pen object.
- Methods FillEllipse and DrawEllipse draw ellipses. For each method, the first argument specifies the drawing object to use. The last four arguments represent the ellipse's bounding box. The ellipse touches the midpoint of each of the four sides of the bounding rectangle.

Section 15.7 Drawing Arcs
- Arcs are portions of ellipses and are measured in degrees, beginning at a starting angle and continuing for a specified number of degrees called the arc angle. Arcs that sweep in a clockwise direction are measured in positive degrees.
- The Point constructor takes as arguments the *x*- and *y*-coordinates of the new point.

- The Location property determines the upper-left corner of the Rectangle.
- The Size property of a Rectangle determines the arc's height and width.

Section 15.8 Drawing Polygons and Polylines
- There are several Graphics methods used to draw polygons—DrawLines draws a series of connected points, DrawPolygon draws a closed polygon and FillPolygon draws a solid polygon.

Section 15.9 Additional Brush Types
- Class LinearGradientBrush (System.Drawing.Drawing2D) enables drawing with a color gradient. One of its constructors takes four arguments—a Rectangle, two Colors and a member of enumeration LinearGradientMode. All linear gradients are defined along a line that determines the gradient endpoints. This line can be specified by either the start and endpoints or the diagonal of a rectangle. The Rectangle argument represents the endpoints of the linear gradient—the upper-left corner is the starting point and the bottom-right corner is the ending point. The second and third arguments specify the colors the gradient will use. The last argument, a type from the enumeration LinearGradientMode, specifies the gradient's direction. LinearGradientMode.ForwardDiagonal creates a gradient from the upper-left to the lower-right corner.
- Class Bitmap can produce images in color and gray scale. Graphics method FromImage retrieves the Graphics object associated with an Image, which may be used to draw on the image.
- A TextureBrush is a brush that fills the interior of a shape with an image rather than a solid color. The TextureBrush constructor takes as an argument an image that defines its texture.
- A GraphicsPath (System.Drawing.Drawing2D namespace) represents a general path. The class provides functionality for creating complex shapes from vector-based primitive graphics objects.
- GraphicsPath method CloseFigure attaches the final vector-graphic object endpoint to the initial starting point for the current figure by a straight line, then starts a new figure. Method StartFigure begins a new figure within the path without closing the previous figure.
- GraphicsPath method AddLine appends a line to the shape.
- Method TranslateTransform sets the origin of a Graphics object.
- Graphics method RotateTransform enables you to rotate drawing positions around the origin.
- Graphics method FillPath draws a filled version of a GraphicsPath.

Section 15.10 Loading, Displaying and Scaling Images
- Graphics method Clear paints the entire Form in the current background color.
- Graphics method DrawImage receives as arguments the image to draw, the x- and y-coordinates of the image's upper-left corner, the width of the image and the height of the image. The image is scaled to fit the specified width and height.

Section 15.11 Windows Media Player
- The Windows Media Player control enables an application to play video and sound in many multimedia formats, including MPEG, AVI, WAV and MIDI.
- To use the Windows Media Player control, you must add the control to the **Toolbox**.
- The Windows Media Player control provides several buttons that allow the user to play the current file, pause, stop, play the previous file, rewind, forward and play the next file. The control also includes a volume control and trackbars to select a specific position in the media file.
- The URL property of a Windows Media Player control object specifies the file that Windows Media Player is currently using.

Section 15.12 Printing

- A `PrintPreviewDialog` displays a dialog in which the user can view the document that will print before it is sent to the printer.

- A `PrintDocument` object allows you to specify how to print a specified document.

- The default event for a `PrintDocument` is the `PrintPage` event, which occurs when the data required to print the current page is needed—that is, when the document is printed or a print preview is generated. In this event handler, you define what will print by using the `Graphics` capabilities presented in this chapter.

- The `MarginBounds` represent the printable area of a page.

- References to all of a Form's controls are stored in its `Controls` property.

- The `TypeOf...Is` operator returns `True` if the variable between `TypeOf` and `Is` refers to an object of the type specified to the right of `Is`.

- A `PrintPreviewDialog`'s `Document` property specifies which `PrintDocument` will be previewed.

- `PrintPreviewDialog` method `ShowDialog` displays the dialog and causes a `PrintPage` event on the `PrintDocument` object specified in the `Document` property.

- `PrintDocument` method `Print` method sends a `PrintDocument` to the printer and causes a `PrintPage` event on the `PrintDocument` object.

Terminology

Self-Review Exercises

15.1 State whether each of the following is *true* or *false*. If *false*, explain why.
   a) A Font object's size can be changed by setting its Size property.
   b) In the GDI+ coordinate system, x-values increase from left to right.
   c) Method FillPolygon draws a solid polygon with a specified Brush.
   d) Method DrawArc allows negative angles.
   e) Font property Size returns the size of the current font in centimeters.
   f) Pixel coordinate (0, 0) is located at the exact center of the monitor.
   g) A HatchBrush is used to draw lines.
   h) A Color is defined by its alpha, red, green and violet content.
   i) Every Control has an associated Graphics object.
   j) Method OnPaint is inherited by every Form.

15.2 Fill in the blanks in each of the following statements:
   a) Class _____ is used to draw lines of various colors and thicknesses.
   b) Classes _____ and _____ define the fill for a shape in such a way that the fill gradually changes from one color to another.
   c) Method _____ of class Graphics draws a line between two points.
   d) ARGB is short for _____, _____, _____ and _____.
   e) Font sizes usually are measured in units called _____.
   f) Class _____ fills a shape using a pattern drawn in a Bitmap.
   g) _____ _____ _____ allows an application to play multimedia files.
   h) Class _____ defines a path consisting of lines and curves.
   i) The FCL's drawing capabilities are part of the namespaces _____ and _____.

Answers to Self-Review Exercises

15.1   a) False. Size is a read-only property. b) True. c) True. d) True. e) False. It returns the size of the current Font in design units. f) False. The coordinate (0,0) corresponds to the upper-left corner of a GUI component on which drawing occurs. g) False. A Pen is used to draw lines, a Hatch-

`Brush` fills a shape with a pattern defined by a member of the `HatchStyle` enumeration. h) False. A color is defined by its alpha, red, green and blue content. i) True. j) True.

15.2 a) `Pen`. b) `LinearGradientBrush`, `PathGradientBrush`. c) `DrawLine`. d) alpha, red, green, blue. e) points. f) `TextureBrush`. g) Windows Media Player h) `GraphicsPath` i) `System.Drawing`, `System.Drawing.Drawing2D`.

Exercises

15.3   *(Concentric Circles)* Write a program that draws eight concentric circles. The circles should be separated from one another by 10 pixels. Use the `DrawArc` method.

15.4   *(Random Lines)* Write a program that draws 100 lines with random lengths, positions, thicknesses and colors.

15.5   *(Pyramid)* Write a program that draws a tetrahedron (a pyramid). Use class `GraphicsPath` and method `DrawPath`.

15.6   *(Simple Drawing Application)* Write a program that allows the user to draw "free-hand" images with the mouse in a `PictureBox`. Allow the user to change the drawing color and width of the pen. Provide a button that allows the user to clear the `PictureBox`.

15.7   *(Image Flasher)* Write a program that repeatedly flashes an image on the screen. Do this by interspersing the image with a plain background-color image.

15.8   **(CheckWriter** *Modified to Print Background Images)* Modify the **Check Writer** application to display and print a background for the check. Users can select one of two background images by clicking the appropriate `RadioButton`. The image should appear in the **Print preview** dialog box and also should print as a background to the check. We've provided wood and brick images in the images folder with this chapter's examples.

15.9   *(Screen Saver Application)* Develop an application that simulates a screen saver. This application should add random-colored, random-sized, solid and hollow shapes at random positions on the `Form`. The `Form` should have a black background and a `Timer` control. Each `Timer` event should display another random shape. Clear the `Form` after every 20 shapes.

Making a Difference Exercises

15.10   *(Large-Type Displays for People with Low Vision)* The accessibility of computers and the Internet to all people, regardless of disabilities, is becoming more important as these tools play increasing roles in our personal and business lives. According to a recent estimate by the World Health Organization (www.who.int/mediacentre/factsheets/fs282/en/), 314 million people worldwide have low vision. To learn more about low vision, check out the GUI-based low vision simulation at www.webaim.org/simulations/lowvision.php. People with low vision might prefer to choose a font and/or a larger font size when reading electronic documents and web pages. Write an application that provides a `TextBox` in which the user can type text. Allow the user to select `Times New Roman`, `Arial` or `Courier New` from a `ComboBox`. Provide a **Bold** `CheckBox`, which, if checked, makes the text bold. Include **Increase Font Size** and **Decrease Font Size** `Button`s that allow the user to scale the size of the font up or down, respectively, by one point at a time. Start with a font size of 18 points. For the purposes of this exercise, set the font size on the `ComboBox`, `Button`s and `CheckBox` to 20 points so that a person with low vision will be able to read the text on them.

15.11   *(Ecofont)* Ecofont (www.ecofont.eu/ecofont_en.html)—developed by SPRANQ (a Netherlands-based company)—is a free, open-source computer font designed to reduce by as much as 20% the amount of ink used for printing, thus reducing also the number of ink cartridges used and the environmental impact of the manufacturing and shipping processes (using less energy, less fuel for shipping, and so on). The font, based on sans-serif Verdana, has small circular "holes" in the letters that are not visible in smaller sizes—such as the 9- or 10-point type frequently used. Download Ecofont, then install the font file `Spranq_eco_sans_regular.ttf` using the instructions from the Ecofont website. Next, develop an application that allows you to type text to be displayed in the Ecofont. Create **Increase Font Size** and **Decrease Font Size** buttons that allow you to scale up or down by one point at a time. Start with a default font size of 9 points. As you scale up, you'll be able to see the holes in the letters more clearly. As you scale down, the holes will be less apparent. What is the smallest font size at which you begin to notice the holes?

Online Content

This book's Companion Website

`www.pearsonhighered.com/deitel/`

contains PDFs of the following:

These files can be viewed in Adobe® Reader® (`get.adobe.com/reader`). Several of the preceding chapters extend those in the print book. All of the preceding chapters cover intermediate and advanced Visual Basic material. Several of the online chapters use console applications. We introduce how to create console applications in the online Appendix F. The online index contains entries for the entire book—the index in the printed book contains entries for only the content in Chapters 1–15 and Appendices A–E.

New copies of this book come with a Companion Website access code that is located on the card inside the book's front cover. If the access code is visible or there is no card, you purchased a used book or an edition that does not come with an access code. In this case, you can purchase access directly from the Companion Website.

Operator Precedence Chart

Operators are shown in decreasing order of precedence from top to bottom, with each level of precedence separated by a horizontal line. Visual Basic operators associate from left to right.

Operator	Type
TypeOf	type comparison
^	exponentiation
+ –	unary plus unary minus
* /	multiplication division
\	integer division
Mod	modulus
+ –	addition subtraction
&	concatenation
<< >> = <> < <= > >= Like Is IsNot	bitwise left shift bitwise right shift relational is equal to relational is not equal to relational less than relational less than or equal to relational greater than relational greater than or equal to pattern matching reference comparison reference comparison
Not	logical negation
And AndAlso	logical AND without short-circuit evaluation logical AND with short-circuit evaluation

Fig. A.1 | Operator precedence chart. (Part 1 of 2.)

Operator	Type
`Or`	logical inclusive OR without short-circuit evaluation
`OrElse`	logical inclusive OR with short-circuit evaluation
`Xor`	logical exclusive OR

Fig. A.1 | Operator precedence chart. (Part 2 of 2.)

Primitive Types

Type	Size in bytes	Value range
SByte	1	−128 to 127, inclusive
Byte	1	0 to 255, inclusive
Boolean	2	True or False
Char	2	0 to 65,535, inclusive (representing the Unicode character set)
Short	2	−32,768 to 32,767, inclusive
UShort	2	0 to 65,535, inclusive
Integer	4	−2,147,483,648 to 2,147,483,647, inclusive
UInteger	4	0 to 4,294,967,295, inclusive
Single	4	negative range: −3.4028235E+38 to −1.401298E−45 positive range: 1.401298E−45 to 3.4028235E+38
Long	8	−9,223,372,036,854,775,808 to 9,223,372,036,854,775,807, inclusive
ULong	8	0 to 18,446,744,073,709,551,615, inclusive
Double	8	negative range: −1.79769313486231570E+308 to −4.94065645841246544E−324 positive range: 4.94065645841246544E−324 to 1.79769313486231570E+308
Date	8	0:00:00 on 1 January 0001 to 23:59:59 on 31 December 9999
Decimal	16	Range with no decimal point: ±79,228,162,514,264,337,593,543,950,335 Range with 28 places to the right of the decimal point: ±7.9228162514264337593543950335 The smallest nonzero number is ±0.0000000000000000000000000001 (±1E−28)
String		Up to approximately 2 billion Unicode characters

Fig. B.1 | Primitive types.

To promote portability, Microsoft uses internationally recognized standards for character formats (Unicode, www.unicode.org) and floating-point numbers (IEEE 754, grouper.ieee.org/groups/754/). We discuss Unicode in Appendix E, Unicode®.

C

Number Systems

Here are only numbers ratified.
—William Shakespeare

Nature has some sort of arithmetic-geometrical coordinate system, because nature has all kinds of models. What we experience of nature is in models, and all of nature's models are so beautiful. It struck me that nature's system must be a real beauty, because in chemistry we find that the associations are always in beautiful whole numbers— there are no fractions.
—Richard Buckminster Fuller

Objectives

In this appendix you'll learn:

- Basic number-systems concepts, such as base, positional value and symbol value.

- How to work with numbers represented in the binary, octal and hexadecimal number systems.

- To abbreviate binary numbers as octal or hexadecimal numbers.

- To convert octal and hexadecimal numbers to binary.

- To convert between decimal values and their binary, octal and hexadecimal equivalents.

- To understand binary arithmetic and how negative binary numbers are represented using two's-complement notation.

C.1 Introduction

In this appendix, we introduce the key number systems that programmers use, especially when they're working on software projects that require close interaction with machine-level hardware. Projects like this include operating systems, computer networking software, compilers, database systems and applications requiring high performance.

When we write an integer such as 227 or –63 in a program, the number is assumed to be in the decimal (base-10) number system. The digits in the decimal number system are 0, 1, 2, 3, 4, 5, 6, 7, 8 and 9. The lowest digit is 0 and the highest is 9—one less than the base of 10. Internally, computers use the binary (base-2) number system. The binary number system has only two digits, namely 0 and 1. Its lowest digit is 0 and its highest is 1—one less than the base of 2.

As you'll see, binary numbers tend to be much longer than their decimal equivalents. Programmers who work in assembly languages and in high-level languages that enable programmers to reach down to the machine level find it cumbersome to work with binary numbers. So, two other number systems—the octal number system (base 8) and the hexadecimal number system (base 16)—are popular primarily because they make it convenient to abbreviate binary numbers.

In the octal number system, the digits range from 0 to 7. Because both the binary and the octal number systems have fewer digits than the decimal number system, their digits are the same as the corresponding digits in decimal.

The hexadecimal number system poses a problem because it requires 16 digits—a lowest digit of 0 and a highest digit with a value equivalent to decimal 15 (one less than the base of 16). By convention, the letters A through F represent the hexadecimal digits corresponding to decimal values 10 through 15. Thus, in hexadecimal, you can have numbers like 876 consisting solely of decimal-like digits, numbers like 8A55F consisting of digits and letters and numbers like FFE consisting solely of letters. Occasionally, a hexadecimal number spells a common word such as FACE or FEED—this can appear strange to programmers accustomed to working with numbers. The digits of the binary, octal, decimal and hexadecimal number systems are summarized in Figs. C.1 and C.2.

Each of these number systems uses positional notation—each position in which a digit is written has a different positional value. For example, in the decimal number 937 (the 9, the 3 and the 7 are referred to as symbol values), we say that the 7 is written in the ones position, the 3 is written in the tens position and the 9 is written in the hundreds position. Each of these positions is a power of the base (base 10) and that these powers begin at 0 and increase by 1 as we move left in the number (Fig. C.3).

Binary digit	Octal digit	Decimal digit	Hexadecimal digit
0	0	0	0
1	1	1	1
	2	2	2
	3	3	3
	4	4	4
	5	5	5
	6	6	6
	7	7	7
		8	8
		9	9
			A (decimal value of 10)
			B (decimal value of 11)
			C (decimal value of 12)
			D (decimal value of 13)
			E (decimal value of 14)
			F (decimal value of 15)

Fig. C.1 | Digits of the binary, octal, decimal and hexadecimal number systems.

Attribute	Binary	Octal	Decimal	Hexadecimal
Base	2	8	10	16
Lowest digit	0	0	0	0
Highest digit	1	7	9	F

Fig. C.2 | Comparing the binary, octal, decimal and hexadecimal number systems.

Positional values in the decimal number system			
Decimal digit	9	3	7
Position name	Hundreds	Tens	Ones
Positional value	100	10	1
Positional value as a power of the base (10)	10^2	10^1	10^0

Fig. C.3 | Positional values in the decimal number system.

For longer decimal numbers, the next positions to the left would be the thousands position (10 to the 3rd power), the ten-thousands position (10 to the 4th power), the hundred-thousands position (10 to the 5th power), the millions position (10 to the 6th power), the ten-millions position (10 to the 7th power) and so on.

In the binary number 101, the rightmost 1 is written in the ones position, the 0 is written in the twos position and the leftmost 1 is written in the fours position. Each position is a power of the base (base 2), and these powers begin at 0 and increase by 1 as we move left in the number (Fig. C.4). So, $101 = 1 * 2^2 + 0 * 2^1 + 1 * 2^0 = 4 + 0 + 1 = 5$.

For longer binary numbers, the next positions to the left would be the eights position (2 to the 3rd power), the sixteens position (2 to the 4th power), the thirty-twos position (2 to the 5th power), the sixty-fours position (2 to the 6th power) and so on.

In the octal number 425, we say that the 5 is written in the ones position, the 2 is written in the eights position and the 4 is written in the sixty-fours position. Each of these positions is a power of the base (base 8) and that these powers begin at 0 and increase by 1 as we move left in the number (Fig. C.5).

For longer octal numbers, the next positions to the left would be the five-hundred-and-twelves position (8 to the 3rd power), the four-thousand-and-ninety-sixes position (8 to the 4th power), the thirty-two-thousand-seven-hundred-and-sixty-eights position (8 to the 5th power) and so on.

In the hexadecimal number 3DA, we say that the A is written in the ones position, the D is written in the sixteens position and the 3 is written in the two-hundred-and-fifty-sixes position. Each of these positions is a power of the base (base 16) and that these powers begin at 0 and increase by 1 as we move left in the number (Fig. C.6).

For longer hexadecimal numbers, the next positions to the left would be the four-thousand-and-ninety-sixes position (16 to the 3rd power), the sixty-five-thousand-five-hundred-and-thirty-sixes position (16 to the 4th power) and so on.

Positional values in the binary number system			
Binary digit	1	0	1
Position name	Fours	Twos	Ones
Positional value	4	2	1
Positional value as a power of the base (2)	2^2	2^1	2^0

Fig. C.4 | Positional values in the binary number system.

Positional values in the octal number system			
Decimal digit	4	2	5
Position name	Sixty-fours	Eights	Ones
Positional value	64	8	1
Positional value as a power of the base (8)	8^2	8^1	8^0

Fig. C.5 | Positional values in the octal number system.

Positional values in the hexadecimal number system			
Decimal digit	3	D	A
Position name	Two-hundred-and-fifty-sixes	Sixteens	Ones
Positional value	256	16	1
Positional value as a power of the base (16)	16^2	16^1	16^0

Fig. C.6 | Positional values in the hexadecimal number system.

C.2 Abbreviating Binary Numbers as Octal and Hexadecimal Numbers

The main use for octal and hexadecimal numbers in computing is for abbreviating lengthy binary representations. Figure C.7 highlights the fact that lengthy binary numbers can be expressed concisely in number systems with higher bases than the binary number system.

Decimal number	Binary representation	Octal representation	Hexadecimal representation
0	0	0	0
1	1	1	1
2	10	2	2
3	11	3	3
4	100	4	4
5	101	5	5
6	110	6	6
7	111	7	7
8	1000	10	8
9	1001	11	9
10	1010	12	A
11	1011	13	B
12	1100	14	C
13	1101	15	D
14	1110	16	E
15	1111	17	F
16	10000	20	10

Fig. C.7 | Decimal, binary, octal and hexadecimal equivalents.

A particularly important relationship that both the octal and the hexadecimal number system have to the binary system is that the bases of octal and hexadecimal (8 and 16, respectively) are powers of the base of the binary number system (base 2). Consider the following 12-digit binary number and its octal and hexadecimal equivalents. See if you can determine how this relationship makes it convenient to abbreviate binary numbers in octal or hexadecimal. The answer follows the numbers.

Binary number	Octal equivalent	Hexadecimal equivalent
100011010001	4321	8D1

To see how the binary number converts easily to octal, simply break the 12-digit binary number into groups of three consecutive bits each and write those groups over the corresponding digits of the octal number as follows:

100	011	010	001
4	3	2	1

The octal digit you have written under each group of three bits corresponds precisely to the octal equivalent of that 3-digit binary number, as shown in Fig. C.7.

The same kind of relationship can be observed in converting from binary to hexadecimal. Break the 12-digit binary number into groups of four consecutive bits each and write those groups over the corresponding digits of the hexadecimal number, as follows:

1000	1101	0001
8	D	1

Notice that the hexadecimal digit you wrote under each group of four bits corresponds precisely to the hexadecimal equivalent of that 4-digit binary number as shown in Fig. C.7.

C.3 Converting Octal and Hexadecimal Numbers to Binary Numbers

In the previous section, you learned how to convert binary numbers to their octal and hexadecimal equivalents by forming groups of binary digits and simply rewriting them as their equivalent octal digit values or hexadecimal digit values. This process may be used in reverse to produce the binary equivalent of a given octal or hexadecimal number.

For example, the octal number 653 is converted to binary simply by writing the 6 as its 3-digit binary equivalent 110, the 5 as its 3-digit binary equivalent 101 and the 3 as its 3-digit binary equivalent 011 to form the 9-digit binary number 110101011.

The hexadecimal number FAD5 is converted to binary simply by writing the F as its 4-digit binary equivalent 1111, the A as its 4-digit binary equivalent 1010, the D as its 4-digit binary equivalent 1101 and the 5 as its 4-digit binary equivalent 0101 to form the 16-digit binary number 1111101011010101.

C.4 Converting from Binary, Octal or Hexadecimal to Decimal

We're accustomed to working in decimal, and therefore it is often convenient to convert a binary, octal, or hexadecimal number to decimal to get a sense of what the number is "really" worth. Our diagrams in Section C.1 express the positional values in decimal. To convert a number to decimal from another base, multiply the decimal equivalent of each digit by its positional value and sum these products. For example, the binary number 110101 is converted to decimal 53, as shown in Fig. C.8.

To convert octal 7614 to decimal 3980, we use the same technique, this time using appropriate octal positional values, as shown in Fig. C.9.

To convert hexadecimal AD3B to decimal 44347, we use the same technique, this time using appropriate hexadecimal positional values, as shown in Fig. C.10.

C.5 Converting from Decimal to Binary, Octal or Hexadecimal

The conversions in Section C.4 follow naturally from the positional notation conventions. Converting from decimal to binary, octal, or hexadecimal also follows these conventions.

Converting a binary number to decimal					
Positional values:	32	16	8	4	2	1
Symbol values:	1	1	0	1	0	1
Products:	1*32=32	1*16=16	0*8=0	1*4=4	0*2=0	1*1=1
Sum:	= 32 + 16 + 0 + 4 + 0s + 1 = 53					

Fig. C.8 | Converting a binary number to decimal.

Converting an octal number to decimal			
Positional values:	512	64	8	1
Symbol values:	7	6	1	4
Products	7*512=3584	6*64=384	1*8=8	4*1=4
Sum:	= 3584 + 384 + 8 + 4 = 3980			

Fig. C.9 | Converting an octal number to decimal.

Converting a hexadecimal number to decimal			
Positional values:	4096	256	16	1
Symbol values:	A	D	3	B
Products	A*4096=40960	D*256=3328	3*16=48	B*1=11
Sum:	= 40960 + 3328 + 48 + 11 = 44347			

Fig. C.10 | Converting a hexadecimal number to decimal.

Suppose we wish to convert decimal 57 to binary. We write the positional values of the columns right to left until we reach a column whose positional value is greater than the decimal number. We don't need that column, so we discard it. Thus, we first write:

Positional values:	64	32	16	8	4	2	1

Then we discard the column with positional value 64, leaving:

Positional values:	32	16	8	4	2	1

Next we work from the leftmost column to the right. We divide 32 into 57 and observe that there is one 32 in 57 with a remainder of 25, so we write 1 in the 32 column. We divide 16 into 25 and observe that there is one 16 in 25 with a remainder of 9 and write 1 in the 16 column. We divide 8 into 9 and observe that there is one 8 in 9 with a remainder of 1. The next two columns each produce quotients of 0 when their positional values are divided into 1, so we write 0s in the 4 and 2 columns. Finally, 1 into 1 is 1, so we write 1 in the 1 column. This yields:

Positional values:	32	16	8	4	2	1
Symbol values:	1	1	1	0	0	1

and thus decimal 57 is equivalent to binary 111001.

To convert decimal 103 to octal, we write the positional values of the columns until we reach a column whose positional value is greater than the decimal number. We do not need that column, so we discard it. Thus, we first write:

Positional values:	512	64	8	1

Then we discard the column with positional value 512, yielding:

Positional values:	64	8	1

Next we work from the leftmost column to the right. We divide 64 into 103 and observe that there is one 64 in 103 with a remainder of 39, so we write 1 in the 64 column. We divide 8 into 39 and observe that there are four 8s in 39 with a remainder of 7, so we write 4 in the 8 column. Finally, we divide 1 into 7 and observe that there are seven 1s in 7 with no remainder, so we write 7 in the 1 column. This yields:

Positional values:	64	8	1
Symbol values:	1	4	7

and thus decimal 103 is equivalent to octal 147.

To convert decimal 375 to hexadecimal, we write the positional values of the columns until we reach a column whose positional value is greater than the decimal number. We do not need that column, so we discard it. Thus, we first write:

Positional values:	4096	256	16	1

Then we discard the column with positional value 4096, yielding:

Positional values:	256	16	1

Next we work from the leftmost column to the right. We divide 256 into 375 and observe that there is one 256 in 375 with a remainder of 119, so we write 1 in the 256 column. We divide 16 into 119 and observe that there are seven 16s in 119 with a remainder of 7, so we write 7 in the 16 column. Finally, we divide 1 into 7 and observe that there are seven 1s in 7 with no remainder, so we write 7 in the 1 column. This yields:

Positional values:	256	16	1
Symbol values:	1	7	7

and thus decimal 375 is equivalent to hexadecimal 177.

C.6 Negative Binary Numbers: Two's-Complement Notation

The discussion so far in this appendix has focused on positive numbers. In this section, we explain how computers represent negative numbers using *two's-complement notation*. First we explain how the two's complement of a binary number is formed, then we show why it represents the negative value of the given binary number.

Consider a machine with 32-bit integers. Suppose

```
Dim value As Integer = 13
```

The 32-bit representation of value is

```
00000000 00000000 00000000 00001101
```

To form the negative of value we first form its *one's complement* by combining value with &H7FFFFFFF using Visual Basic's Xor operator, as in:

```
onesComplement = value Xor &H7FFFFFFF
```

Internally, onesComplement is now value with each of its bits reversed—ones become zeros and zeros become ones, as follows:

```
value:
00000000 00000000 00000000 00001101

onesComplement
11111111 11111111 11111111 11110010
```

To form the two's complement of value, we simply add 1 to value's one's complement, which produces

```
Two's complement of value:
11111111 11111111 11111111 11110011
```

Now if this is in fact equal to −13, we should be able to add it to binary 13 and obtain a result of 0. Let us try this:

```
  00000000 00000000 00000000 00001101
 +11111111 11111111 11111111 11110011
 -----------------------------------
  00000000 00000000 00000000 00000000
```

The carry bit coming out of the leftmost column is discarded and we indeed get 0 as a result. If we add the one's complement of a number to the number, the result will be all 1s. The key to getting a result of all zeros is that the two's complement is one more than the one's complement. The addition of 1 causes each column to add to 0 with a carry of 1. The carry keeps moving leftward until it is discarded from the leftmost bit, and thus the resulting number is all zeros.

Computers actually perform a subtraction, such as

```
x = a - value;
```

by adding the two's complement of value to a, as follows:

```
x = a + (onesComplement + 1);
```

Suppose a is 27 and value is 13, as before. If the two's complement of value is actually the negative of value, then adding the two's complement of value to a should produce the result 14. Let us try this:

```
a (that is, 27)                00000000 00000000 00000000 00011011
+(onesComplement + 1)         +11111111 11111111 11111111 11110011
                              ------------------------------------
                               00000000 00000000 00000000 00001110
```

which is indeed equal to 14.

Summary

- An integer such as 19 or 227 or –63 in a program is assumed to be in the decimal (base-10) number system. The digits in the decimal number system are 0, 1, 2, 3, 4, 5, 6, 7, 8 and 9. The lowest digit is 0 and the highest digit is 9—one less than the base of 10.
- Internally, computers use the binary (base-2) number system. The binary number system has only two digits, namely 0 and 1. Its lowest digit is 0 and its highest digit is 1—one less than the base of 2.
- The octal number system (base 8) and the hexadecimal number system (base 16) are popular primarily because they make it convenient to abbreviate binary numbers.
- The digits of the octal number system range from 0 to 7.
- The hexadecimal number system poses a problem because it requires 16 digits—a lowest digit of 0 and a highest digit with a value equivalent to decimal 15 (one less than the base of 16). By convention, we use the letters A through F to represent the hexadecimal digits corresponding to decimal values 10 through 15.
- Each number system uses positional notation—each position in which a digit is written has a different positional value.
- A particularly important relationship of both the octal number system and the hexadecimal number system to the binary system is that the bases of octal and hexadecimal (8 and 16 respectively) are powers of the base of the binary number system (base 2).
- To convert an octal to a binary number, replace each octal digit with its three-digit binary equivalent.
- To convert a hexadecimal number to a binary number, simply replace each hexadecimal digit with its four-digit binary equivalent.
- Because we're accustomed to working in decimal, it is convenient to convert a binary, octal or hexadecimal number to decimal to get a sense of the number's "real" worth.
- To convert a number to decimal from another base, multiply the decimal equivalent of each digit by its positional value and sum the products.
- Computers represent negative numbers using two's-complement notation.
- To form the negative of a value in binary, first form its one's complement by combining the value with &H7FFFFFFF using Visual Basic's Xor operator. This reverses the bits of the value. To form the two's complement of a value, simply add one to the value's one's complement.

Terminology

base
base-2 number system

base-8 number system
base-10 number system

base-16 number system
binary number system
conversions
decimal number system
digit
hexadecimal number system
negative value

octal number system
one's-complement notation
positional notation
positional value
symbol value
two's-complement notation

Self-Review Exercises

C.1   Fill in the blanks in each of the following statements:

a) The bases of the decimal, binary, octal and hexadecimal number systems are _____, _____, _____ and _____, respectively.

b) The positional value of the rightmost digit of any number in either binary, octal, decimal or hexadecimal is always _____.

c) The positional value of the digit to the left of the rightmost digit of any number in binary, octal, decimal or hexadecimal is always equal to _____.

C.2   State whether each of the following is *true* or *false*. If *false*, explain why.

a) A popular reason for using the decimal number system is that it forms a convenient notation for abbreviating binary numbers simply by substituting one decimal digit per group of four binary bits.

b) The highest digit in any base is one more than the base.

c) The lowest digit in any base is one less than the base.

C.3   In general, the decimal, octal and hexadecimal representations of a given binary number contain (more/fewer) digits than the binary number contains.

C.4   The (octal / hexadecimal / decimal) representation of a large binary value is the most concise (of the given alternatives).

C.5   Fill in the missing values in this chart of positional values for the rightmost four positions in each of the indicated number systems:

decimal	1000	100	10	1
hexadecimal	...	256	...	...
binary	...	...	...	...
octal	512	...	8	...

C.6   Convert binary 110101011000 to octal and to hexadecimal.

C.7   Convert hexadecimal FACE to binary.

C.8   Convert octal 7316 to binary.

C.9   Convert hexadecimal 4FEC to octal. [*Hint:* First convert 4FEC to binary, then convert that binary number to octal.]

C.10   Convert binary 1101110 to decimal.

C.11   Convert octal 317 to decimal.

C.12   Convert hexadecimal EFD4 to decimal.

C.13   Convert decimal 177 to binary, to octal and to hexadecimal.

C.14   Show the binary representation of decimal 417. Then show the one's complement of 417 and the two's complement of 417.

C.15   What is the result when a number and its two's complement are added to each other?

Answers to Self-Review Exercises

C.1   a) 10, 2, 8, 16. b) 1 (the base raised to the zero power). c) The base of the number system.

C.2   a) False. Hexadecimal does this. b) False. The highest digit in any base is one less than the base. c) False. The lowest digit in any base is zero.

C.3   Fewer.

C.4   Hexadecimal.

C.5   Fill in the missing values in this chart of positional values for the rightmost four positions in each of the indicated number systems:

decimal	1000	100	10	1
hexadecimal	4096	256	16	1
binary	8	4	2	1
octal	512	64	8	1

C.6   Octal 6530; Hexadecimal D58.

C.7   Binary 1111 1010 1100 1110.

C.8   Binary 111 011 001 110.

C.9   Binary 0 100 111 111 101 100; Octal 47754.

C.10   Decimal 2 + 4 + 8 + 32 + 64 = 110.

C.11   Decimal 7 + 1 * 8 + 3 * 64 = 7 + 8 + 192 = 207.

C.12   Decimal 4 + 13 * 16 + 15 * 256 + 14 * 4096 = 61396.

C.13   Decimal 177
to binary:

```
256 128 64 32 16 8 4 2 1
128 64 32 16 8 4 2 1
(1*128)+(0*64)+(1*32)+(1*16)+(0*8)+(0*4)+(0*2)+(1*1)
10110001
```

to octal:

```
512 64 8 1
64 8 1
(2*64)+(6*8)+(1*1)
261
```

to hexadecimal:

```
256 16 1
16 1
(11*16)+(1*1)
(B*16)+(1*1)
B1
```

C.14   Binary:

```
512 256 128 64 32 16 8 4 2 1
256 128 64 32 16 8 4 2 1
(1*256)+(1*128)+(0*64)+(1*32)+(0*16)+(0*8)+(0*4)+(0*2)+(1*1)
110100001
```

```
One's complement: 001011110
Two's complement: 001011111
Check: Original binary number + its two's complement
```

```
110100001
001011111
---------
000000000
```

C.15   Zero.

Exercises

C.16   Some people argue that many of our calculations would be easier in the base-12 number system because 12 is divisible by so many more numbers than 10 (for base 10). What is the lowest digit in base 12? What would be the highest symbol for the digit in base 12? What are the positional values of the rightmost four positions of any number in the base-12 number system?

C.17   Complete the following chart of positional values for the rightmost four positions in each of the indicated number systems:

decimal	1000	100	10	1
base 6	...	...	6	...
base 13	...	169	...	...
base 3	27	...	...	...

C.18   Convert binary 100101111010 to octal and to hexadecimal.

C.19   Convert hexadecimal 3A7D to binary.

C.20   Convert hexadecimal 765F to octal. (*Hint:* First convert 765F to binary, then convert that binary number to octal.)

C.21   Convert binary 1011110 to decimal.

C.22   Convert octal 426 to decimal.

C.23   Convert hexadecimal FFFF to decimal.

C.24   Convert decimal 299 to binary, to octal and to hexadecimal.

C.25   Show the binary representation of decimal 779. Then show the one's complement of 779 and the two's complement of 779.

C.26   Show the two's complement of integer value −1 on a machine with 32-bit integers.

ASCII Character Set

ASCII character set										
	0	**1**	**2**	**3**	**4**	**5**	**6**	**7**	**8**	**9**
0	nul	soh	stx	etx	eot	enq	ack	bel	bs	ht
1	lf	vt	ff	cr	so	si	dle	dc1	dc2	dc3
2	dc4	nak	syn	etb	can	em	sub	esc	fs	gs
3	rs	us	sp	!	"	#	$	%	&	'
4	(	)	*	+	,	-	.	/	0	1
5	2	3	4	5	6	7	8	9	:	;
6	<	=	>	?	@	A	B	C	D	E
7	F	G	H	I	J	K	L	M	N	O
8	P	Q	R	S	T	U	V	W	X	Y
9	Z	[	\	]	^	_	`	a	b	c
10	d	e	f	g	h	i	j	k	l	m
11	n	o	p	q	r	s	t	u	v	w
12	x	y	z	{	|	}	~	del		

Fig. D.1 | ASCII character set.

The digits at the left of the table are the left digits of the decimal equivalent (0–127) of the character code, and the digits at the top of the table are the right digits of the character code. For example, the character "F" is in row 7 and column 0, so its character code is 70. Similarly, the character "&" is in row 3 and column 8, so its character code is 38.

Most users of this book are interested in the ASCII character set used to represent English characters on many computers. The ASCII character set is a subset of the Unicode character set used by Visual Basic to represent characters from most of the world's languages. For more information on the Unicode character set, see Appendix E.

E

Unicode®

Objectives

In this appendix you'll learn:

- The mission of the Unicode Consortium.

- The design basis of Unicode.

- The three Unicode encoding forms: UTF-8, UTF-16 and UTF-32.

- Characters and glyphs.

- The advantages and disadvantages of using Unicode.

- About the Unicode Consortium's website.

E.1 Introduction

The use of inconsistent character **encodings** (that is, numeric values associated with characters) in the developing of global software products causes serious problems, because computers process information as numbers. For instance, the character "a" is converted to a numeric value so that a computer can manipulate that piece of data. Many countries and corporations have developed their own encoding systems that are incompatible with the encoding systems of other countries and corporations. For example, the Microsoft Windows operating system assigns the value 0xC0 to the character "A with a grave accent"; the Apple Macintosh operating system assigns that same value to an upside-down question mark. This results in the misrepresentation and possible corruption of data when it is not processed as intended.

In the absence of a widely implemented universal character-encoding standard, global software developers had to **localize** their products extensively before distribution. Localization includes the language translation and cultural adaptation of content. The process of localization usually includes significant modifications to the source code (such as the conversion of numeric values and the underlying assumptions made by programmers), which results in increased costs and delays releasing the software. For example, some English-speaking programmers might design global software products assuming that a single character can be represented by one byte. However, when those products are localized for Asian markets, the programmer's assumptions are no longer valid; thus, the majority, if not the entirety, of the code needs to be rewritten. Localization is necessary with each release of a version. By the time a software product is localized for a particular market, a newer version, which needs to be localized as well, may be ready for distribution. As a result, it is cumbersome and costly to produce and distribute global software products in a market where there is no universal character-encoding standard.

In response to this situation, the **Unicode Standard**, an encoding standard that facilitates the production and distribution of software, was created. The Unicode Standard outlines a specification to produce consistent encoding of the world's characters and symbols. Software products that handle text encoded in the Unicode Standard need to be localized, but the localization process is simpler and more efficient, because the numeric values need not be converted and the assumptions made by programmers about the character encoding are universal. The Unicode Standard is maintained by a nonprofit organization called the **Unicode Consortium**, whose members include Apple, IBM, Microsoft, Oracle, Sun Microsystems, Sybase and many others.

When the Consortium envisioned and developed the Unicode Standard, they wanted an encoding system that was **universal**, **efficient**, **uniform** and **unambiguous**. A universal encoding system encompasses all commonly used characters. An efficient encoding system allows text files to be parsed easily. A uniform encoding system assigns fixed values to all characters. An unambiguous encoding system represents a given character in a consistent manner. These four terms are referred to as the Unicode Standard **design basis**.

E.2 Unicode Transformation Formats

Although Unicode incorporates the limited ASCII character set (that is, a collection of characters), it encompasses a more comprehensive character set. In ASCII each character is represented by a byte containing 0s and 1s. One byte is capable of storing the binary numbers from 0 to 255. Each character is assigned a number between 0 and 255; thus, ASCII-based systems can support only 256 characters, a tiny fraction of world's characters. Unicode extends the ASCII character set by encoding the vast majority of the world's characters. The Unicode Standard encodes all of those characters in a uniform numerical space from 0 to 10FFFF hexadecimal. An implementation will express these numbers in one of several transformation formats, choosing the one that best fits the particular application at hand.

Three such formats are in use, called **UTF-8**, **UTF-16** and **UTF-32**, depending on the size of the units—in bits—being used. UTF-8, a variable-width encoding form, requires one to four bytes to express each Unicode character. UTF-8 data consists of 8-bit bytes (sequences of one, two, three or four bytes depending on the character being encoded) and is well suited for ASCII-based systems, where there is a predominance of one-byte characters (ASCII represents characters as one byte). Currently, UTF-8 is widely implemented in UNIX systems and in databases.

The variable-width UTF-16 encoding form expresses Unicode characters in units of 16 bits (that is, as two adjacent bytes, or a short integer in many machines). Most characters of Unicode are expressed in a single 16-bit unit. However, characters with values above FFFF hexadecimal are expressed with an ordered pair of 16-bit units called **surrogates**. Surrogates are 16-bit integers in the range D800 through DFFF, which are used solely for the purpose of "escaping" into higher-numbered characters. Approximately one million characters can be expressed in this manner. Although a surrogate pair requires 32 bits to represent characters, it is space efficient to use these 16-bit units. Surrogates are rare characters in current implementations. Many string-handling implementations are written in terms of UTF-16. [*Note:* Details and sample code for UTF-16 handling are available on the Unicode Consortium website at www.unicode.org.]

Implementations that require significant use of rare characters or entire scripts encoded above FFFF hexadecimal should use UTF-32, a 32-bit, fixed-width encoding form that usually requires twice as much memory as UTF-16 encoded characters. The major advantage of the fixed-width UTF-32 encoding form is that it expresses all characters uniformly, so it is easy to handle in arrays.

There are few guidelines that state when to use a particular encoding form. The best encoding form to use depends on computer systems and business protocols, not on the data itself. Typically, the UTF-8 encoding form should be used where computer systems and business protocols require data to be handled in 8-bit units, particularly in legacy systems being upgraded, because it often simplifies changes to existing programs. For this reason, UTF-8 has become the encoding form of choice on the Internet. Likewise, UTF-

16 is the encoding form of choice on Microsoft Windows applications. UTF-32 is likely to become more widely used in the future, as more characters are encoded with values above FFFF hexadecimal. Also, UTF-32 requires less sophisticated handling than UTF-16 in the presence of surrogate pairs. Figure E.1 shows the different ways in which the three encoding forms handle character encoding.

Character	UTF-8	UTF-16	UTF-32
Latin Capital Letter A	0x41	0x0041	0x00000041
Greek Capital Letter Alpha	0xCD 0x91	0x0391	0x00000391
CJK Unified Ideograph-4e95	0xE4 0xBA 0x95	0x4E95	0x00004E95
Old Italic Letter A	0xF0 0x80 0x83 0x80	0xDC00 0xDF00	0x00010300

Fig. E.1 | Correlation between the three encoding forms.

E.3 Characters and Glyphs

The Unicode Standard consists of characters, written components (that is, alphabetic letters, numerals, punctuation marks, accent marks, and so on) that can be represented by numeric values. Examples of characters include: U+0041 LATIN CAPITAL LETTER A. In the first character representation, U+*yyyy* is a **code value**, in which U+ refers to Unicode code values, as opposed to other hexadecimal values. The *yyyy* represents a four-digit hexadecimal number of an encoded character. Code values are bit combinations that represent encoded characters. Characters are represented with **glyphs**, various shapes, fonts and sizes for displaying characters. There are no code values for glyphs in the Unicode Standard. Examples of glyphs are shown in Fig. E.2.

Fig. E.2 | Various glyphs of the character A.

The Unicode Standard encompasses the alphabets, ideographs, syllabaries, punctuation marks, **diacritics**, mathematical operators and so on that comprise the written languages and scripts of the world. A diacritic is a special mark added to a character to distinguish it from another letter or to indicate an accent (for example, in Spanish, the tilde "~" above the character "n"). Currently, Unicode provides code values for 94,140 character representations, with more than 880,000 code values reserved for future expansion.

E.4 Advantages/Disadvantages of Unicode

The Unicode Standard has several significant advantages that promote its use. One is its impact on the performance of the international economy. Unicode standardizes the characters for the world's writing systems to a uniform model that promotes transferring and sharing data. Programs developed using such a schema maintain their accuracy, because each character has a single definition (that is, *a* is always U+0061, % is always U+0025). This enables corporations to manage the high demands of international markets by processing different writing systems at the same time. Also, all characters can be managed in an identical manner, thus avoiding any confusion caused by different character-code architectures. Moreover, managing data in a consistent manner eliminates data corruption, because data can be sorted, searched and manipulated via a consistent process.

Another advantage of the Unicode Standard is portability (that is, the ability to execute software on disparate computers or with disparate operating systems). Most operating systems, databases, programming languages and web browsers currently support, or are planning to support, Unicode. Additionally, Unicode includes more characters than any other character set in common use (although it does not yet include all of the world's characters).

A disadvantage of the Unicode Standard is the amount of memory required by UTF-16 and UTF-32. ASCII character sets are 8 bits in length, so they require less storage than the default 16-bit Unicode character set. However, the **double-byte character set** (DBCS) and the **multibyte character set** (MBCS) that encode Asian characters (ideographs) require two to four bytes, respectively. In such instances, the UTF-16 or the UTF-32 encoding forms may be used with little hindrance to memory and performance.

E.5 Using Unicode

Visual Studio uses Unicode UTF-16 encoding to represent all characters. Figure E.3 uses Visual Basic to display the text "Welcome to Unicode!" in eight different languages: English, French, German, Japanese, Portuguese, Russian, Spanish and Traditional Chinese.

```
1   ' Fig. E.3: UnicodeDemo.vb
2   ' Using Unicode encoding.
3   Public Class UnicodeDemo
4      Private Sub UnicodeDemo_Load(ByVal sender As System.Object, _
5         ByVal e As System.EventArgs) Handles MyBase.Load
6         'English
7         englishLabel.Text = ChrW(&H57) & ChrW(&H65) & ChrW(&H6C) & _
8            ChrW(&H63) & ChrW(&H6F) & ChrW(&H6D) & ChrW(&H65) & _
9            ChrW(&H20) & ChrW(&H74) & ChrW(&H6F) & ChrW(&H20) & _
10           "Unicode" & ChrW(&H21)
11
12        ' French
13        frenchLabel.Text = ChrW(&H42) & ChrW(&H69) & ChrW(&H65) & _
14           ChrW(&H6E) & ChrW(&H76) & ChrW(&H65) & ChrW(&H6E) & _
15           ChrW(&H75) & ChrW(&H65) & ChrW(&H20) & ChrW(&H61) & _
16           ChrW(&H75) & ChrW(&H20) & "Unicode" & ChrW(&H21)
```

Fig. E.3 | Windows application demonstrating Unicode encoding. (Part 1 of 2.)

```
17
18          ' German
19          germanLabel.Text = ChrW(&H57) & ChrW(&H69) & ChrW(&H6C) & _
20             ChrW(&H6B) & ChrW(&H6F) & ChrW(&H6D) & ChrW(&H6D) & _
21             ChrW(&H65) & ChrW(&H6E) & ChrW(&H20) & ChrW(&H7A) & _
22             ChrW(&H75) & ChrW(&H20) & "Unicode" & ChrW(&H21)
23
24          ' Japanese
25          japaneseLabel.Text = "Unicode " & ChrW(&H3078) & _
26             ChrW(&H3087) & ChrW(&H3045) & ChrW(&H3053) & _
27             ChrW(&H305D) & ChrW(&H21)
28
29          ' Portuguese
30          portugueseLabel.Text = ChrW(&H53) & ChrW(&HE9) & ChrW(&H6A) & _
31             ChrW(&H61) & ChrW(&H20) & ChrW(&H42) & _
32             ChrW(&H65) & ChrW(&H6D) & ChrW(&H76) & _
33             ChrW(&H69) & ChrW(&H6E) & ChrW(&H64) & _
34             ChrW(&H6F) & ChrW(&H20) & "Unicode" & ChrW(&H21)
35
36          ' Russian
37          russianLabel.Text = ChrW(&H414) & ChrW(&H43E) & ChrW(&H431) & _
38             ChrW(&H440) & ChrW(&H43E) & ChrW(&H20) & _
39             ChrW(&H43F) & ChrW(&H43E) & ChrW(&H436) & _
40             ChrW(&H430) & ChrW(&H43B) & ChrW(&H43E) & _
41             ChrW(&H432) & ChrW(&H430) & ChrW(&H442) & _
42             ChrW(&H44A) & ChrW(&H20) & ChrW(&H432) & _
43             ChrW(&H20) & "Unicode" & ChrW(&H21)
44
45          ' Spanish
46          spanishLabel.Text = ChrW(&H42) & ChrW(&H69) & ChrW(&H65) & _
47             ChrW(&H6E) & ChrW(&H76) & ChrW(&H65) & _
48             ChrW(&H6E) & ChrW(&H69) & ChrW(&H64) & _
49             ChrW(&H61) & ChrW(&H20) & ChrW(&H61) & _
50             ChrW(&H20) & "Unicode" & ChrW(&H21)
51
52          ' Traditional Chinese
53          chineseLabel.Text = ChrW(&H6B22) & ChrW(&H8FCE) & _
54             ChrW(&H4F7F) & ChrW(&H7528) & ChrW(&H20) & _
55             "Unicode" & ChrW(&H21)
56       End Sub ' UnicodeDemo_Load
57    End Class ' UnicodeDemo
```

Fig. E.3 | Windows application demonstrating Unicode encoding. (Part 2 of 2.)

The first welcome message (lines 7–10) contains the hexadecimal codes for the English text. The **Code Charts** page on the Unicode Consortium website contains a document that lists the code values for the **Basic Latin** block (or category), which includes the English alphabet. The hexadecimal codes in lines 7–8 equate to "Welcome." When using Unicode characters in Visual Basic, the format &H*yyyy* is used, where *yyyy* represents the hexadecimal Unicode encoding. For example, the letter "W" (in "Welcome") is denoted by &H57. [*Note:* The actual code for the letter "W" is &H0057, but Visual Studio removes the two zeros.] Line 9 contains the hexadecimal for the *space* character (&H20). The hexadecimal value for the word "to" is on lines 9, and the word "Unicode" is on line 10. "Unicode" is not encoded because it is a registered trademark and has no equivalent translation in most languages. Line 10 also contains the &H21 notation for the exclamation mark (!).

The remaining welcome messages (lines 13–55) contain the hexadecimal codes for the other seven languages. The code values used for the French, German, Portuguese and Spanish text are located in the **Basic Latin** block, the code values used for the Traditional Chinese text are located in the **CJK Unified Ideographs** block, the code values used for the Russian text are located in the **Cyrillic** block and the code values used for the Japanese text are located in the **Hiragana** block.

[*Note:* To render the Asian characters in a Windows application, you would need to install the proper language files on your computer. To do this, open the **Regional Options** dialog from the **Control Panel** (**Start > Control Panel > Clock, Language, and Region**). Under the **Keyboard and Languages** tab, click the **Change Keyboards...** button. At the bottom of the **General** tab is a list of languages. Click **Add...** then search the tree view for the **Japanese** and the **Traditional Chinese** checkboxes and press **OK**. Follow the directions of the install wizard to install the languages. For additional assistance, visit `www.unicode.org/help/display_problems.html`.]

E.6 Character Ranges

The Unicode Standard assigns code values, which range from 0000 (**Basic Latin**) to E007F (**Tags**), to the written characters of the world. Currently, there are code values for 94,140 characters. To simplify the search for a character and its associated code value, the Unicode Standard generally groups code values by **script** and function (that is, Latin characters are grouped in a block, mathematical operators are grouped in another block, and so on). As a rule, a script is a single writing system that is used for multiple languages (for example, the Latin script is used for English, French, Spanish, and so on). The **Code Charts** page on the Unicode Consortium website lists all the defined blocks and their respective code values. Figure E.4 lists some blocks (scripts) from the website and their range of code values.

Script	Range of code values
Arabic	U+0600–U+06FF
Basic Latin	U+0000–U+007F
Bengali (India)	U+0980–U+09FF
Cherokee (Native America)	U+13A0–U+13FF

Fig. E.4 | Some character ranges. (Part 1 of 2.)

Script	Range of code values
CJK Unified Ideographs (East Asia)	U+4E00–U+9FAF
Cyrillic (Russia and Eastern Europe)	U+0400–U+04FF
Ethiopic	U+1200–U+137F
Greek	U+0370–U+03FF
Hangul Jamo (Korea)	U+1100–U+11FF
Hebrew	U+0590–U+05FF
Hiragana (Japan)	U+3040–U+309F
Khmer (Cambodia)	U+1780–U+17FF
Lao (Laos)	U+0E80–U+0EFF
Mongolian	U+1800–U+18AF
Myanmar	U+1000–U+109F
Ogham (Ireland)	U+1680–U+169F
Runic (Germany and Scandinavia)	U+16A0–U+16FF
Sinhala (Sri Lanka)	U+0D80–U+0DFF
Telugu (India)	U+0C00–U+0C7F
Thai	U+0E00–U+0E7F

Fig. E.4 | Some character ranges. (Part 2 of 2.)

Summary

- Before Unicode, software developers were plagued by the use of inconsistent character encoding (that is, numeric values for characters). Most countries and organizations had their own encoding systems, which were incompatible. A good example is the individual encoding systems on the Windows and Macintosh platforms.

- Computers process data by converting characters to numeric values. For instance, the character "a" is converted to a numeric value so that a computer can manipulate that piece of data.

- Without Unicode, localization of global software requires significant modifications to the source code, which results in increased cost and delays in releasing the product.

- Localization is necessary with each release of a version. By the time a software product is localized for a particular market, a newer version, which needs to be localized as well, is ready for distribution. As a result, it is cumbersome and costly to produce and distribute global software products in a market where there is no universal character-encoding standard.

- The Unicode Consortium developed the Unicode Standard in response to the serious problems created by multiple character encodings and the use of those encodings.

- The Unicode Standard facilitates the production and distribution of localized software. It outlines a specification for the consistent encoding of the world's characters and symbols.

- Software products that handle text encoded in the Unicode Standard need to be localized, but the localization process is simpler and more efficient because the numeric values need not be converted.

- The Unicode Standard is designed to be universal, efficient, uniform and unambiguous.

- A universal encoding system encompasses all commonly used characters; an efficient encoding system parses text files easily; a uniform encoding system assigns fixed values to all characters; and an unambiguous encoding system represents the same character for any given value.

- Unicode extends the limited ASCII character set to include all the major characters of the world.

- Unicode makes use of three Unicode Transformation Formats (UTF): UTF-8, UTF-16 and UTF-32, each of which may be appropriate for use in different contexts.

- UTF-8 data consists of 8-bit bytes (sequences of one, two, three or four bytes depending on the character being encoded) and is well suited for ASCII-based systems, where there is a predominance of one-byte characters (ASCII represents characters as one byte).

- UTF-8 is a variable-width encoding form that is more compact for text involving mostly Latin characters and ASCII punctuation.

- UTF-16 is the default encoding form of the Unicode Standard. It is a variable-width encoding form that uses 16-bit code units instead of bytes. Most characters are represented by a single unit, but some characters require surrogate pairs.

- Surrogates are 16-bit integers in the range D800 through DFFF, which are used solely for the purpose of "escaping" into higher-numbered characters.

- Without surrogate pairs, the UTF-16 encoding form can encompass only 65,000 characters, but with the surrogate pairs, this is expanded to include over a million characters.

- UTF-32 is a 32-bit encoding form. The major advantage of the fixed-width encoding form is that it uniformly expresses all characters, so that they're easy to handle in arrays and so forth.

- The Unicode Standard consists of characters. A character is any written component that can be represented by a numeric value.

- Characters are represented with glyphs (various shapes, fonts and sizes for displaying characters).

- Code values are bit combinations that represent encoded characters. The Unicode notation for a code value is U+$yyyy$, in which U+ refers to the Unicode code values, as opposed to other hexadecimal values. The $yyyy$ represents a four-digit hexadecimal number.

- Currently, the Unicode Standard provides code values for 94,140 character representations.

- An advantage of the Unicode Standard is its impact on the overall performance of the international economy. Applications that conform to an encoding standard can be processed easily by computers anywhere.

- Another advantage of the Unicode Standard is its portability. Applications written in Unicode can be easily transferred to different operating systems, databases, web browsers and so on. Most companies currently support, or are planning to support, Unicode.

- To obtain more information about the Unicode Standard and the Unicode Consortium, visit www.unicode.org. It contains a link to the code charts, which contain the 16-bit code values for the currently encoded characters.

- The Unicode Standard has become the default encoding system for XML and any language derived from XML, such as XHTML.

- The Visual Basic IDE uses Unicode UTF-16 encoding to represent all characters.

- In the marking up of Visual Basic documents, the entity reference &H$yyyy$ is used, where $yyyy$ represents the hexadecimal code value.

Terminology

&H$yyyy$ notation
ASCII

block
character

character set	surrogate
code value	symbol
diacritic	unambiguous (Unicode design basis)
double-byte character set (DBCS)	Unicode Consortium
efficient (Unicode design basis)	Unicode design basis
encode	Unicode Standard
entity reference	Unicode Transformation Format (UTF)
glyph	uniform (Unicode design basis)
hexadecimal notation	universal (Unicode design basis)
localization	UTF-8
multibyte character set (MBCS)	UTF-16
portability	UTF-32
script	

Self-Review Exercises

E.1 Fill in the blanks in each of the following.
  a) Global software developers had to _____ their products to a specific market before distribution.
  b) The Unicode Standard is a(n) _____ standard that facilitates the uniform production and distribution of software products.
  c) The four design bases that constitute the Unicode Standard are: _____, _____, _____ and _____.
  d) A(n) _____ is the smallest written component that can be represented with a numeric value.
  e) Software that can execute on different operating systems is said to be _____.
  f) Of the three encoding forms, _____ is currently supported by Internet Explorer 5.5 and Netscape Communicator 6.

E.2 State whether each of the following is *true* or *false*. If *false*, explain why.
  a) The Unicode Standard encompasses all the world's characters.
  b) A Unicode code value is represented as U+*yyyy*, where *yyyy* represents a number in binary notation.
  c) A diacritic is a character with a special mark that emphasizes an accent.
  d) Unicode is portable.
  e) When designing Visual Basic programs, the entity reference is denoted by #U+*yyyy*.

Answers to Self-Review exercises

E.1 a) localize. b) encoding. c) universal, efficient, uniform, unambiguous. d) character. e) portable. f) UTF-8.

E.2 a) False. It encompasses the majority of the world's characters. b) False. The *yyyy* represents a hexadecimal number. c) False. A diacritic is a special mark added to a character to distinguish it from another letter or to indicate an accent. d) True. e) False. The entity reference is denoted by &H*yyyy*.

Exercises

E.3 Navigate to the Unicode Consortium website (www.unicode.org) and write the hexadecimal code values for the following characters. In which block are they located?
  a) Latin letter 'Z.'
  b) Latin letter 'n' with the 'tilde (~).'

    c) Greek letter 'delta.'

    d) Mathematical operator 'less than or equal to.'

    e) Punctuation symbol 'open quote (").'

E.4 Describe the Unicode Standard design basis.

E.5 Define the following terms:

    a) code value.

    b) surrogates.

    c) Unicode Standard.

    d) UTF-8.

    e) UTF-16.

    f) UTF-32.

E.6 Describe a scenario where it is optimal to store your data in UTF-16 format.

E.7 Using the Unicode Standard code values, create a program that prints your first and last name. If you know other writing systems, print your first and last name in those as well. Use a `Label` to display your name.

E.8 Write an ASP.NET program that prints "Welcome to Unicode!" in English, French, German, Japanese, Portuguese, Russian, Spanish and Traditional Chinese. Use the code values provided in Fig. E.3. In ASP.NET, a code value is represented the same way as in a Windows application (&H*yyyy*, where *yyyy* is a four-digit hexadecimal number).

Index